ArtScroll Tanach Series®

A traditional commentary on the Books of the Bible

Rabbi Nosson Scherman / Rabbi Meir Zlotowitz

General Editors

A PROJECT OF THE

Mesorah Heritage Foundation

מיכה
נחום
חבקוק
צפניה
חגי
זכריה
מלאכי

Translation and Commentary by
Rabbi Yitzchok Stavsky

Micah
Nahum
Habakkuk
Zephaniah
Haggai
Zechariah
Malachi

Trei Asar

THE TWELVE PROPHETS Vol. II: / A NEW TRANSLATION WITH A COMMENTARY ANTHOLOGIZED FROM TALMUDIC, MIDRASHIC, AND RABBINIC SOURCES

Published by
Mesorah Publications, ltd

FIRST EDITION
First Impression ... September 2009

Published and Distributed by
MESORAH PUBLICATIONS, LTD.
4401 Second Avenue / Brooklyn, N.Y 11232

Distributed in Europe by
LEHMANNS
Unit E, Viking Business Park
Rolling Mill Road
Jarow, Tyne & Wear, NE32 3DP
England

Distributed in Australia and New Zealand
by **GOLDS WORLDS OF JUDAICA**
3-13 William Street
Balaclava, Melbourne 3183
Victoria, Australia

Distributed in Israel by
SIFRIATI / A. GITLER — BOOKS
6 Hayarkon Street
Bnei Brak 51127

Distributed in South Africa by
KOLLEL BOOKSHOP
Ivy Common
105 William Road
Norwood 2192, Johannesburg, South Africa

THE ARTSCROLL TANACH SERIES®
TREI ASAR / THE TWELVE PROPHETS VOL.II

4401 Second Avenue / Brooklyn, N.Y. 11232 / (718) 921-9000 / www.artscroll.com

ISBN 10: 1-4226-0911-1 / ISBN 13: 978-1-4226-0911-8

Typography by CompuScribe at ArtScroll Studios, Ltd.

Printed in Canada
Bound by Sefercraft, Quality Bookbinders, Ltd., Brooklyn N.Y. 11232

This volume is dedicated in memory of our husband, father, grandfather, and great-grandfather

Israel Schmell ז״ל

ישראל מרדכי בן נפתלי הערץ

ודבורה הדסה ז״ל

נפטר ב׳ אלול תשס״ג

His calm manner, total integrity, and practical wisdom earned Izzy Schmell the respect and confidence of all. His advice and counsel were sought and accepted by family, business associates and the many Jewish institutions that were part of his life. He loved Torah and mitzvos and utilized all his resources both for his personal learning and to realize the desire that every Jewish child – not only his own – receive a Torah education.

In spite of his demanding schedule, his greatest pleasure was spending time with family. His loving relationship and his presence at every family simchah around the globe are cherished memories to us all.

Izzy Schmell's accomplishments were cloaked in humility, making him all the more respected.

We have no greater privilege than to try and live up to his legacy.

Mrs. Gert Schmell

Anita and Yona Seif **Chaim and Sima Schmell**

Moshe and Chavi Schmell **Shlomo and Miriam Ruchoma Schmell**

and their families

⊷§ *Publisher's Preface*

We are privileged to present this final volume of *Trei Asar / The Twelve Prophets.* In it we read how its great protagonists carried God's message to their contemporaries, and — if we read it well and contemplate it seriously — we hear them speaking to us, as well. Of the countless prophecies conveyed to Israel during the First Temple era, the ones preserved in Scripture were only those that were relevant to future generations. Thus, the soaring words and searing experience of these prophets, for example, were meant for us, as well as for their contemporaries. But the words that are so beautiful and laden with meaning are extremely hard to understand; hence the need for this new translation and commentary.

The author of this volume is RABBI YITZCHOK STAVSKY, who earned our respect and gratitude as a contributing editor to the ArtScroll Edition of *Shmuel / Samuel* and *Melachim / Kings.* His work on this volume is testimony to his scholarship and skill. We are also grateful to RABBI MATIS ROBERTS, author of *Trei Asar* Vol. 1, who contributed preliminary scholarship to parts of this volume.

This volume is dedicated by the SCHMELL FAMILY in memory of their husband and father ISRAEL SCHMELL ז״ל. He was a respected friend, role model, and wise supporter of worthy causes, and his family carries on his legacy

Many members of the ArtScroll staff were involved in the exacting task of typing and correcting the manuscript. We are grateful to MRS. DEVOIRY BIDERMAN, MRS. ESTI DICKER, MRS. SURY ENGLARD, MRS. REIZY GANZ, and MRS. CHUMIE LIPSCHITZ for completing the work and paginating the entire volume under the supervision of the acknowledged master of the craft,

our esteemed colleague, REB SHEAH BRANDER. MRS MIRYAM STAVSKY reviewed the final manuscript We are also grateful to RABBI AVROHOM YITZCHOK DEUTSCH and MRS. FAYGIE WEINBAUM for their customarily meticulous proofreading.

This volume ends with the words of Malachi: "*Behold, I send you Elijah the prophet before the coming of the great and awesome day of Hashem and he will turn back [to God] the hearts of fathers with [their] sons and the hearts of sons with their fathers ...*"

May it be Hashem's will that this prophecy be fulfilled speedily, in our time.

Rabbi Meir Zlotowitz / Rabbi Nosson Scherman

Elul 5769 / September 2009

◆§ *Table of Contents*

מיכה / Micah 2

נחום / Nahum 66

חבקוק / Habakkuk 94

צפניה/ Zephania 134

חגי / Haggai 170

זכריה / Zechariah 194

מלאכי / Malachi 310

Micah

א דְּבַר־יְהוָה | אֲשֶׁר הָיָה אֶל־מִיכָה הַמֹּרַשְׁתִּי
בִּימֵי יוֹתָם אָחָז יְחִזְקִיָּה מַלְכֵי יְהוּדָה אֲשֶׁר־
ב חָזָה עַל־שֹׁמְרוֹן וִירוּשָׁלִָם: שִׁמְעוּ עַמִּים
כֻּלָּם הַקְשִׁיבִי אֶרֶץ וּמְלֹאָהּ וִיהִי אֲדֹנָי

I

1. דְּבַר־ה׳ — *The word of* HASHEM. I.e., the prophetic word of G-d. The word דיבור is one of the ten expressions used by Scripture to show how the word of G-d is revealed to man. According to R' Yochanan, it designates a fateful and foreboding prophecy (*Bereishis Rabbah* 44:7).

Micah's prophecies are directed toward both the Northern Kingdom of Israel and the Kingdom of Judah. The prophet chastises the nation for their intolerable actions against one another and for their rebellious behavior against G-d. He predicts the terrible destruction that will befall the people as a result of their sins, foretelling the Babylonian exile 150 years before it actually occurred (4:10), and the devastation of Jerusalem while the great city was yet in its full splendor (3:12).

מִיכָה הַמֹּרַשְׁתִּי — *Micah the Morashite.* Micah was from Mareshah, a city in the Kingdom of Judah (*Radak; Metzudos*). He was a disciple of the prophet Isaiah and received the Oral Tradition from him and his court (*Rambam — Introduction to Mishneh Torah*). He is not to be confused with the prophet Micaiahu ben Yimlah mentioned in *I Kings* 22:8, who prophesied during the days of Ahab, the monarch who ruled over the Northern Kingdom from 3021-3042. Micah the Morashite prophesied during the days of Jotham, Ahaz and Hezekiah, who ruled over Judah from 3168-3228.

Although Scripture does not identify Micah's tribe, *Abarbanel* suggests that the prophet was a member of the tribe of Judah since Mareshah, the city where Micah lived was located in the territory of Judah.

יוֹתָם אָחָז יְחִזְקִיָּה — *Jotham, Ahaz, Hezekiah.* These were the tenth, eleventh and twelfth kings of the Kingdom of Judah; each the son of his predecessor. Jotham reigned for 16 years (*II Kings* 15:33), as did Ahaz (ibid. 16:2), and Hezekiah ruled for 29 years (ibid. 18:2).

Hosea, Isaiah, Amos and Micah all prophesied in one era (*Pesachim* 87a). However, the books of the first three of these prophets mention that they were active during the days of Uziah, the ninth king of Judah, as well. Since this king is not mentioned in the Book of *Micah*, it is assumed that Micah was younger than his contemporaries and did not yet prophesy during the days of Uziah (*Mahari Kara*).

Although the Books of *Hosea* and *Amos* record the names of the monarchs of the Northern Kingdom who were the contemporaries of these prophets (see *Hosea* 1:1; *Amos* 1:1), the Book of *Micah* does not mention the name of any Northern Kingdom monarch. *Metzudos* suggests that since Micah did not utter his prophecies in the cities of the Northern Kingdom of Israel as did Hosea and Amos, Scripture did not find it necessary to mention the names of its kings (*Metzudos*).

Furthermore, *Abarbanel* maintains that the prophets who dwelt in the Kingdom of Judah did not recognize the monarchs of the Northern Kingdom as true kings, as they were not of the Davidic dynasty, and considered them no better than usurpers and enemies of

[1] **T**he word of HASHEM that came to Micah the Morashite, in the days of Jotham, Ahaz, Hezekiah, kings of Judah — that he saw concerning Samaria and Jerusalem:

[2] *Hear, O peoples, all of you! Listen, Be attentive O Land and its fullness! And let the Lord*

G-d. They, therefore, saw no reason to mention them in their books.[1]

חָזָה — *Saw.* I.e., saw in a vision, prophesied (*Metzudos, Amos* 1:1). Whereas ראה is used to describe physical sight, חזה related to חָזֶה, *breast,* the seat of the heart, seems to mean seeing in a spiritual sense, perceiving and comprehending that which is invisible to the physical eye (*R' Hirsch, Genesis* 15:1).

In *Bereishis Rabbah* (44:7), חָזוֹן, *chazon,* too, is enumerated among the ten expressions of prophecy (see above s.v. *The word of HASHEM*). R' Elazar there differs with R' Yochanan and maintains that it is חָזוֹן that introduces the most foreboding prophecy, not דִּיבּוּר. Accordingly, both R' Yochanan and R' Elazar would agree that this verse is introducing a most fateful prophecy.

שֹׁמְרוֹן וִירוּשָׁלָםִ — *Samaria and Jerusalem.* Samaria was the capital of the Northern Kingdom and Jerusalem the capital of the Kingdom of Judah. Although Scripture mentions only the capital cities, it is actually referring to the entire kingdom.

When the Ten Tribes seceded from the House of David after the death of King Solomon (leaving only Judah and Benjamin loyal to Solomon's son, Rehoboam), their first king, Jeroboam son of Nebat, established Shechem as the capital of the newly founded Northern Kingdom (Kingdom of Israel) [see *I Kings*, Chap. 12], while Jerusalem remained the capital of the Kingdom of Judah. Years later, Omri, the sixth king of the Northern Kingdom, moved the capital to Samaria (see *I Kings* 16:24).

◆§ The Call to Micah

2. שִׁמְעוּ עַמִּים כֻּלָּם — *Hear, O peoples, all of you* [lit., *all of them*]. Hear, O tribes of Israel (*Radak; Metzudos*), inhabitants of Samaria and Jerusalem (*Mahari Kara*)! God is warning you and testifying against you because of your evil deeds (*Mahari Kara*). *Da'as Sofrim* suggests that Micah may be addressing all the nations of the world.

The verse seems somewhat ambiguous for it opens by addressing the people (tribes of Israel) directly and yet, in the very same phrase, uses a third-person pronoun — כֻּלָּם, *all of them* [in place of the expected second-person pronoun כֻּלְּכֶם, *all of you*], implying that they are being addressed indirectly. *Radak* and *Abarbanel* maintain that this is a peculiarity of the Scriptural form; *Radak* cites four similar cases. *Ibn Ezra* suggests that the word כֻּלָּם is unique in that it may be used as both a direct and indirect pronoun.

הַקְשִׁיבִי אֶרֶץ וּמְלֹאָהּ — *Be attentive O Land and its fullness.* The land is the Land of Israel, the land par excellence, and its fullness is the Israelite nation that inhabits it (*Radak*). There are three verbs that are used to express the ability to hear — שמע, האזן and הקשב. Although seemingly synonymous, each has its special use. שמע is used to express simple *hearing,* while האזן [from the root אֹזֶן, *ear*] expresses a readiness to *listen* to what is being said, to "incline one's ear" and to show interest. הקשב goes a step further. It expresses an anxiousness to hear more, to activate one's

1. Although Jeroboam, the first monarch of the Northern Kingdom of Israel, had been anointed by Ahijah Hashiloni at the command of God, nevertheless, the kings who reigned over Israel after him did so unjustly, for they created a dynasty other than from the House of David, which is forbidden (*Ramban, Genesis* 49:10) [see also *Rambam* and *Raavad, Hil. Melachim* 1:9; *Derashos Haran* 7].

ג יֱהֹוִ֛ה בָּכֶם֙ לְעֵ֔ד אֲדֹנָ֖י מֵהֵיכַ֥ל קָדְשֽׁוֹ׃ כִּֽי־הִנֵּ֥ה יְהֹוָ֖ה יֹצֵ֣א מִמְּקוֹמ֑וֹ וְיָרַ֥ד וְדָרַ֖ךְ עַל־°במותי אָֽרֶץ׃ ד וְנָמַ֤סּוּ הֶֽהָרִים֙ תַּחְתָּ֔יו וְהָעֲמָקִ֖ים יִתְבַּקָּ֑עוּ ה כַּדּוֹנַג֙ מִפְּנֵ֣י הָאֵ֔שׁ כְּמַ֖יִם מֻגָּרִ֥ים בְּמוֹרָֽד׃ בְּפֶ֤שַׁע יַֽעֲקֹב֙ כָּל־זֹ֔את וּבְחַטֹּ֖אות בֵּ֣ית יִשְׂרָאֵ֑ל מִֽי־פֶ֣שַׁע יַֽעֲקֹ֗ב הֲלוֹא֙ שֹׁמְר֔וֹן וּמִי֙ בָּמ֣וֹת יְהוּדָ֔ה הֲל֖וֹא יְרוּשָׁלִָֽם׃ ו וְשַׂמְתִּ֥י שֹׁמְר֖וֹן לְעִ֣י הַשָּׂדֶ֑ה

°בָּמֳתֵי ק׳

sense of hearing to receive a message fully (*R' Hirsch, Psalms* 5:3). Accordingly, Micah is instructing the nation not to simply hear what he is about to tell them but to be anxiously attentive to every word of the forthcoming prophecy and to understand its implications.

וִיהִי אֲדֹנָי יֱהוִֹה בָּכֶם לְעֵד — *And let the Lord* HASHEM/ELOHIM *be a witness against you.* Let G-d be a witness that I have prophesied in His Name and that I have admonished you and warned you of the consequences of your evil ways (*Rashi*).

The Name אֱלֹהִים is used when God appears as the God of Judgment. The Name יְהֹוָה denotes God as being merciful and compassionate (see ArtScroll *Genesis* 1:1, footnote). Thus, the combined Name of יהוה written as the tetragrammaton but pronounced אֱלֹהִים is interpreted by *Rashi* (*Deut.* 3:24) as רַחוּם בַּדִּין, the One Who is merciful in judgment. According to *Mizrachi* (ibid.), it expresses the plea that even in judgment, God should temper His decree with mercy. Furthermore, although God's action may appear at times as harsh and strict, in essence, it is a manifestation of His love and mercy. His severity is only an instrument of His love by which the foundations of a blissful future are built (*R' Hirsch, Genesis* 15:2).

אֲדֹנָי מֵהֵיכַל קָדְשׁוֹ — *The Lord from His holy Sanctuary.* I.e., from the heavens (*Radak, Ibn Ezra;* see *Psalms* 11:4, *II Chronicles* 30:27). G-d will look down from the heavens at your deeds and will testify regarding them (*Metzudos*). Alternatively, *G-d's sanctuaty* refers to the Holy Temple in Jerusalem [i.e., the place where His presence was continuously felt] (*Abarbanel;* see *Jonah* 2:5 and *Psalms* 5:8).

3. כִּי־הִנֵּה ה׳ יֹצֵא מִמְּקוֹמוֹ — *For behold,* HASHEM *is going forth from His place.*

This verse must be understood allegorically for God does not have any human characteristics and does not physically *go, come* or *tread* upon anything (see *Moreh Nevuchim* 2:29). Micah is prophetically describing the manner in which God's decree will come forth and trample the heights of the land (*Radak*). It will be as if God is leaving His throne of mercy and is ascending His throne of judgment to administer justice to the inhabitants of Samaria and Jerusalem (*Rashi; Metzudos*). *Malbim* sees a similarity to *Exodus* 11:4, where God states that He Himself will slay the Egyptian firstborn. Here too, God Himself will exact the punishment due and will not rely on Divine agents.

4. וְנָמַסּוּ הֶהָרִים תַּחְתָּיו — *The mountains will melt away under Him.* Scripture continues the metaphor introduced in the previous verse as it describes the fall of Samaria. The *mountains* refer to the haughty kings and officers, and the *valleys* refer to the multitudes of the nation (*Metzudos*). These towering mountains, the leaders of the nation, will be destroyed with ease, as fire melts wax (*Abarbanel*), fire metaphorically describing God's wrath (*Ibn Ezra; Abarbanel*).

HASHEM/ELOHIM be a witness against you, the Lord from His holy Sanctuary. [3] *For behold, HASHEM is going forth from His place; He will descend and trample the heights of the land.* [4] *The mountains will melt away under Him and the valleys will split open, like wax before a fire, like water flowing down a slope.* [5] *All this because of the transgression of Jacob, because of the sins of the House of Israel. Who [caused] the transgression of Jacob; was it not Samaria? Who [caused] the high places of Judah; was it not Jerusalem?* [6] *I will make Samaria into a mound in the field,*

כְּמַיִם מֻגָּרִים בְּמוֹרָד — *Like water flowing down a slope.* The suffering and destruction of the nation will be as catastrophic as if the mountains would melt and the valleys would split apart. They will melt so quickly that the molten mass will rush as forcefully as water cascading down a steep incline; their destruction will be swift (*Radak*). Alternatively, the *water flowing down a slope* is not referring to the molten mountains but to the *valleys,* the multitudes of the nation that will be split apart. The people of Israel will be split apart and scattered among the gentile nations like a waterfall whose water sprays in all directions as it hits the ground (*Ibn Ezra; Metzudos*). *Malbim* sees this as a reference to the destruction of the actual land; the mountains and the valleys will be destroyed.

◆§ The Transgressions of Samaria and Jerusalem

5. בְּפֶשַׁע יַעֲקֹב כָּל־זֹאת וּבְחַטֹּאות בֵּית יִשְׂרָאֵל ... — *All this because of the transgression of Jacob, because of the sins of the House of Israel ...*

Jacob and the *House of Israel* are both referring to the Ten Tribes of the Northern Kingdom. *Judah,* mentioned near the end of the verse, is referring to the Kingdom of Judah (*Radak; Metzudos*). Micah declares that the destruction described in the previous verse will take place because of the sins committed by the inhabitants of the two kingdoms. He then accuses the kings of both Samaria and Jerusalem for misleading their people and causing the proliferation of idolatry in their respective kingdoms for if the leaders would have discouraged these illicit practices, the people would have ceased sinning (*Radak*).

The Ten Tribes worshiped the calves of Jeroboam (*Radak*) and were steeped in idolatry (*Metzudos*). The people of Judah offered their sacrifices to God at the *bamos* (high places) rather than at the Temple Altar (*Malbim*) and would even build *bamos* for idolatry (*Metzudos*).

◆§ The Destruction of Samaria

6. וְשַׂמְתִּי שֹׁמְרוֹן לְעִי הַשָּׂדֶה ... — *I will make Samaria into a mound in the field ...* Because Samaria had been the cause of Jacob's sins, I will destroy the city and demolish its building with only heaps of stones remaining. Its ruins will resemble unattended fields full of mounds of earth (*Metzudos*). God's agent of destruction was the Assyrian king Shalmaneser, who captured Samaria after besieging it for three years. He exiled its inhabitants and populated the surrounding cities with foreign nations (*II Kings* 17:5,6,25).[1]

1. The Talmud (*Berachos* 58a) compares the destruction of Babylon to the destruction of Samaria and notes that although Samaria was destroyed and its inhabitants exiled, its land

א/ז־ט

לְמַטָּעֵי כָרֶם וְהִגַּרְתִּי לַגַּי אֲבָנֶיהָ וִיסֹדֶיהָ אֲגַלֶּה׃ ז וְכָל־פְּסִילֶיהָ יֻכַּתּוּ וְכָל־אֶתְנַנֶּיהָ יִשָּׂרְפוּ בָאֵשׁ וְכָל־עֲצַבֶּיהָ אָשִׂים שְׁמָמָה כִּי מֵאֶתְנַן זוֹנָה קִבָּצָה וְעַד־אֶתְנַן זוֹנָה יָשׁוּבוּ׃ ח עַל־זֹאת אֶסְפְּדָה וְאֵילִילָה אֵילְכָה °שילל וְעָרוֹם אֶעֱשֶׂה מִסְפֵּד כַּתַּנִּים וְאֵבֶל כִּבְנוֹת יַעֲנָה׃ ט כִּי אֲנוּשָׁה מַכּוֹתֶיהָ כִּי־בָאָה עַד־יְהוּדָה

°שׁוֹלָל ק׳

לְמַטָּעֵי כָרֶם — *A place to plant vineyards.*

The city of Samaria had been built on a mountain, an ideal location for planting superior vineyards. Micah foretells that Samaria will not be rebuilt but will be used for planting vineyards (*Radak*).

7. וְכָל־פְּסִילֶיהָ ... וְכָל־עֲצַבֶּיהָ — *All of its graven images ... and all of its idols.* A פֶּסֶל is any sculptured or carved image [a relief] that is worshiped (*Rashi, Exodus* 20:14). It is usually carved from wood or stone (*R' Hirsch*, ibid.; *Malbim*) and was often covered with gold or silver (*Radak*). The פֶּסֶל was believed to be the supreme idol while the עֶצֶב [idol] was viewed as the subordinate that carried out the instructions of the פֶּסֶל (*Malbim*).

וְכָל־פְּסִילֶיהָ יֻכַּתּוּ — *All of its graven images will be smashed.*

The attacking Assyrians will smash Samaria's idols and remove their gold and silver plating (*Metzudos*).

וְכָל־אֶתְנַנֶּיהָ יִשָּׂרְפוּ בָאֵשׁ — *And all of its [idolatrous] gifts will be burned in fire.*

When the Assyrians will capture the city they will set it afire and destroy the ornate gifts of gold and silver together with the fine vestments that the Samaritans had brought to their idols (*Radak*).

וְכָל־עֲצַבֶּיהָ אָשִׂים שְׁמָמָה — *And I will make all of its idols desolate.*

The prophecy is referring to the golden calves of Jeroboam among other idols. God will destroy them all (*Abarbanel*). Alternatively, עֲצַבִּים is referring to the *house* of idol worship. Not only will God destroy their idols but He will destroy their houses of idol worship as well (*Targum Yonasan; Radak*).

The word עֶצֶב actually means *worry* or *anger*. It is used as a synonym for idols because when the worshiper realizes that his god cannot offer him salvation, he becomes frustrated and angry (*Metzudos Tzion; Radak Shorashim*).

כִּי מֵאֶתְנַן זוֹנָה קִבָּצָה ... — *For they were collected as harlot's hire ...* Objects of wealth that had been gathered from the entire country and brought to Samaria to be presented as gifts to the idols (*Radak*) and all the valuables that had been donated to the false gods will be hauled away by the Assyrians to be presented to their idols. The previous part of the verse (אתנניה, Lit. harlot's wages) which states that the harlot's wages will be burned refers to items of lesser value which the enemy will not bother to plunder (*Abarbanel, Metzudos*).

Harlotry [זְנוּת] is a metaphor used throughout Scripture to describe turning away from G-d [see *Exodus* 34:15; *Leviticus* 17:7; *Judges* 2:17]. Just as the harlot [זוֹנָה, lit., *the one who turns away*] turns away from moral behavior to seek out the adulterers, so too does the idol worshiper turn away from G-d toward false gods (*Metzudos, Hosea* 1:2).

nevertheless remained a blessing to its neighbors for its fertile fields were used *for planting vineyards*. Babylon, however, remained a wasteland inhabited by wild beasts and birds.

a place to plant vineyards. I will roll away its stones to the valley and lay bare its foundations. [7] *All of its graven images will be smashed and all of its [idolatrous] gifts will be burned in fire, and I will make all of its idols desolate. For they were collected as harlot's hire, and they will revert to harlot's hire.* [8] *For this I will lament and wail; I will go about delirious and naked; I will make lamentation like the jackals and mourning like ostriches.* [9] *For her wound is grievous; for it has come to Judah;*

◆§ The Prophet's Grief

8. עַל־זֹאת אֶסְפְּדָה וְאֵילִילָה — *For this I will lament and wail.* After receiving the fateful prophecy regarding the nation, Micah expresses his grief and says that he will lament and wail over the destruction of the Land of Israel and over the exile of its people (*Radak*). Alternatively, he is lamenting over the destruction of the Kingdom of Judah and its capital, Jerusalem (*Metzudos*). Micah felt that the punishments that had been predicted regarding Samaria were due and just for they had followed the false gods [and did not repent their sins even after the constant pleadings of the prophets]. But his feelings regarding the punishments of the Kingdom of Judah were quite different. For *their* punishments, Micah says, *I will lament and wail,* for during the days of Jotham, idol worship was not practiced in Judah (*Malbim*).

אֵילְכָה שׁוֹלָל וְעָרוֹם — *I will go about delirious and naked.*

He continues to describe his extreme pain and anguish and says that the destruction of his land and people will cause him to act as if he has gone mad, tearing his garments and going naked (*Mahari Kara*). Although Micah's future conduct seems extreme and puzzling, *Metzudos* explains that the prophet never really intended to conduct himself in this bizarre manner. It is only to accentuate the anguish, the terrible pain and mourning that will overcome him that he exaggerated his future behavior. Alternatively, Micah is not describing his own actions, but those of the nation. They will go into exile chained, naked, lamenting and wailing as they are driven from their land (*Targum Yonasan*). [Perhaps the personal pronoun, I, is used by Micah for he, too, was a member of the Kingdom of Judah and identified with them.]

אֶעֱשֶׂה מִסְפֵּד כַּתַּנִּים וְאֵבֶל כִּבְנוֹת יַעֲנָה — *I will make lamentation like the jackals and mourning like ostriches.* תַּנִּים are a species of snake (*Radak, Shorashim* s.v. תנן; *Metzudos*). In Modern Hebrew a תַּן is a jackal. See ArtScroll, *Eichah* 4:3, for further discussion. בְּנוֹת יַעֲנָה are a species of bird (*Metzudos*). The sounds vocalized by these creatures are similar to sounds of wailing and lament (*Radak*).

9. כִּי אֲנוּשָׁה מַכּוֹתֶיהָ כִּי־בָאָה עַד־יְהוּדָה — *For her wound is grievous; for it has come to Judah.* Micah foresaw that the blows that the Ten Tribes will receive during the Assyrian invasion will be terribly severe. Although the subject of the verse מַכּוֹתֶיהָ is plural, and אֲנוּשָׁה is singular, Scripture means that each of the punishments that Samaria will in fact receive, the battles, the famine and the plagues, will be powerful and devastating, so much so that it will spread to the Kingdom of Judah (*Radak; Metzudos*).

י נָגַע עַד־שַׁעַר עַמִּי עַד־יְרוּשָׁלָֽם׃ בְּגַת֙ אַל־תַּגִּידוּ בָּכ֖וֹ אַל־תִּבְכּ֑וּ בְּבֵ֣ית לְעַפְרָ֔ה עָפָ֖ר °התפלשתי׃ יא עִבְרִ֥י לָכֶ֛ם יוֹשֶׁ֥בֶת שָׁפִ֖יר עֶרְיָה־בֹ֑שֶׁת לֹ֣א יָצְאָ֗ה יוֹשֶׁ֙בֶת֙ צַֽאֲנָ֔ן מִסְפַּד֙ בֵּ֣ית הָאֵ֔צֶל

°הִתְפַּלָּֽשִׁי ק׳

Alternatively, *Rashi* sees the Ten Tribes as the subject of the verse and translates כִּי אֲנוּשָׁה, *for she is grievously ill,* מַכּוֹתֶיהָ, *from her wounds,* and explains that this is a description of Israel's weakened condition due to the punishments it will receive. *Mahari Kara* and *Abarbanel* understand that the severity of the punishment was not that it spread and engulfed the Kingdom of Judah but rather that the Ten Tribes of the Northern Kingdom of Israel were exiled from Samaria, never to return.

Malbim maintains that this verse refers not to the exiles and sufferings inflicted by Israel's enemies but rather to the wounds inflicted by the Northern Kingdom upon the Kingdom of Judah during the days of Ahaz. At that time, Pekah ben Remaliah [the nineteenth king of the Ten Tribes] killed one hundred and twenty thousand members of the Kingdom of Judah [see *II Chronicles* 28:6].

נָגַע עַד־שַׁעַר עַמִּי — *It has extended until the gate of My people.* The destruction extended from Samaria through the Kingdom of Judah to the city of Jerusalem. Scripture often uses *gate* when referring to the actual city; see *Deut.* 17:8 (*Metzudos*).

10. בְּגַת אַל־תַּגִּידוּ — *Tell it not in Gath.* Although the inhabitants of Gath undoubtedly knew of the destruction of Samaria and Jerusalem, nevertheless, Micah adopts the phraseology of those who express their grief in dirges [*wishing* that the enemy should not hear of Israel's suffering or their weeping lest the enemy rejoice]. Compare *II Samuel* 1:20 (*Radak*). *Malbim* explains that Micah is saying, "Do not let the Philistines of Gath hear that you have been defeated, for they may then try to overpower you; but go far away, to Aphrah, and mourn there."

The Philistine city of Gath was located between Jerusalem and the Mediterranean coast. It was captured by King David (see *II Samuel* 8:11 and *Rashi*) and later by Uziah, the twelfth monarch of the Kingdom of Judah (*II Chronicles* 26:6). During the interim period it seems to have been under Philistine rule (see *Amos* 6:2). After Uziah's campaign it was under the authority and jurisdiction of the Kingdom of Judah (*Malbim*).

בְּבֵית לְעַפְרָה עָפָר הִתְפַּלָּשִׁי — *In each house of Aphrah, wallow in the dirt.* Rolling in dirt or ashes was common practice among mourners. Hence Micah is lamenting grievously. "For the houses of Aphrah that are no more, roll in the dirt and mourn their destruction" (*Radak*).

Although Micah seems to mourn the destruction of only several Israelite cities, he actually was mourning the desolation of the entire land. These cities were selected because they are phonetically similar to the expressions of mourning that Micah uses — לָשׁוֹן נוֹפֵל עַל לָשׁוֹן — paronomasia, a play on words (*Rashi; Radak; Tosafos Rid*). [עָפָר, *dirt*, being a play on the city עַפְרָה. Some also attribute the written text התפלשתי to a play on פְּלֶשֶׁת, Philistia, of which Gath was a major city.] The use of this device is a common practice among composers of poetry and dirges (*Radak*).

There were two cities in the Land of Israel with the name Aphrah: one in the territory belonging to the tribe of Manasseh (*Rashi* to *Judges* 6:11) and one belonging to the tribe of Benjamin (*Joshua* 18:23). *Rashi* understands Aphrah of our verse to be of Manasseh's territory while *Radak* and *Malbim* cite *Joshua* 18:23 as belongings to the tribe of Benjamin.

11. עִבְרִי לָכֶם יוֹשֶׁבֶת שָׁפִיר — *Pass on [to exile], O inhabitant of Saphir.* The prophet describes the exile of various cities of Israel. Starting with the city of Saphir (*Rashi*), he foretells that its inhabitants will be led into captivity with their nakedness uncovered (*Targum Yonasan*), in torn and tattered clothes (*Da'as Sofrim*).

it has extended until the gate of My people, up to Jerusalem. [10] *Tell it not in Gath; weep not at all; in each house of Aphrah, wallow in the dirt.* [11] *Pass on [to exile], O inhabitant of Saphir, with nakedness uncovered. The inhabitant of Zaanan did not go forth in lamentation for Beth-ezel;*

The exact location of this city is unknown, for it is not mentioned elsewhere in Scripture (*Da'as Sofrim*).

A grammatical irregularity at the opening of the verse warrants clarification. The verb עִבְרִי, *pass on*, is feminine singular, while לָכֶם is male plural. One would expect the grammatically consistent phrase עִבְרִי לָךְ rather than the hybrid עִבְרִי לָכֶם. The commentators explain that Micah uses עִבְרִי to address the entire assemblage of people as one unit [the Hebrew word for assemblage of people (כְּנֵסִיָּה) is a word of feminine gender]. He uses לָכֶם to address each individual (*Rashi; Radak; Tosafos Rid*). *Da'as Sofrim* understands עִבְרִי to be an address to the leaders of the city [the group of leaders also being a כְּנֵסִיָּה].

עֶרְיָה־בֹשֶׁת — *With nakedness uncovered. Metzudos* and *Malbim* again note the use of paronomasia — עֶרְיָה־בֹשֶׁת being a play on שָׁפִיר — for other than being the name of a city, שָׁפִיר is the word usually used for the fetus or placenta that is expelled from a woman's womb after birth. In a similar vein, *Rashi* translates שָׁפִיר as *a stillborn child.*

Radak maintains that Scripture is not employing paronomasia in this verse but a different device often used in poetry and dirges. Translating שָׁפִיר as *beautiful* (see *Genesis* 49:21), he explains that at times Scripture may use a certain word at the onset of the verse and close with a word that conveys a diametrically opposite picture than was originally presented. This tool is employed to give a very descriptive and clear picture of what is being stated. This verse demonstrates how the *beautiful* [שָׁפִיר] nation was ultimately expelled from its land בְּעֶרְיָה בֹשֶׁת [a phrase indicative of ugliness].

לֹא יָצְאָה יוֹשֶׁבֶת צַאֲנָן ... — *The inhabitant of Zaanan did not go forth ...* This translation follows most commentators who join this section with the end of the verse. *Radak* notes that Micah is again employing paronomasia for יָצְאָה and צַאֲנָן have similar sounds.

Zaanan and Beth-ezel were neighboring cities. When the enemy attacked, the inhabitants of Beth-ezel were the first to be exiled, wailing and lamenting their lot. Their neighbors, the inhabitants of Zaanan, did not come to console them. Instead, they remained in their own city, anticipating their own impending doom (*Radak; Metzudos*). Alternatively, *Targum Yonasan* followed by *Rashi* view the last part of the verse as consisting of independent clauses and render לֹא יָצְאָה יוֹשֶׁבֶת צַאֲנָן, *the inhabitants of Zaanan will not escape. Rashi* understands the next part of the verse, בֵּית הָאֵצֶל, not as a proper noun but as the *adjacent house, the house next door* [אֵצֶל translated as *near*]. He maintains that the houses referred to are those that were taken by force from others so that the landowners could extend their properties. He therefore explains that each person will lament the loss of his house together with his neighbor.

The identity of Zaanan is unclear, for there is no other mention of this city in Scripture. A city of similar name, Zanon, is listed in the Book of *Joshua* (15:37) among the cities of Judah. *Malbim* assumes that they are identical. [Perhaps the א is added to make צַאֲנָן sound more similar to יָצְאָה.] *Tosafos Rid* maintains that Zaanan is not the name of a city but is synonymous with the word שַׁאֲנַן, *peaceful;*

יב יִקַּח מִכֶּם עֶמְדָּתוֹ: כִּי־חָלָה לְטוֹב יוֹשֶׁבֶת מָרוֹת כִּי־יָרַד רָע מֵאֵת יהוה לְשַׁעַר יְרוּשָׁלִָם: יג רְתֹם הַמֶּרְכָּבָה לָרֶכֶשׁ יוֹשֶׁבֶת לָכִישׁ רֵאשִׁית חַטָּאת הִיא לְבַת־צִיּוֹן כִּי־בָךְ נִמְצְאוּ פִּשְׁעֵי יִשְׂרָאֵל: יד לָכֵן תִּתְּנִי שִׁלּוּחִים עַל מוֹרֶשֶׁת גַּת

it is a description of the peacefulness of the city. [Since the letters ז,ס,ש,ר,צ are all formed in the same area of the mouth, they may be used interchangeably.]

יִקַּח מִכֶּם עֶמְדָּתוֹ — *[The enemy] will seize [the cost of] his stay from you.* The enemy will demand payment for the time he spent standing in position while besieging the city. He will plunder the city, take all its possessions and send its inhabitants into exile (*Radak*).

Alternatively, since you stood and ignored your neighbors' cries while they were being exiled, יִקַּח מִכֶּם עֶמְדָּתוֹ, the enemy will repay *each of you* for your callous *standing by* and send you into exile (*Metzudos*). *Rashi* explains that the lament and anguish that the land thieves caused [מִסְפַּד בֵּית הָאֵצֶל] will in turn cause the structures that they erected [*that are standing*] to be destroyed.

12. כִּי־חָלָה לְטוֹב יוֹשֶׁבֶת מָרוֹת — *For the inhabitants of Maroth were anguished over [the lost] good.* Most commentators take Maroth to be the name of a city[1] (*Ibn Ezra; Radak; Metzudos*) and explain that as the inhabitants of Maroth were recalling God's benevolence of which they had been the recipients, they were filled with *anguish and pain* for what they had lost. The evil that befell them was entirely from God and not a mere coincidence (*Radak; Metzudos*).

Alternatively, *Rashi* translates מָרוֹת not as a proper noun but as an adjective meaning *rebellious*: the nation had rebelled against the words of the prophets. He also relates חָלָה to יַחֵל (*Psalms* 130:5-7), *to hope* or *to anxiously wait* (*R' Hirsch* ibid.). He explains that although she (Jerusalem) had been at ease and had *hoped for the best*, only evil will descend from Heaven due to her rebellious actions against the prophets. Accordingly, *Rashi* renders the second כִּי in the verse *but* rather than *because*.

לְשַׁעַר יְרוּשָׁלִָם — *To the gate of Jerusalem.* Even if Maroth is not identical with Jerusalem, the meaning of this phrase can be that the evil extended *even* to the gate of Jerusalem — comp. v. 9 (*Radak*). See Comm. ibid.

13. רְתֹם הַמֶּרְכָּבָה לָרֶכֶשׁ יוֹשֶׁבֶת לָכִישׁ — *Fasten the chariot to the swift steed, O inhabitant of Lachish.* רְתֹם is an Arabic word (*Rashi*) meaning to harness or tie (*Targum Yonasan; Rashi; Radak*). Through the idea of the swift animal, Micah is exhorting the inhabitants of Lachish to quickly escape into exile before the enemy overtakes their city (*Rashi; Radak*). *Radak* and *Metzudos* both note that רֶכֶשׁ is a play on words [לָשׁוֹן נוֹפֵל עַל לָשׁוֹן] to לָכִישׁ, for both words have similar sounds.

The classical commentators do not identify רֶכֶשׁ with any particular animal. They merely write, "a swift animal" (*Rashi; Radak; Metzudos*). *Ibn Janach* (*Shorashim* s.v. רכש) translates: good, young horses. *Ralbag* (*I Kings* 5:6) renders: swiftest horses. *Radak* (*Shorashim* s.v. רכש) speculates that רֶכֶשׁ is a species other than horses and cites *I Kings*

1. Some speculate that it may be identified as Jarmuth, a city in the portion of Issachar (*Joshua* 21:29) which is also referred to as רָאמוֹת (*I Chronicles* 6:58) or רָמוֹת (*Joshua* 19:21). *Pardes Yosef* (vol. I p. 226) suggests that perhaps Maroth is the city Ma'arath located in the portion of Judah (see *Joshua* 15:59). The name of the city assumes this variant form due to the anguish and pain portrayed by Micah in his dirge, for מָרוֹת means bitter. *Mahari Kara* takes Maroth to be synonymous with Jerusalem as evidenced by the end of the verse.

[the enemy] will seize [the cost of] his stay from you. [12]*For the inhabitants of Maroth were anguishesd over [the lost] good, but evil came down from before* HASHEM, *to the gate of Jerusalem.* [13]*Fasten the chariot to the swift steed, O inhabitant of Lachish; that was the origin of sin for the people of Zion, for it was in you that the trangressions of Israel were found.* [14]*Therefore, send gifts to Moresheth-gath!*

5:6 as proof. For Scripture writes, "And barley and straw for the horses and *rechesh.*"

רֵאשִׁית חַטָּאת הִיא לְבַת־צִיּוֹן — *That was the origin of sin for the people of Zion.* Lachish, although situated in the territories of the Kingdom of Judah, was in close proximity to the Northern Kingdom and was the first area affected by her evil ways (*Ibn Ezra*) and introduced idol worship to the inhabitants of Zion (*Metzudos*).

Ba'al worship had been introduced to the Northern Kingdom by Jezebel, the Sidonite wife of Ahab [אַחְאָב], the eighth king of Israel, and it was she who influenced him to spread its worship among the people. The inhabitants of Lachish followed their northern neighbors and they too proceeded to worship Ba'al. [They were led by Amatziah, the eleventh monarch of Judah, who had taken refuge there (see *II Kings* 14:19). He was the first of the kings of Judah to embrace idol worship.] They, in turn, introduced this form of worship to their brethren who inhabited the rest of the Kingdom of Judah (*Radak*).

בַּת־צִיּוֹן, lit., *daughter of Zion,* is a term often used by the prophets, most often by Isaiah, as a reference to the inhabitants of Jerusalem. Originally, Zion was a fortress in southeastern Jerusalem that had been inhabited by the Jebusites and was captured by King David [see *II Samuel* 5:7. Note *Psalms* 149:2 where the Jewish people are referred to as the *sons* of Zion].

כִּי־בָךְ נִמְצְאוּ פִּשְׁעֵי יִשְׂרָאֵל — *For it was in you that the transgressions of Israel were found.* The *idols* of the Northern Kingdom were found in Lachish (*Metzudos*). Scripture does not write that the transgressions of Israel were *practiced* in Lachish but were *found* in Lachish, implying that Israel's transgressions were not rampant in Judah. *Da'as Sofrim* suggests that the multitudes of Judah did not practice idol worship. The transgressions were only *found* in Judah; only a small percentage of people actually practiced it.

14. לָכֵן תִּתְּנִי שִׁלּוּחִים עַל מוֹרֶשֶׁת גַּת — *Therefore, send gifts to Moresheth-gath.* שִׁלּוּחִים are large gifts (*Ibn Ezra; Radak; Metzudos*). Micah scornfully addresses the inhabitants of Lachish: "Since you practiced idol worship and you taught this practice to others, you will need the assistance of others to ward off the invading enemy." He therefore suggests that the people send gifts to the inhabitants of Moresheth-gath in the hope that they will be persuaded to assist the people of Judah" (*Radak*).

עַל מוֹרֶשֶׁת גַּת — *To Moresheth-gath.* Although the word עַל is usually translated *on*, there is Scriptural proof that at times it is translated *to* (*Radak*). Moresheth-gath was actually the Philistine city of Gath often mentioned in Scripture. It was renamed Moresheth-gath when the Philistines recaptured it from the Jewish people, thereby making the Philistines the *inheritors of Gath* [Moresheth from the Hebrew word *yerushah*]. It is as if Micah is saying, "Look where your transgressions have gotten you. The city of Gath had been captured by King David and was our inheritance; but due to your sins it has now become a Philistine legacy. You must now humiliate yourselves and try to bribe the Philistines to offer you protection" (*Radak*).

א/טו־טז

טו בָּתֵּי אַכְזִיב לְאַכְזָב לְמַלְכֵי יִשְׂרָאֵל׃ עֹד הַיֹּרֵשׁ אָבִי לָךְ יוֹשֶׁבֶת מָרֵשָׁה עַד־עֲדֻלָּם יָבוֹא כְּבוֹד טז יִשְׂרָאֵל׃ קָרְחִי וָגֹזִּי עַל־בְּנֵי תַּעֲנוּגָיִךְ הַרְחִבִי קָרְחָתֵךְ כַּנֶּשֶׁר כִּי גָלוּ מִמֵּךְ׃

ב/א

א הוֹי חֹשְׁבֵי־אָוֶן וּפֹעֲלֵי רָע עַל־מִשְׁכְּבוֹתָם בְּאוֹר הַבֹּקֶר

Alternatively, *Malbim* explains that Moreshah and Gath were actually two distinct cities, adjacent to each other. The walls of Gath had been destroyed by Uziah [the ninth king of Judah] during his successful campaign to capture the city. Afterward, the inhabitants of neighboring Moreshah protected Gath and saw to it that the Philistines would not retake it from Judah. Hence, the composite name Moresheth-gath.

Rashi understands this verse as an admonishment to the nation for forsaking the Davidic dynasty and defecting to Pekah ben Remaliah, the king of the Northern Kingdom. Micah is saying, "Since you dismissed the Davidic dynasty that bequeathed the city of Gath to you, when Pekah will fall you will suffer from his downfall, as well" [see *Sanhedrin* 102a and *Rashi* thereon].

בָּתֵּי אַכְזִיב לְאַכְזָב — *The houses of Achzib will become a lost cause* [lit., *are a dried-out spring*]. Just as one who had set his hope on getting water to quench his thirst is severely disappointed upon realizing that no water is in fact available, you will also be disillusioned when you realize that you had placed your hope in false gods (*Radak*).

As mentioned earlier, the inhabitants of Achzib rebelled against their king, Ahaz [the eleventh monarch of Judah], and instead followed Pekah ben Remaliah. Micah is telling his fellow members of Judah that their defection to Pekah ben Remaliah was a futile move, for when the enemy will arrive he will destroy the houses of Achzib and tear their ties with the Northern Kingdom (*Rashi; Metzudos*). *Radak*, however, explains that *the houses of Achzib* refer to the houses of idol worship in which the people had placed their hope. With their destruction, the nation will realize that their hope had been placed in *false* (כזב) gods.

The city of Achzib was located in the territories of the land of Judah (*Rashi; Radak*) [see *Joshua* 15:44]. *Ibn Ezra* and *Radak* maintain that it is identical with the Biblical city of Kezib [see *Genesis* 38:5].

לְמַלְכֵי יִשְׂרָאֵל — *To the kings of Israel.* According to *Rashi*, the meaning of this phrase is that the people of Achzib would realize their mistake of defecting *to the kings of Israel.* According to *Radak*, however, who explained that the sin of the people of Achzib was idol-worship, what is the connection to *the kings of Israel*? Citing many verses of Scriptural proof, *Radak* explains that the monarchs of the Kingdom of Judah are often referred to as the Kings of Israel [for Judah, too, was one of the Twelve Tribes of Israel].

Scripture again employs paronomasia, אַכְזָב being a play on אַכְזִיב (*Rashi; Radak*).

15. עֹד הַיֹּרֵשׁ אָבִי לָךְ יוֹשֶׁבֶת מָרֵשָׁה — *I will yet bring a dispossessor against you, O inhabitant of Mareshah.* The enemy dispossessor is the Assyrian army led by Sennacherib [see *II Kings* 18:13 — Sennacherib had captured all the fortified cities of Judah during the fourteenth year of Hezekiah's reign] (*Radak*). Alternatively, *Metzudos* identifies Nebuchadnezzar as the dispossessor [see *II Kings* Chap. 25].

Rashi, citing a Midrashic source, explains that the enemy is the Chaldeans and the descendants of Shem's firstborn son, Elam [identified by R' Saadiah Gaon as the inhabitants of Persia and Media]. According to this Midrash, the Land of Israel was originally to be given to the descendants of Elam but due to the love God had for our ancestors, it was given to the descendants of Arpachshad, Shem's third

The houses of Achzib will become a lost cause to the kings of Israel. [15] *I will yet bring a dispossessor against you, O inhabitant of Mareshah; the glory of Israel will withdraw to Adullam.* [16] *Make yourself bald and pull out your hair for the children of your delight; make your baldness broad like an eagle's, for they have departed from you.*

[1] *Woe to those who devise iniquity and plan evil upon their beds; at the morning's light*

son [see *Genesis* (Chs.10,11) where the Patriarch Abraham's lineage is traced to Eber, Arpachshad's second son]. Now that the nation had sinned, God says, "I will bring the Chaldeans and the descendants of Elam [הַיֹּרֵשׁ, *the original inheritor*] upon them. [*Ibn Ezra* rejects this explanation without citing any source or giving any reason.]

The commentators again note the לָשׁוֹן נוֹפֵל עַל לָשׁוֹן: Mareshah [מָרֵשָׁה] being a play on יוֹרֵשׁ (*Rashi; Radak*).

עַד־עֲדֻלָּם יָבוֹא כְּבוֹד יִשְׂרָאֵל — *The glory of Israel will withdraw to Adullam.* The dispossessor will remove the glory of Israel even as far as the city of Adullam; for he will plunder the wealth of the entire land (*Metzudos*).

Radak identifies Adullam as a city of Judah. [See *Joshua* 15:34 where Adullam is mentioned as a city of the northern lowlands of Judah.]

16. קָרְחִי וָגֹזִּי — *Make yourself bald and pull out your hair.* The prophet is figuratively addressing the actual cities and land of Judah and telling them to mourn for their exiled inhabitants. He pictures the land as tearing out its hair.

Some say that קָרְחִי is *to make one's head bald* and גֹּזִּי is *to tear out one's hair* (*Rashi; Mahari Kara*). Others say that קָרְחִי is *to tear out one's hair* while גֹּזִּי is *to cut with scissors* (*Radak; Metzudos*).

Although the Torah explicitly prohibits the making of bald patches (*Deut.* 14:1), this prohibition applies only when the bald patches are made as an expression of grief over death. When done for any other reason, it is permitted (*Rambam, Mishneh Torah, Hilchos Avodah Zarah* 12:15; *Shulchan Aruch* Y.D. 180:9).

עַל־בְּנֵי תַּעֲנוּגָיִךְ — *For the children of your delight.* Our translation follows *Radak* who cities *Lamentations* 4:2 as his source. According to this view, Micah is referring to the nation as it appeared in its former glory, i.e., the precious, beloved nation.

Alternatively, *Targum Yonasan* and *Metzudos* translate *your pampered [delicate] children.* [This would seem to refer to the nation that had become spoiled and accustomed to having all the enjoyments and delights that they wished.]

הַרְחִבִי קָרְחָתֵךְ כַּנֶּשֶׁר — *Make your baldness broad like an eagle's.* At times, the eagle sheds much of his feathers (*Rashi; Radak*). [*Radak* explains that this occurs once in ten years.]

II

◈ Micah Rebukes the Nation

1. הוֹי חֹשְׁבֵי־אָוֶן וּפֹעֲלֵי רָע עַל־מִשְׁכְּבוֹתָם ... — *Woe to those who devise iniquity and plan evil upon their beds ...* Micah now points out the depths to which the nation had fallen. Not only do they rob and steal during the daylight hours but even while lying in bed at night, a time reserved for reflection [see *Psalms* 4:5], they scheme and plan to do evil (*Radak*).

ב יַעֲשׂוּהָ כִּי יֶשׁ־לְאֵל יָדָם: וְחָמְדוּ שָׂדוֹת וְגָזָלוּ וּבָתִּים וְנָשָׂאוּ וְעָשְׁקוּ גֶּבֶר וּבֵיתוֹ וְאִישׁ וְנַחֲלָתוֹ: ג לָכֵן כֹּה אָמַר יהוה הִנְנִי חֹשֵׁב עַל־הַמִּשְׁפָּחָה הַזֹּאת רָעָה אֲשֶׁר לֹא־תָמִישׁוּ מִשָּׁם צַוְּארֹתֵיכֶם וְלֹא תֵלְכוּ רוֹמָה כִּי עֵת רָעָה הִיא: ד בַּיּוֹם הַהוּא יִשָּׂא עֲלֵיכֶם מָשָׁל וְנָהָה נְהִי נִהְיָה אָמַר שָׁדוֹד נְשַׁדֻּנוּ חֵלֶק עַמִּי יָמִיר אֵיךְ יָמִישׁ לִי לְשׁוֹבֵב שָׂדֵינוּ יְחַלֵּק:

Although the evil actions were only in the planning stage, and God does not usually punish a Jew for merely thinking of committing a sin, this did not apply to the people of Micah's generation, for their sinful acts were sure to occur the very next morning (*Malbim*). They have the ability to carry out their evil plan, for there is no one to stop them (*Metzudos*).

אֵל is a non-sacred noun denoting power (*Ibn Ezra*).

2. וְחָמְדוּ שָׂדוֹת וְגָזָלוּ — *They covet fields and they rob [them].* If one desired a particular field or house, he would offer to buy it from its owner. However, if the owner refused to sell it, he would take it by force (*Radak*).

R' Hirsch differentiates between תַּאֲוָה and חֶמְדָּה and explains that תַּאֲוָה is an inner longing or lust. חֶמְדָּה, however, is a longing which proceeds to action (*Exodus* 20:14). Hence, Scripture does not write הִתְאַוּוּ שָׂדוֹת but חָמְדוּ שָׂדוֹת וְגָזָלוּ — they followed their longing with action. They stole fields and houses for which they had longed.

According to *Rambam* (*Mishneh Torah, Hil. Gezeilah* 1:9), one who covets his friend's possessions, and pesters him incessantly until he acquires them from him, transgresses the injunction of לֹא תַחְמֹד even if he pays a high price for them. However, see *Tosafos* to *Sanhedrin* 25b who states a different view.

וְעָשְׁקוּ גֶּבֶר וּבֵיתוֹ — *They oppress a man and his household.*

Our translation of עֹשֶׁק follows *Radak* and *Metzudos*. If the landowner refused to relinquish his property, he would be severely beaten and held captive, thereby oppressing him both physically and economically (*Radak*). Other translations are to defraud or to take cunningly (*Ibn Ezra*) or to hold back that which was initially and willingly given by the owner (*Rambam — Mishneh Torah, Hil. Gezeilah* 1:3,4). *R' Hirsch* (*Deuteronomy* 28:25) explains that גֶּזֶל is to rob one of his possessions while עֹשֶׁק is to rob one of his rights. Scripture may then be saying: Not only did these people steal their neighbors' properties but they stole their rights as well by not allowing them to live peacefully.

3. לָכֵן כֹּה אָמַר ה׳ הִנְנִי חֹשֵׁב עַל־הַמִּשְׁפָּחָה הַזֹּאת רָעָה — *Therefore, thus said* H*ASHEM*: *Behold, I am devising evil against this family.* [Micah is foretelling that the nation will receive a severe punishment for the crimes they have committed.]

Although the nation had already sinned, G-d is not quick to execute evil against His nation. It is yet in the "planning stage" [perhaps the nation will repent and forestall its arrival] (*Da'as Sofrim*). Others note the similarity of this verse to verse 1 [*devise iniquity and plan evil*] pointing out that G-d repays His creatures measure for measure — מִדָּה כְּנֶגֶד מִדָּה.

עַל־הַמִּשְׁפָּחָה הַזֹּאת, *against this family*, means against the Jewish people. [See *Genesis* 12:2; *Jeremiah* 10:25 where *nations* are referred to as *families*] (*Radak; Metzudos*). Alternatively, *Targum Yonasan* renders דָּרָא הָדֵין, *this*

they carry it out, for there is power in their hand. [2]*They covet fields and they rob [them], [they covet] houses and they take [them]; they oppress a man and his household, a person and his heritage.*

[3]*Therefore, thus said* HASHEM:

Behold, I am devising evil against this family, from which you will not extricate your necks; you will not walk erect, for it will be a bad time. [4]*On that day he will recite a parable about you; he will lament, "A lament has come to be!" He will say, "We have been utterly plundered! [God] is exchanging the portion of my people! How could He return what was mine when our field is apportioned to the enemy?"*

generation, for God is planning evil against the entire generation.

לֹא־תָמִישׁוּ מִשָּׁם צַוְּארֹתֵיכֶם — *You will not extricate your necks.* Scripture is portraying the nation's suffering and punishment as a crushing yoke upon their necks. God's punishment of the nation will be such that they will not be able to save themselves from it (*Radak; Metzudos*). Times will be so terrible that one will not even be capable of lifting his head due to the burden and yoke of suffering (*Radak*). *Malbim* notes that if times are peaceful and calamity strikes a particular area, one can still hope that he will be spared. But, if *it will be a bad time* — if the entire world is engulfed in a catastrophic upheaval — then there is no hope for any area.

4. בַּיּוֹם הַהוּא יִשָּׂא עֲלֵיכֶם מָשָׁל — *On that day he will recite a parable about you.* On the day that G-d will exact punishment from you, the one who laments over you will recite a dirge about you (*Metzudos*). This is referring to a false prophet whose advice and predictions had not materialized and he therefore laments and recites dirges. It is referred to as a parable, because he expresses his lamentations in parables (*Radak*)

Throughout the days of the monarchy there were false prophets who contested the words of the true prophets. While the prophets of God had been demanding self-examination of the people and warning them of imminent destruction, the false prophets were reinforcing the wishes and hopes of the people, persuading them that just as previous dangers had passed, so would the present ones [see *I Kings* Chap. 22; *Jeremiah* 28:2-4, ibid. 29:26,27; *Behold a People*, pp. 356,357].

וְנָהָה נְהִי נִהְיָה — *He will lament, "A lament has come to be!"* Our translation follows *Rashi* who relates נִהְיָה to הָיָה, *to be.* Accordingly, the translation of the verse is וְנָהָה, *and he will lament,* נְהִי נִהְיָה, *a lament has come to be.* Alternative translations are *and mourn a bitter lament* (*Radak*) or *to moan* as one does when ill (quoted by *Radak* and *Ibn Ezra*).

שָׁדוֹד נְשַׁדֻּנוּ ... — *We have been utterly plundered!* ... As he laments, he expresses his despair. The enemy has plundered our land and oppressed us. The land that had been apportioned to our nation has now been given to the enemy. How will He ever *return to me* the fields that have been divided by the enemy? (*Rashi*). The false prophet declares that he thought God was going to return the fields that the enemy had plundered. But he saw that he was mistaken. The enemy has strengthened his hold on the fields and has divided them among his own nation (*Radak; Ibn Ezra*).

ה לָכֵן לֹא־יִהְיֶה לְךָ מַשְׁלִיךְ חֶבֶל בְּגוֹרָל
ו בִּקְהַל יהוה: אַל־תַּטִּפוּ יַטִּיפוּן לֹא־יַטִּפוּ
ז לָאֵלֶּה לֹא יִסַּג כְּלִמּוֹת: הֶאָמוּר בֵּית־יַעֲקֹב
הֲקָצַר רוּחַ יהוה אִם־אֵלֶּה מַעֲלָלָיו הֲלוֹא
ח דְבָרַי יֵיטִיבוּ עִם הַיָּשָׁר הוֹלֵךְ: וְאֶתְמוּל עַמִּי
לְאוֹיֵב יְקוֹמֵם מִמּוּל שַׂלְמָה אֶדֶר תַּפְשִׁטוּן

5. לָכֵן לֹא־יִהְיֶה לְךָ — *Therefore, you will have no one.* Micah is addressing the subjects of verse 2. Since they robbed the people of their fields and homes, they will leave no descendant that will repossess the land when God will eventually bring the nation back to the Land of Israel (*Ibn Ezra*). Alternatively, *Radak,* who identifies the lamenters as the false prophets, explains that Micah is addressing these false prophets. Since it is only due to their false prophecies of hope and comfort that the enemy was sent to seize the land, no descendant of theirs will remain to inherit the land (*Radak*).

מַשְׁלִיךְ חֶבֶל בְּגוֹרָל — *One who casts [the surveyor's] line for the lot.* When one wished to divide or apportion his property, he measured its boundaries with a cord [see *Bava Basra,* Chapter 7, Mishnah 3].

בִּקְהַל ה׳ — *In the congregation of Hashem.*

Although the Ten Tribes had sinned grievously, they still did not lose their unique status of being קְהַל ה׳, the nation of Hashem (*Da'as Sofrim*).

6. אַל־תַּטִּפוּ יַטִּיפוּן — *"Do not preach!" those who preach.* Micah is instructing his fellow prophets to refrain from reprimanding the nation lest the prophets be the objects of mockery (*Rashi*).

Alternatively, *Ibn Ezra* and *Radak* translate *"Do not preach!" they preach,* and explain that these words are being uttered by the people. *They* are instructing the prophet to cease preaching, for they have no interest in what God has to say. *Abarbanel* explains that the poor and oppressed, whose causes the prophets champion, are advising the prophets to refrain from speaking the word of God, for the nation will show no embarrassment or shame at the prophetic rebuke.

לֹא־יַטִּפוּ לָאֵלֶּה — *They shall not preach to these [people].* Indeed, the prophets will not continue to preach and admonish the nation as they previously had, for now they would only be objects of mockery and shame (*Radak*).

לֹא יִסַּג כְּלִמּוֹת — *[So that] shame shall not overtake them.*

יִסַּג is the same as יַשִּׂג, *to encounter* (*Radak, Metzudos*).

Scripture uses כְּלִמָּה and not בּוּשָׁה to describe the shame of the prophets. בּוּשָׁה is the humiliation felt when one's hopes are frustrated; כְּלִמָּה is related to גֹּלֶם, *a shapeless body, an object devoid of form.* It is used to express the shame felt when one realizes his unworthiness (*R' Hirsch, Psalms* 35:4).

Yerushalmi (*Berachos* 1:4) notes that the words of the elders are more important than the words of the prophets [חֲמוּרִים דִּבְרֵי זְקֵנִים מִדִּבְרֵי נְבִיאִים]. For God told the prophets to cease preaching their prophetic words because the nation had no interest in them, but we never find God instructing the elders to cease their preaching. [See commentary of *Pnei Moshe* thereon.]

7. הֶאָמוּר בֵּית־יַעֲקֹב — *Should this be said by the House of Jacob?* When the people hear the foreboding prophetic words predicting the punishments that

[5]Therefore, you will have no one who casts [the surveyor's] line for the lot in the congregation of HASHEM. [6]"Do not preach!" those who preach, "They shall not preach to these [people], [so that] shame shall not overtake them." [7]Should this be said by the House of Jacob? Has HASHEM become short spirited? Are these His deeds? Behold, My ways are benevolent with the one who walks with uprightness. [8] Yesterday My people arose as an enemy [to its fellows]; for the sake of a garment, a mantle, you would strip them, [making] innocent passersby fugitives of war. [9]You

will befall the nation for their evil actions, they turn an accusing finger toward God and reply, הֲקָצַר רוּחַ ה׳, *"Has Hashem become short-spirited* — has God lost His patience? Or, perhaps He has lost the ability to bestow goodness and can now only inflict punishment?" The prophet expresses amazement upon hearing these complaints and retorts, "How can the House of Jacob truly utter these words?" (*Rashi*).

הֲלוֹא דְבָרַי יֵיטִיבוּ עִם הַיָּשָׁר הוֹלֵךְ — *Behold, My ways are benevolent with the one who walks with uprightness.* Do they not realize that God is conducting Himself in this manner because of their sinful actions? It is only evildoers and sinners who God punishes with such severity, but He bestows goodness upon the righteous (*Rashi*).

Alternatively, the *spirit of HASHEM* is referring to His prophetic words (*Ibn Ezra; Mahari Kara*). G-d's prophetic words are never "short." They always speak the truth (*Ibn Ezra*). Is it proper that they should be held back and not be uttered by the prophet? (*Mahari Kara*).

8. וְאֶתְמוּל — *Yesterday. Ibn Ezra* and *Radak* translate אֶתְמוּל as *yesterday*, as if the word were vowelized אֶתְמוֹל. *Radak* explains: The foreign enemy attack against you today is measure for measure for your having risen up against your weak and defenseless brothers yesterday [just a short time ago, too recently for you to be able to deny your guilt (*Metzudos*)]. Accordingly, לְאוֹיֵב, *as an enemy*, refers not to God but to the nation.

Alternatively, *Rashi* and *Mahari Kara* view וְאֶתְמוּל as a compound consisting of the words וְאֶת מוּל, lit., *that for which* (*Abarbanel*).

In the previous verse, Micah had stated that God is benevolent and kind and wishes to bestow goodness upon His nation if they conduct themselves in a righteous manner. The prophet now continues and explains, "But because they have acted wickedly, they have caused God to rise up as an enemy to His nation" (ibid.).

עַמִּי — *My people.* A term usually reserved to express God's affection for the Israelite nation (*Rashi, Numbers* 11:1). [Although Micah is reproaching the nation for their wicked actions, perhaps Scripture chose to use עַמִּי to emphasize the reproach by contrasting the status of Israel from what it actually was to what it should have been.]

מִמּוּל שַׂלְמָה אֶדֶר תַּפְשִׁטוּן — *For the sake of a garment, a mantle, you would strip them.* The people would steal the clothing and precious garments from unsuspecting travelers. This is one of the reasons that God does not bestow His goodness upon the nation (*Rashi*).

ט מְעֹבְרִים בֶּטַח שׁוּבֵי מִלְחָמָה: נְשֵׁי עַמִּי תְּגָרְשׁוּן מִבֵּית תַּעֲנֻגֶיהָ מֵעַל עֹלָלֶיהָ תִּקְחוּ הֲדָרִי לְעוֹלָם: י קוּמוּ וּלְכוּ כִּי לֹא־זֹאת הַמְּנוּחָה בַּעֲבוּר טָמְאָה תְּחַבֵּל וְחֶבֶל נִמְרָץ: יא לוּ־אִישׁ הֹלֵךְ רוּחַ וָשֶׁקֶר כִּזֵּב אַטִּף לְךָ לַיַּיִן וְלַשֵּׁכָר וְהָיָה מַטִּיף הָעָם הַזֶּה:

מֵעֹבְרִים בֶּטַח שׁוּבֵי מִלְחָמָה — *[Making] innocent passersby fugitives of war.* Instead of passing by confidently, they are left without food and clothing as people vanquished in battle who return home after having lost all to the enemy (*Rashi*).

The literal translation of מִמּוּל is *in front* or *opposite.* Before actually stealing the garment the thief stands *in front of it* and then removes it from his victim (*Metzudos*). *Tosafos Rid* renders מִמּוּל, *from on top of;* שַׂלְמָה, *the shirt;* אֶדֶר תַּפְשִׁטוּן, *you remove his mantle;* and leave him wearing his shirt.

[See ArtScroll *Jonah* 3:6 for additional translations of אֶדֶר.]

9. Scripture continues to list the sins of the nation for which God has refrained from bestowing His goodness upon them.

נְשֵׁי עַמִּי תְּגָרְשׁוּן מִבֵּית תַּעֲנֻגֶיהָ — *You evict [each of] the women of My people from the home of her delight.* The wicked drive the women from their pleasant homes by murdering their husbands and causing the women to be widowed. Alternatively, since the evildoers have robbed the men of all their possessions, they live distressful and unpleasant lives and cannot bring happiness to their wives (*Rashi*). *Metzudos* explains that the wicked drive away *all* the home-owners, including the prosperous women who delightfully bask in the shade of their homes. The thieves then take possession of these homes.

Although Scripture mentions the women of the nation, the verse is metaphorically referring to the general unhappiness of the entire nation (*Targum Yonasan*).

Citing *Exodus* 22:24 where עַמִּי is a specific reference to the poor, *Radak* renders, "The wicked have caused the poor of My nation to drive away their wives from their homes (through their constant acts of thievery)." When the husband returned home and found the thief in his house he suspected his wife of adultery and drove her out (divorced her) from his home. *Malbim* explains that the women were taken hostage from the homes of their husbands and defiled.

מֵעַל עֹלָלֶיהָ תִּקְחוּ הֲדָרִי לְעוֹלָם — *From her young children you remove My glory forever.* The glory of honor and wealth that I have bestowed upon her (*Rashi*) and that I have given her to adorn her children, they have taken for themselves forever, never to return it (*Metzudos*).

Alternatively, a conjugal relationship that results in the fulfillment of God's command to be fruitful and bear children glorifies God's Name. By causing the wives to be driven away from their homes, they have hindered My glory and honor from being publicized (*Radak*).

Abarbanel translates עֹלָלֶיהָ as *deeds* and renders, "After committing these wicked deeds how will the people ever merit to possess My eternally glorious land?"

10. ... קוּמוּ וּלְכוּ — *Arise and go [into exile]* ... [As a result of their degenerate actions they cannot remain in this land] they must be expelled and sent into exile.

כִּי לֹא־זֹאת הַמְּנוּחָה — *Because not for this [purpose] is the Resting Place [given to you].*

The Resting Place is the Land of Israel. See *Deut.* 12:9. God declares that He has not given the land to anyone as a resting place on these terms (*Rashi; Radak*).

evict [each of] the women of My people from the home of her delight; from her young children you remove My glory forever. [10] *Arise and go [into exile], because not for this [purpose] is the resting place [given to you]. Because it has become defiled, it will destroy [you] absolutely.* [11] *If a man would be going about, deceiving with wind and falsehood, [and would say,] "I will preach to you to [drink] wine and liquor," he would be an [approved] preacher for this people!*

בַּעֲבוּר טָמְאָה — *Because it has become defiled.* Our translation follows *Radak* and *Ibn Ezra* who translate טָמְאָה as it is written in our texts — without a מַפִּיק[1] in the ה — *it* [the land] *has become defiled with your evil deeds* (*Ibn Ezra; Metzudos*). *Targum Yonasan* and *Rashi* translate טָמְאָה as if it were written with a מַפִּיק — *in order to defile it* ... See *Minchas Shai* on this verse for further discussion.

The Land of Israel cannot tolerate sinners (*Sifra, Leviticus* 18:28). The Torah writes (*Leviticus*, ibid.) that Israel must not defile the Land they are inheriting. If they do, the Land would spew them out as it has cast out its previous inhabitants for their abominable acts.

R' Hirsch (ibid.) explains: As long as sins remain confined to individuals while God's law of morality finds supporters and avengers among the main body of the nation, the sinners would be purged from their midst and the nation could then continue to find the land as a source of blessing for its development. But if sins become the general practice of the community and wrongdoing becomes excusable and even approved of as right, then, as the body vomits forth anything that is irreconcilable to it, so does the land then eject its inhabitants.

תְּחַבֵּל וְחֶבֶל נִמְרָץ — *It will destroy [you] absolutely.* Our translation follows *Radak* and *Ibn Ezra* who relate the root חבל to וְחִבֵּל אֶת־מַעֲשֵׂה יָדֶיךָ, *and he shall destroy the work of your hands* (*Ecclesiastes* 5:5). *Rashi*, however, explains חֶבֶל as a group or band (see *I Samuel* 10:5; *Psalms* 119:61). The evildoers banded together to defile the Land and commit their sins. When they banded together their intent was clear (נִמְרָץ, *clear*; see *Job* 6:25). According to *Rashi*, the verse would be rendered: in order to defile it you have banded together with clear intent.

11. Verse 6 described how the nation mocked the prophets of G-d. In contrast, this verse describes how the false prophets were praised and honored by the people.

לוּ־אִישׁ הֹלֵךְ ... — *If a man would be going about* ... If a deceitful person, the false prophet, would tell the nation, "Drink wine and intoxicate yourselves; be merry for you have nothing to fear," he would be the respected prophet; the one to whom the nation would listen (*Rashi*).

אַטִּף לְךָ לַיַּיִן וְלַשֵּׁכָר — *I will preach to you to [drink] wine and liquor.* Our translation follows *Rashi*. Others, however, translate *I will preach to you for wine,* and explain that upon receipt of drinks of wine as payment, the deceitful person would prophesy assurances of peace (*Radak; Mahari Kara*).

1. A מַפִּיק is a dot that indicates that the word is a third-person female possessive.

יב אָסֹף אֶאֱסֹף יַעֲקֹב כֻּלָּךְ קַבֵּץ אֲקַבֵּץ שְׁאֵרִית
יִשְׂרָאֵל יַחַד אֲשִׂימֶנּוּ כְּצֹאן בָּצְרָה כְּעֵדֶר בְּתוֹךְ
הַדָּבְרוֹ תְּהִימֶנָה מֵאָדָם׃ יג עָלָה הַפֹּרֵץ לִפְנֵיהֶם
פָּרְצוּ וַיַּעֲבֹרוּ שַׁעַר וַיֵּצְאוּ בוֹ וַיַּעֲבֹר מַלְכָּם
לִפְנֵיהֶם וַיהוָה בְּרֹאשָׁם׃

א וָאֹמַר שִׁמְעוּ־
נָא רָאשֵׁי יַעֲקֹב וּקְצִינֵי בֵּית יִשְׂרָאֵל הֲלוֹא
לָכֶם לָדַעַת אֶת־הַמִּשְׁפָּט׃ ב שֹׂנְאֵי טוֹב וְאֹהֲבֵי

12-13. The commentators differ in the interpretation of the next two verses. *Targum Yonasan* and *Rashi* explain that they are words of consolation and encouragement. God is assuring the people that although they will be punished and exiled from their Land, in the end of days He will gather them together and bring them back to the Land of Israel whose cities will teem with people. *Radak*, however, sees these verses to be a continuation of the foreboding prophecies foretelling the catastrophic events that the Jewish people will endure. The people will flee and take refuge in their strongholds due to the fear of the attacking enemy. Alternatively, these verses are a continuation of the false prophecies introduced in the previous verse. The false prophets fabricated that God will not punish the people but will gather them together, remove the yoke of Torah from them and treat them like any other nation (*Malbim*).

12. אָסֹף אֶאֱסֹף ... קַבֵּץ אֲקַבֵּץ — *I will surely gather ... I will surely assemble.* Although Scripture often uses different phrases to describe or emphasize the same idea (*Metzudos*), *Malbim* sees a clear distinction between אָסֹף and קַבֵּץ. אָסֹף is used when something is gathered from one particular area and is brought into another area. קַבֵּץ, however, is used when gathering objects that are scattered all about. אָסֹף, therefore, may be a reference to the Ten Tribes of the Northern Kingdom who were all exiled into the land of כוש [see *Malbim, Isaiah* 11:12] while קַבֵּץ refers to the Kingdom of Judah who were scattered across the four corners of the earth.

כְּצֹאן בָּצְרָה — *Like a flock in a fold.* I will gather the nation together into My land and protect them as the shepherd gathers his sheep into a fold (*Rashi; Metzudos*). Others see בָּצְרָה as a proper noun and render *as sheep in Bozrah,* an Edomite city that had an abundance of sheep (*Ibn Ezra; Radak; Mahari Kara*). The people fleeing from the enemy will resemble sheep being herded into their folds (*Radak*).

תְּהִימֶנָה מֵאָדָם — *They will teem with people.* The land that had been left desolate for so many years will again be filled with people. Noise and commotion will therefore fill its cities. Alternatively, the noise that will be heard will be caused by the pursuing enemy (*Radak*).

13. הַפֹּרֵץ — *The one who breaks forth.*
The Messiah will break through all the barriers that have been restraining Israel's return to the land (*Mahari Kara*). He will wage war with Israel's enemies and will capture many of their cities (*Targum Yonasan*). Alternatively, the פֹּרֵץ is Elijah the Prophet who will arrive prior to the final redemption to usher in the new era. He will break through to the hearts of the people, persuade them to repent and encourage them to turn their hearts to God — see *Malachi* 3:24 (*Metzudos*).

[12] *I will surely gather all of you, O Jacob. I will surely assemble the remnant of Israel; I will place them together like a flock in a fold; like a herd in its pen, they will teem with people.* [13] *The one who breaks forth will go before them; they will break forth and pass through the gate, and go out through it; their king will pass in front of them, with HASHEM at their head.*

[1] *I said, "Listen, now, [you] leaders of Jacob and officers of the House of Israel! Is it not up to you to know the law?* [2] *[But you] hate good and love*

פָּרְצוּ ... וַיֵּצְאוּ בוֹ — *They will break forth ... and go out through it.* The people will be receptive to the prophet's encouragement and will stir themselves to repent their sins. It will be as if they will break through the walls that imprison them and pass through the gateways they have made (*Metzudos*).

וַיַּעֲבֹר מַלְכָּם לִפְנֵיהֶם — *Their king will pass in front of them.* When they will return to their Land they will be led by the Messianic king and God will precede them all by returning His presence to Zion (*Metzudos*). *Radak*, however, interprets this verse as a foreboding prophecy, foretelling the destruction of the first temple. הַפֹּרֵץ, *the one who breaks forth,* is referring to King Zedekiah [20th monarch of the Kingdom of Judah] who tried to escape from Jerusalem by breaching through the wall of the city when it was besieged by the Babylonians [see *II Kings* 25; *Ezekiel* 12; the entire episode is detailed in *Jeremiah* 12 vv. 10-14]. *And their king passed before them* — King Zedekiah ran from the city followed by his army.

וַה׳ בְּרֹאשָׁם — *With HASHEM at their head.* Prior to the exile of Israel, God had already removed His presence from Jerusalem.

III

◆§ Micah Rebukes the Leaders

1. וָאֹמַר שִׁמְעוּ־נָא רָאשֵׁי יַעֲקֹב וּקְצִינֵי בֵּית יִשְׂרָאֵל — *I said, "Listen now, [you] leaders of Jacob and officers of the House of Israel."*

In the previous chapter, Micah admonished the entire nation for the evils they had committed against the poor. Now, he specifically addresses the leaders of the nation and holds them responsible for the actions of the people. They are to be blamed, for it is their responsibility to know the law, administer justice and return to the poor that which had been seized by their oppressors (*Radak*). Even if the leaders were to claim that they were ignorant of the injustices that had been committed by the people, they would still be accountable, for it is their responsibility to investigate whether justice has been administered (*Abarbanel*).

Malbim adds that Micah is answering the complaints of the people [2:7: הֲקָצַר רוּחַ ה׳] who had claimed that the punishments foretold by the prophet were too severe for the sins they had committed and that God was dealing with them unjustly and unfairly. He therefore answers, "Judge yourselves, leaders of Israel! You should have known what justice is!"

רעה° גֹּזְלֵי עוֹרָם מֵעֲלֵיהֶם וּשְׁאֵרָם מֵעַל עַצְמוֹתָם׃ ג וַאֲשֶׁר אָכְלוּ שְׁאֵר עַמִּי וְעוֹרָם מֵעֲלֵיהֶם הִפְשִׁיטוּ וְאֶת־עַצְמֹתֵיהֶם פִּצֵּחוּ וּפָרְשׂוּ כַּאֲשֶׁר בַּסִּיר וּכְבָשָׂר בְּתוֹךְ קַלָּחַת׃ ד אָז יִזְעֲקוּ אֶל־יהוה וְלֹא יַעֲנֶה אוֹתָם וְיַסְתֵּר פָּנָיו מֵהֶם בָּעֵת הַהִיא כַּאֲשֶׁר הֵרֵעוּ מַעַלְלֵיהֶם׃ ה כֹּה אָמַר יהוה עַל־הַנְּבִיאִים הַמַּתְעִים אֶת־עַמִּי הַנֹּשְׁכִים בְּשִׁנֵּיהֶם וְקָרְאוּ

°רָעק׳

The name *Israel* conveys a higher spiritual state than the name *Jacob.* Hence, *[you] leaders of Jacob* is referring to the self-appointed leaders of the Ten Tribes who had forcibly gained their positions of leadership. In contrast, *officers of the House of Israel* refers to the leaders of the Kingdom of Judah who were men of stature and royal ancestry, and were qualified for their positions of honor (*Malbim*).

2. שֹׂנְאֵי טוֹב וְאֹהֲבֵי רָע — *[But you] hate good and love evil.* Not only do the leaders fail to guide the people to do that which is good and just but they commit evil themselves by oppressing the poor and seizing their money and food (*Radak*).[1]

גֹּזְלֵי עוֹרָם מֵעֲלֵיהֶם — *You rob [people's] skin from upon them.* Scripture metaphorically describes the rampant thievery (*Metzudos*). Since the poor have been deprived of their means of sustenance, it is as if their oppressors have flayed the skin from their bodies and removed the flesh from their bones, for without nourishment the body wastes away (*Radak*).

3. וַאֲשֶׁר אָכְלוּ שְׁאֵר עַמִּי — *[You] have eaten the flesh of My people.* Scripture elaborates on the metaphor introduced in the previous verse, describing the oppression that had been rendered to the poor and indigent [שְׁאֵר עַמִּי] (*Radak*). Alternatively, שְׁאֵר עַמִּי is referring to the righteous members of the nation (*Ibn Ezra*). Not only do the leaders oppress the poor, but they oppress the righteous as well.

וְאֶת־עַצְמֹתֵיהֶם פִּצֵּחוּ — *You have broken open their bones.* Although *Radak* merely translates פִּצֵּחוּ as *and they broke* [עִנְיָן שְׁבִירָה], most commentators (*Rashi; Mahari Kara; Malbim*) translate *and they opened.* Accordingly, the idea being conveyed by Scripture is that the bones were broken open to empty them of their marrow. See *Numbers* 13:19 where *Onkelos* translates הַבְּמַחֲנִים [*open cities*] as הַבְּפַצְחִין (*Mahari Kara*).

וּפָרְשׂוּ כַּאֲשֶׁר בַּסִּיר וּכְבָשָׂר בְּתוֹךְ קַלָּחַת — *And you have sliced them [into pieces] like that which is in a pot and like meat in a cauldron.*

A סִיר is a small pot and קַלָּחַת in Old French is קלדיירא, *caldiera* [that is, a large pot, cauldron (*Marpei Lashon*)] (*Malbim*). Scripture metaphorically describes the extent of the evil that the wealthy leaders do to the poor by comparing the poor to bones that have been stripped of its meat and its marrow removed (*Radak*). These bones were then chopped and cooked in a pot or cauldron (*Metzudos*).

1. The commentators note that the prophet Amos [5:15] besought the people to hate evil, love good and establish justice. But they did not heed his words for they hated good, loved evil and did not know what justice was.

evil; you rob [people's] skin from upon them and their flesh from upon their bones; [3] *[you] have eaten the flesh of My people, you have stripped their skin from upon them, you have broken open their bones; and you have sliced them [into pieces] like that which is in a pot and like meat in a cauldron.* [4] *Then they will cry out to HASHEM but He will not answer them; He will hide His face from them at that time, just as they had done evil with their deeds."*

[5] *Thus said HASHEM about the prophets who mislead My people, who chew with their teeth and declare*

4. אָז יִזְעֲקוּ אֶל־ה׳ וְלֹא יַעֲנֶה אוֹתָם — *Then they will cry out to HASHEM but He will not answer them.* When God will come to rescue His nation and gather them from exile (see 2:12), the wicked will cry out to Him pleading that they too wish to be the recipients of His benevolence. They too wish to be rescued from exile. But their pleas will be ignored (*Rashi*). Alternatively, *Radak* and *Metzudos* explain that the evildoers will cry out to G-d *upon the arrival of the enemy* that has been sent to inflict their deserved punishment upon them.[1]

וְיַסְתֵּר פָּנָיו מֵהֶם בָּעֵת הַהִיא — *He will hide His face from them at that time.* God will remove His Divine Presence from their midst (*Targum Yonasan*). He will hide His face as if He does not see their troubles (*Rashi — Deuteronomy* 31:17) and will withdraw His special care from them (*Sifsei Chachamim* ibid.). If they will call out to Him, He will not answer them (*Ibn Ezra* ibid.). For just as they have ignored the cries of the poor, so too will God ignore their cries, measure for measure (*Radak; Abarbanel*).

Malbim, who maintains that this chapter is answering the complaints of 2:7 [*Has HASHEM become short-spirited? Are these His deeds* ... see comm. to v. 1], explains that these are not God's doings but the result of their own evil deeds.

◆§ Micah Rebukes the False Prophets

5-8. Throughout the days of the monarchy there were false prophets who contested the words of the true prophets [see footnote 1 to 2:4 above]. Micah now admonishes them for their evil deeds.

5. כֹּה אָמַר ה׳ עַל־הַנְּבִיאִים הַמַּתְעִים אֶת־עַמִּי — *Thus said HASHEM about the prophets who mislead My people.* This prophecy is concerning the *false* prophets (*Metzudos*). Although the word נָבִיא is usually reserved for one who speaks or reveals the true word of God, Scripture may be using נָבִיא in a borrowed sense, since the false prophets had claimed they were נְבִיאִים (*Ramban, Deuteronomy* 13:2).

הַנֹּשְׁכִים בְּשִׁנֵּיהֶם וְקָרְאוּ שָׁלוֹם — *Who chew with their teeth and declare peace.* The people presented gifts of meat delicacies

1. [It is of utmost importance that we realize that although Scripture continuously rebukes the nation for their corruption and evil acts that had been committed among themselves, they were, nevertheless, believers in God and never denied His existence, for these same wicked people were the ones that were now crying out and pleading with Him for mercy.

For this very same reason — realizing that God oversees all actions yet arrogantly ignoring this realization and proceeding to follow the dictates of one's own desires — for this lack of fear of Heaven, God will not answer any plea for mercy. Throughout Scripture we find that the prophets rebuked the people in a similar manner — see *I Samuel* 8:18; *Isaiah* 1:15; *Proverbs* 1:28.]

שָׁלוֹם וַאֲשֶׁר לֹא־יִתֵּן עַל־פִּיהֶם וְקִדְּשׁוּ עָלָיו
ו מִלְחָמָה׃ לָכֵן לַיְלָה לָכֶם מֵחָזוֹן וְחָשְׁכָה לָכֶם
מִקְּסֹם וּבָאָה הַשֶּׁמֶשׁ עַל־הַנְּבִיאִים וְקָדַר עֲלֵיהֶם
ז הַיּוֹם׃ וּבֹשׁוּ הַחֹזִים וְחָפְרוּ הַקֹּסְמִים וְעָטוּ עַל־
ח שָׂפָם כֻּלָּם כִּי אֵין מַעֲנֵה אֱלֹהִים׃ וְאוּלָם אָנֹכִי
מָלֵאתִי כֹחַ אֶת־רוּחַ יהוה וּמִשְׁפָּט וּגְבוּרָה לְהַגִּיד
ט לְיַעֲקֹב פִּשְׁעוֹ וּלְיִשְׂרָאֵל חַטָּאתוֹ׃ שִׁמְעוּ־
נָא זֹאת רָאשֵׁי בֵּית יַעֲקֹב וּקְצִינֵי בֵּית
יִשְׂרָאֵל הַמְתַעֲבִים מִשְׁפָּט וְאֵת כָּל־הַיְשָׁרָה
י יְעַקֵּשׁוּ׃ בֹּנֶה צִיּוֹן בְּדָמִים וִירוּשָׁלַםִ בְּעַוְלָה׃

to the false prophets and in return, the well-fed "prophets" foretold a future of peace and tranquility (*Targum Yonasan; Rashi; Mahari Kara*). But against those people who have not offered any gifts, the false prophets wage campaigns (*Rashi; Radak*) or prophesy that war is imminent (*Mahari Kara; Metzudos*). Isn't it clear that they are false prophets since their predictions are always in proportion to the gifts which they receive from their seekers? (*Abarbanel*).

6. לָכֵן לַיְלָה לָכֶם מֵחָזוֹן — *Therefore, it shall be night for you because of such vision.* The false prophecies will result in night and darkness to those who had uttered them. For when the enemy will arrive, it will be obvious to all that the predictions had been false (*Radak*).

לַיְלָה ... וְחָשְׁכָה ... וּבָאָה הַשֶּׁמֶשׁ ... וְקָדַר ... — *Night ... dark ... the sun will set ... blackened ...* These are all metaphors describing the troubles and anguish that will befall the false prophets (*Radak; Metzudos*).

The prophet is referring to the three categories of people who claimed to foretell the future: seers, diviners and false prophets. Seers claimed to see their visions at night; but instead of the night ushering in a vision, the vision will usher in the night. Diviners usually practiced their divinations in a dark place; instead of the darkness bringing the divination, the divination will bring on the darkness. The false prophets prophesied by day. Their punishment will be that the sun will set for them and their day will become dark (*Malbim*).

7. וּבֹשׁוּ הַחֹזִים וְחָפְרוּ הַקֹּסְמִים — *The seers will be ashamed and the diviners disgraced.* When the false prophets see that their predictions did not materialize they will be ashamed and disgraced for the people will now realize that all they had been told by their "prophets" was not the word of God but a fabrication (*Radak; Metzudos*).

וְעָטוּ עַל־שָׂפָם כֻּלָּם — *And all of them will wear veils over their lips.* Veiling the upper lip was the traditional sign of mourning — see *Mishneh Torah, Hil. Aveilus* 5:19; *Yoreh Deah* 386:1. The false prophets will hide their faces in shame in the manner practiced by a mourner (*Radak*). Alternatively, the false prophets will actually mourn their fate when the terrible punishments occur (*Metzudos*).

Like בֹּשֶׁת, חָפַר is a term that denotes shame (*Metzudos*) but is more degrading than בֹּשֶׁת (*Malbim*). The actual translation of חָפַר is *to dig*. *Da'as Sofrim* suggests that it is used as a term

peace, but whoever does not put [food] into their mouths, they prepare war against him:

[6]Therefore, it shall be night for you because of such vision, and it shall be dark for you because of such divination; the sun will set upon the prophets and the daylight will be blackened for them. [7]The seers will be ashamed and the diviners disgraced and all of them will wear veils over their lips, for [they] had no word of God.

[8]But as for me, I was filled with strength by the spirit of HASHEM, and [with] justice and might, to inform Jacob of his transgression and Israel of his sin.

[9]Listen, now, to this, O leaders of the House of Jacob and officers of the House of Israel, who detest justice and who twist all that is straight, [10]who build Zion with blood and Jerusalem with iniquity:

denoting shame, for the person feels like "digging a hole in the ground" to hide his reddened face.

R' Hirsch (*Psalms* 34:6) explains that the basic meaning of חָפַר is, "to expose something that has been hidden heretofore." It is therefore at times translated *to dig* (*Genesis* 26:15,18,19) and at times *to explore unknown territory* (*Joshua* 2:2,3). In our case it is used to express the feelings of shame that one experiences when an unpleasant fact, that he would have rather kept concealed, is brought into the open.

8. וְאוּלָם אָנֹכִי מָלֵאתִי כֹחַ אֶת־רוּחַ ה' ... — *But as for me, I was filled with strength by the spirit of HASHEM ...* Micah declares, "I am unlike false prophets who fear the nation and bribe the people with false prophecies. The spirit of G-d fills me with the *strength* [כֹּחַ] of *justice* [מִשְׁפָּט] and *courage* [גְבוּרָה]. Therefore, the words I speak are true and just, and I do not fear to rebuke the people for their sins" (*Radak*).

לְהַגִּיד לְיַעֲקֹב פִּשְׁעוֹ וּלְיִשְׂרָאֵל חַטָּאתוֹ — *To inform Jacob of his transgression and Israel of his sin.* One of the tasks of God's prophet is to prevent the people from committing evil deeds — see *Rambam, Mishneh Torah, Hil. Yesodei HaTorah* 8:7.

9. שִׁמְעוּ־נָא זֹאת רָאשֵׁי בֵּית יַעֲקֹב וּקְצִינֵי בֵּית יִשְׂרָאֵל — *Listen, now, to this, O leaders of the House of Jacob and officers of the House of Israel.* Micah again turns to the leaders of the nation and rebukes them for their corrupt ways (*Radak*). They corrupt justice (*Targum Yonasan*) and cause it to be despised in the eyes of the people (*Da'as Soferim*). They distort all the just and straight words that come forth from my mouth (*Ibn Ezra*).

The Talmud (*Shabbos* 139a) explains that Micah is rebuking the judges of the nation: "R' Yose ben Elisha says: If you see a generation overwhelmed by many troubles, go forth and examine the judges of Israel, for all retribution that comes to the world comes only because of the judges of Israel." The Talmud then cites vv. 9-11 of this chapter.

10. בֹּנֶה צִיּוֹן בְּדָמִים — *Who build Zion with blood.* The word דָּמִים may be translated either *blood* or *money. Metzudos*

יא רָאשֶׁיהָ | בְּשֹׁחַד יִשְׁפֹּטוּ וְכֹהֲנֶיהָ בִּמְחִיר יוֹרוּ וּנְבִיאֶיהָ בְּכֶסֶף יִקְסֹמוּ וְעַל־יהוה יִשָּׁעֵנוּ לֵאמֹר הֲלוֹא יהוה בְּקִרְבֵּנוּ לֹא־תָבוֹא עָלֵינוּ רָעָה: יב לָכֵן בִּגְלַלְכֶם צִיּוֹן שָׂדֶה תֵחָרֵשׁ וִירוּשָׁלַםִ עִיִּין תִּהְיֶה וְהַר הַבַּיִת לְבָמוֹת יָעַר: א וְהָיָה | בְּאַחֲרִית הַיָּמִים יִהְיֶה הַר בֵּית־יהוה נָכוֹן בְּרֹאשׁ הֶהָרִים וְנִשָּׂא הוּא מִגְּבָעוֹת וְנָהֲרוּ עָלָיו עַמִּים:

writes that all of the leaders *murder* and use the wealth of their victims to build homes in Zion. Alternatively, *Ibn Ezra* renders that the leaders build Zion with *money* stolen from the poor. *Radak* combines both explanations. *Stealing* from the poor is comparable to *murder*, for they have only meager means with which to sustain themselves.

Although the words בֹּנֶה צִיּוֹן [lit., *who builds Zion*] is in singular form, these commentators explain that the term is referring to the leaders of the previous verse. They justify use of the singular form by maintaining that the prophet is addressing each individual leader. *Mahari Kara*, however, explains that בֹּנֶה צִיּוֹן refers to God and the sentence is interrogative. Do they really think God will build Zion while iniquity is yet in their hands?

11. רָאשֶׁיהָ בְּשֹׁחַד יִשְׁפֹּטוּ וְכֹהֲנֶיהָ בִּמְחִיר יוֹרוּ — *Her leaders judge for bribes and her Kohanim teach for a fee.* The leaders of Jerusalem, the kings (*Ibn Ezra*) or possibly the Sanhedrin [judges of the High Court that was situated in the Temple] (*Radak*), would rule in favor of the one who offered him a bribe, in direct opposition to the words of the Torah, *Do not take bribery* (*Exodus* 23:8).

The Kohanim were responsible for disseminating Torah scholarship and for answering questions of Torah law (see *Deut.* 33:10; *Malachi* 2:7).[1] Micah rebukes the Kohanim for their corrupt practices of tailoring their rulings to the desires of the people who paid them fees (*Radak; Metzudos*).

וּנְבִיאֶיהָ בְּכֶסֶף יִקְסֹמוּ — *And her prophets divine for money.* Her false prophets (*Ibn Ezra; Radak*) foresaw good tidings for those who paid them their price (*Metzudos*).

וְעַל־ה׳ יִשָּׁעֵנוּ לֵאמֹר הֲלוֹא ה׳ בְּקִרְבֵּנוּ ... — *Yet they rely on* HASHEM, *saying, "Is not* HASHEM *in our midst ...?"* Although they committed these sins they had the audacity to assume that as long as God's presence dwelled in the Holy Temple which was in their midst, He would allow no harm to befall them or His Temple (*Radak; Metzudos*). This distortion was contested in later times by Jeremiah (Chap. 7) and Ezekiel (Chap. 4:11). [See *Ezekiel*, ArtScroll edition, p. 71 footnote 1.] God instructed Jeremiah to tell the people that their protection was dependent only on their actions and good deeds. It was not at all dependent on whether His Divine Presence was in their midst or not.

12. לָכֵן בִּגְלַלְכֶם צִיּוֹן שָׂדֶה תֵחָרֵשׁ וִירוּשָׁלַםִ עִיִּין תִּהְיֶה — *Therefore, because of you, Zion will be plowed over like a field and Jerusalem will become heaps of rubble.* Because of the numerous sins of the people, God will disregard His honor

1. In a lengthy essay, *R' Z.H. Chajes* (*Toras Nevi'im*, Chap. 1) maintains that the Kohanim and the prophets each had their exclusive tasks in leading the nation. The Kohanim were to teach Torah and judge the people; the prophets were to deliver the word of God, whatever it might be, to the people. He cites our verse among the many passages he uses to prove his point.

3/6-10

[11] *Her leaders judge for bribes and her Kohanim teach for a fee and her prophets divine for money — yet they rely on HASHEM, saying, "Is not HASHEM in our midst? No evil can befall us!"* [12] *Therefore, because of you, Zion will be plowed over like a field and Jerusalem will become heaps of rubble and the Temple Mount will become like stone heaps in the forest.*

4/1

[1] *It will happen in the end of days that the mountain of the Temple of HASHEM will be firmly established as the head of the mountains, and it will be exalted up above the hills, and peoples will stream to it.*

and will destroy His holy city (*Radak; Metzudos*). Zion, that had been built בְּדָמִים [see comm. to v. 10], will now become devoid of its structures and will resemble a plowed field.[1] Jerusalem, which had been built through iniquity, will be destroyed. The enemy will heap the stones of its structures into mounds (*Radak*).

[In the first chapter (v. 6), Micah had foretold that Samaria, the capital city of the Northern Kingdom, would be transformed into a heap of stones. He now declares that Jerusalem, the capital city of the Kingdom of Judah, will suffer a similar fate.] The Talmud (*Shabbos* 139a) explains that due to the three sins listed in v. 11, the nation will be punished in a threefold manner.

וְהַר הַבַּיִת לְבָמוֹת יָעַר — *And the Temple Mount will become like stone heaps in the forest.* Once the Temple will be destroyed, its mount will become overgrown with weeds and trees. The plural לְבָמוֹת includes the desolation of Mount Olives which is in close proximity to the Temple Mount or to the many heaps of stones that will be the ruins of the Temple (*Radak*).

Metzudos translates בָּמוֹת יַעַר as *high places of the forest* and explains that they are the tree stumps that remain after the trees have been cut. Scripture refers to them as high places [בָּמוֹת] for they resemble the high places upon which sacrifices had been offered. The ruins on the Temple Mount will be piled into many small heaps resembling a forest full of tree stumps.

Micah was the first of the prophets to foretell the destruction of the Holy Temple (*Da'as Soferim*). His prophecy was later quoted by the elders of Israel in defense of the prophet Jeremiah (*Jeremiah* 26:18). From their words it is clear that Micah uttered this prophecy during the days of Hezekiah's reign.

IV

◈ Jerusalem and Zion of the Future

Micah had just foretold the destruction of the Temple Mount and the Holy City of Jerusalem (3:12). This chapter opens with words of encouragement and hope, predicting that Jerusalem and its Temple will not forever remain desolate for a

1. *Rambam* (*Mishneh Torah, Hil. Taaniyos* 1:3) writes that this prophecy was fulfilled when the wicked Turnus Rufus plowed the Temple grounds and its surrounding areas.

ד/ב

ב וְהָלְכוּ גּוֹיִם רַבִּים וְאָמְרוּ לְכוּ | וְנַעֲלֶה אֶל־הַר־יהוה וְאֶל־בֵּית אֱלֹהֵי יַעֲקֹב וְיוֹרֵנוּ מִדְּרָכָיו וְנֵלְכָה בְּאֹרְחֹתָיו כִּי מִצִּיּוֹן תֵּצֵא תוֹרָה וּדְבַר יהוה מִירוּשָׁלָם׃

time will come when they will both be rebuilt and regain their original status. The prophecies of this chapter (vv. 1-3) are also written in the Book of *Isaiah* (2:2-4) with minor differences (*Radak; Abarbanel*).

Isaiah and his disciple Micah were both granted the same prophetic vision, albeit at different times. When Micah articulated his prophecy to the nation, he chose to use the basic text that had been uttered previously by Isaiah because he was well acquainted with it (*Abarbanel*). As for the minor differences, most commentators explain that although two prophets may be granted the same prophecy, its articulation varied from prophet to prophet — סִגְנוֹן אֶחָד עוֹלֶה לְכַמָּה נְבִיאִים וְאֵין שְׁנֵי נְבִיאִים מִתְנַבְּאִים בְּסִגְנוֹן אֶחָד (*Sanhedrin* 89a).

1. וְהָיָה בְּאַחֲרִית הַיָּמִים — *It will happen in the end of days.*

This refers to the Messianic era (*Radak*) after the doers of evil will be destroyed (*Rashi* to *Isaiah*). Some translate בְּאַחֲרִית הַיָּמִים, *in days to come*, because the term *end of days* may erroneously imply that upon the arrival of the Messiah, time will end — see *The Living Nach — Isaiah*. However, the end of days actually means the end result, the culmination of all of world history which is flowing toward this point of time — see *R' M. Eisemann, Yechezkel* 38:8, ArtScroll edition.

יִהְיֶה הַר בֵּית־ה׳ נָכוֹן בְּרֹאשׁ הֶהָרִים — *The mountain of the Temple of Hashem will be firmly established as the head of the mountains.*

This is Mount Moriah, the mountain on which the Holy Temple was constructed (*Radak* to *Isaiah*). Since the nations of the world had worshiped their strange gods upon the high mountains and hills, the prophet confirms that in Messianic times the Temple Mount will be established above all other mountains as the religious metropolis of the world, esteemed and respected by all nations (*Radak*). Alternatively, the mountains and hills metaphorically represent the great miracles that took place on mountains throughout the history of the Jewish people. On Mt. Sinai the nation received the Torah — see *Exodus* 19:16; on Mt. Carmel, the prophet Elijah proved God's omnipotence through the descent of a heavenly fire — see *I Kings* Chapter 19; and on Mt. Tabor, the Jewish armies defeated the armies of Sisera — see *Judges* 4:15,16. The miracles that will occur on the Temple Mount in Messianic times will greatly surpass these miracles (*Rashi* to *Isaiah*).

וְנָהֲרוּ עָלָיו עַמִּים — *And peoples will stream to it.* The nations of the world will gather together and stream to the Temple as rivers gather together and swiftly flow into the sea (*Rashi*). They will run swiftly for they will realize that Hashem is the true God (*Radak; Abarbanel*).

Vilna Gaon suggests that the nations will travel by way of ships and boats over the rivers and stream to the Temple (*Aderes Eliyahu, Isaiah* 2:2). Alternatively, the word נהר is not only the streaming forth of water but is the streaming forth of light, as well — see *R' Hirsch, Psalms* 34:6. The nations of the world will swiftly travel toward the spiritual light that streams forth from the Temple (*Tos. Rid*).

4/2

[2] *Many nations will go and say, "Come, let us go up to the Mountain of HASHEM and to the Temple of the God of Jacob, and He will teach us of His ways and we will walk in His paths." For from Zion will the Torah come forth, and the word of HASHEM from Jerusalem.*

2. וְהָלְכוּ גּוֹיִם רַבִּים וְאָמְרוּ לְכוּ וְנַעֲלֶה אֶל־הַר־ה׳ ... — *Many nations will go and say, "Come, let us go up to the Mountain of HASHEM* ... The nations will encourage one another (*Metzudos*) to go up to the *mountain of Hashem* so that they too may be at His Temple (*Abarbanel*) for they too will feel drawn to it as the source of all their light and life (*R' Hirsch*).

וְאֶל־בֵּית אֱלֹהֵי יַעֲקֹב — *And to the Temple of the God of Jacob.*

The commentators wonder why Micah refers to the Temple as the *Temple of the God of Jacob.* Why not the God of Abraham or the God of Isaac? *Rashi* (*Isaiah* 2:3) explains that it was Jacob who gave Mt. Moriah the distinguished name of Beth-el [בֵּית־אֵל — *Genesis* 28:19], *the House of God*, while Abraham and Isaac did not. Abraham referred to it as the Mountain of God [הַר ה׳ — ibid. 22:14] and Isaac referred to it as a field [שָׂדֶה — ibid. 24:63]. Micah therefore credits Jacob by referring to the Temple, the House of God, as the Temple of the God of Jacob — see *Pesachim* 88a.

וְיוֹרֵנוּ מִדְּרָכָיו וְנֵלְכָה בְּאֹרְחֹתָיו — *And He will teach us of His ways and we will walk in His paths."* God will teach the people through those who are knowledgeable of the Torah (*Metzudos*). Alternatively, he is not referring to God but to the king Messiah who will teach them the ways of G-d and will judge disputes among the nations (*Radak*). [Accordingly, the H of *He* and *His* would be lower case since it is not referring to God.]

דְּרָכִים are the main roads and אֹרְחוֹת are its branches. [In this verse, both words are used figuratively.] The nations will say, "Although we have only been taught the דְּרָכִים — the fundamentals of the religion — nevertheless we will strive to learn its details on our own — וְנֵלְכָה בְּאֹרְחֹתָיו (*Malbim, Isaiah* 2:3).

כִּי מִצִּיּוֹן תֵּצֵא תוֹרָה וּדְבַר ה׳ מִירוּשָׁלָםִ — *For from Zion will the Torah come forth, and the word of HASHEM from Jerusalem.* Torah law that comes forth from Zion is the most authoritative (*Metzudos*), for the לִשְׁכַּת הַגָּזִית, the *Chamber of Hewn Stone*, where the Sanhedrin sit in judgment is located there (*Malbim, Isaiah* 2:3).

Some say that these are the words of the prophet who is explaining that the nations will aspire to go to the Temple Mount because it is from there that Torah law and moral instruction will come forth (*Radak*). Alternatively, the nations are explaining their reason for traveling to the Temple Mount (*Mahari Kara*).

But is not Zion a section of Jerusalem and is not the Torah the *word of Hashem?* What then is being added with the words וּדְבַר ה׳ מִירוּשָׁלָםִ that has not been expressed by the words כִּי מִצִּיּוֹן תֵּצֵא תוֹרָה? *R' Ovadiah* in his *Perush* to *Mishnah Torah, Hil. Kiddush HaChodesh* 1:8 explains that nothing is being added for they indeed are the same — for Zion is in Jerusalem and Torah is *the word of Hashem* — but it is common for Scripture to be repetitive and use different terminology to elaborate on ideas that have already been conveyed earlier in the verse. *Malbim*, however, maintains that תּוֹרָה and דְּבַר ה׳ are not synonymous, and neither are Zion and Jerusalem. דְּבַר ה׳, *the word of HASHEM*, is referring to prophecy which unlike the Torah did not come forth from Zion but from the prophets who assembled in Jerusalem. *Rambam* writes that the king Messiah will be wiser than even King Solomon and almost as great a prophet as Moses (*Mishnah Torah — Hil. Teshuvah* 9:2). Accordingly, it is he who will teach the Torah that will come forth from Zion and it is he who will prophesy the word of Hashem from Jerusalem (*Rinas Yitzchak*).

ג וְשָׁפַ֗ט בֵּ֚ין עַמִּ֣ים רַבִּ֔ים וְהוֹכִ֛יחַ לְגוֹיִ֥ם עֲצֻמִ֖ים עַד־רָח֑וֹק וְכִתְּת֨וּ חַרְבֹתֵיהֶ֜ם לְאִתִּ֗ים וַחֲנִיתֹֽתֵיהֶם֙ לְמַזְמֵר֔וֹת לֹא־יִשְׂא֞וּ גּ֤וֹי אֶל־גּוֹי֙ ד חֶ֔רֶב וְלֹא־יִלְמְד֥וּן ע֖וֹד מִלְחָמָֽה׃ וְיָשְׁב֗וּ אִ֣ישׁ תַּ֧חַת גַּפְנ֛וֹ וְתַ֥חַת תְּאֵנָת֖וֹ וְאֵ֣ין מַחֲרִ֑יד כִּי־פִ֛י ה יְהוָ֥ה צְבָא֖וֹת דִּבֵּֽר׃ כִּ֚י כָּל־הָ֣עַמִּ֔ים יֵלְכ֕וּ אִ֖ישׁ בְּשֵׁ֣ם אֱלֹהָ֑יו וַאֲנַ֗חְנוּ נֵלֵ֛ךְ בְּשֵׁם־יְהוָ֥ה אֱלֹהֵ֖ינוּ ו לְעוֹלָ֥ם וָעֶֽד׃ בַּיּ֨וֹם הַה֜וּא נְאֻם־יְהוָ֗ה אֹֽסְפָה֙ הַצֹּ֣לֵעָ֔ה וְהַנִּדָּחָ֖ה אֲקַבֵּ֑צָה

3. וְשָׁפַט בֵּין עַמִּים רַבִּים וְהוֹכִיחַ לְגוֹיִם עֲצֻמִים עַד־רָחוֹק — *He will judge between many peoples and will settle the arguments of mighty nations from far away.* Our translation of עַד־רָחוֹק, *from far away,* follows *Mahari Kara* and is the simple translation of the verse. The king Messiah will arbitrate the disputes (*Radak; Ibn Ezra*) and will clarify the law to the mighty nations who dwell in distant places (*Metzudos*). Alternatively, the inhabitants of Mount Zion, those who dwell on the Mountain of Hashem (*Mahari Kara, Isaiah* 2:4) or the Sanhedrin who sit in judgment on the Temple Mount, will judge the nations (*Abarbanel*).

Targum Yonasan, however, translates עַד עָלְמָא, *forever,* which is a measurement of time and not of distance.

וְכִתְּתוּ חַרְבֹתֵיהֶם לְאִתִּים וַחֲנִיתֹתֵיהֶם לְמַזְמֵרוֹת — *They will beat their swords into plowshares and their spears into pruning hooks.*

אִתִּים are sharp blades that attach to the beam of the plow and cut into the ground (*Rashi, I Samuel* 13:20). *Radak* translates מָרָא, *a shovel.* מַזְמֵרוֹת are implements used for pruning vines and trees (*Radak*). The people will beat their now useless weapons and form farming equipment from them (*Metzudos*).

לֹא־יִשְׂאוּ גּוֹי אֶל־גּוֹי חֶרֶב וְלֹא־יִלְמְדוּן עוֹד מִלְחָמָה — *Nation will not lift sword against nation, nor will they learn war anymore.*

Since all the decisions of the king Messiah will be accepted by all, no nation will again resort to war as a way of settling their disputes (*Radak* to *Isaiah*). Moreover, once the nations join together to acknowledge that Hashem is the One and Only God, there will be no reason for war, since most wars are rooted in religious disputes (*Abarbanel*).

4. וְיָשְׁבוּ אִישׁ תַּחַת גַּפְנוֹ וְתַחַת תְּאֵנָתוֹ ... — *They will sit, each man under his vine and under his fig tree* ... [The term לָשֶׁבֶת תַּחַת גַּפְנוֹ וְתַחַת תְּאֵנָתוֹ is used throughout Scripture to describe a time of peace and prosperity — see *I Kings* 5:5; *Zechariah* 3:10.] All the inhabitants of the world will live together peacefully (*Ibn Ezra*) without fear for there will be no need to go to war.

כִּי־פִי ה׳ צְבָאוֹת דִּבֵּר — *For the mouth of Hashem, Master of Legions, has spoken.*

God has promised that *there will be peace in the land and you will lie down with none to frighten you* — see *Leviticus* 26:6 (*Rashi*). Since it is Hashem, Master of Legions, Who has made this promise it will surely occur because He is sure to keep His word (*Radak*).

5. כִּי כָּל־הָעַמִּים יֵלְכוּ אִישׁ בְּשֵׁם אֱלֹהָיו וַאֲנַחְנוּ נֵלֵךְ בְּשֵׁם־ה׳ אֱלֹהֵינוּ לְעוֹלָם וָעֶד — *For all the peoples will go forth, each man in the name of his god, but we go forth with the Name of Hashem, our God, forever and ever.* The prophet declares that all

[3]He will judge between many peoples and will settle the arguments of mighty nations from far away. They will beat their swords into plowshares and their spears into pruning hooks; nation will not lift sword against nation, nor will they learn war anymore. [4]They will sit, each man under his vine and under his fig tree, and none will make them afraid, for the mouth of H*ASHEM*, *Master of Legions, has spoken. [5]For all the peoples will go forth, each man in the name of his god, but we go forth with the Name of* H*ASHEM*, *our God, forever and ever.*

[6]On that day — the word of H*ASHEM — I will assemble the lame one and gather in the one driven away*

this honor will be bestowed upon Israel because unlike the nations of the world who worshiped the gods of their choice, Israel remained faithful to Hashem and followed His teachings through their long exile and will forever continue to do so (*Metzudos*). *Radak* adds that although the nations will ultimately leave their idolatrous ways and follow the ways of Hashem, they will not do so until the king Messiah will motivate them to penitence after the war of Gog and Magog.[1]

Alternatively, *Targum Yonasan* translates יֵלְכוּ as יְהָרוֹן לַאֲבַדּוֹן, *will go to destruction*, and renders *all the nations will be destroyed for worshiping foreign gods.*

6. בַּיּוֹם הַהוּא נְאֻם־ה׳ אֹסְפָה הַצֹּלֵעָה — *On that day — the word of* H*ASHEM — I will assemble the lame one.*

Our translation follows *Radak* who explains that on the day of the ingathering of the exiles which will take place at the end of days, God will gather in the Israelite nation, who, due to their torturous exile is likened to one who is ill, lame and suffering. Alternatively, *Rashi* and *Mahari Kara* cite *II Kings* 5:6 and translate אֹסְפָה as *heal* — I will heal Israel from that which it suffered in exile.

וְהַנִּדָּחָה אֲקַבֵּצָה — *And gather in the one driven away.* I will gather in Israel who has been cast among the nations of the world (*Metzudos*) and is far from its destined place (*Radak*). Alternatively, אוֹסְפָה הַצֹּלֵעָה is referring specifically to the members of the Northern Kingdom and וְהַנִּדָּחָה אֲקַבֵּצָה is referring to the members of the Kingdom of Judah (*Abarbanel; Malbim*).

Although *Abarbanel* and *Malbim* arrive at the same conclusion, they differ in their reasoning. *Abarbanel* explains that בֵּית יַעֲקֹב, *the House of Jacob*, is generally referring to the Northern Kingdom. In the Book of *Genesis* (32:25-33), Scripture relates that the patriarch Jacob had wrestled with a man who the Rabbis relate was the שָׂרוֹ שֶׁל עֵשָׂו, *the Guardian Angel of Esau*, in a human guise. The "man" struck the socket of Jacob's hip and caused him to become lame. Hence, the *lame* of our verse is referring to the House of Jacob — the Northern Kingdom of Israel. The נִדָּחָה is referring to the Kingdom of Judah who elected to flee to אֶרֶץ הַנִּדָּחִים, the far-off lands of Greece and Rome.

1. For a detailed study of the wars of Gog and Magog, see ArtScroll *Yechezkel*, comm. to Chapters 38 and 39.

ז וַאֲשֶׁר הֲרֵעֹתִי׃ וְשַׂמְתִּי אֶת־הַצֹּלֵעָה לִשְׁאֵרִית וְהַנַּהֲלָאָה לְגוֹי עָצוּם וּמָלַךְ יהוה עֲלֵיהֶם ח בְּהַר צִיּוֹן מֵעַתָּה וְעַד־עוֹלָם׃ וְאַתָּה מִגְדַּל־עֵדֶר עֹפֶל בַּת־צִיּוֹן עָדֶיךָ תֵּאתֶה וּבָאָה הַמֶּמְשָׁלָה הָרִאשֹׁנָה מַמְלֶכֶת לְבַת־ ט יְרוּשָׁלָםִ׃ עַתָּה לָמָּה תָרִיעִי רֵעַ הֲמֶלֶךְ אֵין־ בָּךְ אִם־יוֹעֲצֵךְ אָבָד כִּי־הֶחֱזִיקֵךְ חִיל כַּיּוֹלֵדָה׃

Malbim first differentiates between אָסַף and קִבֵּץ: אָסַף is used when transfering object from one specific area to another. קִבֵּץ is to gather objects that have been scattered around. Hence, regarding the ten tribes of the Northern Kingdom who were all driven to one far-off land, Scripture uses אָסַף but regarding the members of the Kingdom of Judah who had been scattered to the far corners of the world, Scripture uses קִבֵּץ.

[For a lengthy discussion of the return of the Ten Tribes of the Northern Kingdom see *Yechezkel*, ArtScroll edition, comm. to 37:15-22.]

וַאֲשֶׁר הֲרֵעֹתִי — *And whomever I have harmed.* I will assemble those whom I have punished for the sins of the nation (*Rashi*) and have been disgraced among the nations (*Ibn Ezra*). Just as I treated them harshly I will now deal well with them (*Radak*); measure for measure (*Metzudos*). Alternatively, this is a prophetic reference to those of the nation who will be exiled during the destruction of the Second Temple (*Abarbanel; Malbim*).

7. וְשַׂמְתִּי אֶת־הַצֹּלֵעָה לִשְׁאֵרִית וְהַנַּהֲלָאָה לְגוֹי עָצוּם — *And I will make the lame one into a remnant and the one forced to wander into a mighty nation.* The lame nation will not become extinct while in exile (*Radak*) for a remnant will return to its Land and become a mighty nation (*Metzudos*).

As explained previously, *the lame one* is referring to the Ten Tribes of the Northern Kingdom who had been driven to a far-off land and seem to have either disappeared forever or abandoned their faith and intermingled with the nations of the world. Regarding them God says, *"I will make the lame one into a remnant."* The Kingdom of Judah, who had been cast from place to place and from nation to nation and had become few in number during the exile, *will become a mighty nation* upon its return to the land (*Malbim*).

וּמָלַךְ ה׳ עֲלֵיהֶם בְּהַר צִיּוֹן מֵעַתָּה וְעַד־עוֹלָם — *And* HASHEM *will reign over them at Mount Zion from now and forever.* From that time on the heathen nations will never again rule over Israel for God will be their ruler with His kingdom situated on Mount Zion. His glory will never again depart from that place (*Abarbanel; Metzudos*).

8. וְאַתָּה מִגְדַּל־עֵדֶר — *And you, Migdal-eder* (Tower of the Flock). The prophet continues to describe Israel's future return from exile, the restoration of Jerusalem, its Temple and the return of the Davidic kingdom. As it often does — see 2:13 — Scripture refers to the Congregation of Israel as a flock of sheep (*Radak*).

What does the Tower represent? *Targum Yonasan* understands the מִגְדַּל to be מְשִׁיחָא דְיִשְׂרָאֵל, *the Messiah of Israel*, or it may be the Holy Temple [where Israel had flocked to observe its festivals] (*Rashi; Mahari Kara*). *Radak* writes that the מִגְדַּל is מִגְדַּל דָּוִד, *the Tower of David* [*Berachos* 30a implies that מִגְדַּל דָּוִד is synonymous with the Holy Temple], and *Ibn Ezra* maintains that the מִגְדַּל is the City of Jerusalem. Alternatively, מִגְדַּל־עֵדֶר is the name of a town that was located in close proximity to Bethlehem (*Rashbam* to *Genesis* 35:21). It is in this town that

and whomever I have harmed, [7] *and I will make the lame one into a remnant and the one forced to wander into a mighty nation; and HASHEM will reign over them at Mount Zion from now and forever.* [8] *And you, Migdal-eder (Tower of the Flock), Ophel of the daughter of Zion, they will come [back] to you; and the original kingdom will arrive, the kingdom of the daughter of Jerusalem.* [9] *Now, why do you seek [foreign] alliance? Is there not a king in your midst? Has your counselor become lost, that pains have gripped you like a woman in childbirth?*

the Messianic king will initially reveal himself (*Targum Yonasan* ibid.).

In the city of Migdal-eder, the number of tribes was completed at twelve, for the youngest of the twelve tribes, Benjamin, was born there. The prophet is therefore foretelling that in the end of days, the nation that had been divided into two kingdoms will be unified and the nation will again be complete as it originally had been at Migdal-eder (*R' Bachya, Genesis* ibid.).

עֹפֶל בַּת־צִיּוֹן עָדֶיךָ תֵּאתֶה — *Ophel of the daughter of Zion, they will come [back] to you.* Like *migdal, ophel* is a tower or fortress (*Metzudos*). The remnant of the lame and the weak will come back to you — the *migdal* [the Messianic king, the Temple, or Jerusalem] (*Rashi*). Alternatively, *Targum Yonasan* interprets the verse as if the word עֹפֶל would be written with an א — אֹפֶל — *darkness,* and translates "the Messiah of Israel that had been *concealed* — דִּטְמִיר [that was held in darkness] due to the sins of those who assembled in Zion."

Although the cantillation to the word תֵּאתֶה indicates a pause, *Ibn Ezra* and *Radak* join עָדֶיךָ תֵּאתֶה with the latter section of the verse with understanding that תֵּאתֶה and וּבָאָה both translate as *come. Ibn Ezra* cites *Psalms* 72:20 where a similar situation exists.

וּבָאָה הַמֶּמְשָׁלָה הָרִאשֹׁנָה... — *And the original kingdom will arrive ...* The kingdom in its entirety — both the Kingdom of Judah and the Northern Kingdom — will again be under the reign of the Davidic House as it had been before the division of the monarchy (*Rashi*).

9. עַתָּה לָמָּה תָרִיעִי רֵעַ — *Now, why do you seek [foreign] alliance?* Our translation of תָרִיעִי רֵעַ follows *Rashi* who explains that Micah is reprimanding the people for seeking the friendship and aid of the kings of Egypt and Assyria (*Rashi*). He also warns them not to enter into a friendship with the Chaldeans and not to worship their deities (*Mahari Kara*). Alternatively, *Radak* relates תָרִיעִי רֵעַ to תְּרוּעָה, to *cry out in anguish,* and renders now that you will soon be exiled why do you mourn and weep; remember the day of your salvation.

הֲמֶלֶךְ אֵין־בָּךְ אִם־יוֹעֲצֵךְ אָבָד — *Is there not a king in your midst? Has your counselor become lost?* There is no need to seek alliances with other kings for God is the King and His prophets are the counselors who counsel the people to return to Him (*Metzudos*).

כִּי־הֶחֱזִיקֵךְ חִיל כַּיּוֹלֵדָה — *That pains have gripped you like a woman in childbirth.* The people tremble and shudder as a woman in labor, for they fear the heathen nations that are ready to attack them (*Metzudos*). *Malbim* explains the analogy. Just as the woman shudders and trembles when she is about to expel her child from her body, so too is it with Israel whose people are about to be expelled from their cities into exile.

י חֽוּלִי וָגֹחִי בַּת־צִיּוֹן כַּיּוֹלֵדָה כִּֽי־עַתָּה תֵצְאִי מִקִּרְיָה וְשָׁכַנְתְּ בַּשָּׂדֶה וּבָאת עַד־בָּבֶל שָׁם תִּנָּצֵלִי שָׁם יִגְאָלֵךְ יהוה מִכַּף אֹיְבָיִךְ׃ יא וְעַתָּה נֶאֶסְפוּ עָלַיִךְ גּוֹיִם רַבִּים הָאֹמְרִים תֶּחֱנָף וְתַחַז בְּצִיּוֹן עֵינֵינוּ׃ יב וְהֵמָּה לֹא יָֽדְעוּ מַחְשְׁבוֹת יהוה וְלֹא הֵבִינוּ עֲצָתוֹ כִּי קִבְּצָם כֶּעָמִיר גֹּרְנָה׃ יג קוּמִי וָדוֹשִׁי בַת־צִיּוֹן כִּֽי־קַרְנֵךְ אָשִׂים בַּרְזֶל וּפַרְסֹתַיִךְ אָשִׂים נְחוּשָׁה וַהֲדִקּוֹת עַמִּים רַבִּים

10. חוּלִי וָגֹחִי בַּת־צִיּוֹן כַּיּוֹלֵדָה — *Be in pain and groan like a woman in childbirth, O daughter of Zion.* Because the people had placed their trust in foreign monarchs, they will indeed suffer and sigh for those monarchs will be of no assistance to them (*Metzudos*).

כִּי־עַתָּה תֵצְאִי מִקִּרְיָה וְשָׁכַנְתְּ בַּשָּׂדֶה — *For now you will leave the city and dwell in the field.* The enemy will rout the people from all the cities in the Land of Israel (*Radak*) or from the city par excellence: Jerusalem (*Rashi; Mahari Kara*). They will gather the people together and, as captives, assemble them in the fields and then lead them into exile (*Radak*). Alternatively, many will actually *dwell* in the fields of Egypt and other surrounding lands (*Malbim*).

Talmud Yerushalmi (*Succah* 4:3) encounters difficulty with the use of וְשָׁכַנְתְּ, *and you will dwell*, for it seems to indicate a peaceful time rather than the turmoil of exile. It would seem that מִטַּלְטֵל, *to be mixed*, or גָּלוּת, *to be exiled*, would be a more appropriate word. R' Zachai therefore explains that וְשָׁכַנְתְּ is not referring to the Israelite nation but to God's Divine Presence [שְׁכִינָה]. His Divine Presence will accompany the nation into exile.

וּבָאת עַד־בָּבֶל שָׁם תִּנָּצֵלִי — *You will come to Babylonia and there you will be rescued.* Nebuchadnezzar will exile the people to Babylonia (*Radak; Ibn Ezra*) where they will remain until the day that it falls. They will then be set free, without the aid of the heathen kings (*Metzudos*).

Malbim notes that only those who had been exiled to Babylonia returned to Israel during the days of Cyrus. Those who became inhabitants of the "fields" surrounding Israel were killed by the Chaldeans.

11. וְעַתָּה נֶאֶסְפוּ עָלַיִךְ גּוֹיִם רַבִּים — *And now, many nations have assembled against you.* Although the prophet introduces this prophecy with the word וְעַתָּה, *and now*, implying that he is discussing events that are taking place then, during his time, most commentators (*Ibn Ezra; Radak; Metzudos*) understand this as a prophecy foretelling events that will ultimately take place during Messianic times. Micah uses עַתָּה to assure the nation that this will indeed occur although it may be a long way off (*Radak*). Accordingly, the *many nations that have assembled against you, Israel*, are Gog and Magog and the multitude of nations who have assembled with him (*Metzudos*). Other opinions are the armies of Sennacherib (*Tos. Rid*) or the Romans (*Abarbanel*). *Malbim* sees this passage as a prophetic overview spanning the period after the days of Cyrus [when the Israelite nation returned to Israel and built the Second Sanctuary] until the end of days. The *many nations* are those who oppressed the Jewish people through the ages: Greece, Rome and Gog and Magog.

הָאֹמְרִים תֶּחֱנָף וְתַחַז בְּצִיּוֹן עֵינֵינוּ — *Who say, "Let her be [proclaimed] guilty, and let our eyes behold Zion."* The nations

[10] Be in pain and groan like a woman in childbirth, O daughter of Zion; for now you will leave the city and dwell in the field; you will come to Babylonia and there you will be rescued; there HASHEM *will redeem you from the palms of your enemies. [11] And now, many nations have assembled against you, who say, 'Let her be [proclaimed] guilty, and let our eyes behold Zion!' [12] But they do not know the thoughts of* HASHEM *and do not understand His counsel — for He has gathered them like sheaves to the threshing floor. [13] Arise and thresh, O daughter of Zion! For I will make your horn [like] iron and I will make your hooves [like] copper, and you will grind many peoples.*

think that Zion will be held liable for her sins (*Rashi; Metzudos*) and that she will be destroyed for committing them (*Radak*). They gaze at her jubilantly and gloat over her degradation for it is the fulfillment of all their hopes (*Rashi*).

Malbim translates תֶּחֱנָף as *to flatter* and תַּחַז as *to prophesy,* and offers a unique explanation of this passage: Scripture is alluding to the two approaches that the nations used throughout history in their persecution of the Jews. Under the Greeks and Romans, Israel was a satellite nation, subservient and paying tribute to their mighty master. This is alluded to with תֶּחֱנָף, *to flatter.* As the slave flatters his master, Israel, the slave nation, flatters his master nation. Other nations, such as the Arabs, believed that Israel had lost its unique status of being God's chosen people and had been replaced by them, a new chosen nation. This is *Malbim's* translation of וְתַחַז בְּצִיּוֹן עֵינֵינוּ — that which had been prophesied regarding Zion is upon *our* eyes — they claim that all the prophecies written in Scripture regarding Israel actually concerns them, not Israel.

12. וְהֵמָּה לֹא יָדְעוּ מַחְשְׁבוֹת ה׳ וְלֹא הֵבִינוּ עֲצָתוֹ כִּי קִבְּצָם כֶּעָמִיר גֹּרְנָה — *But they do not know the thoughts of* HASHEM *and do not understand His counsel — for He has gathered them like sheaves to the threshing floor.* The nations think that they are assembled to wage a campaign against Jerusalem but do not realize that God is bringing them together to be trampled (*Radak*). In the same manner that sheaves are brought to the threshing floor, God will gather them in the Valley of Jehoshaphat and around Jerusalem to be beaten and threshed like sheaves (*Rashi; Radak*).

13. קוּמִי וָדוֹשִׁי בַת־צִיּוֹן כִּי־קַרְנֵךְ אָשִׂים בַּרְזֶל וּפַרְסֹתַיִךְ אָשִׂים נְחוּשָׁה וַהֲדִקּוֹת עַמִּים רַבִּים — *Arise and thresh, O daughter of Zion! For I will make your horn [like] iron and I will make your hooves [like] copper, and you will grind many peoples.* Since the nations were compared to sheaves of grain that were about to be threshed, Israel is now compared to the ox that will facilitate the threshing (*Ibn Ezra*). Although the long exile will weaken Israel's strength, the prophet assures the people that God will give them the necessary strength to defeat the nations who will wage war with them. He will make the horn of the nation strong like iron to gore and kill its enemies (*Metzudos*) and its hooves like copper to thresh (*Radak*) and trample its oppressors (*Metzudos*). *Targum Yonasan* relates the horn and hooves to different sections of the nation indicating that the *entire* nation will be revitalized with renewed vigor.

יד וְהַחֲרַמְתִּי לַיהוה בִּצְעָם וְחֵילָם לַאֲדוֹן כָּל־הָאָרֶץ: עַתָּה תִּתְגֹּדְדִי בַת־גְּדוּד מָצוֹר שָׂם עָלֵינוּ בַּשֵּׁבֶט יַכּוּ עַל־הַלְּחִי אֵת שֹׁפֵט יִשְׂרָאֵל:

א וְאַתָּה בֵּית־לֶחֶם אֶפְרָתָה צָעִיר לִהְיוֹת בְּאַלְפֵי יְהוּדָה מִמְּךָ לִי יֵצֵא לִהְיוֹת מוֹשֵׁל בְּיִשְׂרָאֵל וּמוֹצָאֹתָיו מִקֶּדֶם מִימֵי עוֹלָם: ב לָכֵן יִתְּנֵם עַד־עֵת יוֹלֵדָה יָלָדָה

וְהַחֲרַמְתִּי לַה׳ בִּצְעָם וְחֵילָם לַאֲדוֹן כָּל־הָאָרֶץ — *I will consecrate unto* HASHEM *all their ill-gotten riches, and their wealth unto the Lord of the entire earth.* בֶּצַע is the riches that the enemy acquired from others through thievery and violence. חַיִל is the wealth that had actually belonged to them — their possessions (*Rashi*). All the treasures that Israel will capture they will consecrate to G-d (*Malbim*). Alternatively, Israel will keep a portion of the captured treasures and consecrate a portion to God (*Radak*).

14. עַתָּה תִּתְגֹּדְדִי בַת־גְּדוּד — *Now, muster yourself, O daughter of the armed band!* Our translation of תִּתְגֹּדְדִי follows *Rashi, Mahari Kara* and *Radak* who relate תִּתְגֹּדְדִי to גְּדוּד, *troops.* Micah now "returns from the distant future" and foretells events of the present. Israel will not be successful in her campaigns at this time, for her sins have increased. Therefore muster yourself, O Chaldeans (*Rashi*) or Assyrians (*Mahari Kara*) and send your troops for you will be successful (*Rashi*).

Others explain that Micah continues to foretell events of Messianic times. Israel will be surrounded by troops when Gog and Magog will unsuccessfully attempt to besiege Jerusalem (*Radak*). Alternatively, *Metzudos* translates תִּתְגֹּדְדִי, *cut yourself,* and explains that Micah is addressing the nations that will join Gog and Magog. The verse is a play on words: תִּתְגֹּדְדִי, *cut yourself,* you nation בַת־גְּדוּד, *of many troops,* because you will be punished severely for laying siege to Jerusalem prior to the destruction of the Second Temple.

Malbim writes that this verse is pointing out the nations that will be crushed by Israel. They will be descendants — בַת־גְּדוּד — "daughters" of the armed bands, of the very nations who had besieged Jerusalem and destroyed her Temple through the ages.

בַּשֵּׁבֶט יַכּוּ עַל־הַלְּחִי אֵת שֹׁפֵט יִשְׂרָאֵל — *With a stick they strike on the cheek the judges of Israel.*

Because Israel had struck its prophets and judges on the cheek and was guilty of disgracing and humiliating them, it will not succeed in its battles against its enemies (*Rashi*). Alternatively, the nations who will attack Israel in Messianic times will be punished for disgracing and humiliating Israel's judges throughout the exile (*Metzudos*).

V

In the previous chapter Micah foretold that ultimately Jerusalem and its Temple will be rebuilt and the nations of the world will follow the Messianic king. He now discusses the Messianic king. Unlike most commentators however, *Tos. Rid* maintains that the descendant of the Davidic house discussed in this chapter is King Hezekiah.

4/14

I will consecrate unto Hashem *all their ill-gotten riches, and their wealth unto the Lord of the entire land.*

[14] *'Now, muster yourself, O daughter of the armed band!' He has laid siege against us; with a stick they strike on the cheek the judges of Israel.*

5/1-2

[1] *Bethlehem — Ephratah, you are too small to be among the thousands of Judah, but from you someone will emerge for Me to be a ruler over Israel; and his origins will be from early times, from days of old.* [2] *Therefore, He will deliver them [to their enemies] until the time that a woman in childbirth gives birth;*

1. וְאַתָּה בֵּית־לֶחֶם אֶפְרָתָה צָעִיר לִהְיוֹת בְּאַלְפֵי יְהוּדָה — *Bethlehem — Ephratah, you are too small to be among the thousands of Judah.* Bethlehem-Ephratah of Judah was the birthplace of King David — see *I Samuel* 17:12. Since there was another Bethlehem located in the territory of the tribe of Zebulun — see *Joshua* 19:15 — Scripture writes Bethelehem-Ephratah of Judah to distinguish between the two (*Metzudos*). Micah addresses the Davidic house and declares that due to their descent from Ruth the Moabite, it really would have been more proper that they be the least prominent members of the tribe of Judah. However, it is from this family that the Messianic king will emerge (*Rashi*). Alternatively, the prophet is not directing his words to the Davidic house but to the city of Bethlehem which was one of the smallest cities of Judah. Nevertheless it merited that one of its sons, King David, would have a descendant who would lead the nation (*Radak*). In any event, Scripture does not mean that the Messiah's birthplace will be the city of Bethlehem [as the Christian writers propose] but that the Messianic king will be a descendant of the House of David which originated in Bethlehem (*Metzudos*). [See "Awake My Glory" by R' A. Miller par. 218-219.]

וּמוֹצָאֹתָיו מִקֶּדֶם מִימֵי עוֹלָם — *And his origins will be from early times, from days of old.* The origin or roots of the Messiah are from ancient times, from the days of his ancestor King David (*Radak*). Alternatively, his name was known [to Me] from long ago (*Targum Yonasan*). Citing the verse לִפְנֵי־שֶׁמֶשׁ יִנּוֹן שְׁמוֹ, *before the sun [was created] Yinon was his name* (*Psalms* 72:17), the Talmud explains that the name of the Messiah was one of the seven things that God created before He created the world (*Rashi; Mahari Kara* from *Pesachim* 54a). [See also *Pirkei D'Rabbi Eliezer* Chap. 3.] *Ran* (*Nedarim* 39b) explains that the existence of the world is dependent on these seven things. God therefore created them before He created the world. *Malbim* adds that the entire purpose of creation is the perfection of the human race which will not occur until Messianic times.

2. לָכֵן יִתְּנֵם עַד־עֵת יוֹלֵדָה יָלָדָה — *Therefore, He will deliver them [to their enemies] until the time that a woman in childbirth gives birth.* Micah had previously foretold that God will deliver the inhabitants of Zion into the hands of their enemies. The people will be in pain and will tremble and groan terribly like a woman who is about to give birth (4:9,10). This will continue until the appropriate time for redemption will arrive (*Rashi*). For just as a woman must endure the pangs of labor prior to the delivery of her child, so too, must Israel endure

ג וְיֶתֶר אֶחָיו יְשׁוּבוּן עַל־בְּנֵי יִשְׂרָאֵל׃ וְעָמַד וְרָעָה בְּעֹז יהוה בִּגְאוֹן שֵׁם יהוה אֱלֹהָיו וְיָשָׁבוּ כִּי־עַתָּה ד יִגְדַּל עַד־אַפְסֵי־אָרֶץ׃ וְהָיָה זֶה שָׁלוֹם אַשּׁוּר | כִּי־יָבוֹא בְאַרְצֵנוּ וְכִי יִדְרֹךְ בְּאַרְמְנֹתֵינוּ וַהֲקֵמֹנוּ ה עָלָיו שִׁבְעָה רֹעִים וּשְׁמֹנָה נְסִיכֵי אָדָם׃ וְרָעוּ אֶת־אֶרֶץ אַשּׁוּר בַּחֶרֶב וְאֶת־אֶרֶץ נִמְרֹד בִּפְתָחֶיהָ

suffering and pain to atone for their sins (*Mahari Kara*). *Radak* points to the prophecies of *Daniel* (12:1) that foretell of suffering so terrible that they can be compared to none that had ever occurred.

Scripture often metaphorically compares the suffering of the Messianic era to the pain of a woman in childbirth. Rav taught (*Sanhedrin* 98b) that the Messiah will come only after the wicked kingdom [Rome — see *Yoma* 10a] has extended its dominion over Israel for nine months. According to *Rashi* (ibid.) it will extend its dominion over all parts of the world to which Jews are dispersed. *Abarbanel* notes that the Talmudic sages had a tradition handed down to them from the prophets that the war of the nations will last for exactly nine months.

Alternatively, the subject of this prophecy is not Israel, but Gog and Magog. *They* will suffer terribly when they will be defeated by the Messianic king (*Metzudos*). *Tos. Rid*, however, explains that the entire verse is referring to Sennacherib who will suffer and fall to Hezekiah.

וְיֶתֶר אֶחָיו יְשׁוּבוּן עַל־בְּנֵי יִשְׂרָאֵל — *Then the rest of his brothers will return with the Children of Israel.* Although the people must endure intense hardship and terrible suffering, it will end with the rebirth of the Jewish nation (*Mahari Kara*) and the return of the Messiah's brethren. The rest of the tribe of Judah (*Rashi*) together with the tribe of Benjamin (*Radak*) will join the Messianic king and unite with the other tribes in a united kingdom never again to be divided (*Rashi; Radak*). *Abarbanel* maintains that the Ten Tribes of the Northern Kingdom will be the first to return to Israel. They will battle the Christians with other Eastern and Northern nations and will be joined with the tribes of Judah and Benjamin. Alternatively, the brothers of Gog and the remainder of his nation will return to be subservient to Israel (*Metzudos*).

3. וְעָמַד וְרָעָה בְּעֹז ה׳ — *He will stand up and lead with the strength of* HASHEM. The Messianic king will lead the nation with the strength granted to him by God (*Metzudos*) and thereby bring the people back from exile (*Targum Yonasan; Rashi*). They will then dwell in peace (*Radak; Metzudos; Malbim*), for once the wicked are punished, the name of the Messiah will be exalted and publicized for his fame will spread over the entire face of the earth (*Radak*). The nations will even pay tribute to him with horses and chariots (*Rashi*). Alternatively, it is the Name of God that will be exalted and publicized over the entire earth (*Metzudos*).

בִּגְאוֹן שֵׁם ה׳ אֱלֹהָיו — *With the majesty of the Name of* HASHEM *his God.* Although *Metzudos* does not differentiate between *the strength of* HASHEM and *the majesty of the Name of* HASHEM and understands it as a repetitive feature of Scripture, *Malbim* sees a difference between the two. עֹז is used to describe physical might and strength — primarily in battle. גְאוֹן is used to describe majestic supernatural strength, Divinely inspired by the name of HASHEM/ELOHIM. Scripture is stating that the Messianic king will lead Israel with these God-given powers.

then the rest of his brothers will return with the Children of Israel. [3]*He will stand up and lead with the strength of* HASHEM, *with the majesty of the Name of* HASHEM *his God. They will settle [in peace], for at that time he will be great to the ends of the earth,* [4]*and this will [assure] peace. If Assyria will come into our land, and if he will tread upon our palaces, we will set up seven shepherds and eight officers against him,* [5]*and they will pound the land of Assyria with the sword, and the land of Nimrod at its gateways;*

4. וְהָיָה זֶה שָׁלוֹם — *And this will [assure] peace.* Unlike previous times, when the victories brought only a temporary peace, under the Messianic king there will be an everlasting peace (*Rashi*). All the nations of the world will accept his laws and his dominion and will not resort to violence or war. His greatness will be realized through the peace he will bring (*Malbim*).

אַשּׁוּר כִּי־יָבוֹא בְאַרְצֵנוּ וְכִי יִדְרֹךְ בְּאַרְמְנֹתֵינוּ ... — *If Assyria will come into our land, and if he will tread upon our palaces ...* If the Assyrians will not be interested in peace even after the arrival of the Messiah and will wish to invade our land at that time, we will confront them with seven shepherds and eight officers who will stand up against them and smite them (*Radak*).

Who are the seven shepherds and eight officers? *Radak* writes that they are the officers of the Messianic king who will assist him in leading Israel. He explains that the numbers seven and eight are not exact and refers us to *Koheles* (11:2) where a similar phrase is used to express abundance. Accordingly, Scripture is simply stating that many officers will confront the enemy. The Sages (*Succah* 52b), however, identify the seven shepherds and eight officers. The seven shepherds are: David in the center, Adam, Seth and Methuselah on his right; Abraham, Jacob and Moses on his left. The eight officers are: Jesse, Saul, Samuel, Amos, Zephaniah, Zedekiah [some glosses have Hezekiah], Elijah and the Messiah.

Rashi, both in his Talmudic and Scriptural commentaries, writes that he is unaware of the source or reason that these righteous men were specifically chosen.

Although the Sages list these men as the seven shepherds and eight princes of men, *Malbim* offers his own interpretations of this subject: one reflecting on ancient times and another foretelling events of the Messianic era.

(a) The eight princes are the last eight monarchs [excluding Shalum ben Yavesh who only reigned for one month] who ruled the Northern Kingdom prior to the Assyrian invasion. They are Jehoachaz, Joash, Jeroboam, Zechariah, Menahem, Pekachiah, Pekach and Hoshea.

The seven princes are Hezekiah, Manasseh, Amon [*Malbim* does not include Josiah in this listing], Jehoachaz, Jehoyakim, Jehoyachin and Zedekiah.

(b) During Messianic times (as described in *Ezekiel*, Chapters 32 and 38) many nations will join Gog and Magog in battle. Seven are mentioned in *Ezekiel* 32: Egypt, Elam, Meshech, Tuval, Edom, princes of the North and the Zidoni. According to *Malbim* they are the seven shepherds.

The eight princes are those nations listed in *Ezekiel* Chapter 38: Gog the leader of Magog, Meshech, Tuval, Persia, Cush, Put, Gomer and Beth-Togramah.

5. וְרָעוּ אֶת־אֶרֶץ אַשּׁוּר בַּחֶרֶב וְאֶת־אֶרֶץ נִמְרוֹד בִּפְתָחֶיהָ — *And they will pound the land of Assyria with the sword, and the land of Nimrod at its gateways.* The shepherds will pound Assyria with the sword (*Radak*) and the land

וְהִצִּיל֙ מֵֽאַשּׁ֔וּר כִּֽי־יָב֣וֹא בְאַרְצֵ֔נוּ וְכִ֥י יִדְרֹ֖ךְ בִּגְבוּלֵֽנוּ׃ ו וְהָיָ֣ה ׀ שְׁאֵרִ֣ית יַעֲקֹ֗ב בְּקֶ֙רֶב֙ עַמִּ֣ים רַבִּ֔ים כְּטַל֙ מֵאֵ֣ת יהוה כִּרְבִיבִ֖ים עֲלֵי־עֵ֑שֶׂב אֲשֶׁ֤ר לֹֽא־יְקַוֶּה֙ לְאִ֔ישׁ וְלֹ֥א יְיַחֵ֖ל לִבְנֵ֥י אָדָֽם׃ ז וְהָיָה֩ שְׁאֵרִ֨ית יַעֲקֹ֜ב בַּגּוֹיִ֗ם בְּקֶ֙רֶב֙ עַמִּ֣ים רַבִּ֔ים כְּאַרְיֵה֙ בְּבַהֲמ֣וֹת יַ֔עַר כִּכְפִ֖יר בְּעֶדְרֵי־צֹ֑אן ח אֲשֶׁ֧ר אִם־עָבַ֛ר וְרָמַ֥ס וְטָרַ֖ף וְאֵ֥ין מַצִּֽיל׃ תָּרֹ֥ם ט יָדְךָ֖ עַל־צָרֶ֑יךָ וְכָל־אֹיְבֶ֖יךָ יִכָּרֵֽתוּ׃ וְהָיָ֤ה

of Nimrod — Babylonia[1] — (*Rashi; Radak; Ibn Ezra*) will be broken within the gateways of her cities, before she has a chance to leave the city for battle (*Rashi*). These nations will never again invade the Land of Israel nor tread onto its borders (*Radak*).

Our translation of פְּתָחֶיהָ, *its gateways*, follows *Rashi*. *Radak* and *Ibn Ezra* translate *swords* [as they do in *Psalms* 55:22. *Rashi* there quotes *Menachem ben Saruk* who also translates פְּתָחֶיהָ of our verse as *swords*]. Accordingly, the verse means that the inhabitants of the land of Nimrod will be killed by the sword.

6. וְהָיָה שְׁאֵרִית יַעֲקֹב בְּקֶרֶב עַמִּים — *The remnant of Jacob will be in the midst of many peoples.* The remnant of Jacob — the righteous Jews who will survive the sufferings of exile — will be among the forces of Gog when he will converge upon Jerusalem (*Radak; Abarbanel*) and will then seek salvation only from God and will wait for Him to deliver them from their enemy (*Rashi; Radak*).

כְּטַל מֵאֵת ה׳ ... וְלֹא יְיַחֵל לִבְנֵי אָדָם — *Like dew from HASHEM ... and not awaited from a human being.* This is a metaphor describing Israel's hope for salvation. One cannot beseech any mortal for dew or rain for they are both gifts from God. So too, will Israel seek help only from God (*Rashi; Radak*).

כְּטַל מֵאֵת ה׳ — *Like dew from HASHEM.*

Unlike rain, dew is never withheld by God, even if Israel sins and is undeserving. Similarly, God's goodness will not be withheld from Israel (*Talmud Yerushalmi* 5:2, see commentary of *Pnei Moshe*).

In Midrashic literature, טַל is symbolic of blessings. In Messianic times, Israel will be a source of blessings to the world (*Abarbanel*). With its true teachings, Israel will be like dew and rain to the nations, transforming "the desert of humanity into a place of blossoming beauty and flourishing prosperity" (*R' Mendel Hirsch*).

כִּרְבִיבִים עֲלֵי־עֵשֶׂב — *Like raindrops upon grass.*

The word רְבִיבִים is related to רבה, *to shoot* [רֹבֶה קַשָּׁת, *an archer* (*Gen.* 21:20)]. It is the rain that shoots down into the earth as an arrow (*Rashi, Deut.* 32:2). *Ibn Ezra* (ibid.) maintains that the root of רְבִיבִים is רב, *abundance*. It is an abundance of rain (*Radak*).

7. וְהָיָה שְׁאֵרִית יַעֲקֹב בַּגּוֹיִם בְּקֶרֶב עַמִּים רַבִּים — *And the remnant of Jacob will be among the nations, in the midst of many peoples.*

Although the opening phrase of this verse is similar to that of the previous passage, *Abarbanel* notes the addition of the word בַּגּוֹיִם and explains that the עַמִּים רַבִּים, the *many peoples* of this verse are the enemies of Israel whom the

1. *Ramban* (*Genesis* 10:11) identifies the land of Nimrod as Assyria.

and he will rescue [us] from Assyria when they enter our land and when they tread onto our borders. [6] *The remnant of Jacob will be in the midst of many peoples like dew from* HASHEM, *like raindrops upon grass, which is not hoped for from man and not awaited from a human being.*

[7] *And the remnant of Jacob will be among the nations, in the midst of many peoples, like a lion among the beasts of the forest and like a lion's whelp among flocks of sheep, who, when he passes by, tramples and tears apart, and there is no rescuer.* [8] *Your hand will be raised over your oppressors, and all your enemies will be eliminated.*

Torah refers to as גּוֹי אֲשֶׁר לֹא־יָדַעְתָּ — גּוֹי, *a nation you never knew* (*Deut.* 28:36) and גּוֹי עַז פָּנִים, *a brazen nation* (ibid. v. 50). He identifies these nations as Edom and Yishmael.

כְּאַרְיֵה בְּבַהֲמוֹת יַעַר — *Like a lion among the beasts of the forest.*

Our translation of בְּבַהֲמוֹת as *beasts* follows *Radak* and *Metzudos*, the latter citing *Deut.* 32:24 where וְשֶׁן־בְּהֵמֹת אֲשַׁלַּח־בָּם is translated *the teeth of beasts shall I dispatch against them.*[1] Israel, led by the king Messiah, will overpower the nations that have assembled against Jerusalem and will rule over them as the lion rules over the powerful beasts of the forest (*Rashi; Radak; Mahari Kara*). Even the leopard, the bear and the wolf are no match for the mighty lion as he tramples and tears them apart (*Radak*).

כִּכְפִיר בְּעֶדְרֵי־צֹאן — *Like a lion's whelp among flocks of sheep.*

The כְּפִיר, *the young lion,* is not as strong as the אַרְיֵה and cannot overpower the beasts of the forest, but is strong enough to trample and tear apart the flocks of sheep (*Radak*).

וְרָמַס וְטָרַף — *Tramples and tears apart.*

רָמַס is the lion's trampling and clawing upon his prey when he is famished; devouring it at that very spot. טָרַף is when the lion kills his prey and takes it to his den for his whelps and mate to eat [see *Nahum* 2:13] (*Rashi*).

8. תָּרֹם יָדְךָ עַל־צָרֶיךָ וְכָל־אֹיְבֶיךָ יִכָּרֵתוּ — *Your hand will be raised over your oppressors and all your enemies will be eliminated.* יָד רָמָה, *a raised hand,* is an expression used to denote victory or superiority — see *Deut.* 32:27; *Psalms* 89:14. Micah is foretelling that under the leadership of the Messiah, the hand of the nation will be raised to overpower and destroy their enemies (*Metzudos*). Alternatively, this is to be understood metaphorically: God's hand will be raised and will smite the enemies of the Israelite nation (*Yalkut Shimoni*).

צָרֶיךָ ... אֹיְבֶיךָ — *Your oppressors ... your enemies ...*

Malbim differentiates between צַר and אוֹיֵב. A צַר actively oppresses and outwardly attacks his adversary. The אוֹיֵב has a deep-rooted hatred for his

1. *Abarbanel*, however, lists as examples of בַּהֲמֹת יַעַר: בָּקָר, *cattle;* אַיִל, *ram* [or אַיָּל, *hart*]; צְבִי, *deer;* יַחְמוּר, *roebuck;* which seem to imply that the בַּהֲמֹת יַעַר are actually animals rather than beasts.

בַיּוֹם־הַהוּא֙ נְאֻם־יְהוָ֔ה וְהִכְרַתִּ֥י סוּסֶ֖יךָ
י מִקִּרְבֶּ֑ךָ וְהַאֲבַדְתִּ֖י מַרְכְּבֹתֶֽיךָ׃ וְהִכְרַתִּ֖י עָרֵ֣י
יא אַרְצֶ֑ךָ וְהָרַסְתִּ֖י כָּל־מִבְצָרֶֽיךָ׃ וְהִכְרַתִּ֥י כְשָׁפִ֖ים
יב מִיָּדֶ֑ךָ וּמְעוֹנְנִ֖ים לֹ֥א יִֽהְיוּ־לָֽךְ׃ וְהִכְרַתִּ֥י פְסִילֶ֛יךָ
וּמַצֵּבוֹתֶ֖יךָ מִקִּרְבֶּ֑ךָ וְלֹא־תִשְׁתַּחֲוֶ֥ה ע֖וֹד לְמַעֲשֵׂ֥ה
יג יָדֶֽיךָ׃ וְנָתַשְׁתִּ֥י אֲשֵׁירֶ֖יךָ מִקִּרְבֶּ֑ךָ וְהִשְׁמַדְתִּ֖י
יד עָרֶֽיךָ׃ וְעָשִׂ֜יתִי בְּאַ֧ף וּבְחֵמָ֛ה נָקָ֖ם אֶת־הַגּוֹיִ֑ם
ו/א א אֲשֶׁ֖ר לֹ֥א שָׁמֵֽעוּ׃ שִׁמְעוּ־

opponent and wishes him bad but does not actively attack him. The prophet therefore says, *Your hand will be raised over your oppressors*, and you will be victorious over them in battle, *and all your enemies will be eliminated* — they will destroy themselves. *Pirkei D'Rabbi Eliezer* identifies *your oppressors* as the descendants of Esau [Edom] and *your enemies* as the descendants of Yishmael.

9-14. In the verses that follow, Micah seems to censure Israel in an extremely harsh manner. The prophet's intent, however, is to assure Israel that peace will prevail forever and therefore the objects mentioned will never again be needed (*Radak*). Alternatively, this prophecy is not being directed toward Israel but toward the nations of the world — *their* horses, *their* chariots etc. will be destroyed (*Targum Yonasan*).

9. וְהָיָה בַיּוֹם־הַהוּא נְאֻם־ה׳ וְהִכְרַתִּי סוּסֶיךָ מִקִּרְבֶּךָ וְהַאֲבַדְתִּי מַרְכְּבֹתֶיךָ — *It will be on that day — the word of* HASHEM — *I will eliminate your horses from your midst and I will destroy your chariots.* After the war of Gog and Magog, Israel will never again need horses and chariots because peace will prevail (*Radak; Ibn Ezra*). *Rashi* suggests that the horses symbolize the assistance of Egypt upon which Israel depended for its supply of horses. Alternatively, *during* these wars you will not be saved through your horses and chariots but through the help of God (*Abarbanel; Metzudos*). *Targum Yonasan* renders, God will destroy the horses and chariots of the nations from the midst of Israel.

10. וְהִכְרַתִּי עָרֵי אַרְצֶךָ וְהָרַסְתִּי כָּל־מִבְצָרֶיךָ — *I will eliminate the [walled] cities from your land and I will tear down all your fortifications.* Walled and fortified cities will no longer be needed for peace will prevail (*Rashi; Radak*). The blessing of peace that I will give will be tantamount to tearing down the protective walls of the cities (*Radak*).

An עִיר is a city that is surrounded by a wall. An עִיר פְּרוּז is an unwalled city (*Metzudos*).

Radak notes that living in an unwalled city is healthier than living in a walled city for the air is fresher.

11. וְהִכְרַתִּי כְשָׁפִים מִיָּדֶךָ וּמְעוֹנְנִים לֹא יִהְיוּ־לָךְ — *I will eliminate witchcraft from your domain and there will be no diviners among you.* There will be no one practicing witchcraft in all the land as is done today (*Radak*), for when the people will realize that My Divine Providence is upon them, they will not seek to know the future through witchcraft (*Metzudos*).

מְעוֹנְנִים, *diviners*, are the topic of a Talmudic dispute. According to R' Akiva, מְעוֹנְנִים are those who calculate times and hours and predict that "today is a good day for departure" or "tomorrow is a good day for purchases." The Sages, however, explain that מְעוֹנְנִים are those who seize the eye — אֲחִיזַת הָעֵינַיִם, those who delude by optical deception (*Radak* from *Sanhedrin* 65b). *Ibn Ezra*

5/9-14

[9]*It will be on that day — the word of* HASHEM *— I will eliminate your horses from your midst and I will destroy your chariots.* [10]*I will eliminate the [walled] cities from your land and I will tear down all your fortifications.* [11]*I will eliminate witchcraft from your domain and there will be no diviners among you.* [12]*I will eliminate your graven images and your pillars from your midst, and you will no longer prostrate yourselves to your own handiwork.* [13] *I will uproot your Asherah trees from your midst, and I will destroy those who hate you.* [14]*And with anger and wrath I will carry out revenge against the nations, because they did not listen.*

maintains that they gaze at the clouds, עֲנָנִים, to predict the future.

12. וְהִכְרַתִּי פְסִילֶיךָ וּמַצֵּבוֹתֶיךָ מִקִּרְבֶּךָ וְלֹא־ תִשְׁתַּחֲוֶה עוֹד לְמַעֲשֵׂה יָדֶיךָ — *I will eliminate your graven images and your pillars from your midst, and you will no longer prostrate yourselves to your own handiwork.* The people will no longer prostrate themselves before their idols carved from wood or stone (*Ibn Ezra*), for they will then realize that there is no other God besides Me (*Metzudos*).

The מַצֵּבָה was an altar made of one stone and was used for idolatrous purposes (*Rashi, Deut.* 12:3).

13. וְנָתַשְׁתִּי אֲשֵׁירֶיךָ מִקִּרְבֶּךָ — *I will uproot your Asherah trees from your midst.*

An *Asherah* is a tree that is designated for worship (*Metzudos; Rashi, Deut.* 12:3). It seems to have been a tree which one imagined to be under the special protection of a god whose presence and influence one believed could be obtained by tending and looking after it (*R' Hirsch, Exodus* 34:13). The people will never again prostrate themselves before these trees (*Metzudos*).

וְהִשְׁמַדְתִּי עָרֶיךָ — *And I will destroy those who hate you.* I will destroy your enemies (*Radak*). *Rashi* cites *Isaiah* 14:21 and *I Samuel* 28:16 where עָר is a reference to enemies. In an alternative explanation, *Radak* renders, *and I will destroy your cities,* as explained in verse 10. *Ibn Ezra* and *Malbim* explain: I will destroy the cities that contain the Asherah.

14. וְעָשִׂיתִי בְּאַף וּבְחֵמָה נָקָם אֶת־הַגּוֹיִם אֲשֶׁר לֹא שָׁמֵעוּ — *And with anger and wrath I will carry out revenge against the nations because they did not listen.* I will pour forth My anger upon the nations who refused to obey the teachings of the Torah (*Targum Yonasan*) or the true religion (*Malbim*). Alternatively, I will wreak wrathful vengeance upon the nations in a manner that the world has never before heard (*Metzudos*).

Sifrei (*Deut.* 33:2) relates that God first offered the Torah to the nations of the world but they refused to accept it. Only Israel accepted it by saying, "All that Hashem has said we will do and we will listen." *Sifrei* cites this verse as proof.

R' Mendel Hirsch explains that verses 9-14 are directed toward Israel who had lost its glorious power and had suffered in exile but nevertheless had, at the ultimate redemption, won its victories in a supernatural manner ordained by God. The nations of the world, upon seeing the collapse of the nation of Israel, should have understood that they too were threatened and should have changed their evil ways, but they did not. God therefore says, "I will pour forth My anger in vengeance upon the nations who have not paid attention."

ו/ב־ד

נָא אֵת אֲשֶׁר־יהוה אֹמֵר קוּם רִיב אֶת־
ב הֶהָרִים וְתִשְׁמַעְנָה הַגְּבָעוֹת קוֹלֶךָ: שִׁמְעוּ
הָרִים אֶת־רִיב יהוה וְהָאֵתָנִים מֹסְדֵי אָרֶץ
כִּי רִיב לַיהוה עִם־עַמּוֹ וְעִם־יִשְׂרָאֵל יִתְוַכָּח:
ג עַמִּי מֶה־עָשִׂיתִי לְךָ וּמָה הֶלְאֵתִיךָ עֲנֵה בִי:
ד כִּי הֶעֱלִתִיךָ מֵאֶרֶץ מִצְרַיִם וּמִבֵּית עֲבָדִים
פְּדִיתִיךָ וָאֶשְׁלַח לְפָנֶיךָ אֶת־מֹשֶׁה אַהֲרֹן וּמִרְיָם:

VI

Micah now calls to the mountains and hills on God's behalf and instructs them to listen to a suit between God and Israel. He calls their attention to the kindness and benevolence that God displayed to His people throughout history and their ungrateful response. He then admonishes Israel for not following the ways of the Torah (*Yalkut Me'am Loez*).

1. שִׁמְעוּ־נָא אֵת אֲשֶׁר־ה׳ אֹמֵר קוּם רִיב אֶת־הֶהָרִים וְתִשְׁמַעְנָה הַגְּבָעוֹת קוֹלֶךָ — *Listen, now, [to] what HASHEM is saying [to me]: "Arise, contend before the mountains and let the hills hear your voice."* God said to me (*Ibn Ezra*), "Go out to the mountains and hills and plead your case before them for they have heard all that God has spoken" (*Radak*). Raise your voice loudly and publicize the iniquities of the nation in a manner that even the inanimate mountains and hills will hear what is being said (*Abarbanel; Metzudos*). In Chapter 3, Micah had called upon the leaders of Jacob to act as judges of Israel but they failed to listen to his words. He therefore chooses new judges: the mountains and hills (*Malbim*). Alternatively, the mountains represent the Patriarchs: Abraham, Isaac and Jacob; and the hills represent the Matriarchs: Sarah, Rebecca, Rachel and Leah (*Rashi; Radak*). They should be aware of the ungracious reactions their children had to God's goodness (*Radak*). *Mahari Kara* maintains that the mountains represent the kings of the nations of the world and the hills are their officers. They should take to heart God's warning to Israel and thereby ensure their own future (*R' Mendel Hirsch*).

2. שִׁמְעוּ הָרִים אֶת־רִיב ה׳ וְהָאֵתָנִים מֹסְדֵי אָרֶץ — *Listen, you mountains, to the grievance of HASHEM and you mighty ones, the foundations of the earth!* This is the speech that God instructed Micah to deliver on His behalf. "Listen, you mountains ..." (*Metzudos*). The mighty ones of this verse are synonymous with the mountains and hills of verse 1 (*Radak*).

The Sages (*Rosh Hashanah* 11a) say that הָאֵתָנִים מֹסְדֵי אָרֶץ, *you mighty ones, the foundations of the earth,* is a reference to our Patriarchs Abraham, Isaac and Jacob, in whose merit the world exists. *R' Mendel Hirsch* adds that it is actually the ideal Israel who is described as מוֹסְדֵי אָרֶץ, *the foundations of the earth.* Because Israel's mission is to bring mankind to the recognition of God which is the true calling of human beings, they are the real foundations of the formation of human happiness.

כִּי רִיב לַה׳ עִם־עַמּוֹ וְעִם־יִשְׂרָאֵל יִתְוַכָּח — *For HASHEM has a grievance with His people, and He will contend with Israel. Malbim* differentiates between רִיב and וִיכּוּחַ. A רִיב is a heated argument resolved by strength and power. A וִיכּוּחַ is a calm disagreement that is resolved logically. Therefore, with the multitudes of the nations there is a רִיב, a powerful argument, but with the great people of Israel the argument is of a logical nature.

[1] *Listen, now, [to] what HASHEM is saying [to me]: "Arise, contend before the mountains, and let the hills hear your voice!"* [2] *Listen, you mountains, to the grievance of HASHEM, and you mighty ones, the foundations of the earth! For HASHEM has a grievance with His people, and He will contend with Israel:*

[3] *My people, what [wrong] did I do to you and how did I tire you? Testify against Me!* [4] *For I brought you up from the land of Egypt and redeemed you from the house of bondage; and I sent Moses, Aaron and Miriam before you.*

3. עַמִּי מֶה־עָשִׂיתִי לְךָ — *My people! What [wrong] did I do to you.* God challenges His nation through Micah and asks, "My dear nation [see comm. to 2:8]! What wrong have I done to you (*Radak*)? Take heed and realize all the goodness I have done for you (*Rashi*). Although you have been punished for your sins, you must realize that you were actually deserving of much worse" (*Chida, Chomas Anoch*).

וּמָה הֶלְאֵתִיךָ עֲנֵה בִּי — *And how did I tire you? Testify against Me!* Micah continues and asks the people, "Which of My commandments do you find wearisome? (*Rashi; Radak*). If I have wronged you (*Radak*) or wearied you (*Metzudos*) then testify against Me!"

The Rabbis note that God did not command Israel to bring sacrifices from the wild beasts of the field but only from domesticated animals, those that are easily accessible such as cattle, sheep and goats because He did not wish to weary His nation with His service (*Bamidbar Rabbah* 20:5). Indeed, *Rambam* writes that the intent of all of God's commandments is to facilitate the service of God and lessen one's burden in His service (*Moreh Nevuchim* 3:47).

R' Yitzchak explained this idea with a parable. A king issued a decree to a certain country. Upon receiving the decree the people rose and stood upon their feet, bared their heads and read the decree with awe and fear, shuddering at every word. But God is different. He didn't require His nation to stand or bare their heads when they recite the *Shema*. It may be read, "when you are sitting in your house or when you are going on the road, when you lie down or when you rise," for God does not wish to weary His people with the observance of His commandments (*Vayikra Rabbah* 27:6).

4. The prophet now tells of the goodness that God bestowed upon His nation throughout its existence.

כִּי הֶעֱלִתִיךָ מֵאֶרֶץ מִצְרַיִם וּמִבֵּית עֲבָדִים פְּדִיתִיךָ — *For I brought you up from the land of Egypt and redeemed you from the house of bondage.* The people were slaves to Pharaoh in Egypt where they were subjected to hard and rigorous labor, yet God redeemed them (*Mahari Kara*) although it was a land from which slaves never escaped (*Abarbanel*).

מִבֵּית עֲבָדִים is usually translated *from the house of bondage* and is referring to the land of Egypt — the place where the Israelites were slaves (*Radak*). An alternative translation may be from the house of *slaves* and is referring to the *Egyptian people* who are descendants of Ham (*Genesis* 10:6) and were destined to become slaves (see ibid. 9:25-27) (*Radak*).

וָאֶשְׁלַח לְפָנֶיךָ אֶת־מֹשֶׁה אַהֲרֹן וּמִרְיָם — *And I sent Moses, Aaron and Miriam before you.* God sent Moses to teach the nation the laws, Aaron to atone for their sins and Miriam to instruct the women (*Targum Yonasan*). Furthermore, He sent them with tidings of redemption while the people were yet in bondage so that they may be relieved of their anguish (*Radak*).

ה עַמִּי זְכָר־נָא מַה־יָּעַץ בָּלָק מֶלֶךְ מוֹאָב וּמֶה־עָנָה אֹתוֹ בִּלְעָם בֶּן־בְּעוֹר מִן־הַשִּׁטִּים עַד־הַגִּלְגָּל
ו לְמַעַן דַּעַת צִדְקוֹת יהוה: בַּמָּה אֲקַדֵּם יהוה אִכַּף לֵאלֹהֵי מָרוֹם הַאֲקַדְּמֶנּוּ בְעוֹלוֹת בַּעֲגָלִים בְּנֵי
ז שָׁנָה: הֲיִרְצֶה יהוה בְּאַלְפֵי אֵילִים בְּרִבְבוֹת נַחֲלֵי־שָׁמֶן הַאֶתֵּן בְּכוֹרִי פִּשְׁעִי פְּרִי בִטְנִי חַטַּאת נַפְשִׁי:

5. עַמִּי זְכָר־נָא מַה־יָּעַץ בָּלָק מֶלֶךְ מוֹאָב וּמֶה־עָנָה אוֹתוֹ בִּלְעָם בֶּן־בְּעוֹר — *My people, remember now what Balak, king of Moab, schemed, and what Balaam son of Beor answered him.* The prophet now recalls the lovingkindness God bestowed upon His nation when [Balak and] Balaam had attempted to destroy them (*Ibn Ezra*).

Hoping to bring about their destruction, Balak had sent emissaries to Balaam and solicited him to curse Israel [see *Numbers* Chapters 22-24] (*Mahari Kara*). Balaam, however, was firmly instructed by God not to curse His nation (ibid. 22:12) and therefore replied, מָה אֶקֹּב לֹא קַבֹּה אֵל, *How can I curse [if] God has not cursed* (ibid. 23:8). Furthermore, Balaam also informed Balak that God did not feel any real anger against Israel and he is therefore unable to invoke God's anger against them — מָה אֶזְעֹם לֹא זָעַם ה׳, *How can I anger [if] Hashem is not angry* (ibid.), for God did not get angry at Israel during the entire time that Balaam was seeking to curse Israel[1] (*Rashi*). Ultimately, Balaam told Balak, "*Behold! Now I have come to you — am I empowered to say anything? Whatever word God puts into my mouth, that shall I speak*" [*Numbers* 22:38] (*Mahari Kara*), referring to all the prophetic blessings that God forced Balaam to utter against his will (*Abarbanel*).

מִן־הַשִּׁטִּים — *From Shittim.* Encouraged by Balaam, the daughters of Moab lured the Israelites into immorality and idolatry at Shittim (*Numbers* Chapter 25). Although the entire nation should have been destroyed, the death of a small number of sinners who perished in a plague [24,000 people] was sufficient to atone for the entire nation (*Radak*).

עַד־הַגִּלְגָּל — *To Gilgal.* Despite their having sinned at Shittim, God in His great mercy did not withhold His goodness nor His help from them (*Rashi*) and miraculously brought them through the Jordan River (*Radak*) to Gilgal and conquered the land [of Canaan] for them (*Rashi*).

It appears that Gilgal later became a place of disgraceful idol worship — see *Hosea* 4:15, 9:15 and *Amos* 4:4. Micah, then, is rebuking the nation, "Although your history has been a continuous defection from God, from Shittim long ago to Gilgal where you still now sin," God's patience and lovingkindness toward you has known no end (*R' M. Hirsch*).

לְמַעַן דַּעַת צִדְקוֹת ה׳ — *In order to recognize the righteous acts of* HASHEM. God did all this so that the nation may have the opportunity to realize all the goodness that He performed for them (*Ibn Ezra*) and how He extended Himself for them (*Metzudos*). The people should recall all this through oral tradition or from what is written in the Torah so that they may recognize the righteous acts of Hashem (*Radak*).

6. בַּמָּה אֲקַדֵּם ה׳ אִכַּף לֵאלֹהֵי מָרוֹם הַאֲקַדְּמֶנּוּ בְעוֹלוֹת בַּעֲגָלִים בְּנֵי שָׁנָה — *[If you ask,]*

1. Balaam had the ability to calculate the exact moment of God's wrath (*Berachos* 7a). God was therefore careful to "contain His anger" during that entire period. This does not mean that God angers in the literal sense of the word, for that would be giving God anthropomorphic characteristics; but rather that God did not judge the Israelite nation with מִדַּת הַדִּין, *strict justice*, during that time but with מִדַּת הָרַחֲמִים, *leniency* (*Abarbanel*).

6/5-7

[5] My people, remember now what Balak, king of Moab, schemed, and what Balaam son of Beor answered him, [and all the events] from Shittim to Gilgal — in order to recognize the righteous acts of HASHEM.

[6] [If you ask,] With what shall I approach HASHEM, *humble myself before God on high? Shall I approach Him with burnt-offerings or with calves in their first year? [7] Will* HASHEM *be appeased by thousands of rams or with tens of thousands of streams of oil? Shall I give my firstborn [to atone for] my transgression, or the fruit of my belly [for] the sin of my soul?*

With what shall I approach HASHEM, *humble myself before God on high? Shall I approach Him with burnt-offerings or with calves in their first year?* Should one of the people ask, "What offerings shall I bring before God and with what will I humble myself before Him?" (*Radak*). "With what will I be accepted by Him Who bestowed such kindness on my forefathers?" (*Ibn Ezra*). "Would there be any purpose for me to bring burnt-offerings? What would He gain from them?" (*Metzudos*).

לֵאלֹהֵי מָרוֹם — *God on high.*

This reference to God should impress upon one who has sinned and rebelled against Him the degree of subordination and humility that he must have as he returns to God; for one who has rebelled against God has rebelled against the One Who is most high. It is therefore imperative that he lower and humble himself (*Shaarei Teshuvah* 1:25).

בַּעֲגָלִים בְּנֵי שָׁנָה — *With calves in their first year.*

Abarbanel notes that the choicest calves are those within their first year. Even though they make the finest offerings, God does not need them (*Metzudos*).

7. הֲיִרְצֶה ה׳ בְּאַלְפֵי אֵילִים בְּרִבְבוֹת נַחֲלֵי־שָׁמֶן הַאֶתֵּן בְּכוֹרִי פִּשְׁעִי פְּרִי בִטְנִי חַטַּאת נַפְשִׁי — *Will* HASHEM *be appeased by thousands of rams or with tens of thousands of streams of oil? Shall I give my firstborn [to atone for] my transgression, or the fruit of my belly [for] the sin of my soul?* Does God desire thousands of rams for sacrifices or tens of thousands of streams of oil to pour on meal-offerings (*Metzudos*) as payment for His lovingkindness? (*Shaarei Teshuvah* 1:25). Perhaps God does not want meal-offerings or animals but what is dearest to man: his firstborn child. Shall he be offered to God to atone for his sins? (*Radak*).

The question raised in the last two verses summarizes the pagan outlook toward religion which believes that one can appease God with offerings and please Him by sacrificing dear ones (*R' Mendel Hirsch*). God does not need man's generosity nor does He want his twisted concept of self-sacrifice. God wants man's obedience.

[Although some critics wish to understand these verses as stating that God has abolished the precepts of sacrificial service, it is obvious to the careful reader that this was never the case. God only wishes that we be sincere in our service to Him. All the sacrifices in the world mean nothing to God if those who bring them are insincere in His service.]

פֶּשַׁע, *transgression,* is an offense that constitutes a rebellion and is worse than חֵטְא, *sin.* The prophet therefore states in the name of the people of Israel, "Shall I give *my firstborn* to atone for *my transgression* and the *fruit of my belly — any of my children — for the sin of my soul?*" (*Shaarei Teshuvah* 1:25).

ח הִגִּיד לְךָ אָדָם מַה־טּוֹב וּמָה־יהוה דּוֹרֵשׁ מִמְּךָ
כִּי אִם־עֲשׂוֹת מִשְׁפָּט וְאַהֲבַת חֶסֶד וְהַצְנֵעַ
לֶכֶת עִם־אֱלֹהֶיךָ׃ ט קוֹל יהוה לָעִיר
יִקְרָא וְתוּשִׁיָּה יִרְאֶה שְׁמֶךָ שִׁמְעוּ מַטֶּה וּמִי
יְעָדָהּ׃ י עוֹד הַאִשׁ בֵּית רָשָׁע אֹצְרוֹת רֶשַׁע

8. הִגִּיד לְךָ אָדָם מַה־טּוֹב ... — *He has told you, O man, what is good ...* This is in reply to the question of *With what shall I approach* HASHEM [v. 6] (*Rashi*). God informed the nation long ago through the prophet Samuel that He has no desire for sacrifices but only that the people do what is good and just — see *I Samuel* 15:22 (*Radak*).

כִּי אִם־עֲשׂוֹת מִשְׁפָּט — *But to do justice.* This includes all the commandments that govern man's conduct with his fellow man: נִזְקֵי מָמוֹן, *financial laws,* and עֲרָיוֹת, *laws of immorality* (*Radak*).

וְאַהֲבַת חֶסֶד — *To love kindness.* These are acts of benevolence and kindness (*Radak*). One should always try to be more kind to others, even more than his neighbor actually desires. Perseverance for the welfare of one's people and for the betterment of his neighbor, whether poor or rich, is among the most stringent and essential demands made of a person (*Shaarei Teshuvah* 3:13). However, one must realize that it is not enough to simply do acts of kindness in fulfillment of an obligation. One must learn to *love* to do kindness, and do it with his entire heart (*Chafetz Chaim, Ahavas Chesed* 2:1).

וְהַצְנֵעַ לֶכֶת עִם־אֱלֹהֶיךָ — *And to walk modestly with your God.* Fear God in a discreet manner (*Targum Yonasan*). Fulfill His commandments in an unassuming manner, privately and without great publicity. Do not perform them only for the sake of gaining honor (*Metzudos*), for there is nothing dearer to God than one who is humble (*Tos. Rid*). Alternatively, this is a description of man's belief in the unity of God and the fulfillment of loving Him with all one's heart and soul. Since these sentiments are felt within the confines of one's heart and is hidden from others, Micah uses the term הַצְנֵעַ לֶכֶת, *to walk modestly or discreetly* (*Radak*). *Rashi* maintains that Micah is teaching us the method we should use when repenting our sins before God. Unlike a human who, if embarrassed publicly, demands a public apology, God does not demand that we admit our sins publicly. We must admit them before no one but God — in a private manner [see also *Rambam, Hil. Teshuvah* 2:5 and comments of *Ohr Sameach* thereon].

The Sages (*Succah* 49a) explain that Micah's instructions of וְהַצְנֵעַ לֶכֶת עִם־אֱלֹהֶיךָ, *and to walk discreetly with your God,* are specifically referring to the commandments of הַלְוָיַת הַמֵּת, *attending a funeral,* and הַכְנָסַת כַּלָּה, *attending a wedding ceremony,* both usually performed publicly. If these commandments should be observed discreetly, we must surely observe all other commandments in a discreet manner.

R' Mendel Hirsch notes that the three ideals of this verse were fundamental essentials put forth by the three prophets of verse 4, Moses, Aaron and Miriam. *Doing justice* was the fundamental tone of Moses' character, as is apparent by his killing of the Egyptian and his behavior at the well in Midian. *Lovingkindness* was the essence of Aaron who always strove to bring kindness and peace to the nation. *Walking modestly* was the quality of Miriam whose task was to preserve chastity and purity among the women.

One should not think that merely by doing justice, lovingkindness and walking discreetly one may come close to God. The prophet is stating that these social and rational ideas are absolutely necessary, for one

[8] He has told you, O man, what is good! What does H*ASHEM require of you but to do justice, to love kindness and to walk modestly with your God?*

[9] The voice of H*ASHEM calls out to the [people of the] city, and the [man of] wisdom recognizes Your Name: Listen [O Israel,] to the rod [of punishment] and to the One Who has ordained it! [10] Are there still stores of wickedness in the house of the wicked one,*

cannot properly fulfill the Divinely ordained laws unless he first observes the basic rational laws of ethics (*Kuzari* 2:48).

9. Since the prophet had instructed the nation to do justice, he now rebukes them for their lack of justice and for using false weights and measures (*Ibn Ezra*).

קוֹל ה׳ לָעִיר יִקְרָא — *The voice of* H*ASHEM calls out to the [people of the] city.* The voice of the prophets of God who are summoning the nation to repentance (*Rashi; Radak*) calls out to the people of the city par excellence, to the people of Jerusalem (*Mahari Kara; Metzudos*). Others suggest that *the city* is a reference to Samaria (*Ibn Ezra; Radak*). In an alternative explanation, *Radak* cites others who translate לָעִיר, *to awaken*, like לְהָעִיר. Thus the voice of Hashem calls out to *awaken* the people to repent.

וְתוּשִׁיָּה יִרְאֶה שְׁמֶךָ — *And [the man of] wisdom recognizes Your Name.* The prophet calls out to all the people of the city but it is only the man of wisdom who reacts positively to the words of the prophet and sees God's Name in his heart (*Radak; Ibn Ezra*). Alternatively, it is the prophet who is the man of wisdom for he is the one who is perceptive to see God's ways (*Rashi*). Accordingly, the translation of the passage is "The voice of Hashem calls out to the [people of the] city *through* the man of wisdom ..."

תוּשִׁיָּה means *wisdom* based on Torah scholarship and is related to the word יֵשׁ, *there is* (*Metzudos*), expressing the idea that nothing in this material world other than wisdom has any permanence (*Radak*).

שִׁמְעוּ מַטֶּה וּמִי יְעָדָהּ — *Listen [O Israel,] to the rod [of punishment] and to the One Who has ordained it.* The people are told to bend their ear and hearken to the words of the prophets who have been rebuking them (*Rashi*) and to clearly understand the severity of the decree that has been placed upon them (*Radak*). Perceive Who is the One Who has decreed these punishments. Has He not the ability to implement His decree? (*Rashi; Radak*).

Alternatively, *Abarbanel* translates *Listen, O corrupt ones* [מַטֶּה may be translated to *twist* or to *corrupt* — see *Deut.* 16:19]. Accordingly, the prophet is addressing those people who have corrupted justice, have been unkind or have not walked modestly with God.

10. עוֹד הַאִשׁ בֵּית רָשָׁע אֹצְרוֹת רֶשַׁע — *Are there still stores of wickedness in the house of the wicked one.* After all that had been stated by the prophets in God's Name, can there still be stolen treasures in the houses of the wicked? (*Radak*). Alternatively, can the house of the wicked that is filled with stolen treasures last for a long time? (*Targum Yonasan*).

The ה of הַאִשׁ is vowelized with a *pasach* for it is the ה׳ הַשְּׁאֵלָה, *interrogative* ה (*Rashi; Radak*). The word הַאִשׁ is the equivalent of הֲיֵשׁ for at times the י is substituted with an א — see *II Samuel* 14:19; *I Chron.* 2:13 (*Rashi*). Alternatively, *Ibn Ezra* renders הָאִישׁ, *the man.* The honorable man of the city continues in his evil ways by keeping stolen treasures and a lean measure.

יא וְאֵיפַת רָזוֹן זְעוּמָה: הַאֶזְכֶּה בְּמֹאזְנֵי רֶשַׁע
יב וּבְכִיס אַבְנֵי מִרְמָה: אֲשֶׁר עֲשִׁירֶיהָ מָלְאוּ חָמָס
וְיֹשְׁבֶיהָ דִּבְּרוּ־שָׁקֶר וּלְשׁוֹנָם רְמִיָּה בְּפִיהֶם:
יג וְגַם־אֲנִי הֶחֱלֵיתִי הַכּוֹתֶךָ הַשְׁמֵם עַל־חַטֹּאתֶךָ:
יד אַתָּה תֹאכַל וְלֹא תִשְׂבָּע וְיֶשְׁחֲךָ בְּקִרְבֶּךָ וְתַסֵּג
טו וְלֹא תַפְלִיט וַאֲשֶׁר תְּפַלֵּט לַחֶרֶב אֶתֵּן: אַתָּה
תִזְרַע וְלֹא תִקְצוֹר אַתָּה תִדְרֹךְ־זַיִת וְלֹא־תָסוּךְ
טז שֶׁמֶן וְתִירוֹשׁ וְלֹא תִשְׁתֶּה־יָּיִן: וְיִשְׁתַּמֵּר חֻקּוֹת
עָמְרִי וְכֹל מַעֲשֵׂה בֵית־אַחְאָב וַתֵּלְכוּ בְּמֹעֲצוֹתָם

וְאֵיפַת רָזוֹן זְעוּמָה — *Or a lean measure that angers [God]?* These are the fraudulent weights that the wealthy use to deceive the poor and cause them to become *lean,* to starve. These items are condemned by God and bring forth His anger (*Rashi*). *Malbim* translates רָזוֹן as the officers who are responsible to set honest weights — רוֹזֵן. The weights set by these officers cause God's anger to grow because they are falsely measured.

11. הַאֶזְכֶּה בְּמֹאזְנֵי רֶשַׁע וּבְכִיס אַבְנֵי מִרְמָה — *Can I be judged righteous with scales of wickedness, or with a pouch of deceitful weights?* Each person should have asked himself, "Can I be judged righteous with scales of wickedness or with a pouch of deceitful weights?" (*Radak*). Alternatively, Micah is speaking about himself. "Even I, a prophet of God and a completely righteous man, would never merit in judgment had I sinned with false measures," for using deceitful weights is a terrible sin as it destroys any moral perfection that one may have achieved (*Abarbanel*).

וּבְכִיס אַבְנֵי מִרְמָה — *Or with a pouch of deceitful weights?* Possessing different size weights is prohibited by Torah Law — see *Deut.* 25:13. When purchasing goods he uses the large weight but when offering goods for sale he uses the smaller weight (*Radak*).

12. אֲשֶׁר עֲשִׁירֶיהָ מָלְאוּ חָמָס וְיֹשְׁבֶיהָ דִּבְּרוּ־שָׁקֶר וּלְשׁוֹנָם רְמִיָּה בְּפִיהֶם — *For its rich men are full of thievery, and its inhabitants speak falsehood; their tongue is guile in their mouth.* The wealthy who live in Jerusalem or Samaria have homes filled with stolen goods, and her poorer inhabitants speak falsehood (*Radak*). Their simple talk is replete with blatant lies and their intelligent conversations [לְשׁוֹנָם] are deceitful; the lies are cunningly subtle (*Malbim*).

Its rich men are full of thievery violates the command to *love kindness* (v. 8) and *their tongue is guile in their mouth* violates to *walk modestly with God,* for the people deceitfully say that God's providence is no longer over the land (*Abarbanel*).

13. וְגַם־אֲנִי הֶחֱלֵיתִי הַכּוֹתֶךָ הַשְׁמֵם עַל־חַטֹּאתֶךָ — *I have hurt you, as well, by smiting you, bringing desolation for your sins.* Micah addresses the wealthy men of the previous verse: "Just as you have hurt the poor and defenseless with your guile, so have I smitten you with severe blows, measure for measure" (*Ibn Ezra; Radak*).

14. אַתָּה תֹאכַל וְלֹא תִשְׂבָּע וְיֶשְׁחֲךָ בְּקִרְבֶּךָ — *You will eat but not be satisfied, and you will stoop over [because of sickness] in your innards.* "Your food will be cursed that it will not satisfy you (*Radak*). In addition to being insufficient, it will make you ill and you will walk stooped over" (*Rashi*).

6/11-16 *or a lean measure that angers [God]? [11] Can I be judged righteous with scales of wickedness, or with a pouch of deceitful weights? [12] For its rich men are full of thievery, and its inhabitants speak falsehood; their tongue is guile in their mouth. [13] I have hurt you, as well, by smiting you, bringing desolation for your sins. [14] You will eat but not be satisfied, and you will stoop over [because of sickness] in your innards; you will conceive but you will not deliver, and those you do deliver I will give to the sword. [15] You will sow, but not reap; you will trample olives, but not smear oil; [trample] wine-grapes, but not drink wine. [16] The decrees of Omri and all the deeds of the house of Ahab are preserved, and you follow their counsels,*

Eating and not being satisfied is the result of a special curse that takes effect on the bread that is already in one's stomach (*Rashi, Lev.* 26:26).

Alternatively, וְיֶשְׁחֲךָ בְּקִרְבֶּךָ, *"and you will be humbled, made to walk in a stooped manner, in your midst" (Radak). Metzudos* renders *"Due to the hunger that is within your innards, you will become humbled,"* for when one is satiated he tends to become proud and defiant.

וְתַסֵּג וְלֹא תַפְלִיט — *"You will conceive but you will not deliver.* Your wife will conceive [lit., will reach pregnancy, from the word תַּשִּׂיג] but the fetus will not be born at term [תַּפְלִיט, *to eject*] for it will die in its mother's womb. Those who will be born will bring you no happiness for they will soon be killed by the enemy" (*Ibn Ezra; Radak*). Alternatively, "You will overtake your enemies but you will be unable to rescue your sons and daughters from captivity. Those who will be rescued will only be killed" (*Rashi*).

Abarbanel translates וְתַסֵּג as *closed off,* as with a barrier [see *Shir HaShirim* 7:3, סוּגָה בַּשּׁוֹשַׁנִּים] and renders the wombs of the women will be sealed and they will not conceive.

15. ... אַתָּה תִזְרַע וְלֹא תִקְצוֹר — *You will sow, but not reap ...* "Not only will your bodies be cursed but your produce will be cursed as well" (*Malbim*). "You will sow your field but you will not reap, for the enemy will harvest it for himself. You will trample olives to extract their oil but you will not anoint yourself with it. You will trample wine grapes but you won't drink the wine, for it will all be taken by the nations" (*Metzudos*).

16. וְיִשְׁתַּמֵּר חֻקּוֹת עָמְרִי וְכֹל מַעֲשֵׂה בֵית־אַחְאָב וַתֵּלְכוּ בְּמֹעֲצוֹתָם — *The decrees of Omri and all the deeds of the house of Ahab are preserved and you follow their counsels.* "I know that you will not hearken to Me because all the decrees of Omri and Ahab are being observed by you and your children" (*Rashi*). "Even with all the evil that I bring upon you, you continue to keep the decrees of Omri instead of My decrees" (*Radak*).

The decrees of Omri and all the deeds of the house of Ahab are references to the golden calves and the worship of the Baal (*Tos. Rid*).

Omri was the sixth monarch of the Northern Kingdom and reigned for twelve years. Scripture describes him as *more wicked than all those who preceded him* (*I Kings* 16:25).

לְמַ֫עַן תִּתִּי אֹתְךָ לְשַׁמָּה וְיֹשְׁבֶיהָ לִשְׁרֵקָה
ז/א־ג א וְחֶרְפַּת עַמִּי תִּשָּׂאוּ׃ אַלְלַי לִי
כִּי הָיִיתִי כְּאָסְפֵּי־קַיִץ כְּעֹלְלֹת בָּצִיר אֵין־
ב אֶשְׁכּוֹל לֶאֱכוֹל בִּכּוּרָה אִוְּתָה נַפְשִׁי׃ אָבַד
חָסִיד מִן־הָאָרֶץ וְיָשָׁר בָּאָדָם אָיִן כֻּלָּם לְדָמִים
ג יֶאֱרֹבוּ אִישׁ אֶת־אָחִיהוּ יָצוּדוּ חֵרֶם׃ עַל־הָרַע
כַּפַּיִם לְהֵיטִיב הַשַּׂר שֹׁאֵל וְהַשֹּׁפֵט בַּשִּׁלּוּם

He went in the entire path of Jeroboam son of Nebat and in his sin [the golden calves — *Radak*] (v. 26). Ahab, Omri's son, succeeded him to the throne and reigned for twenty-two years. He too *did what was evil in the eyes of HASHEM, more than all who had preceded him. The least of his evils was going in the way of the sins of Jeroboam ... and he went and worshiped the Baal ... and he erected an altar for the Baal ... and Ahab made an Asherah-tree; and Ahab did more to anger HASHEM, God of Israel, than all the kings of Israel who had preceded him* (ibid. vv. 30-33).

לְמַעַן תִּתִּי אֹתְךָ לְשַׁמָּה ... — *So that I will give you over to [be an] astonishment ...* Everyone will be astonished at the extent of the destruction that will befall Jerusalem and its inhabitants. The nations will whistle as people do when viewing a horrible sight (*Metzudos*).

וְחֶרְפַּת עַמִּי תִּשָּׂאוּ — *And you will bear [the punishment of] the shame of My nation.* Because you transgress the commandment of possessing false weights and measures, you will be a disgrace in the eyes of the nations (*Rashi*). Alternatively, because you disgraced the poor, you will be disgraced by the nations (*Radak*).

עַמִּי, *My nation,* is referring to the poor and oppressed of the nation (*Radak*); or to עוֹבְדֵי ה׳, *those who worship HASHEM* (*Ibn Ezra*); or to the Ten Tribes of the Northern Kingdom — the Kingdom of Judah will be exiled as were the ten tribes, for they followed in their ways (*Abarbanel; Metzudos*).

VII

Micah laments over Israel's moral decline and unethical practices and bemoans the retribution that is in store for them.

1. אַלְלַי לִי כִּי הָיִיתִי כְּאָסְפֵּי־קַיִץ כְּעֹלְלֹת בָּצִיר — *Woe is me, for I am like the last pickings of the summer fruit, like the gleanings of the grape harvest.* Micah compares the small number of righteous people of his generation to the sparse number of summer fruit (*Metzudos*) or to the unripe figs of inferior quality that remain on the trees after the harvest (*Rashi*). He laments over his predicament and cries out, "Woe is me, for I have been designated to be a prophet in a generation where righteous men cannot be found" (*Rashi*). Alternatively, he is lamenting over Israel who refused to hearken to his rebuke. He grieves over the extent of their wickedness and the retribution God has prepared for them (*Radak*).

אֵין־אֶשְׁכּוֹל לֶאֱכוֹל — *There is no cluster to eat,* The metaphor continues: There is no man whose deeds are good (*Targum Yonasan*), or there are no pious men from whom to learn to do good deeds (*Radak*).

בִּכּוּרָה אִוְּתָה נַפְשִׁי — *My soul yearns for a ripe fruit.* My soul yearns for someone of this generation who will teach piety and integrity (*Radak*).

so that I will give you over to [be an] astonishment, and its inhabitants [to be a cause for] whistling; and you will bear [the punishment of] the shame of My people.

7/1-3

[1] *Woe is me, for I am like the last pickings of the summer fruit, like the gleanings of the grape harvest; there is no cluster to eat; my soul yearns for a ripe fruit.* [2]*The devout one has disappeared from the land; and one upright among men is no more. They all lie in ambush [to shed] blood; they trap, each man his brother, with a net.* [3]*[Do they expect] to benefit from the evil of their hands? The official asks [for bribes]; the judge [has a share] in the payment;*

2. אָבַד חָסִיד מִן־הָאָרֶץ וְיָשָׁר בָּאָדָם אָיִן — *The devout one has disappeared from the land; and one upright among men is no more.* This is the explanation of the parable of the previous verse (*Metzudos*). There are no more righteous or upright men in Israel; only murderers and wicked people (*Mahari Kara*).

The devout person [חָסִיד] is one who is meticulous in observing both precepts that are בֵּין אָדָם לַמָּקוֹם, *between man and God*, and בֵּין אָדָם לַחֲבֵרוֹ, *between man and his fellow*. The upright person [יָשָׁר] is meticulous in his dealings with his fellow man (*Malbim*).

אִישׁ אֶת־אָחִיהוּ יָצוּדוּ חֵרֶם — *They trap, each man his brother, with a net.*

Each one traps the other with the intent to kill, as a hunter traps birds with a net (*Radak*). Although רֶשֶׁת is the more common word used for net, the word חֵרֶם is used where destruction is implied (*Radak, Ezekiel* 32:3).

3. עַל־הָרַע כַּפַּיִם לְהֵיטִיב — *[Do they expect] to benefit from the evil of their hands?* Do the evil and corrupt expect God to reward them for the evil that they commit? (*Rashi*). Alternatively, they intensify their evil ways by taking bribes — the word לְהֵיטִיב expressing intensification (*Radak*). *Ibn Ezra* renders, "All this will come upon them because their hands are full of evil *instead* of good" — the ל of לְהֵיטִיב translated as *instead* (see *Gen.* 11:3).

For various reasons, *Abarbanel* is dissatisfied with these explanations. He therefore joins this section of the verse to the next section and renders, "When the people come to the official, judge or nobleman לְהֵיטִיב, to rectify the evil they committed, the officials ask for payment." *Malbim* explains the verse by rearranging the words — עַל־הָרַע כַּפַּיִם הַשַּׂר שֹׁאֵל וְהַשֹּׁפֵט לְהֵיטִיב בַּשִּׁלּוּם. Although the officer and judge search for the evil that they had committed, it is not being done to punish the guilty but to do good to those who have given payments.

הַשַּׂר שֹׁאֵל ... — *The official asks [for bribes]* ... The official, the judge and the nobleman braid their strands of evil into a strong rope of iniquity. The official asks for bribes; the judge, if he is found to be a thief, asks his fellow judge to accept payment and declare his innocence and he will return the favor in a different case. The king utters his heart's desire and praises whatever verdicts please him and are for his benefit (*Rashi*). Alternatively, it is the king that is behind it all, but it is demeaning of him to ask for payment. So he sends an official in his stead. The judge turns the case for the favors the king offers through the nobleman (*Radak*).

וְהַגָּדוֹל דֹּבֵר הַוַּת נַפְשׁוֹ הוּא וַיְעַבְּתוּהָ: ד טוֹבָם כְּחֵדֶק יָשָׁר מִמְּסוּכָה יוֹם מְצַפֶּיךָ ה פְּקֻדָּתְךָ בָאָה עַתָּה תִהְיֶה מְבוּכָתָם: אַל־ תַּאֲמִינוּ בְרֵעַ אַל־תִּבְטְחוּ בְּאַלּוּף מִשֹּׁכֶבֶת ו חֵיקֶךָ שְׁמֹר פִּתְחֵי־פִיךָ: כִּי־בֵן מְנַבֵּל אָב בַּת קָמָה בְאִמָּהּ כַּלָּה בַּחֲמֹתָהּ אֹיְבֵי ז אִישׁ אַנְשֵׁי בֵיתוֹ: וַאֲנִי בַּיהוָה אֲצַפֶּה אוֹחִילָה לֵאלֹהֵי יִשְׁעִי יִשְׁמָעֵנִי אֱלֹהָי:

וְהַגָּדוֹל דֹּבֵר הַוַּת נַפְשׁוֹ — *And the nobleman expresses his selfish desires.*

The translation of הַוַּת נַפְשׁוֹ is the *desires of his soul* [in our context, *his selfish desires*] (*Targum Yonasan, Rashi, Tos. Rid*). Alternatively, *Radak* translates שִׁבְרוֹן נֶפֶשׁ, *misfortune*. The nobleman speaks of the misfortune that will occur if the bribe is not paid and coerces the person into payments.

הַוַּת may be related to הָיָה, *to be*. It is the constant planning of bringing something into being and generally indicates brooding over something (*R' Hirsch, Psalms* 5:10).

4. טוֹבָם כְּחֵדֶק יָשָׁר מִמְּסוּכָה — *The best of them is like a thorn, the upright are [worse] than a thorn hedge.* The best of them is like a thorn that causes pain to anyone who touches it (*Radak; Metzudos*). It is as hard for one to extricate oneself from the clutches of their hands, and is as difficult as removing thorns that are embedded in wool (*Rashi*). Even the good that they do is tainted with evil (*Da'as Sofrim*).

A מְסוּכָה is a hedge of thornbushes that surrounds a vineyard (*Radak*). The ס of מְסוּכָה is interchanged with a שׂ [see *Isaiah* 5:5 where the word מְשׂוּכָּתוֹ is used] (*Rashi; Ibn Ezra*).

Abarbanel explains that the prophet is comparing the official, judge and king of the previous verse to thorns and thornbushes, for just as it is impossible to get to the grapes of the vineyard without first getting injured by the thornbush, so too, is it impossible to receive a verdict from the judges without first suffering by paying the bribe.

יוֹם מְצַפֶּיךָ פְּקֻדָּתְךָ בָאָה — *On the day of your expectation, your punishment will come.* On the very day that you expect good fortune, punishment will come in its place (*Rashi*). Alternatively, יוֹם מְצַפֶּיךָ is *the day* of *your false prophets* who would instill false hopes in the nation; now we will see whether good or evil will befall you on that day (*Radak*). *Malbim* maintains that מְצַפֶּיךָ are the heathen nations who have hoped for Israel's downfall. On the day that had been designated for their downfall, *your* punishments will arrive.

עַתָּה תִהְיֶה מְבוּכָתָם — *Now you will become perplexed.* On that day you will become perplexed and confused by the severity of the punishments and will not know what to do (*Metzudos*). Alternatively, you will become confused by the inaccurate "prophecies" of the false prophets (*Radak*).

5. אַל־תַּאֲמִינוּ בְרֵעַ אַל־תִּבְטְחוּ בְּאַלּוּף מִשֹּׁכֶבֶת חֵיקֶךָ שְׁמֹר פִּתְחֵי־פִיךָ — *Do not trust a friend; do not rely on an official; guard the doorways of your mouth from the one who lies in your bosom.* Micah is describing the low moral standards of his time. In this generation one cannot trust his friend or one who is in an official position, people who usually keep their word. One must even guard

and the nobleman expresses his selfish desires; and they plait them together. [4]*The best of them is like a thorn, the upright are [worse] than a thorn hedge. On the day of your expectation, your punishment will come; now you will become perplexed.* [5]*Do not trust a friend; do not rely on an official; guard the doorways of your mouth from the one who lies in your bosom.* [6]*For a son disparages [his] father; a daughter rises up against her mother, a daughter-in-law against her mother-in-law; a man's enemies are the people of his household.* [7]*As for me, I put my hope in HASHEM and await the God of my salvation; my God will hear me.*

his words from his wife because she, too, will reveal his secrets (*Metzudos*). Alternatively, Micah is instructing the women not to place their confidence in their husbands — see *Proverbs* 2:17, אַלּוּף נְעוּרֶיהָ, *the husband of their youth* (*Ibn Ezra*). *Radak* translates אַלּוּף as *older brother;* one cannot even trust his older brother during these times. The Sages (*Chagigah* 16a) explain that the רֵעַ of this verse is referring to God. Do not sin with the intent that God is our Beloved and He will forgive us, for your soul that lies in your bosom will testify against you.

Chafetz Chaim notes the use of פִּתְחֵי־פִיךָ, *the doorways of your mouth.* One must always realize that just as the doors of one's house are not constantly kept open, so too must one's mouth open only for words of Torah and other important matters, and stay closed for trivial matters (*Shmiras HaLashon* 2:2).

6. ... כִּי־בֵן מְנַבֵּל אָב ... — *For a son disparages [his] father.* Micah continues to describe the low moral character of his generation. Normally, a son exalts his father and honors him, but in this generation, the son disgraces and humiliates him. The daughter rises up against her mother to scorn and insult her and the daughter-in-law does the same (*Radak*). Even his own household has become his enemy and one must be suspicious of his servants and slaves (*Abarbanel*).

7. וַאֲנִי בַּה׳ אֲצַפֶּה אוֹחִילָה לֵאלֹהֵי יִשְׁעִי יִשְׁמָעֵנִי אֱלֹהָי — *As for me, I put my hope in HASHEM and await the God of my salvation; my God will hear me.* Micah addresses the nation: "Although you have committed all these sinful acts, I will nevertheless hope for G-d's salvation and that He will listen to our prayers" (*Mahari Kara*). Alternatively, he is speaking *on behalf* of the nation: Although I will be exiled from my land as punishment for the sins I have committed, I still place my hope in G-d and He will take me out of exile (*Rashi*).

Malbim maintains that during the days of Micah the nation had become far too depraved to merit salvation and therefore explains that Micah's hope could only be fulfilled בְּאַחֲרִית הַיָּמִים, *in the End of Days,* when the ultimate redemption will take place. He further explains that the ultimate redemption could either come at its destined time — at the End of Days which is expressed with the words אוֹחִילָה לֵאלֹהֵי יִשְׁעִי, *I await the God of my salvation* — or through prayer and repentance, which will bring the redemption at an earlier time, expressed with the words יִשְׁמָעֵנִי אֱלֹהָי, *My God will hear me.*

ח אַל־תִּשְׂמְחִי אֹיַבְתִּי לִי כִּי נָפַלְתִּי קָמְתִּי כִּי־אֵשֵׁב
ט בַּחֹשֶׁךְ יהוה אוֹר לִי׃ זַעַף יהוה אֶשָּׂא כִּי
חָטָאתִי לוֹ עַד אֲשֶׁר יָרִיב רִיבִי וְעָשָׂה מִשְׁפָּטִי
י יוֹצִיאֵנִי לָאוֹר אֶרְאֶה בְּצִדְקָתוֹ׃ וְתֵרֶא אֹיַבְתִּי
וּתְכַסֶּהָ בוּשָׁה הָאֹמְרָה אֵלַי אַיּוֹ יהוה אֱלֹהָיִךְ עֵינַי
תִּרְאֶינָּה בָּהּ עַתָּה תִּהְיֶה לְמִרְמָס כְּטִיט חוּצוֹת׃
יא־יב יוֹם לִבְנוֹת גְּדֵרָיִךְ יוֹם הַהוּא יִרְחַק־חֹק׃ יוֹם הוּא
וְעָדֶיךָ יָבוֹא לְמִנִּי אַשּׁוּר וְעָרֵי מָצוֹר וּלְמִנִּי מָצוֹר

8. אַל־תִּשְׂמְחִי אֹיַבְתִּי לִי כִּי נָפַלְתִּי קָמְתִּי — *Do not rejoice over me, my enemy, for though I fell, I will rise!* Micah now foretells the exchange that will take place between a contrite Israel and its oppressor nations (*Rashi*). Babylonia (*Rashi*) and Rome (*Rashi; Radak; Abarbanel*), do not rejoice over me, for though I have fallen into exile I will yet rise (*Radak*).

Although קָמְתִּי is past tense and should really be translated *I have risen*, prophetic verses often substitute the past for future tense, for whatever God predicts is as though it has already taken place (*Radak*). Alternatively, I have fallen so many times in the past: I was exiled into Egypt and into Babylonia and *I have risen* from those places; I will rise from this exile as well (*Metzudos*).

Divrei Shmuel (*Miketz*) renders *because* I have fallen I shall rise; because I perceived that I have fallen so low, I am encouraged to rise again to attain spiritual heights.

כִּי־אֵשֵׁב בַּחֹשֶׁךְ ה׳ אוֹר לִי — *Though I sit in the darkness,* HASHEM *is a light unto me!* If I now sit in exile, in deep trouble as if in darkness, I have faith in G-d that He will take me out of the darkness and bring me into the light (*Radak*).

Talmud Yerushalmi (*Berachos* 1:1) cites this verse and compares the redemption of Israel to the light of day. Just as the light of day slowly increases after dawn until sunrise, so too, will the redemption start slowly and bit by bit increase until it is complete, for the exile is the darkness and the redemption is the light (*Pnei Moshe* ibid.).

9. זַעַף ה׳ אֶשָּׂא כִּי חָטָאתִי לוֹ — *I shall bear the fury of* HASHEM *for I have sinned unto Him.* The Jewish people will bear the fury of G-d Who was incensed with them and delivered them into the hands of the nations because they sinned against Him (*Mahari Kara*). By bearing G-d's anger they will purge themselves from the sins they committed and will be forgiven (*Malbim*).

עַד אֲשֶׁר יָרִיב רִיבִי ... — *until He will take up my cause ...*

Until God will plead my cause and execute justice against those nations who oppressed the Jewish people (*Mahari Kara*).

This will occur during the time of the redemption (זְמַן הַגְּאוּלָּה). During the exile, however, the nation sits in darkness, unable to see the light of God's righteousness; but at the time of the redemption, God will bring them out into the light and they will all behold His righteousness. They will then realize the righteousness and kindness that He did for the nation during their entire stay in exile for it was all for their benefit (*Malbim*).

10. וְתֵרֶא אֹיַבְתִּי וּתְכַסֶּהָ בוּשָׁה... — *Then my enemy will see and shame will cover her ...* When the enemy will see the kindness that God showed the Jewish people, she will bear her shame for confronting them during the exile and asking, "Where is Hashem your God?" (*Radak; Metzudos*).

Throughout Israel's exile, the nations have taunted the Jews and have asked, "Why has your God abandoned you?" In the future,

[8] *"Do not rejoice over me, my enemy, for though I fell, I will rise! Though I sit in the darkness, HASHEM is a light unto me!* [9] *I shall bear the fury of HASHEM for I have sinned unto Him, until He will take up my cause and execute judgment for me; He will bring me out into the light; I will behold His righteousness.* [10] *Then my enemy will see and shame will cover her, she who said to me, 'Where is HASHEM your God?' My eyes will behold her: now she will be for trampling, like mud in the streets."*

[11] *"The day to rebuild your fences, that day is far away in a distant time."*

[12] *"That day exists! And he will come against you: from Assyria to the fortified cities; from Egypt*

however, it will become evident to all that God was always with His nation and that all the hardships the people experienced were for their ultimate benefit (*Malbim*).

עַתָּה תִּהְיֶה לְמִרְמָס כְּטִיט חוּצוֹת — *Now she will be for trampling, like mud in the streets.* Just as she beheld us when our people were down, so too, will we behold her now that she is like the mud that is trampled upon in the street (*Mahari Kara*). *Malbim* sees the word עַתָּה, *now*, as the key word of this phrase. Now, even during the time of *exile*, our people gaze upon the enemy with scornful eyes for they realize that all her success is only to magnify her future destruction.

11. יוֹם לִבְנוֹת גְּדֵרָיִךְ יוֹם הַהוּא יִרְחַק־חֹק — *The day to rebuild your fences, that day is far away in a distant time.* This is a continuation of the previous verse. The enemy had chided Israel, "The day that you hope to rebuild your fences — the day of your salvation — will never come." For this, too, she will be overcome with shame (*Rashi*). The rebuilding of your fences is a reference to *Amos* 9:11: *On that day I will raise up the fallen booth of David; and I will repair their breaches, and its ruins I will raise up and I will build it up as in days of old* (*Mahari Kara*).

Targum Yonasan understands this verse as a pledge to Israel. There will indeed be a day that the nation will be rebuilt and the decrees of its enemies will be nullified. Alternatively, Micah is addressing the enemy: The day that you thought you would build your fences and establish your presence in the Land of Israel, when you will come with Gog and Magog, that day will never come (*Radak*).

Abarbanel offers a novel interpretation of this verse. After Titus destroyed Jerusalem, Israel was ruled by Edom (the Christians). In later years the Ishmaelites (Arabs) captured Jerusalem and took it from them. This prophecy is addressed to Edom who will attempt to recapture the city. This, says the prophet, will not occur for they will be unsuccessful in their campaign.

12. יוֹם הוּא וְעָדֶיךָ יָבוֹא לְמִנִּי אַשּׁוּר וְעָרֵי מָצוֹר ... — *That day exists! And he will come against you: from Assyria to the fortified cities* ... Micah replies to the enemy's mockery. That day of redemption will indeed come but your fate will be that the enemy will come to you to destroy you. They will first destroy our principal oppressor, Assyria, and then reach out to all the fortified cities (*Rashi; Radak*). From the fortified cities they will go to

יג וְעַד־נָהָר וְיָם מִיָּם וְהַר הָהָר: וְהָיְתָה הָאָרֶץ
יד לִשְׁמָמָה עַל־יֹשְׁבֶיהָ מִפְּרִי מַעַלְלֵיהֶם: רְעֵה
עַמְּךָ בְשִׁבְטֶךָ צֹאן נַחֲלָתֶךָ שֹׁכְנִי לְבָדָד
יַעַר בְּתוֹךְ כַּרְמֶל יִרְעוּ בָשָׁן וְגִלְעָד כִּימֵי
טו עוֹלָם: כִּימֵי צֵאתְךָ מֵאֶרֶץ מִצְרָיִם אַרְאֶנּוּ
טז נִפְלָאוֹת: יִרְאוּ גוֹיִם וְיֵבֹשׁוּ מִכֹּל גְּבוּרָתָם

the Euphrates River, the [northeastern] boundary of the Land of Israel, and then to those who dwell along the sea which is in the west [the Mediterranean] (*Rashi*), the western boundary of the Land of Israel (*Metzudos*) and then to those who dwell in the mountains (*Rashi*).

Alternatively, the עָרֵי מָצוֹר are cities of different eastern nations, בְּנֵי מִזְרָח, who had been driven into the mountains by Alexander the Great. They will join the Assyrians and battle the Christians at this time. The Ten Tribes of Israel who had been near the Euphrates River will also join the battle against the Christians which will be fought both on land and sea (*Abarbanel*).

Our translation of וְהַר הָהָר, *and the dwellers of the mountain*, follows *Rashi*. Alternatively, *Ibn Ezra* translates *from mountain to mountain* — from the mountains of the south to the mountains in the north. *Radak* translates *Hor Hahar*, the burial site of Aaron, which was also one of the boundaries of the Land of Israel (see *Numbers* 34:8[1]).

Alternatively, Micah is not foretelling the destruction of Israel's enemies but the ingathering of the exiles that will take place on *that day* from the four corners of the earth (*Targum Yonasan*). From Assyria and Egypt, מִנִּי אַשּׁוּר וְעָרֵי מָצוֹר, Sennacherib had exiled the nation to these countries; וְיָם מִיָּם, and those who had been exiled by the Romans to the west will now return from the west; וְהַר הָהָר, and those who were exiled to the north will now return from Har Hahar which was at the northern tip of Israel (*Malbim*).

13. וְהָיְתָה הָאָרֶץ לִשְׁמָמָה עַל־יֹשְׁבֶיהָ ... — *And the land will be desolate with its inhabitants.*

The land of the heathen nations (*Rashi; Radak*) will become desolate together with its inhabitants because of the evil they did to Israel (*Metzudos*). Alternatively, the Land of Israel will become devoid of its inhabitants — the nations who dwelt there ... (*Abarbanel*). *Malbim* suggests that at the End of Days, the entire earth, כְּדוּר הָאָרֶץ כּוּלוֹ, will be in desolation for God will then recall the sins of its inhabitants.

14-20. Prior to his death, Moses gathered the entire nation and admonished them with harsh words of reproof (see *Deut.* Chapters 1 and 32). His very last words, however, were of a comforting nature (see ibid. Chapter 33 וְזֹאת הַבְּרָכָה, *And this is the blessing*). Micah and many other prophets followed suit and tempered their harsh reproof by ending their admonishment with words of comfort and hope (*Sifre, Deut.* 33:1). Although *Sifre* cites the last three verses of this chapter as proof, *Abarbanel* adapts *Sifre's* concept to verses 14-20.

14. רְעֵה עַמְּךָ בְשִׁבְטֶךָ צֹאן נַחֲלָתֶךָ שֹׁכְנִי לְבָדָד — *Shepherd Your people with Your staff, the flock of Your heritage; [let them] dwell [in secure] isolation.* Micah prays to God that He have mercy on the Jewish people and take them out of exile. He beseeches God to guide them with His staff as the shepherd leads his flock (*Radak*) and that He protect them so they should not be driven by the rod

1. *Radak's* source, *Numbers* 34:8, poses difficulty for the Hor Hahar of Aaron's burial place was located *outside* of the southern border of the Land of Israel, for it bordered the land of Edom [see *Numbers* 33:37, 38], while Hor Hahar of *Numbers* 34:8 was Israel's northwestern border.

to the [Euphrates] River; from the Western (Mediterranean) Sea; and the dwellers of the mountain. [13]*"And the land will be desolate with its inhabitants, as the fruit of their actions."*

[14]*"Shepherd Your people with Your staff, the flock of Your heritage; [let them] dwell [in secure] isolation, in forest as in fertile field; [let them] graze in Bashan and Gilead as in days of old."*

[15]*"As in the days when you left the land of Egypt I will show him wonders.* [16]*The nations will see and be ashamed of all their [unavailing] power;*

of their enemies (*Abarbanel*). He prays that Israel should dwell in secure isolation (*Rashi*), for one dwells alone only when he is secure. Those who live in fear of an enemy dwell together so that one may assist and protect the other. Alternatively, may Israel be the exclusive nation that will dwell in the land (*Radak*).

יַעַר בְּתוֹךְ כַּרְמֶל — *In forest as in fertile field.* May Israel dwell securely in the forest, a place frequented by wild beasts, as they dwell in the fertile field and inhabited areas (*Rashi; Radak; Metzudos*). [The prophet is not specifically referring to the area of Mt. Carmel] for any inhabited area, with fields, vineyards and trees is called Carmel (*Metzudos*). *Abarbanel* suggests that Carmel of this verse is a reference to Jerusalem and the land of Israel, for Israel will eventually be a land flourishing with greenery.

יִרְעוּ בָשָׁן וְגִלְעָד כִּימֵי עוֹלָם — *[Let them] graze in Bashan and Gilead as in days of old.* The Bashan and Gilead were very fertile pasture areas located on the eastern bank of the Jordan (*Radak*) and were inhabited in ancient times by the tribes of Reuben, Gad and half of the tribe of Manasseh (*Abarbanel*). יְמֵי עוֹלָם, *days of old*, are the days of Moses, for it was he who allocated these portions to them (*Metzudos*).

15. כִּימֵי צֵאתְךָ מֵאֶרֶץ מִצְרָיִם אַרְאֶנּוּ נִפְלָאוֹת — *As in the days when you left the land of Egypt I will show him wonders.* God responds to Micah's prayer: Tell the nation that I will perform wonders for them[1] as I previously did during the exodus from Egypt (*Radak*). Although the generation of the forthcoming redemption will not be the actual generation that took part in the exodus from Egypt, nevertheless they are referred to as such — *when you left* — for it is as if they too went out of Egypt (ibid.). This is restated every year at the Passover Seder. "Not only our fathers did the Holy One, Blessed is He, redeem, but He also redeemed us with them" (*Passover Haggadah*). Citing this passage, the Midrash (*Shemos Rabbah* 15:12) writes that the future redemption will occur during the month of Nissan as did our redemption from Egypt.

16. יִרְאוּ גוֹיִם וְיֵבֹשׁוּ מִכֹּל גְּבוּרָתָם — *The nations will see and be ashamed of all their [unavailing] power.* This is a continuation of God's reply. This is what will occur at the time of the redemption (*Ibn Ezra*). The nations that will assemble with Gog and Magog against Jerusalem will see the miracles that God will perform and will be put to shame for they had relied on their own might to attack Jerusalem but were instantly shattered (*Radak; Abarbanel*).

1. Scripture writes אַרְאֶנּוּ נִפְלָאוֹת, *I will show him wonders*, for the pronoun *him* is referring to the entire nation collectively (*Abarbanel*).

יז יָשִׂימוּ יָד עַל־פֶּה אָזְנֵיהֶם תֶּחֱרַשְׁנָה: יְלַחֲכוּ עָפָר כַּנָּחָשׁ כְּזֹחֲלֵי אֶרֶץ יִרְגְּזוּ מִמִּסְגְּרֹתֵיהֶם אֶל־יהוה אֱלֹהֵינוּ יִפְחָדוּ וְיִרְאוּ מִמֶּךָּ: יח מִי־אֵל כָּמוֹךָ נֹשֵׂא עָוֹן וְעֹבֵר עַל־פֶּשַׁע לִשְׁאֵרִית נַחֲלָתוֹ

יָשִׂימוּ יָד עַל־פֶּה — *They will place a hand over [their] mouth.* They will be so astonished at the extent of the miracles that God will perform that they will be unable to vocalize the unbelievable sights they will see (*Malbim*).

אָזְנֵיהֶם תֶּחֱרַשְׁנָה — *Their ears will become deaf.* They will ignore the tidings of Israel's success as if they are deaf, for it distresses them (*Metzudos*).

17. יְלַחֲכוּ עָפָר כַּנָּחָשׁ כְּזֹחֲלֵי אֶרֶץ — *They will lick the dust like the snake, like creatures that crawl on the ground.* The prophet describes the final humbling of the nations and their awe and reverence for God and Israel (*Radak*). The nations will prostrate themselves before Israel and it will seem as though they are licking the dust of their feet as the snake licks the dust, which he eats as his food (*Metzudos*). *Creatures that crawl on the ground* are either snakes (*Rashi*) or worms and similar creatures (*Radak*). Alternatively, the prophet may be describing the fall of the nations in battle: they will fall to the ground mortally wounded and writhe in pain and lick the dust as snakes and worms. Only then, when God will avenge Israel's suffering, will they realize how they wronged her in exile (*Abarbanel*).

יִרְגְּזוּ מִמִּסְגְּרֹתֵיהֶם — *They will tremble from their places of confinement.* They will tremble because of their cramped places of imprisonment and captivity (*Rashi*). Those who took refuge in the cities due to their fear of Israel will tremble in those cities (*Radak*). *Their places of confinement* may also be their palaces (*Ibn Ezra*). Alternatively, the nations tremble for having held the Jewish people in captivity (*Metzudos*). Citing *Isaiah* 24:22, *Abarbanel* maintains that מַסְגֵּר is a term used for exile. The nations will suffer for oppressing Israel while they were in exile.

אֶל־ה׳ אֱלֹהֵינוּ יִפְחָדוּ וְיִרְאוּ מִמֶּךָּ — *They will fear* Hashem *our God and be afraid of you.* They will fear Hashem our God for they will know that there is no other God but He (*Radak*), and they will be afraid of you because He is with you (*Malbim*).

פַּחַד is the fear of something unknown, while יִרְאָה is fear of a given subject. When referring to the greatness of God and the fear His eminence instills, Scripture uses פַּחַד. When referring to the fear the nations will have of Israel, it uses יִרְאָה (*Malbim*).

18-20. The following three passages occupy special status in Jewish liturgy as they are quoted numerous times during the services of the High Holy Days season: at the close of each *Selichos* service, at the end of the *Haftaros* of *Shabbos Shuvah* and of *Minchah* on Yom Kippur. They also form the very core of the *Tashlich* service of Rosh Hashanah. According to Sephardic custom, they are also recited each day after the recitation of the *Akeidah*. In addition, verse 20, תִּתֵּן אֱמֶת לְיַעֲקֹב, *Give truth to Jacob,* is recited at the end of the *Uva LeTzion* prayer every morning.

According to the Kabbalah, these three verses correspond to the Thirteen Attributes of Mercy that God had taught Moses after the sin of the Golden Calf. See ArtScroll *Tashlich* for further discussion of this concept.

Micah, who has been the recipient of good tidings regarding Israel's future (*Metzudos*) and has been told that the nation will be forgiven for its sins (*Malbim*), now offers praise to God.

they will place a hand over [their] mouth; their ears will become deaf."

[17] *"They will lick the dirt like the snake and like creatures that crawl on the ground; they will tremble from their places of confinement; they will fear* HASHEM *our God and be afraid of you."*

[18] *Who is a God like You, Who pardons iniquity and overlooks transgression for the remnant of His heritage?*

18. מִי־אֵל כָּמוֹךָ — *Who is a God like You.* The prophet addresses God (*Radak*) and praises Him for His promise of good fortune (*Metzudos*). There is no one but You, You alone are God (*Targum Yonasan*); Who, Almighty One, is like You? (*Malbim; R' Mendel Hirsch*).

God is unlike any other power in the world. He patiently bears insult and sustains life that is used against Him, in the hope that man will repent. One should strive to emulate His Creator by training himself to be patient, to bear insult and even to bestow kindness upon those who abuse him (*Tomer Devorah*). Indeed, it is told that when one wronged R' Yisrael Salanter, he would immediately strive to act with kindness to his offender to fulfill the commandment of וְהָלַכְתָּ בִּדְרָכָיו, *and you shall follow in His ways* (*Ohr Yisrael*). Alternatively, the word אֵל is non-sacred, meaning god or power. The nations are stating there is no god who bestows so much goodness upon his heritage as You (*Ibn Ezra*).

נֹשֵׂא עָוֹן — *Who pardons iniquity.* According to the strict letter of the law, we are not worthy of the goodness that You plan to bestow upon us for we have grievously sinned; but who is a God like You that pardons sins? (*Metzudos*). Alternatively, God does not punish the evildoer immediately but *bears* [lit., translation of נֹשֵׂא] *the iniquity* until a further occasion for punishment arises [giving the sinner an opportunity to repent] (*Malbim*).

Both explanations find their source in *Rosh Hashanah* (17a). The school of R' Yishmael taught that God pardons the sins first, before they are placed on the scale, thereby giving the sinner more merits than sins. Rabbah explained that the sin itself is not erased but is kept on the side to be included if the sins outweigh the merits (see *Rashi* ad loc.).

One must learn to be tolerant of others. Even when offended by another and the results of the offense are still in existence, the victim should not harm his offender but rather wait patiently for the wrong to be righted (*Tomer Devorah*).

וְעֹבֵר עַל־פֶּשַׁע — *And overlooks transgression.*

God does not "stop" by the transgression to demand retribution from the one who committed it but passes it by as if He never saw it (*Metzudos*). Furthermore, it is He alone Who cleanses the sin (see *Yechezkel* 36:25) and grants forgiveness (*Tomer Devorah*).

The Talmud (*Rosh Hashanah* 17a) cites this verse and explains that God overlooks the transgressions only of one who does not insist upon his rights.

לִשְׁאֵרִית נַחֲלָתוֹ — *For the remnant of His heritage.*

The remnant of His heritage is referring to those who will survive the sufferings of the Messianic age (*Metzudos*) and will be present when the redeemer arrives (*Radak*). Alternatively, שְׁאֵר may be translated as שְׁאֵר בָּשָׂר, *blood relative.* Throughout Scripture, Israel is referred to as God's close relative (see *Psalms* 148:14). God says, "How can I possibly punish Israel? It would be as if I would be hurting Myself," if one may so say regarding G-d (*Tomer Devorah*).

One should learn to love his fellow man and emulate the love God shows to His nation (*Tomer Devorah*).

יט לֹא־הֶחֱזִיק לָעַד אַפּוֹ כִּי־חָפֵץ חֶסֶד הוּא: יָשׁוּב יְרַחֲמֵנוּ יִכְבֹּשׁ עֲוֹנֹתֵינוּ וְתַשְׁלִיךְ בִּמְצֻלוֹת יָם כָּל־חַטֹּאתָם: כ תִּתֵּן אֱמֶת לְיַעֲקֹב חֶסֶד לְאַבְרָהָם אֲשֶׁר־נִשְׁבַּעְתָּ לַאֲבֹתֵינוּ מִימֵי קֶדֶם:

לֹא־הֶחֱזִיק לָעַד אַפּוֹ — *He does not retain His wrath forever.* Although this remnant is unworthy of redemption for the people continue to do the very same sins for which their fathers were exiled, nevertheless, God does not eternally retain His wrath against them (*Radak*). *R' M. Hirsch* notes that God's aim in showing His anger by sending suffering is only for the purpose of doing away with the cause of that anger.

Even when one has the right to rebuke his neighbor, he should emulate His Creator and not persist in his rebuke nor continue his anger (*Tomer Devorah*).

כִּי־חָפֵץ חֶסֶד הוּא — *For He desires kindness.* The Torah writes that God is רַב־חֶסֶד, *abundant kindness* (*Exodus* 34:6). When the time for Israel's redemption will arrive, God's kindness will overwhelm its sins (*Radak*). Acts of kindness that Jews perform to one another are so dear to God that He recalls this aspect of their character even when they are guilty in other respects (*Tomer Devorah*).

When hurt or provoked, one should look at the offender's good and admirable qualities, emulate the kindness of his Creator and ignore his neighbor's provocative behavior (*Tomer Devorah*).

19. יָשׁוּב יְרַחֲמֵנוּ — *He will once again show us mercy.* God will be merciful to us as in previous times (*Metzudos*) and He will pardon us through His mercy (*Malbim*). When one returns to God and repents his sins, God reciprocates by showing him *more* mercy, for the status of the penitent is higher than that of the perfectly righteous (*Tomer Devorah*).

If an offender seeks reconciliation, one should emulate his Creator and show him a greater degree of kindness than he did previously, even more than he would show a perfectly righteous acquaintance who had never offended him (*Tomer Devorah*).

יִכְבֹּשׁ עֲוֹנֹתֵינוּ — *He will suppress our iniquities.* God will hide our sins (*Mahari Kara*) so that punishment will not be exacted (*Metzudos; Malbim*). Other translations of יִכְבֹּשׁ are *to tread underfoot* (*Radak*) and *to grasp* in a strong manner (*Metzudos*); whatever the translation may be, the idea conveyed in the verse is the same.

One should suppress the memory of any evil which was done to him, but remember every kindness and sincerely appreciate it (*Tomer Devorah*).

וְתַשְׁלִיךְ בִּמְצֻלוֹת יָם כָּל־חַטֹּאתָם — *You will cast all their sins into the depths of the sea.* God will not recall our sins to exact punishment for them. It is as if they have been cast into the depths of the sea and are not seen (*Metzudos*). Furthermore, by sinking their sins into the depths of the sea, God causes them to disappear without leaving any trace or having any effect on Israel (*R' Mendel Hirsch*).

[It is from these words that the *Tashlich* prayer recited on Rosh Hashanah (*Rema, Orach Chaim* 583:2) derives its name.]

Alternatively, it is the wicked who are likened to the deep sea (see *Isaiah* 57:20). Micah, in essence, is stating that God will cast all of Israel's sins upon the wicked who are likened to the muddy depths of the sea (*Tomer Devorah*).

If one notices that his neighbor is crushed by suffering as a result of his sins, he should not disdain him for it. Rather, he should be compassionate and befriend him and realize that suffering cleanses one of sin (*Tomer Devorah*).

20. תִּתֵּן אֱמֶת לְיַעֲקֹב — *Grant truth to Jacob.* In Beth-el God swore to Jacob

He does not retain His wrath forever, for He desires kindness. [19] *He will once again show us mercy, He will suppress our iniquities. You will cast all their sins into the depths of the sea.* [20] *Grant truth to Jacob, kindness to Abraham, as You swore to our forefathers in the days of old.*

that He will never forsake him nor his descendants — see *Radak* to *Genesis* 28:15. Micah now beseeches God to confirm the oath that He adjured to Jacob (*Rashi*). Furthermore, it was in Beth-el that Jacob was granted the prophetic vision of angels ascending and descending a ladder, which was a revelation of the exile and ultimate redemption of his descendants. Micah is stating that when the redemption will ultimately occur, God will have fulfilled the promise that He assured the Patriarch Jacob (*Abarbanel*).

Although Jacob was the last of the Patriarchs, he is mentioned first because it was to him that God foretold the ultimate redemption. Alternatively, Jacob is symbolic of the average, ordinary person who upholds the letter of the law, for Jacob was a symbol of exact honesty. One should treat his neighbor with truth and refuse to pervert justice so that even the average person will be perfected in accordance with the quality of truth (*Tomer Devorah*).

חֶסֶד לְאַבְרָהָם — *Kindness to Abraham.* Confirmation of the promise that You assured Jacob will be payment of the reward for the quality of kindness that Abraham possessed-exemplified by commanding his descendants to keep the ways of God: to do kindness and justice [*Genesis* 18:19] (*Rashi*).

Alternatively, the redemption of Israel will be an act of kindness to Abraham, for the Assyrians and Ishmaelites, both descendants of Abraham,[1] will accept God's Torah at that time and will dwell in peace, subservient to Israel (*Abarbanel*).

Alternatively, Abraham is symbolic of the righteous people who go beyond the letter of the law. God reciprocates and acts toward these people with kindness beyond the letter of the law. When dealing with these people, one should exceed the requirements of the law and strive to be exceptionally patient with them (*Tomer Devorah*).

The commentators are troubled by Micah's omission of the Patriarch Isaac's name. *Ibn Ezra* maintains that since Isaac was also the father of Esau from whom Edom descended, he did not wish to mention him in his praise of God. Similarly, *Abarbanel* explains that unlike Assyria and Ishmael, Edom will not live peacefully and will not accept God's Torah, for there will be no remnant of Esau's descendants at the time of Israel's redemption. Micah therefore did not mention Isaac's name.

אֲשֶׁר־נִשְׁבַּעְתָּ לַאֲבֹתֵינוּ מִימֵי קֶדֶם — *As You swore to our forefathers in the days of old.* After Abraham bound Isaac on the altar and was prepared to sacrifice his son to God, He swore, *Because you have done this thing and have not withheld your son, your only one, that I shall surely bless you and greatly increase your offspring* (*Genesis* 22:16-18) (*Rashi*). This was repeated to Isaac [ibid. 26:3-5] and to Jacob (ibid. 28:13-15); so in essence, this part of the verse is referring to all three Patriarchs (*Radak*).

If the merit of the forefathers is ever exhausted and Israel is unworthy, God will recall all the good deeds that Israel performed from the day of its inception and merit God's mercy (*Tomer Devorah*).

1. The Assyrians were of the offspring of Abraham's wife Keturah — see *Genesis* 25:1-3; the Ishmaelites of Hagar — see ibid. 16:15.

nahum

א־ב מַשָּׂא נִינְוֵה סֵפֶר חֲזוֹן נַחוּם הָאֶלְקֹשִׁי: אֵל קַנּוֹא

Introduction

Nahum was a disciple of the prophet Joel (*Rambam*, intro. to *Yad HaChazakah*) and prophesied during the days of Manasseh, king of Judah, about 70 years before the destruction of the First Temple (*Seder Olam* Ch. 20). Scripture does not mention this, however, because it did not wish to associate the name of the righteous prophet with the evil Manasseh. It appears, however, that some commentators do not subscribe to this chronology, and put Nahum in the time of Sennacherib, several decades earlier. [See 1:14 and commentary there.]

In any event, by the time Nahum appeared on the scene, the Assyrian Empire had been the region's greatest power for nearly a century. It was the mission of this prophet to warn the Assyrians that their utter destruction was sure to come if they did not change their wicked ways. Indeed, these prophecies were fulfilled over 40 years later when the Babylonians and Medes triumphantly marched into Nineveh, the Assyrian capital. The entire Book of *Nahum* focuses on these prophecies that foretell the destruction of the Assyrian Empire.

Many years earlier, God had sent the prophet Jonah to Nineveh to advise them of their impending destruction if they would not repent their evil ways [see *Jonah* 3:4]. The Ninevites accepted the words of the prophet and the city was spared, as related in the Book of *Jonah*. In the course of time, however, they reverted to their evil ways, and some hundred years later, God sent the prophet Nahum to rebuke them (*Rashi*). It was during that time that the Assyrians invaded the Northern Kingdom of Israel (the Ten Tribes) and exiled its inhabitants to a distant province. God was now preparing to avenge the great harm that the Assyrians had inflicted upon the people of Israel by sending Nebuchadnezzar to destroy Assyria (*Radak*). The following prophecies are directed at the dynasty of Sennacherib, Assyria's monarch (*Rashi*).

Malbim divides the Book of *Nahum* into two sections. The first, which encompasses Chapters 1 and 2, called "The Prophecy of Nineveh," describes the destruction of Nineveh that had occurred prior to or during the days of the prophet. The second section, Chapter 3, called "The Vision of Nahum," foretells Nineveh's future destruction by Nebuchadnezzar. Although Rabbinical sources record only Nebuchadnezzar's campaign against Nineveh, its previous destruction is described extensively in secular historical records. [See *Malbim* for a brief synopsis of these records.]

I.

1. מַשָּׂא — *A prophecy.* מַשָּׂא, lit., *burden*, is used synonymously for prophecy because the prophet *carries* the prophetic word in his mouth (*Metzudos* to *Isaiah* 13:1). It is one of the ten expressions of prophecy enumerated in *Bereishis Rabbah* (44:7) and usually introduces a fateful and foreboding prophecy. Indeed, *Targum Yonasan* paraphrases *the prophecy of the cup of torment that will be given to Nineveh to drink.* Most prophecies directed to the nations of the world are introduced by this term.

נִינְוֵה — *Nineveh.*

Nineveh was the principal city of Assyria and was situated on the eastern bank of the Tigris River. It was settled by Sennacherib (*II Kings* 19:36) who ultimately made it the capital of Assyria. In the time of Jonah, its population exceeded one hundred and twenty thousand people (*Jonah* 4:11).

סֵפֶר חֲזוֹן נַחוּם הָאֶלְקֹשִׁי — *The book of the vision of Nahum the Elkoshite.* Whereas ראה is used to describe physical sight,

[1] A *prophecy regarding Nineveh. The book of the vision of Nahum the Elkoshite:*

[2] *HASHEM is a jealous and vengeful God; HASHEM*

חָזוֹן (derived from חזה) related to חָזֶה, *breast*, the seat of the heart, seems to mean seeing in a spiritual sense, perceiving and comprehending that which is invisible to the physical eye (*R' Hirsch, Genesis* 15:1).

In our text, the ח of חֲזוֹן is vowelized with a חֲטַף פַּתַּח which grammatically joins the word חֲזוֹן with נַחוּם. Accordingly, the passage is translated: *The book of the vision of Nahum the Elkoshite* (*Ibn Ezra; Radak*). However, in *Rashi's* text this ח was vowelized חָזוֹן indicating that the words חָזוֹן and נַחוּם are grammatically independent of each other. Accordingly, *Rashi* explains: *A prophecy regarding Nineveh; a book of vision,* [the section of] *Nahum the Elkoshite.*[1] The Book of *Jonah* had already recorded the prophecy regarding the threatened destruction of Nineveh because of its sins. When Nineveh had repented, God suspended their punishment. Now that they reverted to their evil ways, their doom was again foretold by Nahum. His book, therefore, is a continuation of the book of visions concerning Nineveh begun by Jonah (*Rashi* from *Targum Yerushalmi*).

The Book of *Nahum* is the only prophetic work that Scripture itself refers to as a book [סֵפֶר חֲזוֹן]. In a novel explanation, *Abarbanel* suggests that unlike other prophets who confronted their audiences, Nahum did not travel to Nineveh to publicly proclaim his prophecy but wrote it in a book and sent the prophetic message to the people.

נַחוּם הָאֶלְקֹשִׁי — *Nahum the Elkoshite.* Elkosh was either the name of Nahum's city (*Rashi*) or the name of one of his ancestors (*Ibn Ezra; Radak*).

2. אֵל קַנּוֹא וְנֹקֵם ה׳ — *Hashem is a jealous and vengeful God.* Although God is the All-merciful One, He is vengeful for Israel's sake. He is vengeful for the welfare of His people for He sees that they are in great distress in exile. Although Assyria had fulfilled God's wishes by exiling Israel from their land (*Isaiah* 10:5), God held them accountable for they intensified and increased Israel's punishment and caused them undue suffering — see *Zechariah* 1:15 (*Radak*). Furthermore, Assyria never intended to fulfill God's wishes by attacking Israel but did so only because of its own evil and wicked intentions. It was for this reason that God's vengeance descended upon them (*Abarbanel;* see also *Ramban's* commentary to *Genesis* 15:14 for a lengthy discussion of this issue).

Rambam (*Moreh Nevuchim* 1:36) maintains that Scriptural references to wrath [anger, jealousy, vengeance] when applied to God are only found in regard to idolatry. God's enemies are none other than the idolaters. So as not to attribute any corporeal characteristics to God, *Rambam* further explains that these characteristics are not the result of any emotion or passion, for God is above all defect. They are merely described in a manner that, when performed by humans, originate in certain mental dispositions (*Moreh Nevuchim* 1:54). In a similar vein, Rabbi Yehudah Halevi writes that we perceive God only through His various deeds and He therefore appears different to us on different occasions. In reality, however, He never changes from one attribute to another (*Kuzari* 2:2).

1. *Mahari Kara* notes that the cantillation under the word חָזוֹן, indicative of a pause in the passage, lends support to *Rashi's* explanation. *Abarbanel*, too, maintains that the accurately written texts of Spain were written as *Rashi's* text, חָזוֹן. But *Minchas Shai* reports that all the texts that he had obtained were written as our text, חֲזוֹן.

וְנֹקֵם יהוה נֹקֵם יהוה וּבַעַל חֵמָה נֹקֵם יהוה לְצָרָיו

ג וְנוֹטֵר הוּא לְאֹיְבָיו׃ יהוה אֶרֶךְ אַפַּיִם °וגדול־כֹּחַ

וְנַקֵּה לֹא יְנַקֶּה יהוה בְּסוּפָה וּבִשְׂעָרָה דַּרְכּוֹ וְעָנָן

ד אֲבַק רַגְלָיו׃ גּוֹעֵר בַּיָּם וַיַּבְּשֵׁהוּ וְכָל־הַנְּהָרוֹת הֶחֱרִיב

°וּגְדָל־ק׳

נֹקֵם ה׳ וּבַעַל חֵמָה — *Hashem is vengeful and full of wrath.* *Malbim* suggests that אַף is an anger which is actually being displayed. In contrast, חֵמָה denotes anger which is being contained until a future time. It is thus an inner resentment, a wrath that boils inside (*R' Hirsch — Gen.* 49:7, *Psalms* 37:8).

נֹקֵם ה׳ לְצָרָיו — *Hashem is vengeful to His adversaries.* G-d is taking vengeance upon His enemies because they destroyed His land and exiled His people (*Rashi*). God's vengeance is directed only against *His adversaries,* i.e., the heathen nations, but not against His nation Israel (*Metzudos*). [See *Avodah Zarah* 4a.]

Although vengeance is a despicable character trait and is prohibited by the Torah, see *Lev.* 19:18, this is only so when directed against a fellow Jew. It is permitted however, when directed against enemies and oppressors (*Abarbanel*).

וְנוֹטֵר הוּא לְאֹיְבָיו — *And reserves hostility for His enemies.* God does not always avenge the deeds of His enemies immediately following their evil actions, but often retains His animosity for a future time and then directs His vengeance upon them or their descendants (*Radak*).

The three seemingly redundant expressions of נֹקֵם ה׳, *God is vengeful,* refer to God acting in this capacity in the past, present and future (*Rashi,* based on *Seder Olam*). Some explain that God will avenge the Assyrians for the three waves of exile they inflicted upon the Northern Kingdom of Israel (*Rashi; Radak*).[1]

3. ה׳ אֶרֶךְ אַפַּיִם וּגְדָל־כֹּחַ — *Hashem is slow to anger, but He has great power.* God patiently restrains His anger and delays punishment thereby giving the sinner a chance to reconsider and repent his evil way (*Rashi, Exodus* 34:6 based on *Sanhedrin* 111a). The Talmud (*Bava Kamma* 50a-b) notes the use of the plural form אַפַּיִם [lit., *angers*] rather than the singular form אַף, and explains that God is not only slow to anger at righteous people who have sinned, but He even contains His anger against the wicked.

One should not mistake God's patience for weakness, for God has *great power* and has the ability to execute His vengeance immediately. He delays executing His vengeance only because He is slow to anger (*Rashi*). Human beings, however, are incapable of such forbearance. Therefore, any delay in reaction is usually the result of their present impotence (*Mahari Kara*). Furthermore, God's patience is an expression of His great strength. Impatience denotes weakness, an inability to control one's impulses and desires. Patience, however, is really a display of strength. Actually, Moses acted upon this teaching when God was ready to destroy the nation for sinning and following the evil report of the spies — see *Numbers* 14:17,18. At that time, the people were prepared to appoint a new leader and return to Egypt and thereby proved themselves unworthy of their God-given mission. God, therefore, proposed to destroy the entire Israelite nation and start a new nation with Moses. The humble Moses pleaded with God on behalf of his people and pointed out that God's Name would be desecrated if He would indeed destroy Israel, for none of the nations would believe that Israel was to blame for its own downfall. The nations of the world would misinterpret God's actions and would say that God destroyed

1. The first Israelites to be exiled were the tribes who dwelt in Transjordan [Reuben, Gad and half of the Tribe of Manasseh] (*I Chronicles* 5:26). The second were those who dwelt in the land of Naftali [the cities of Ijon, Abel-beth maacah, etc., see *II Kings* 15:29]. The third group to be exiled were the inhabitants of Samaria and its neighboring cities [see ibid. 17:6]. See ArtScroll *I Chronicles* 5:25-26.

is vengeful and full of wrath; HASHEM *is vengeful to His adversaries and reserves hostility for His enemies.* [3] HASHEM *is slow to anger, but He has great power and He will not absolve [iniquity].* HASHEM, *His path is in a storm and in a tempest, and clouds are the dust of His feet.* [4] *He rebukes the sea and makes it dry, and makes all the rivers parched.*

the nation in the desert for He did not have the ability to lead them victoriously against the powerful kings of Canaan. Therefore, said Moses, "Let the *strength of Hashem be* magnified as You had previously proclaimed by saying that *Hashem is slow to anger*" (*Ibn Ezra; Radak*).

R' Hirsch (*Numbers* 14:17) adds that it is not through God's *destructive might* that we can perceive the true greatness of God, but rather through His strength (כֹּחַ); that in spite of the nations's rebellious actions, He contains His anger and achieves His goal by changing their rebelliousness into agreement with His plans.

וְנַקֵּה לֹא יְנַקֶּה — *And He will not absolve [iniquity].* Although God is slow to anger, He is sure to punish the guilty (*Rashi; Radak*). Though He has not yet punished the Assyrians, they will eventually receive their due (*Abarbanel*).

ה׳ בְּסוּפָה וּבִשְׂעָרָה דַּרְכּוֹ — *Hashem, His path is in a storm and in a tempest. Rashi* interprets the verse literally. The elements enumerated here are God's emissaries for bringing retribution upon His enemies [see *Exodus* 14:21; *Job* 4:9; *Ezekiel* 27:26] (*Rashi*). *Radak,* however, interprets the verse figuratively. When God finally does punish His enemies, His retribution descends with the sudden swiftness of a whirlwind.

The word for whirlwind, שְׂעָרָה, is usually spelled סְעָרָה, with the first letter a ס rather than a שׂ. *Da'as Sofrim* suggests that with this variation Scripture may be intimating that even during God's wrath [סְעָרָה], He exacts punishment to the most minute detail [כְּחוּט הַשְּׂעָרָה, *like a hair strand*].

וְעָנָן אֲבַק רַגְלָיו — *And clouds are the dust of His feet.* The *clouds* represent the darkness that will enshroud the enemy as a result of the heavenly punishment that will befall him. The *dust* of his feet are the decrees that God will place upon the enemy. Hence, the interpretation of the verse is: the decrees that God will place upon His enemies will bring them darkness (*Radak*). *Ibn Ezra* explains this as a continuation of the first part of the verse. God's heavenly decrees will come with the swiftness of the clouds that travel at the foot of the heavens.

◆§ God's Dominion Over the Waters

4. גּוֹעֵר בַּיָּם וַיַּבְּשֵׁהוּ — *He rebukes the sea and makes it dry.* This verse is to be understood both literally and allegorically (*Rashi; Radak*). The imagery of the drying of the seas is a reference to the future destruction of Assyria and the other nations of the region at the hand of Nebuchadnezzar, whom God will bring to power in the days of King Jehoiakim — see *Isaiah* 17:12 where the nations are described as mighty waters (*Rashi*). Alternatively, the prophecy is specifically referring to the downfall of the Assyrian monarchs (*Radak*). If God demands the mightiest of His creations, the seas, to change their nature and become dry land as He did at the Sea of Reeds, is it beyond Him to cause the downfall of empires, a process which does not violate natural law? (*Radak*).

וְכָל־הַנְּהָרוֹת הֶחֱרִיב — *And makes all the rivers parched.* If God can dry the seas He can surely dry the rivers for they are not as mighty as the seas. God can do

ה אֻמְלַל בָּשָׁן֙ וְכַרְמֶ֔ל וּפֶ֥רַח לְבָנ֖וֹן אֻמְלָֽל׃ הָרִים֙ רָעֲשׁ֣וּ מִמֶּ֔נּוּ וְהַגְּבָע֖וֹת הִתְמֹגָ֑גוּ וַתִּשָּׂ֤א הָאָ֙רֶץ֙
ו מִפָּנָ֔יו וְתֵבֵ֖ל וְכָל־י֥וֹשְׁבֵי בָֽהּ׃ לִפְנֵ֤י זַעְמוֹ֙ מִ֣י יַֽעֲמ֔וֹד וּמִ֥י יָק֖וּם בַּחֲר֣וֹן אַפּ֑וֹ חֲמָתוֹ֙ נִתְּכָ֣ה כָאֵ֔שׁ
ז וְהַצֻּרִ֖ים נִתְּצ֥וּ מִמֶּֽנּוּ׃ ט֣וֹב יְהֹוָ֔ה לְמָע֖וֹז בְּי֣וֹם צָרָ֑ה
ח וְיֹדֵ֖עַ חֹ֥סֵי בֽוֹ׃ וּבְשֶׁ֣טֶף עֹבֵ֔ר כָּלָ֖ה יַעֲשֶׂ֣ה מְקוֹמָ֑הּ

this in a miraculous manner, as when the Israelite nation crossed the Jordan River on dry land [see *Joshua* 3:16], or even in a natural manner, by holding back rain (*Radak*).

God uses His two emissaries of the previous verse to dry the seas and rivers. The winds dry the seas and the clouds hold back their rain (*Abarbanel*).

☙ God's Dominion Over Vegetation

אֻמְלַל בָּשָׁן וְכַרְמֶל — *Bashan and Carmel become devastated.* Bashan and Carmel were fertile pasture lands; Bashan in the east and Carmel in the west. When God withholds rain and dries the rivers, there is no vegetation in these normally productive areas. This refers allegorically to the destruction of the kings and common people of the nations (*Radak*).

וּפֶרַח לְבָנוֹן אֻמְלָל — *And the flower of Lebanon becomes devastated.* I.e., the *trees* of Lebanon will wither (*Targum Yonasan*). The Lebanon was a forest located in the northern area of the Land of Israel — see *I Kings* 5:20.

According to the Talmud (*Yoma* 39b), Lebanon is a reference to Solomon's Temple and the flower is a reference to the golden fruit that miraculously grew within it. When Solomon built the Temple, he planted golden fruit trees that miraculously bore fruit of gold in their appointed times. When the wind would blow, the fruit would fall off the tree and the Kohanim would sell them and support themselves with the proceeds. When the conquering enemies entered the Temple, these trees dried up and their fruit withered (*Rashi*).

☙ God's Dominion Over the Land

5. הָרִים רָעֲשׁוּ מִמֶּנּוּ — *Mountains quake because of Him.* Even the firm mountains quake and crumble at God's will (*Radak*). Metaphorically, this refers to kings and nobles (*Rashi*).

וַתִּשָּׂא הָאָרֶץ מִפָּנָיו — *The earth smolders from before Him.* The word וַתִּשָּׂא means *to raise up* (*Rashi*) or *to burn* — see *II Samuel* 5:21 (*Radak*). In any event, the imagery is of smoke rising from the ground after the land has suffered fiery destruction (*Rashi; Mahari Kara; Radak*). Alternatively *Malbim* translates וַתִּשָּׂא, *to lift up*, and explains that although land is ordinarily not capable of movement on its own it nevertheless lifts itself up before God, in a display of honor and respect toward Him.

וְתֵבֵל וְכָל־יוֹשְׁבֵי בָהּ — *The world and all who dwell in it.* תֵּבֵל, as opposed to אֶרֶץ, denotes the inhabited portion of the world (*Metzudos*).

6. לִפְנֵי זַעְמוֹ מִי יַעֲמוֹד — *Who can stand before His fury.* The prophet continues to describe the anger displayed by God against Nineveh (*Ibn Ezra*).

Malbim differentiates between the expressions used here for anger. חֵמָה is inner anger that is contained in one's heart. When the anger is expressed and displayed it is referred to as אַף — see comm. to v.2. The punishment that is decreed through the anger is זַעַם. Accordingly, *Malbim* explains: Before His punishment, who can stand? And who can rise up in the fierce glow of His anger that has not yet even decreed any punishment? And even the anger that has not yet been displayed — that is yet contained — is, nevertheless, fierce.

Bashan and Carmel become devastated, and the flower of Lebanon becomes devastated. [5] *Mountains quake because of Him and the hills melt; the earth smolders from before Him, the world and all who dwell in it.* [6] *Who can stand before His fury, and who can rise against His burning wrath? His wrath is poured out like fire and rocks become shattered because of Him.* [7] *HASHEM is beneficent, a stronghold on the day of distress, and mindful of those who take refuge in Him.* [8] *With a sweeping flood He puts an end to its place,*

חֲמָתוֹ נִתְּכָה כָאֵשׁ — *His wrath is poured out like fire.* His wrath has descended from Heaven and has *reached* the earth (*Rashi*). [See *Rashi, Exodus* 9:33.] The unusual metaphor *poured out like fire* is variously explained to describe either solid objects heated to such a high temperature that they have been melted by the fire (*Targum Yonasan*), the speedy descent of bolts of fiery lightning from heaven to earth (*Radak*), or volcanic eruptions in which the earth spews forth fire and lava from its bowels (*Malbim*).

וְהַצֻּרִים נִתְּצוּ מִמֶּנּוּ — *And rocks become shattered because of Him.* צוּר is the hardest of rocks (*R' Hirsch* to *Psalms* 114:8). Thus, when God will focus His wrath upon them, even this most powerful and mighty of nations will be smashed and destroyed (*Metzudos*).

7. טוֹב ה׳ ... — *Hashem is beneficent ...* At the very same time that He exacts punishment from His enemies, God, the Omnipotent, is merciful to those who revere Him (*Rashi*), protecting His nation in times of distress. Although the Assyrian Empire will be destroyed, the people of Israel who dwell in exile in their land will be spared the sword of Nebuchadnezzar (*Radak*).

לְמָעוֹז — *A stronghold.* [Scripture often refers to God as a stronghold or fortress. See *Psalms* 31:3; 37:39; *Jeremiah* 16:19.]

וְיֹדֵעַ חֹסֵי בוֹ — *And mindful of those who take refuge in Him.* I.e., He is mindful of the needs of those who take refuge in Him (*Rashi*). Alternatively, He is a stronghold to those who take refuge in Him, for He alone knows the secrets of men's hearts and recognizes those who really take refuge — i.e., trust — in Him (*Ibn Ezra*).

Radak compares וְיֹדֵעַ of our verse to *Psalms* 1:6: כִּי־יוֹדֵעַ ה׳ דֶּרֶךְ צַדִּיקִים, *For Hashem knows the way of the righteous,* i.e., He supervises their lives and grants them continuous protective care (*R' Hirsch, Psalms* ibid.; cf. *Exodus* 2:25 and *Rashi* there). Thus: *Hashem is beneficent — a stronghold on the day of distress — guarding those who take refuge in Him.*

The prophet previously declared (v. 5) that the land will be destroyed. Scripture now describes the manner of destruction (*Rashi*).

8. וּבְשֶׁטֶף עֹבֵר כָּלָה יַעֲשֶׂה מְקוֹמָהּ — *With a sweeping flood He puts an end to its place.* Just as a turbulent river overflows its banks and sweeps through the surrounding area utterly destroying everything in its path, so too, God's wrath (*Rashi*) — in the person of Nebuchadnezzar — will rage over Nineveh until no remnant is left (*Radak; Mahari Kara*). In contrast to Israel's exile at the hands of the Assyrians, which took place in shifts (see above footnote 1 to v. 2), Nineveh's destruction would take place in one destructive sweep (*Abarbanel*).

Malbim explains this verse literally

א/ט־יב ט וְאֹיְבָיו יְרַדֶּף־חֹשֶׁךְ׃ מַה־תְּחַשְּׁבוּן֙ אֶל־יהוֹה כָּלָ֖ה ה֣וּא
י עֹשֶׂ֑ה לֹא־תָק֥וּם פַּעֲמַ֖יִם צָרָֽה׃ כִּ֚י עַד־סִירִ֣ים סְבֻכִ֔ים
יא וּכְסָבְאָ֖ם סְבוּאִ֑ים אֻכְּל֕וּ כְּקַ֥שׁ יָבֵ֖שׁ מָלֵֽא׃ מִמֵּ֣ךְ יָצָ֔א
יב חֹשֵׁ֥ב עַל־יהוָ֖ה רָעָ֑ה יֹעֵ֖ץ בְּלִיָּֽעַל׃ כֹּ֣ה ׀ אָמַ֣ר יהוֹה
אִם־שְׁלֵמִים֙ וְכֵ֣ן רַבִּ֔ים וְכֵ֥ן נָגֹ֖זּוּ וְעָבָ֑ר וְעִנִּתִ֕ךְ לֹ֥א

and maintains that the verse is referring to the first time that Nineveh was destroyed — see commentary to v. 1. During its first siege, the king of Nineveh was trapped in the city by his enemies. Nineveh was surrounded by the Tigris River and soothsayers had assured the king that as long as the river maintained its natural boundaries he had nothing to fear for it would serve as a natural barrier against his enemies. This situation existed for three years until the river overflowed its banks. When this occurred, the king lost heart and ordered his family and wealth burned in his palace, where he too committed suicide.

וְאֹיְבָיו יְרַדֶּף־חֹשֶׁךְ — *And darkness will pursue His enemies.* Our translation follows *Ibn Ezra* and *Metzudos.* Alternatively, *Radak* translates *And His enemies He will pursue with darkness* and explains that darkness here is figurative, referring to the general troubles with which God will pursue the Ninevites.

In an additional explanation, *Ibn Ezra* writes that the Ninevites will be pursued into a dark place so that they will not be aware of the destruction that is about to befall them. Alternatively, *Targum Yonasan* interprets that the dark place is Gehinnom, where they will be punished even after death.

9. מַה־תְּחַשְּׁבוּן אֶל־ה׳ — *What can you devise against Hashem?* Nahum is addressing the inhabitants of Nineveh. What plan do you propose to devise to escape God's decree of destruction? (*Metzudos*). Alternatively, *Radak* renders: *What do you think of Hashem?* Do you think that He is unable to fulfill the word He has spoken against you? — see *II Kings* 18:35 where the blasphemous words that were uttered by Sennacherib to Hezekiah are recorded.

לֹא־תָקוּם פַּעֲמַיִם צָרָה — *Misfortune will not arise twice.* The initial destruction of Nineveh will be so complete that it will be unnecessary for God to bring punishment against them a second time (*Rashi; Radak*). *Malbim*, who maintains that Nineveh was indeed destroyed twice [see commentary to v. 1], explains the trouble [צָרָה] — Assyria — will only rise once, but not a second time. They will be destroyed by Nebuchadnezzar, never to rise again.

10. כִּי־עַד סִירִים סְבֻכִים — *While they are still like tangled thorns.* The thorns metaphorically represent the strength (*Rashi*) and unity (*Metzudos*) of the Assyrian people. The prophet foretells that the Assyrians will be utterly destroyed in spite of their power and unity. Furthermore, tangled thorns are impossible to uproot and remove [because there is no point on the bush where one can insert his hand to grasp it and pull it up without sustaining injury]. These thorns represent the Assyrians: a thorn stabbing painfully at the flesh of many nations, but firmly entrenched and impossible to uproot (*Radak*).

וּכְסָבְאָם סְבוּאִים — *And while they are drunk in their swilling.* Their destruction will take place while they still carouse in their drunken revelry (*Rashi*), totally unprepared for the enemy attack (*Metzudos*). Alternatively, this is an analogy for the feeble military resistance that the Assyrians will muster against the invading armies (*Radak*).

and darkness will pursue His enemies. [9] *What can you devise against* HASHEM? *He is making an end [of you]; misfortune will not arise twice.* [10] *While they are still like tangled thorns and while they are drunk in their swilling, they will be consumed like fully grown dried straw.* [11] *From you has come forth a plotter of evil against* HASHEM, *a lawless counselor.*

[12] *Thus said* HASHEM *[to Nineveh]: Even if [your troops] are united and also numerous — even so they will be cut down and pass on.*

אֻכְּלוּ כְּקַשׁ יָבֵשׁ מָלֵא — *They will be consumed like fully grown dried straw.* The Assyrians will not lose their powerful position step by step in a gradual decline, but — while they are yet entrenched as thorns and reveling in their drink — they will fall suddenly and swiftly as fully grown dried straw which has been put to the torch (*Rashi*). [Indeed, the only effective method for eradicating tangled thorn bushes is to burn them to the ground (*Radak*).] Furthermore, when thorns and straw have been thoroughly burnt, they leave very little ash and are easily blown away by the wind. So too, the Assyrians will be so thoroughly destroyed that no remnant of them will remain (*Radak*).

11. מִמֵּךְ יָצָא חֹשֵׁב עַל־ה׳ רָעָה ... — *From you has come forth a plotter of evil against Hashem* ... From you, Nineveh, has come forth Sennacherib with his evil plot to destroy God's Holy Temple (*Rashi*) or His nation, Israel (*Radak*), and his wicked counsel to blaspheme God (*Rashi; Metzudos*).

When Sennacherib set out to conquer the kingdom of Judah, he sent an army under Rabshakeh to surround Jerusalem. Rabshakeh called on Jerusalem to surrender, boasting of the irresistible might of Assyria and mocking Gd's power to save Jerusalem from the hands of her king, Sennacherib. This blasphemy was repeated in a message sent by Sennacherib to Hezekiah, king of Judah (see *II Kings* Chs. 18 and 19).

חֹשֵׁב ... יֹעֵץ בְּלִיָּעַל — *A plotter ... a lawless counselor.*

Malbim maintains that חֹשֵׁב is used when the advice given is of a philosophical nature while יֹעֵץ is used for pragmatic advice. Accordingly, חֹשֵׁב עַל־ה׳ רָעָה would be referring to Sennacherib's blasphemy while יֹעֵץ בְּלִיָּעַל would be his plan to destroy the Temple.

בְּלִיָּעַל — *Lawless.*

The word בְּלִיָּעַל is a combination of the words בְּלִי עוֹל — without the yoke of Heaven (*Metzudos*).

12. אִם־שְׁלֵמִים וְכֵן רַבִּים וְכֵן נָגֹזּוּ וְעָבָר — *Even if [your troops] are united and also numerous — even so they will be cut down and pass on.* If the inhabitants of Nineveh should become even more powerful and more numerous and prestigious than they are today, it will only serve to magnify their fall and destruction at the hands of G-d (*Rashi*). Their great might and numbers will not save them from being so thoroughly destroyed that they will pass from the stage of history, as G-d has decreed (*Metzudos*).

Radak relates the word שְׁלֵמִים to שָׁלוֹם, *peace*, and renders: Even though the Assyrians will arrive in Jerusalem at ease and unafraid, having conquered all the surrounding nations, they will nevertheless be destroyed.

א/יג־יד	יג	אֲעַנֵּךְ עוֹד׃ וְעַתָּה אֶשְׁבֹּר מֹטֵהוּ מֵעָלָיִךְ וּמוֹסְרֹתַיִךְ
	יד	אֲנַתֵּק׃ וְצִוָּה עָלֶיךָ יהוה לֹא־יִזָּרַע מִשִּׁמְךָ עוֹד
		מִבֵּית אֱלֹהֶיךָ אַכְרִית פֶּסֶל וּמַסֵּכָה אָשִׂים קִבְרֶךָ כִּי
ב/א	א	קַלּוֹתָ׃ הִנֵּה עַל־הֶהָרִים רַגְלֵי מְבַשֵּׂר מַשְׁמִיעַ
		שָׁלוֹם חָגִּי יְהוּדָה חַגַּיִךְ שַׁלְּמִי נְדָרָיִךְ כִּי לֹא יוֹסִיף

וְעִנִּתִךְ לֹא אֲעַנֵּךְ עוֹד — *I will afflict you, and I will not [need to] afflict you again.* I will thoroughly destroy you, Assyria — so thoroughly that it will be unnecessary for Me ever to afflict you again (*Rashi*). [See v. 9 where the prophet states that the *misfortune will not arise twice* (*Metzudos; Abarbanel*).] Alternatively, these words are addressed to Israel. If I afflicted you, Jerusalem, through Assyria, I will never again afflict you through them, for they will be totally destroyed (*Ibn Ezra; Radak*).

Rashi cites *Targum Yonasan* who phrases the entire verse differently: *Even if they* [the various factions of Nineveh] *will be united and even more numerous, and even if they will cut through* [וְכֵן נָגוֹזּוּ] the Tigris River *and cross* [וְעָבָר] the Euphrates to capture Jerusalem, they will be unsuccessful in their campaign, *for I have afflicted you* [with them once] *and I will not afflict you* [with them] *any more.*

13. וְעַתָּה אֶשְׁבֹּר מֹטֵהוּ מֵעָלָיִךְ — *And now, I will break his yoke from upon you.* The Divine Presence addresses Israel — "I will break the Assyrian yoke [the forced servitude and tribute (*Malbim*)] from upon you" (*Rashi*). Alternatively, *Abarbanel* sees the prophet addressing Nineveh. "I will break the yoke of your king from upon you; and the bonds with which you [Nineveh] imprisoned all the nations you ruled, I will tear asunder" — i.e., bring the empire to collapse.

מוֹטוֹת are the wooden poles of the animal yoke while מוֹסְרוֹת are the straps with which it is tied to the plow (*Metzudos*).

God Decrees

14. וְצִוָּה עָלֶיךָ ה׳ — *And Hashem will decree upon you.* This decree is being foretold against the king of Assyria (*Rashi*) or against the king of Nineveh (*Ibn Ezra*). From *Radak* and *Ibn Ezra*, it seems that the prophecy is specifically referring to Sennacherib. However, from *Rashi's* remarks it is apparent that his understanding is that God is not addressing Sennacherib but a later Assyrian king. See also *Abarbanel*.

לֹא־יִזָּרַע מִשִּׁמְךָ עוֹד — *That your name will never again be sown.* None of your descendants will ascend the throne (*Rashi*) and your name will not be perpetuated (*Ibn Ezra*). Sennacherib was murdered by his sons Adrammelech and Sarezer who fled to the land of Ararat (*Radak*).

מִבֵּית אֱלֹהֶיךָ אַכְרִית פֶּסֶל וּמַסֵּכָה — *I will eliminate idol and molten image from the temple of your gods.* Sennacherib's murder occurred while he was praying in the temple of Nisroch (*II Kings* 19:37). Due to his murder, this temple was subsequently abandoned. Since it was God who inspired Adrammelech and Sarezer to murder their father which resulted in the abandonment of the temple, it is as if God Himself cut off the graven and molten images of the temple (*Radak*).

Malbim remarks that it was the custom of the Assyrian kings to install images of themselves in their temples. When the line of Sennacherib would end in disgrace, these images would be removed [marking the final humiliation of these kings].

אָשִׂים קִבְרֶךָ כִּי קַלּוֹתָ — *I will make your grave [there], because you have become abhorrent [to Me].* You have made yourself despicable in My eyes (*Rashi*). You have become degraded

I will afflict you, and I will not [need to] afflict you again.

[13] *And now, I will break his yoke from upon you, [O Israel,] and I will snap your bonds.* [14] *And HASHEM will decree upon you that your name will never again be sown. I will eliminate idol and molten image from the temple of your gods; I will make your grave [there], because you have become abhorrent [to Me].*

[1] *Behold on the mountains the feet of the herald proclaiming peace! Celebrate your feasts, O Judah, fulfill your vows; for the lawless one will never again pass*

and disgraced for you will be assassinated by your own sons, and in your own temple. Your downfall is a punishment because you have derided Me with the words of blasphemy that you uttered against Me (see *II Kings* 18:35).

Instead of a monument in your honor, a plaque stating that you have become despised will be placed on your grave (*Abarbanel*).

II.

◆§ News of Judah's salvation

1. הִנֵּה עַל־הֶהָרִים רַגְלֵי מְבַשֵּׂר מַשְׁמִיעַ שָׁלוֹם — *Behold on the mountains the feet of the herald proclaiming peace!* Nahum tells that the news of Sennacherib's[1] death will soon be announced throughout the Kingdom of Judah and those who had been expelled from the land should return to their homes for Assyria has fallen (*Radak; Metzudos*). [Bearers of tidings stood upon mountains so that their words may be heard from afar (see *Judges* 9:7; *Isaiah* 40:9). See also *Isaiah* 52:7 where the prophet employs similar imagery.] The intent of the imagery is that salvation of the nation is imminent (*Abarbanel*).

חָגִּי יְהוּדָה חַגַּיִךְ — *Celebrate your feasts, O Judah.* During the cruel Assyrian occupation, the people were denied access to the Holy Temple in Jerusalem and were forbidden to celebrate their festivals. Now that Sennacherib is dead, the people are urged to resume their former way of life and again celebrate the festivals (*Mahari Kara*).

שַׁלְּמִי נְדָרָיִךְ — *Fulfill your vows.* Throughout the years of oppression, the people had vowed to offer sacrifices at the Temple if God would only drive away their cruel enemy. Nahum exhorts the people to fulfill their vow for God has now delivered them from the hands of Sennacherib (*Rashi*).

כִּי לֹא יוֹסִיף עוֹד ... — *For the lawless one will never again ...* For Sennacherib and his descendants will never again oppress the nation, for they have been utterly destroyed (*Rashi; Metzudos*).

1. Most commentators maintain that Sennacherib is the subject of this prophecy. If these commentators subscribe to the chronology of *Seder Olam*, that Nahum prophesied several decades after Sennacherib's death (see prologue), the prophet's words must then be interpreted as a description of past events. The implication is, just as Sennacherib fell in the past, so will the Assyrian nation in its entirety be routed in the future. *Abarbanel*, however, maintains that it is the fall of Sennacherib's son, the king of Assyria, to whom Scripture is referring.

ב/ב־ה °לְעֲבָרק׳ ב

עוֹד °לעבור־בָּךְ בְּלִיַּעַל כֻּלֹּה נִכְרָת: עָלָה מֵפִיץ עַל־פָּנַיִךְ נָצוֹר מְצֻרָה צַפֵּה־דֶרֶךְ חַזֵּק

ג מָתְנַיִם אַמֵּץ כֹּחַ מְאֹד: כִּי שָׁב יהוה אֶת־גְּאוֹן יַעֲקֹב כִּגְאוֹן יִשְׂרָאֵל כִּי בְקָקוּם בֹּקְקִים

ד וּזְמֹרֵיהֶם שִׁחֵתוּ: מָגֵן גִּבֹּרֵיהוּ מְאָדָּם אַנְשֵׁי־חַיִל מְתֻלָּעִים בְּאֵשׁ־פְּלָדוֹת הָרֶכֶב בְּיוֹם הֲכִינוֹ

ה וְהַבְּרֹשִׁים הָרְעָלוּ: בַּחוּצוֹת יִתְהוֹלְלוּ הָרֶכֶב

2. עָלָה מֵפִיץ עַל־פָּנַיִךְ נָצוֹר מְצֻרָה — *The scatterer has left your presence, he is beset with a siege.* Nahum continues to address the inhabitants of Judah. The kingdom of Sennacherib, who had scattered you into exile during the days of Hezekiah, is now besieged by Nebuchadnezzar, king of Babylonia (*Rashi; Mahari Kara*). Alternatively, *Radak* translates the words נָצוֹר מְצֻרָה as *guard the fortress* — see *II Chronicles* 14:5, and renders *the scatterer that has come against you* is destroyed; therefore, *guard the fortresses* — inhabit the fortified cities that had been captured and made desolate by the Assyrian king; do not abandon them. *Ibn Ezra* maintains that the prophet is addressing Nineveh, and advising them to prepare for the invasion of Nebuchadnezzar who will scatter them.

צַפֵּה־דֶרֶךְ — *Look out at the road.* Eventually, the Assyrian Empire will be besieged and conquered by the Babylonians. Nahum instructs the people of Judah to "look out" at the crossroads and see the approaching invaders of Assyria, for they will receive much strength and satisfaction as they watch the invasion of their enemy (*Rashi*).

Strength conveys not only physical power but also strength of conviction and unshakable belief in God. The people should therefore be strengthened by their salvation from the Assyrians and be of good heart and trust in G-d [see *Proverbs* 24:5, וְאִישׁ־דַּעַת מְאַמֶּץ־כֹּחַ, *a man of knowledge fortifies his strength*] (*Radak*).

3. כִּי שָׁב ה׳ אֶת־גְּאוֹן יַעֲקֹב כִּגְאוֹן יִשְׂרָאֵל — *For Hashem has restored the pride of Jacob like the [former] pride of Israel.* The glory of Israel will be restored to its previous status (*Rashi; Targum Yonasan*). Alternatively, with the death of Sennacherib, *Hashem will make the glory of Jacob tranquil and restful* [from their enemies] as they had been in earlier times (*Radak; Metzudos*). [See *Radak* (*Shorashim* שׁוּב) where numerous words with the root שׁוּב are cited from various verses and are translated *rest* or *tranquil*.]

The "pride and glory of Jacob" is referring to Jerusalem and the land of Judah [see *Psalms* 47:5] (*Radak*) or to the Holy Temple (*Metzudos, Psalms* ibid.).

The names "Jacob" and "Israel" describe the Israelite nation in exile [Jacob] and in their homeland [Israel] (*Ibn Ezra*).

Malbim maintains that when the names "Jacob" and "Israel" are used in the same verse, "Jacob" refers to the Ten Tribes of the Northern Kingdom and "Israel" refers to the Kingdom of Judah. [See commentary to *Micah* 1:5 for further discussion of this topic.]

Unlike the other commentators who explain this verse as a description of the salvation of Israel, *Abarbanel* writes that it is foretelling Israel's destruction. The pride of Jacob — Jerusalem and the land of Judah — will end as did the pride of Israel — the Northern Kingdom — in exile and destruction; for after the destruction of Nineveh, Nebuchadnezzar will arrive in Israel to destroy Jerusalem.

כִּי בְקָקוּם בֹּקְקִים וּזְמֹרֵיהֶם שִׁחֵתוּ — *For plunderers have laid them bare and have destroyed their vine branches.* For

by you; he is completely cut off. [2]*The scatterer has left your presence, he is beset with a siege. Look out at the road; gird your loins and gather much strength.* [3]*For* HASHEM *has restored the pride of Jacob like the [former] pride of Israel; for plunderers have laid them bare and have destroyed their vine branches.* [4]*The shields of his mighty men are reddened; his soldiers are colored scarlet; the chariots [glisten] with the fire of torches on the day he is readied; and the cypress trees are bedecked.* [5]*The chariots careen in the streets;*

their [Israel's] enemies have emptied the land of all her good and have continuously plundered her vegetation (*Radak*). *Targum Yonasan* relates זְמֹרֵיהֶם to זִמְרַת הָאָרֶץ, *the best of the land* — see *Genesis* 43:11, and renders: *and they destroyed their best cities.* Alternatively, *Metzudos* explains that the plunderers are the Babylonians who plundered *Assyria* and took *their* wealth and murdered *their* mighty warriors. Israel, therefore, need not fear Assyria any more.

◆§ The Babylonians Prepare to Attack

4. מָגֵן גִּבֹּרֵיהוּ ... מְתֻלָּעִים — *The shields of his mighty men ... colored scarlet.* Scripture is referring to the shields of the mighty men of the Babylonian king Nebuchadnezzar who will lay siege to Assyria (*Rashi; Radak*). Their shields and clothing are red and scarlet either as a symbol of their high rank or due to their custom of going to battle in bright colors to frighten their opponents (*Radak*). Alternatively, the red color on their shields and clothes is due to the blood of the Assyrians that the Babylonians have killed. [Red clothes is a term used by the prophets to describe a large-scale killing — see *Isaiah* 63:2.] (*Metzudos; Abarbanel*).

בְּאֵשׁ־פְּלָדוֹת הָרֶכֶב בְּיוֹם הֲכִינוֹ — *The chariots [glisten] with the fire of torches on the day he is readied.* The chariots are polished on the day that they prepare for battle [and glow like fire] (*Rashi*). Alternatively, on the day that Nebuchadnezzar will prepare his soldiers for battle, the chariots will be driven very swiftly and their metal wheels will cause sparks to fly as they race over the rocks and stones on the road (*Radak; Ibn Ezra; Metzudos*). Or, the chariots race like sparks of fire (*Mahari Kara*).

Some explain the word פְּלָדוֹת to be an inverted form of the word לַפִּיד [a torch] (*Rashi; Ibn Ezra; Metzudos*).

וְהַבְּרֹשִׁים הָרְעָלוּ — *And the cypress trees are bedecked.* The tall and stately cypress trees metaphorically represent the leaders of Nebuchadnezzar's army who are wrapped in special colorful garments (*Targum Yonasan; Rashi*).

Other interpretations have been offered:

Radak quotes his father who translates הָרְעָלוּ as *trembling* [synonymous with רָעֲדוּ] and renders "the officers of Nineveh are trembling," for they fear the Babylonian armies. *Radak* and *Metzudos* relate הָרְעָלוּ to רַעַל, *poison*, and translate, "the javelins (which were made of cypress wood) have their tips covered with poison." *Mahari Kara* explains that the metal tips of the spears were kept wrapped in cloth until the time of battle.

◆§ Assyria Prepares for War

5. בַּחוּצוֹת יִתְהוֹלְלוּ הָרֶכֶב — *The chariots careen in the streets.* The Assyrian horsemen panic, and run madly in the streets of Nineveh. They dare not leave the safety of the city to battle the

יְשְׁתַּקְשְׁקוּן בָּרְחֹבוֹת מַרְאֵיהֶן כַּלַּפִּידִם כַּבְּרָקִים
ו יְרוֹצֵצוּ׃ יִזְכֹּר אַדִּירָיו יִכָּשְׁלוּ °בהלכותם
ז יְמַהֲרוּ חוֹמָתָהּ וְהֻכַן הַסֹּכֵךְ׃ שַׁעֲרֵי הַנְּהָרוֹת
ח נִפְתָּחוּ וְהַהֵיכָל נָמוֹג׃ וְהֻצַּב גֻּלְּתָה הֹעֲלָתָה
וְאַמְהֹתֶיהָ מְנַהֲגוֹת כְּקוֹל יוֹנִים מְתֹפְפֹת
ט עַל־לִבְבֵהֶן׃ וְנִינְוֵה כִבְרֵכַת־מַיִם מִימֵי הִיא

°בַּהֲלִיכָתָם ק׳

enemy, since they are greatly outnumbered by the Babylonian forces (*Radak*). Alternatively, the armies of Nebuchadnezzar are so overjoyed at going to battle that they madly run about in the streets of their city [see *Jeremiah* 46:9] (*Abarbanel*).

יִשְׁתַּקְשְׁקוּן בָּרְחֹבוֹת — *They clang in the city squares.* יִשְׁתַּקְשְׁקוּן means *to make noise* — see *Joel* 2:24; *Isaiah* 33:4 (*Rashi*). The sound of the clattering of their weapons can be heard in the city squares (*Targum Yonasan*). Alternatively, the word יִשְׁתַּקְשְׁקוּן is related to שׁוֹק, *a leg.* Since everyone is running in a frenzy they collide and bang their legs [שׁוֹק] into one another (*Ibn Ezra; Radak*).

מַרְאֵיהֶן כַּלַּפִּידִם — *Their appearance is like flames.* The faces of the Assyrians redden in shame for they are not strong enough to go to battle against their enemies (*Radak*).

כַּבְּרָקִים יְרוֹצֵצוּ — *They dash like lightning.* They run all around the city not knowing what to do (*Radak*). The root of יְרוֹצֵצוּ is thus רָץ, *to run* (*Ibn Ezra*) or *to hasten* (see *R' Hirsch, Genesis* 25:22).

Following *Targum Yonasan, Rashi* renders, "[the clattering of their weapons cause] those who hear it to become frightened as when one sees bolts of lightning." According to this interpretation, the word יְרוֹצֵצוּ means יְרוֹעֲעוּ, *to be frightened* or *discomfited* (ibid.).

The Weakened Assyrian Nation

6. ... יִזְכֹּר אַדִּירָיו — *He will [then] remember his mighty men ...* The Assyrian monarch will recall the former glory of his mighty forces, and will wish to take them to battle against the invading Babylonians but they will stumble and falter on the way (*Rashi*).

יְמַהֲרוּ חוֹמָתָהּ — *They will hasten [to defend] its wall.*

Our texts have a מַפִּיק in the ה [a dot indicating that the word is third person female possessive] and is translated "[her] *its* wall," i.e., the wall of the city of Nineveh [see *Radak*]. *Rashi*'s text did not have the מַפִּיק. He therefore translates "*to* the wall," for the prefix ל, *to,* may be interchanged with the suffix ה. [See *Yevamos* 13b.] Accordingly, the verse means that the Assyrians will flee *to the city's wall* to protect it from the invading Babylonians (*Rashi; Metzudos*). *Minchas Shai* notes that although *Radak's* reading appears in our editions, *Rashi's* reading seems to concur with *Targum Yonasan* [see also *Ibn Ezra*].

וְהֻכַן הַסֹּכֵךְ — *But the covering will have been set up.*

Our translation follows *Radak* who maintains that the סֹכֵךְ was a protective roof built of wood and skins to protect the besiegers from the projectiles of the defenders. It allowed the soldiers to advance to an area immediately in front of the city and tunnel under its wall. Alternatively, it was one of the several fortified towers that were built along the wall to protect the defenders of the city (*Rashi, Targum Yonasan* — see *Ibn Ezra*). Citing *Ezekiel* 28:14, *Rashi* suggests that סֹכֵךְ may be an expression of *ruling* and renders "the monarch [who protects his subjects] has armed himself."

they clang in the city squares; their appearance is like flames; they dash like lightning. [6] *He will [then] remember his mighty men — but they will stumble as they go. They will hasten [to defend] its wall, but the covering will have been set up.*

[7] *The gates of the rivers have been opened, and the palace is melting.* [8] *The queen has been exposed and carried off [into captivity]; her handmaids moan, like the sounding of doves, beating upon their hearts.* [9] *Nineveh had been like a pool of [still] water, from her [earliest] days —*

◆§ The Fall of Nineveh

7. שַׁעֲרֵי הַנְּהָרוֹת נִפְתָּחוּ — *The gates of the rivers have been opened.* The gates of the city that are near the rivers have been breached by the enemy (*Rashi*) leaving the palace open for invasion (*Radak*). *Targum Yonasan* renders "the bridges of the rivers have been severed."

וְהַהֵיכָל נָמוֹג — *And the palace is melting.* Nineveh's palace has quivered and quaked from the stone missiles that have battered its walls (*Rashi*). Alternatively, the king trembles in his palace (*Targum Yonasan*).

8. וְהֻצַּב גֻּלְּתָה הֹעֲלָתָה — *The queen has been exposed and carried off [into captivity].* וְהֻצַּב is a reference to the queen who stands [הַנִּצֶּבֶת] at the king's right side. The queen, who generally remained secluded in her royal chambers (*Radak*), will publicly be taken captive and will be brought from the city (*Rashi*). Alternatively, the queen's name was Hutzab. She will be brought up (הֹעֲלָתָה) onto a wagon and taken captive (*Ibn Ezra*). *Radak* quotes his father who renders "the palace [mentioned just previously] that had stood [הֻצַּב] peacefully in Nineveh for many years will be cut [הֹעֲלָתָה] to the ground."

וְאַמְהֹתֶיהָ מְנַהֲגוֹת כְּקוֹל יוֹנִים — *Her handmaids moan, like the sounding of doves.* Her handmaids moan in a mournful tone, like the sound of lamenting doves (*Rashi*). *Ibn Ezra* relates מְנַהֲגוֹת to נהג, *to lead*, and renders "the handmaids who lead her [the queen] sound like moaning doves."

In numerous places (*Isaiah* 38:14 ibid. 59:11; *Jeremiah* 48:28) Scripture uses the dove as a picture of lamenting, moaning and suffering. Birds, in general, are used metaphorically to picture a fugitive existence, threatened by danger and defenseless. *R' Hirsch* (*Lev.* 1:17) speculates that perhaps for this reason only birds are offered as sacrifices in cases of conditions of bodily suffering or illness (מְצוֹרָע, זָב, זָבָה, יוֹלֶדֶת).

Radak quotes his father who translates אַמְהֹתֶיהָ as *her noble women.* They are referred to as handmaids for they will be as lowly handmaids when exiled.

מְתֹפְפֹת עַל־לִבְבֵהֶן — *Beating upon their hearts.* They beat their hearts [in anguish] as one beats a drum [תֹּף] (*Rashi*).

9. וְנִינְוֵה כִבְרֵכַת־מַיִם מִימֵי הִיא — *Nineveh had been like a pool of [still] water, from her [earliest] days.* From the time Nineveh was founded, its inhabitants had always dwelt in peace and tranquility, as still as a pond whose water does not move (*Rashi*). Alternatively, the prophecy metaphorically describes the wealth and prosperity with which Nineveh had been endowed since its early days. It had always been filled

י וְהֵ֥מָּה נָסִ֖ים עִמְד֣וּ עֲמֹ֑דוּ וְאֵ֖ין מַפְנֶֽה׃ בֹּ֥זּוּ כֶ֖סֶף בֹּ֣זּוּ זָהָ֑ב וְאֵ֥ין קֵ֙צֶה֙ לַתְּכוּנָ֔ה כָּבֹ֕ד מִכֹּ֖ל כְּלִ֥י חֶמְדָּֽה׃ יא בּוּקָ֥ה וּמְבוּקָ֖ה וּמְבֻלָּקָ֑ה וְלֵ֨ב נָמֵ֜ס וּפֵ֣ק בִּרְכַּ֗יִם וְחַלְחָלָה֙ בְּכָל־מָתְנַ֔יִם וּפְנֵ֥י כֻלָּ֖ם קִבְּצ֥וּ פָארֽוּר׃ יב אַיֵּה֙ מְע֣וֹן אֲרָי֔וֹת וּמִרְעֶ֥ה ה֖וּא לַכְּפִרִ֑ים אֲשֶׁ֣ר הָלַךְ֩ אַרְיֵ֨ה לָבִ֥יא שָׁ֛ם גּ֥וּר אַרְיֵ֖ה וְאֵ֥ין מַחֲרִֽיד׃ יג אַרְיֵ֤ה טֹרֵף֙ בְּדֵ֣י גֹרוֹתָ֔יו וּמְחַנֵּ֖ק לְלִבְאֹתָ֑יו

with the best as the pond is filled with water (*Radak*). Its wealth was so great that all nations came to benefit from it (*Mahari Kara*). *Abarbanel* explains this literally. Nineveh was built along the Tigris River and its soil was always moist [like a pool of water]. The continuous moisture caused its inhabitants to become unhealthy and weak.

וְהֵמָּה נָסִים — *But [now] they flee!* But now, due to the great stress and oppression caused by their enemies, they flee their land (*Rashi*), leaving their wealth behind (*Metzudos*). *Abarbanel*, following his interpretation of the previous phrase, explains that since the people were weak, they fled when the enemy came and they did not remain to fight.

עִמְדוּ עֲמֹדוּ וְאֵין מַפְנֶה — *"Halt! Halt!" But no one pays attention.* When its inhabitants are told to stop fleeing the city and to stand up against the enemy, no one turns his heart to listen (*Rashi; Mahari Kara*). Alternatively, when the enemy orders them to stop, they do not heed his order and continue to flee the city (*Radak*).

10. בֹּזּוּ כֶסֶף בֹּזּוּ זָהָב וְאֵין קֵצֶה לַתְּכוּנָה — *"Plunder silver, plunder gold; the amount is limitless!"* The prophet addresses the Babylonians, "Plunder the endless amount of silver and gold that the Assyrians have amassed in their treasuries" (*Rashi; Metzudos*). Alternatively, it is the Ninevites that are addressing the Babylonians and pleading with them. "Take all the wealth that you wish but do not kill us" (*Mahari Kara*).

[The word קֵצֶה is synonymous with the word קֵץ, *end*, and is often interchanged in Scripture. See 3:3 and *Isaiah* 2:7.]

The word תְּכוּנָה [*that which was accounted for*] is used to denote a treasury because one carefully counts that which is stored there [see *II Kings* 12:12, *and they gave the money that was counted* (הַכֶּסֶף הַמְתֻכָּן)] (*Rashi*).

כָּבֹד מִכֹּל כְּלִי חֶמְדָּה — *"Sweep [it] clean of every precious vessel."* The word כָּבוֹד is the infinitive form (which often serves as an imperative, as in זָכוֹר, שָׁמוֹר) of the word הַכְבָּדָה, *to sweep clean.* Nahum is instructing the Babylonians to sweep Nineveh clean of all its precious objects (*Rashi*). Alternatively, הִתְכַּבְּדִי is related to כָּבוֹד, *honor*. This phrase, then, is the enemy's reply to the pleas of Nineveh's inhabitants. "No, we do not care to keep you alive, the honor of victory is more valuable to us than any treasures that we may take" (*Mahari Kara*).

11. בּוּקָה וּמְבוּקָה וּמְבֻלָּקָה — *She is emptied, emptied and breached.* Nineveh's enemies will thoroughly empty her of her wealth and will break open her walls (*Rashi*).

The compounded form of the root בוק (the addition of the prefix "מ") is used to reinforce the idea of *total* waste. This form is often used by Scripture (see *Jeremiah* 16:19; *Ezekiel* 6:14). The word מְבֻלָּקָה literally means *to be cut off* (*Radak*). *Rashi* elsewhere (*Isaiah* 24:1) translates *destroyed*.

וְלֵב נָמֵס וּפֵק בִּרְכַּיִם ... — *With melted*

but [now] they flee! "Halt! Halt!" but no one pays attention.

[10] *"Plunder silver, plunder gold; the amount is limitless! Sweep [it] clean of every precious vessel!"* [11] *She is emptied, emptied and breached; with melted heart, buckled knees, pain in all the loins, and all of their faces have gathered blackness.* [12] *Where is the lions' den which was the feeding place of the young lions, where the lion [and] lioness went about, [leaving] the lion whelp there, with none to make them afraid?* [13] *The lion would tear prey to provide for his cubs, choking [prey] for his lionesses.*

heart, buckled knees ... Scripture describes the terror and fear of Nineveh's inhabitants (*Mahari Kara; Metzudos*). They will be so terrified that their knees will buckle under them (*Rashi*). *Radak* explains that when one is in great fear his knees knock together [see *Daniel* 5:6 — when Belshazzar saw the handwriting on the wall he became frightened, "and his knees knocked together"].

וּפְנֵי כֻלָּם קִבְּצוּ פָארוּר — *And all of their faces have gathered blackness.* And their faces are as black as the soot that forms on a pot [פָּרוּר — see *Numbers* 11:8] (*Rashi*). *Ibn Ezra* (*Joel* 2:6) explains that פָּארוּר is related to פְּאֵר, *beauty*. All faces will withdraw their beauty due to the fear of the invading Babylonians.

12. אַיֵּה מְעוֹן אֲרָיוֹת וּמִרְעֶה הוּא לַכְּפִרִים — *Where is the lions' den which was the feeding place of the young lions.* The prophet "laments" the downfall of Nineveh and recites a dirge for the great and powerful city. "Nineveh, the city that was inhabited by fierce kings, who were as powerful as lions [where are your lions now...]" (*Rashi; Metzudos*). Alternatively, *Radak* and *Ibn Ezra* explain that it is the nations of the world who are expressing their amazement at Nineveh's destruction. In previous times, warriors who were as powerful as lions would go forth from Nineveh to devour and plunder other nations and bring back their prey, as a lion brings his prey back to his den (*Radak*).

אֲשֶׁר הָלַךְ אַרְיֵה לָבִיא שָׁם ... — *Where the lion [and] lioness went about ...* The lion and lioness came and went from their dwelling place and left their cubs, without fear of injury. This again refers to the kings and officers of Nineveh who fearlessly went to battle leaving their families behind (*Targum Yonasan; Rashi; Metzudos*).

Our translation of לָבִיא as lioness follows *Malbim* who does not make a distinction between לָבִיא and לְבִיָּא (*Ezekiel* 19:2) which is obviously a lioness [see *Radak* there]. *Metzudos* here is unclear but *Ezekiel* ibid. translates לְבִיָּא, *lioness*, as in *Job* 4:11, where the word לָבִיא is used, implying that לָבִיא, too, is a lioness. *Radak* (*Judges* 14:5), however, defines לָבִיא as a lion older than an אַרְיֵה. How true are the words of R' Hirsch (*Genesis* 49:9): "It is regrettable that the actual meaning of לָבִיא is unknown." [He relates it to לבה and להב and translates *the excited inflamed lion.*]

13. אַרְיֵה טֹרֵף בְּדֵי גֹרוֹתָיו ... — *The lion would tear prey to provide for his cubs ...* [The imagery of the fearless powerful lion continues.] The kings [of Nineveh] brought back much spoils, enough for their households (*Targum Yonasan; Rashi*).

ב/יד יד וַיְמַלֵּא־טֶרֶף חֹרָיו וּמְעֹנֹתָיו טְרֵפָה׃ הִנְנִי אֵלַיִךְ נְאֻם יְהוָה צְבָאוֹת וְהִבְעַרְתִּי בֶעָשָׁן רִכְבָּהּ וּכְפִירַיִךְ תֹּאכַל חָרֶב וְהִכְרַתִּי מֵאֶרֶץ טַרְפֵּךְ וְלֹא־יִשָּׁמַע עוֹד קוֹל מַלְאָכֵכֵה׃

ג/א־ג א הוֹי עִיר דָּמִים כֻּלָּהּ ב כַּחַשׁ פֶּרֶק מְלֵאָה לֹא יָמִישׁ טָרֶף׃ קוֹל שׁוֹט וְקוֹל ג רַעַשׁ אוֹפָן וְסוּס דֹּהֵר וּמֶרְכָּבָה מְרַקֵּדָה׃ פָּרָשׁ מַעֲלֶה וְלַהַב חֶרֶב וּבְרַק חֲנִית וְרֹב חָלָל וְכֹבֶד פָּגֶר

וַיְמַלֵּא־טֶרֶף חֹרָיו — *He would fill up his lairs with prey.* As the lion filled his lairs with the prey that he had captured, so too, will the kings and officers fill their treasuries with what they had carried away (*Targum Yonasan; Rashi*).

14. הִנְנִי אֵלַיִךְ נְאֻם ה׳ צְבָאוֹת — *Behold I am against you — the word of Hashem, Master of Legions.* G-d is addressing Nineveh. "Behold I am turning My face against you to destroy you" (*Radak*), or "Behold I am going to war against you" (*Metzudos*).

The term *Hashem, Master of Legions* [ה׳ צְבָאוֹת], expresses the idea that G-d takes the infinite number of forces and conditions of the universe and harmonizes them to perform His will (*Rav Hirsch, Siddur*). [Scripture continues to describe how God will use the forces of nature to destroy Nineveh.]

וְהִבְעַרְתִּי בֶעָשָׁן רִכְבָּהּ — *I will burn her chariots in smoke.* I will burn her chariots in a great fire whose smoke will be seen from afar (*Radak*). *Rashi* renders, "and I will burn many chariots into smoke"; the idea of many is indicated by the extra ה of רִכְבָּה. [Apparently in *Rashi*'s text the ה was written without the מַפִּיק (רִכְבָּה). In our text, however, the ה does have the מַפִּיק and would thus be translated *her* chariots.]

וּכְפִירַיִךְ תֹּאכַל חָרֶב — *And the sword will devour your cubs.* The cubs refer to the soldiers (*Radak*) or to the children of the kings (*Metzudos*).

וְהִכְרַתִּי מֵאֶרֶץ טַרְפֵּךְ — *I will eliminate your prey from the earth.* You will never again maraud through the land to take the spoils of the nations (*Metzudos*).

וְלֹא־יִשָּׁמַע עוֹד קוֹל מַלְאָכֵכֵה — *And the voice of your messengers will be heard no more!* Prior to the invasion of a country to be conquered, the Assyrian kings sent their officers to instill terror and fear among its inhabitants. Scripture is referring to these messengers (*Radak*). See *II Kings* 18:19 and *Isaiah* 36:13 where Sennacherib sent Rabshakeh who arrogantly taunted Israel (*Rashi; Radak*).

III.

The Doom of Nineveh

1. הוֹי — *Woe.* Nahum continues his rebuke of Nineveh and explains the reasons for its severe punishment (*Abarbanel*). Our translation of הוֹי follows *Targum Yonasan* who translates הוֹי as וַי — *Woe, city of blood.* Alternatively, *Ibn Ezra* and *Radak* suggest that it is a word signifying direct address — *O city of blood.*

עִיר דָּמִים — *City of blood.* Nineveh is a city full of murder for its inhabitants have shed the blood of many nations (*Metzudos*).

כֻּלָּהּ כַּחַשׁ ... — *It is all deceit* ... Its inhabitants are deceitful to one another and thievery is rampant (*Radak*). The word פֶּרֶק, *robbery*, literally means *to remove* or *cast off* (cf. *Genesis* 27:40). It is used to indicate robbery, for a robber

2/14

He would fill up his lairs with prey and his dens with torn carcasses. [14] *Behold I am against you — the word of* HASHEM, *Master of Legions — I will burn her chariots in smoke, and the sword will devour your cubs. I will eliminate your prey from the earth, and the voice of your messengers will be heard no more!*

3/1-3

[1] *Woe to the city of blood; it is all deceit, full of robbery; prey departs not [from it];* [2] *the sound of the whip and the sound of rattling wheel; galloping horse and bounding chariot;* [3] *the horseman raises a flashing sword and a glittering spear; numerous slain and heaps of corpses;*

removes the object from its owner's hand (*Rashi; Radak*). Alternatively, *Ibn Ezra* translates "crossroad" and renders *each crossroad is full of lies.*

לֹא יָמִישׁ טָרֶף — *Prey departs not [from it].* She is constantly filled with prey and booty, for its people constantly attack and destroy other nations (*Radak; Metzudos*).

Malbim explains this verse differently: הוֹי עִיר דָּמִים — *Woe, murderous city;* כֻּלָּהּ כַּחַשׁ — *Whose inhabitants all deny the existence of God;* פֶּרֶק מְלֵאָה — *although it is full of corpses;* לֹא יָמִישׁ טָרֶף — *nevertheless, their preying continues;* i.e., they are never sated of murder and rapaciousness.

2. קוֹל שׁוֹט וְקוֹל רַעַשׁ אוֹפָן — *The sound of the whip and the sound of rattling wheel.* In the city of Nineveh one always hears the crack of whips and the rattling sound of the chariot wheels [for her inhabitants are always preparing for war] (*Rashi*). Alternatively, *Radak* and *Tos. Rid* explain that the prophet is describing the battle sounds of the approaching enemy.

וְסוּס דֹּהֵר וּמֶרְכָּבָה מְרַקֵּדָה — *Galloping horse and bounding chariot.* Due to the speed of the galloping horses the chariots are tossed about and appear to be dancing (*Radak*). [Similar imagery is recorded in *Judges* 5:22 and *Joel* 2:5.]

3. פָּרָשׁ מַעֲלֶה וְלַהַב חֶרֶב וּבְרַק חֲנִית — *The horseman raises a flashing sword and a glittering spear.* Our translation follows *Radak* who interprets וְלַהַב as if there were no conjunctive ו, i.e., as if the word was written לַהַב. Hence, it is the sword that is raised by the horseman. *Metzudos*, however, explains that it is the horseman who raises *himself* as his horse gallops. *Malbim* maintains that מַעֲלֶה is not a verb at all, but means "heights." The verse is referring to the mountainous regions, where the chariots cannot go. There you will find only the horsemen.

The word לַהַב, literally *flame*, is often used to refer to the blade of the sword (*Rashi*), for it flashes like a flame of fire (*Radak Shorashim; Metzudos*). Similarly, the word בָּרָק, literally, *lightning*, is used for the iron portion of the spear, for it glistens like a bolt of lightning (*Rashi*).

וְרֹב חָלָל וְכֹבֶד פָּגֶר ... — *Numerous slain and heaps of corpses* ... The prophet continues to describe the cruelty of the Assyrians whose horsemen would slay many, resulting in many corpses, so numerous that people stumble over them because there is no room to walk (*Rashi; Metzudos*). Alternatively, the phrase is referring to the corpses of the Ninevites who were slain by the invading Babylonians (*Ibn Ezra; Radak*).

The word פֶּגֶר is used exclusively to

°וכשלו ק׳ ד וְאֵין קֵ֫צֶה לַגְּוִיָּה °יכשלו בִּגְוִיָּתָם: מֵרֹב זְנוּנֵי זוֹנָה טוֹבַת חֵן בַּעֲלַת כְּשָׁפִים הַמֹּכֶרֶת גּוֹיִם
ה בִּזְנוּנֶיהָ וּמִשְׁפָּחוֹת בִּכְשָׁפֶיהָ: הִנְנִי אֵלַיִךְ נְאֻם יהוה צְבָאוֹת וְגִלֵּיתִי שׁוּלַיִךְ עַל־פָּנָיִךְ וְהַרְאֵיתִי
ו גוֹיִם מַעְרֵךְ וּמַמְלָכוֹת קְלוֹנֵךְ: וְהִשְׁלַכְתִּי עָלַיִךְ
ז שִׁקֻּצִים וְנִבַּלְתִּיךְ וְשַׂמְתִּיךְ כְּרֹאִי: וְהָיָה כָל־רֹאַיִךְ יִדּוֹד מִמֵּךְ וְאָמַר שָׁדְּדָה נִינְוֵה מִי יָנוּד
ח לָהּ מֵאַיִן אֲבַקֵּשׁ מְנַחֲמִים לָךְ: הֲתֵיטְבִי מִנֹּא אָמוֹן הַיֹּשְׁבָה בַּיְאֹרִים מַיִם סָבִיב לָהּ אֲשֶׁר־

describe a dead body while גְוִיָּה may refer to a live person as well (*Radak*).

4. מֵרֹב זְנוּנֵי זוֹנָה — *[All this] because of the many harlotries of the harlot.* The concepts of harlotries and harlot used in this verse are metaphoric terms (*Ibn Ezra*). The violent deeds listed in verse 3 were accomplished by Nineveh through her harlot-like conduct. She would first entice and befriend the kings of the land to gain their confidence and would then attack them and conquer them (*Rashi*). *Radak*, who interpreted verse 3 to be acts of violence committed *against* the Ninevites, explains that all the punishments of verse 3 occurred to Nineveh because she conducted herself unscrupulously, like a harlot.

טוֹבַת חֵן בַּעֲלַת כְּשָׁפִים ... — *Rich in grace, practitioner of witchcraft ...* Those nations who were not influenced by Nineveh's enticing actions, she captured through witchcraft (*Malbim*).

וּמִשְׁפָּחוֹת — *And families.* [The word "families" is used by Scripture synonymously for nations — see *Jeremiah* 1:15.]

5. הִנְנִי אֵלַיִךְ — *Behold, I am against you.* Scripture continues the imagery of the harlot by comparing the destruction of Nineveh to the disgrace of the harlot (*Radak*).

וְגִלֵּיתִי שׁוּלַיִךְ עַל־פָּנָיִךְ ... — *And I will pull up your skirts over your face ...* The word שׁוּלַיִךְ actually means *your hem.* It was customary to disgrace the harlot by having her publicly stand unclothed. Her skirt was lifted over her face thereby exposing its hem [שׁוּלַיִם] (*Metzudos*). [See *Hosea* 2:5; *Jeremiah* 13:26; *Ezekiel* 16:37 where this idea is reiterated.]

The word מַעְרֵךְ literally means "your uncoveredness" — see *Micah* 1:11 (*Rashi*), *Lev.* 20:18 [הֶעֱרָה] (*Tos. Rid*).

6. וְהִשְׁלַכְתִּי עָלַיִךְ שִׁקֻּצִים וְנִבַּלְתִּיךְ — *And I will cast repulsive things upon you and make you disgusting.* The imagery of the harlot continues. The repulsive things are filthy garments that will cause the harlot to be disgraced (*Rashi*). That is, the enemy will slaughter many Ninevites and will take the remainder into captivity in a disgraceful manner (*Metzudos*).

וְשַׂמְתִּיךְ כְּרֹאִי — *I will make you like dung.* Our translation of כְּרֹאִי, *like dung*, follows *Rashi*, *Ibn Ezra* and *Radak* who relate רֹאִי to מֻרְאָתוֹ, *its crop* (*Lev.* 1:16), the organ containing the dung of the bird. Alternatively, *Mahari Kara* relates רֹאִי to רְאִיָּה, *to be seen*, and explains that Nineveh will be left open for all to see her disgrace, as reiterated in the following verse.

7. וְהָיָה כָל־רֹאַיִךְ יִדּוֹד מִמֵּךְ וְאָמַר שָׁדְּדָה נִינְוֵה — *And it will be that all who see you will move away from you and say, "Nineveh has been ravaged."* Whoever will see you in your degradation

there is no end to the bodies, and they stumble over their bodies. [4] *[All this] because of the many harlotries of the harlot, rich in grace, practitioner of witchcraft, who sells nations through her harlotries and families through her witchcraft.*

[5] *Behold, I am against you — the word of* HASHEM, *Master of Legions — and I will pull up your skirts over your face; and I will show the nations your nakedness and the kingdoms your shame.* [6] *And I will cast repulsive things upon you and make you disgusting; I will make you like dung.* [7] *And it will be that all who see you will move away from you and say, 'Nineveh has been ravaged; who will bemoan her?' From where can I seek comforters for you?*

[8] *Are you better than No-amon, which sits by*

and disgrace will keep their distance from you as from a disgusting object (*Metzudos*). Scripture is referring to those who have sided with Nineveh in the past. Now they, too, will move away from her (*Mahari Kara*) and say, "Nineveh, who had ruled over the nations, has now been made desolate" (*Radak*).

מִי יָנוּד לָהּ — *"Who will bemoan her?" From where can I seek comforters for you,* for everyone is rejoicing at your downfall because of the evil that you committed against them (*Radak*).

Although we translated the word יָנוּד, *bemoan,* its actual translation is *to move,* for in earlier times, one who came to comfort the mourner would shake his head before him (*Metzudos*). [Some say that this was a way of sharing the sorrow with the mourner for he would shake his head in grief and then the comforter would do the same. See *Jeremiah* 22:10; *Job* 2:11.]

◆§ The Destruction of the Great City of No

8. הֲתֵיטְבִי מִנֹּא אָמוֹן — *Are you better than No-amon.* The prophet admonishes the people of Nineveh for relying on the impregnability of their city since No-amon shared physical similarities with Nineveh yet was destroyed by Nebuchadnezzar when he conquered Egypt (*Rashi; Radak*). Although many commentators see Amon as part of the name of the city No-amon, *Rashi* translates אָמוֹן as *pedagogue,* for No was the city where the Egyptian kings were trained and anointed.

Targum Yonasan identifies No-amon as Alexandria. *Abarbanel* points out that this explanation is problematic because Alexandria was not built until several centuries later, by Alexander the Great! He therefore maintains that No was a different Egyptian city that was conquered by Nebuchadnezzar. Perhaps *Targum* means that Alexandria was built on the site of the former great city, No.

בַּיְאֹרִים — *By the rivers. Metzudos* renders *canals.* [Egypt had numerous canals branching off from the Nile. In fact, Scripture refers to her as יְאֹרִים, translated by *Rashi* as the *land of rivers.* See *Rashi, Ezekiel* 30:12.]

ט חֵ֣יל יָ֔ם מִיָּ֖ם חוֹמָתָֽהּ׃ כּ֥וּשׁ עָצְמָ֛ה וּמִצְרַ֖יִם
י וְאֵ֣ין קֵ֑צֶה פּ֣וּט וְלוּבִ֔ים הָי֖וּ בְּעֶזְרָתֵֽךְ׃ גַּם־הִ֗יא
לַגֹּלָה֙ הָלְכָ֣ה בַשֶּׁ֔בִי גַּ֥ם עֹלָלֶ֛יהָ יְרֻטְּשׁ֖וּ בְּרֹ֣אשׁ
כָּל־חוּצ֑וֹת וְעַל־נִכְבַּדֶּ֙יהָ֙ יַדּ֣וּ גוֹרָ֔ל וְכָל־גְּדוֹלֶ֖יהָ
יא רֻתְּק֥וּ בַזִּקִּֽים׃ גַּם־אַ֣תְּ תִּשְׁכְּרִ֔י תְּהִ֖י נַעֲלָמָ֑ה
יב גַּם־אַ֛תְּ תְּבַקְשִׁ֥י מָע֖וֹז מֵאוֹיֵֽב׃ כָּ֨ל־מִבְצָרַ֔יִךְ
תְּאֵנִ֖ים עִם־בִּכּוּרִ֑ים אִם־יִנּ֕וֹעוּ וְנָפְל֖וּ עַל־פִּ֥י
יג אוֹכֵֽל׃ הִנֵּ֨ה עַמֵּ֤ךְ נָשִׁים֙ בְּקִרְבֵּ֔ךְ לְאֹ֣יְבַ֔יִךְ פָּת֥וֹחַ
נִפְתְּח֖וּ שַׁעֲרֵ֣י אַרְצֵ֑ךְ אָכְלָ֥ה אֵ֖שׁ בְּרִיחָֽיִךְ׃

חֵיל ... חוֹמָתָהּ — *Rampart ... wall.* The חֵיל was the small inner wall that surrounded the city while the חוֹמָה was the large outer wall (*Mahari Kara*).

9-10. Scripture continues to list the nations who offered assistance to No, but to no avail.

9. כּוּשׁ עָצְמָה וּמִצְרַיִם וְאֵין קֵצֶה פּוּט וְלוּבִים הָיוּ בְּעֶזְרָתֵךְ — *Powerful Cush and endless Egypt, Put and Lubim were your helpers.* The forebears of these nations were all relatives of Ashur, the founder of Nineveh and progenitor of Assyria — see *Genesis* 10:6-13. They came to the aid of No-amon but to no avail (*Mahari Kara*). The Cushites were the strength of No-amon for they came to her aid together with the Egyptians. In fact, there was no end to those who came to help her (*Metzudos*). Alternatively, the words וְאֵין קֵצֶה, *without end*, are modifying only Egypt [מִצְרַיִם]. The Egyptians, a nation that was so numerous [without end] ... nevertheless fell to Nebuchadnezzar (*Radak*).

Cush is usually identified with Ethiopia. The identity of Put and Lubim is uncertain. Some identify Lubim as Libya. *Abarbanel*, however, identifies Put as Libya.

הָיוּ בְּעֶזְרָתֵךְ — *Were your helpers.* Put and Lubim who had come to your [Nineveh's] assistance had also furnished men for No-amon's army and, with all their combined strength, they were nevertheless exiled (*Metzudos*).

10. גַּם־הִיא לַגֹּלָה הָלְכָה בַשֶּׁבִי — *Yet each of them too went into exile in captivity.* No-amon, Kush and Egypt — each one of them were exiled. Nineveh, you too will be exiled for you are no better than they (*Radak*). *Ibn Ezra*, however, identifies Egypt alone as the subject of the verse.

Although the words in captivity [בַשֶּׁבִי] and into exile [לַגֹּלָה] portray the same idea and seem repetitious, Scripture often employs this manner to strengthen the idea it is conveying (*Radak*). Alternatively, *Malbim* notes that one may be exiled from one area without being deprived of his freedom. Scripture is stressing that these nations went into exile *in captivity*.

גַּם עֹלָלֶיהָ יְרֻטְּשׁוּ ... — *Its babies were also smashed ...* [Scripture continues to describe the destruction.]

The word יְרֻטְּשׁוּ means to split or dash into pieces, see *Isaiah* 13:18 (*Metzudos*).

וְעַל־נִכְבַּדֶּיהָ יַדּוּ גוֹרָל — *And they cast lots over her noblemen.* The lots were cast over her noblemen to decide who would receive whom as a slave (*Metzudos, Malbim*).

וְכָל־גְּדוֹלֶיהָ רֻתְּקוּ בַזִּקִּים — *And all her great men were bound in chains.* The word רַתּוּקוֹת means *chains* [see *I Kings* 6:21] as does the word זִקִּים [see *Psalms*

the rivers, with water surrounding it, whose rampart was the sea, and whose wall was of the sea? [9] *Powerful Cush and endless Egypt, Put and Lubim were your helpers.* [10] *Yet each of them too went into exile in captivity, its babies were also smashed at the head of every street; and they cast lots over her noblemen, and all her great men were bound in chains.* [11] *You too will become drunk; you will become unknown; you will also seek refuge from the enemy.* [12] *All your fortresses will be [like] fig trees with newly ripened fruit, when they are shaken, they fall into the mouth of the eater.* [13] *Behold, your nation is [like] women in your midst. The gates of your land have been opened*

149:8]. The composite translation of both words together, רֻתְּקוּ בַזִּקִּים, lit., *chained in chains,* is *bound in chains* (*Radak*).

11. גַּם־אַתְּ תִּשְׁכְּרִי תְּהִי נַעֲלָמָה — *You too will become drunk; you will become unknown.* You too, Nineveh, with all your greatness, will become drunk from the cup of God's fury as did the great city of No. You will vanish and will become unknown, for your destruction will be so complete that it will seem as though you never existed (*Rashi; Radak*). Alternatively, Scripture uses drunkenness metaphorically, for the drunk's loss of rationality renders him as if he never existed (*Ibn Ezra*).

גַּם־אַתְּ תְּבַקְשִׁי מָעוֹז מֵאוֹיֵב — *You will also seek refuge from the enemy.* The prophet foretells that Nineveh will share the same fate as No. Just as No sought aid and refuge from her enemy, so will Nineveh; but, as with No, it will be to no avail (*Metzudos*).

12. כָּל־מִבְצָרַיִךְ תְּאֵנִים עִם־בִּכּוּרִים — *All your fortresses will be [like] fig trees with newly ripened fruit.* All of Assyria's impregnable fortresses will easily be conquered and plundered by Nebuchadnezzer, like the fig tree, which, when shaken, drops its newly ripened fruit into the mouth of one who wishes to eat them (*Rashi; Radak*). *Mahari Kara* adds that just as one who covets the figs catches them in his mouth so that they will not fall to the ground, so too, do all the nations long to march against Assyria and destroy it.

Although the word בִּכּוּרִים is usually translated *first fruit,* in the context of our verse it is translated *fully ripened fruit* (*Metzudos*).

13. הִנֵּה עַמֵּךְ נָשִׁים בְּקִרְבֵּךְ — *Behold, your nation is [like] women in your midst.* Nahum addresses Assyria: Your nation is weak. They are like women who have not the strength to wage war (*Radak; Mahari Kara*).

לְאֹיְבַיִךְ פָּתוֹחַ נִפְתְּחוּ שַׁעֲרֵי אַרְצֵךְ ... — *The gates of your land have been opened wide to your enemies ...* It will appear as if the gates of the city have opened themselves and as if the bolts have been burned for the enemy will quickly smash through the gates of the land (*Radak*).

בְּרִיחָיִךְ — *Your bolts.*

The בְּרִיחִים were wooden bars that bolted the gates of the city (*Metzudos*).

יד מֵי מָצוֹר שַׁאֲבִי־לָךְ חַזְּקִי מִבְצָרָיִךְ בֹּאִי בַטִּיט
טו וְרִמְסִי בַחֹמֶר הַחֲזִיקִי מַלְבֵּן: שָׁם תֹּאכְלֵךְ אֵשׁ
תַּכְרִיתֵךְ חֶרֶב תֹּאכְלֵךְ כַּיָּלֶק הִתְכַּבֵּד כַּיֶּלֶק
טז הִתְכַּבְּדִי כָּאַרְבֶּה: הִרְבֵּית רֹכְלַיִךְ מִכּוֹכְבֵי הַשָּׁמָיִם
יז יֶלֶק פָּשַׁט וַיָּעֹף: מִנְּזָרַיִךְ כָּאַרְבֶּה וְטַפְסְרַיִךְ כְּגוֹב
גֹּבָי הַחוֹנִים בַּגְּדֵרוֹת בְּיוֹם קָרָה שֶׁמֶשׁ זָרְחָה וְנוֹדַד
יח וְלֹא־נוֹדַע מְקוֹמוֹ אַיָּם: נָמוּ רֹעֶיךָ מֶלֶךְ אַשּׁוּר
יִשְׁכְּנוּ אַדִּירֶיךָ נָפֹשׁוּ עַמְּךָ עַל־הֶהָרִים וְאֵין מְקַבֵּץ:

14. מֵי מָצוֹר שַׁאֲבִי־לָךְ — *Draw water for the siege.* Cities that haven't any cisterns to store water must fill numerous barrels so that they may have an adequate supply of water during a siege. Nahum advises the people of Nineveh to prepare water for drinking for they are about to be besieged by the Babylonians (*Rashi*). Alternatively, Nahum mockingly addresses the people and instructs them to draw water before the Babylonians arrive for then they will be besieged and unable to do so (*Ibn Ezra*).

בֹּאִי בַטִּיט ... — *Come into the clay* ... Go into the clay and tread upon it to make bricks to strengthen the sections of the wall that need repair (*Rashi*). *Malbim* sees this too, as a mockery of Nineveh, for he renders *come into the clay and trample as if it were mortar.* Bricks that are formed from טִיט will crumble to dust. It is only from חֹמֶר which they did not have that they can be made to last.

הַחֲזִיקִי מַלְבֵּן — *Grasp the brick mold.* Grasp the brick mold so that bricks may be formed (*Rashi*). *Radak*, however, translates מַלְבֵּן as *the kiln where the bricks are formed and made* and renders *take hold of the kiln used for baking the bricks.*

15. שָׁם תֹּאכְלֵךְ אֵשׁ — *There fire will consume you.* Your preparations will be futile, for the fire of the enemy will consume you there; in your fortresses and strongholds.

תַּכְרִיתֵךְ חֶרֶב תֹּאכְלֵךְ כַּיָּלֶק — *A sword will cut you down. It will consume you like the chewing-locust.* You will be cut down by the sword, and as the chewing-locust devours the field and destroys its vegetation, so too, will you be destroyed by the enemy (*Metzudos*).

הִתְכַּבֵּד כַּיֶּלֶק הִתְכַּבְּדִי כָּאַרְבֶּה — *You will be swept away as [by] the chewing-locust; you will be swept away as [by] the abundant-locust.* Our translation of הִתְכַּבֵּד follows *Rashi* and *Metzudos* who translate, the land will be *swept*, as it were, by the broom of destruction. Others relate כבד to *heavy* or *many* and render, if you will gather an army as *plentiful* as a swarm of locusts it will be to no avail (*Ibn Ezra; Radak*). *Yelek* and *arbeh* are species of locusts. Scripture mentions both species to strengthen the idea of total destruction through the double expression. Just as locusts clear the field through their destruction, so too, will the Assyrians be cleared from their land (*Metzudos*).

Malbim explains the phrase differently. *Yelek* refers to a locust which is still in its worm-like infant stage. It then forms a cocoon and eventually matures. The imagery portrayed is that the inhabitants of Nineveh now may enjoy remaining in the city as the crawling worm (הִתְכַּבֵּד כַּיֶּלֶק), but they will soon flee as the flying locust (הִתְכַּבְּדִי כָּאַרְבֶּה).

16. הִרְבֵּית רֹכְלַיִךְ מִכּוֹכְבֵי הַשָּׁמָיִם ... — *You had more merchants than the*

wide to your enemies; fire has consumed your bolts. [14] *Draw water for the siege, bolster your fortresses. Come into the clay and trample the mortar; grasp the brick mold.* [15] *There fire will consume you; a sword will cut you down. It will consume you like the chewing-locust — you will be swept away as [by] the chewing-locust; you will be swept away as [by] the abundant-locust.* [16] *You had more merchants than the stars of the sky, [like] the chewing-locust that spreads out and then flies away.* [17] *Your princes are like abundant-locusts and your captains are as swarms of locusts which settle on the fences on a cold day; when the sun shines they move away, and their place is unknown — Where are they?* [18] *Your shepherds are asleep, O king of Assyria, your mighty men are at rest. Your nation is scattered*

stars of the sky ... Of what value are your merchants who were as numerous as the stars in the sky; for just as the locust spreads out over the earth and then quickly flies away, so too, will they quickly be destroyed and their wealth will not save them from their fate (*Radak*). Alternatively, to what avail are your merchants who had conducted their trade with ease — as the locust spreads its wings and flies (*Rashi*).

17. מִנְּזָרַיִךְ כָּאַרְבֶּה ... — *Your princes are like abundant-locusts* ... The prophet continues the imagery of the locusts. During the cold hours of the day, locusts generally attach themselves to a wall or fence and wait for the temperature to rise. As the sun begins to shine and the day becomes warmer, they fly away leaving no trace of ever having been at that place. So too [declares the prophet], will your entire nation (*Rashi*), even your princes (*Radak*), be exiled, and no one will ever realize that you existed in this very place (*Rashi; Radak*).

כְּגוֹב גֹּבָי — *As swarms of locusts. Rashi* renders *as armies of locusts.*

Targum's translation of אַרְבֶּה is גּוֹבָא. The term גוֹב גֹּבָי is similar to מֶלֶךְ מְלָכִים [king of kings] and would literally be translated the locust of locusts, i.e., the largest genus of locusts (*Radak*).

18. נָמוּ רֹעֶיךָ מֶלֶךְ אַשּׁוּר — *Your shepherds are asleep, O king of Assyria.* Your officers are powerless against the enemy; it is as if they are asleep (*Radak*).

יִשְׁכְּנוּ אַדִּירֶיךָ — *Your mighty men are at rest.* Your mighty men are at rest and cannot rise up [to fight the enemy] (*Rashi*). Alternatively, it is as if your mighty men have died (at rest in their grave), for nothing will help them against their enemies (*Radak*).

נָפֹשׁוּ עַמְּךָ עַל־הֶהָרִים וְאֵין מְקַבֵּץ — *Your nation is scattered upon the mountains with no one to gather them.* The word נָפֹשׁוּ is similar to the word נָפוֹצוּ, *scattered* (*Rashi*).

Since Scripture compared the officers to shepherds, it compares the nation to sheep that are scattered upon the mountains for they have no shepherd to lead them (*Radak*).

יט אֵין־כֵּהָה לְשִׁבְרֶךָ נַחְלָה מַכָּתֶךָ כֹּל | שֹׁמְעֵי שִׁמְעֲךָ תָּקְעוּ כַף עָלֶיךָ כִּי עַל־מִי לֹא־עָבְרָה רָעָתְךָ תָּמִיד:

Letters formed in the same area of the mouth may occasionally be interchanged. The letters צ׳, ס׳, ש׳, ז׳ are all formed by placing the tip of the tongue against the teeth. The צ׳ of נָפֹצוּ can therefore be interchanged with the ש of נָפֹשׁוּ (*Rashi*).

Alternatively, נָפֹשׁוּ may also be translated *to increase*. The translation of the verse would then be: Your nation who is scattered upon the mountains has increased (*Radak*). *Metzudos* maintains that נָפֹשׁוּ should be translated *to rest*, and renders, "your nation is at rest upon the mountains and there is no one to gather them to battle."

19. אֵין־כֵּהָה לְשִׁבְרֶךָ — *No one is pained over your fracture.* Our translation follows *Targum Yonasan* and *Rashi*. כֵּהָה is an expression used for something

upon the mountains with no one to gather them. [19]*No one is pained over your fracture [though] your wound is grievous. All who hear the report about you clap their hands over you; for over whom has your wickedness not passed constantly?*

that has darkened (*Rashi*). When one is distressed the shining countenance of his face fades and darkens (*Metzudos*). Alternatively, *Radak* explains that כֵּהָה indicates the healing or abatement of a wound. Accordingly, the verse means there is no *cure* for your fracture.

כֹּל שֹׁמְעֵי שִׁמְעֲךָ — *All who hear the report about you.* All who hear the report of your defeat (*Metzudos*) applaud and rejoice (*Radak; Metzudos*).

כִּי עַל־מִי לֹא־עָבְרָה רָעָתְךָ תָּמִיד — *For over whom has your wickedness not passed constantly?* Since Assyria acted wickedly toward *all the nations,* now that she is defeated *all the nations* rejoice (*Mahari Kara*).

Habakkuk

א/א־ג

א־ב הַמַּשָּׂא אֲשֶׁר חָזָה חֲבַקּוּק הַנָּבִיא: עַד־אָנָה יהוה שִׁוַּעְתִּי וְלֹא תִשְׁמָע אֶזְעַק אֵלֶיךָ חָמָס וְלֹא תוֹשִׁיעַ: ג לָמָּה תַרְאֵנִי אָוֶן וְעָמָל תַּבִּיט וְשֹׁד וְחָמָס לְנֶגְדִּי וַיְהִי רִיב וּמָדוֹן יִשָּׂא:

☙ Introduction

Little is known regarding the background of the prophet Habakkuk, for Scripture mentions neither his generation nor his lineage (*Radak*). According to *Seder Olam* (Ch. 20), he was a contemporary of the prophets Joel and Nahum and prophesied during the days of Manasseh, king of Judah. However, this is not mentioned by Scripture for it did not wish to associate the name of the righteous prophet with the evil Manasseh. He was a disciple of the prophet Nahum (*Rambam — Introduction to Yad HaChazakah*). He prophesied regarding the rise and fall of the Babylonian Empire under the leadership of its king, Nebuchadnezzar, and foretold of the harm that he would inflict on the people of Judah. He also foretold of the eventual downfall and destruction of Nebuchadnezzar's descendants at the hands of the Persians and Medes (*Radak; Ibn Ezra*).

Sefer Yossifon [Ch. 3] claims that Habakkuk was a contemporary of the prophet Daniel and miraculously sustained him while he was imprisoned in the lions' den. *Abarbanel* rejects this view as being anachronistic: Manasseh reigned more than 90 years prior to Nebuchadnezzar and Daniel was thrown into the lions' den after Nebuchadnezzar had reigned for 70 years. Accordingly, Habakkuk would have been well over 160 years old when this miracle took place (if the opinions of *Seder Olam* and *Yossifon* are both accepted). According to the Sages, Habakkuk was the son born to the Shunammite woman who had been blessed by the prophet Elisha (*II Kings* 4:16) — see *Zohar, B'shalach*. He was called Habakkuk, an expression of embracing to recall the words the prophet used in his blessing: לַמּוֹעֵד הַזֶּה ... אַתְּ **חוֹבֶקֶת בֵּן**, *at this season next year ... you will be embracing a son* (*Abarbanel*). Accordingly, Habakkuk lived approximately two centuries before Manasseh. *Da'as Sofrim* links the two opinions and suggests that Habakkuk was only a *descendant* of the Shunammite woman's son and not her actual son.

I

1. הַמַּשָּׂא — *The prophecy.* The term מַשָּׂא, lit., *burden*, is one of the ten expressions of prophecy enumerated in *Bereishis Rabbah* 44:7. According to the Sages, it introduces a fateful and foreboding prophecy. It is most often used to introduce a prophecy that is directed to the nations of the world [see comm. to *Nahum* 1:1]. *Abarbanel* maintains that the term מַשָּׂא is used when the prophecy is being directed to just *one* person or just *one* nation.

אֲשֶׁר חָזָה חֲבַקּוּק הַנָּבִיא — *That Habakkuk the prophet saw.* The prophecy that Habakkuk received through Divine Inspiration (*Rashi*). Whereas רָאָה is used to describe physical sight, חָזוֹן (derived from חזה) related to חָזֶה, *breast*, the seat of the heart, seems to mean seeing in a spiritual sense, perceiving and comprehending that which is invisible to the physical eye (*R' Hirsch, Genesis* 15:1).

☙ The Prophet Questions God

2. עַד־אָנָה ה׳ שִׁוַּעְתִּי וְלֹא תִשְׁמָע — *How long, O Hashem, will I cry out and You*

[1] *The prophecy that Habakkuk the prophet saw:* [2] *How long, O* H*ASHEM*, *will I cry out and You not hear me; [how long] will I cry out to You [regarding] injustice and You not save?* [3] *Why do You allow me to see iniquity and You look at evil deeds, with robbery and injustice before me, while the one who carries strife and contention still remains?*

not hear me. Habakkuk grieved and entreated God because he prophetically saw that Nebuchadnezzar would rule over the entire world and would severely oppress Israel (*Rashi*). He was troubled by the success of these wicked oppressors and entreated God on behalf of the righteous people who would be afflicted by Nebuchadnezzar in the future (*Radak*). *Abarbanel* points out that it was not the oppression of the Jewish people that troubled the prophet as much as the success of the wicked Babylonians. For although the Jewish people were guilty of committing serious sins and were deserving of punishment, the Babylonians were guilty of continuously desecrating the Name of God and were therefore undeserving of success. Habakkuk's protest was thus not about the sight of the suffering of the righteous (צַדִּיק וְרַע לוֹ), but of the thriving of the wicked (רָשָׁע וְטוֹב לוֹ).

שִׁוַּעְתִּי — *Will I cry out.* The term שַׁוְעָה denotes prayer emanating from a grievous heart. It is one of the ten expressions of prayer enumerated in *Sifrei, Va'eschanan.*

אֶזְעַק אֵלֶיךָ חָמָס וְלֹא תוֹשִׁיעַ — *[How long] will I cry out to You [regarding] injustice and You not save?* I cry to You because of the injustices that have been done to Israel but You do not save them (*Radak*).

Malbim differentiates between שַׁוְעָה, a cry for help (יְשׁוּעָה), and זְעָקָה, a cry expressing one's feeling that an injustice has been committed against him.

3. Again Habakkuk asserts himself and pleads with God to thwart the success of the Babylonians (*Malbim*).

לָמָּה תַרְאֵנִי אָוֶן וְעָמָל תַּבִּיט — *Why do You allow me to see iniquity and You look at evil deeds.* Why do You show me the spoils and robbery plundered by the Babylonians? You are aware of these evil deeds and yet You offer no salvation (*Rashi*). Furthermore, since God's Providence [הַשְׁגָּחָה] is maintained over the entire world and He observes the good and evil deeds of all mankind, why, then, does He allow this evil nation to succeed for such a long time? (*Radak*).

וְשֹׁד וְחָמָס לְנֶגְדִּי — *With robbery and injustice before me.* In my prophetic vision, the success of Babylonia is before my eyes and I have not been shown its downfall (*Malbim*). Alternatively, the *iniquity and evil deeds* are not referring to the evil deeds committed by the Babylonians but to the iniquities committed by *Israel*, which were shown to Habakkuk in a prophetic vision. Robbery and injustice refer to the punishment they will receive. The prophet thus speaks out plaintively to God and says, "Why must I see the sins and punishments of my nation? Why must I be pained so? Why must my prophecy be one of revelation of sin and punishment, destruction and exile of my nation?" (*Abarbanel; Metzudos*).

וַיְהִי רִיב וּמָדוֹן יִשָּׂא — *While the one who carries strife and contention.* The evil [Nebuchadnezzar] continues to exist and is not eliminated (*Rashi*).

ד עַל־כֵּן֙ תָּפ֣וּג תּוֹרָ֔ה וְלֹֽא־יֵצֵ֥א לָנֶ֖צַח מִשְׁפָּ֑ט כִּ֤י רָשָׁע֙ מַכְתִּ֣יר אֶת־הַצַּדִּ֔יק עַל־כֵּ֛ן יֵצֵ֥א מִשְׁפָּ֖ט מְעֻקָּֽל׃ ה רְא֤וּ בַגּוֹיִם֙ וְֽהַבִּ֔יטוּ וְהִֽתַּמְּה֖וּ תְּמָ֑הוּ כִּי־פֹ֙עַל֙ פֹּעֵ֣ל ו בִּֽימֵיכֶ֔ם לֹ֥א תַאֲמִ֖ינוּ כִּ֥י יְסֻפָּֽר׃ כִּֽי־הִנְנִ֤י מֵקִים֙ אֶת־הַכַּשְׂדִּ֔ים הַגּ֖וֹי הַמַּ֣ר וְהַנִּמְהָ֑ר הַֽהוֹלֵךְ֙ לְמֶרְחֲבֵי־ ז אֶ֔רֶץ לָרֶ֖שֶׁת מִשְׁכָּנ֥וֹת לֹּא־לֽוֹ׃ אָיֹ֥ם וְנוֹרָ֖א ה֑וּא

4. עַל כֵּן־תָּפוּג תּוֹרָה — *That is why the Torah is weakened.* Our translation of תָּפוּג תּוֹרָה, *the Torah is weakened,* follows *Radak* and *Metzudos* who explain that Habakkuk complained that since God allows wickedness to prevail and the righteous to suffer, Israel's commitment to the Torah slackens due to the weakening of their resolve. Alternatively, *Rashi* translates פוג as חלף, *to be transformed, to turn away* — see *Rashi* to *Genesis* 45:26. Due to Nebuchadnezzar's success, the observance of the Torah slips away from Israel and instead, they obey his command of prostrating themselves before the image in Bikath Dura (*Rashi*).[1]

Ibn Ezra translates "silenced." The laws of the Torah have been silenced as if the Torah ceases to exist.

וְלֹא־יֵצֵא לָנֶצַח מִשְׁפָּט — *And justice never emerges. Malbim* differentiates between *Torah* and מִשְׁפָּט (justice). *Torah* is referring to philosophical beliefs and opinions and commandments that are between man and God. מִשְׁפָּט, *justice,* refers to the civil laws that govern relations between man and his neighbor. Both will cease to be observed, due to the success of the wicked and the suffering of the Jews.

כִּי רָשָׁע מַכְתִּיר אֶת־הַצַּדִּיק — *Since the wicked surround the righteous.* The root of מַכְתִּיר is כֶּתֶר, "a crown" (*Ibn Ezra*). The wicked Nebuchadnezzar surrounds the righteous Israel as the crown encircles the head (*Metzudos*). He surrounds them so that he may continuously oppress them (*Radak*). Although the Kingdom of Judah was deserving of punishment at this time, Scripture refers to them as "the righteous" when compared to Nebuchadnezzar (*Metzudos*).

עַל־כֵּן יֵצֵא מִשְׁפָּט מְעֻקָּל — *Therefore justice emerges distorted.* Since Israel does not see the wicked punished for their wrongdoing, they begin to think that there is no heavenly judgment or justice from God, and they too act unjustly (*Metzudos*). Alternatively, since Israel has been oppressed they cannot judge in a proper manner (*Mahari Kara*). *Malbim* interprets מַכְתִּיר to mean "crowning" or "appointing to a high position." Since it is the wicked king who appoints the judge [רָשָׁע מַכְתִּיר אֶת־הַצַּדִּיק], the righteous judge must perform according to the wishes of the wicked king; therefore, even the most honest judgments must be tainted with inaccuracy [עַל־כֵּן יֵצֵא מִשְׁפָּט מְעֻקָּל] to appease the evil king.

5. ... רְאוּ בַגּוֹיִם וְהַבִּיטוּ — *Look among the nations and observe ...* At this point, Habakkuk addresses Israel and explains the reasons for his anxieties. Look and realize (*Malbim*) the extent of the destruction that Nebuchadnezzar will inflict on the nations of the world and you will surely realize that he has been sent by God (*Radak*). Although there have been many victorious nations throughout history, one cannot compare their victories to the exceptional conquests of Nebuchadnezzar whose unbelievable

1. The story of the golden image in Bikath Dura is recounted in *Daniel* Ch. 3. For further study, see introduction to ArtScroll *Daniel* Ch. 3.

[4]*That is why the Torah is weakened and justice never emerges. Since the wicked surround the righteous, therefore justice emerges distorted.*

[5]*Look among the nations and observe, and be utterly astounded; for [God] is bringing about an occurrence in your days that you will not believe when it is related.* [6]*For behold, I am establishing the Chaldeans, that bitter and impetuous nation that will go across the breadth of the earth to possess dwelling places that are not its own.* [7]*It is awesome and terrifying;*

success was accomplished in an unnatural manner. He was not a member of the royal family and was unaided by others, and yet he conquered the entire civilized world of that time without opposition (*Abarbanel, Malbim*).

וְהִתַּמְּהוּ תְּמָהוּ — *And be utterly astounded.* [The use of the double form of a verb is common in Scripture to emphasize the point being made.] The double form of תמה is used to express the utter astonishment displayed at the evil deeds (*Radak*) and success (*Abarbanel; Metzudos*) of Nebuchadnezzar.

כִּי־פֹעַל פֹּעֵל בִּימֵיכֶם — *For [God] is bringing about an occurrence in your days.* For God [Who causes all occurrences] (*Radak*) will make Nebuchadnezzar victorious in your days (*Metzudos*). God's name is not mentioned in the verse for it is understood that He is the prime cause of all (*Ibn Ezra*).

Radak cites this verse as proof that Habakkuk and Nebuchadnezzar were contemporaries [see Prologue].

לֹא תַאֲמִינוּ כִּי יְסֻפָּר — *That you will not believe when it is related.* You will be astonished when you will be told about the wicked and terrible deeds of Nebuchadnezzar (*Radak*). If you would only be *told* about the success of Nebuchadnezzar's wicked campaigns you would never believe it. Surely then, when you will see it with your very eyes you will be utterly astonished (*Metzudos; Malbim*).

6. כִּי־הִנְנִי מֵקִים ... הַגּוֹי ... וְהַנִּמְהָר — *For behold, I am establishing ... impetuous nation.* Although Habakkuk uses the first person singular *I am establishing ...*, these are not his own words but the exact words he heard from God (*Radak;* cf. *Abarbanel*). Chaldea is synonymous with Babylon (see *Isaiah* 47:1,5). The Chaldeans were considered the lowest and most worthless of the nations. [See ibid. 23:13.] *Rashi* writes that this nation was one of the three creations [see *Succah* 52: where four are mentioned] that God (as it were) regretted that He created. The Chaldeans are a nation of embittered spirit, cruel and impulsive (*Metzudos*).

Scripture uses the word מֵקִים, lit., *to raise up,* to indicate that God will now raise the Chaldeans from their low status [to serve His purpose] (*Metzudos*).

הַהוֹלֵךְ לְמֶרְחֲבֵי־אֶרֶץ ... — *That will go across the breadth of the earth ...* The Chaldeans will travel the world over to conquer מִשְׁכָּנוֹת, inhabited places that are not theirs (*Metzudos*). They are particularly impetuous to conquer Israel's land (*Mahari Kara*).

7. אָיֹם וְנוֹרָא הוּא — *It is awesome and terrifying. Malbim* explains that אָיֹם (awesome) refers to fear inspired by the mere enormity of an object, person or force; נוֹרָא (terrifying) describes the fear

ח מִמֶּנּוּ מִשְׁפָּטוֹ וּשְׂאֵתוֹ יֵצֵא: וְקַלּוּ מִנְּמֵרִים סוּסָיו וְחַדּוּ מִזְּאֵבֵי עֶרֶב וּפָשׁוּ פָּרָשָׁיו וּפָרָשָׁיו מֵרָחוֹק יָבֹאוּ יָעֻפוּ כְּנֶשֶׁר חָשׁ לֶאֱכוֹל: ט כֻּלֹּה לְחָמָס יָבוֹא מְגַמַּת פְּנֵיהֶם קָדִימָה וַיֶּאֱסֹף כַּחוֹל שֶׁבִי: י וְהוּא בַּמְּלָכִים יִתְקַלָּס וְרֹזְנִים מִשְׂחָק לוֹ הוּא לְכָל־מִבְצָר יִשְׂחָק וַיִּצְבֹּר עָפָר וַיִּלְכְּדָהּ:

of the evil and destructive potential of that thing. The Chaldean force will be awesome in its enormity and terrifying in its wickedness.

מִמֶּנּוּ מִשְׁפָּטוֹ וּשְׂאֵתוֹ יֵצֵא — *Its judgment and its burden go forth from it.* From the Chaldean nation unassisted by others [מִמֶּנּוּ — from him only] (*Radak*) come judges and rulers who impose judgments and burdens and instill fear upon the people (*Rashi*). Alternatively, the word מִמֶּנּוּ is not referring to the Chaldeans, but to God. The judgment and majesty of the Chaldeans go forth from God, for it is He who appointed them to conquer and destroy other kingdoms (*Abarbanel*).

8. וְקַלּוּ מִנְּמֵרִים סוּסָיו — *Its horses are swifter than leopards.* [The prophet now describes the Chaldeans by comparing them to fierce beasts and birds of prey.] The horses of the Chaldeans are swifter in battle than leopards (*Metzudos; Abarbanel*).

וְחַדּוּ מִזְּאֵבֵי עֶרֶב — *And fiercer than wolves of the evening.* The Chaldeans (*Metzudos; Abarbanel*) or their *horses* (*Malbim*) are fiercer than the evening wolves.

Evening wolves that haven't eaten all day are fiercer than the wolves of the morning that first start to stalk their prey (*Mahari Kara*). An alternative translation of עֶרֶב offered by *Malbim* is "wilderness" (from the word עֲרָבָה).

וּפָשׁוּ פָּרָשָׁיו — *And its horsemen increase.* Our translation of פָּשׁוּ, *increase,* follows *Targum Yonasan* who translates וְיִרְבִּין פְּרָשׁוֹהִי. The [Chaldean] horsemen increase each day and do not lessen, for none of them fall in battle (*Metzudos*). Alternatively, *Ibn Ezra* relates פָּשׁוּ to פשט, *to spread out.* The horsemen spread themselves out in their fearless attack against the Israelites.

וּפָרָשָׁיו מֵרָחוֹק יָבֹאוּ . . . — *Its horsemen will come from afar . . .* Although the [Chaldean] horsemen come from afar, they do not grow weary or tired from their journey but like the eagle[1] that swoops down on its prey, they race after their enemies and immediately attack them (*Metzudos; Abarbanel; Malbim*).

The prophet mentions the eagle because it flies higher than other birds and flies very swiftly (*Radak*). It is interesting to note that the prophet Ezekiel referred to Nebuchadnezzar as the *Great Eagle*, an appropriate simile for the conqueror of the world — see *Mahari Kara* to *Ezekiel* 17:3.

9. כֻּלֹּה לְחָמָס יָבוֹא — *It comes entirely for plunder.* Unlike the Romans who went to battle so that they may gain honor and glory, the Chaldeans went to battle only to rob and plunder (*Rashi; Metzudos; Abarbanel*). Consequently, the devastation caused by their invasion is much worse than the invader who wishes to annex the newly conquered land (*Metzudos*).

מְגַמַּת פְּנֵיהֶם קָדִימָה — *The eagerness of their faces is like the east wind.*

The word מְגַמַּת is related to הַגְמִיאֵנִי, *let me please gulp* (*Genesis* 24:17), a phrase which denotes eagerness and

1. [The נֶשֶׁר is usually identified as the eagle. But see *Tos. Chullin* 63a ד״ה נץ who disagrees.]

its judgment and its burden go forth from it. [8] *Its horses are swifter than leopards and fiercer than wolves of the evening, and its horsemen increase. Its horsemen will come from afar; they will fly like an eagle hastening to eat.* [9] *It comes entirely for plunder; the eagerness of their faces is like the east wind; and it will gather captives like the sand.* [10] *He scoffs at kings, and officers are sport to him. He laughs at every stronghold; heaping up earth and capturing it.*

haste. The Chaldeans conquer territory with such haste that it appears as if they swallowed and gulped the land (*Rashi*).

קָדִימָה — *The east wind.* Our translation follows *Rashi* who explains that the east wind is the harshest of all winds. Scripture is then describing the strength and haste of the Chaldeans through an additional metaphor. Alternatively, *Abarbanel* and *Malbim* translate מְגַמַּת פְּנֵיהֶם קָדִימָה as the *direction of their faces is eastward* and explain that although Babylonia is east of the Land of Israel and a Chaldean going toward Israel would thus be going westward, nevertheless the intent of the Chaldeans was not to settle their captured land but to destroy, plunder and bring their spoils back east to Babylonia. Hence, Scripture writes that *the direction of their faces is eastward* to describe the intent of the Chaldean attackers.

וַיֶּאֱסֹף כַּחוֹל שֶׁבִי — *And it will gather captives like the sand.* The Chaldeans will gather many captives and leave over no one (*Metzudos*). The captives referred to are Israelites (*Mahari Kara*). [Scripture often uses the sand of the sea to describe an exceedingly great number.]

10. וְהוּא בַּמְּלָכִים יִתְקַלָּס — *He scoffs at kings.* Scripture now describes the impudent self-assurance of Nebuchadnezzar, the Chaldean king (*Abarbanel*). Our translation of יִתְקַלָּס, *scoffs,* follows *Rashi, Radak* and *Ibn Ezra. Rashi* adds that the word קלס is used to describe any spoken word regarding a particular subject: positive or negative. Hence קלס is sometimes translated "praise" or "glory" [see *Ezekiel* 16:31 and *Rashi* thereon] and sometimes "scorn" or "mockery" [see *II Kings* 2:23]. Alternatively, *Mahari Kara,* citing *Jeremiah* 27:8, interprets יִתְקַלָּס in its positive sense and renders *and he is praised through kings*: all the kingdoms are under his [Nebuchadnezzar's] dominion, and this is a source of glorification for him.

וְרֹזְנִים מִשְׂחָק לוֹ — *And officers are sport to him.* For his awe is upon them all (*Mahari Kara*).

R' Hirsch (*Psalms* 2:2) relates רֹזְנִים to רסן — harness [for the rulers lead the nation as the rider leads his horse with its reins].

הוּא לְכָל־מִבְצָר יִשְׂחָק — *He laughs at every stronghold.* If the enemy is in a stronghold or fortress, he mockingly laughs at him (*Rashi*), bragging that he can easily capture the stronghold (*Metzudos*).

וַיִּצְבֹּר עָפָר וַיִּלְכְּדָהּ — *Heaping up earth and capturing it.* Nebuchadnezzar's many soldiers carry earth and heap it before the enemy's stronghold until it becomes a high mound from which they attack the enemy and storm the fortress (*Rashi*) [see *II Samuel* 20:15]. *Radak,* however, interprets this section figuratively. *He gathers a multitude of soldiers (as numerous as the dust of the earth) and captures the stronghold.*

א/יא־יג יא־יב אָז חָלַף רוּחַ וַיַּעֲבֹר וְאָשֵׁם זוּ כֹחוֹ לֵאלֹהוֹ: הֲלוֹא אַתָּה מִקֶּדֶם יהוה אֱלֹהַי קְדֹשִׁי לֹא נָמוּת יהוה
יג לְמִשְׁפָּט שַׂמְתּוֹ וְצוּר לְהוֹכִיחַ יְסַדְתּוֹ: טְהוֹר עֵינַיִם מֵרְאוֹת רָע וְהַבִּיט אֶל־עָמָל לֹא תוּכָל לָמָּה תַבִּיט בּוֹגְדִים תַּחֲרִישׁ בְּבַלַּע רָשָׁע צַדִּיק מִמֶּנּוּ:

11. ... אָז חָלַף רוּחַ וַיַּעֲבֹר — *Then a spirit will come and pass over [him]. ...* The word רוּחַ, *spirit,* of this verse is actually referring to one's thoughts (*Metzudos*) or personality characteristics such as arrogance, anger and cruelty (*Malbim*). Seeing his great success and accomplishments, a sinful thought of extreme arrogance possesses Nebuchadnezzar (*Abarbanel*) and he ascribes his might to his heathen god (*Rashi; Mahari Kara*). *Malbim* maintains that the Chaldean king, Belshazzar — see *Daniel* 5:23 — is the subject of this verse and that he imagined that his heathen god has invested itself in his own might so that his might in essence is his heathen god.

12-17. Habakkuk pleads with God on behalf of Israel. [After receiving the vision of the Chaldean victories, Habakkuk offers the following prayer to God.]

12. ... הֲלוֹא אַתָּה מִקֶּדֶם — *Are You not from the beginning of time ...* Habakkuk says to God, "I understand that the Chaldeans were appointed to punish those [Israel] who rebelled against You, but are You not my Holy God from past times? Do not deliver us into their hands to die" (*Rashi; Mahari Kara*).

In the previous verse Scripture wrote that Nebuchadnezzar attributed his success and victories to his heathen gods. Habakkuk now voices his opposition to this erroneous claim. He wonders, "How can he attribute all this to his god that he himself made? We, Your nation Israel, know that it is only *You* Who has given Nebuchadnezzar his power and success. May it be Your will that he not be given the power to kill us and annihilate us. For, after all, has he not been appointed only to punish those who rebel against You and to chastise the nations of the world?"(*Radak*)

קְדֹשִׁי — *My Holy One.* The term *Holy* [קָדוֹשׁ] — when used as a description of Hashem — expresses the concept of God's spirituality, that He is incorporeal and never assumes or resembles a corporeal form (*Kuzari* 4:3; see comm. of *Otzar Nechmad*).

The *Kuzari* (ibid.) continues to explain the terms *The Holy One of Israel* [קְדוֹשׁ יִשְׂרָאֵל] and *My Holy One* [קְדוֹשִׁי]. *The Holy One of Israel* is an expression of the Divine Influence [God's providence and guidance] that had cleaved unto the Patriarch Jacob [who was also named Israel] and onto his descendants [the Israelite nation]. The term *My Holy One* [in its singular form] should not be used by anyone other than a prophet or pious person who has experienced this Divine Influence [in an extraordinary manner].

לֹא נָמוּת — *Let us not die!* The verse should actually read **לֹא תָמוּת**, "*You,* Hashem, will never die." This is one of the variations occurring in Scripture, such as writers make [תִּיקּוּנֵי סוֹפְרִים], for the purpose of enhancing an expression (*Rashi*).[1]

The commentators differ as to the exact meaning of תִּיקּוּן סוֹפְרִים [lit., "emendations of the scribes"].

Aruch, עֶרֶךְ כָּבוֹד, writes that Ezra and the Men of the Great Assembly, אַנְשֵׁי כְּנֶסֶת

1. *Midrash Tanchuma* (*Exodus* 23:16), *Mechilta* (*B'shalach, Parshah* 6, v. 7) and *Sifra* (*Numbers* 10:35) list many of the passages where the word that seemingly should have been used by Scripture would have been offensive to the dignity of God and תִּיקּוּנֵי סוֹפְרִים therefore have been applied.

[11] *Then a spirit will come and pass over [him], and he will incur guilt [by saying] that his god gave him strength.*

[12] *Are You not from the beginning of time, O* HASHEM *my God, my Holy One? Let us not die! O* HASHEM, *You have ordained him for judgment; and [You,] O Rock, You have established him to chasten [us].* [13] *[Your eyes] are too pure to see evil and You cannot look upon wrongdoing. Why then do You look upon betrayers? [Why do] You remain silent when a wicked man swallows up one more righteous than he?*

הַגְּדוֹלָה, felt that the word originally used by Scripture was offensive to God's dignity and therefore they altered the Scriptural text and substituted the original word with another word, thereby "improving" the text. *Radak* seems to have understood this term in a similar manner for he writes that this is one of the eighteen *Tikunei Sofrim,* for it had previously been written *you* will not die, כִּי לֹא תָּמוּת הָיָה כָּתוּב. This view seems to be supported by *Midrash Tanchuma* (פ׳ בְּשַׁלַּח) where it is written that these are "emendations of the scribes of the *Men of the Great Assembly.*" The commentator *Etz Yosef* on the *Tanchuma* quotes both the *Tzedah LaDerech* and the *Meor Einayim* who write that this line in the *Tanchuma* was the erroneous addition of an inferior student or scribe, and was not in the original texts of the *Tanchuma. Minchas Shai* (*Zechariah* 2:12) sarcastically comments regarding the above explanation, "Such would not be called the 'emendation of scribes' but the 'emendation of fools,' for no Jewish person would have the gall to alter even one letter of the Torah." He therefore follows the view of *Rashba* and *Ikarim* (3:22), who maintain that our text is indeed the original text, which employed certain words to avoid writing an irreverent expression. The Sages revealed to us that the Scriptural text is not to be *interpreted* as it is *worded* but rather as a euphemism for the proper wording. Accordingly, the intent of the term *emendation of the scribes,* תִּיקּוּנֵי סוֹפְרִים, is that just as a scribe or secretary substitutes a more proper word than that which was related to him, so too *did God Himself* substitute a more reverent term than the text would seem to have required (*Mizrachi, Numbers* 11:15; *Gur Aryeh, Gen.* 18:22).

וְצוּר — *And [You,] O Rock.* This term is a reference to God, for He is the strength of the worlds (*Metzudos*). When the term *Rock* is referring to God, it is portraying the idea that He is the origin and cause of everything (*Rambam, Moreh Nevuchim* 1:16).

◆§ Habakkuk's Second Point

13. טְהוֹר עֵינַיִם מֵרְאוֹת רָע ... — *Your eyes are too pure to see evil* ... [Habakkuk continues his appeal to God and adds the following argument.] You, God, are the epitome of goodness. You favor those who do good and despise those who commit evil. How do You permit that which is contrary to Your wisdom and goodness to take place? Why do You permit the Chaldeans to do evil to Israel? (*Radak*).

לָמָּה תַבִּיט בּוֹגְדִים — *Why [then] do You look upon betrayers?* Why then do You provide for those who rebel against You by granting them the rule over such a vast kingdom? (*Metzudos*).

תַּחֲרִישׁ בְּבַלַּע רָשָׁע צַדִּיק מִמֶּנּוּ — *[Why do] You remain silent when a wicked man swallows up one more righteous than he?* Although the Israelites were not completely righteous, they were surely more righteous than the wicked Chaldeans. Habakkuk therefore wonders [How do You] remain silent regarding the destruction that the wicked Nebuchadnezzar will inflict upon Israel? (*Mahari Kara*).

וַתַּעֲשֶׂה אָדָם כִּדְגֵי הַיָּם כְּרֶמֶשׂ לֹא־מֹשֵׁל בּוֹ: כֻּלֹּה בְּחַכָּה הֵעֲלָה יְגֹרֵהוּ בְחֶרְמוֹ וְיַאַסְפֵהוּ בְּמִכְמַרְתּוֹ

טז עַל־כֵּן יִשְׂמַח וְיָגִיל: עַל־כֵּן יְזַבֵּחַ לְחֶרְמוֹ

Using this verse as its source, the Talmud (*Berachos* 7b) states that the wicked have no command over one that is flawlessly just (צַדִּיק גָּמוּר), but may have command over one who is "more just than they." Israel, even with their sins, were superior than Nebuchadnezzar and his nation but their sins left them open to attack. Therefore Habakkuk pleaded with God, *"Why do You remain silent while a wicked man swallows a man more righteous than he?"* (*Radak; Abarbanel*).

Metzudos notes that Habakkuk did not wish to free Israel from all punishment for they were indeed guilty of many sins. His question was rather why *Nebuchadnezzar* should be God's agent of punishment. Was he not more wicked than they? Habakkuk clearly understood that Nebuchadnezzar was being utilized as God's implement of punishment, God's rod to punish Israel as he said in v. 12. He was only concerned that one who would observe the punishment of the righteous through the wicked might think that God punishes unjustly. Habakkuk therefore declared, *"You Who are too pure ..."*(*Ikkarim* 4:15, 2:3). He also continues to explain that at times God may permit the success of the wicked over the righteous so that the wicked may ultimately be punished with total destruction, while the righteous person merits his portion of the World to Come. This, too, was the case of Nebuchadnezzar and Israel. Nebuchadnezzar's descendants were all destroyed and Israel returned to its land.

Alternatively, the *wicked man* of this verse is Nebuchadnezzar and the *righteous man*, King Zedekiah [the last king of Judah, who reigned from 3327-3338] (*Rashi*). It was Nebuchadnezzar who ordered the blinding of Zedekiah [see *II Kings* 25:7] before he was brought to Babylon in chains. Habakkuk foresees this tragedy and questions God regarding it.

[For analysis of the blindness of Zedekiah see Overview to ArtScroll *Yechezkel* Ch. VIII, Yehoyakim and Zidkiyahu.]

14-17. A new argument is introduced by Habakkuk regarding the removal of God's Providence from mankind or, as some explain, the removal of His special care from His nation. He compares mankind to fish and insects and says:

14. וַתַּעֲשֶׂה אָדָם כִּדְגֵי הַיָּם — *You have made man like the [helpless] fish of the sea.* Habakkuk argues before God that He has abandoned mankind before the wicked man [Nebuchadnezzar] as the fish of the sea who may be caught by anyone who wishes (*Rashi; Radak*). Furthermore, the prophet points out that like fish, the larger ones devour the smaller; so too, do the Chaldeans devour Israel whom Scripture refers to as Adam (אָדָם) (*Ezekiel* 34:31) [see *Yevamos* 61a, "You are called Adam, but the nations of the world are not called Adam"] (*Mahari Kara*).

See comm. to 2:8 for an in-depth discussion of the "Adam" concept.

כְּרֶמֶשׂ לֹא־מֹשֵׁל בּוֹ — *Like creeping things without a ruler.* [The analogy introduced at the beginning of the verse is repeated in a similar manner.]

There is no one that rules over the insects and therefore anyone who wishes can catch them. So too, have You placed mankind before this evil man (*Radak*). In addition, since there is no ruler over the insects, each one devours the other (*Mahari Kara*). *Malbim* maintains that Scripture is introducing a new analogy. Fish are at least protected by the sea that covers them so that if someone wishes to catch them he must use either nets or hooks, but you have made mankind to be as the creeping insects that are completely exposed to its captors.

The Talmud (*Avodah Zarah* 3b) aggadically interprets that man may indeed be compared to the fish of the sea: "R' Yehudah said in the name of Shmuel, Just as fish, when placed upon dry land, immediately die, so is it with the Jew; as soon as he departs from

[14] You have made man like the [helpless] fish of the sea, like creeping things without a ruler. [15] He brings them all up with a fishhook; He catches them in his net and he gathers them in his trawl; therefore he rejoices and exults. [16] Therefore he sacrifices to his net

the Torah and mitzvos he, too, immediately dies."

Rambam (*Moreh Nevuchim* 3:17) quotes the last two verses as support of his view of the nature of Divine Providence. According to *Rambam*, God's Providence exists on an individual basis only upon rational beings. Divine Providence examines all their deeds with the intent of rewarding or punishing them. Other living things are only governed in relation to their species and not individually. Hence, one may say that insects and fish are abandoned and unprotected and have no ruler.

15. [Scripture continues with the analogy of fish being caught by the fisherman.]

כֻּלֹּה בְּחַכָּה הֵעֲלָה — *He brings them all up with a fishhook.* The wicked person mentioned in v. 13 brings up all of mankind with his fishhook (*Rashi*). Since Habakkuk compared mankind to the fish of the sea, he compares Nebuchadnezzar to the great fisherman who raises all the fish of the sea with his fishhook (*Radak; Abarbanel*).

Radak and *Minchas Shai* note the unusual form of the word הֵעֲלָה which is usually written הֶעֱלָה.

יְגֹרֵהוּ בְחֶרְמוֹ וְיַאַסְפֵהוּ בְּמִכְמַרְתּוֹ — *He catches them in his net and he gathers them in his trawl.* Although we translated יְגֹרֵהוּ, *he catches them*, it actually means *to gather* (*Rashi*). *Malbim* differentiates between אגר and אסף. אגר is used when one gathers individual objects while אסף is used when one gathers many different types of objects at one time.

מִכְמוֹרֶת and חֶרֶם are both words that mean "nets" or "traps" (*Metzudos*). Scripture often uses several terms with similar meaning for emphasis (*Radak*).

Malbim discusses the differences between חַכָּה, חֶרֶם and מִכְמוֹרֶת and their implications in understanding the analogy. The חַכָּה is used for capturing the great fishes (see *Job* 40:25). The חֶרֶם is a net used for capturing the average-size fish en masse by spreading many of these nets in different places. The מִכְמוֹרֶת is also a type of net but it is spread across the water thereby trapping all the fish who encounter it and through its use multitudes may be gathered at one time. In a similar manner, first Nebuchadnezzar captured individual countries, one by one, in a display of great power. Next, he captured many of the smaller countries that were spread around [as is done with the net]. Finally, he captured all the remaining nations [as by way of the trawl].

עַל־כֵּן יִשְׂמַח וְיָגִיל — *Therefore he rejoices and exults.* Since he is successful in all his ways and captures everything at his will, he rejoices (*Radak*).

Malbim notes the difference between שִׂמְחָה and גִּילָה. שִׂמְחָה is joy over a continuing pleasure, while גִּילָה is used to express the joy of a new experience. Scripture is saying that Nebuchadnezzar rejoices for both his old and new conquests.

16. [Habakkuk adds another argument to those that he previously stated. Look unto whom Nebuchadnezzar attributes his success.]

עַל־כֵּן יְזַבֵּחַ לְחֶרְמוֹ — *Therefore he sacrifices to his net.* Therefore he sacrifices to his *idol* for he says that it is the idol that conquered all before him (*Rashi*).

Nebuchadnezzar believes that his god is his net with which he has managed to ensnare all his adversaries and he therefore offers sacrifices to the net [see *Mahari Kara*]. Alternatively, *Rashi* is using a play on words. Idols are referred to as חֵרֶם [*that which is banned*] [see *Deut.* 7:26]. In essence Scripture is stating that Nebuchadnezzar shows his allegiance to his actual idol but it uses the expression חֵרֶם for idol due to its double

א/יז וְיקַטֵּר לְמִכְמַרְתּוֹ כִּי בָהֵמָּה שָׁמֵן חֶלְקוֹ
יז וּמַאֲכָלוֹ בְּרִאָה: הַעַל כֵּן יָרִיק חֶרְמוֹ וְתָמִיד
ב/א־ב א לַהֲרֹג גּוֹיִם לֹא יַחְמוֹל: עַל־מִשְׁמַרְתִּי אֶעֱמֹדָה
וְאֶתְיַצְּבָה עַל־מָצוֹר וַאֲצַפֶּה לִרְאוֹת מַה־
ב יְדַבֶּר־בִּי וּמָה אָשִׁיב עַל־תּוֹכַחְתִּי: וַיַּעֲנֵנִי יהוה
וַיֹּאמֶר כְּתוֹב חָזוֹן וּבָאֵר עַל־הַלֻּחוֹת לְמַעַן יָרוּץ

entendre, thereby connecting this statement to the analogy of the fisherman's net used in the previous two verses [see *Metzudos*].

[*R' Hirsch, Lev.* 27:28, relates the word חֵרֶם, "banned," to חֶרֶם, "a net." One that is "banned" is in a condition of being trapped away from all other relationships.]

Radak sees יְזַבֵּחַ לְחֶרְמוֹ as really sacrificing to himself. Nebuchadnezzar does not acknowledge that it is God Who gives him his strength, but thinks that he conquered many nations and gained military victories with his own ingenuity (as represented by the "net") and power.

וִיקַטֵּר לְמִכְמַרְתּוֹ — *And burns incense to his trawl.* Our translation follows *Targum Yonasan* who translates וִיקַטֵּר, *to burn incense. Malbim* explains that the primary form of service to the idol was the זְבִיחָה, while the secondary form was הַקְטָרָה. The prophet therefore states that the זְבִיחָה was performed to the חֶרֶם, the "net" that destroyed the many nations. The הַקְטָרָה was performed to מַכְמוֹרֶת, the "trawl" that only took nations captive.

כִּי בָהֵמָּה שָׁמֵן חֶלְקוֹ וּמַאֲכָלוֹ בְּרִאָה — *For through them his portion is fat and his food is healthful.* He offers sacrifices and incense to his net and trawl because he thinks that it is through their strength that he acquired his rich portions (*Radak*).

Malbim explains that there are foods that are fat [rich] but that are not sound for the body. Scripture is noting that Nebuchadnezzar's portion [his conquests] were both fat and sound.

17. הַעַל כֵּן יָרִיק חֶרְמוֹ — *Shall he therefore empty his net.* Our translation of יָרִיק as *empty* follows *Radak* who renders, *Is it because he attributes his power to his god that he succeeds in emptying his net each day?* The prophet is actually asking why God rewards him with success each day when he denies His existence and worships idols (*Radak*). Although *Rashi* translates יָרִיק חֶרְמוֹ to *gird* or *arm himself with his net*, the intent of the verse is basically the same. *Rashi* adds that the prophet is asking a rhetorical question. Is it proper in God's eyes that he should think that his continuous success is due to his worship of idols? Of course not! Alternatively, *Metzudos* explains: Will he ever empty his net and release his captives if he experiences continuous success?

II

⊰§ God's Reply

In the previous chapter Habakkuk questioned God's justice: the success of the wicked and the distressing conditions of the righteous. The prophet now awaits God's reply.

1. עַל־מִשְׁמַרְתִּי אֶעֱמֹדָה ... — *I will stand upon my watch* ... As the sentinel stands guard and does not move from his place and as soldiers who besiege a city do not leave it until it is captured, so too, will Habakkuk not move from

1/17 *and burns incense to his trawl, for through them his portion is fat and his food is healthful.* [17] *Shall he therefore empty his net, to slay nations continuously, without compassion?*

2/1-2 [1] *I will stand upon my watch and take my place at the siege, and I will wait to see what He will speak to me and what I can answer my reproof.*

[2] *And* HASHEM *answered me and said, "Write the vision and clarify it upon tablets, so that a reader*

his place and will not retract his complaints (*Metzudos*). The Sages (*Taanis* 23a), however, translate the word מִשְׁמָר as *prison* or *dungeon* [as in *Numbers* 15:34 — see also *Rashi, Taanis* ibid. ד״ה כדרך], and understand that Habakkuk demanded an explanation from God: "He drew a circle and stood inside it and declared that he would not leave it until God explained why the wicked often succeed and the righteous often suffer" (*Rashi*). Alternatively, *Radak* translates מִשְׁמַרְתִּי as *my waiting* and renders *I anxiously wait for God's answer as to why the wicked are successful.*

In a novel interpretation, *Abarbanel* translates מִשְׁמֶרֶת as a session of deep spiritual meditation in which a prophet would engage as a prerequisite for experiencing a prophetic revelation. Habakkuk is saying that during his meditative sessions he would continuously focus his thoughts [אֶתְיַצְּבָה] toward the forthcoming siege [מָצוֹר] of Jerusalem and the apparent injustice of it all, so that he might receive prophetic inspiration from God [מַה־יְדַבֶּר־בִּי] and be able to explain it to those who questioned him [וּמָה אָשִׁיב עַל־תּוֹכַחְתִּי].

Malbim differentiates between מִשְׁמָר [guard, post] and מָצוֹר [siege, attack]. The מִשְׁמָר is used to protect those who are being guarded while the מָצוֹר is used for conquering and besieging the opposing forces. Accordingly, Habakkuk used the word מִשְׁמָר in reference to the protection that Israel needed, for he was pleading with God that although Israel may not be deserving, God should nevertheless remove the evil decree that had been placed upon them. The prophet used the word מָצוֹר because he had confronted God and demanded that He explain the reason that He permitted the evil Chaldeans to achieve such unbounded success.

מַה־יְדַבֶּר־בִּי — *What He will speak to me.* I.e., what God will convey to Habakkuk through a spirit of prophecy (*Radak*).

וּמָה אָשִׁיב עַל־תּוֹכַחְתִּי — *And what I can answer my reproof.* Habakkuk hoped that he would be given an answer that he could convey to those who come to contend with him and criticize God's strict justice (*Rashi*). Alternatively, Habakkuk hoped that he would have an answer for Israel who continuously questioned him as to when the terrible Babylonian exile will finally end (*Mahari Kara*).

2. וַיַּעֲנֵנִי ה׳ וַיֹּאמֶר — *And Hashem answered me and said.* God answered Habakkuk by implying to him that Nebuchadnezzar's success is only temporary and would not prevail. His blasphemous attitude will be broken and he will acknowledge that Hashem is God (*Radak*).

כְּתוֹב חָזוֹן וּבָאֵר עַל־הַלֻּחוֹת לְמַעַן יָרוּץ קוֹרֵא בוֹ — *"Write the vision and clarify it upon tablets, so that a reader may read it swiftly.* Habakkuk is instructed to write down the vision that will be revealed to him and clearly explain it upon tablets so that it may be read swiftly, without stumbling (*Rashi*), and one would not

ג קוֹרֵא בוֹ: כִּי עוֹד חָזוֹן לַמּוֹעֵד וְיָפֵחַ לַקֵּץ וְלֹא יְכַזֵּב אִם־יִתְמַהְמַהּ חַכֵּה־לוֹ כִּי־בֹא יָבֹא לֹא יְאַחֵר: ד הִנֵּה עֻפְּלָה לֹא־יָשְׁרָה נַפְשׁוֹ בּוֹ

need to study it to understand it (*Abarbanel; Metzudos*). The prophecy is to be written on tablets, and not in a scroll, for tablets were used by the masses, and the prophecy would thereby be made known to multitudes of people. Scrolls were read only by individuals (*Malbim*). Alternatively, *Radak* maintains that the vision is to be recorded twice: once on a scroll, and a second time on tablets. The scroll was to be written in the actual cryptic manner that the prophecy was granted [כְּתוֹב חָזוֹן], ambiguous and in riddles, only alluding to its true meaning.[1] The tablets were to be written in a clear manner describing and explaining that which the prophet foresaw [וּבָאֵר עַל־הַלֻּחוֹת]. The scroll would be preserved for many years to come and when the *appointed time* would arrive, the people of that future generation will have the ability to interpret and understand the vision that had been recorded. The tablets, on the other hand, were for Habakkuk's contemporaries to read and therefore were to be written in a manner whereby everything that would eventually occur to the wicked Chaldeans would be clearly explained so that no one of his day would be led astray by the enemy's success.

Translating the word כְּתוֹב as a passive participle, as if it would read כָּתוּב, *Targum Yonasan* explains that God told Habakkuk that the answer to his question had long ago been written in the Torah, but in a vague cryptic manner. Habakkuk should now write it onto tablets and clearly explain that the vision will yet be revealed at its proper time.

Targum Yonasan's reference is to *Lev.* 26:34: אָז תִּרְצֶה הָאָרֶץ אֶת־שַׁבְּתֹתֶיהָ, *Then the land will be appeased for its sabbaticals.* Due to Israel's neglect of seventy sabbatical years [61 sabbatical years and nine jubilee years], they were to endure seventy years of exile. See also *II Chronicles* 36:21 and *Ezekiel* 4:5 (*Rashi*).

◆§ The Prophecy

3. ...כִּי עוֹד חָזוֹן לַמּוֹעֵד — *For there is yet another vision about the appointed time ...*

There is another prophecy regarding the appointed time of the destruction of Babylon and the redemption of Israel which will be revealed at a future date to a different prophet (*Rashi*). God is alluding to the prophecy of Jeremiah (*Jeremiah* 29:10) where he foretold the exact date that Babylon will fall: 70 years after the destruction of the First Temple (*Rashi*). The Chaldean Kingdom was destroyed during the days of Belshazzar, Nebuchadnezzar's grandson after he blasphemed God (as did his grandfather), and profaned the vessels of the Holy Temple (*Radak*). Others maintain that in addition to the prophecy of the fall of Babylon and the destruction of the Chaldean Kingdom, Habakkuk was also granted a prophetic vision of the ultimate redemption that will take place during the Messianic era (*Abarbanel; Metzudos*); for when one will witness the destruction of the Chaldeans, he will then trust in the prophecy of the redemption that will ultimately occur during Messianic times (*Metzudos*).

וְיָפֵחַ לַקֵּץ וְלֹא יְכַזֵּב — *It will speak of the End and it will not deceive.*

The prophecy that will be revealed to the later prophet will be regarding the *end* of Babylonia (*Rashi*). Alternatively, *Abarbanel* maintains that the word קֵץ, *end*, is used by Scripture only when

1. See *Yad HaChazakah* 7:3, *Hil. Yesodei HaTorah* regarding the visions of prophets.

may read it swiftly. [3] *For there is yet another vision about the appointed time; it will speak of the End and it will not deceive. Though it may tarry, await it, for it will surely come; it will not delay.*
[4] *Behold, his soul is defiant; it is unsettled in him.*

referring to the ultimate redemption that will take place during the Messianic era. Jeremiah was granted a vision of the destruction of the Chaldeans and Daniel prophesied regarding the Messianic era (*Malbim*).

Although the root הפח generally means *to blow air*, it is often translated *speaks* for when one speaks, air is discharged from the mouth (*Rashi*). Alternatively, *Malbim* suggests that וְיָפֵחַ is used when the spoken word of God is not granted in a clear vision but through allusions and hints that warrant clarification.

... אִם־יִתְמַהְמַהּ חַכֵּה־לוֹ ... — *Though it may tarry, await it ...*

Habakkuk addresses those who will be exiled to Babylon and encourages them not to give up hope. Although their captivity will seem to be exceedingly long and the appointed time will seem to tarry, they should wait for it, for it will surely come. The exile will not last even one moment longer than the seventy years foretold by Jeremiah (*Rashi*).

Although *Rashi* and *Radak* explain the verse as referring to the end of the Babylonian exile, the Talmud (*Sanhedrin* 97b) interprets it as alluding to the final redemption. לֹא יְכַזֵּב, *it will not deceive;* the latest date for redemption will not pass without the redemption arriving. אִם־יִתְמַהְמַהּ חַכֵּה־לוֹ — *Though it may tarry, await it;* if the date seems long in arriving, wait for it. כִּי־בֹא יָבֹא לֹא יְאַחֵר — *for it will surely come; it will not delay,* because once that day arrives, the Messiah will surely come and will not delay.

חַכֵּה־לוֹ — *Await it.*

The *Chafetz Chaim* interprets this phrase homiletically. חַכֵּה־לוֹ, *wait for His sake,* for God's honor. When one prays for the coming of the Messiah, he should not do so with the intent that the troubles of the Jewish people should come to an end for in essence that would be only for his benefit and the benefit of the Jewish people. Rather his intent should be for God's sake, that the glory of God should be revealed through the entire universe. That would inevitably result in an end to the troubles of the nation, as well.

4-10. Habakkuk now explains the vision he was granted regarding the downfall of Babylonia and the destruction of Nebuchadnezzar's descendants (*Metzudos*).

4. ... הִנֵּה עֻפְּלָה — *Behold, his soul is defiant ...* Our translation of עֻפְּלָה ... follows *Rashi* who translates לְשׁוֹן עַזּוּת, *an expression of insolence and defiance,* and explains that the soul of this wicked person, Nebuchadnezzar, is continuously wrathful and lustful and only aspires to devour others. He is never satisfied nor content with that which he already possesses and is therefore deserving of punishment (*Rashi*). *Radak* translates עֻפְּלָה as arrogant and also explains this passage as a reference to Nebuchadnezzar and his grandson Belshazzar who were faithless and arrogant, fearless of God's punishments.

Alternatively, *Mahari Kara* translates עֻפְּלָה as רשע, *wicked,* and explains that the verse is referring to the Babylonian kingdom in general, who acted more wickedly than any other kingdom and is infamously unique — see *Targum Onkelos, Numbers* 14:44 where וַיַּעְפִּלוּ is translated וְאַרְשַׁעוּ — *and they acted wickedly. R' Moshe Kimchi* relates the word עֻפְּלָה to עֹפֶל וָבַחַן — a *citadel or fortress* — and explains that one whose "soul is not upright" would place himself in a fortress to seek refuge from his enemy rather than turn toward God and beseech Him for salvation. The righteous person, however, is different for his soul is humble

ב/ה

ה וְצַדִּיק בֶּאֱמוּנָתוֹ יִחְיֶה: וְאַף כִּי־הַיַּיִן בּוֹגֵד גֶּבֶר יָהִיר וְלֹא יִנְוֶה אֲשֶׁר הִרְחִיב כִּשְׁאוֹל נַפְשׁוֹ וְהוּא כַמָּוֶת וְלֹא יִשְׂבָּע וַיֶּאֱסֹף אֵלָיו כָּל־הַגּוֹיִם וַיִּקְבֹּץ אֵלָיו כָּל־הָעַמִּים:

and he always fears God. He will therefore always live by his faith in God and avoid the evil that befalls the *wicked* (*Radak*). In a novel interpretation, *Malbim* sees the verse addressing those individuals who attempt to calculate the exact date of the ultimate redemption. When their calculation is proven wrong, they still try to convince others that the redemption has, in fact, arrived. If they are unsuccessful, then they abandon the ways of the Torah. Scripture admonishes these people and blames them for postponing the redemption.

וְצַדִּיק בֶּאֱמוּנָתוֹ יִחְיֶה — *But the righteous person shall live through his faith.* The righteous person lives with steadfast faith that all that occurs is from God. He does not credit his own merits or strength for his success (*Metzudos*). He surrenders himself totally to God and places his complete trust in Him, not deviating at all from His ways (*Maharal, Nesiv HaEmunah* 2).

Scripture is referring to Jeconiah [also knows as Jehoiachin, the fifteenth monarch of the Kingdom of Judah], who was exiled by Nebuchadnezzar — see *II Kings* 24:8-16 — and remained righteous while he was in exile. Upon Nebuchadnezzar's death, his successor, Evil Merodach, released Jeconiah from imprisonment and elevated him above all the kings who were with him in Babylon — see ibid. 25:27-29 (*Rashi*). Alternatively, the righteous man is referring to the Israelites, who were exiled to Babylon together with King Zedekiah, who refused to be coerced into worshiping idols. When King Cyrus of Persia conquered Babylon, he spared the Jews and even granted them permission to rebuild the Holy Temple (*Radak*).

Targum Yonasan translates the word אֱמוּנָה as *honesty*. Unlike the wicked *whose soul is not upright, the righteous person lives with honesty.*

The Talmud (*Makkos* 23b) expounds on this verse. R' Simlai commented, "six hundred and thirteen commandments were related to Moses. King David came and established eleven ethical requirements for the fulfillment of these commandments. Isaiah came and reduced them to six ... Micah came and reduced them to three ... then came Habakkuk and reduced them to one, namely, 'The righteous person lives through his faith.' "

This cannot mean that each of the aforementioned prophets reduced the requirements of mitzvah observance from the original 613 to eleven, six, three or one, for one of the basic tenets of Judaism is that the commandments of the Torah are eternal and no commandment may be discarded. *Rivan* (*Makkos* ibid.) explains that originally the entire nation was on a high-enough spiritual level to perform all six hundred and thirteen commandments with the proper intensity, thereby meriting the World to Come. As time went on, the spiritual level of the nation declined and people were not able to fulfill all the commandments in the desired manner. King David therefore set forth these eleven ethical requirements through which one would merit the World to Come.

The *Chafetz Chaim* (*Prophets — Habakkuk* 2:4) explains that the prophets never intended to reduce the requirement of mitzvah observance. Their intent was to pinpoint the *mitzvah* that the people of that specific generation needed to reinforce and diligently observe. But the basic idea common to all of these prophets is that one must live with אֱמוּנָה, with faith and trust in G-d. He must realize that anything that ever occurred and all that is now taking place and all that will ever take place is all the will of God. [For further discussion see *Maharsha; Makkos* 24b; *Maharal, Nesiv HaEmunah* Ch. 2.]

Malbim sees this verse as a praise to the righteous person who knows that God will some day send His redeemer. He does not

But the righteous person shall live through his faith. [5]The wine also betrayed him; the arrogant man, his house will not stand. He has widened his soul like the grave and, like death, he is not satisfied. He gathered unto himself all the nations and assembled unto himself all the peoples.

place his faith in false prophets or in those who have claimed to calculate the proper date of the coming of the End of Days (mentioned in v. 3). The righteous person faithfully waits for God to send the Messiah.

5. Scripture now relates the vision of the fall of Babylonia (*Malbim*).

וְאַף כִּי־הַיַּיִן בּוֹגֵד — *The wine also betrayed him.* This is a reference to Belshazzar, the grandson of Nebuchadnezzar, who, while under the influence of wine, desecrated the holy vessels of the Temple and profaned God's Name (*Rashi*) [see *Daniel* 5:1-4]. This provoked God's wrath and he ordered the immediate destruction of the Babylonian Empire (*Malbim*). Alternatively, *Radak* translates *and surely the drunken traitor,* and sees this verse as a description of Nebuchadnezzar who, in his intoxicated state, acted haughtily and recklessly. He mercilessly murdered and betrayed his allies. God punishes all wicked men; and certainly He will punish this treacherous, unscrupulous Nebuchadnezzar.

גֶּבֶר יָהִיר וְלֹא יִנְוֶה — *The arrogant man, his house will not stand. Rashi* translates יִנְוֶה figuratively, *his royal house.* Belshazzar's wicked actions resulted in his death and the end of the Babylonian Empire. The royal house of Nebuchadnezzar was cut down leaving no descendants to carry on his dynasty (*Rashi*). The word נָוֶה, however, actually means *residence* or *dwelling place.* Belshazzar will no longer dwell in his palace, for his kingdom will be removed from him and given over to Darius the Mede for the Babylonian Empire was divided between the Persians and Medes (*Mahari Kara*).

Alternatively, the verse is foretelling that Nebuchadnezzar will be driven from his palace — see *Daniel* 4:30. Nebuchadnezzar, later in his life, lost his sanity to the point where he thought he was an animal. He ate grass like oxen, washed his body with dew and was driven from mankind (*Radak*). Alternatively, Nebuchadnezzar is like a man whose confidence is bolstered by alcohol. He continuously leaves his home to embark on ambitious expeditions of conquest in foreign lands (*Ibn Ezra*). *Metzudos* interprets that the arrogant person does not confine himself to his own dwelling place but usurps from others that which is theirs.

אֲשֶׁר הִרְחִיב כִּשְׁאוֹל נַפְשׁוֹ ... — *He has widened his soul like the grave ...* [Scripture now relates the wickedness of Nebuchadnezzar.]

Nebuchadnezzar's insatiable lusts are metaphorically described by Scripture as a wide grave and as the angel of death, who are never satisfied with what they have. So too, Nebuchadnezzar gathered nation upon nation to be subservient to him and was not satisfied with what he acquired (*Rashi; Radak*). Furthermore, just as no one can escape death, so too, no one could escape from Nebuchadnezzar (*Abarbanel*).

Metzudos sees the verse as a continuation of the description of the wicked arrogant man who surely deserves punishment. He lusts for everything and wishes that all should be subservient to him. One who acts in this way must surely receive retribution.

ו הֲלוֹא־אֵלֶּה כֻלָּם עָלָיו מָשָׁל יִשָּׂאוּ וּמְלִיצָה חִידוֹת לוֹ וְיֹאמַר הוֹי הַמַּרְבֶּה לֹּא־לוֹ עַד־מָתַי וּמַכְבִּיד עָלָיו עַבְטִיט׃ ז הֲלוֹא פֶתַע יָקוּמוּ נֹשְׁכֶיךָ וְיִקְצוּ מְזַעְזְעֶיךָ וְהָיִיתָ לִמְשִׁסּוֹת לָמוֹ׃ ח כִּי־אַתָּה שַׁלּוֹתָ גּוֹיִם רַבִּים יְשָׁלּוּךָ כָּל־יֶתֶר עַמִּים מִדְּמֵי אָדָם

6-19. The prophet now enumerates the punishments of the Chaldeans in general and Nebuchadnezzar in particular. *Rashi* continues to explain that the subject of the verse is Nebuchadnezzar's descendant Belshazzar.

6. ... הֲלוֹא־אֵלֶּה כֻלָּם עָלָיו מָשָׁל יִשָּׂאוּ — *Shall all of these not take up a parable about him ...* Will not all the nations that he had assembled and enslaved take up parables and mock him at the time of his downfall? (*Rashi; Radak; Mahari Kara*).

The commentators explain the difference between מְלִיצָה and חִידָה. מְלִיצָה is used when referring to statements made in a clear language. חִידוֹת are riddles — sayings that are more profound or esoteric (*Metzudos*). Alternatively, the מְלִיצָה is the explanation of what the parable represents. In our case, the explanation was given in riddle (חִידָה) form (*Malbim*).

וְיֹאמַר — *One will say.* Either the one reciting the *melitzah* will say (*Rashi*) or each and every person assembled will say (*Radak; Metzudos*).

הוֹי הַמַּרְבֶּה לֹּא־לוֹ — *"Woe to him who amasses that which is not his."* This is the *melitzah* (saying). "Woe to the one who has amassed his wealth and broadened his kingdom but it will not even remain his" — for the king of the Medes will come and take it all from him (*Rashi*). Alternatively, *Radak* and *Mahari Kara* explain, "Woe to the one who amasses his wealth from that which was not his." He plundered and robbed many nations (*Radak*) and took the vessels of the Holy Temple (*Mahari Kara*). *Ibn Ezra* notes that Scripture previously wrote regarding the wicked Chaldeans that they are a nation *that will go across the breadth of the earth to possess dwelling places that are not its own* — see 1:6.

עַד־מָתַי וּמַכְבִּיד עָלָיו עַבְטִיט — *"How long [can he go on]? He burdens himself heavily with thick mud."* How long will he continue to increase [his wealth] and thereby add to his heavy burden of sin? (*Rashi*). Alternatively, how long will he continue to increase his wealth which has become as weighty as thick mud? (*Radak*).

Radak quotes his father who explains that the verse is referring to the thick mud that will be piled on Nebuchadnezzar's grave. In a similar vein, *Mahari Kara* explains that he will die and *become* thick mud. *Ibn Ezra* writes that he will act as one who is mad and throw mud upon himself. [This is a reference to *Daniel* 4:30, cited in comm. to v. 3.]

The word עַבְטִיט is composed of the two words עַב (thick) and טִיט (mud) (*Radak*). *Rashi* interprets the two words differently: עַב is a heavy beam or pillar; טִיט, in this case, one made of mud or clay (brick). *Targum Yonasan* relates the word עַבְטִיט to עֲבַט — to borrow [see also *Malbim* to this verse]. Everything the Chaldeans have taken from their neighbors is in reality "on loan," and must be repaid. These debts have become tremendous burdens and the Chaldeans haven't the ability to repay them.

7. ... הֲלוֹא פֶתַע יָקוּמוּ נֹשְׁכֶיךָ — *Will those who would bite you not rise up suddenly?* Suddenly your attackers ("biters"), the kings of Persia and Media, will awaken and rise up against you (*Metzudos*). Similarly, *Mahari Kara* explains that the biters are a reference to Darius and his army who attacked Belshazzar

[6] Shall all of these not take up a parable about him and a metaphor; [and] riddles regarding him? One will say, "Woe to him who amasses that which is not his. How long [can he go on]? He burdens himself heavily with thick mud." [7] Will those who would bite you not rise up suddenly? And [will] those who would cause you to tremble [not] awaken? You will be plunder for them! [8] Because you have expelled many nations, all the remnants of the nations will expel you, for the blood of men [that you spilt]

and killed him. Alternatively, the attackers are the descendants of those whom Nebuchadnezzar had murdered. It will be as if the dead themselves will awaken [וְיִקְצוּ] and rise up from their grave to attack him (*Ibn Ezra*).

Scripture describes the attackers as "biters" [נֹשְׁכֶיךָ] and not simply "avengers" so that we may visualize the fury and anger with which they attacked (*Da'as Sofrim*). *Radak* again quotes his father who understands the "biters" to be the worms that will devour Nebuchadnezzar's corpse in its grave. Scripture is in effect saying to him, "Nebuchadnezzar! In your arrogance you never stopped to think that one day you will be a corpse lying in a grave with worms needling through your flesh." *Malbim* translates נֶשֶׁךְ in its other meaning — "creditors" — continuing the parable of the previous verse. Nebuchadnezzar was compared to someone who leads a wealthy lifestyle by constantly borrowing (on interest) large sums of money from others (הַמַּרְבֶּה לֹּא־לוֹ). Does he not realize that eventually his creditors will one day arise and suddenly seize all his belongings?

וְיִקְצוּ מְזַעְזְעֶיךָ — *And [will] those who would cause you to tremble [not] awaken.* The word וְיִקְצוּ is synonymous with וְיָקִיצוּ — *and they will awaken* (*Rashi*). The Persian and Median kings who were under the rule of Nebuchadnezzar and were subservient to his nation will suddenly rebel during the days of Belshazzar, as one who suddenly awakens from his slumbers (*Abarbanel*).

וְהָיִיתָ לִמְשִׁסּוֹת לָמוֹ — *You will be plunder for them!* The prophet is either referring to Nebuchadnezzar who was exhumed from his grave — see *Isaiah* 14:19 — or to Belshazzar who was suddenly attacked by the Persian army and slain (*Radak*).

8. כִּי־אַתָּה שַׁלּוֹתָ גּוֹיִם רַבִּים ... — *Because you have expelled many nations ...* Our translation follows *Rashi* who relates the words שַׁלּוֹתָ and יְשָׁלּוּךָ to the word נָשַׁל, *to cast away.* Because you have expelled many nations from their lands, the remaining nations, those who have not been driven out from their lands, will expel you from yours (*Rashi; Mahari Kara*). Alternatively, *Radak* and *Ibn Ezra* relate שַׁלּוֹתָ to the word שָׁלָל, "spoils," and render, "because you have despoiled many nations the remnant of the nations will despoil you."

R' Hirsch (*Deut.* 7:1) writes that the word נשל is a term used specifically for fruit that suddenly fall from the trees long before they have ripened [see *Deut.* 28:40]. In our context, וְנָשַׁל is used because the inhabitants of the land have suddenly been denied the use of their land.

מִדְּמֵי אָדָם ... — *For the blood of men ...* These punishments will befall you to avenge the blood of the many nations that you have spilled (*Radak; Ibn Ezra*). *Rashi*, however, explains that דְּמֵי אָדָם, the *blood of men*, is referring specifically to the blood of the Israelite nation for Scripture refers to Israel as אָדָם, *man* — see *Ezekiel* 34:31. *Mahari Kara*

ט וַחֲמַס־אֶרֶץ קִרְיָה וְכָל־יֹשְׁבֵי בָהּ׃ הוֹי
בֹּצֵעַ בֶּצַע רָע לְבֵיתוֹ לָשׂוּם בַּמָּרוֹם קִנּוֹ
י לְהִנָּצֵל מִכַּף רָע׃ יָעַצְתָּ בֹּשֶׁת לְבֵיתֶךָ קְצוֹת־
יא עַמִּים רַבִּים וְחוֹטֵא נַפְשֶׁךָ׃ כִּי־אֶבֶן מִקִּיר תִּזְעָק
יב וְכָפִיס מֵעֵץ יַעֲנֶנָּה׃ הוֹי בֹּנֶה עִיר בְּדָמִים

cites *Jeremiah* 52:10 which records the slaughter of the sons of Zedekiah and the princes of Judea by the king of Babylon as an example of this bloodshed.

The Talmud writes: *You [Israel] are called Adam but the nations of the world are not called Adam* (*Yevamos* 61a). When God created Adam, the first man, He created him utterly perfect in body, intellect and spirit but not all of his descendants could attain this lofty spirituality. It was only the descendants of Jacob who achieved that level of Godliness and became the true heirs of the spirit of Adam and the ones privileged to bear his name — see *Kuzari* 1:95. *Radak* (*Ezekiel* 34:31) writes that when one permits himself to be drawn to the physical desires of this world he is called animal, not man. However, when one serves G-d with all his heart, then he is worthy of the title Adam. [For further discussion of the title *Adam* see *Yechezkel* — ArtScroll ed. Overview IV.]

וַחֲמַס־אֶרֶץ — *And the violence against the land. Radak* and *Ibn Ezra* render, to avenge the violence that had been committed against the world in general. *Rashi* and *Metzudos* follow *Targum Yonasan* who translates *against the Land of Israel.* The violence against the land was its devastation and destruction (*Mahari Kara*).

קִרְיָה וְכָל־יוֹשְׁבֵי בָהּ — *The city and all its inhabitants.* [And to avenge the violence that had been committed against] the city of Jerusalem [and to avenge the violence that had been committed against all her inhabitants] (*Rashi*). *Abarbanel* and *Malbim,* however, maintain that the subject of the verse is the land of Babylon. *Abarbanel* explains that the violence and treachery with which Nebuchadnezzar maintained his rule over the land will result in the rebellion of his Persian and Median subjects. According to *Malbim,* Babylonia will be plundered due to the debts and interest for which its creditors are now demanding payment. The "debts and interest" are the blood of the people and the violence against the land.

9. הוֹי בֹּצֵעַ בֶּצַע רָע לְבֵיתוֹ — *Woe to him who gains evil profit for his house.* Our translation follows *Radak.* The profit is described as being evil for it has come through an evil deed. *Rashi,* however, understands that the word רַע, *evil,* is describing the fate of Nebuchadnezzar and is not modifying "profits." He translates, "Woe to him who has robbed people of their wealth; for it will only cause him disaster [evil]." The money that Nebuchadnezzar obtained through thievery will cause his downfall.

According to *R' Hirsch* (*Exodus* 18:21) the word בֶּצַע is related to פֶּצַע — to wound. It is an advantage gained at the expense of another.

לְבֵיתוֹ — *For his house.* The stolen money was used to erect great structures for Nebuchadnezzar's personal use (*Rashi; Radak*). *Metzudos* translates *his household,* i.e., his descendants will be cut down because he profited unjustly [see *Gen.* 30:30]. *Ibn Ezra* sees the entire country of Babylonia as *his house.*

לָשׂוּם בַּמָּרוֹם קִנּוֹ ... — *So that he may set his nest up high ...* As a precaution against the invasion of neighboring enemies, Nebuchadnezzar erected a great and powerful fortress in Babylon with the wood and stones of the cities he had captured and destroyed (*Radak; Mahari Kara*).

[Scripture often metaphorically uses the *nest up high* to portray the conceit and ambitiousness of the wicked. (See *Obadiah* 1:4.)]

and the violence against the land, the city and all its inhabitants.

[9] *Woe to him who gains evil profit for his house, so that he may set his nest up high to be rescued from the grasp of evil.* [10] *You have counseled shame for your house by cutting off many peoples, and you have sinned against your soul.* [11] *For a stone will cry out from the wall and a sliver will answer it from the beams.*

[12] *Woe to him who builds a city with bloodshed*

[The money that Nebuchadnezzar had gathered through the plundering of the nations caused his downfall, for Scripture (*Daniel* 4:26-28) writes that when Nebuchadnezzar was walking atop his royal palace in Babylon, he exclaimed, "Is this not the great Babylon, which I have built up . . . with *my* powerful strength and for glorification of *my* splendor!" and he was immediately punished (*Rashi*).]

10. יָעַצְתָּ בֹּשֶׁת לְבֵיתֶךָ ... — *You have counseled shame for your house* ... Your counsel of destroying many nations and using the wealth that you captured from them to build your palaces and fortresses was ill advice, for it will only bring your destruction (*Rashi; Radak*).

קְצוֹת־עַמִּים רַבִּים — *By cutting off many peoples.* Our translation follows *Radak* and *Metzudos.* The word קְצוֹת means "to cut off" as in *Deut.* 25:12, וְקַצֹּתָה אֶת־כַּפָּהּ (*Metzudos*). Alternatively, קְצוֹת means "to scrape," as in *Lev.* 14:43, וְאַחֲרֵי הִקְצוֹת אֶת הַבַּיִת (*Rashi*). In any event, the intent of Scripture is to describe the destruction of the many nations.

וְחוֹטֵא נַפְשֶׁךָ — *And you have sinned against your soul.* You have sinned and caused your own destruction (*Rashi*).

11. כִּי־אֶבֶן מִקִּיר תִּזְעָק — *For a stone will cry out from the wall.* The stones [of the buildings you plundered] will cry out from the wall [that you built and exclaim that they had been stolen by Nebuchadnezzar] (*Rashi; Metzudos*). The singular אֶבֶן, *stone,* is used to illustrate that *each and every* stone will publicize its origin (*Metzudos*).

וְכָפִיס מֵעֵץ יַעֲנֶנָּה — *And a sliver will answer it from the beams.* Our translation follows *Targum Yonasan* cited by *Rashi.* The chip of wood answers the call of the stone and says, "I too, have been stolen by Nebuchadnezzar." Both the stone and the wood of the building will cry out together (*Rashi; Metzudos*). Alternatively, *Radak* translates כָּפִיס as "beam" and עֵץ as the roofing of the entire building. Scripture intends to metaphorically portray that *everyone* knew that Nebuchadnezzar's structures were built with stolen goods (*Radak; Abarbanel*).

Mahari Kara sees this verse referring to the stones and wood of the Holy Temple that was destroyed by Nebuchadnezzar. Even if only one stone of the Temple would remain, it would cry out to God and mourn the destruction of the Temple.

The Talmud (*Taanis* 11a; *Chagigah* 16a) learns from this verse that the walls and beams of one's house testify before God of the evil actions he commits in the privacy of his home.

12. הוֹי בֹּנֶה עִיר בְּדָמִים ... — *Woe to him who builds a city with bloodshed* ... Woe to Nebuchadnezzar who built the city of Babylon with properties he seized through murder and established it with properties acquired through iniquity (*Mahari Kara*) [see v. 9]. Although *Radak* and *Mahari Kara* explain this verse as a repetition of v. 9, *Metzudos* maintains that this verse is introducing prophecies that relate to the ultimate

יג וְכוֹנֵן קִרְיָה בְּעַוְלָה: הֲלוֹא הִנֵּה מֵאֵת יהוה צְבָאוֹת וְיִיגְעוּ עַמִּים בְּדֵי־אֵשׁ יד וּלְאֻמִּים בְּדֵי־רִיק יִעָפוּ: כִּי תִּמָּלֵא הָאָרֶץ לָדַעַת אֶת־כְּבוֹד יהוה כַּמַּיִם יְכַסּוּ עַל־

redemption of Israel during the Messianic era and the downfall of the nations who destroyed the Second Temple. *Abarbanel*, too, maintains that verses 12-20 are a prophecy in which Habakkuk foresaw the ultimate destruction of Rome, the leader of the Edomite kingdom who destroyed the Second Temple, and are not a prophecy describing the downfall of Nebuchadnezzar.

See also *Radak's* alternative explanation of v. 14 where he, too, is of the opinion that these verses are referring to the Messianic era.

וְכוֹנֵן קִרְיָה בְּעַוְלָה — *And establishes a city with iniquity.*

Scripture uses the words בנה and כנן to describe the construction of Babylonia. בּוֹנֶה is used when describing the onset of the building's construction. כּוֹנֵן is used when refering to the finishing touches. Since קִרְיָה refers to the placing of the roof [תִּקְרָה], and is done upon completion of the structure, the word כּוֹנֵן is used (*Malbim*).

13. הֲלוֹא הִנֵּה מֵאֵת ה' צְבָאוֹת — *Behold, is it not from Hashem, Master of Legions.* Scripture is referring to the retribution of the wicked (*Rashi*). Are not punishments decreed by God? They are not simply coincidental occurrences (*Metzudos*). *Radak* understands that this verse is referring to Nebuchadnezzar and his descendants. *Abarbanel* and *Metzudos* explain this verse as referring to the heathen nations who will wage war against the people of Israel prior to the Messianic era.

The Name *"Hashem, Master of Legions"* expresses the idea that He rules over the entire world. It is Hashem Who has formed all His creatures; He commands them, leads them and guides them (*R' Hirsch, Psalms* 24:10).

וְיִיגְעוּ עַמִּים בְּדֵי־אֵשׁ — *That the peoples will toil for the fire.* The fire to which Scripture is referring is the fire of God's anger. God is saying that the nations will become weary and ragged before they will have had their measure of God's wrath (*Rashi*).

Alternatively, *Radak* explains that the nations who have allied themselves with Nebuchadnezzar will come to the realization that all their toil [יְגִיעָה] has been for naught, for the structures that they built will be destroyed or burned. All their toil will bring them only to the fire of Gehinnom (*Mahari Kara*). [Accordingly, the verse would be translated, and the toil of the nations [will end] in fire and the nations' weariness [will end] in nothingness].

וּלְאֻמִּים בְּדֵי־רִיק יִעָפוּ — *And the nations will weary themselves for nothingness?* When Babylon will fall, the wooden structures of the city (its roofs) will burn and then the stone wall will be attacked. Its inhabitants will try to put out the fires (יִיגְעוּ בְּדֵי־אֵשׁ) and to save the stone walls, but to no avail (בְּדֵי־רִיק יִעָפוּ) (*Malbim*). The prophet Jeremiah, a contemporary of Habakkuk, prophesied the downfall of Babylon in similar terms. [See *Jeremiah* 51:58.] Alternatively, all the nations that will try to defend themselves during the wars that will take place during Messianic times will toil in vain for God's decrees are always fulfilled (*Abarbanel; Metzudos*).

The phrases בְּדֵי־אֵשׁ and בְּדֵי־רִיק are to be translated as if written בְּאֵשׁ — *in fire*, and בְּרִיק — *in nothing*. The word די [usually translated as "enough"] denotes a continuously intensifying state (*Radak, Jeremiah* 51:58).

14. כִּי תִּמָּלֵא הָאָרֶץ לָדַעַת אֶת־כְּבוֹד ה' — *For the earth will be filled with knowledge of Hashem's glory.* In our

and establishes a city with iniquity. [13] *Behold, is it not from* H*ASHEM*, *Master of Legions, that the peoples will toil for the fire, and the nations will weary themselves for nothingness?* [14] *For the earth will be filled with knowledge of* H*ASHEM's glory, as the waters cover the seabed.*

commentary to v. 12 we noted that there are two views as to the explanation of vv. 12-20. The first, is that Scripture is referring to the downfall of Nebuchadnezzar and the Chaldean kingdom. The second, is that Scripture is dealing with the downfall of the nations during the Messianic era. Although he explains these verses according to the first view, *Radak* notes that this verse [v. 14] seems to lend credence to the latter view.

According to the first approach, the verse is telling us that at the time of the downfall of the Chaldean kingdom, all will realize the greatness of G-d (*Radak*). When Nebuchadnezzar arrogantly blasphemed Hashem, God immediately punished him with madness [see *Daniel* 4:28-30]. King Belshazzar, Nebuchadnezzar's grandson, was also punished immediately after he had desecrated the holy vessels of the Temple in Jerusalem. He was killed the very night that Daniel foretold of his downfall when he interpreted the writing on the wall [see ibid. 5:24-30]. After Belshazzar's death, Cyrus the Mede conquered Babylon and exclaimed, "All the kingdoms of the land did Hashem the God of the heavens give to me." [See *II Chronicles* 36:23.] It seems quite clear, then, that all the nations of the world at that time realized that the downfall of Babylon was brought by God and that His providence is over mankind and grants each person his due (*Radak; Malbim*).

The prophet Isaiah [11:9] used almost identical words when he foretold the events of the Messianic era. The prophet Jeremiah [31:33], too, prophesied in a similar manner. Due to the implications of this verse, *Radak*, as mentioned earlier, is inclined to explain vv. 12-20 as a vision of the Messianic era.

Accordingly, the explanation of v. 13 is: Although the people of this generation have witnessed God's vengeance against Babylon, a greater phenomenon will be witnessed some time in the future, when God will take vengeance on all the nations who will join forces with Gog and Magog against Jerusalem. Then will their toil end in fire and be for naught as explained in the prophecies of Ezekiel (Ch. 39) and Zechariah (Ch. 14) (*Radak*).

This verse cannot be referring to the era of the Second Temple for the earth did not know the glory of G-d at the time. It was an era filled with Sadducees, Boethusians, heretics and skeptics. This verse can only be referring to the era of the ultimate redemption (*Abarbanel*).

כַּמַּיִם יְכַסּוּ עַל־יָם — *As the waters cover the seabed.* What point is Scripture trying to make by comparing the knowledge of God in Messianic times to waters that cover the sea?

The *Chafetz Chaim* (*Isaiah* 11:9) remarks that when one travels the oceans, he only sees a vast expanse of water but the mountains and the valleys of the ocean floor remain undetected. So too, will it be with the knowledge mankind will have of God. Nowadays, there are many different beliefs and opinions regarding the knowledge of God; as numerous as the mountain and valleys of the ocean floor. But in Messianic times when all will recognize that it is only Hashem Who is the God over the universe, the knowledge of God will be like the expanse of ocean where only its waters are seen.

טו יָם: הוֹי מַשְׁקֵה רֵעֵהוּ מְסַפֵּחַ חֲמָתְךָ
טז וְאַף שַׁכֵּר לְמַעַן הַבִּיט עַל־מְעוֹרֵיהֶם: שָׂבַעְתָּ
קָלוֹן מִכָּבוֹד שְׁתֵה גַם־אַתָּה וְהֵעָרֵל תִּסּוֹב
יז עָלֶיךָ כּוֹס יְמִין יהוה וְקִיקָלוֹן עַל־כְּבוֹדֶךָ: כִּי־
חֲמַס לְבָנוֹן יְכַסֶּךָּ וְשֹׁד בְּהֵמוֹת יְחִיתַן מִדְּמֵי
יח אָדָם וַחֲמַס־אֶרֶץ קִרְיָה וְכָל־יֹשְׁבֵי בָהּ: מָה־
הוֹעִיל פֶּסֶל כִּי פְסָלוֹ יֹצְרוֹ מַסֵּכָה וּמוֹרֶה שָּׁקֶר

15. ... הוֹי מַשְׁקֵה רֵעֵהוּ — *Woe to him who gives his fellow to drink ...* The subject of this verse is the wicked Nebuchadnezzar whose habit it was to forcibly intoxicate the kings that he had captured so that he could mock them and act immorally with them (*Rashi; Radak*). Alternatively, *Seder Olam* sees Belshazzar as the subject. For it was he who gave his officers wine in the vessels of the Holy Temple and intoxicated them.

Metzudos sees the heathen nations that distressed Israel as the verse's subject. [In what seems to be an uncensored version of *Metzudos*, אֱדוֹם, *Rome*, is written instead of עַכּוּם, *heathen nations.*] Because they first befriended Israel and then treacherously "intoxicated" her with a potent brew of suffering, the prophet uses the word רֵעֶה, *friend*. Alternatively, Scripture is literally using the word רֵעֶה in this verse since those whom Nebuchadnezzar oppressed were kings like he (*Radak*).

מְסַפֵּחַ חֲמָתְךָ וְאַף שַׁכֵּר — *You gather your anger and intoxicate [them].* Through giving the captive kings the wine to drink, you, Nebuchadnezzar, amass your anger upon them and intoxicate them with your fury (*Rashi*). Alternatively, it is *God*'s anger that is increased with Nebuchadnezzar's actions (*Mahari Kara*).

לְמַעַן הַבִּיט עַל־מְעוֹרֵיהֶם — *So that you may look upon their nakedness.* This is referring to Nebuchadnezzar's sodomizing of the captive kings (*Rashi*). Alternatively, it is meant figuratively: you did this in order to see them in their shame, for the Babylonians had nothing to gain by afflicting the Israelites. Their only intent was to gloat over the shame that they imposed upon them.

16. שָׂבַעְתָּ קָלוֹן מִכָּבוֹד — *You are sated more with shame than with glory.* You derived more pleasure from the shame of the heathen kings than from the honor displayed to you (*Radak*). Alternatively, you will receive more shame than the honor you previously were given, for the time of your punishment has arrived (*Ibn Ezra*).

שְׁתֵה גַם־אַתָּה וְהֵעָרֵל — *You too, will drink and become confounded.* You too Nebuchadnezzar will drink the "cup of shame" that you gave to others (*Radak*). Nebuchadnezzar was stricken with madness and was driven from mankind and lived among the beasts of the field; see *Daniel* 4:3 (ibid.).

The word וְהֵעָרֵל is actually the reflexive form of the verb ערל, *to be closed up*. Nebuchadnezzar will be closed up [in his senses] because of the destruction and confusion (*Rashi*).

תִּסּוֹב עָלֶיךָ כּוֹס יְמִין ה׳ — *The cup of Hashem's right hand is turned upon you.* The intoxication caused by the cup of curse that God's right hand will turn upon you will cause you to become confused (*Rashi, Exodus* 6:12).

וְקִיקָלוֹן עַל־כְּבוֹדֶךָ — *And the vomit of shame will cover your glory.* You will be as repulsive as vomit and covered with shame (*Metzudos*). *Radak* notes

[15] *Woe to him who gives his fellow to drink: You gather your anger and intoxicate [them] so that you may look upon their nakedness.* [16] *You are sated more with shame than with glory. You too, will drink and become confounded; the cup of* HASHEM*'s right hand is turned upon you, and the vomit of shame will cover your glory.* [17] *For the violence against Lebanon will cover you, and the plunder [done] by [your] animals will destroy you, because of the blood of men [that you spilt] and the robbery of the land, the city and all its inhabitants.*

[18] *Of what avail is the graven image that its maker has carved, the molten image and teacher of falsehood,*

that the word קִיקָלוֹן is a combination of the words קִיא, *vomit*, and קָלוֹן, *shame.*

17. כִּי־חֲמַס לְבָנוֹן יְכַסֶּךָּ — *For the violence against Lebanon will cover you.* The violence that you committed against the Holy Temple will be the cause of your shame (*Rashi; Mahari Kara*).

[The Talmud (*Yoma* 39b) explains that the Holy Temple is referred to as Lebanon for it whitens [לָבָן] the sins of Israel.] *Radak* and *Metzudos* say that לְבָנוֹן is a poetic name for the Land of Israel. *Ibn Ezra* takes Lebanon literally (referring to the area by that name, known for its cedar forests): Because you cut down the cedars of Lebanon for your buildings, you will be covered with shame.

וְשֹׁד בְּהֵמוֹת יְחִיתַן — *And the plunder [done] by [your] animals will destroy you.* The plunder of your beasts and your armies who plundered My nation Israel will cause you to be broken (*Rashi*). Alternatively, since Scripture referred to Israel as the Lebanon, a forested area in northern Biblical Israel, he refers to Israel's inhabitants as beasts, for beasts inhabit the forests. The plunder perpetrated against the people of Israel will be the downfall of the Chaldeans (*Radak; Metzudos*). [See *Jeremiah* 50.]

מִדְּמֵי אָדָם ... — *Because of the blood of men [that you spilt] ...* All the punishments that will befall you are due to the blood of Israel that you have spilled. Israel is referred to as Adam (*Metzudos*). [See comm. to v. 8.]

18. מָה־הוֹעִיל פֶּסֶל כִּי פְסָלוֹ יֹצְרוֹ — *Of what avail is the graven image that its maker has carved.* To what avail is the idol with which the Babylonian king prided himself, saying his god was the source of his strength (cf. 1:11) — to what avail will the man-made image be on the day of his destruction? (*Radak*).

מַסֵּכָה וּמוֹרֶה שָּׁקֶר — *The molten image and teacher of falsehood.* And to what avail, too, is the molten image [on the day of destruction]? The images only teach falsehood to those who worship them (*Radak*). The *teacher of falsehood* is the idol's priest (*Ibn Ezra; Mahari Kara*). *Abarbanel* [who maintains that vv. 12-20 are referring to the downfall of Rome — see comm. to v. 12] explains that this verse is not only referring to Pagan Rome, whose people were idol worshipers, but also to Christian Rome whose practice it is to erect statues in the image of the founder of its religion and its so-called saints.

ב/יט־כ

כִּי־בָטַ֞ח יֹצֵ֤ר יִצְרוֹ֙ עָלָ֔יו לַעֲשׂ֖וֹת אֱלִילִ֥ים אִלְּמִֽים׃ יט הֹ֣וי אֹמֵ֤ר לָעֵץ֙ הָקִ֔יצָה ע֖וּרִי לְאֶ֣בֶן דּוּמָ֑ם ה֣וּא יוֹרֶ֔ה הִנֵּה־ה֗וּא תָּפוּשׂ֙ זָהָ֣ב וָכֶ֔סֶף וְכָל־ר֖וּחַ אֵ֥ין בְּקִרְבּֽוֹ׃ כ וַיהוָ֖ה בְּהֵיכַ֣ל קָדְשׁ֑וֹ הַ֥ס מִפָּנָ֖יו כָּל־הָאָֽרֶץ׃

ג/א־ב

א תְּפִלָּ֖ה לַחֲבַקּ֣וּק הַנָּבִ֑יא עַ֖ל שִׁגְיֹנֽוֹת׃ ב יהוה

כִּי־בָטַח יֹצֵר יִצְרוֹ עָלָיו ... — *That its maker should place his trust in it* ... To what avail are the idols that cannot speak and do not answer those who call to them that their maker places his trust and salvation in his own handicraft? (*Rashi; Radak*). *Metzudos* notes that the word אֱלִיל (*idol*) is a contraction of the word אַל וְלֹא — something that has no use.

19. הוֹי אֹמֵר לָעֵץ הָקִיצָה . . . — *Woe to him who says to wood, 'Wake up ...'* [Scripture continues admonishing the idol-worshiping Babylonians.] Woe to the one who says to the wooden idol, "Wake up from your slumber," and to the silent stone, "Arise" (*Metzudos*). How can you, who call to it, possibly think that it can teach you what to do (*Radak*)?

הִנֵּה־הוּא תָּפוּשׂ זָהָב וָכֶסֶף ... — *Behold, it is coated with gold and silver* ... It is not even made of flesh and blood that can receive a spirit of life; it is made only of gold and silver (*Radak*). Although it may be beautiful to the sight, it hasn't any spirit in it (*Metzudos*). Not only do the images of wood and stone lack *human* spirit וְכָל־רוּחַ אֵין בְּקִרְבּוֹ, *but it has no spirit at all in its midst*. They do not even possess the *animal* spirit of life (*Radak; Metzudos*).

20. וַה׳ בְּהֵיכַל קָדְשׁוֹ — *But Hashem is in His holy Sanctuary*. [Scripture is contrasting the Omnipotence of God with the impotence of the idols.]

Although God is in His heavenly abode His Providence is over all mankind (*Radak; Metzudos*). He is ready to punish the wicked (*Rashi*). [See *Micah* 1:2; *Psalms* 11:4; *II Chronicles* 30:27; *Jonah* 2:8.] Others translate, "When God will reveal His glory in His Holy Temple" (*Mahari Kara; Abarbanel*). [See *Jonah* 2:5; *Isaiah* 5:8.]

הַס מִפָּנָיו כָּל־הָאָרֶץ — *Let all the world be silent, before Him.*" Let all of mankind be filled with awe, for He sees your every move (*Radak*). Alternatively, when God will punish the wicked and destroy their land, silence will prevail (*Rashi*).

[Verses 2:20-3:19 are read as the *Haftarah* of the second day of *Shavuos*.]

III

1. תְּפִלָּה לַחֲבַקּוּק הַנָּבִיא — *A prayer of Habakkuk the prophet.*

In the previous two chapters, Habakkuk stated that the insolence of the growing Chaldean power had taken on such extraordinary dimensions that an intervention of Divine judgment seemed absolutely necessary to save mankind from their hands lest men begin to doubt God's justice. Missing this Divine intervention, the prophet turned to God in the first chapter with his plea of "Why?" In the second chapter, the prophet received the answer to his question. True, the final universal judgment of God [קֵץ] is slow in coming. God's ultimate decree is yet distant and can be seen only in the spirit of "*A vision for the appointed time*" [חָזוֹן לַמּוֹעֵד], and the words *And it speaks of the end*

that its maker should place his trust in it to make mute idols?

[19] *Woe to him who says to wood, 'Wake up!' and to silent stone, 'Arise!' Will it teach? Behold, it is coated with gold and silver but it has no spirit at all in its midst.* [20] *But HASHEM is in His holy Sanctuary; let all the world be silent before Him."*

[1] *A prayer of Habakkuk the prophet, for erroneous utterances:*

[וְיָפֵחַ לַקֵּץ] gives an ominous intimation of this ultimate goal, yet this does not mean that we have been deceived [לֹא יְכַזֵּב] (2:3). He who puts his trust in God must patiently await the final coming of justice [אִם־יִתְמַהְמַהּ חַכֵּה־לוֹ] and must draw renewed vigor from this unshakable faith [וְצַדִּיק בֶּאֱמוּנָתוֹ יִחְיֶה]. Moreover, even before the coming of that day of judgment, the world will not succumb to the violence of the wicked because all evil, all insolence and violence, will eventually bring about its own destruction (*R' Hirsch, Psalms* 7:1).

The following, Habakkuk's prayer, is the lesson derived עַל שִׁגְיֹנוֹת, from his previous erroneous doubts.

Malbim divides this chapter into three sections. The first section (until the words מֵהַר־פָּארָן סֶלָה of v.3) is a general prayer that God should protect Israel while they are in their lengthy exile. Section Two (until the word סֶלָה of v. 13) is an elaboration of the prayers of Section One, with the addition of a prayer for God's revelation at the time of Israel's redemption. Section Three (until the end of the chapter) is a prayer regarding the tribulations that will take place in the pre-Messianic times.

תְּפִלָּה... שִׁגְיֹנוֹת — *A prayer ... erroneous utterances.*

Habakkuk now realizes that he erred [שִׁגָּיוֹן] when he impudently entreated God regarding His delay in punishing the Babylonians — see 1:4, 1:14; 2:1 (*Rashi; Mahari Kara*). He therefore beseeches God to have mercy on him and forgive his unintentional transgression (*Metzudos*).

Alternatively, *Targum Yonasan* explains that Habakkuk composed this prayer when he received the revelation that the sins of the wicked are considered as if they were merely committed unintentionally after their wholehearted repentance. Habakkuk now understood that God does not always punish the wicked immediately for their sins and gives them an opportunity to repent and therefore prayed that Israel's sins should be considered as if committed unintentionally (*Radak*).

Radak observes that the word שִׁגְיֹנוֹת is found only in one other place in all of Scripture: *Psalms* 7:1. He also notes the use of the word *selah* [סֶלָה], a word used only in *Psalms*. He therefore maintains that this prayer is a poetic song (similar to those of the *Psalms*) in which the prophet both prays that Israel will endure the hardships of exile and praises God for the miracles He has performed for them throughout their history. [שִׁגְיֹנוֹת is a technical term used for a specific form of poetic song (*Radak, Psalms* 7:1), or a type of musical instrument (*Meiri* ibid.) used in Biblical times to accompany prayer (*Rashi* to *Psalms* 7:1).

ג/ג

שָׁמַעְתִּי שִׁמְעֲךָ יָרֵאתִי יהוה פָּעָלְךָ בְּקֶרֶב שָׁנִים חַיֵּיהוּ בְּקֶרֶב שָׁנִים תּוֹדִיעַ בְּרֹגֶז רַחֵם תִּזְכּוֹר:

ג אֱלוֹהַ מִתֵּימָן יָבוֹא וְקָדוֹשׁ מֵהַר־פָּארָן סֶלָה

2. ה׳ שָׁמַעְתִּי שִׁמְעֲךָ יָרֵאתִי — *O Hashem! I have heard Your reputation [and] I became afraid.* Our translation follows *Rashi* who explains that Habakkuk was concerned and worried about the fate of his people because he had heard that since ancient times[1] God always metes out punishment to those who anger Him; however, that has not been the case with Nebuchadnezzar.[2] The prophet therefore became afraid, realizing to what depths Israel must have sunk for God to have suspended this attribute of Strict Justice against their tormentors (*Rashi*). Alternatively, *Radak* translates the word שמע as *prophecy* [see *Hosea* 7:12] and explains that Habakkuk saw through a prophetic vision that Israel will endure a lengthy and difficult exile and he feared for them. He could not understand how they could possibly survive while being in the midst of their enemies for such a length of time. According to *Ibn Ezra,* Habakkuk foresaw that a terrible famine had been decreed for the Land of Israel that would leave them incapable of defending themselves against their enemies. He therefore prayed that God have mercy and revoke the harsh decree.

ה׳ פָּעָלְךָ בְּקֶרֶב שָׁנִים חַיֵּיהוּ — *O Hashem! Your work — in the midst of the years revive it.* Habakkuk prayed that God revive His original practice and mete out swift punishment to His enemies during these years of trouble (*Rashi; Mahari Kara*). Alternatively, *Radak* translates פָּעָלְךָ as *Your handiwork,* referring to the Israelite nation, and sees this verse as the prophet's prayer on behalf of Israel: Let Israel live during their long and lengthy exile, and do not allow them to be destroyed among their enemies.

בְּקֶרֶב שָׁנִים תּוֹדִיעַ — *In the midst of the years, make it known.*

During these years [of Nebuchadnezzar's oppression] make known Your method of punishing the wicked (*Rashi*). Make known Your testimony of *Lev.* 26:44, *But despite all this, while they will be in the land of their enemies, I will not have been revolted by them nor will I have rejected them to obliterate them* (*Radak*).

Malbim understands פָּעָלְךָ to refer to the way God oversees the events of the world. He differentiates between the phrases פָּעָלְךָ בְּקֶרֶב שָׁנִים חַיֵּיהוּ and בְּקֶרֶב שָׁנִים תּוֹדִיעַ. There are two methods that God uses while His Providence oversees the Jewish people. One is in a concealed manner, בְּדֶרֶךְ נִסְתָּר, in which the world proceeds according to natural law. The second is where God performs miracles and everyone realizes that God's Providence oversees them. פָּעָלְךָ בְּקֶרֶב שָׁנִים חַיֵּיהוּ is Habakkuk's prayer that although God's Providence is not realized during the years of exile [בְּקֶרֶב שָׁנִים], it should nevertheless not cease [חַיֵּיהוּ]. בְּקֶרֶב שָׁנִים תּוֹדִיעַ is his prayer that at times God should also perform miracles for Israel so that His Providence may be known [תּוֹדִיעַ].

R' Mendel Hirsch (Haftaros) explains that God's great work [פָּעָלְךָ] of educating the human race requires the course of whole periods of time for it to become a reality [בְּקֶרֶב שָׁנִים חַיֵּיהוּ]. It is only in the course of time that God makes it known [תּוֹדִיעַ] to mankind, and makes men understand exactly what He has done.

בְּרֹגֶז רַחֵם תִּזְכּוֹר — *In wrath, remember to be merciful.*

1. *Mahari Kara* points specifically to the generation of the Great Deluge, the generation of Enosh, the generation of the Dispersion [דּוֹר הַפְּלָגָה], to Sodom and Gomorah and to Egypt, where wicked actions were immediately punished.

2. King Solomon, the builder of the great Temple, reigned for only 40 years, while the wicked Nebuchadnezzar, the destroyer of the Temple, reigned for 45 years (*Mahari Kara*).

[2] O HASHEM, I have heard Your reputation [and] I became afraid. O HASHEM! Your work — in the midst of the years revive it; in the midst of the years, make it known. In wrath, remember to be merciful.

[3] God came from Teman; the Holy One from Mount Paran, Selah!

In Your wrath that You display against the wicked, be compassionate to Israel (*Rashi*). Alternatively, "Even if, in Your wrath, You wish to deliver Israel into the hands of their enemies, be compassionate with them and save them" (*Mahari Kara*). *Radak* sees the *time of wrath* as the time of exile and explains, "during the years that Israel is in exile, recall the love of their forefathers." (See *Lev.* 26:45, *and I will remember for them the covenant of the ancients.*)[1]

3-6. The prophet now enumerates the many miracles God performed for Israel during their sojourn through the desert before leading them into the Land of Israel. It is the prophet's prayer that God again revive this love for Israel and redeem them from the present exile with miracles that are just as great and awesome as those performed in the wilderness (*Radak*).

3. ... אֱלוֹהַ מִתֵּימָן יָבוֹא — *God came from Teman ...*

This verse is referring to the revelation on Sinai when God came to give the Torah (*Rashi; Radak*). The Talmud (*Avodah Zarah* 2b) writes that before God came to Israel to offer them the Torah, He first approached every nation of the world but it was only Israel who was willing to accept it. Alternatively, Habakkuk is referring to the miracles that God performed for Israel when they circumvented the territory of Edom and fought against the two powerful Canaanite kings, Sichon and Og — see *Deut.* 2:31, 3:3 (*Metzudos*). According to *Malbim* verses 4-13 are foretelling events that will occur at the time of the ultimate redemption of Israel, with this verse acting as an introduction. He explains that during the last exile, Israel will be oppressed by two kingdoms, the Edomites and the Ishmaelites. As He did in the days of Moses, God will again confront the Edomites [referred to in Scripture as *Teman*] and the Ishmaelites [referred to as *Mount Paran*], but this time to reprimand them and show them that the religions they accepted upon themselves are far from that which He offered at Sinai.

As in *Deut.* 33:2, Scripture specifically enumerates the Edomites and Ishmaelites for they dwelt near Mount Sinai (*Radak*). Although the word תֵּימָן actually means south — see *Targum Yonasan* — it is also a proper noun, for Teman was the name of one of Esau's grandsons — see *Gen.* 36:11 — and it may have therefore become synonymous with Seir and Edom — see *Amos* 1:12; *Obadiah* 1:9; *Jeremiah* 49:20. Paran is a reference to Ishmael for it was he who settled in Paran — see *Gen.* 21:21 (*Rashi*).

סֶלָה — *Selah!*

Many translations and explanations of *selah* are offered by the commentators. *Targum Yonasan* translates *forever* or *everlasting* [לְעָלְמִין], referring to God's everlasting strength. *Ibn Ezra*

1. *Radak* explains homiletically that the numerical value of רַחֵם is identical to the numerical value of the name אַבְרָהָם, the Patriarch Abraham [248]. The prophet is saying, "During the time of Your wrath remember רַחֵם [248], the covenant made with the Patriarch Abraham."

ד כִּסָּה שָׁמַיִם הוֹדוֹ וּתְהִלָּתוֹ מָלְאָה הָאָרֶץ: וְנֹגַהּ כָּאוֹר תִּהְיֶה קַרְנַיִם מִיָּדוֹ לוֹ וְשָׁם חֶבְיוֹן עֻזֹּה: ה־ו לְפָנָיו יֵלֶךְ דָּבֶר וְיֵצֵא רֶשֶׁף לְרַגְלָיו: עָמַד | וַיְמֹדֶד אֶרֶץ רָאָה וַיַּתֵּר גּוֹיִם וַיִּתְפֹּצְצוּ הַרְרֵי־עַד

maintains that *selah* is synonymous with אֱמֶת [truth]. *Radak* (*Psalms* 3:3) notes that other than in this song of praise, the word *selah* is found only in the Book of *Psalms*. Using *Isaiah* 62:10 as his source, *Radak* translates the word *selah* as *elevate*. It is an instruction for the one reciting the psalm [or praise] to elevate his voice at that point. *Malbim* writes that *selah* is used in Scripture to signify the conclusion of a certain idea. [At times it may also be used to indicate that part of a verse is parenthetic.] Here, *selah* indicates the conclusion of Section one of Habakkuk's prayer — see intro. to Chapter 3.

כִּסָּה שָׁמַיִם הוֹדוֹ ... — *His glory covered the heavens . . .*

When Israel accepted the Torah at Sinai, God's Glory covered the heavens and His Praise filled the earth (*Rashi; Mahari Kara*). This is a reference to the flames, לַפִּידִים, that lit up the heavens and earth on the day the Torah was given [see *Exodus* 20:15] (*Radak*).

Malbim renders, Although His Glory is concealed by the heavens (for the world seems to be governed by natural law), nevertheless, the inhabitants of the earth have started to recognize that all of nature is governed by Divine Law and for this they praise Him.

4. וְנֹגַהּ כָּאוֹר תִּהְיֶה — *A glow was like the light [of day].* The light of the day of the Sinaitic Revelation was as brilliant as the supernal light of the seven days of Creation (*Rashi*). [See *Rashi, Genesis* 1:4;14.] Alternatively, *Radak* sees this verse referring to *Exodus* 24:17 where Scripture writes that the sight of God's Glory [on Mount Sinai] was like a consuming fire on the top of the mountain. According to *Ibn Ezra* and *Metzudos*, Scripture is referring to the pillar of fire that guided the Israelite nation in the desert. The pillar of fire was as bright as the light of midday.

R' Mendel Hirsch understands this figuratively and renders *and the gleam will then become like bright light.* The knowledge and understanding of God which is now only a yearning in people's hearts [only a weak gleam or glimmer] will become a bright light radiating throughout the world.

קַרְנַיִם מִיָּדוֹ לוֹ — *Rays of light [came] from His hand to [Israel].*

The word קֶרֶן, which literally means *horn*, is used to describe the light that shines through a hole and gives the appearance of horns — i.e., rays of light. The phrase means that the light of that day came to the Israelite nation from the hands of God, i.e., directly from God (*Rashi*). Alternatively, this section of the verse is referring to the luminescence of Moses' face. This luminescence came from the hand of God (*Radak*).

Metzudos understands the verse figuratively and translates קֶרֶן as *horn*. The horn is symbolic of power (cf. *Devarim* 33:17) for the animals use their horns to gain power over one another. Scripture is stating that the dominion and increasing strength that Israel acquired was granted directly from God's hands.

וְשָׁם חֶבְיוֹן עֻזֹּה — *And there His hidden strength [was revealed].*

And there, at Sinai, He revealed His power that was previously hidden (*Rashi*).

The commentators however differ in their interpretations of עֻזֹּה, *His strength*. *Radak* explains that עֻזֹּה is referring to God's Glory. At no other time did God reveal His Glory as He did at Sinai. Alternatively, God's strength is referring to the Tablets of

His glory covered the heavens His praise filled the earth.

[4] A glow was like the light [of day]; rays of light [came] from His hand to [Israel]; and there His hidden strength [was revealed].

[5] Before Him goes pestilence; and fire went forth at His feet.

[6] He stood and measured out the land; He looked and dispersed nations. Everlasting mountains were smashed,

the Commandments, which were previously concealed in the heavens and were afterwards placed in the Ark — see *Psalms* 132:8 where the tablets are referred to as עֹז (*Metzudos*). *Mahari Kara* writes that עֻזֹּה is the Torah that had been kept hidden for 2000 years prior to the Sinaitic Revelation.

5. לְפָנָיו יֵלֶךְ דָּבֶר — *Before Him goes pestilence.*

Just as when the Israelite nation observed God's commandments He performed miracles for them, so too, when they disobeyed His word during their 40 years in the desert, He inflicted them with pestilence and other punishments (*Radak; Abarbanel*). Alternatively, this is referring to the capturing of the land of Canaan. The pestilence and other forms of destructive agents went before God's Glory or before the Holy Ark to punish the heathen nations — see *Exodus* 23:28 (*Ibn Ezra*).

In a Midrashic interpretation, *Rashi* writes that when God gave the Torah to Israel, He distracted the Angel of Death and occupied him with other matters so that he should not complain and question His decision to give the Torah to the nation who would, in forty days, be guilty of heresy through the worship of the Golden Calf. Similarly, *Targum Yonasan* translates מִן קֳדָמוֹהִי מִשְׁתַּלַּח מַלְאַךְ מוֹתָא, *the Angel of Death was banished before Him.*

וְיֵצֵא רֶשֶׁף לְרַגְלָיו — *And fire went forth at His feet.* Fiery angels came with Him to Sinai (*Rashi*) to destroy the world if Israel would not accept the Torah (*Mahari Kara*). Alternatively, *Radak* and *Ibn Ezra* understand רֶשֶׁף as a synonym for דֶּבֶר and translate both words as *pestilence.*

6. עָמַד וַיְמֹדֶד אֶרֶץ — *He stood and measured out the land.* Our translation follows *Rashi* who understands that Habakkuk is praising God for the manner in which He exacts punishment from the wicked, measure for measure. He waited to exact punishment from the generation of the Great Flood, measure for measure. For they sinned with heat, by arousing themselves to sin, and were therefore similarly punished with the boiling waters of the flood — see *Sanhedrin* 108b (*Rashi*).

רָאָה וַיַּתֵּר גּוֹיִם — *He looked and dispersed nations.*

He looked at the generation of the Tower of Babel and saw that since all the people communicated with one another in a common language, a unanimous rebellion against God resulted. He therefore exacted punishment from them by dispersing the nations through the development of seventy languages (*Rashi*).

וַיִּתְפֹּצְצוּ הַרְרֵי־עַד... — *Everlasting mountains were smashed ...*

The *everlasting mountains* are an allegorical reference to the officers of the nations (*Rashi*). *Mahari Kara* specifically notes Pharaoh and the king of Sodom. God smashed them and humiliated them.

ז שַׁחוּ גִּבְעוֹת עוֹלָם הֲלִיכוֹת עוֹלָם לוֹ: תַּחַת אָוֶן רָאִיתִי אָהֳלֵי כוּשָׁן יִרְגְּזוּן יְרִיעוֹת אֶרֶץ
ח מִדְיָן: הֲבִנְהָרִים חָרָה יהוה אִם בַּנְּהָרִים אַפֶּךָ אִם־בַּיָּם עֶבְרָתֶךָ כִּי תִרְכַּב
ט עַל־סוּסֶיךָ מַרְכְּבֹתֶיךָ יְשׁוּעָה: עֶרְיָה תֵעוֹר קַשְׁתֶּךָ שְׁבֻעוֹת מַטּוֹת אֹמֶר סֶלָה נְהָרוֹת
י תְּבַקַּע־אָרֶץ: רָאוּךָ יָחִילוּ הָרִים זֶרֶם

הֲלִיכוֹת עוֹלָם לוֹ — *For the ways of the world are His.*

He showed them that the conduct of the entire universe is only according to what He orders (*Rashi*).

Alternatively, *Radak* translates *He stood and measured out the land* and identifies the Holy Ark as the subject of the verse. The Ark tarried in Gilgal for fourteen years until the Israelite nation captured the land [of Canaan] and accurately distributed it. *He looked and dispersed nations* — from there [Gilgal] the Ark was victorious in its battle over the nations; as if it merely looked at the nations and caused their downfall. *Everlasing mountains were smashed* — He smashed and scattered the mighty Canaanite kings. *The ways of the world are His* — God does to the nations of the world as He desires, elevating one nation and humbling another, driving one nation out of its territory and giving its land to another.

7-13. Habakkuk continues his review of Israel's history. He points out that although God often did miracles for them, at times He displayed His anger toward His nation; when they sinned against Him and did not follow His Torah. But as soon as they returned to Him, He again miraculously delivered their enemies into their hands (*Abarbanel*).

7. תַּחַת אָוֶן רָאִיתִי אָהֳלֵי כוּשָׁן — *Because of [our] iniquity I saw the tents of Cushan.*

Because the Israelite nation worshiped heathen gods, God punished them by delivering them into the hands of the armies of Cushan-rishathaim [see *Judges* Ch. 3] (*Targum Yonasan; Rashi*).

יִרְגְּזוּן יְרִיעוֹת אֶרֶץ מִדְיָן — *The curtains of the land of Midian trembled.* But when Israel repented and returned to God, He miraculously saved them through the judge Gideon [see *Judges* 6-8] who attacked the Midianites (*Targum Yonasan*). The *curtains of the land of Midian* are their tents, for, in essence, tents are the spreading of hangings [over poles] (*Radak*).

According to *Malbim* [see comm. to v. 3] vv. 7-14 are referring to the miracles that will take place at the time of the future redemption of Israel. The first miracle listed is the return of the Ten Tribes of Israel who, in *Malbim's* opinion, were exiled to the land of Cush. The Ten Tribes will leave the land of Cush and will wage war with the Ishmaelites on the way back to Israel. [*Malbim* maintains that the land of Ishmael is synonymous with the land of Midian — see *Genesis* Ch. 37: 28, 36.]

8. הֲבִנְהָרִים חָרָה ה׳ ... — *Was Hashem angry with the rivers ...* The "הֲ" of הֲבִנְהָרִים designates a question [ה הַשְּׁאֵלָה].

During the days of Joshua, God miraculously dried up the Jordan River [נְהָרִים][1] enabling the Israelite nation to cross into Canaan on dry land. So too, in the days of Moses, He split the Sea of Reeds [בַּיָּם] and the nation crossed on dry land (*Radak*). Can it be that God's wrath and anger was directed against

1. *Radak* notes that Scripture does not list the miracles in historical order.

eternal hills were laid low; for the ways of the world are His.

[7] Because of [our] iniquity I saw the tents of Cushan; the curtains of the land of Midian trembled.

[8] Was HASHEM *angry with the rivers; was Your wrath with the rivers, or Your fury against the Sea? Rather You rode upon Your horses, Your chariots were [our] salvation.*

[9] Your bow bared itself; the oaths to the tribes, an enduring word. You split open the earth with rivers. [10] Mountains saw You and shuddered; a stream of

the rivers and seas when He performed miracles with them?

כִּי תִרְכַּב עַל־סוּסֶיךָ מַרְכְּבֹתֶיךָ יְשׁוּעָה — *Rather You rode upon Your horses, Your chariots were [our] salvation.* Rather it is because You wished to bring salvation and victory to Your nation that You performed these miracles (*Metzudos*). The horses and chariots are used figuratively as symbols of God's glory that fought and brought victory for Israel against Pharaoh at the Sea of Reeds (*Radak*).

Alternatively, *Targum Yonasan* and *Rashi* explain: God's wrath was directed upon the kings and armies of the nations who were as abundant as the waters of a river. The revelation of Your miracles on behalf of Israel demonstrated Your strength and salvation. *Ibn Ezra* sees the prophet extolling God's greatness in His ability to bring rain to Israel. The prophet expresses wonder at the formation of clouds that develop from the rivers and seas and then travel to the area that God designates.

9. עֶרְיָה תֵעוֹר קַשְׁתֶּךָ — *Your bow bared itself.* God's might is portrayed as if He is a warrior grasping a bow and is preparing to shoot an arrow (*Rashi*). In the previous verse the prophet figuratively used horses [סוּסֶיךָ] to symbolize victory. Here, the analogy of a bow is used to describe God's strength (*Radak*).

שְׁבֻעוֹת מַטּוֹת — *The oaths to the tribes.* God's strength was revealed so that He may fulfill the oaths that He swore to the forefathers when He proclaimed that He would give the Land of Israel to their descendants, the Tribes of Israel (*Radak*).

According to *Ibn Ezra* who explained the previous verse as a prayer thanking God for plentiful rain, the קֶשֶׁת is referring to the rainbow that follows a rain. The מַטּוֹת ("rods") are the bolts of lightning that follow God's command.

אֹמֶר סֶלָה — *An enduring word.* The word אֹמֶר is vowelized with a סֶגּוֹל and is accented on the first syllable as it is a noun [and not a verb] (*Rashi*). The word *selah* in this verse means everlasting [see comm. to v. 3] (*Rashi; Radak*). The oath that God made to the forefathers will last forever.

נְהָרוֹת תְּבַקַּע־אָרֶץ — *You split open the earth with rivers.* You split the dry earth to give Your nation water. [The water that God gave Israel in the desert was in such great abundance that it appeared like rivers flowing in the desert — see *Psalms* 78:16] (*Radak*).

10. רָאוּךָ יָחִילוּ הָרִים ... — *Mountains saw You and shuddered ...* When the mountains on each side of the Arnon brook saw Your glory leading the Israelite nation, they trembled and miraculously moved closer to each other and thereby crushed the Amorites who were

מַיִם עָבָר נָתַן תְּהוֹם קוֹלוֹ רוֹם יָדֵיהוּ נָשָׂא׃
יא שֶׁמֶשׁ יָרֵחַ עָמַד זְבֻלָה לְאוֹר חִצֶּיךָ יְהַלֵּכוּ
יב לְנֹגַהּ בְּרַק חֲנִיתֶךָ׃ בְּזַעַם תִּצְעַד־אָרֶץ בְּאַף
יג תָּדוּשׁ גּוֹיִם׃ יָצָאתָ לְיֵשַׁע עַמֶּךָ לְיֵשַׁע אֶת־מְשִׁיחֶךָ
מָחַצְתָּ רֹּאשׁ מִבֵּית רָשָׁע עָרוֹת יְסוֹד עַד־צַוָּאר
יד סֶלָה׃ נָקַבְתָּ בְמַטָּיו רֹאשׁ °פרזו יִסְעֲרוּ

°פְּרָזָיו ק׳

hiding in caves waiting to attack the unsuspecting Israelites (*Rashi; Metzudos* [see *Rashi, Numbers* 21:15]). *Targum Yonasan*, however, sees this phrase as referring to the revelation at Sinai.

Alternatively, *Radak* understands this verse figuratively. The mountains symbolize the Canaanite kings who became terrified and trembled when they heard about the great miracles that God performed for Israel in the desert. [A confirmed report, although only *heard*, may be described as "seen." Hence, the use of the word ראה instead of שמע (see *Gen.* 42:1).]

זֶרֶם מַיִם עָבָר — *A stream of water flowed. Rashi* sees this phrase as referring to the miraculous interruption of the flowing waters of the Jordan River that allowed the Israelite nation to cross over a dry riverbed [see *Joshua* Ch. 3]. Surging waters passed downstream while the water from upstream, which would normally have flowed into its place, miraculously rose up in a column. *Metzudos*, however, sees this as a continuation of the miracle described at the onset of the verse. After the mountains of Arnon crushed the Amorites, the waters of the well that had traveled with the Israelite nation through the desert passed through the two mountains and brought forth the limbs and bodies of the enemy so that Israel would realize the miracle that had taken place (as described in *Rashi* to *Numbers* 21:16).

נָתַן תְּהוֹם קוֹלוֹ — *The depth raised its voice.* The mortal inhabitants of the earth praised God [for the miracle at the Jordan River] (*Rashi*). Alternatively, *Metzudos* explains that the waters of the well that had publicized the miracle [by bringing up the limbs of the enemies] caused the people to praise God for their salvation. *Radak* says that it refers to the sound that the waters of the Jordan River emitted when it was split.

רוֹם יָדֵיהוּ נָשָׂא — *And the heights [of Heaven] raised their hands.* The heavenly hosts as well raised their hands in praise of God [upon witnessing this great miracle] (*Rashi*). Alternatively, *Radak* sees this phrase as another description of the miracle of the Jordan River. The river was full with water and it rose and towered in a tall column. It was as if the depths of water rose up and lifted its hands up high.

11. שֶׁמֶשׁ יָרֵחַ עָמַד זְבֻלָה — *The sun and the moon stood still in their abodes.* The sun and the moon temporarily ceased their heavenly orbit when Joshua led the Israelite nation against the Canaanite kings in Gibeon (*Rashi; Radak*) [see *Joshua* 10:13].

לְאוֹר חִצֶּיךָ יְהַלֵּכוּ ... — *[Israel] would travel by the light of Your arrows ...* Israel pursued her enemies (*Rashi*) to the light of the glistening metal of God's arrows (*Metzudos*). This is a figurative way of saying that Israel was victorious due to Divine intervention and not their own military strength (*Metzudos*). Alternatively, *Radak* explains that God's arrows are bolts of lightning, for together with the hailstones that fell upon the Canaanite kings [see *Joshua* 10:11], there were bolts of lightning.

water flowed. The depth raised its voice, and the heights [of Heaven] raised their hands.

[11]*The sun and the moon stood still in their abodes. [Israel] would travel by the light of Your arrows, by the lightning flash of Your spear.*

[12]*In fury You trod the earth; in anger You trampled nations.*

[13]*You went forth to save Your people, to save Your anointed one. You crushed the head of the house of the wicked, laying bare from the foundation to the neck, Selah!*

[14]*With his own staffs You pierced the head of his outspread troops, who came storming to*

Malbim, who interprets these verses as a reference to the future redemption of Israel, explains that just as in the days of Joshua the sun and moon ceased their orbit, so too, will this miracle occur again when Israel will battle with her enemies.

12. בְּזַעַם תִּצְעַד־אָרֶץ ... — *In fury You trod the earth* ... In rage You trod upon the land of Canaan to drive out the seven nations who inhabited it (*Rashi; Radak*).

This verse is proof to what was said earlier [v. 8]. It was not that God vented His anger against the rivers or seas, but against the heathen nations (*Mahari Kara*).

13. יָצָאתָ לְיֵשַׁע עַמֶּךָ — *You went forth to save Your people.* [You always led Your nation in battle and performed miracles on their behalf, for You wished to save Your nation from their enemies.]

לְיֵשַׁע אֶת־מְשִׁיחֶךָ — *To save Your anointed one.* [You went forth] for the salvation of Kings Saul and David [who were anointed as kings] (*Rashi*).

עָרוֹת יְסוֹד עַד־צַוָּאר — *Laying bare from the foundation to the neck.* You laid bare the foundations of the walls of their enemies and together with their "necklike" tall towers, they were destroyed (*Rashi*).

Alternatively, just as God came to the salvation of His nation when they entered the land of Canaan, so too, will He come to their salvation and take them out of exile and bring them to the Land of Israel. Accordingly, *Your anointed one* (מְשִׁיחֶךָ) is referring to the Messiah and *the head of the house of the wicked* is the head of the army of the wicked Gog (*Radak*). *Mahari Kara* sees this verse as recalling the exodus from Egypt. God went forth [see *Ex.* 11:4] to save His nation Israel [Your anointed one] and smote the firstborn of Pharaoh [the head of the house of the wicked]. According to *Metzudos,* the *anointed* one is referring to Hezekiah, king of Judah, and the victory God wrought for him over the wicked Sennacherib [see *II Kings* 18-19].

14-19. Again, the commentators differ in the explanation of this verse. *Rashi* and *Metzudos* see Sennacherib and his officers as the subject of God's punishment, while *Radak* maintains that the verse is referring to Messianic times and that Gog is the subject. *Mahari Kara* sees the verse referring to Pharaoh.

14. נָקַבְתָּ בְמַטָּיו רֹאשׁ פְּרָזָיו — *With his own staffs You pierced the head of his outspread troops.* [This is an expression describing the fall of Sennacherib.] God did to Sennacherib that which the

לְהֲפִיצֵנִי עֲלִיצֻתָם כְּמוֹ־לֶאֱכֹל עָנִי בַּמִּסְתָּר׃

טו־טז דָּרַכְתָּ בַיָּם סוּסֶיךָ חֹמֶר מַיִם רַבִּים׃ שָׁמַעְתִּי | וַתִּרְגַּז בִּטְנִי לְקוֹל צָלֲלוּ שְׂפָתַי יָבוֹא רָקָב בַּעֲצָמַי וְתַחְתַּי אֶרְגָּז אֲשֶׁר אָנוּחַ לְיוֹם צָרָה לַעֲלוֹת

יז לְעַם יְגוּדֶנּוּ׃ כִּי־תְאֵנָה לֹא־תִפְרָח וְאֵין יְבוּל

wicked king intended to do to Israel. He attempted to destroy the inhabitants of Jerusalem but instead it was he that was killed (*Metzudos*). Alternatively, when Gog will rise up to conquer Jerusalem, God will cause terror and panic to overtake his armies and they will strike one another's head in confusion (*Radak*).

Mahari Kara interprets *Pharaoh, king of Egypt, was struck by Moses' staff*, but this is to be understood figuratively [because Moses would never strike the king]. Moses hit the sea with his staff *causing* Pharaoh to drown.

רֹאשׁ פְּרָזָיו — *The head of his outspread troops. Rashi* renders רֹאשׁ פְּרָזָיו as the leaders of the cities [פְּרָזִים being unwalled cities]. Alternatively, *Radak* and *Metzudos* translate רֹאשׁ literally, *the head of the body*. They interpret פְּרָזָיו to mean *armies*, for armies usually come in large numbers and camp out in the open terrain around the city. Thus, the meaning of the phrase is, *The heads of the soldiers will be smashed.*

יִסְעֲרוּ לַהֲפִיצֵנִי — *Who came storming to scatter me.* A רוּחַ סְעָרָה is a whirlwind. It was Sennacherib's intent to scatter the nation of Israel into other lands (see *II Kings* Ch. 36 and *Isaiah* Ch. 19) as a whirlwind scatters everything in its path (*Metzudos*).

עֲלִיצֻתָם — *Their joy.* The only joy of Sennacherib and his armies is that they are capable of destroying Israel (*Rashi*).

Radak explains: Just as Pharaoh had intended to destroy the Israelite nation and joyfully pursued them thinking that God could not stop him for He has no power over the seas, so too, does the nation of Gog rejoice at the thought of scattering Israel.

The עָנִי [poor man] of this verse is Israel who is referred to as the poor nation (*Rashi*) [see *Isaiah* 54:11].

15. דָּרַכְתָּ בַיָּם סוּסֶיךָ — *You trampled [them] in the sea with Your horses.* This verse is to be understood figuratively. God trampled Sennacherib's army that was as numerous as the sand of the sea (*Rashi*). Alternatively, just as in the days of Pharaoh it was God who fought for Israel at the Sea of Reeds [see *Ex.* 14:28], so too, will God fight for Israel against the armies of Gog (*Radak*).

חֹמֶר מַיִם רַבִּים — *With mountains of abundant water.* The word חֹמֶר means heaps as in *Exodus* 8:10 (*Rashi*). [According to *Rashi*, the reference is again referring to the vast army of Sennacherib and according to *Radak* the waters of the Sea of Reeds — see *Exodus* 15:8.]

16. שָׁמַעְתִּי וַתִּרְגַּז בִּטְנִי — *I heard and my innards shuddered.* After hearing about the punishments that God had wrought upon the Egyptians, Babylonia trembled (*Targum Yonasan; Rashi*). Alternatively, *Radak* interprets that it is the prophet who is trembling, for he has prophetically heard of the suffering that the Jews will endure on the day Gog will come upon them. According to *Mahari Kara*, Habakkuk heard that God will again bring salvation to Israel with the fall of Babylonia, and his insides trembled, personifying the terror that would grip the defeated Babylonians.

לְקוֹל צָלֲלוּ שְׂפָתַי — *My lips quivered at the report. Rashi* relates צָלֲלוּ to מְצִלּוֹת הַסּוּס (*Zechariah* 14:20), the clanging

scatter me. Their joy came when they could devour a poor man in secret.

[15]*You trampled [them] in the sea with Your horses, with mountains of abundant water.*

[16]*I heard and my innards shuddered; my lips quivered at the report. Rot came into my bones and I shuddered in my place; because the time I should have rested will become a day of distress, for a people to come up with its troops.*

[17]*For the fig tree blossoms not; there is no fruit*

bells that ornamented the horses. He therefore explains צָלְלוּ as the lips *made noise,* i.e., as bells, and renders, "I trembled at the report that I heard until my lips quivered so violently that they made noise" (*Rashi; Radak*).

This symbolizes that all who will hear of the fall of Babylonia, their ears will tingle (*Mahari Kara*).

יָבוֹא רָקָב בַּעֲצָמַי — *Rot came into my bones.* Even my bones, the hardest material found in the human body, rotted, as it were, at the news [of that which will occur on that day] (*Radak*).

This is symbolizing that the Babylonians will not be able to move at all (*Mahari Kara*).

וְתַחְתַּי אֶרְגָּז — *And I shuddered in my place.* I trembled in *every* place that I stood. Wherever I stood I could not remove the report from my mind (*Metzudos*).

אֲשֶׁר אָנוּחַ לְיוֹם צָרָה ... — *Because the time I should have rested will become a day of distress ...* Babylonia is trembling at the thought of her destruction and proclaims that her calm rest is only a preparation for her day of trouble, the day that God will take Israel up from Babylonia and return her with her troops to her land (*Rashi*). Alternatively, it is Israel who is speaking. Israel thought that she would dwell in tranquility after she returned to her land, but that day of rest has become a day of distress (*Radak*). The day that Gog will rise up against Israel is referred to throughout Scripture as a day of great distress — see *Daniel* 12:1, *And there shall be a time of trouble such as never was* (*Radak*).

Mahari Kara renders, "When the day of distress will fall upon Babylonia, then will Israel rest." [This is referring to the defeat of Belshazzar, king of Babylonia, by the Median king Darius.]

17. כִּי־תְאֵנָה לֹא־תִפְרָח — *For the fig tree blossoms not.* The commentators explain this verse figuratively. *Rashi* sees the verse referring to the Babylonians. From this day on the Babylonians will not be successful in anything they attempt to do. *Targum Yonasan* understands that the verse is referring to many different nations: the Babylonians, the Medes, the heathen nations in general and the Romans. They all will ultimately be unsuccessful in their attempts to prevail against Israel and Jerusalem. According to *Radak* many nations will ally themselves with Gog and Magog in the Messianic era to destroy Israel but they will not be successful. *Metzudos* sees the fig tree as representing the thus far unblossomed Israelite nation. They haven't yet the power and strength to stand up in battle against Gog. Habakkuk therefore prays that God assist Israel in their fight against Gog.

בַּגְּפָנִים כִּחֵשׁ מַעֲשֵׂה־זַיִת וּשְׁדֵמוֹת לֹא־עָשָׂה
יח אֹכֶל גָּזַר מִמִּכְלָה צֹאן וְאֵין בָּקָר בָּרְפָתִים: וַאֲנִי
יט בַּיהוָה אֶעְלוֹזָה אָגִילָה בֵּאלֹהֵי יִשְׁעִי: יֱהֹוִה אֲדֹנָי
חֵילִי וַיָּשֶׂם רַגְלַי כָּאַיָּלוֹת וְעַל בָּמוֹתַי יַדְרִכֵנִי
לַמְנַצֵּחַ בִּנְגִינוֹתָי:

וְאֵין יְבוּל בַּגְּפָנִים ... — *There is no fruit on the grapevines ...* The entire verse is figuratively describing Israel's lack of strength and lack of understanding of strategic warfare (*Metzudos*).

18. וַאֲנִי בַּה׳ אֶעְלוֹזָה ... — *But as for me, in Hashem will I rejoice.* I, the Israelite nation, will rejoice with God's help at the destruction of Babylon (*Rashi; Mahari Kara*), or when the armies of Gog will perish (*Radak*).

Malbim differentiates between אֶעְלוֹזָה and אָגִילָה. עָלַז is the physical expression of joy through dancing. גִילָה is the emotional feeling of joy felt in one's heart.

19. יֱהֹוִה אֲדֹנָי חֵילִי — *Hashem/Elohim, the Lord is my strength.* Although we [the Jewish people] are the minority, God will take the place of a large army (*Metzudos*).

The unusual Name of God, "יֱהֹוִה", which has the spelling of the four-letter Name but the punctuation of *Elohim* combines God's attribute of mercy, יהוה, with His attribute of Judgment, אֱלֹהִים, implying the plea that even in judgment, God should temper His decree with mercy — see ArtScroll *Bereishis* 15:8.

וַיָּשֶׂם רַגְלַי כָּאַיָּלוֹת — *He makes my legs [as swift] as harts.* He makes me

on the grapevines; the labor of the olive trees has failed and the fields do not yield food; the sheep are cut off from the fold and no cattle are in the stall.

[18] *But as for me, in* HASHEM *will I rejoice; I will exult in the God of my salvation.*

[19] HASHEM/ELOHIM, *the Lord, is my strength. He makes my legs [as swift] as harts; and upon my high places He leads me. To the conductor, [for accompaniment] with my songs.*

fleetfooted to pursue my enemies (*Radak*). Harts are known for their swiftness (*Mahari Kara*).

וְעַל בָּמוֹתַי יַדְרִכֵנִי — *And upon my high places He leads me.*

The high places are referring to places in the Land of Israel in general and to Jerusalem in particular. Habakkuk is pleading on behalf of Israel, "Help me tread upon the high places of my country and help me destroy my enemies" (*Radak*).

לַמְנַצֵּחַ בִּנְגִינוֹתָי — *To the conductor, [for accompaniment] with my songs.* Habakkuk instructs the Levites who played musical instruments in the Temple to accompany the reading of this prayer with a particular tune chosen by the prophet (*Metzudos*).

I will sing praises to Hashem for the miraculous victory He granted me (*Radak*).

The word מְנַצֵּחַ literally means "a victor." It is used when describing group singing for it is common for each person involved to outsing [sing louder than] his colleagues (*Metzudos*).

Zephaniah

א/א־ג

א דְּבַר־יְהוָ֣ה ׀ אֲשֶׁ֣ר הָיָ֗ה אֶל־צְפַנְיָה֙ בֶּן־כּוּשִׁ֣י בֶן־גְּדַלְיָ֔ה בֶּן־אֲמַרְיָ֖ה בֶּן־חִזְקִיָּ֑ה בִּימֵ֛י יֹאשִׁיָּ֥הוּ
ב בֶן־אָמ֖וֹן מֶ֥לֶךְ יְהוּדָֽה׃ אָסֹ֨ף אָסֵ֜ף כֹּ֗ל מֵעַ֛ל פְּנֵ֥י
ג הָאֲדָמָ֖ה נְאֻם־יְהוָֽה׃ אָסֵ֨ף אָדָ֜ם וּבְהֵמָ֗ה אָסֵ֤ף
עוֹף־הַשָּׁמַ֙יִם֙ וּדְגֵ֣י הַיָּ֔ם וְהַמַּכְשֵׁל֖וֹת אֶת־הָרְשָׁעִ֑ים

I

1. דְּבַר־ה׳ ... — *The word of Hashem.*

[These are the prophetic words of God that were issued to the Jewish people through Zephaniah.] The introductory phrase דְּבַר־ה׳, *the word of Hashem,* prefaces many of the Scripture books. According to R' Yochanan (*Bereishis Rabbah* 44:7), דִּבּוּר introduces a fateful and foreboding prophecy. Zephaniah tells of the terrible destruction that will befall the Land of Israel in general, her heathen neighbors and the Land of the Judean Kingdom in particular.

אֲשֶׁר הָיָה אֶל־צְפַנְיָה — *That came to Zephaniah.*

Zephaniah was a disciple of the prophet Habakkuk and was the mentor of the prophet Jeremiah (*Rambam — Introduction to Mishneh Torah*). He was one of three prophets who prophesied during the reign of Josiah: Jeremiah, Zephaniah and Huldah. Jeremiah prophesied in the streets, Zephaniah in the synagogues and houses of study, and Huldah directed her words to the women. Nevertheless, the people did not heed their words (*Pesikta,* cited by *Yalkut*).

בֶּן־כּוּשִׁי ... בֶּן־חִזְקִיָּה — *Son of Cushi ... son of Hezekiah.*

Although nothing is mentioned regarding Cushi, the prophet's father, he probably was a prophet as well, for as is the rule throughout Scripture, when the name of the prophet's father is mentioned together with him, it indicates that the father, too, was a prophet of G-d (*Megillah* 15a).

The identity of Zephaniah's ancestor Hezekiah is the subject of a dispute among the commentators. *Ibn Ezra* contends that this refers to Hezekiah, king of Judah. Thus, Amariah was the brother of Manasseh, Hezekiah's successor, and Gedaliah was a first cousin to Amon. This would make Zephaniah a generation younger than King Josiah. Nevertheless, it is not incomprehensible that they should have lived at the same time, since it was over one hundred years from the time Hezekiah reached adulthood until Josiah assumed the throne. *Abarbanel* contests this theory, arguing that neither Scripture nor the Sages would have allowed so vital a fact to go unmentioned. *Radak* is uncertain on this issue. In any event, although Hezekiah, Zephaniah's ancestor, may not have been the king of Judah, he was nevertheless a prominent person who was held in esteem by the people (*Radak*). *Abarbanel* thinks that he, too, may have been a prophet.

בִּימֵי יֹאשִׁיָּהוּ בֶן־אָמוֹן מֶלֶךְ יְהוּדָה — *In the days of Josiah son of Amon, king of Judah.*

Josiah became king at the age of eight (*II Kings* 22:1) after his father, the wicked Amon, had been assassinated by his servants. In contrast to his father, he did what was *proper in the eyes of God* (ibid. v.2). *Before him there had never been a king like him who returned to Hashem with all his heart, with all his soul ...* (ibid. 23:25). The Sages disagree [only] as to whether Josiah had first sinned and then repented or whether he was righteous from the start (*Shabbos* 56b).

[1] *The word of HASHEM that came to Zephaniah, son of Cushi, son of Gedaliah, son of Amariah, son of Hezekiah, in the days of Josiah son of Amon, king of Judah:*

[2] *I will utterly destroy everything from upon the face of the land — the word of HASHEM.* [3] *I will destroy man and animal; I will destroy the bird of the sky and the fish of the sea and the stumbling blocks of the wicked;*

The precise timing of Zephaniah's prophecy is a matter of contention. Despite Josiah's righteousness, Zephaniah continued to prophesy during his reign concerning the nation's defeat and exile. Although Josiah followed G-d wholeheartedly, the decree of the Jewish nation's exile remained intact due to the abundance and magnitude of the sins that had been committed before his time. However, because of Josiah's merit, it did not occur in his lifetime (*Mahari Kara*). Others maintain that Zephaniah prophesied during the early years of Josiah's reign, prior to his repentance and return to righteousness. Indeed, it is possible that these prophecies were instrumental in bringing about that repentance (*Radak; Abarbanel*).[1]

2. ... אָסֹף אָסֵף כֹּל — *I will utterly destroy everything ...*

I will destroy all life from upon the face of the Land of Israel (*Radak*), particularly from the Land of Judah (*Abarbanel*). The prophet begins with this general declaration and then goes on to specify [in great detail] (*Radak*). The verse is alluding to the future conquest of the area by Nebuchadnezzar (*Malbim*).

3. אָסֵף אָדָם וּבְהֵמָה אָסֵף עוֹף־הַשָּׁמַיִם וּדְגֵי הַיָּם — *I will destroy man and animal; I will destroy the bird of the sky and the fish of the sea.*

[So great will be the destruction I bring upon them that not only will man be obliterated from the land but even the animals, the birds and the fish of the sea.] The prophet may be describing the upcoming destruction in exaggerated terms in order to drive home the magnitude of the calamity that will occur or he may be describing that which will actually come to pass. Animals, birds and fish tend to settle in inhabited areas where they can find food. Since the land will become desolate and there will be no source of food, they will abandon the land (*Radak*).

Abarbanel understands this verse metaphorically. The different species represent different classes of society. The animals of the field represent the lower class of people, the farmers who work the fields together with the animals; the birds of the heavens represent the upper classes of kings and princes, who rise above the rest of society. The fish of the sea represent those people who are immersed in adultery and robbery, like the fish of the sea who live in totally unstructured groups. All those not cited among these groups are included in the final phrase, *and I will cut off mankind from the face of the land.*

וְהַמַּכְשֵׁלוֹת אֶת־הָרְשָׁעִים — *And the stumbling blocks of the wicked.*

These are the false gods with whom the wicked stumble in transgression

1. The statement of *Pesikta* cited above would seem to support the view of *Mahari Kara,* since it states explicitly that Zephaniah's words were not heeded. However, it is possible that *Pesikta* means that the people did not heed all the words of the prophets and did not return to God with a full heart, and therefore could not completely abolish the decree of destruction.

וְהִכְרַתִּי אֶת־הָאָדָם מֵעַל פְּנֵי הָאֲדָמָה נְאֻם־יהוה:
ד וְנָטִיתִי יָדִי עַל־יְהוּדָה וְעַל כָּל־יוֹשְׁבֵי יְרוּשָׁלָם
וְהִכְרַתִּי מִן־הַמָּקוֹם הַזֶּה אֶת־שְׁאָר הַבַּעַל אֶת־
ה שֵׁם הַכְּמָרִים עִם־הַכֹּהֲנִים: וְאֶת־הַמִּשְׁתַּחֲוִים
עַל־הַגַּגּוֹת לִצְבָא הַשָּׁמָיִם וְאֶת־הַמִּשְׁתַּחֲוִים
הַנִּשְׁבָּעִים לַיהוה וְהַנִּשְׁבָּעִים בְּמַלְכָּם:

(*Rashi; Malbim*).[1] Others render *the stumbling blocks with the wicked* — those items with which the wicked cause others to stumble will be destroyed together with the evildoers themselves (*Metzudos*). Alternatively, *Radak* and *Ibn Ezra* understand that this is a new statement in itself rather than a continuation of the list of those who will be destroyed: *And stumbling blocks will befall the wicked* — they will encounter troubles upon which they will stumble and die. *Targum* renders: [the massive destruction will take place] because of the many *stumbling blocks of the wicked.*

וְהִכְרַתִּי אֶת־הָאָדָם מֵעַל פְּנֵי הָאֲדָמָה — *And I will cut off mankind from the face of the land.*

This is a repetition of the first general statement (*Radak*). Although it is only the thoroughly wicked who will actually perish, the remainder of the nation, even those who are truly righteous, will nevertheless be banished from the land and sent into exile (*Radak*). According to *Ibn Ezra*, this refers only to the wicked mentioned in the previous phrase. Alternatively, *mankind* is referring to the numerous gentile nations who were destroyed by Nebuchadnezzar in his campaign to conquer the Middle East (*Malbim*).

R' Eliezer of Beaugency offers an entirely different approach to these two verses: Due to the multitude and magnitude of the iniquities of the people, God really wished to destroy the entire land with all its inhabitants, even the animals, the birds and the fish. But since it was only man who actually sinned, He felt that it would suffice to only cut off mankind from upon the face of the land.[2]

1. [This interpretation is supported by the words of the Gemara, cited below.]

2. This is similar to the approach of the Sages, who relate as follows: A philosopher once asked R' Gamliel, "It says in your Torah, *'Hashem, your God, — He is a consuming fire, a jealous God'* (*Deut.* 4:24). Why is He vengeful of those who worship idols? Let Him take revenge against the idols themselves!" R' Gamliel replied, "I will answer you with a parable. There was once a king who told his son to take care of the king's dog. After some time, the son began showing more respect for the dog than for his father, until one day the king overheard his son say, 'I swear by the life of my father's dog!' " R' Gamliel continued, "With whom do you think the king was angry: with the dog or his son?" After successfully making his point, R' Gamliel asked the philosopher what had prompted him to ask his question. The philosopher replied that he had once seen a raging fire in his town and the only building that was left standing was the temple used for idol worship. "Instead of destroying the idol worshipers, let him destroy the idols," asked the philosopher. To this R' Gamliel said, "You are right about objects that are unnecessary for the existence of the world, but why should God destroy the world because some people worship the sun, the moon, the stars, the constellations, the rivers and the valleys? Should He destroy His world because of some fools?!" So is it taught in verse 2, [should] *I utterly destroy everything from upon the face of the land?* [Should] I destroy man and beast; the birds of the heavens and the fish of the sea, and the stumbling blocks of the wicked? Because the wicked stumble upon them, should I remove them from the world? No! Instead I will cut off mankind from the face of the earth" (*Avodah Zarah* 54b).

and I will cut off mankind from the face of the land — the word of H*ASHEM.* [4]*I will stretch out My hand against Judah and against all the inhabitants of Jerusalem; and I will cut off from this place any remnant of the Baal and the memory of the ministers with the priests;* [5]*and those who prostrate themselves on the roofs to the heavenly host, and those who bow down and swear to* H*ASHEM and [then] swear by their king;*

4. וְנָטִיתִי יָדִי עַל־יְהוּדָה ... — *I will stretch out My hand against Judah ...*

I will stretch out My hand to strike a powerful blow against the people of Judah and the inhabitants of Jerusalem (*Targum Yonasan*), and I will remove every vestige of the Baal until there will be no remnant to serve as his remembrance (*Rashi*). Although Josiah had broken the hold of Baal worship from upon the nation and eradicated it from Judah — see *II Kings* Ch. 23 — there remained some areas where the idol was still served. These, too, declared the Almighty, will be obliterated completely, until there is no trace left of its existence (*Mahari Kara*). Alternatively, this prophecy was issued before Josiah eradicated the worship of Baal from among the Jewish people (*Radak;* cf. comm. to v. 1).

אֶת־שֵׁם הַכְּמָרִים עִם־הַכֹּהֲנִים — *The memory of the ministers with the priests.*

Our translation follows *Radak* and most commentators who maintain that both כְּמָרִים and כֹּהֲנִים are priests. *Rashi* follows *Targum Yonasan* and translates כְּמָרִים as פָּלְחֵיהוֹן, *their worshipers.*

Radak explains that the כְּמָרִים were priests who wore black vestments in honor of the idols and the כֹּהֲנִים were those who actually performed the service. *Metzudos* also identifies כְּמָרִים and כֹּהֲנִים as two different categories of priests of idolatry. Others contend that the word כֹּהֲנִים always means *Kohanim* of Hashem unless otherwise indicated. Thus: The priests of idolatry will be cut off from the land along with the Kohanim, for the Almighty's retribution will be all inclusive (*Abarbanel; Malbim*). *Alshich* renders: *And the name of the priests [who were mentioned] along with the Kohanim* — people would refer to both categories of priests in one breath, as if both served legitimate deities and were thus comparable in their elevated status.

5. וְאֶת־הַמִּשְׁתַּחֲוִים עַל־הַגַּגּוֹת ... — *And those who prostrate themselves on the roofs ...*

I will also strike down those who climb up to the rooftops to worship the heavenly bodies (*Metzudos*). Similarly, I will strike down those who swear to the Almighty and then repeat their oath in the name of their idol (*Rashi*).

הַנִּשְׁבָּעִים לַה׳ וְהַנִּשְׁבָּעִים בְּמַלְכָּם — *And swear to Hashem and [then] swear by their king.*

מַלְכָּם, *their king,* is referring to the idol that they worship because the people accept its rule over themselves as if it were a monarch (*Radak*). By swearing first to the Almighty and then repeating the oath to their idol they gave more validity to their idols than to G-d for they are implying that "If you do not believe my oath by G-d's Name, surely you can trust my oath in the name of the idol" (*Rashi*).

Mahari Kara explains: When they would swear falsely they would do so in the name of the Almighty; if their oath was true it would be issued in the name of their false god. *Radak* interprets: Sometimes they would swear by G-d's Name and other times in the name of their idols, thereby giving their false

ו וְאֶת־הַנְּסוֹגִים מֵאַחֲרֵי יהוה וַאֲשֶׁר לֹא־בִקְשׁוּ אֶת־
ז יהוה וְלֹא דְרָשֻׁהוּ׃ הַס מִפְּנֵי אֲדֹנָי יֱהֹוִה כִּי קָרוֹב יוֹם
ח יהוה כִּי־הֵכִין יהוה זֶבַח הִקְדִּישׁ קְרֻאָיו׃ וְהָיָה
בְּיוֹם זֶבַח יהוה וּפָקַדְתִּי עַל־הַשָּׂרִים וְעַל־
בְּנֵי הַמֶּלֶךְ וְעַל כָּל־הַלֹּבְשִׁים מַלְבּוּשׁ נָכְרִי׃
ט וּפָקַדְתִּי עַל כָּל־הַדּוֹלֵג עַל־הַמִּפְתָּן בַּיּוֹם הַהוּא

deities equal status with the Almighty, a violation of the prohibition (*Exodus* 20:20): *You shall not make* [images of what is] *with Me; gods of silver and gods of gold shall you not make for yourselves.*

Others understand וְהַנִּשְׁבָּעִים בְּמַלְכָּם literally, *they swear by their human king*. These people worship neither the Almighty nor do they worship idols. When they must take an oath, they do so in the name of their king. G-d's punishment will extend to these people as well. The previous phrase, הַנִּשְׁבָּעִים לַה׳, refers to those who loyally serve the Almighty. They, too, will be exiled, for G-d's retribution shall include the entire nation (*Abarbanel; Metzudos*). According to *R' Eliezer of Beaugency*, מַלְכָּם is referring to the *Molech*, the idol to whom human sacrifice was offered.

6. וְאֶת־הַנְּסוֹגִים מֵאַחֲרֵי ה׳ — *And those who have turned back from following Hashem.*

I will also punish those who did not follow the ways of the Almighty and did not keep His Torah. Alternatively, this is referring to those who once followed the ways of the Almighty but subsequently abandoned Him and His ways (*Metzudos*).

וַאֲשֶׁר לֹא־בִקְשׁוּ אֶת־ה׳ ... — *And those who have not sought Hashem ...*

Although these people did not abandon the Torah to worship idols, they see no point in seeking G-d or turning to Him in times of need, for in their hearts, they refuse to acknowledge that He is the source of all good and evil that befalls them (*Radak; R' Eliezer of Beaugency*).

Alternatively, these are people who never sought G-d in the first place (*Metzudos*). God will exact punishment from them, as well.

7. הַס מִפְּנֵי אֲדֹנָי יֱהֹוִה כִּי קָרוֹב יוֹם ה׳ — *Be silent before the Lord Hashem/Elohim, for the day of Hashem is near!*

Those of you who maintain that the Almighty does not look at your deeds, be silent (*Radak*). And those who contend that there is still a great deal of time left before He will exact retribution, do not express that opinion (*Metzudos*). [For the day of G-d's retribution is drawing near] and He will soon exile you in the days of King Jehoiakim, son of Josiah (*Mahari Kara*). Alternatively, *Targum Yonasan* translates הַס, *to remove* or *destroy* — see comm. to *Amos* 6:10 — and renders *all the wicked are destroyed before the Lord Hashem Elohim.*

The unusual combination of the names of God, אֲדֹנָי יֱהֹוִה, is explained by *Mizrachi* (*Deut.* 3:24). The name אֲדֹנָי means My Master. The name יֱהֹוִה, which has the spelling of the four-letter Name but the punctuation of Elohim, combines God's attribute of Mercy [י־ה־ו־ה] with His attribute of Judgment [אֱלֹהִים] implying that even in judgment, God should temper His decree with mercy [see ArtScroll *Bereishis* 15:8].

כִּי־הֵכִין ה׳ זֶבַח הִקְדִּישׁ קְרֻאָיו — *For Hashem has prepared a slaughter; He has invited His guests.*

The prophet metaphorically describes the death of the wicked as a slaughter for a feast (*Ibn Ezra* to v.8). Indeed, God has already set in motion the sequence of events which will culminate in His slaughter of the wicked and He has

[6] *and those who have turned back from following* Hashem *and those who have not sought* Hashem *nor inquired after Him.*

[7] *Be silent before the Lord* Hashem/Elohim, *for the day of* Hashem *is near! For* Hashem *has prepared a slaughter; He has invited His guests.* [8] *And it will happen on the day of* Hashem*'s slaughter that I will deal with the officials and the king's sons and all who wear foreign garments.* [9] *And I will deal with all those who leap over the threshold on that day, [and with]*

called together the mighty hordes of Nebuchadnezzar to participate in that event (*Rashi; Mahari Kara*). Others interpret: He has invited the animals of the field and the birds of the heavens to consume the corpses of those who will be slaughtered, as foretold by the Torah (*Deut.* 28:26) (*Radak*).

8. וְהָיָה בְּיוֹם זֶבַח ה׳ ... — *And it will happen on the day of Hashem's slaughter ...*

On the day of the slaughter, God will extend His wrath primarily upon the officials and the king's sons. It is they who, due to their power, have oppressed the poor and humble, and it is they who will fall by the sword on the day of slaughter. This refers specifically to Zedekiah and his sons, along with the princes of Judah who were slaughtered in Riblah — see *II Kings* 25:7,21 (*Radak*). Alternatively, it alludes to the death of the three kings of Judah [at the hands of the Babylonians]; Jehoiakim, Jeconiah and Zedekiah (*Mahari Kara*).

Alshich understands this verse as alluding to the righteous among the officers and princes. Because they were in a position to protest the wanton wickedness and they did not, they, too, will be slaughtered.

וְעַל כָּל־הַלֹּבְשִׁים מַלְבּוּשׁ נָכְרִי — *And all who wear foreign garments.*

My wrath will also be directed at those who wear the ornaments of the idols (*Rashi*), i.e., the priestly garments of those who serve the false gods (*Mahari Kara*). Others interpret מַלְבּוּשׁ נָכְרִי as *strange* [i.e., unusual] *garments.* The verse is referring to those who haughtily don special clothing in order to distinguish themselves from the common folk (*Ibn Ezra*), or to demonstrate their pretended piety (*Radak*). Alternatively, this is a further reference to men of power. These people dress uniquely in special royal garments because they serve in the vicinity of the king (*Abarbanel; Malbim*). Another interpretation is *the garments of strangers.* If they see someone wearing unusually fine clothing, they would confiscate it and take it for themselves (*Radak*, citing his father). *R' Eliezer of Beaugency* understands this to refer to men who wear women's clothing and vice versa, all in pursuit of immoral behavior.

9. וּפָקַדְתִּי עַל כָּל־הַדּוֹלֵג עַל־הַמִּפְתָּן ... — *And I will deal with all those who leap over the threshold ...*

I will also demand retribution from those who follow the practice of the Philistines who refrain from stepping upon the threshold of the temple of the idol Dagon (*Targum Yonasan; Rashi*).

As related in Scripture (*I Samuel* 5:1-5), when the Philistines captured the Holy Ark and took it to the temple of their idol Dagon in Ashdod, the idol fell to the ground before the Ark of Hashem. When they returned it to its place, it fell again and was broken, with its head and two hands severed from its body.

י הַֽמְמַלְאִ֛ים בֵּ֥ית אֲדֹנֵיהֶ֖ם חָמָ֥ס וּמִרְמָֽה׃ וְהָיָ֣ה בַיּוֹם֩ הַה֨וּא נְאֻם־יְהוָ֜ה ק֤וֹל צְעָקָה֙ מִשַּׁ֣עַר הַדָּגִ֔ים וִֽילָלָ֖ה מִן־הַמִּשְׁנֶ֑ה וְשֶׁ֥בֶר גָּד֖וֹל
יא מֵהַגְּבָעֽוֹת׃ הֵילִ֖ילוּ יֹשְׁבֵ֣י הַמַּכְתֵּ֑שׁ כִּ֤י נִדְמָה֙
יב כָּל־עַ֣ם כְּנַ֔עַן נִכְרְת֖וּ כָּל־נְטִ֥ילֵי כָֽסֶף׃ וְהָיָה֙

At that point, it was left lying on the threshold. In deference to their god, the priests of Dagon refrained from that time onward from stepping upon the threshold of the house of Dagon in Ashdod. Indeed, the Jews were even stricter in this practice than the Philistines themselves: the latter merely refrained from actually stepping upon the threshold; the Jews deliberately jumped over it in order to show their respect (*Midrash Shmuel* 11:5, cited by *Radak*). Furthermore, whereas the Philistines treated only the threshold at the temple of Dagon with sanctity, the Israelites treated every threshold that idols had passed over with sanctity and would refrain from stepping on every one of them (*Jerusalem Talmud — Avodah Zarah* 3:2).

According to this interpretation, the second half of the verse, הַמְמַלְאִים בֵּית אֲדֹנֵיהֶם חָמָס וּמִרְמָה, must be interpreted independently of the first half: [Not only will I deal with all those who leap over the threshold, but] I will also deal with those who fill the house of their masters with injustice and deceit.

R' Eliezer of Beaugency offers a slightly different interpretation, which clarifies the flow of the verse: Just as the Philistines refrain from treading upon the threshold of Dagon, so do you show respect for God by jumping over the threshold of His house of worship. However, although you attempt thereby to show that you are truly God-fearing, the truth is quite different. For you throw off the yoke of fear of the Almighty when you fill the houses of your masters with your plunder and robbery. Others directly connect the phrase כָּל־הַדּוֹלֵג עַל־הַמִּפְתָּן, *all those who leap over the threshold*, with the phrase הַמְמַלְאִים בֵּית אֲדֹנֵיהֶם חָמָס וּמִרְמָה, *those who fill the house of their masters with injustice and deceit*. They maintain that leaping over the threshold has nothing to do with idol worship but is an expression used by Scripture to describe joy and eagerness. The ministers of wealthy Israelites felt such great joy in delivering the wealth and treasures they plundered that it was as if they would jump over the threshold in their eagerness to bring it into the house of their master (*Ibn Ezra*). Similarly, *Radak* explains that when the people robbed the poor, they did so with such enthusiasm that it was as if they leaped over the threshold as they entered the poor man's house.

10. ... וְהָיָה בַיּוֹם הַהוּא — *On that day ...*

On the day of God's wrath (*Abarbanel*), a great outcry will be heard throughout the city of Jerusalem that will emanate from the Fish Gate as well as from הַמִּשְׁנֶה, the gate second to it, the Bird Gate (*Rashi*). Along with this outcry will come a great destruction in the hills of Jerusalem (*Targum Yonasan; Rashi*).

The Fish Gate is mentioned in *Nehemiah* 12:39. *Radak* suggests that the fishermen may have marketed their fish near that particular gate giving it its unique name. Similarly, fowl was probably sold near the Bird Gate giving it its name (*Mahari Kara*).

Other interpretations of הַמִּשְׁנֶה are: the palace of the assistant (second) to the king (*Ibn Ezra*) or the area where the officers of the king dwelt (*Malbim*). *Radak* refers us to *II Kings* 22:14 where מִשְׁנֶה is identified as the *study hall* [see *Targum Yonasan* there]. It is where Huldah the Prophetess was sitting when she was asked to interpret the significance of the Torah found rolled to *Deut.* 28:36. *Metzudos* defines מִשְׁנֶה

those who fill the house of their masters with injustice and deceit.

[10] On that day — the word of HASHEM — there will be a sound of an outcry from the Fish Gate and a wail from the second gate, and of a great catastrophe from the hills. [11] Wail, O inhabitants of Maktesh, for the entire people of Canaan has been destroyed; all those laden with silver have been cut off.

as the space between the two walls that surround Jerusalem.

The Sages interpret the verse in the following manner: *From the Fish Gate* — this is referring to the ancient port city of עַכּוֹ, *Acre,* which is situated in the bosom of the sea, where many fish are caught. *From the mishneh* — this is the city of לוּד, *Lod,* the second most important city in the Land of Israel after Jerusalem. *From the hills* — this is the city of צִיפּוֹרִי, *Sepphoris,* which was located in the hills (*Pesikta Rabbasi,* cited by *Yalkut, Rashi* et al.). When the enemy shall fall upon the nation of Israel, an outcry of anguish will be heard from *Acre,* located on one end of the kingdom, on the Mediterranean coast and from *Lod,* located at the other end, near Jerusalem, for these will be the targets of the enemy's two-pronged assault. Thus, *Sepphoris,* situated between these cities, will be caught in the lock-vise of enemy troops and will thereby be destroyed (*Alshich*).

11. הֵילִילוּ יֹשְׁבֵי הַמַּכְתֵּשׁ — *Wail, O inhabitants of Maktesh.*

Wail over your fate, inhabitants of Maktesh, because the enemy will conquer and destroy the entire area of Jerusalem and the sound of crying and wailing will be heard.

The proper noun Maktesh is related to the word מַכְתֶּשֶׁת, *mortar,* a deep vessel used for crushing herbs (*Metzudos Tzion*). Wherever Maktesh was located, it was probably situated in an area that was lower than the rest of the city. According to *Targum Yonasan* cited by *Rashi,* Maktesh is referring to the Kidron Valley, an area deeply indented, like a mortar. *Radak* explains that it was in an area of Jerusalem that was situated in a depression. Alternatively it is the city of טְבֶרְיָה, *Tiberias,* which is situated in the region with the lowest altitude in the entire Land of Israel (*Rashi* from *Pesikta*).

כִּי נִדְמָה כָּל־עַם כְּנַעַן — *For the entire people of Canaan has been destroyed.*

I.e., the entire Jewish people, whose deeds have come to resemble those of the decadent Canaanite nations (*Targum Yonasan; Rashi*), or all of Israel, who dwell in the Land of Canaan (*Mahari Kara*), has been destroyed. Alternatively, [*the people of Israel*] *will resemble the people of Canaan.* Just as the Canaanites were banished from the land, leaving no remnant behind, so too, will there be no vestige left of the Israelite people (*Abarbanel*).

נִכְרְתוּ כָּל־נְטִילֵי כָסֶף — *All those laden with silver have been cut off.*

All those who are wealthy with possessions and laden with gold and silver have been cut off (*Targum Yonasan; Rashi*); even their great wealth could not ward off their downfall and disaster (*Abarbanel*). Others interpret: Those who mint coins of silver and are thus laden with abundant silver (*Mahari Kara*). According to *Abarbanel,* only silver is mentioned among all of the precious metals, because that was the only metal used for coins in ancient Israel.

Ibn Ezra sees כְּנַעַן as a synonym for merchants — see *Gen.* 38:2; *Hosea* 12:8 — and offers an entirely different interpretation to this verse. Wail, O those who live in the area known as Maktesh, where the merchants and barterers are situated. For the entire "nation" of merchants has been destroyed, all those who are laden with silver.

בָּעֵת הַהִיא אֲחַפֵּשׂ אֶת־יְרוּשָׁלַם בַּנֵּרוֹת וּפָקַדְתִּי עַל־הָאֲנָשִׁים הַקֹּפְאִים עַל־שִׁמְרֵיהֶם הָאֹמְרִים בִּלְבָבָם לֹא־יֵיטִיב יהוה וְלֹא יָרֵעַ׃ יג וְהָיָה חֵילָם לִמְשִׁסָּה וּבָתֵּיהֶם לִשְׁמָמָה וּבָנוּ בָתִּים וְלֹא יֵשֵׁבוּ וְנָטְעוּ כְרָמִים וְלֹא יִשְׁתּוּ אֶת־יֵינָם׃ יד קָרוֹב יוֹם־יהוה הַגָּדוֹל קָרוֹב וּמַהֵר מְאֹד קוֹל יוֹם יהוה מַר צֹרֵחַ שָׁם גִּבּוֹר׃ טו יוֹם עֶבְרָה הַיּוֹם הַהוּא יוֹם צָרָה וּמְצוּקָה יוֹם שֹׁאָה וּמְשׁוֹאָה יוֹם חֹשֶׁךְ וַאֲפֵלָה יוֹם עָנָן וַעֲרָפֶל׃

12. וְהָיָה בָּעֵת הַהִיא אֲחַפֵּשׂ אֶת־יְרוּשָׁלַם בַּנֵּרוֹת — *It will be at that time that I will search Jerusalem with candles.*

At that time I will search Jerusalem to seek out and exact punishment from each and every last one of her sinners. I will search thoroughly, like one who searches by candlelight in every nook and cranny, leaving no spot unexamined (*Radak*).

וּפָקַדְתִּי עַל־הָאֲנָשִׁים הַקֹּפְאִים עַל־שִׁמְרֵיהֶם — *And I will deal with the men who are settled on their lees.*

And I will exact retribution from those who dwell securely in their homes and rely on their wealth and possessions (*Targum Yonasan; Ibn Ezra*). Others interpret: Those who still dwell calmly in their homelands, because they think they will not be exiled (*Mahari Kara; R' Eliezer of Beaugency*). Scripture compares the complacency that they felt due to their false security to wine that calmly rests upon its lees.[1]

הָאֹמְרִים בִּלְבָבָם לֹא־יֵיטִיב ה׳ וְלֹא יָרֵעַ — *Who say in their heart, "Hashem will not do good and will not do evil."*

These people contend that God does not bestow good upon those who follow His will nor does He inflict harm upon those who transgress it (*Rashi*). Indeed, they deny that He providentially oversees events of earthly beings, and thus is not the source of any good or evil that occurs (*Radak*).

The Sages offer the following homiletic interpretation to this verse: Said R' Acha: Do not pronounce the word אֲחַפֵּשׂ with a שׂ, *I will search*, but אֲחַפֵּשׁ with a שׁ: *I will set free*, i.e., God wishes to set Jerusalem free. Said the Holy One, Blessed is He: Did I not write in My Torah (*Exodus* 21:26): *If a man shall strike the eye of his slave or the eye of his maidservant and destroy it, he shall set him free in return for his eye. I must surely set Jerusalem free for I have struck both of Israel's eyes*, as it is stated (*Isaiah* 29:10): *For Hashem has poured upon you a spirit of deep sleep and He has closed your eyes.* Is it not proper that I should set it free? (*Yalkut Shimoni* from *Pesikta*).

13. וְהָיָה חֵילָם לִמְשִׁסָּה וּבָתֵּיהֶם לִשְׁמָמָה ... — *Their wealth will give way to plunder and their houses to desolation ...*

All of their wealth will fall to the invading enemy as spoils of war (*Targum Yonasan*),[2] and their houses will be left desolate when they are banished from them and sent into exile. [Thus,] they will never inhabit the houses that they

1. Anything that is gathered together, such as frozen water or curdled milk, is called קִפָּאוֹן (*Radak*). Others render: *that float upon their lees* (*Rashi; Metzudos*).

2. *Metzudos* translates מְשִׁסָּה as *trampling* — their wealth will be trampled under the feet of the enemy.

[12] *It will be at that time that I will search Jerusalem with candles and I will deal with the men who are settled on their lees, who say in their heart, "HASHEM will not do good and will not do evil."* [13] *Their wealth will give way to plunder and their houses to desolation; they will build houses, but will not dwell in them; they will plant vineyards, but not drink their wine.* [14] *The great day of HASHEM is near, it is near and hastens greatly, the sound of the day of HASHEM, when the mighty warrior cries out bitterly.* [15] *A day of fury is that day, a day of trouble and distress, a day of destruction and desolation, a day of darkness and blackness, a day of cloud and thick cloud,*

toil to erect, nor will they enjoy the fruits of the vineyards that they plant, for the enemy will come and confiscate them all (*Metzudos*).

Alshich sees this verse as describing a sequence of events: First, the wealth and homes of the nation will fall plunder to the enemy, with the exile of kings Jehoiakim and Jehoiachin. Those who remain behind will then seek to rebuild the land, erecting houses and planting vineyards. However, they, too, will soon be exiled, never to enjoy the fruits of their labors.

14. קָרוֹב יוֹם־ה׳ הַגָּדוֹל ... — *The great day of Hashem is near ...*

That day of great magnitude, when the Almighty will exact retribution from His people, is near and it is drawing closer very swiftly (*Metzudos*). On that day of Hashem there will be heard a great clamor and noise (*Abarbanel*), the sound of mighty warriors crying bitterly in their misfortune (*Rashi; Ibn Ezra; Mahari Kara*). Alternatively: The sound on that day will be so great that it will melt the heart of even the mighty warrior, who will cry out in battle with a bitter shriek (*Metzudos*).

Others render: *The sound of the day of Hashem will call out bitterly;* it is as if the day is calling out due to the calamity taking place. *There is the mighty warrior* — i.e., the mighty warriors who will decimate the Jewish nation will come there. Alternatively, the mighty warriors who will be destroyed by the enemy will come there (*Radak*).

15. יוֹם עֶבְרָה הַיּוֹם הַהוּא ... — *A day of fury is that day ...*

That fateful day will be one of misfortune and disaster, bringing in its wake darkness and gloom, for the Almighty will vent His wrath upon the Jewish nation (*Metzudos*).

Alshich interprets this verse as alluding to the five major calamities which occurred to the Jewish nation on the day designated for misfortune: the ninth of Av. *A day of fury* refers to the day that it was decreed upon the Israelites in the wilderness that they would not be allowed to enter the Holy Land. *A day of trouble and distress* alludes to the destruction of the First Temple and *a day of destruction and desolation* to the destruction of the Second Temple. With the destruction of Beitar, where they had lit candles for the destruction of Jerusalem, it was turned into *a day of darkness and blackness* and when Apostimus burned the Torah scroll written by Moses, it made the day into *a day of cloud and thick cloud.*

טז יוֹם שׁוֹפָר וּתְרוּעָה עַל הֶעָרִים הַבְּצֻרוֹת וְעַל
הַפִּנּוֹת הַגְּבֹהוֹת׃ יז וַהֲצֵרֹתִי לָאָדָם וְהָלְכוּ כַּעִוְרִים
כִּי לַיהוָה חָטָאוּ וְשֻׁפַּךְ דָּמָם כֶּעָפָר וּלְחֻמָם
כַּגְּלָלִים׃ יח גַּם־כַּסְפָּם גַּם־זְהָבָם לֹא־יוּכַל לְהַצִּילָם
בְּיוֹם עֶבְרַת יהוה וּבְאֵשׁ קִנְאָתוֹ תֵּאָכֵל כָּל־הָאָרֶץ
כִּי־כָלָה אַךְ־נִבְהָלָה יַעֲשֶׂה אֵת כָּל־יֹשְׁבֵי הָאָרֶץ׃

16. יוֹם שׁוֹפָר וּתְרוּעָה ... — *A day of trumpet and battle cries ...*

On that day, the invading hordes will blow their trumpets and sound their battle cries as they descend upon the Holy Land. They will conquer her fortified cities, along with its lofty towers (*Radak*). Alternatively, it is Israel who will blow the trumpets as an alarm and warning that the enemy is approaching (*Malbim*).

הַפִּנּוֹת הַגְּבֹהוֹת — *The high towers.*

Our translation follows *Radak*. Although the word פִּנּוֹת literally means *corners*, Scripture uses it as a synonym for *towers* because the towers usually stood at the corners of the fortifications (*Metzudos Tzion*). Alternatively, *Targum Yonasan* followed by *Ibn Ezra* translate פִּנּוֹת as *hills*, apparently referring to mountaintop fortresses (*The Living Nach*).

17. וַהֲצֵרֹתִי לָאָדָם ... — *I will lay siege against the people ...*

I will lay siege against the people of Israel who will be within those fortified cities (*Radak; Ibn Ezra*). Our translation follows *Radak* and *Ibn Ezra* who follow *Targum Yonasan* and understand that אָדָם is an idiomatic expression meaning *the people*. Here, it is referring to the Israelites who sought refuge from their enemies in their fortified cities. *Rashi* and *Metzudos*, however, explain that אָדָם, *Adam*, is a specific reference to the Israelite nation for Scripture refers to Israel as אָדָם, *Adam* — see *Ezekiel* 34:31. Indeed, the Talmud (*Yevamos* 61a) writes that Israel is called *Adam* but the nations of the world are not called *Adam*. See also comm. to *Habakkuk* 2:8 and overview IV to *Ezekiel* ArtScroll ed.

וְהָלְכוּ כַּעִוְרִים כִּי לַה׳ חָטָאוּ — *And they will go about like the blind for they have sinned against Hashem.*

And they will go about confused and in chaos, like blind men (*R' Eliezer of Beaugency*), unable to extricate themselves from their plight (*Mahari Kara; Abarbanel*). For they have sinned against the Almighty God, against Whom there is no defense or recourse (*Mahari Kara*).

וְשֻׁפַּךְ דָּמָם כֶּעָפָר... — *Their blood will be spilled out like dust ...*

So extensive will the slaughter be that their blood will be spilled like dust that is thrown out without any care, and their flesh will be dumped into heaps like dung (*Radak*) — left to rot without being buried (*R' Eliezer of Beaugency*).

וּלְחֻמָם כַּגְּלָלִים — *And their flesh like dung.*

Our translation follows *Rashi* and *Ibn Ezra* who maintain that לְחֻמָם is an Arabic word meaning *flesh. Abarbanel* disagrees for there is no reason for the prophet to use an Arabic word rather than the Hebrew. He renders *And their bread like dung;* while in a state of siege, they will be forced to partake of food that is *tamei* — ritually unclean — like dung.

Malbim sees this verse as describing a series of events. Even after G-d will punish the people, they will still refuse to acknowledge that He is the source of their misfortune, and that

[16] a day of trumpet and battle cries against the fortified cities and against the high towers. [17] I will lay siege against the people, and they will go about like the blind for they have sinned against HASHEM. Their blood will be spilled out like dust and their flesh like dung. [18] Even their silver, even their gold will not be able to rescue them on the day of HASHEM's fury; in the fire of His zeal the entire land will be consumed; for He will make an end, an abrupt one, of all the inhabitants of the land.

it has befallen them because they have sinned against Him. They will walk like blind men, unable to see what is before them. Therefore, G-d will bring the enemy upon them a second time, and he will slaughter them wantonly and cruelly.

18. גַּם־כַּסְפָּם גַּם־זְהָבָם ... — *Even their silver, even their gold ...*

Not only will their might and power be helpless in the face of the enemy's onslaught but their gold and silver will prove to be worthless as well, for the Chaldeans will not be bribed into sparing the lives of the Israelites (*Metzudos*). *Abarbanel* explains that with all their gold and silver, they will not be able to procure for them even the basic necessities of food and drink.

וּבְאֵשׁ קִנְאָתוֹ תֵּאָכֵל כָּל־הָאָרֶץ — *In the fire of His zeal the entire land will be consumed.*

The Almighty will bring sudden destruction upon the land amidst great confusion and chaos thereby precluding the possibility of escape (*Radak*). Alternatively, for the confusion shall bring only destruction upon the inhabitants of the land (*Metzudos*).

Alshich interprets these verses as describing how the Almighty vented His wrath upon the structures and fortifications of the land rather than upon its inhabitants, for had He struck at them, they would have been totally annihilated, for that is what they actually deserved. Thus, it shall be a day of *trumpet and battle cries against the fortified cities and against the high towers* [rather than the people themselves], for if God were to punish the people, they would go around like blind men, with no hope for salvation, since they have sinned against Him. Even the gold and silver that they will give to charity would not help them at that time, for it would be too late to save them from that which had already been decreed. However, by destroying the land, the destruction that was fitting to befall the people will be limited to chaos.[1]

II

In the previous chapter Zephaniah described the devastation and destruction that was to befall the people of Judah for the iniquities they had committed. The prophet now exhorts the people to repent their evil ways before the punishments arrive so that they may thereby gain God's mercy.

1. The Sages write that the Almighty vented His wrath upon wood and stone, thereby sparing the people themselves. The glory of Jerusalem and Eretz Yisrael demanded a standard of excellence beyond that which would otherwise be expected, due to the opportunities for spiritual greatness that it afforded and the inspiration that it provided. Therefore, with the destruction of the land, the scope of Israel's potential was lessened and, with it, the prosecution for their unwillingness to live up to it (see *Ramban* to *Lev.* 18:28 and *Michtav MeEliyahu* vol. 2).

א־ב הִתְקוֹשְׁשׁוּ וָקוֹשּׁוּ הַגּוֹי לֹא נִכְסָף׃ בְּטֶרֶם לֶדֶת חֹק
כְּמֹץ עָבַר יוֹם בְּטֶרֶם | לֹא־יָבוֹא עֲלֵיכֶם חֲרוֹן אַף־
ג יהוה בְּטֶרֶם לֹא־יָבוֹא עֲלֵיכֶם יוֹם אַף־יהוה׃ בַּקְּשׁוּ
אֶת־יהוה כָּל־עַנְוֵי הָאָרֶץ אֲשֶׁר מִשְׁפָּטוֹ פָּעָלוּ
בַּקְּשׁוּ־צֶדֶק בַּקְּשׁוּ עֲנָוָה אוּלַי תִּסָּתְרוּ בְּיוֹם אַף יהוה׃

1. הִתְקוֹשְׁשׁוּ וָקוֹשׁוּ — *Gather yourselves together and correct [your deeds].*

Our translation follows *Rashi* who renders הִתְקוֹשְׁשׁוּ, *gather and assemble together,* וָקוֹשׁוּ, *and align your deeds with the will of your Creator.* The Sages (*Sanhedrin* 18a) understand both words as an expression of aligning or straightening, for they expound הִתְקוֹשְׁשׁוּ, *correct [straighten] yourself,* וָקוֹשׁוּ, *and then correct others.* Alternatively, *Radak* maintains that both words mean to *search and gather* and explains the dictum of the Sages accordingly. *Seek out your faults and gather them together so that you may eradicate them. Afterward do the same for others.* Similarly, *Ibn Ezra* interprets *chastise yourself and then castigate others. Abarbanel* relates הִתְקוֹשְׁשׁוּ to קַשׁ, *straw,* and adds: accept upon yourselves the afflictions due to you for your misdeeds, until you will be like straw that has been beaten down and refined [see *Rashbam Baba Basra* 60b].

הַגּוֹי לֹא נִכְסָף — *O nation without desire.*

I.e., the nation that does not desire to study the Torah (*Targum Yonasan; Rashi*) nor to be close to the Almighty (*Mahari Kara*). *Radak* interprets: The nation that does not desire to do that which the prophet requested of them: to seek out and eradicate its faults.[1]

2. בְּטֶרֶם לֶדֶת חֹק — *Before the decree is born.*

The Almighty has decreed that His wrath and fury be poured out upon His people. It is therefore of utmost importance that they improve their ways and repent their evil deeds immediately before His decree comes to pass (*Abarbanel*).

כְּמֹץ עָבַר יוֹם — *When you will become like chaff [that is blown away by the wind and as smoke] that passes from before the sun.*

Our translation follows *Rashi* who understands this verse as an ellipsis. Accordingly, the verse is forewarning that the people should immediately change their evil ways for once the decree is carried out, they will be rendered like the chaff that is blown away by the wind and like smoke that passes from before the sun[light of the day].

Rashi bases his explanation on *Targum Yonasan.* Our version of *Targum Yonasan,* however, has *like the shadow* ... instead of *like smoke* ...

Alternatively, this verse is to be understood as if it were written in inverted order, as is common in Scripture. בְּטֶרֶם לֶדֶת חֹק יוֹם כְּמֹץ עָבַר, *Before the decree of the day is born when you shall be as passing chaff* (*Radak; Metzudos*).

Other commentators follow the literal translation of the verse. *Mahari Kara*

1. *Alshich* notes that this verse is directed to those whose transgressions are still light like straw, not to the truly wicked whose sins weigh heavily like beams or to the righteous who are basically without sin. Nevertheless, they are described as a nation that does not desire. Although they are not guilty of truly reprehensible behavior, they lack the quality or the quest for self-improvement.

Others render: *A nation undesired* — despised and unloved by the rest of the world (*Ibn Ezra; Abarbanel*). Still others translate: *A nation without shame* — that is not embarrassed by its wicked deeds (*Radak,* citing his father).

[1] *Gather yourselves together and correct [your deeds], O nation without desire:* [2] *before the decree is born, when you will become like chaff [that is blown away by the wind and as smoke] that passes from before the sun; before* H*ASHEM's burning wrath comes upon you; before the day of* H*ASHEM's anger comes upon you.* [3] *Seek* H*ASHEM, all humble of the land who have fulfilled His law; seek righteousness; seek humility. Perhaps you will be concealed on the day of* H*ASHEM's anger.*

renders, improve your ways before you will be strewn among the lands *like chaff that passes* due to the winds of *the day. R' Eliezer of Beaugency* interprets *Just like chaff; so shall pass the day* of your prosperity and life (see also *Abarbanel, Malbim*).

בְּטֶרֶם לֹא־יָבוֹא עֲלֵיכֶם חֲרוֹן אַף־ה׳ בְּטֶרֶם לֹא־יָבוֹא עֲלֵיכֶם יוֹם אַף־ה׳ — *Before Hashem's burning wrath comes upon you; before the day of Hashem's anger comes upon you.*

If the people will repent before that fateful day arrives, neither that dark day nor its decrees will materialize for G-d's burning anger will have abated (*Abarbanel*).

3. The prophet now turns to the righteous among the nation and delivers the word of G-d that is directed specifically to them. Although the majority of the people were sinful, there remained a significant number of God-fearing individuals within the nation. Yet, despite their righteousness, they too were slain and decimated by the sword of the enemy (*Radak; Abarbanel;* see *Alshich,* cited below).

בַּקְּשׁוּ אֶת־ה׳ כָּל־עַנְוֵי הָאָרֶץ אֲשֶׁר מִשְׁפָּטוֹ פָּעָלוּ בַּקְּשׁוּ־צֶדֶק בַּקְּשׁוּ עֲנָוָה — *Seek Hashem, all humble of the land who have fulfilled His law; seek righteousness; seek humility.*

Those who have remained steadfast in their righteousness and fidelity to G-d's laws should continue their course of action and reinforce their deeds. They should pursue their righteousness and humility even further (*Ibn Ezra; R' Eliezer of Beaugency; Malbim*). *Abarbanel* interprets the phrase, *Seek Hashem,* as exhorting the righteous to seek the Almighty through their prayers; beseech G-d.

Radak interprets בַּקְּשׁוּ־צֶדֶק בַּקְּשׁוּ עֲנָוָה to mean *pursue righteousness and humility.* I.e., strive with all of your might to inspire the rest of the nation to repent. Others see these words as being directed again to the common folk: The rest of you, who have hitherto indulged in sin, improve your ways and seek righteousness and humility (*Abarbanel; Metzudos*).

Alshich interprets this verse as alluding to the punishment imposed upon the righteous of the nation for their lack of protest against the misdeeds of the masses. This was a result of their great humility, which led them to believe that their words would be totally ignored.

אוּלַי תִּסָּתְרוּ בְּיוֹם אַף ה׳ — *Perhaps you will be concealed on the day of Hashem's anger.*

The prophet advises them that if they will heed his words, they may yet arouse a sufficient measure of Divine mercy to spare them from the wrath of the enemy's sword. He does not tell them that they will not go into exile, because that had already been decreed during the days of Manasseh — see *II Kings* 21:12-14, 22:20 (*Radak*).

ד כִּ֤י עַזָּה֙ עֲזוּבָ֣ה תִֽהְיֶ֔ה וְאַשְׁקְל֖וֹן לִשְׁמָמָ֑ה
ה אַשְׁדּ֗וֹד בַּֽצָּהֳרַ֙יִם֙ יְגָ֣רְשׁ֔וּהָ וְעֶקְר֖וֹן תֵּעָקֵֽר׃ ה֗וֹי
יֹשְׁבֵ֛י חֶ֥בֶל הַיָּ֖ם גּ֣וֹי כְּרֵתִ֑ים דְּבַר־יהוָ֣ה
עֲלֵיכֶ֗ם כְּנַ֙עַן֙ אֶ֣רֶץ פְּלִשְׁתִּ֔ים וְהַאֲבַדְתִּ֖יךְ
ו מֵאֵ֥ין יוֹשֵֽׁב׃ וְֽהָ֨יְתָ֜ה חֶ֣בֶל הַיָּ֗ם נְוֺ֛ת כְּרֹ֥ת
ז רֹעִ֖ים וְגִדְר֥וֹת צֹֽאן׃ וְהָ֣יָה חֶ֗בֶל לִשְׁאֵרִ֛ית
בֵּ֥ית יְהוּדָ֖ה עֲלֵיהֶ֣ם יִרְע֑וּן בְּבָתֵּ֣י אַשְׁקְל֗וֹן

The Sages relate: When R' Ami would come to this verse he would cry ... He said, "All this [spiritual accomplishment] and only perhaps," i.e., even with all this repentance, there is no assurance of survival (*Chagigah* 4b).

Others interpret this phrase as expressing a new idea entirely. If the people will pursue righteousness and humility, the exile will last only for a short while, as if to keep the people hidden away until the wrath of the Almighty passes and then they would be able to return to their homeland in safety (*Abarbanel*).

4-15. In the following verses, the prophet describes the destruction of Israel's neighbors. He declares that if Israel will only repent, the Almighty will bring retribution upon her wicked neighbors: Philistia, Ammon and Moab (*Rashi*). Some say that this means that He will remove His wrath from over the Jewish people and direct it against the gentiles instead (*Mahari Kara*). Others contend, as cited above, that it was too late for the people of Judah to avoid the Almighty's fury. However, if they would seek G-d, He would pour out His wrath upon the heathen nations as well, thereby preventing them from rejoicing at Israel's destruction (*Radak*). According to *Abarbanel* and *Metzudos*, this verse continues the theme expressed at the end of the previous verse. Whereas Israel will return to its land after a short time of exile, the banishment of her neighbors will last for a much longer time. Thus, when Israel returns, she will find their lands in a state of desolation.

◆§ The Destruction of the Philistine Cities

In this verse, Zephaniah resorts to paranomasia, a play on words to relate each nation's punishment to its name (*Ibn Ezra; Radak*)

4. עַזָּה ... וְאַשְׁקְלוֹן ... אַשְׁדּוֹד ... וְעֶקְרוֹן — *Gaza ... Ashkelon ... Ashdod ... Ekron ...*

The verse lists four of the largest Philistine cities whose destruction Israel would witness if they would rectify their ways. Gaza, עַזָּה, will become deserted, עֲזוּבָה, bereft of her inhabitants (*Metzudos*). Ashkelon, אַשְׁקְלוֹן, will be laid waste, for invading nations shall take (שְׁקוּלוֹ) her inhabitants by force and exile them from their land (*Mahari Kara*). Ashdod, אַשְׁדּוֹד, too, will be conquered by her enemies. Just as the שֵׁד, *demon*, named *Ketev* is said to wreak havoc (יָשׁוּד) at noon — see *Rashi* to *Psalms* 91:6 — so too, will the residents of Ashdod be suddenly driven out of their city at noon (*Rashi*). Ekron, עֶקְרוֹן, too, will be uprooted, תֵּעָקֵר, with no one remaining in the land (*Metzudos*). Scripture does not mention the future destruction of Gath, a major Philistine city, because it had already been conquered by the people of Judah (*Radak*). Alternatively: Ashdod, which was [filled with] sheep pastures, will be driven out at noon, a time when it is especially difficult for sheep to be outside (*Rashi*).

5. הוֹי יֹשְׁבֵי חֶבֶל הַיָּם גּוֹי כְּרֵתִים — *Woe to the inhabitants of the seacoast, the nation of the Cherethites!*

[4] *For Gaza will be deserted; and Ashkelon become a wasteland; they will drive out Ashdod's residents at noon; and Ekron will be uprooted.*

[5] *Woe to the inhabitants of the seacoast, the nation of the Cherethites! The word of* HASHEM *is against you, O Canaan, land of the Philistines, and I will destroy you, without an inhabitant.* [6] *The seacoast will be an abode for shepherds and sheepfolds.* [7] *It will be a portion for the remnant of the House of Judah; upon which they will graze. In the houses of Ashkelon*

The Cherethites were Philistines who lived along the Mediterranean coast[1] in an area of Philistia called Cherethi (*Rashi*). Some say that it is another name for the Philistine nation (*Radak; Metzudos*). Zephaniah calls out to them, "Woe," for just as their name כְּרֵתִים means *cut off*, so too, are they deserving of destruction (*Rashi*).

דְּבַר־ה׳ עֲלֵיכֶם כְּנַעַן אֶרֶץ פְּלִשְׁתִּים ... — *The word of Hashem is against you, O Canaan, land of the Philistines ...*

Therefore, Canaanite nation of Philistines (see *Joshua* 13:3), you will be totally destroyed without a single inhabitant remaining (*Metzudos*). You will thereby suffer the same fate as the other Canaanite nations who were totally destroyed when the Jewish people first conquered the Land of Israel (*R' Eliezer of Beaugency; Abarbanel*). *Malbim* interprets *The word of Hashem is already against you*: God has already declared through the earlier prophecies of Joel, Amos and Hosea that you are to be destroyed.

6. ... וְהָיְתָה חֶבֶל הַיָּם נְוֹת כְּרֹת רֹעִים ... — *The seacoast will be an abode for shepherds ...*

[Some commentators see this verse too as a play on words. The region of the Cherethites, כְּרֵתִים, will be an abode for shepherds, נְוֹת "כְּרֹת" רֹעִים.] After its destruction, that same seacoast will become a temporary shelter for shepherds, where they will eat their morning meal (*Rashi*) and it will become a dwelling place for flocks of sheep, as well. Its cities, however, will lay in ruins and will not be rebuilt (*Abarbanel*). Others relate כְּרֹת to כְּרִיָּה, *digging*, and explain נְוֹת כְּרֹת רֹעִים as a place where shepherds will dig shelters for their sheep (*Radak*), or a place where they will dig wells for their flocks (*R' Eliezer of Beaugency*).

7. וְהָיָה חֶבֶל לִשְׁאֵרִית בֵּית יְהוּדָה — *It will be a portion for the remnant of the House of Judah.*

Although *Targum Yonasan* translated חֶבֶל הַיָּם of the previous two verses as סְפַר יַמָּא, *border of the sea* or *seacoast*, here he translates עַדְבָא, synonymous with *lot* or *portion*. Zephaniah is foretelling, when the remnant of Judah will return from their exile in Babylonia they will occupy these desolate seacoast cities for they will now become a part of the portion of the House of Judah (*Rashi*).

... עֲלֵיהֶם יִרְעוּן — *Upon which they will graze ...*

Since these great cities will lie in ruins, the returning Judeans will use the area

1. The word חֶבֶל means *a portion*. חֶבֶל הַיָּם means *the portion of land that is close to the sea* (*Ibn Ezra; Radak*). *Rashi* explains that the word חֶבֶל actually means *a rope*. It became an expression used for a measure of land because they would measure their territory with a rope that was of a standard length.

בָּעֶ֫רֶב יִרְבָּצ֔וּן כִּ֤י יִפְקְדֵם֙ יהוה אֱלֹהֵיהֶ֖ם וְשָׁ֥ב °שבותם׃ ח שָׁמַ֙עְתִּי֙ חֶרְפַּ֣ת מוֹאָ֔ב וְגִדּוּפֵ֖י בְּנֵ֣י עַמּ֑וֹן אֲשֶׁ֤ר חֵֽרְפוּ֙ אֶת־עַמִּ֔י וַיַּגְדִּ֖ילוּ עַל־גְּבוּלָֽם׃ ט לָכֵ֣ן חַי־אָ֡נִי נְאֻם֩ יהוה צְבָא֜וֹת אֱלֹהֵ֣י יִשְׂרָאֵ֗ל כִּֽי־מוֹאָב֙ כִּסְדֹ֣ם תִּֽהְיֶ֗ה וּבְנֵ֤י עַמּוֹן֙ כַּעֲמֹרָ֔ה מִמְשַׁ֥ק חָר֛וּל וּמִכְרֵה־מֶ֥לַח וּשְׁמָמָ֖ה עַד־עוֹלָ֑ם שְׁאֵרִ֤ית עַמִּי֙ יְבָזּ֔וּם וְיֶ֥תֶר °גוי יִנְחָלֽוּם׃

°שְׁבִיתָם ק׳

°גּוֹיִי ק׳

as pasture land for their flocks (*Radak*). Alternatively, the expressions referring to the flocks of sheep are to be understood metaphorically representing the Judeans who are returning from exile. They will rebuild the Philistine ruins and dwell there in peace (*Targum Yonasan; Radak*).

כִּי יִפְקְדֵם ה׳ אֱלֹהֵיהֶם — *For Hashem, their God, will remember them.*

Although the Judeans and Philistines will both be exiled and their lands laid to waste, their lot will not be the same, for God will have the Judeans return to their land and also possess the lands of the Philistines (*Abarbanel*).

◆§ The Destruction of Moab and Ammon

8. שָׁמַעְתִּי חֶרְפַּת מוֹאָב וְגִדּוּפֵי בְּנֵי עַמּוֹן ... — *I have heard the taunt of Moab and the jeers of the children of Ammon ...*

When the Israelites were being led northward to the land of the Chaldeans,[1] they passed through the lands of their neighbors, Moab and Ammon. God announces that Moab and Ammon will suffer severe retribution for their wicked taunting of the Israelites as they went into exile. Seeing the despondent Jews sobbing, groaning and weeping in their anguish, these wicked people taunted them and called out, "Why do you sob and weep so? Are you not returning to the land of your forefathers who dwelt on the other side of the Euphrates from earliest times?" — see *Joshua* 24:2 (*Rashi, Mahari Kara* from *Midrash*). Furthermore, when the heathens entered the Holy of Holies, Ammonites and Moabites entered with them and removed the Cherubs. Marching through the streets with the Cherubs held high, they proclaimed, "The Israelites always claimed that they did not worship idols. What, then, were they doing with these? They were worshiping these images all the time!" (*Yalkut* from *Pesikta*).

וַיַּגְדִּילוּ עַל־גְּבוּלָם — *And became haughty on their border.*

Our translation follows *Rashi* and *Targum Yonasan* who understand that the Moabites arrogantly mocked and taunted the Israelites as they passed their border. *Radak* renders: *They expanded* their mouths and tongues, they opened their mouths wide to mock the children of Israel as the latter crossed *over their border* [into their land]. Alternatively, they taunted the Israelites regarding *the border of Israel which was destroyed* and in ruins (ibid.; *R' Eliezer of Beaugency*). Others interpret: *They extended their borders* — by annexing portions of the conquered Land of Israel (*Abarbanel; Malbim*).[2] *Ibn Ezra*

1. The Chaldeans dwelt north of the Euphrates River.

2. *Malbim* interprets גִּדּוּף to refer specifically to the profaning of that which is sanctified. Thus Moab ridiculed My nation, but Ammon profaned that which is holy when they annexed portions of the Holy Land for their use.

they will lie down in the evening, for HASHEM, their God, will remember them and will return their captivity.

[8] I have heard the taunt of Moab and the jeers of the children of Ammon who taunted My people, and became haughty on their border. [9] Therefore, as I live — the word of HASHEM, Master of Legions, God of Israel — [I swear] that Moab will be like Sodom and the children of Ammon like Gomorrah, a rustling thornbush, a salt mine, a desolate wasteland forever. The remnant of My people will loot them and the remainder of My nation will inherit them.

renders: *While they were still on their borders* — before they [too] were exiled.

9. מוֹאָב כִּסְדֹם תִּהְיֶה וּבְנֵי עַמּוֹן כַּעֲמֹרָה — *Moab will be like Sodom and the children of Ammon like Gomorrah.*

Because Moab mockingly told My people in their hour of agony that they are merely returning to the land of their forefathers, so shall I return you to the state of your forefathers' land. Was not your progenitor, Lot, from Sodom? Indeed, I swear that your land will be destroyed forever as was Sodom, the land of your forefather (*Rashi; Mahari Kara; Abarbanel* from *Midrash*).

The fate of Ammon shall be even more severe for they profaned the sanctity of the Holy Land and the sanctity of God's Name. Whereas Lot and his daughters survived the destruction of Sodom, Ammon's end will be like that of the city of Gomorrah, from which no one survived (*Malbim*).

Pesikta states that at the very moment that Ammon paraded the Cherubs in the streets, the Almighty swore, "Moab shall be like Sodom and the children of Ammon like Gomorrah."

מִמְשַׁק חָרוּל — *A rustling thornbush.*

Because of the absence of any passerby, the only sound that will be heard is the sound of thornbushes and thistles rattling against each other (*Rashi*). Others render *a land abandoned to thornbushes (Targum Yonasan; Radak,* citing his father) or *desolate place, which breeds thornbushes* (*Mahari Kara; Radak*). *Ibn Ezra* interprets *a permanent home for thornbushes.*

וּמִכְרֵה־מֶלַח — *A salt mine.*

Rashi relates the word מִכְרֵה to כְּרִיַּת, *to dig. Radak* adds that it may be related to כְּרִי, *a mound.* In any event, the lands of Moab and Ammon will become full of salt mines (*Rashi*) or mounds of salt (*Radak*). Furthermore, wherever one digs he will find salt (*Abarbanel; Metzudos*), just like the cities of the plains that were destroyed together with Sodom (*Malbim*). *Mahari Kara* adds that in the places where salt is mined nothing will ever grow.

שְׁאֵרִית עַמִּי יְבָזּוּם וְיֶתֶר גּוֹיִי יִנְחָלוּם — *The remnant of My people will loot them and the remainder of My nation will inherit them.*

When the people return from the Babylonian exile, they will plunder and inherit the conquered lands of Ammon and Moab (*Radak; Metzudos*). *Radak* suggests that this may also refer to Messianic times.

י זֹאת לָהֶם תַּחַת גְּאוֹנָם כִּי חֵרְפוּ וַיַּגְדִּלוּ עַל־עַם
יא יהוה צְבָאוֹת: נוֹרָא יהוה עֲלֵיהֶם כִּי רָזָה אֵת כָּל־
אֱלֹהֵי הָאָרֶץ וְיִשְׁתַּחֲווּ־לוֹ אִישׁ מִמְּקוֹמוֹ כֹּל אִיֵּי
יב־יג הַגּוֹיִם: גַּם־אַתֶּם כּוּשִׁים חַלְלֵי חַרְבִּי הֵמָּה: וְיֵט
יָדוֹ עַל־צָפוֹן וִיאַבֵּד אֶת־אַשּׁוּר וְיָשֵׂם אֶת־נִינְוֵה
יד לִשְׁמָמָה צִיָּה כַּמִּדְבָּר: וְרָבְצוּ בְתוֹכָהּ עֲדָרִים כָּל־
חַיְתוֹ־גוֹי גַּם־קָאַת גַּם־קִפֹּד בְּכַפְתֹּרֶיהָ יָלִינוּ קוֹל

Malbim interprets עַם as referring to the notables among the nation and גּוֹי to the common folk. He also maintains that שְׁאֵרִית applies to those who remain behind of their own volition, whereas יֶתֶר are those who are forced by others to remain. Thus, the notables among the nation, who chose to remain in the Holy Land, as described in the first chapter of *Daniel*, will plunder the lands of Ammon and Moab but will not settle there [for they would rather settle in the Holy Land itself]. The common people, who were forced to remain in the land, will inhabit those lands as well.

10. זֹאת לָהֶם תַּחַת גְּאוֹנָם ... — *This they shall have in place of their haughtiness ...*

Although these gentile nations are guilty of murder, idolatry and adultery, the three cardinal sins, this punishment will befall them only because they taunted and mocked the Children of Israel in their time of anguish (*Malbim*).

וַיַּגְדִּלוּ עַל־עַם ה׳ צְבָאוֹת — *And boasted over the people of Hashem, Master of Legions.*

They taunted Israel, the people who worship Hashem, Master of Legions, by claiming that they worshiped idols (*Abarbanel*).

11. נוֹרָא ה׳ עֲלֵיהֶם ... — *Hashem will be fearsome unto them ...*

Although the nations of the world now mock and jeer the Children of Israel and the God of Israel, a time will come when He will be feared by all the nations and they will be afraid to harm His people (*Radak*). Alternatively, on that day the *people of Israel* will fear God (*Targum Yonasan; Radak*).

כִּי רָזָה אֵת כָּל־אֱלֹהֵי הָאָרֶץ ... — *For He will enfeeble all the powers of the earth ...*

When the nations will witness the destruction of their deities and how they were powerless against Him and His people, they will prostrate themselves before Him, the Almighty God, from their own land, wherever they live, even from the most distant islands (*Rashi, Metzudos*). *Targum Yonasan* understands that this is referring to the Children of Israel who will be inspired to fear God when they will witness His destruction of the heathen gods.

◆§ The Destruction of the Cushites

12. גַּם־אַתֶּם כּוּשִׁים חַלְלֵי חַרְבִּי הֵמָּה — *You, too, Cushites, you are slain by My sword.*

People of Cush, you also deserve punishment because you taunted the Children of Israel when they were led into exile and were taken to the other side of the rivers of Cush (*Rashi; Malbim*). Although you dwell far from the Land of Israel, you nevertheless found the means to harm the Jewish people and you shall therefore be slain by God's sword (*Radak*).

The prophet switches from the second person אַתֶּם, *you*, to the third person הֵמָּה, *they*, in midverse, as is prevalent throughout Scripture (*Radak*). Alternatively, חַלְלֵי חַרְבִּי הֵמָּה should be understood as if Scripture would have written כְּהֵמָּה, *like* them; you are

[10] This they shall have in place of their haughtiness, for they taunted and boasted over the people of HASHEM*, Master of Legions. [11]* HASHEM *will be fearsome unto them, for He will enfeeble all the powers of the earth. And they will prostrate themselves to Him, each man from his place, all the islands of the nations.*

[12] You, too, Cushites, you are slain by My sword.

[13] He will stretch out His hand toward the north and He will destroy Assyria; he will make Nineveh a wasteland, arid as the desert. [14] Herds will lie down in its midst, every nation's beasts; both owls and bitterns will lodge in its capitals, [their] voice

to be slain by My sword *like* them, i.e., like the nations of Ammon and Moab (*Yapheth*, cited by *Ibn Ezra; Radak*). *Abarbanel* writes that this will take place during Messianic times.

☙§ The Destruction of Assyria

13. וְיֵט יָדוֹ עַל־צָפוֹן וִיאַבֵּד אֶת־אַשּׁוּר... — *He will stretch out His hand toward the north and He will destroy Assyria ...*

This prophecy is regarding Assyria exclusively for it is she who lies north of the Land of Israel (*Rashi*). Alternatively, עַל־צָפוֹן, *against the north*, is referring to a northern nation not mentioned by name, i.e., Babylonia (*Radak*). The Babylonians will be destroyed for destroying Judea, Jerusalem and the Holy Temple; the Assyrians, for exiling the Ten Tribes of the Northern Kingdom (*Radak; Abarbanel*).

וְיָשֵׂם אֶת־נִינְוֵה לִשְׁמָמָה צִיָּה כַּמִּדְבָּר ... — *He will make Nineveh a wasteland ...*

Nineveh, the capital city of Assyria (*Rashi*), will be a desolate wasteland fit only for sheep grazing, unfit for human habitation (*Abarbanel*).

14. וְרָבְצוּ בְתוֹכָהּ עֲדָרִים כָּל־חַיְתוֹ־גוֹי ... — *Herds will lie down in its midst, every nation's beasts ...*

Although we have translated חַיְתוֹ according to its common meaning *beasts*, in this verse it actually means *cattle* (*Rashi*). *Metzudos* notes that it is not uncommon for Scripture to refer to cattle as חיות — see *Psalms* 78:50.

Scripture describes the extent of Nineveh's destruction. No longer will the city be inhabited by people, but by herds of cattle and flocks of sheep that the residents of the surrounding nations will bring to graze on the site of the once mighty city (*Metzudos*).

גַּם־קָאַת גַּם־קִפֹּד... — *Both owls and bitterns ...* These are desert birds that inhabit ruins when in civilized areas (*Metzudos*). They will lodge in all of the beautiful buildings that are lying desolate (*Abarbanel*), and the songs of the birds will be heard through the windows (*Rashi*).

כַּפְתֹּרֶיהָ — *Its capitals.*

These are the rounded knobs on the tops of the roofs (*Rashi*). *Radak* explains that it is a term used for the door lintels because they were often covered with pictures of flowers and knobs.

ב/טו

טו יְשׁוֹרֵר בַּחַלּוֹן חֹרֶב בַּסַּף כִּי אַרְזָה עֵרָה׃ זֹאת הָעִיר הָעַלִּיזָה הַיּוֹשֶׁבֶת לָבֶטַח הָאֹמְרָה בִּלְבָבָהּ אֲנִי וְאַפְסִי עוֹד אֵיךְ | הָיְתָה לְשַׁמָּה מַרְבֵּץ לַחַיָּה כֹּל עוֹבֵר עָלֶיהָ יִשְׁרֹק יָנִיעַ יָדוֹ׃

ג/א־ג

א הוֹי מֹרְאָה וְנִגְאָלָה הָעִיר הַיּוֹנָה׃ ב לֹא שָׁמְעָה בְּקוֹל לֹא לָקְחָה מוּסָר בַּיהוה לֹא בָטָחָה אֶל־אֱלֹהֶיהָ לֹא קָרֵבָה׃ ג שָׂרֶיהָ בְקִרְבָּהּ אֲרָיוֹת שֹׁאֲגִים שֹׁפְטֶיהָ זְאֵבֵי עֶרֶב לֹא גָרְמוּ לַבֹּקֶר׃

חֹרֶב בַּסַּף ... — *Desolation will be in its doorway ...*

The doorposts[1] will corrode and rot from the destruction, for the enemy will strip bare the cedar ceilings above them, thus exposing them to the destructive elements (*Targum Yonasan; Radak*). *Rashi* renders: *For its cedarwork has been destroyed* — i.e., He will have uprooted and totally destroyed its cedars.

15. זֹאת הָעִיר הָעַלִּיזָה ... — *This is the exultant city ...*

This mighty city of Nineveh at one time was joyful, happy and prosperous. She sat astride the entire world in its incomparable might, and considered itself unique and alone in its greatness (*Metzudos*).

אֵיךְ הָיְתָה לְשַׁמָּה ... — *How did it become desolate ...*

It, too, will fall and become desolate until all who pass by shall whistle in wonderment over its destruction and wave their hands in sympathy for its fate (*Abarbanel*).

III

Zephaniah's first prophecy, as recorded in Chapter One, foretold the destruction of the Kingdom of Judah and its capital city, Jerusalem — see 1:1-2:3. The prophet then foretold the destruction of Israel's neighbors: the Philistines, Moabites, Ammonites, Cushites and Assyrians, with special attention given to Nineveh, the Assyrian capital. He now returns to his original theme and directs his words to the city of Jerusalem. He begins by describing the faults and sins of the city, for which it is to be conquered and destroyed, but continues on to prophesy about its ultimate redemption and restoration to glory (*Rashi; Radak; Ibn Ezra*). In a novel approach, *Abarbanel* maintains that this chapter is describing the glory of Israel in the times of the Second Temple as well as its eventual destruction. According to *Malbim*, the prophet is foretelling events of the future redemption.

1. הוֹי מֹרְאָה וְנִגְאָלָה הָעִיר הַיּוֹנָה — *Woe to the filthy and polluted one, the dove-like city.*

Our translation of הָעִיר הַיּוֹנָה, *the dove-like city*, follows *Rashi* who renders *woe to the city of Jerusalem which has been polluted with the filth of her sins.* She behaves like a foolish dove without the intelligence to know what is good for her and what is not. Others relate the word הַיּוֹנָה to לֹא תוֹנוּ, *you shall not aggrieve* — *Lev.* 25:17 (*Radak; Ibn Ezra*) — and explain that the prophet refers to Jerusalem as the City of Oppression because of the corruption and oppression that prevailed in the city — see v. 3. הָעִיר הַיּוֹנָה may also be interpreted as *the city that is similar to a dove in her beauty* (*Ibn Ezra*).

1. Some commentators understand these doorposts to be those of the houses of Nineveh (*Rashi; Mahari Kara; Malbim*). Others interpret this as referring to the doorposts of the city gates (*Radak; Abarbanel; Metzudos*).

2/15 *will sing out in the window; desolation will be in its doorway, for the cedarwork will be removed.* [15] *This is the exultant city that dwelt in security; that said in its heart, "Only I, and besides me, nothing." How did it become desolate, a resting place for the beast? Everyone who passes by it will whistle and wave his hand.*

3/1-3

[1] *Woe to the filthy and polluted one, the dovelike city.* [2] *She did not listen to the voice [of the prophets]; she did not accept chastisement; she did not trust in* HASHEM; *she did not draw near to her God.* [3] *Her princes in her midst are roaring lions; her judges are wolves of the evening, they do not leave a bone for the morning;*

מֹרְאָה — *Filthy.*

Rashi relates the word מֹרְאָה to מֻרְאָתָה, *the [bird's] crop — Lev.* 1:16 and to רֹאִי, *dung — Nahum* 3:6. Others understand this verse as noting the former glory of Jerusalem which has now been lost. They translate מֹרְאָה as *fearsome* and render *the city that had been feared by all other nations is now sullied with her blood* (*Mahari Kara*). According to *R' Yeshayah* cited by *Ibn Ezra*, מֹרְאָה means *rebellious*, as in בֵּן סוֹרֵר וּמוֹרֶה.

The Sages see the entire verse as a description of the former glory of the Jewish nation, and interpret it as a preface to the prophecy that foretells of its destruction: Woe to the nation whose fear I had placed upon the entire world when I redeemed them from Egypt and woe to the city that I considered outstanding in her mitzvah observance and performance of good deeds, like a dove (*Yalkut* from *Eichah Rabbasi*).

2. ... לֹא שָׁמְעָה בְּקוֹל — *She did not listen to the voice [of the prophets] ...*

Our translation follows *Targum Yonasan*. She did not listen to the voice of the prophets who reprimanded the people (*Ibn Ezra*) and instructed them [to follow in God's way] (*Radak*).

לֹא לָקְחָה מוּסָר — *She did not accept chastisement.*

Even after witnessing the destruction of the Northern Kingdom and the exile of the Ten Tribes, the people of Judah did not learn a lesson and change their evil ways (*Metzudos*).

... בַּה' לֹא בָטָחָה — *She did not trust in Hashem ...*

She turned to foreign powers for military assistance and did not place her faith in God and draw near to Him to seek His assistance (*Metzudos*).

3. ... שָׂרֶיהָ בְקִרְבָּהּ אֲרָיוֹת שֹׁאֲגִים — *Her princes in her midst are roaring lions ...*

The prophet describes the ruthlessness of the Judean leaders. Like roaring lions the princes terrorize the people (*Metzudos*). They rob them and prey upon them like lions who roar over their prey (*Mahari Kara*).

שֹׁפְטֶיהָ זְאֵבֵי עֶרֶב — *Her judges are wolves of the evening.*

Her judges seize bribes from the people and swiftly consume them as do hungry wolves who have not eaten all day (*Metzudos*).

לֹא גָרְמוּ לַבֹּקֶר — *They do not leave a bone for the morning.*

So thorough and swift was the treachery of the Judean judges that Scripture compares them to the wolves who leave nothing of their kill for the morning, not even the bones to gnaw (*Metzudos*).

ד נְבִיאֶ֙יהָ֙ פֹּֽחֲזִ֔ים אַנְשֵׁ֖י בֹּֽגְד֑וֹת כֹּהֲנֶ֙יהָ֙ חִלְּלוּ־קֹ֔דֶשׁ חָמְס֖וּ
ה תּוֹרָֽה׃ יְהוָ֤ה צַדִּיק֙ בְּקִרְבָּ֔הּ לֹ֥א יַעֲשֶׂ֖ה עַוְלָ֑ה בַּבֹּ֨קֶר
בַּבֹּ֜קֶר מִשְׁפָּט֨וֹ יִתֵּ֤ן לָאוֹר֙ לֹ֣א נֶעְדָּ֔ר וְלֹֽא־יוֹדֵ֥עַ עַוָּ֖ל
ו בֹּֽשֶׁת׃ הִכְרַ֣תִּי גוֹיִ֗ם נָשַׁ֙מּוּ֙ פִּנּוֹתָ֔ם הֶחֱרַ֥בְתִּי חֽוּצוֹתָ֖ם
מִבְּלִ֣י עוֹבֵ֑ר נִצְדּ֧וּ עָרֵיהֶ֛ם מִבְּלִי־אִ֖ישׁ מֵאֵ֥ין יוֹשֵֽׁב׃

Malbim crystallizes the analogy. The princes brazenly rob and steal for they fear no one and need not conceal their treachery. Scripture therefore compares them to the lion who publicly emits a mighty roar over his kill. The judges who are not as powerful must take their bribery secretly and quickly, like the wolf who slaughters his prey in the darkness of the night and leaves no remnant, for he even devours the bones.

4. נְבִיאֶיהָ פֹּחֲזִים — *Her prophets are impetuous.*

Her false prophets (*Targum Yonasan; Radak*) are impulsive (*Rashi* to *Judges* 9:4), frivolous (*Radak*) and are void of any substance (*Ibn Ezra*). *R' Hirsch* adds they are of unstable character (*Genesis* 49:4). They feign prophecy only because they have no food to eat and the people feed them for the prophecies they claim to foretell (*Ibn Ezra*).

אַנְשֵׁי בֹּגְדוֹת — *Men of rebellion.*

Ibn Ezra as well as *Malbim* note that the word בֹּגְדוֹת is the female form of the adjective *rebellious* and בֹּגְדִים would seem more correct. They therefore explain that אַנְשֵׁי בֹּגְדוֹת actually means *men of unfaithful women*, the women are disloyal to their husbands. The false prophets had illicit relations with the Judean women.

כֹּהֲנֶיהָ חִלְּלוּ־קֹדֶשׁ חָמְסוּ תּוֹרָה — *Her priests have desecrated the sacred; they have robbed the Torah.*

The priests who are charged with the mission of teaching the nation to distinguish between the sacred and the profane — see *Lev.* 10:10 (*Mahari Kara*) — have themselves desecrated that which is sacred (*Radak*). In addition, they, who are responsible for teaching Torah to the people — see *Deut.* 33:10 — robbed them of their rightful heritage by withholding it from those who sought its knowledge (*Rashi*). *Radak* adds that these priests themselves transgressed the precepts of the Torah. Others explain that they robbed the Torah by issuing rulings that are inconsistent with its teachings (*Mahari Kara*).

5. ה׳ צַדִּיק בְּקִרְבָּהּ לֹא יַעֲשֶׂה עַוְלָה — *Hashem, the Righteous One, is in her midst; He commits no corruption.*

Despite their wickedness, the Almighty has permitted His Divine Presence to reside in their midst. However, because He is absolutely righteous, He cannot tolerate their evil deeds (*Rashi*). Any punishment they receive, they deserve, for He commits no injustice (*Radak*). Unlike *Rashi* and *Radak* who understand the words *He commits no injustice* as a reference to God, *Ibn Ezra* maintains that these words are referring to the inhabitants of Jerusalem. Because God Who is righteous is in their midst, the people should have never committed any injustice. *Malbim* explains Hashem is the Righteous One in their midst, for He alone has remained steadfast in His righteousness.

בַּבֹּקֶר בַּבֹּקֶר מִשְׁפָּטוֹ יִתֵּן לָאוֹר... — *Morning after morning, He brings His judgment to light ...*

Although God judges an absolutely true judgment every morning and His Divine Presence dwells in the midst of the city, the unjust judges are not ashamed to act in the manner that they do (*Rashi*). Alternatively, although Israel continuously witnesses God's judgment

[4] her prophets are impetuous, men of rebellion; her priests have desecrated the sacred; they have robbed the Torah. [5] HASHEM, the Righteous One, is in her midst; He commits no corruption. Morning after morning, He brings His judgment to light, it does not fail, but the corrupt one knows no shame. [6] I have eliminated nations, their towers have become desolate; I have destroyed their streets without passerby; their cities have become ruins, without people, so there is no inhabitant.

against the nations, he, Israel, is not ashamed to continue in his unjust ways (*Ibn Ezra*). Some see this as a continuation of the first portion of the verse. The Almighty is just in His punishment, for He has consistently sent His prophets every morning to warn the people of their punishment if they continue to persist in their wicked ways (*R' Eliezer of Beaugency*).

R' Joseph Kimchi explains this verse differently. From the time that God created light, He gives the light its מִשְׁפָּט, *its authority to shine every morning,* בַּבֹּקֶר בַּבֹּקֶר מִשְׁפָּטוֹ יִתֵּן לָאוֹר לֹא נֶעְדָּר; and although mankind may anger God through his evil deeds and be undeserving, He does not allow it to fail and it continues to shine. The unjust person does not have the sense of shame to realize that just as God keeps His faith upon us, so should we reciprocate and place our faith in Him.

6-7. Generally, God allows the gentile nations to follow their chosen paths in this world and exacts retribution for their misdeeds in the World to Come. However, there are times when He alters this approach and brings punishment upon an idolatrous nation so that the Jews who are witnesses to this retribution will be fearful of being punished themselves and will thus be moved to repent their own sins. In the following two verses, the prophet describes how the Almighty brought destruction upon the idolatrous nations in order to arouse Israel to repent — see *Yevamos* 63a.

6. הִכְרַתִּי גוֹיִם ... — *I have eliminated nations ...*

I have brought retribution upon the nations so that the Israelites will see and be struck with fear and will hasten to repent their ways (*Rashi*). *R' Eliezer of Beaugency* adds: I have shown the Jewish people the severity of My judgment by eliminating entire nations through the conquests of Sennacherib and Nebuchadnezzer.

נָשַׁמּוּ פִּנּוֹתָם — *Their towers have become desolate.*

See comm. to 1:16.

מֵאֵין יוֹשֵׁב — *So there is no inhabitant.*

Metzudos renders there is no one passing by or visiting because there are no inhabitants. *Mahari Kara* writes that this may be compared to a father who must punish his loving son for a wrongdoing that he committed. Instead of punishing his son, he punishes his slave [for his wrongdoing] so that the son may see the punishment and thereby learn his lesson.

Malbim interprets this verse as describing the gradual destruction of these nations in three distinct steps. First, God laid waste to their corners, פִּנּוֹתָם, the edges and borders of the nations. Next, He turned their roads and highways, which run outside the main cities and through the smaller villages, into ruins. Finally, He allowed the conquering enemy to complete his conquest, capturing and destroying even the mighty cities.

ג/ז־ט

ז אָמַ֨רְתִּי אַךְ־תִּירְאִ֤י אוֹתִי֙ תִּקְחִ֣י מוּסָ֔ר וְלֹֽא־יִכָּרֵ֣ת מְעוֹנָ֔הּ כֹּ֥ל אֲשֶׁר־פָּקַ֖דְתִּי עָלֶ֑יהָ אָכֵן֙ הִשְׁכִּ֣ימוּ הִשְׁחִ֔יתוּ כֹּ֖ל עֲלִילוֹתָֽם׃ ח לָכֵ֤ן חַכּוּ־לִי֙ נְאֻם־יְהוָ֔ה לְי֖וֹם קוּמִ֣י לְעַ֑ד כִּ֣י מִשְׁפָּטִי֩ לֶאֱסֹ֨ף גּוֹיִ֜ם לְקָבְצִ֣י מַמְלָכ֗וֹת לִשְׁפֹּ֨ךְ עֲלֵיהֶ֤ם זַעְמִי֙ כֹּ֚ל חֲר֣וֹן אַפִּ֔י כִּ֚י בְּאֵ֣שׁ קִנְאָתִ֔י תֵּאָכֵ֖ל כָּל־הָאָֽרֶץ׃ ט כִּי־אָ֛ז אֶהְפֹּ֥ךְ אֶל־עַמִּ֖ים שָׂפָ֣ה בְרוּרָ֑ה לִקְרֹ֤א כֻלָּם֙ בְּשֵׁ֣ם יְהוָ֔ה לְעָבְד֖וֹ שְׁכֶ֥ם אֶחָֽד׃

7. אָמַרְתִּי אַךְ־תִּירְאִי אוֹתִי תִּקְחִי מוּסָר — *I said, "Just fear Me, accept chastisement.*

I assumed that upon witnessing the destruction wrought upon the gentile nations the people would learn to fear Me and would surely improve their ways (*Metzudos*).

Malbim interprets the phrase *just fear Me* as referring to the awe of G-d's greatness. However, declares the Almighty, even if you will not reach that lofty level, you should at least be frightened from the punishments I may bring upon you.

וְלֹא־יִכָּרֵת מְעוֹנָהּ ... — *So that her abode will not be terminated ..."*

If Israel will react in this manner, her dwellings will not be destroyed from upon the land that houses My Divine Presence, nor will all the good that I have ordained to bring upon her be cut off from her (*Targum; Rashi*). Our translation, however, follows *Radak* and *Metzudos* who explain that מְעוֹנָהּ, *her abode*, is referring specifically to the city of Jerusalem (*Radak*) or to the Holy Temple, the dwelling place of the Divine Presence on earth (*Metzudos*). Had the Israelites repented, the First Temple would have stood for all eternity and all the blessings associated with the Third Temple would have been fulfilled through it (*Alshich*).

אָכֵן הִשְׁכִּימוּ הִשְׁחִיתוּ כֹּל עֲלִילוֹתָם — *But [instead] they arose early and corrupted all their deeds.*

[Despite all My hopes and endeavors] the Children of Israel have been zealous in pursuing every conceivable form of corruption and debasement (*Radak*).

8. לָכֵן חַכּוּ־לִי נְאֻם־ה׳ — *Therefore, wait for Me — the word of Hashem.*

After waiting in vain for Israel to repent, God informs the people that now it will be *their* turn to wait (*Malbim*). Since you refuse to heed My rebuke and return to Me, I will not hasten your redemption as I had wished, and you will have to wait for its designated day (*Mezudos*). Nevertheless, although it may take many years for this to come about, do not despair. Continue to await and seek it, for in the end it will certainly take place (*Abarbanel*).

לְיוֹם קוּמִי לְעַד — *For the day when I will arise to plunder [them].*

Our translation follows *Radak, Ibn Ezra* and *Metzudos* who relate לְעַד to בַּבֹּקֶר יֹאכַל עַד, *in the morning he will devour prey (Genesis* 49:27). On the day that God will plunder the nations that oppressed the Jewish people, that is when your salvation will arrive. *Rashi,* however, relates לְעַד to לְהִתְוַעֵד, *to meet,* and renders *for the day when I will arise to meet with you* [apparently referring to the day that God's Presence will return and dwell among His people]. According to *Abarbanel,* לְעַד is an uncommon form of לָעַד, *forever.* When that long-awaited day finally arrives, it shall not herald a temporary redemption like the redemption from Egypt and Babylonia. The redemption that will take place at the end of days will be full and final. It will be forever: as long as the world exists (*Abarbanel; Malbim*).

כִּי מִשְׁפָּטִי לֶאֱסֹף גּוֹיִם לְקָבְצִי מַמְלָכוֹת ... — *For*

[7] I said, "Just fear Me, accept chastisement, so that her abode will not be terminated, despite all that I have ordained upon her." But [instead] they arose early and corrupted all their deeds.

[8] Therefore, wait for Me — the word of HASHEM — for the day when I will arise to plunder [them]. For My judgment will be to assemble nations, to gather kingdoms, to pour My fury upon them, all My burning wrath; for with the fire of My jealousy the entire earth will be consumed. [9] For then I will change the nations [to speak] a pure language, so that they all will proclaim the Name of HASHEM, to worship Him with a united resolve.

My judgment will be to assemble nations, to gather kingdoms ...

At that time, I will bring about the war of Gog and Magog, in which I will assemble nations and gather kingdoms against Jerusalem so that I may exact My retribution from them (*Radak*). *Abarbanel* maintains that גּוֹיִם, *nations,* is referring to the Christians and מַמְלָכוֹת, *kingdoms,* is referring to the many kingdoms of the Arab world. During the war of Gog and Magog, the Christian nations will battle the Arab world and devastate each other in their war over the Holy Land.

כִּי בְּאֵשׁ קִנְאָתִי תֵּאָכֵל כָּל־הָאָרֶץ — *For with the fire of My jealousy the entire earth will be consumed.*

In the flames of My fury I will destroy most of the inhabitants of the earth (*Radak*) because they worshiped idols (*Ibn Ezra*) and mistreated the Children of Israel (*R' Eliezer of Beaugency*).

9. כִּי־אָז אֶהְפֹּךְ אֶל־עַמִּים שָׂפָה בְרוּרָה — *For then I will change the nations [to speak] a pure language.*

After the war of Gog and Magog, the surviving nations will no longer utter the impure names of their heathen gods but will speak a pure language, i.e., they will call out together in the Name of the true God (*Radak*). *Malbim* notes although some nations may have worshiped the true God, it was not בְּשָׂפָה בְרוּרָה, *in a pure language,* for those religions had false and idolatrous concepts of the unity of God. Alternatively, all the nations will then speak in the Holy Tongue of Hebrew, the most perfect of all languages (*Mahari Kara*). It is only in Hebrew that God's venerable Name can be expressed correctly (*Ibn Ezra*).

The word אֶהְפֹּךְ can also mean *I will turn* implying that the nations will turn back and again speak a language that they had previously spoken. *Abarbanel* explains that before the sin of the Tower of Babel, all the nations of the world spoke one common language, Hebrew — see *Rashi* to *Gen.* 11:1. Because of the sin, God confounded their speech which resulted in the dispersion of the nations and the evolution of different languages and religions. After witnessing the great wonders of God that will take place during this war, they will all call out in the Name of the true God in the very language that they originally spoke.

לִקְרֹא כֻלָּם בְּשֵׁם ה׳ לְעָבְדוֹ שְׁכֶם אֶחָד — *So that they all will proclaim the Name of Hashem, to worship Him with a united resolve.*

They will all unite in full-hearted devotion to the service of G-d (*Radak*),

י מֵעֵבֶר לְנַהֲרֵי־כוּשׁ עֲתָרַי בַּת־פּוּצַי יוֹבִלוּן
יא מִנְחָתִי׃ בַּיּוֹם הַהוּא לֹא תֵבוֹשִׁי מִכֹּל עֲלִילֹתַיִךְ
אֲשֶׁר פָּשַׁעַתְּ בִּי כִּי־אָז | אָסִיר מִקִּרְבֵּךְ עַלִּיזֵי
גַּאֲוָתֵךְ וְלֹא־תוֹסִפִי לְגָבְהָה עוֹד בְּהַר קָדְשִׁי׃
יב וְהִשְׁאַרְתִּי בְקִרְבֵּךְ עַם עָנִי וָדָל וְחָסוּ בְּשֵׁם
יג יְהוָה׃ שְׁאֵרִית יִשְׂרָאֵל לֹא־יַעֲשׂוּ עַוְלָה וְלֹא־
יְדַבְּרוּ כָזָב וְלֹא־יִמָּצֵא בְּפִיהֶם לְשׁוֹן תַּרְמִית

serving Him in the manner required by the Torah, rather than each group choosing its own form of worship (*Malbim*). Some say that שְׁכֶם means *shoulder* and explain that the nations of the world will all turn their shoulders together to bear the burden of serving the Almighty (*R' Eliezer of Beaugency*). *Mahari Kara* translates שְׁכֶם אֶחָד as *one group* and suggests that the nations of the world will all convert together to Judaism in order to serve Hashem.

The unprecedented unity among the nations to call out in the Name of G-d will follow the great miracle of תְּחִיַּת הַמֵּתִים, *the resurrection of the dead*, which will take place at that time. The resurrection will occur in every location and the resurrected will call out in the Name of God. Upon witnessing this most amazing occurrence, the nations, too, will call out in the Name of God (*Abarbanel*).

10. מֵעֵבֶר לְנַהֲרֵי־כוּשׁ עֲתָרַי בַּת־פּוּצַי יוֹבִלוּן מִנְחָתִי — *From the other side of the rivers of Cush, My supplicants, groups of My scattered ones, will bring My tribute.*

Our translation follows *Rashi* who understands that עֲתָרַי, *My supplicants*, and בַּת־פּוּצַי, *My scattered ones*, are referring to the Children of Israel (*Abarbanel*). The Children of Israel, who beseech Me with prayer and whom I have exiled, will bring Me My tribute (*Ibn Ezra*). Alternatively, עֲתָרַי בַּת־פּוּצַי is the name of a nation who dwelt beyond the rivers of Cush. The recognition of God will be so complete that even this distant nation will be moved to bring a great tribute to God, i.e., they will bring the exiled Children of Israel who live among them — see *Isaiah* 66:20 (*Radak*).

11. בַּיּוֹם הַהוּא לֹא תֵבוֹשִׁי מִכֹּל עֲלִילֹתַיִךְ אֲשֶׁר פָּשַׁעַתְּ בִּי — *On that day, you will not be ashamed of all your deeds by which you have wantonly sinned against Me.*

When the final redemption will come, the Children of Israel will have no reason to be ashamed because they will have already been sufficiently punished for their misdeeds and their sins will have surely been atoned (*Rashi*). Others interpret: the Children of Israel will no longer perform deeds from which they will suffer embarrassment (*Radak*). The majority of their sins had been due to the influence of their idolatrous neighbors. Now that all the nations devote themselves wholeheartedly to the service of God, the Children of Israel will no longer be influenced (*Malbim*).

כִּי־אָז אָסִיר מִקִּרְבֵּךְ עַלִּיזֵי גַּאֲוָתֵךְ — *For then I will remove from your midst those who exult in your arrogance.*

No longer will the nation suffer from those in their midst who are haughty and arrogant, and even jubilant in these character flaws (*Radak*). *Mahari Kara* adds: those who are haughty and arrogant and have no regard or respect for others. [Haughty people eventually remove their focus entirely from others and ultimately give them no consideration whatsoever.]

וְלֹא־תוֹסִפִי לְגָבְהָה עוֹד בְּהַר קָדְשִׁי — *And you will no longer continue to be haughty on My holy mountain.*

[10] From the other side of the rivers of Cush, My supplicants, groups of My scattered ones, will bring My tribute. [11] On that day, you will not be ashamed of all your deeds by which you have wantonly sinned against Me. For then I will remove from your midst those who exult in your arrogance, and you will no longer continue to be haughty on My holy mountain. [12] And I will leave in your midst a humble and submissive people, and they will take shelter in the Name of HASHEM. [13] The remnant of Israel will not commit corruption, they will not speak falsehood, and a deceitful tongue will not be found in their mouth;

God will remove those who are haughty because of their presence on the mountain of G-d (*Ibn Ezra*). Alternatively, this is referring to those who are inordinately proud of their spiritual achievements. They will be removed together with those who are haughty in an evil way (*Abarbanel*).

The Talmud teaches that arrogance is so evil in nature that (if one may say) it pushes away the Divine Presence — see *Sotah* 5a.

12. וְהִשְׁאַרְתִּי בְקִרְבֵּךְ עַם עָנִי וָדָל — *And I will leave in your midst a humble and submissive people.*

Our translation follows *Radak* who relates the word עָנִי to עָנָיו, *humble,* and translates דָל, *low in spirit.* When all of the proud and haughty ones of the nation will be removed, only those who are humble and submissive, submitting even to humiliation, will remain (*Targum; Rashi; Mahari Kara; Radak*). [It is only the humble person who is truly placing his trust in the Almighty rather than in his own strength and glory.]

Others translate this phrase literally, i.e., *a poor and destitute people.* Due to their wanderings and tribulations in exile, even the wealthy among the nation will lose their riches, and in this condition they will be redeemed (*Abarbanel*).

Abarbanel notes that unlike the redemption from Egypt, at which time the Israelite nation left with the wealth of the Egyptians, the future redemption will find the nation poor due to their travels from country to country.

וְחָסוּ בְּשֵׁם ה׳ — And *they will take shelter in the Name of Hashem.*

Although the people will be financially poor and destitute, they will be rich in their knowledge and belief in God and will therefore take shelter in the Name of Hashem (*Abarbanel*).

13. שְׁאֵרִית יִשְׂרָאֵל לֹא־יַעֲשׂוּ עַוְלָה וְלֹא־יְדַבְּרוּ כָזָב וְלֹא־יִמָּצֵא בְּפִיהֶם לְשׁוֹן תַּרְמִית — *The remnant of Israel will not commit corruption, they will not speak falsehood, and a deceitful tongue will not be found in their mouth.*

The prophet points to the superior character of the remnant of Israel and declares that those who survive the destruction of the arrogant and haughty will be men of great integrity and will not perform any corrupt or deceitful deeds nor speak any words of falsehood, not even words that are remotely deceitful (*Abarbanel*). *Malbim* adds even their thoughts will be truthful. Scripture uses the tongue to describe one's thoughts for it is only with the tongue that one makes his thoughts known.

יד כִּי־הֵמָּה יִרְעוּ וְרָבְצוּ וְאֵין מַחֲרִיד: רָנִּי בַּת־
צִיּוֹן הָרִיעוּ יִשְׂרָאֵל שִׂמְחִי וְעָלְזִי בְּכָל־לֵב
טו בַּת יְרוּשָׁלָם: הֵסִיר יהוה מִשְׁפָּטַיִךְ פִּנָּה אֹיְבֵךְ
מֶלֶךְ יִשְׂרָאֵל | יהוה בְּקִרְבֵּךְ לֹא־תִירְאִי רָע
טז עוֹד: בַּיּוֹם הַהוּא יֵאָמֵר לִירוּשָׁלַםִ אַל־
יז תִּירָאִי צִיּוֹן אַל־יִרְפּוּ יָדָיִךְ: יהוה אֱלֹהַיִךְ
בְּקִרְבֵּךְ גִּבּוֹר יוֹשִׁיעַ יָשִׂישׂ עָלַיִךְ בְּשִׂמְחָה

כִּי־הֵמָּה יִרְעוּ וְרָבְצוּ וְאֵין מַחֲרִיד — *For they will graze and lie down with none to make them afraid.*

Since Israel is likened to flocks of sheep, Scripture metaphorically uses terminology befitting sheep. As a reward for doing no wrong, they will merit living in peace and security (*Radak*).

14-20. When the Almighty will have exacted retribution from the wicked and evil, and only the righteous will remain, the Divine Presence will once again reside in Jerusalem but at a level never before revealed. The Kingdoms of Judah and Israel will once again be reunited as one nation dedicated to the service of G-d (*Abarbanel*). The prophet portrays that era and the emotions and exultation it will bring.

14. רָנִּי בַּת־צִיּוֹן הָרִיעוּ יִשְׂרָאֵל ... — *Sing, O daughter of Zion! Shout for joy, O Israel ...*

When Israel will finally dwell without fear of any nation, the community of Zion and Israel will shout for joy (*Metzudos*). *Israel* is a reference to the Ten Tribes and *daughter of Zion* is synonymous with Jerusalem (*Radak*) and the Kingdom of Judah (*Abarbanel*). They will both shout for joy at this time because they will no longer be separate kingdoms but will now be united into one nation. Alternatively, all of the tribes of Israel are urging the capital city of Jerusalem to rejoice and be jubilant (*Abarbanel*).

Malbim explains this verse differently. Zion is the place where the Sanhedrin sat and judged the nation. Jerusalem is the city of the royal residence and Israel is referring to the nation in general. All will rejoice at this time because the corrupt judges of Zion and the evil kings of Jerusalem will be no more. God Himself will be King of Israel — see next verse — and will dwell in their midst and guide them. Therefore, no nation will oppress Israel.

15. הֵסִיר ה׳ מִשְׁפָּטַיִךְ — *Hashem has removed your afflictions.*

Our translation follows *Rashi* who translates מִשְׁפָּטַיִךְ as יְסוּרַיִךְ, *your afflictions.* God says, well may you rejoice (*Abarbanel*), for the pain and affliction that have been your lot throughout the years of your exile have been removed forever, never to return again (*Rashi; Mahari Kara; Abarbanel; Metzudos*). Alternatively, *God has removed your judgments* — i.e., the laws that the nations have imposed upon you while you were in exile (*Radak*). *Targum Yonasan* renders God has removed the false judges from among you.

פִּנָּה אֹיְבֵךְ — *He has cleared away your enemy.*

God has swept your enemies out of your land, and they can no longer cause you any harm (*Radak*). Alternatively, their destruction itself is cause for celebration, for a righteous man rejoices when vengeance is taken from the wicked (*Abarbanel*).

The Sages see these two phrases as describing a pattern of cause and effect: Once your false judges have been removed, your enemies will be swept away (*Shabbos* 139a).

for they will graze and lie down with none to make them afraid.

[14] Sing, O daughter of Zion! Shout for joy, O Israel! Be glad and exult with all your heart, O daughter of Jerusalem! [15] HASHEM has removed your afflictions; He has cleared away your enemy. The King of Israel, HASHEM, is in your midst; you will never again fear evil.

[16] On that day, it will be said to Jerusalem, "Have no fear! O Zion, do not despair!" [17] HASHEM, your God, is in your midst, the Mighty One Who will save. He will rejoice over you with gladness;

Abarbanel notes Scripture's use of the singular form of אֹיְבֵךְ, *your enemy*, rather than אֹיְבַיִךְ, *your enemies*, and suggests that Scripture is referring to the Edomites, Israel's foremost enemy.

מֶלֶךְ יִשְׂרָאֵל ה׳ בְּקִרְבֵּךְ לֹא־תִירְאִי רָע עוֹד — *The King of Israel, Hashem, is in your midst; you will never again fear evil.*

The Divine Presence resides once more among the people, never to be removed. Now it is only God Who is the King of Israel for its people are not under the dominion of any other king (*Radak* to *Isaiah* 44:6). Consequently, they are guaranteed that no evil can ever again befall them (*Radak; Abarbanel*).

Some texts have תִרְאִי without the first *yud*, which means *see*. The translation of the verse would then be *Hashem is in your midst; you will never again see evil* — see *Minchas Shai*.

16. בַּיּוֹם הַהוּא יֵאָמֵר יְרוּשָׁלַםִ אַל־תִּירָאִי — *On that day it will be said to Jerusalem, "Have no fear!*

The prophets of G-d shall declare to Zion and Jerusalem at that time: You need no longer fear that any enemy or misfortune may befall you (*Radak; Metzudos*). Alternatively, others interpret this as the declaration of the enemies of Israel, particularly Edom and Ishmael (*Abarbanel*), who will acknowledge that it is no longer within their ability to wage war against God's people (*Ibn Ezra; Radak*).

Radak suggests a third approach, that these words will be expressed among the Jewish people themselves, for they will say this to one another.

צִיּוֹן אַל יִרְפּוּ יָדָיִךְ — *Zion do not despair."*

Literally, this phrase means *do not let your hands become weak*, i.e., do not despair; do not give up hope (*Metzudos*). The verse is urging the people not to be dissuaded from striving for spiritual perfection by fears that God has abandoned them due to their numerous sins (*Malbim*).

17. ה׳ אֱלֹהַיִךְ בְּקִרְבֵּךְ גִּבּוֹר יוֹשִׁיעַ — *Hashem, your God, is in your midst, the Mighty One Who will save.*

This is a continuation of the words of encouragement expressed to Israel in the previous verse (*Ibn Ezra; Radak; Malbim*). G-d has allowed His Divine Presence to dwell in the midst of the people (*Targum*) and they therefore have nothing to fear. God is a mighty King Who is capable of protecting His people from the mighty kings of the nations, and indeed, His will to protect you is in effect (*Radak*).

יָשִׂישׂ עָלַיִךְ בְּשִׂמְחָה — *He will rejoice over you with gladness.*

Do not be concerned that He may still be angry with you for your previous misdeeds, for He is happy with you and rejoicing over you (*Abarbanel*).

יח יַחֲרִישׁ בְּאַהֲבָתוֹ יָגִיל עָלַיִךְ בְּרִנָּה: נוּגֵי
מִמּוֹעֵד אָסַפְתִּי מִמֵּךְ הָיוּ מַשְׂאֵת עָלֶיהָ
יט חֶרְפָּה: הִנְנִי עֹשֶׂה אֶת־כָּל־מְעַנַּיִךְ בָּעֵת
הַהִיא וְהוֹשַׁעְתִּי אֶת־הַצֹּלֵעָה וְהַנִּדָּחָה אֲקַבֵּץ
וְשַׂמְתִּים לִתְהִלָּה וּלְשֵׁם בְּכָל־הָאָרֶץ בָּשְׁתָּם:
כ בָּעֵת הַהִיא אָבִיא אֶתְכֶם וּבָעֵת קַבְּצִי אֶתְכֶם

Malbim interprets שִׂמְחָה to mean inner happiness and שָׂשׂוֹן to refer to its outward manifestation. Thus: Do not be concerned that the signs of happiness He is showing you may be superficial, for they are true indications of the great joy which He takes in you.

יַחֲרִישׁ בְּאַהֲבָתוֹ — *He will be silent with His love.*

Because of His love for you He will remain silent and will not mention the sins that you have previously committed. In His great love for you, He will cover them up (*Targum Yonasan; Rashi*), as *love covers over all misdeeds* (*Mahari Kara* from *Mishlei* 10:12). Others translate יַחֲרִישׁ, *He shall think.* He shall constantly contemplate His great love for you (*R' Eliezer of Beaugency*) and seek ways to increase His kindness and goodness to you (*Malbim*).

יָגִיל עָלַיִךְ בְּרִנָּה — *He will be joyful over you with glad song.*

Abarbanel notes the double expressions of joy used in this verse: *He will rejoice over you with gladness* and *He will be joyful over you with glad song,* and explains that they represent the redemption from the two exiles that the nation experienced.

18. נוּגֵי מִמּוֹעֵד אָסַפְתִּי מִמֵּךְ הָיוּ מַשְׂאֵת עָלֶיהָ חֶרְפָּה — *I have gathered together those who have mourned for the appointed time, they came from you, who had carried a burden of shame over her.*

Our translation follows most commentators who relate the word נוּגֵי to יָגוֹן, *grief* — see *Lamentations* 1:4. According to *Radak,* the appointed time is referring to the time of the redemption. The prophet declares in the Name of G-d to Zion and Jerusalem: I have gathered together those righteous sons of Israel who have grieved and mourned over the extended duration of the exile, and who bore the shame of Jerusalem before the mocking gentiles among whom they lived. And I have returned them to you, Zion, for you are the place from which they came (*Radak; Abarbanel; Metzudos*). This refers either to the descendants of those people or to those people themselves, at the time of resurrection (*Radak*). Others see the appointed time as referring to the festivals: I have gathered together those people who grieved over the loss of the proper celebration of the festivals [in *Eretz Yisrael*] (*Ibn Ezra; R' Eliezer of Beaugency*).

According to *Malbim,* Scripture is referring to those of the nation who were unable to withstand the pressures and tests of faith endured during the years of exile and succumbed to other faiths. Since their decision was made under duress and they anguished over their poor commitment to their faith, they are still counted among the Children of Israel.

Alternatively, *Rashi* relates the word נוּגֵי to הגה, *removed,* and follows an entirely different approach to this verse. *I have gathered in,* i.e., destroyed, [*those who were excluded*] *from My festivals* because they did not keep the Sabbath and the festivals. *These* [*evildoers*] *were from you* — from your people — and *for that* [*sin*], *you have borne a burden of shame.*

The Sages (*Berachos* 28a) translate נוּגֵי as *delay* and understand the appointed times as the specific times of the day when prayers should be said. Accordingly, the explanation

He will be silent with His love; He will be joyful over you with glad song. [18] *I have gathered together those who have mourned for the appointed time, they came from you, who had carried a burden of shame over her.* [19] *Behold, at that time I will crush all those who afflict you. I will save the cripple, and gather the castoff; and I will make them for praise and a good name throughout the land of their shame.* [20] *At that time I will bring you [in], and at [that] time I will gather you;*

of the verse is that those who delay the specific times of prayer will be destroyed.

19. הִנְנִי עֹשֶׂה אֶת־כָּל־מְעַנַּיִךְ בָּעֵת הַהִיא — *Behold, at that time I will crush all those who afflict you.*

Our translation follows *Rashi* and *Mahari Kara* who interpret עֹשֶׂה as an expression of *crushing* — see *Malachi* 3:21. The prophet is foretelling that at the time of the redemption (*Metzudos*), God will crush all those who afflict the Jewish people. Others translate עֹשֶׂה in its usual sense, to *do* or to *make*, and render *I will make [an end] to all who afflict you* (*Ibn Ezra*). Alternatively, *Targum Yonasan* translates *I will cause destruction ...*

וְהוֹשַׁעְתִּי אֶת־הַצֹּלֵעָה וְהַנִּדָּחָה אֲקַבֵּץ — *I will save the cripple, and gather the castoff.*

I will save the Israelite nation who, like a cripple, cannot move from her place and has been banished from her land by the heathen nations (*Metzudos*). Alternatively, הַצֹּלֵעָה, *the cripple*, refers to the Ten Tribes of the Northern Kingdom who have been exiled by the Assyrians, and הַנִּדָּחָה, *the castoff*, refers to the Kingdom of Judah (*Abarbanel*). According to *Malbim*, הַצֹּלֵעָה are those of the nation who are *spiritually* crippled and have strayed from their faith because they had been oppressed by the gentile nations. הַנִּדָּחָה are those who remained steadfast in their faith and were scattered across the globe.

וְשַׂמְתִּים לִתְהִלָּה וּלְשֵׁם בְּכָל־הָאָרֶץ בָּשְׁתָּם — *And I will make them for praise and a good name throughout the land of their shame.*

In the very same places of exile where they had been sent to be shamed and humiliated, there I will make them be honored with praise and renown (*Rashi; Radak*). Alternatively, this is alluding to the gentiles. Throughout the land, the gentiles shall be shamed when they witness how the cripple have become praised (*Ibn Ezra*).

20. בָּעֵת הַהִיא אָבִיא אֶתְכֶם — *At that time I will bring you [in].*

Scripture is addressing the Ten Tribes and informing them, "Although you did not return to your land when the Second Temple was built, when the future redemption will take place, בָּעֵת הַהִיא, *at that time*, I will bring you to your land."

וּבָעֵת קַבְּצִי אֶתְכֶם — *And at [that] time I will gather you.*

This phrase is to be understood as if the word הַהִיא would be written after וּבָעֵת as it is in the beginning of the verse (*Radak*). This part of the verse is addressing the Kingdom of Judah. Unlike when the Second Temple was built and only some of Judah returned to the land, at the time of the future redemption, all of you will return (*Metzudos*).

ג/כ

כִּֽי־אֶתֵּ֨ן אֶתְכֶ֜ם לְשֵׁ֣ם וְלִתְהִלָּ֗ה בְּכֹל֙ עַמֵּ֣י הָאָ֔רֶץ בְּשׁוּבִ֧י אֶת־שְׁבוּתֵיכֶ֛ם לְעֵינֵיכֶ֖ם אָמַ֥ר יְהוָֽה׃

כִּי־אֶתֵּן אֶתְכֶם לְשֵׁם וְלִתְהִלָּה בְּכֹל עַמֵּי הָאָרֶץ — *For I will make you into a good name and praise among all the peoples of the earth.*

No one will remain in exile, for these nations will not only praise Israel but they will even bring Israel back to Jerusalem (*Metzudos*). According to *Malbim*, Israel will be praised for the might they displayed during the war of God and Magog.

בְּשׁוּבִי אֶת־שְׁבוּתֵיכֶם — *When I return your captives.*

3/20 *for I will make you into a good name and praise among all the peoples of the earth, when I return your captives before your eyes, said HASHEM.*

All this will occur when I return the captives of the nation: those of the Ten Tribes of Israel and those of the Kingdom of Judah (*Abarbanel*).

לְעֵינֵיכֶם — *Before your eyes.*

You will witness with your very eyes all the great events God promised He would do (*Ibn Ezra*). This is alluding to the great miracle of the resurrection of the dead, for Zephaniah is addressing his contemporaries and saying, "*You* will rise from your grave and witness before *your* eyes the ingathering of the exiles" (*Metzudos*).

Haggai

א/א א בִּשְׁנַת שְׁתַּיִם לְדָרְיָוֶשׁ הַמֶּלֶךְ בַּחֹדֶשׁ הַשִּׁשִּׁי בְּיוֹם אֶחָד לַחֹדֶשׁ הָיָה דְבַר־יהוה בְּיַד־חַגַּי הַנָּבִיא אֶל־זְרֻבָּבֶל בֶּן־שְׁאַלְתִּיאֵל פַּחַת יְהוּדָה וְאֶל־יְהוֹשֻׁעַ בֶּן־יְהוֹצָדָק הַכֹּהֵן הַגָּדוֹל לֵאמֹר:

☙ Introduction

Jeremiah, the prophet who foretold that Jerusalem will be destroyed and the Jews would be exiled from their land, also foretold that their exile would be only temporary. כִּי־כֹה אָמַר ה׳ כִּי לְפִי מְלֹאת לְבָבֶל שִׁבְעִים שָׁנָה אֶפְקֹד אֶתְכֶם וַהֲקִמֹתִי עֲלֵיכֶם אֶת־דְּבָרִי הַטּוֹב לְהָשִׁיב אֶתְכֶם אֶל־הַמָּקוֹם הַזֶּה — *For thus said Hashem: After seventy years for Babylonia have been completed I will attend to you and I will fulfill for you My favorable promise, to return you to this place* (*Jeremiah* 29:10). And, in fact, seventy years from the rise of Babylon, Cyrus the Mede authorized the Jewish people to return to their homeland and to begin rebuilding the Holy Temple (*Ezra* 1:3).[1] However, the Samaritans, great enemies of the Jews (*Rashi, Ezra* 4:1), convinced the Persian monarchy to revoke the Jews' permission to build, and construction of the Temple was halted (*Ezra* 4:24). Actually, the seventy years mentioned by Jeremiah did not begin from the *rise* of Babylon but rather from the destruction of Jerusalem and the Holy Temple, as explicated by *Daniel* (9:2): אֲנִי דָּנִיֵּאל בִּינֹתִי בַּסְּפָרִים מִסְפַּר הַשָּׁנִים אֲשֶׁר הָיָה דְבַר־ה׳ אֶל־יִרְמְיָה הַנָּבִיא לְמַלֹּאות לְחָרְבוֹת יְרוּשָׁלַם שִׁבְעִים שָׁנָה — *I, Daniel, contemplated the calculation, the number of years about which the word of Hashem had come to the prophet Jeremiah to complete the seventy years from the ruins of Jerusalem* (see *Rashi* to v. 2). This destruction took place eighteen years after the rise of Babylon. Thus, for eighteen years following the first wave of Jewish settlers who returned to the Holy Land, the Temple remained unbuilt. This was the situation for three years under the reign of Cyrus, fourteen under Ahasuerus and through the first year of the rule of Darius (*Rashi*). Finally, in the second year of Darius' rule, seventy years after the First Temple had been destroyed, the time had come for the Jewish people to rebuild the Temple and rededicate themselves to the service of Hashem.

Had the people returned to God wholeheartedly and responded to the words of His prophets with full devotion, the entire nation would have returned to the Holy Land and the Davidic kingdom would have been reinstated under the reign of the Messiah. However, the nation did not seize the opportunity and the era of the Second Commonwealth was therefore one of only partial redemption, limited in scope both qualitatively and quantitatively. Total independence was achieved only briefly, in the era of the Hasmonean kings, and spiritual sanctity never flowered completely. In addition, only a minority of the Jewish people returned to the Holy Land to participate in the Jewish Commonwealth (*Abarbanel; Malbim*).

I

1. בִּשְׁנַת שְׁתַּיִם לְדָרְיָוֶשׁ הַמֶּלֶךְ ... — *In the second year of King Darius ...*

This is Darius the Persian who ruled Persia after Ahasuerus. According to the Sages, he was the son of Queen Esther — see *Lev. Rabbah* 13:4 (*Rashi; Ibn Ezra*). He should not be confused with Darius, son of Ahasuerus the Mede who defeated Belshazzar and ruled Persia before Cyrus (*Rashi, Daniel* 9:1).

1. This refers not to the ascent of Nebuchadnezzar to the throne of Babylonia but rather to the following year when he conquered Judah and relegated it to a vassal state (*Mahari Kara* to v. 2; *Megillah* 11b; for further elaboration, see Overview to ArtScroll *Megillas Esther; Otzar HaIggeres*).

1/1 [1] *In the second year of King Darius, in the sixth month, on the first day of the month, the word of* HASHEM *came through Haggai the prophet to Zerubbabel son of Shealtiel, the governor of Judah, and to Joshua son of Jehozadak, the Kohen Gadol, saying:*

בַּחֹדֶשׁ הַשִּׁשִּׁי בְּיוֹם אֶחָד לַחֹדֶשׁ — *In the sixth month, on the first day of the month.*

This is Rosh Chodesh Elul (*Mahari Kara*). Dates of prophecies are rarely noted by Scripture since they generally serve no purpose and do not add any important information to the prophetic message. In this case, however, Scripture wishes to show how Haggai's prophecy of commanding the Jewish people to rebuild the Temple coincided with the very time that King Darius granted the Jewish people permission to do so, indicating that both of these events were initiated simultaneously by Divine Providence. The date, *Rosh Chodesh Elul,* is also significant, for it was on that day that Moses had ascended Mt. Sinai to receive the Second Tablets from God after the First Tablets were shattered, and it was on that very day that Haggai received the prophecy to construct the Second Temple after the First Temple had been destroyed (*Abarbanel* to *Zechariah* 1:1).

הָיָה דְבַר־ה׳ בְּיַד־חַגַּי הַנָּבִיא — *The word of Hashem came through Haggai the prophet.*

Haggai prophesied during the second year of the reign of Darius, king of Persia, and exhorted the Jews to rebuild the Holy Temple (1:8). He was a member of the Beth Din of Ezra — more commonly referred to as the *Anshei Knesses Hagedolah,* the men of the Great Assembly (*Ramban, Introduction to Mishneh Torah*). He was a contemporary of the prophets Zechariah and Malachi and it was with their demise that prophecy was withdrawn from the Jewish people (*Sanhedrin* 11a). Little is known regarding Haggai's background as Scripture does not mention the name of his tribe nor the name of his father.

אֶל־זְרֻבָּבֶל בֶּן־שְׁאַלְתִּיאֵל — *To Zerubbabel son of Shealtiel.*

Actually, Zerubbabel was the grandson of Shealtiel and the son of Pedaiah — see *I Chronicles* 3:17, 18. *Radak* suggests that Shealtiel may have been a more prominent figure than Pedaiah, so Scripture therefore traces the prophet's lineage back to his grandfather. Alternatively, Zerubbabel may have been raised by Shealtiel and he is therefore referred to as Zerubbabel's father (*Abarbanel*). *Ibn Ezra* contends that Shealtiel was actually Zerubbabel's uncle.

The Talmud (*Sanhedrin* 38a) identifies Zerubbabel as Nehemiah ben Hachaliah, the author and leading personality of the Book of *Nehemiah.* The name Zerubbabel is a contraction of the words נִזְרַע בְּבָבֶל, *conceived* (lit. implanted) *in Babylon.* Nehemiah was designated Zerubbabel to commemorate his birth in Babylon.[1] (See Ezra ArtScroll ed. p.76 and *I Chronicles* ArtScroll ed. p. 47 for further discussion.)

פַּחַת יְהוּדָה — *The governor of Judah.* The Jewish rulers of the Second Temple era were not called "kings" because the Jews were then under the authority of other nations (*Radak*).

וְאֶל־יְהוֹשֻׁעַ בֶּן־יְהוֹצָדָק הַכֹּהֵן הַגָּדוֹל — *And to Joshua son of Jehozadak, the Kohen Gadol.*

Jehozadak, the brother of Ezra the scribe, was the last Kohen Gadol to serve in the First Temple and went into exile when

[1] We must note that *Rambam* in his *Introduction to Mishneh Torah* assumes that Nehemiah and Zerubbabel are two different people. See *B'Shaar HaMelech* by *R' Chaim Kanievsky* who cites *Targum* to *Shir HaShirim* in support of *Rambam's* view.

ב כֹּה אָמַר יְהוָה צְבָאוֹת לֵאמֹר הָעָם הַזֶּה אָמְרוּ
ג לֹא עֶת־בֹּא עֶת־בֵּית יְהוָה לְהִבָּנוֹת׃ וַיְהִי
ד דְּבַר־יְהוָה בְּיַד־חַגַּי הַנָּבִיא לֵאמֹר׃ הַעֵת
לָכֶם אַתֶּם לָשֶׁבֶת בְּבָתֵּיכֶם סְפוּנִים וְהַבַּיִת
ה הַזֶּה חָרֵב׃ וְעַתָּה כֹּה אָמַר יְהוָה צְבָאוֹת
ו שִׂימוּ לְבַבְכֶם עַל־דַּרְכֵיכֶם׃ זְרַעְתֶּם
הַרְבֵּה וְהָבֵא מְעָט אָכוֹל וְאֵין־לְשָׂבְעָה

Hashem exiled Judah and Jerusalem through Nebuchadnezzar — see *I Chron.* 5:41. Since the *Kehunah Gedolah* had already passed to Jehozadak, his son Joshua had first claim to that office rather than the more illustrious Ezra because the *Kehunah Gedolah* is passed from father to son (*Ibn Ezra; Radak*). *Rambam*, however (*Introduction to Mishneh Torah*), writes that Ezra did indeed serve as Kohen Gadol — see *I Chron.* 5:40 ArtScroll ed. note 1 for further discussion.

Although Zerubbabel was not actually the king, the prophet mentions his name before Joshua because (*Ibn Ezra* to 2:2) Zerubbabel was of royal descent, a descendant of Jeconiah, king of Judah, and royalty takes precedence over *Kehunah*.

◆§ Haggai's First Prophecy

2. כֹּה אָמַר ה׳ צְבָאוֹת לֵאמֹר — *Thus said Hashem, Master of Legions, saying:*

Haggai is instructed to tell Zerubbabel and Joshua that they should inform the nation that the time for rebuilding the Temple has arrived (*Radak*).

הָעָם הַזֶּה אָמְרוּ לֹא עֶת־בֹּא — *This people has said, "The time has not yet come!"*

In the fifty-second year after the destruction of Jerusalem, King Cyrus granted the Jews permission to resettle the Land of Israel and rebuild the Holy Temple (*Ezra* 1:3). That year coincided with the seventieth year of the Babylonian Empire's rise to power. Thinking that this was the fulfillment of Jeremiah's prophecy, when Cyrus revoked his decision and the construction was halted — see *Ezra* 4:5, 24 — the people became terribly disheartened and were convinced that God would not keep His word and the Temple will never be rebuilt (*Rashi*).

עֶת־בֵּית ה׳ לְהִבָּנוֹת — *The time for the Temple of Hashem to be rebuilt.*

The nation has erred for they have miscalculated. The seventy years are not to be calculated from the year that Babylonia rose to power, but from the year that the First Temple was actually destroyed. Now that seventy years have passed, the time has indeed come for the Temple to be rebuilt (*Rashi; Mahari Kara*).

This prophecy was transmitted to the Jewish people before Darius granted them permission to rebuild the Temple (*Abarbanel*). They should have realized that God did not take them from exile and bring them back to Eretz Yisrael for naught; and they surely should have understood that their failed efforts to sow the land (see v. 6) were a punishment for failing to rebuild the Temple (*Radak*). Thus, although previous Persian monarchs had prohibited the rebuilding of the Temple, the rise of a new monarch should have moved them to petition for permission to build (*R' Eliezer of Beaugency*). Since they did not do so on their own initiative, the Almighty sent His prophet Haggai to move them to action (*Radak*).

Malbim explains that the people understood that the time was ripe for a full redemption and the advent of the kingdom of the Messiah (see preface). They were also

[2] *"Thus said HASHEM, Master of Legions, saying: This people has said, 'The time has not yet come!' [But I say,] 'It is the time for the Temple of HASHEM to be rebuilt!'"*

[3] *And the word of HASHEM came through Haggai the prophet saying:*

[4] *Is this a time for you yourselves to sit in your paneled houses while this House is in ruins?* [5] *So now, thus said HASHEM, Master of Legions: Set your heart to [consider] your ways!* [6] *You have sown much*

aware that before this will take place there will be signs from the Almighty in heaven and earth (see *Joel* 3:3) along with the wars of Gog and Magog. Since none of this had occurred, they assumed that the time had not yet come for the rebuilding of the Temple.

◆§ Haggai's Second Prophecy

3. וַיְהִי דְּבַר־ה׳ בְּיַד־חַגַּי הַנָּבִיא לֵאמֹר — *And the word of Hashem came through Haggai the prophet saying:*

Following the first prophecy, which was directed at Zerubbabel and Joshua, another prophecy was transmitted through Haggai to the populace at large (*Radak*).

4. הַעֵת לָכֶם אַתֶּם לָשֶׁבֶת בְּבָתֵּיכֶם סְפוּנִים וְהַבַּיִת הַזֶּה חָרֵב — *Is this a time for you yourselves to sit in your paneled houses while this House is in ruins?*

The ה of הַעֵת is vowelized with a פַּתַּח, הַ, because it is an interrogative ה, a ה הַשְּׁאֵלָה (*Rashi; Radak*). To arouse the people so they should take responsibility to build the Temple, Haggai challenges them and asks, "Is it only the right time for *you* to sit in houses with paneled roofs? What about the House of Hashem; will it remain in ruins? (*Metzudos*). You claim that the time for building the Temple has not yet arrived but has the time arrived for you, that you sit in paneled houses which you ventured forth to build? Are you not ashamed?" (*Radak*)

Alshich interprets the double language of לָכֶם אַתֶּם, *for you, you,* as conveying that the criticism is directed to both of the aforementioned listeners: the people at large and the two leaders of the nation.

5. וְעַתָּה כֹּה אָמַר ה׳ צְבָאוֹת שִׂימוּ לְבַבְכֶם עַל־דַּרְכֵיכֶם — *So now, thus said Hashem, Master of Legions: Set your heart to [consider] your ways!*

If you persist in defending your position that the time for rebuilding has not yet arrived (*Abarbanel*), stop and consider your ways. Look at your economic conditions and note that all of your endeavors have proven futile. Know that this is only because My Temple has been neglected and still lies in ruins (*Rashi*).

6. To prove his point, the prophet lists five unnatural occurrences that befell Israel. He admonishes the people in amazement and asks, "How can you fail to realize that these abnormalities are punishments for neglecting to rebuild God's Temple?" (*Radak*).

זְרַעְתֶּם הַרְבֵּה וְהָבֵא מְעָט — *You have sown much but bring in little.*

One generally reaps far more produce than the measure he used for planting but you have been plagued by such unsuccessful harvests that you reap even less than you planted (*Radak; Abarbanel*). This is your due because you ceased bringing the בִּכּוּרִים, the first fruits of the field, to the Temple (*Rashi*).

אָכוֹל וְאֵין־לְשָׂבְעָה ... — *Eating without being satisfied ...*

שָׁתוֹ וְאֵין־לְשָׁכְרָה לָבוֹשׁ וְאֵין־לְחֹם לוֹ
ז וְהַמִּשְׂתַּכֵּר מִשְׂתַּכֵּר אֶל־צְרוֹר נָקוּב: כֹּה
אָמַר יהוה צְבָאוֹת שִׂימוּ לְבַבְכֶם עַל־דַּרְכֵיכֶם:
ח עֲלוּ הָהָר וַהֲבֵאתֶם עֵץ וּבְנוּ הַבָּיִת וְאֶרְצֶה־
ט בּוֹ °ואכבד אָמַר יהוה: פָּנֹה אֶל־הַרְבֵּה
וְהִנֵּה לִמְעָט וַהֲבֵאתֶם הַבַּיִת וְנָפַחְתִּי בוֹ

°וְאֶכָּבְדָה ק׳

Even that little food or drink that you bring into your homes does not bring its expected satiation (*Radak*). For you sinned by ceasing to bring the meal-offerings (*Rashi*) and did not offer the showbread (*Abarbanel*).

שָׁתוֹ וְאֵין־לְשָׁכְרָה — *Drinking without quenching thirst.*

The taste of the wine has been removed because you ceased to bring the wine libations (*Rashi*). *Abarbanel* suggests that the quality of the wine has become poor and hasn't the ability to make one drunk. *Radak*, however, explains that לְשָׁכְרָה does not necessarily imply drunkenness. It is merely the parallel of the word לְשָׂבְעָה, but refers to drink. שִׁכְּרוּת is used to describe drunkenness because a שִׁכּוֹר is one who has had his fill of wine to a degree that it has made him confused.

לָבוֹשׁ וְאֵין־לחם לו — *Dressing, yet no one is warmed.*

The clothing you make does not give the warmth it is naturally capable of providing (*Radak*). For you ceased to wear the priestly garments (*Rashi*).

וְהַמִּשְׂתַּכֵּר מִשְׂתַּכֵּר אֶל־צְרוֹר נָקוּב — *And whoever earns money earns it for a purse with a hole.*

Those who earn money either through business ventures or by offering themselves or their animals for hire never manage to benefit from their earnings for they suffer immeasurable losses. It is as if they place their money into a cloth bundle full of holes from which it eventually falls (*Radak*). This misfortune was due to the cessation of giving charity (*Yalkut Shimoni*).

7. כֹּה אָמַר ה׳ צְבָאוֹת שִׂימוּ לְבַבְכֶם עַל־דַּרְכֵיכֶם — *Thus said Hashem, Master of Legions: Set your heart to [consider] your ways.*

Having considered your affairs and recognized the failure of all your endeavors, now contemplate your ways and your deeds so that you may rectify your wrongdoings (*Abarbanel; Metzudos*).

8. ... עֲלוּ הָהָר וַהֲבֵאתֶם עֵץ וּבְנוּ הַבָּיִת — *Ascend the mountain and bring wood and build the Temple ...*

This is what you should do [to rectify your wrongdoings]: ascend the mountain (*Metzudos*). Do not tarry and delay in order to consider the finest and most lavish way to build the Temple. Rather, hasten immediately to do My bidding and build the Temple with the materials available to you (*Alshich*). Even if it will be small and simple and seemingly inappropriate for My honor, I will be pleased and glorified with it. For it is not the external splendor of the structure that is important but the intent and devotion of its builder (*Abarbanel; Metzudos*).

The word וְאֶכָּבְדָה, *and I will be honored,* is written in this verse without the final *hei* [whose numerical value is five]. This is to teach that there were five things that were missing from the Second Temple that had been present in the first: the Holy Ark,[1]

1. The Talmud actually cites the Ark, its cover and the *cherubim*. However, these are all considered one unit [since they served a single purpose] (*Rashi* ad loc.). These were concealed

but bring in little; eating without being satisfied, drinking without quenching thirst, dressing, yet no one is warmed; and whoever earns money earns it for a purse with a hole.

[7]Thus said HASHEM, *Master of Legions: Set your heart to [consider] your ways! [8]Ascend the mountain and bring wood and build the Temple; I will be pleased with it and I will be honored — said* HASHEM. *[9]You looked for much [produce]*

Urim VeTumim,[2] the fire from heaven,[3] the Divine Presence[4] and Divine Inspiration[5] (*Rashi* from *Yoma* 21b). Although there were additional items missing as well — see *Yoma* 52b — these five are cited by the Sages because of their fundamental role in the level of sanctity of the Temple (*Abarbanel; Maharsha, Chidushei Aggados,* loc. cit.).

9. פָּנֹה אֶל־הַרְבֵּה וְהִנֵּה לִמְעָט — *You looked for much [produce] but, behold, it is little.*

This verse is reiterating that which had been stated previously. You expected to reap far more from your fields than they actually produced (*Rashi; Ibn Ezra*). Alternatively, if you will only heed My call [of v. 8], the curse that is presently upon you will be removed; but until then, although you expect a large and abundant crop, it will only be small and insignificant (*Radak*).

וַהֲבֵאתֶם הַבַּיִת וְנָפַחְתִּי בוֹ — *You bring it home and I blow upon it.*

I will place My curse upon it (*Targum Yonasan*) and infect it with decay and worms (*Rashi*) so that even the little that you gather (*Ibn Ezra*) will be destroyed effortlessly, as something that disappears by merely blowing on it (*Radak*).

by King Josiah before the destruction of the First Temple, because he feared that they would be captured by the invading Babylonians and thereby be desecrated (ibid. 52b). [See *Mishneh Yoma* 5:2 ArtScroll ed. comm. of *Yad Avraham.*]

2. According to *Rashi* (*Exodus* 28:30). The *Urim VeTumim* were a slip of parchment upon which the שֵׁם הַמְפוֹרָשׁ, *ineffable four-letter Name,* was written. Accordingly, it was this parchment that was missing during the Second Temple. Alternatively, *Rambam* (*Klei HaMikdash* 10:10; *Beis HaBechirah* 4:1) seems to hold that the *Urim VeTumim* is synonymous with the breastplate (חֹשֶׁן) or the precious stones affixed to it [see *Mishnah Yoma* 7:5 ArtScroll ed. com. of *Yad Avraham*]. This could not have been actually missing during the Second Temple period, for the Kohen Gadol would be lacking the proper vestments and would therefore be unfit to perform the Temple service! *Rambam* (*Klei HaMikdash* ibid.) explains that they nevertheless did not inquire of them since there was no Divine Inspiration, which was needed by the Kohen for inquiry. [See *Mishnah Yoma* ArtScroll ed. Appendix II for further discussion of this topic.]

3. This was a fiery ember that descended upon the Altar from heaven during the days of King Solomon. During the First Temple era, the fire sat crouched like a lion and miraculously consumed all of the sacrifices brought there. During the days of the Second Temple, the heavenly fire existed, but it resembled a crouched dog and did not function (*Yoma* ad loc., *Rashi* ad loc.; cf. *Abarbanel*).

4. The absence of the Divine Presence was manifested by the absence of the Cloud of Glory which had filled the Tabernacle in the desert as well as the Holy of Holies during the First Temple era (*Abarbanel*).

5. According to *Rambam* (*Moreh Nevuchim* 2:45), this was the Holy Spirit that inspired King David to compose the *Psalms* and King Solomon the Books of *Proverbs, Ecclesiastes* and *Song of Songs.*

יַ֗עַן מֶ֚ה נְאֻם֙ יְהוָ֣ה צְבָא֔וֹת יַ֗עַן בֵּיתִי֙ אֲשֶׁר־ה֣וּא
י חָרֵ֔ב וְאַתֶּ֣ם רָצִ֔ים אִ֖ישׁ לְבֵיתֽוֹ׃ עַל־כֵּ֣ן עֲלֵיכֶ֔ם
כָּלְא֥וּ שָׁמַ֖יִם מִטָּ֑ל וְהָאָ֖רֶץ כָּלְאָ֥ה יְבוּלָֽהּ׃
יא וָאֶקְרָ֨א חֹ֜רֶב עַל־הָאָ֣רֶץ וְעַל־הֶהָרִ֗ים וְעַל־
הַדָּגָן֙ וְעַל־הַתִּיר֣וֹשׁ וְעַל־הַיִּצְהָ֔ר וְעַ֛ל אֲשֶׁ֥ר
תּוֹצִ֖יא הָאֲדָמָ֑ה וְעַל־הָֽאָדָם֙ וְעַל־הַבְּהֵמָ֔ה וְעַ֖ל
יב כָּל־יְגִ֥יעַ כַּפָּֽיִם׃ וַיִּשְׁמַ֣ע זְרֻבָּבֶ֣ל ׀
בֶּן־שַׁלְתִּיאֵ֡ל וִיהוֹשֻׁ֣עַ בֶּן־יְהוֹצָדָק֩ הַכֹּהֵ֨ן הַגָּד֜וֹל
וְכֹ֣ל ׀ שְׁאֵרִ֣ית הָעָ֗ם בְּקוֹל֙ יְהוָ֣ה אֱלֹהֵיהֶ֔ם וְעַל־
דִּבְרֵי֙ חַגַּ֣י הַנָּבִ֔יא כַּאֲשֶׁ֥ר שְׁלָח֖וֹ יְהוָ֣ה אֱלֹהֵיהֶ֑ם
יג וַיִּֽירְא֥וּ הָעָ֖ם מִפְּנֵ֥י יְהוָֽה׃ וַ֠יֹּאמֶר
חַגַּ֞י מַלְאַ֧ךְ יְהוָ֛ה בְּמַלְאֲכ֥וּת יְהוָ֖ה לָעָ֣ם לֵאמֹ֑ר

Abarbanel and *Malbim* explain the imagery of וְנָפַחְתִּי as "I will fan the flames of My anger against the meager amount that you manage to gather."

יַעַן מֶה נְאֻם ה׳ צְבָאוֹת יַעַן בֵּיתִי אֲשֶׁר־הוּא חָרֵב וְאַתֶּם רָצִים אִישׁ לְבֵיתוֹ — *Why is this? — the word of Hashem, Master of Legions — because of My Temple which is ruined, while you run, each to his own house.*

If you will ask, "Why does this great misfortune befall us?" God will answer, "Because you neglect to rebuild My Temple and you concern yourselves with your own private matters" (*Metzudos*).

10. עַל־כֵּן עֲלֵיכֶם כָּלְאוּ שָׁמַיִם מִטָּל ... — *Therefore, because of you the heavens withhold from [giving] dew ...*

I.e., because of your sins God will cause the Heavens to hold back its dew (*Targum Yonasan; Rashi*). Alternatively, you will witness an amazing phenomenon (*Abarbanel*). In all the lands inhabited by the gentile nations, rain and dew will fall normally, in their usual amount, but עֲלֵיכֶם, *upon you*, in your land, the heavens will withhold even the dew, which is normally not withheld (*Radak*).

11. וָאֶקְרָא חֹרֶב עַל־הָאָרֶץ — *I have declared a drought upon the land.*

I.e., I have decreed (*Radak; Ibn Ezra*) a drought upon the Land of Israel (*Abarbanel*). Not only will the drought be upon the land, but even the air will be dry, devoid of the moisture that it would normally draw from the underground waters (*Radak*).

Ibn Ezra notes that Scripture is using a play on words to describe the punishment of drought that will befall the land. The word חֹרֶב, *drought*, is the same word used for destruction [see v. 9, *because of My Temple which is ruined* — יַעַן בֵּיתִי אֲשֶׁר־הוּא חָרֵב], as if Scripture is stating that the drought is a punishment for leaving the Temple in ruins (*Abarbanel*).

וְעַל־הֶהָרִים — *And upon the mountains.*

The drought has been decreed upon the mountains as well, for some mountains normally produce good fruit-bearing trees and good vegetation (*Radak*).

וְעַל־הַדָּגָן וְעַל־הַתִּירוֹשׁ וְעַל־הַיִּצְהָר ... — *And upon the grain and upon the wine and upon the oil ...*

The decree was upon these three items for they are the staples of a person's diet (*Radak*).

but, behold, it is little; you bring it home and I blow upon it. Why is this?! — the word of HASHEM, *Master of Legions — because of My Temple which is ruined, while you run, each to his own house.* [10] *Therefore, because of you the heavens withhold from [giving] dew, and the land withholds its produce.* [11] *I have declared a drought upon the land and upon the mountains and upon the grain and upon the wine and upon the oil and upon whatever the earth brings forth and upon man and upon animal and upon all the toil of [your] hands.*

[12] *And so Zerubbabel son of Shealtiel and Joshua son of Jehozadak, the Kohen Gadol, and the entire remnant of the people listened to the voice of* HASHEM *their God and to the words of Haggai the prophet, according to what* HASHEM *their God had sent him [to prophesy], and the people feared before* HASHEM. [13] *And Haggai, the agent of* HASHEM,

The curse was placed upon the grain, for they ceased bringing the meal-offerings in the Temple; upon the wine, for they ceased the wine libation; upon the oil for they ceased using the oil of the Menorah (*Mahari Kara*). Ultimately, the curse included all kinds of vegetation (*Metzudos*) because they did not bring their first fruits to the Temple (*Mahari Kara*).

וְעַל־הָאָדָם וְעַל־הַבְּהֵמָה — *And upon man and upon the animal.*

The dry air causes illness in man and animal (*Radak*).

וְעַל כָּל־יְגִיעַ כַּפָּיִם — *And upon all the toil of [your] hands.*

All of their labors to alleviate the situation will be to no avail for their wells will dry up before they can water their crops (*Ibn Ezra; Radak*). Alternatively, they will not succeed in any of their endeavors, for My curse will be upon them (*Metzudos*).

☙ The Nation Reacts

12. וַיִּשְׁמַע זְרֻבָּבֶל ... וְעַל־דִּבְרֵי חַגַּי הַנָּבִיא ... — *And so Zerubbabel ... listened ... and to the words of Haggai the prophet ...*

Zerubbabel, Joshua and the entire remnant of the people were inspired by Haggai. They now realized that the unnatural misfortunes that they were experiencing should have moved them to examine their deeds and search them for any shortcomings. Furthermore, Haggai's prophetic message now inspired them to rebuild the Holy Temple (*Radak*).

וַיִּירְאוּ הָעָם מִפְּנֵי ה׳ — *And the people feared before Hashem.*

Malbim identifies the *remnant of the people,* שְׁאֵרִית הָעָם, as the leaders of the nation and *the people,* הָעָם, as the common people. The leaders were inspired by the word of God but the common people reacted only for fear of retribution.

13. וַיֹּאמֶר חַגַּי מַלְאַךְ ה׳ בְּמַלְאֲכוּת ה׳ לָעָם לֵאמֹר — *And Haggai, the agent of Hashem, in the agency of Hashem, spoke to the people, saying.*

This translation of the word מַלְאַךְ is offered by all of the commentators. *Targum Yonasan,* however, translates

א/יד־טז

יד אֲנִי אִתְּכֶם נְאֻם־יְהוָה׃ וַיָּעַר יְהוָה אֶת־רוּחַ זְרֻבָּבֶל בֶּן־שַׁלְתִּיאֵל פַּחַת יְהוּדָה וְאֶת־רוּחַ יְהוֹשֻׁעַ בֶּן־יְהוֹצָדָק הַכֹּהֵן הַגָּדוֹל וְאֶת־רוּחַ כֹּל שְׁאֵרִית הָעָם וַיָּבֹאוּ וַיַּעֲשׂוּ מְלָאכָה בְּבֵית־
טו יְהוָה צְבָאוֹת אֱלֹהֵיהֶם׃ בְּיוֹם עֶשְׂרִים וְאַרְבָּעָה לַחֹדֶשׁ בַּשִּׁשִּׁי בִּשְׁנַת שְׁתַּיִם לְדָרְיָוֶשׁ
א הַמֶּלֶךְ׃ בַּשְּׁבִיעִי

ב/א־ג

בְּעֶשְׂרִים וְאֶחָד לַחֹדֶשׁ הָיָה דְּבַר־יְהוָה בְּיַד־
ב חַגַּי הַנָּבִיא לֵאמֹר׃ אֱמָר־נָא אֶל־זְרֻבָּבֶל בֶּן־שַׁלְתִּיאֵל פַּחַת יְהוּדָה וְאֶל־יְהוֹשֻׁעַ בֶּן־יְהוֹצָדָק
ג הַכֹּהֵן הַגָּדוֹל וְאֶל־שְׁאֵרִית הָעָם לֵאמֹר׃ מִי בָכֶם הַנִּשְׁאָר אֲשֶׁר רָאָה אֶת־הַבַּיִת הַזֶּה בִּכְבוֹדוֹ הָרִאשׁוֹן וּמָה אַתֶּם רֹאִים אֹתוֹ עַתָּה

נְבִיָא — *prophet*, following the statement of the Sages (*Lev. Rabbah* 1:1) that the prophets are referred to as angels.

אֲנִי אִתְּכֶם נְאֻם־ה׳ — *"I am with you — the word of Hashem."*

Since the people had not received permission from the king, they were afraid to begin construction of the Temple. God therefore encouraged them and told them not to be afraid and to begin construction immediately, even without the permission of the king, for He is with them, and their efforts will therefore be successful (*Metzudos; Abarbanel; Malbim*). Although the last time they had wanted to rebuild they were hampered and eventually stopped by the neighboring gentiles, that was because the time was not yet ripe for its construction (*Mahari Kara*). [Now, however, the time has come, and nothing will stand in their way.]

14. וַיָּעַר ה׳ אֶת־רוּחַ זְרֻבָּבֶל ... — *Hashem aroused the spirit of Zerubbabel ...*

The Almighty strengthened the spirit of the people with resolve against the efforts of their oppressors who plotted to obstruct their work (*Radak*).

15. בְּיוֹם עֶשְׂרִים וְאַרְבָּעָה לַחֹדֶשׁ בַּשִּׁשִּׁי... — *On the twenty-fourth day of the month, in the sixth [month] ...*

This verse is actually connected with the previous verse. Thus, on the twenty-fourth day of the sixth month they began the labor of cutting stones and sawing down trees (*Rashi*) in preparation for the actual work of building, which began three months later (*Radak* from 2:18).

II

☙ Haggai's Third Prophecy

Having begun the work of erecting the new Temple, those who had seen and remembered the First Temple in all of its resplendent glory were struck by the small size and diminished splendor of the one they were in the process of building. They therefore became discouraged and their enthusiasm for the project began to wane.

1/14-15 *in the agency of HASHEM, spoke to the people, saying, "I am with you — the word of HASHEM."*

[14] HASHEM aroused the spirit of Zerubbabel son of Shealtiel, the governor of Judah, and the spirit of Joshua son of Jehozadak, the Kohen Gadol, and the spirit of the entire remnant of the people, and they came and did work on the Temple of HASHEM, Master of Legions, their God, [15] on the twenty-fourth day of the month, in the sixth [month], in the second year of King Darius.

2/1-3

[1] In the seventh [month], on the twenty-first of the month, the word of HASHEM came through Haggai the prophet, saying: [2] "Speak, now, to Zerubbabel son of Shealtiel, the governor of Judah, and to Joshua son of Jehozadak, the Kohen Gadol, and to the rest of the people, saying:

[3] Who is left among you who remembers this Temple

For this reason, the Almighty issued a prophecy through Haggai urging them to disregard their emotions and to continue pursuing their great undertaking with the same original enthusiasm (*Abarbanel*).

1. בַּשְּׁבִיעִי בְּעֶשְׂרִים וְאֶחָד לַחֹדֶשׁ... — *In the seventh [month], on the twenty-first of the month ...*

The date of the prophecy is specified because of its significance to the issue involved. The seventh month is the month of Tishrei and the twenty-first of Tishrei is the seventh day of the festival of *Succos, Hoshana Rabbah,* which had been a day of great rejoicing during the days of the First Temple. It was the memory of this day of joyous celebration that moved the elders of the nation to depression over the contrast between the two Temples (*Abarbanel* to *Zechariah* 1:1).

2. אֶל־זְרֻבָּבֶל בֶּן־שַׁלְתִּיאֵל פַּחַת יְהוּדָה וְאֶל־יְהוֹשֻׁעַ בֶּן־יְהוֹצָדָק הַכֹּהֵן הַגָּדוֹל — *To Zerubbabel son of Shealtiel, the governor of Judah, and to Joshua son of Jehozadak, the Kohen Gadol.*

Zerubbabel was a descendant of King Jeconiah and was an heir to the throne. He is therefore mentioned before Joshua for Scripture always grants honor to royalty before *Kehunah* and prophecy (*Ibn Ezra*).

3. מִי בָכֶם הַנִּשְׁאָר אֲשֶׁר רָאָה אֶת־הַבַּיִת הַזֶּה בִּכְבוֹדוֹ הָרִאשׁוֹן... — *Who is left among you who remembers this Temple in its original glory ...*

Since it has been only seventy years since the destruction of the First Temple, many among you can still recall the beauty and grandeur (*Mahari Kara*) of the great Temple that stood on this very spot. Consequently, when you compare the two structures, the present one fades into insignificance (*Abarbanel; Metzudos*).

ד הֲלוֹא כָמֹהוּ כְּאַיִן בְּעֵינֵיכֶם: וְעַתָּה חֲזַק זְרֻבָּבֶל | נְאֻם־יהוה וַחֲזַק יְהוֹשֻׁעַ בֶּן־יְהוֹצָדָק הַכֹּהֵן הַגָּדוֹל וַחֲזַק כָּל־עַם הָאָרֶץ נְאֻם־יהוה וַעֲשׂוּ ה כִּי־אֲנִי אִתְּכֶם נְאֻם יהוה צְבָאוֹת: אֶת־הַדָּבָר אֲשֶׁר־כָּרַתִּי אִתְּכֶם בְּצֵאתְכֶם מִמִּצְרַיִם וְרוּחִי ו עֹמֶדֶת בְּתוֹכְכֶם אַל־תִּירָאוּ: כִּי כֹה אָמַר יהוה צְבָאוֹת עוֹד אַחַת מְעַט הִיא וַאֲנִי מַרְעִישׁ אֶת־הַשָּׁמַיִם וְאֶת־הָאָרֶץ וְאֶת־הַיָּם וְאֶת־הֶחָרָבָה:

הַבַּיִת הַזֶּה — *This Temple.* This is actually referring to the First Temple. The prophet refers to it as *this Temple* because it originally stood at this very site where the new Temple was about to be constructed (*Metzudos*).

הֲלוֹא כָמֹהוּ כְּאַיִן בְּעֵינֵיכֶם — *Is it not like nothing in your eyes?*

The literal translation of כָמֹהוּ כְּאַיִן is *like it, like nothing.* When compared to the First Temple, the Second Temple is so insignificant that *it,* the Second Temple, and *nothing* are equal in your eyes (*Rashi*). According to *Radak,* כָמֹהוּ is referring to the First Temple. If you will compare this one to the first, to be כָמֹהוּ, *like it,* it will [instead] seem כְּאַיִן בְּעֵינֵיכֶם, *like nothing in your eyes.*

4. וְעַתָּה חֲזַק זְרֻבָּבֶל נְאֻם־ה׳ ... — *So now, be strong, O Zerubbabel — the word of Hashem ...*

God encourages the entire nation to build the Temple even though it will be inferior to the first. Be strong, Zerubbabel, leader of the nation! Be strong, Joshua, the second in stature! And be strong, all of the citizens of the land, each according to his own level (*Abarbanel*). Continue to do that which you have begun (*Alshich*) and work on the rebuilding of this house. For the aid and assistance of the Almighty is with you in your endeavor (*Abarbanel*). Although this is but a shadow of the First Temple it shall nevertheless bring upon you the blessing of Hashem that you seek through it (*Metzudos*).

וַעֲשׂוּ ... — *And do ...*

Our translation follows *Metzudos* who explains that the people should continue to do that which they have been doing until now, i.e., continue to build the new Temple. Others, however, connect this verse with the following verse and translate וַעֲשׂוּ, *and fulfill,* i.e., fulfill the covenant that I executed with you when you went out of Egypt. If you will do so, I will be with you, and you will continue to thrive and be strengthened (*Radak*). Alternatively, for I am with you now, just as I was with you when I took you out of Egypt (*Malbim*).

5. אֶת־הַדָּבָר אֲשֶׁר־כָּרַתִּי אִתְּכֶם בְּצֵאתְכֶם מִמִּצְרַיִם — *The matter [of the covenant] that I sealed with you when you went forth from Egypt.*

This verse is to be understood as if the word עֲשׂוּ of the previous verse is connected to this verse as well. You must keep the Torah and do the mitzvos over which we established a covenant when you went forth from Egypt (*Abarbanel; Metzudos*), for the true measure of the Temple does not depend upon its size and splendor but rather on the degree of sanctity and commitment to the laws of the Torah that pervades it (*Abarbanel*).

אֲשֶׁר־כָּרַתִּי אִתְּכֶם — *That I sealed with you.*

Although the covenant was actually sealed with your forefathers, it applies to your generation as well, as if you had

in its original glory, and how do you view it now? Is it not like nothing in your eyes? [4] So now, be strong, O Zerubbabel — the word of HASHEM — and be strong, Joshua son of Jehozadak, the Kohen Gadol, and be strong, the entire people of the land — the word of HASHEM — and do, for I am with you — the word of HASHEM, Master of Legions — [5] the matter [of the covenant] that I sealed with you when you went forth from Egypt. My spirit remains in your midst; do not be afraid. [6] For thus said HASHEM, Master of Legions: There will be one more; it is a small one. I will shake the

been standing there when it was executed — see *Deut.* 5:3 (*Radak*). *R' Eliezer of Beaugency* understands this verse to flow from the previous one. For I am with you through the covenant that I executed with you when you went out of Egypt.

וְרוּחִי עֹמֶדֶת בְּתוֹכְכֶם אַל־תִּירָאוּ — *My spirit remains in your midst; do not be afraid.*

This is My spirit of prophecy that still exists in your midst and is experienced by your prophets (*Targum Yonasan; Rashi; Ibn Ezra; Metzudos*). Therefore, you need not fear the designs of your enemies (*Mahari Kara*) nor the possibility of a lack of success and blessing in your endeavors (*Metzudos*), for I am still with you. *Malbim* adds: Although My spirit is no longer manifest among you through overt miracles, it nevertheless remains in your midst, concealed behind the veil of natural events.

Abarbanel interprets: If you will fulfill the Torah and mitzvos that I commanded you to do when you went out of Egypt, My spirit of prophecy and My Divine Presence will remain in your midst, never to be removed. Indeed, you now have the opportunity to bring about the final redemption with your deeds (see preface to 1:1).

Rashi interprets this verse independent of the previous one: *[As long as] you heed My Torah, My spirit will dwell among you, and this you need not fear.* However, once the people sinned and transgressed the Torah, the spirit of prophecy was removed from them (*Radak*).

6. עוֹד אַחַת מְעַט הִיא — *There will be one more; it is a small one.*

Haggai foretells that after the fall of the Persian Empire that now rules over Israel, there will be one more kingdom that will extend its authority over Israel and oppress them — that of the Greek/Hellenist Empire — but their domination will last only a short time (*Rashi*).

וַאֲנִי מַרְעִישׁ אֶת־הַשָּׁמַיִם וְאֶת־הָאָרֶץ וְאֶת־הַיָּם וְאֶת־הֶחָרָבָה — *I will shake the heavens and the earth and the sea and the dry land.*

I will cause a major upheaval with the miracles that I will perform for the Hasmoneans, during their revolt against the Greeks — a reference to the miracles of Chanukah (*Rashi*). Alternatively, the shaking of heaven and earth refers to the harsh decrees that the Hellenists will impose upon the Jewish nation (*R' Eliezer of Beaugency*).

Others take a totally different approach to this verse. God is assuring Israel that His blessing will not end with all He has already bestowed upon them for He will add slightly to that blessing. Scripture refers to it as a small favor since it is simple for God to

ז וְהִרְעַשְׁתִּי֙ אֶת־כָּל־הַגּוֹיִ֔ם וּבָ֖אוּ חֶמְדַּ֣ת כָּל־הַגּוֹיִ֑ם וּמִלֵּאתִ֞י אֶת־הַבַּ֤יִת הַזֶּה֙ כָּב֔וֹד אָמַ֖ר יְהוָ֥ה צְבָאֽוֹת׃ ח לִ֥י הַכֶּ֖סֶף וְלִ֣י הַזָּהָ֑ב נְאֻ֖ם יְהוָ֥ה צְבָאֽוֹת׃ ט גָּד֣וֹל יִֽהְיֶ֡ה כְּבוֹד֩ הַבַּ֨יִת הַזֶּ֜ה הָאַחֲרוֹן֙ מִן־הָ֣רִאשׁ֔וֹן אָמַ֖ר יְהוָ֣ה צְבָא֑וֹת

accomplish. God says, "Although at this time you are yet plagued by your enemies, there will come a time when you will be entirely free of oppression, during the days of the Hasmoneans and again under the reign of Herod. I will then figuratively "shake the heavens and the earth; for the nations will express an appreciation of the glory and stature of the Holy Temple and will honor it with gifts of gold and silver." The verse may also be understood somewhat literally for, in fact, there was an earthquake that shook the land during the days of Herod, as attested to in the writings of Yossipon (*Radak; Ibn Ezra*).

7. וְהִרְעַשְׁתִּי אֶת־כָּל־הַגּוֹיִם וּבָאוּ חֶמְדַּת כָּל־הַגּוֹיִם וּמִלֵּאתִי אֶת־הַבַּיִת הַזֶּה כָּבוֹד אָמַר ה׳ צְבָאוֹת — *I will shake all the nations, and the precious things of all the nations will arrive here, and I will fill this Temple with glory, said Hashem, Master of Legions.*

I will inspire the nations of the world to hasten and come to witness the glory of the Temple and to bring gifts of gold and silver. As recorded in the works of Yoseph ben Gurion (*Rashi*), this occurred during the days of Herod (*Radak*). *R' Eliezer of Beaugency* interprets: The gentile nations will submit to your power; this occurred in the times of the Hasmoneans and of Herod. And I will fill this house with glory; this, too, occurred in the time of Herod, when the Temple was rebuilt with great splendor.

Mahari Kara interprets these two verses as referring to an earlier period during the days of the Second Temple: *One more; it is a small one* — the oppression under which you now live, that of the kingdom of Persia,[1] shall remain just a bit longer after this Temple is built. *I will shake the heavens and the earth* — this refers to Alexander the Great, who conquered the Persians and the Medes and all the nations under their rule. וּבָאוּ חֶמְדַּת כָּל־הַגּוֹיִם, *And come [to] the desire of all the nations* — they will turn to conquer Eretz Yisrael — the land coveted by all the nations, and to destroy the Temple. *And I will fill this Temple with glory* — this occurred at that time. When Alexander approached Jerusalem, he fell asleep, and an angel appeared to him in a dream and began to strike him. Alexander cried out, "Why do you strike me? Leave me be and I will do whatever you ask of me." Whereupon the angel said to him, "This is my command to you. Tomorrow when you arrive at your destination, you will be met by an elderly man coming from the Temple with the same appearance as my own. This is Joshua the Kohen Gadol.[2] Obey his every command."

Upon encountering Joshua, Alexander descended from his chariot and prostrated himself before the sage. Joshua said to him, "Have you come to destroy the Temple?" Alexander responded, "I will not destroy it if you permit me to place within it an image to serve as a memorial to me." Whereupon Joshua replied, "The silver and gold you would use for the image give instead to the poor and orphaned who returned destitute from their exile in Babylonia and as a memorial to you, every boy born this year will be named Alexander in your honor."

Some say that these two verses are not only foretelling the building of the Second

1. In the version of *Mahari Kara* printed in the Lublin *Nach*, the kingdom of Babylonia is cited. However, this is clearly a printer's error, as by the time of the Second Temple, Babylonia had long since passed from the scene.

2. According to the Talmud (*Yoma* 69b), this was Simon the Just [who was Kohen Gadol later than Joshua].

heavens and the earth and the sea and the dry land. [7] I will shake all the nations, and the precious things of all the nations will arrive here, and I will fill this Temple with glory, said HASHEM, Master of Legions. [8] Mine is the silver and mine is the gold — the word of HASHEM, Master of Legions. [9] The glory of this latter Temple will be greater than [that of] the first, said

Temple but also allude to the ultimate redemption and the building of the Third and final Temple. The prophet is describing the series of events leading to that end: In addition to the First Temple that had already been destroyed, there will be one more that will last for a relatively short span of time: the Second Temple. God will then shake the heavens and earth by bringing destruction upon that one as well. Eventually, however, He will inspire all of the gentile nations to come to Jerusalem to participate in the battle of Gog and Magog, bringing along with them all their wealth and riches. At that time, all these nations will be decimated and their wealth inherited by the nation of Israel, and the Temple will thereby be filled with glory (*Abarbanel; Metzudos*).

Alternatively, the prophet exhorts the nation to be faithful to the laws of the Torah, so that this very Temple will be the final one, rebuilt for eternity. Thus, *A bit more, for it is little* — the extent of My spirit of prophecy which prevails at this time is relatively little. To reach the desired end, the nation must intensify its commitment to the Torah and its commandments. When that will occur, *I will shake the heavens and the earth* and transcend the laws of nature and bring about the full and final glory of My land, My Temple and My nation (*Malbim*).

8. לִי הַכֶּסֶף וְלִי הַזָּהָב נְאֻם ה׳ צְבָאוֹת — *Mine is the silver and Mine is the gold — the word of Hashem, Master of Legions.*

Wherever it may be found (*Ibn Ezra*), and whoever may have it in his possession (*Radak*), all of the silver and gold in existence is Mine. Thus it is in My power, as well as within My rights, to bestow it upon whomever I wish (*Rashi; Radak*). Accordingly, I shall inspire the nations to bring all their silver and gold to the Temple (*Radak*). *Malbim*, following his approach to the previous two verses (see above), interprets: At that time, all will recognize that the silver and gold is Mine, and they will therefore bring it to Jerusalem to present it to the Master of Creation.

The Sages derive from this verse that even if one pursues his livelihood aggressively as well as honestly, to be sure of success, he must also pray for wealth from Him to Whom all wealth belongs (*Niddah* 70b).

9. גָּדוֹל יִהְיֶה כְּבוֹד הַבַּיִת הַזֶּה הָאַחֲרוֹן מִן־הָרִאשׁוֹן — *The glory of this latter Temple will be greater than [that of] the first.*

The nature of this glory is the subject of a dispute between Rav and Shmuel: According to one, it refers to the height[1] of the Temple edifice. [The *Heichal* of the Second Temple was 40 cubits high while that of the first was only 30 cubits.] According to the other, it alludes to its years of existence [four hundred and twenty years, ten years longer than the First Temple] (*Rashi* from *Bava Basra* 3a). Yoseph ben Gurion reports that Herod's renovations of the Second

1. *Rashi* (ad loc.) explains that the *Heichal* of the Second Temple stood 100 cubits tall. However, *Tosafos Yom Tov* (*Yoma* 5:1, s.v. לְבֵין שְׁתֵּי) concludes that this is a printer's error. Originally *Rashi* wrote מ, 40, and it was misinterpreted to mean מֵאָה, 100.

וּבַמָּקוֹם הַזֶּה אֶתֵּן שָׁלוֹם נְאֻם יְהוָה צְבָאוֹת:
י בְּעֶשְׂרִים וְאַרְבָּעָה לַתְּשִׁיעִי בִּשְׁנַת
שְׁתַּיִם לְדָרְיָוֶשׁ הָיָה דְּבַר־יְהוָה °אֶל־חַגַּי
יא הַנָּבִיא לֵאמֹר: כֹּה אָמַר יְהוָה צְבָאוֹת שְׁאַל־
יב נָא אֶת־הַכֹּהֲנִים תּוֹרָה לֵאמֹר: הֵן | יִשָּׂא־אִישׁ
בְּשַׂר־קֹדֶשׁ בִּכְנַף בִּגְדוֹ וְנָגַע °בִּכְנָפוֹ אֶל־
הַלֶּחֶם וְאֶל־הַנָּזִיד וְאֶל־הַיַּיִן וְאֶל־שֶׁמֶן וְאֶל־
כָּל־מַאֲכָל הֲיִקְדָּשׁ וַיַּעֲנוּ הַכֹּהֲנִים וַיֹּאמְרוּ לֹא:

°נ״א בְּיַד

Temple transformed it into the most magnificent building on earth (*Radak*). Indeed the Talmud writes that it was said that whoever did not see the Temple building that was erected by Herod has not seen a truly beautiful building in his lifetime (*Bava Basra* 4a).

וּבַמָּקוֹם הַזֶּה אֶתֵּן שָׁלוֹם — *And I will grant peace to this place.*

Although there were many wars during the days of the Second Temple, there was a long period of time in which peace prevailed (*Radak*). This is in contrast to the First Temple period, which was plagued incessantly by wars and oppression after the death of King Rehoboam, son of Solomon (*Mahari Kara*).[1]

☙ Haggai's Fourth Prophecy

10-11. בְּעֶשְׂרִים וְאַרְבָּעָה לַתְּשִׁיעִי ... — *On the twenty-fourth of the ninth [month]...*

This is the twenty-fourth of Kislev, the ninth month of the Jewish calendar. Preparation for the construction of the Temple began in Elul, the sixth month, but actual construction did not begin until the twenty-fourth of Kislev. It was on this day that Haggai was instructed by the Almighty to test the Kohanim regarding the laws of ritual purity (*Radak*). Since these laws are essential to the functioning of the Temple and many were not relevant in Babylonia, they may have been forgotten (*Rashi; Metzudos*).

Actually, the first returnees from the Babylonian exile had built the altar immediately upon their return to Israel. Sacrifices had been offered and the Kohanim had officiated for nineteen years prior to the actual rebuilding of the Temple. However, the prophet had not been instructed to test them until now, as the sacrifices were about to be offered on a permanent basis (*Radak*).

12-14. In order to understand the dialogue between Haggai and the Kohanim, the following information concerning the laws of *tumah*, ritual defilement, is necessary. Torah law defines several different degrees of *tumah*: A human corpse is classified as an *avi avos hatumah* — a primary source of *tumah* [lit. a father of fathers of *tumah*] and renders anything that comes in contact with it as an *av hatumah* — a source of *tumah* [lit. a father of *tumah*]. A carcass [נְבֵלָה] of an animal or a dead reptile or rodent [שֶׁרֶץ; lit. creeping creature] is also classified as an *av hatumah*. Any object that comes in direct contact with an *av hatumah* becomes a *rishon letumah* — the first level of *tumah* and renders any object that comes in contact with it a *sheni letumah* — a second level of *tumah*. When dealing with *terumah* (the portion of produce given to the Kohen), there is an additional level of *tumah*: if a *sheni* touches *terumah* it renders it a *shlishi letumah;* a third level of tumah. The *terumah* is defiled and is prohibited

1. [In our editions of *Mahari Kara* this is included in his commentary to verses 6,7, but it seems clear that it is a printer's error.]

HASHEM, Master of Legions; and I will grant peace to this place — the word of HASHEM, Master of Legions."

[10]*On the twenty-fourth of the ninth [month], in the second year of Darius, the word of HASHEM came to Haggai the prophet, saying:* [11]*"Thus said HASHEM, Master of Legions: Inquire, now, for a ruling from the Kohanim, saying,* [12]*'If a person carries ritually defiled flesh in the corner of his garment, and then he touches bread with his [garment's] corner, and [the bread touches] stew, and [the stew touches] wine or oil or any other food — does [that food] become defiled?'"*

The Kohanim answered and said, "No."

for consumption. With *kodashim* [that which has been sanctified for Temple use or service], there is another level of *tumah* — a *revii letumah* — a fourth level of *tumah*.

12. הֵן יִשָּׂא־אִישׁ בְּשַׂר־קֹדֶשׁ — *If a person carries ritually defiled flesh.*

Our translation of בְּשַׂר־קֹדֶשׁ follows *Rashi* and *Metzudos.* Although the word קֹדֶשׁ is usually used to describe that which is sanctified or hallowed, its literal translation is *separated,* מוּבְדָל. It can therefore also refer to something that is separated because it is *tamei,* ritually defiled — see *Deut.* 22:9 (*Metzudos*).

Ibn Ezra, Radak and others maintain that בְּשַׂר־קֹדֶשׁ is indeed referring to *sanctified* flesh [see below].

The ritually defiled flesh of our verse is a creeping creature (*Rashi* to *Pesachim* 16b). *Rashi* (ibid.) explains that a creeping creature had become enveloped in a person's garment and the *creeping creature*[1] [not the garment] touched the bread which in turn touched the stew. The stew then touched the wine which in turn touched the oil. Haggai questioned the Kohanim regarding the ritual purity status of the last item.

וַיַּעֲנוּ הַכֹּהֲנִים וַיֹּאמְרוּ לֹא — *The Kohanim answered and said, "No."*

The food will not become ritually defiled (*Rashi*).

Rav and Shmuel (*Pesachim* 17a) disagree in the interpretation of this verse. Rav maintains that Haggai questioned the Kohanim concerning sanctified food that became a *revii letumah.* The creeping creature, an *av hatumah,* touched the bread rendering it a *rishon* which touched the stew, a *sheni* which touched the wine, a *shlishi,* which touched the oil, a *revii.* Accordingly, the Kohanim, who permitted the food, erred, for sanctified food *is* rendered ritually impure even if it is merely a *revii letumah.* Shmuel suggests that Haggai's question was regarding a *chamishi letumah,* a fifth level. According

1. *Rashi's* explanation here is unclear. Although he translates בְּשַׂר־קֹדֶשׁ as he does in *Pesachim,* he nevertheless interprets וְנָגַע בִּכְנָפוֹ to mean that "it (the bread) touched the *garment* which is a *rishon* but it did not touch the creeping creature." [It is interesting to note that the *Rashi* with the heading וְנָגַע בִּכְנָפוֹ is not printed in the Mechon Hamoar Edition of *Mikraos Gedolos.*] This seems to contradict his explanation of *Pesachim* 16b unless we assume that he is explaining the verse according to Shmuel, which seems unlikely since he doesn't mention the disagreement of Rav and Shmuel until later. *Parshandasa* states that *Rashi's* explanation here corresponds with the view of *Rabbeinu Tam* cited by *Tosafos Pesachim* 17a.

יג וַיֹּאמֶר חַגַּי אִם־יִגַּע טְמֵא־נֶפֶשׁ בְּכָל־אֵלֶּה הֲיִטְמָא וַיַּעֲנוּ הַכֹּהֲנִים וַיֹּאמְרוּ יִטְמָא: יד וַיַּעַן חַגַּי וַיֹּאמֶר כֵּן הָעָם־הַזֶּה וְכֵן־הַגּוֹי הַזֶּה לְפָנַי נְאֻם־יהוה וְכֵן כָּל־מַעֲשֵׂה יְדֵיהֶם וַאֲשֶׁר יַקְרִיבוּ שָׁם טָמֵא הוּא: טו וְעַתָּה שִׂימוּ־נָא לְבַבְכֶם מִן־הַיּוֹם הַזֶּה וָמָעְלָה מִטֶּרֶם שׂוּם־אֶבֶן אֶל־אֶבֶן בְּהֵיכַל יהוה:

to Shmuel וְנָגַע בִּכְנָפוֹ אֶל־הַלֶּחֶם means the garment, not the creeping creature, touched the bread. The creeping creature touched the garment making *it* a *rishon* and thereby adding one more step to the sequence of events. Accordingly, the Kohanim were correct by responding that the food is not ritually impure (*Rashi*).

Although *Metzudos* translates בְּשַׂר־קֹדֶשׁ as *Rashi, defiled flesh,* he interprets the verse differently. The creeping creature touched the garment, a *rishon*, which touched the bread, a *sheni,* which touched the stew, a *shlishi,* which touched *either* the wine or the oil making the last item a *revii.* Wine cannot transfer *tumah* according to Torah law even if it were a *rishon* since it is a liquid.

As noted above, *Radak* translates בְּשַׂר־קֹדֶשׁ literally, *sanctified flesh,* i.e., flesh of a sacrifice. His understanding is that the garment had been in contact with a creeping creature, an *av hatumah,* which rendered it a *rishon.* The sanctified flesh was carried in the folds of the garment rendering the flesh a *sheni.* The flesh in turn touched either bread, stew, wine or oil, a *shlishi,* which in turn touched other food rendering it a *revii* (see also *R' Chananel* to *Pesachim* 17a; *Aruch, Erech* רבע).

Another view maintains that Haggai's question was not regarding ritual defilement but regarding sanctification. The Kohanim responded that it does not become sanctified since it merely touched its surface but did not absorb any of its essence (*Ibn Ezra, R' Eliezer of Beaugency, Malbim*).

13. וַיֹּאמֶר חַגַּי אִם־יִגַּע טְמֵא־נֶפֶשׁ בְּכָל־אֵלֶּה הֲיִטְמָא וַיַּעֲנוּ הַכֹּהֲנִים וַיֹּאמְרוּ יִטְמָא — *Haggai said, "If one who touched a human corpse would touch all of these, would it become defiled?" And the Kohanim answered and said, "It would become defiled."*

The process previously described had occurred, but the original source of *tumah* was not a creeping creature but a corpse. As explained earlier, a corpse is an *avi avos hatumah,* a primary source of *tumah,* and renders that which it touches an *av hatumah* (*Rashi*). Thus, the objects touched last in the cycle described above would be only a *shlishi letumah* and not a *revii.* This time, the Kohanim responded that it would be *tamei,* as they were aware of the law that *kodoshim* become *tamei* when they are a *shlishi* (*Metzudos*).

This follows the view of Rav. According to Shmuel, this case is one of a *revii,* and the Kohanim thus showed their expertise in these laws by rendering the *revii tamei* but the *chamishi tahor* (*Rashi*).

14. וַיַּעַן חַגַּי וַיֹּאמֶר כֵּן הָעָם־הַזֶּה וְכֵן־הַגּוֹי הַזֶּה לְפָנַי נְאֻם־ה׳ וְכֵן כָּל־מַעֲשֵׂה יְדֵיהֶם וַאֲשֶׁר יַקְרִיבוּ שָׁם טָמֵא הוּא — *Haggai spoke up and said, "So is this people and so is this nation before Me — the word of Hashem — and so is all their handiwork; what they offer there will be defiled.*

So is this people of Kohanim and so is the entire nation (*Ibn Ezra; Malbim*). Just as they err in regard to the laws of *tumah,* so are they ignorant of many other laws of the Torah (*Rashi*). Thus, all that they sacrifice upon the Altar will be *tamei* if they do not take the necessary steps to learn the laws properly (*Rashi*).

This follows the view of Rav. According to Shmuel, Haggai was saying:

[13] *Haggai said, "If one who touched a human corpse would touch all of these, would it become defiled?"*

And the Kohanim answered and said, "It would become defiled."

[14] *Haggai spoke up and said:*

"So is this people and so is this nation before Me — the word of HASHEM *— and so is all their handiwork: what they offer there will be defiled.* [15] *But nevertheless, consider [the situation] from this day and previously, before stone was placed upon stone in the Sanctuary of* HASHEM*,*

Because they have corrupted their deeds, the Almighty considers the sacrifices they had offered as if they are *tamei* (*Pesachim* 17a). I.e., by delaying the construction of the Temple, they have shown no concern for the honor of the Almighty. He therefore considers these sacrifices as if they were *tamei* (*Radak*).

Rashi to *Pesachim* (17a) interprets this as a prediction of the future: The day will soon come when the people will corrupt their deeds and their offerings will then become despicable in the eyes of the Almighty, as if they were *tamei.*

Others explain the previous two verses as an allegory, leading up to its interpretation in this verse: An object does not become sanctified through mere contact with another sanctified object unless it absorbs from the essence of the latter. So, too, the sacrifices you offer on the Altar without first rebuilding the Temple are incapable of generating sanctity to you or evoking the Almighty's blessings upon you. Thus, both you and your deeds remain void of sanctity before G-d (*R' Eliezer of Beaugency;* cf. *Abarbanel*). Furthermore, all that you sacrifice there is considered *tamei* (*R' Eliezer Beaugency*) because your laziness in honoring G-d defiles your souls and effects the sacrifices you bring, just as the *tumah* of one object spreads to whatever item it touches (*Abarbanel;* cf. *Ibn Ezra; Malbim*).

15. וְעַתָּה — *But nevertheless.* Consider all that has occurred to you in the years that have passed prior to your return to rebuild the Temple (*Rashi*). *Abarbanel* notes that this prophecy took place on the twenty-fourth of Elul, the day the reconstruction of the Temple resumed and was therefore a time to reflect on the past.

שִׂימוּ־נָא לְבַבְכֶם — *Consider [the situation].*

Haggai urges the people to recognize and rectify two of their past sins, i.e., delaying the reconstruction of the Temple and their ignorance of laws pertaining to the *Kehunah* (*Rashi*). Alternatively, the people should focus their hearts upon doing *teshuvah,* repenting their sins, before they place a stone on the foundation that was laid eighteen years ago (*Mahari Kara's* version to *Rashi*).

מִן־הַיּוֹם הַזֶּה וָמָעְלָה — *From this day and previously.*

Our translation follows *Rashi* who explains וָמָעְלָה as *the years that have passed.* Alternatively, *Ibn Ezra* and *Radak* translate *from this day and onward.* Haggai exhorts the people to note and consider the deeds they did prior to the rebuilding of the Temple and what will occur after it is completed (*Radak*). Others interpret: *Pay attention to that which will occur from today and onward,* and note the success and blessing that will be your lot once you begin rebuilding (*R' Eliezer of Beaugency; Malbim*).[1]

1. *Malbim* sees in this verse an allusion to yet another exhortation: See to it that your rebuilding of the Temple shall not be merely a physical exertion. It must also include your שִׂימַת לֵב — your focus and emotional involvement in the sanctity involved.

טז מִהְיוֹתָם בָּא אֶל־עֲרֵמַת עֶשְׂרִים וְהָיְתָה עֲשָׂרָה בָּא אֶל־הַיֶּקֶב לַחְשֹׂף חֲמִשִּׁים פּוּרָה וְהָיְתָה עֶשְׂרִים׃ יז הִכֵּיתִי אֶתְכֶם בַּשִּׁדָּפוֹן וּבַיֵּרָקוֹן וּבַבָּרָד אֵת כָּל־מַעֲשֵׂה יְדֵיכֶם וְאֵין־אֶתְכֶם אֵלַי נְאֻם־יהוָה׃ יח שִׂימוּ־נָא לְבַבְכֶם מִן־הַיּוֹם הַזֶּה וָמָעְלָה מִיּוֹם עֶשְׂרִים וְאַרְבָּעָה לַתְּשִׁיעִי לְמִן־הַיּוֹם אֲשֶׁר־יֻסַּד הֵיכַל־יהוָה שִׂימוּ לְבַבְכֶם׃ יט הַעוֹד הַזֶּרַע בַּמְּגוּרָה וְעַד־הַגֶּפֶן וְהַתְּאֵנָה וְהָרִמּוֹן וְעֵץ הַזַּיִת לֹא נָשָׂא

16. מִהְיוֹתָם בָּא אֶל־עֲרֵמַת עֶשְׂרִים וְהָיְתָה עֲשָׂרָה — *When they would come to a grain heap of [what should have been] twenty [measures] but there were [only] ten.*

The people are told to involve themselves in rebuilding the Temple and learning its laws so that their crops would not be afflicted by a curse as they had been until now (*Rashi*). They should realize that the curse that caused their produce to yield far less than expected is clearly the hand of the Almighty Who was taking them to task for not rebuilding the Temple (*Radak; R' Eliezer of Beaugency; Metzudos*).

בָּא אֶל־הַיֶּקֶב לַחְשֹׂף חֲמִשִּׁים פּוּרָה וְהָיְתָה עֶשְׂרִים — *[When one would] come to the winepress to draw out fifty [measures] from the pit, but there were [only] twenty:*

יֶקֶב is the pit in front of the winepress into which the wine flows and פּוּרָה is the term used for a measure of wine taken from the press (*Rashi*). Alternatively, *Metzudos* translates פּוּרָה as the actual winepress [גַּת] and renders fifty measures of wine that flowed from the פּוּרָה.

The prophet uses a larger measure of wine with a greater percentage of loss [one would expect fifty measures and find only twenty] than it does of grain [one would expect twenty and find only ten] not because a greater curse had been placed on the wine than on the grain; but since wine lies within the deep wine pit it is harder to measure and people therefore tend to assess it incorrectly (*Rashi*).

According to the Sages (*Avos DeRav Nassan*, Ch. 4), Scripture uses a larger measure of wine [fifty measures] than it does regarding grain [twenty measures] because it is teaching that wine is an extra measure for the world and if wine is afflicted then it is a sign of a curse for the entire world. Since the wine must be plentiful, the prophet uses a larger measure (*Rashi*).[1] Others understand that the Sages are explaining the reason the wine produced less than fifty percent of its expected yield, unlike the grain that had produced half. Wine is meant primarily for indulgence in rejoicing. Thus, when G-d's intent is to minimize rejoicing, He lessens the wine to a greater degree than anything else (*Mahari Kara*).

17. הִכֵּיתִי אֶתְכֶם בַּשִּׁדָּפוֹן וּבַיֵּרָקוֹן וּבַבָּרָד אֵת כָּל־מַעֲשֵׂה יְדֵיכֶם וְאֵין־אֶתְכֶם אֵלַי נְאֻם־ה׳ — *I had struck you with blast and blight and hail upon all your handiwork, yet you are not [returning] to Me — the word of Hashem.*

Haggai continues to describe the situation of the people before they began the reconstruction of the Temple. He declares in the name of the Almighty, "I have smitten your standing stalks with blast and caused the seeds of your crops to empty out of the plants (*Ibn Ezra; Abarbanel*), and I have brought down hail upon your crops, as well. Indeed, I have smitten all of the work of your hands (*Radak*) and you have nevertheless not returned to Me and to My service (*Targum Yonasan; Ibn Ezra; Abarbanel*)

1. *Rashi's* version of the *Avos DeRav Nassan* differs from ours which reads *when wine is afflicted, it is an evil sign for the entire year.*

[16] *when they would come to a grain heap of [what should have been] twenty [measures] but there were [only] ten; [when one would] come to the winepress to draw out fifty [measures] from the pit, but there were [only] twenty.* [17] *I had struck you with blast and blight and hail upon all your handiwork, yet you are not [returning] to Me — the word of* HASHEM. [18] *Set now your heart [to consider] from this day and onward, from the twenty-fourth of the ninth [month], from the day when the foundations of the Sanctuary were laid; set your heart [to consider]:* [19] *Is there any more seed in the silo? And the grapevine and the fig tree and the pomegranate tree and the olive tree have not borne [their fruit].*

and therefore cannot be described as Mine" (*Radak*). *R' Eliezer of Beaugency* interprets: And you cannot be brought close to Me, for your deeds have rendered you despicable in My eyes.

18. שִׂימוּ־נָא לְבַבְכֶם ... — *Set now your heart [to consider] ...*

Now that you have begun to build upon the foundation of the Temple that was laid in the times of Cyrus (*Rashi*) [set your hearts to note the contrast between what will now occur with you and your crops and that which has occurred until now].

מִן־הַיּוֹם הַזֶּה וָמָעְלָה — *From this day and onward.*

Although we translated וָמָעְלָה in v. 15 as *previously*, in this verse it should be translated *onward* — see *Metzudos*. *Rashi* does not offer any insight on the matter.

שִׂימוּ־נָא לְבַבְכֶם ... שִׂימוּ לְבַבְכֶם — *Set now your heart [to consider]... set your heart [to consider].*

Malbim interprets the repetition of the phrase *set your heart* to mean a second idea: Set your heart upon your work and build with the proper intentions and devotion, and you will then witness how the Almighty will again bestow His blessings upon you.

19. הַעוֹד הַזֶּרַע בַּמְּגוּרָה — *Is there any more seed in the silo?*

The prophet continues to describe the curse that had been placed upon the people until now, the day that they started reconstruction of the Temple. Most commentators understand this as a rhetorical question. Are there any more seeds in the silo? In truth, only very few remain, as you have already planted most of them only to see them ruined by the Almighty's curse (*Ibn Ezra; Radak*). *Rashi*, however, understands this as a statement. The seeds are still in the silo because you have not yet planted them this year [because you are afraid that they will again be destroyed].

וְעַד־הַגֶּפֶן וְהַתְּאֵנָה ... — *And the grapevine and the fig tree ...*

In addition, the time has not yet come for the blossoming of your grapes, figs, pomegranates and olives (*Rashi; Radak*). Others translate וְעַד as *even*. Even the fruit trees have not given forth their proper yield (*Abarbanel; Metzudos*). [The point is that you really do not have too much to eat (*Rashi; Radak*).]

Radak writes that Scripture specified these trees because they are abundant in Eretz Yisrael (*Radak*). But he wonders why Scripture mentions the olive tree at all, for its season to bear fruit is in Mar Cheshvan and Kislev. He suggests that perhaps the fruit was delayed because of the earlier curse.

כ מִן־הַיּוֹם הַזֶּה אֲבָרֵךְ: כא וַיְהִי דְבַר־יְהוָה | שֵׁנִית אֶל־חַגַּי בְּעֶשְׂרִים וְאַרְבָּעָה לַחֹדֶשׁ לֵאמֹר: אֱמֹר אֶל־זְרֻבָּבֶל פַּחַת־יְהוּדָה לֵאמֹר אֲנִי מַרְעִישׁ אֶת־הַשָּׁמַיִם וְאֶת־הָאָרֶץ: כב וְהָפַכְתִּי כִּסֵּא מַמְלָכוֹת וְהִשְׁמַדְתִּי חֹזֶק מַמְלְכוֹת הַגּוֹיִם וְהָפַכְתִּי מֶרְכָּבָה וְרֹכְבֶיהָ וְיָרְדוּ סוּסִים וְרֹכְבֵיהֶם אִישׁ בְּחֶרֶב אָחִיו: כג בַּיּוֹם הַהוּא נְאֻם־יְהוָה צְבָאוֹת אֶקָּחֲךָ זְרֻבָּבֶל בֶּן־שְׁאַלְתִּיאֵל עַבְדִּי נְאֻם־יְהוָה וְשַׂמְתִּיךָ כַּחוֹתָם כִּי־בְךָ בָחַרְתִּי נְאֻם יְהוָה צְבָאוֹת:

מִן־הַיּוֹם הַזֶּה אֲבָרֵךְ — *But from this day on I will provide blessing.*

However, from this day on I will bless the seeds in the silo and the fruit in the field because you have resumed reconstructing the Temple (*Radak*).

☙ Haggai's Fifth Prophecy

20. וַיְהִי דְבַר־ה׳ שֵׁנִית אֶל־חַגַּי בְּעֶשְׂרִים וְאַרְבָּעָה לַחֹדֶשׁ לֵאמֹר — *The word of Hashem came to Haggai a second time on the twenty-fourth of the month, saying:*

Haggai received a second prophecy on that same day (*Ibn Ezra; Radak*). The majority of commentators interpret this prophecy as describing events which were to take place during the days of the Second Temple. Due to these events G-d will raise the status of Zerubbabel and he will be held in high esteem. Others contend that it is a prophecy foretelling the final redemption.

21. אֱמֹר אֶל־זְרֻבָּבֶל פַּחַת־יְהוּדָה לֵאמֹר אֲנִי מַרְעִישׁ אֶת־הַשָּׁמַיִם וְאֶת־הָאָרֶץ — *Speak to Zerubbabel, the governor of Judah, saying: I am shaking the heavens and the earth.*

This verse is to be understood figuratively. I am going to shake the very heavens and earth with the wars I shall bring upon the Persian Empire. Haggai is to inform Zerubbabel that his esteem would not fall because of these wars but on the contrary, he will be held in greater esteem (*Radak*).

אֲנִי מַרְעִישׁ אֶת־הַשָּׁמַיִם וְאֶת־הָאָרֶץ — *I am shaking the heavens and the earth.* This refers to wars which took place during the reign of Darius or during the reign of Artahshasta his successor. Alternatively, it may allude to the Greek conquest of the Persian Empire which occurred thirty-four years after the rebuilding of the Temple (*Radak*). Others interpret this as a prophecy foretelling the Hasmoneans' wars, when the Jewish people defeated the Syrian-Greeks and peace reigned throughout the land (*Mahari Kara*). Some commentators see these verses as foretelling the ultimate redemption: I shall shake all of the tranquil nations who participated in the oppression of the Jewish people (*R' Eliezer of Beaugency*), with the advent of the wars of Gog and Magog (*Alshich; Malbim*). Still others, following the same general approach to these three verses, see this as an unfavorable prophecy toward Israel because it is foretelling the destruction of the Second Temple and the Jewish Commonwealth, ultimately resulting in the eventual redemption of the Jewish people (*Abarbanel; Metzudos*).

22. וְהָפַכְתִּי כִּסֵּא מַמְלָכוֹת וְהִשְׁמַדְתִּי חֹזֶק מַמְלְכוֹת הַגּוֹיִם ... — *I will upset the thrones of kingdoms and destroy the strength of kingdoms of the nations ...*

I shall overturn the throne of Persia and replace it with that of Greece (*Radak*) thereby destroying the might of the

But from this day on I will provide blessing."

[20]*The word of* HASHEM *came to Haggai a second time on the twenty-fourth of the month, saying,* [21]*"Speak to Zerubbabel, the governor of Judah, saying:*

I am shaking the heavens and the earth. [22]*I will upset the thrones of kingdoms and destroy the strength of kingdoms of the nations; I will turn over a chariot and its drivers, and horses and their riders will fall down, one by the sword of the other.* [23]*On that day — the word of* HASHEM, *Master of Legions — I will take you, Zerubbabel son of Shealtiel, my servant — the word of* HASHEM *— and I shall make you like a signet ring; for you have I chosen — the word of* HASHEM, *Master of Legions."*

Persian Empire that presently rules the entire world (*Rashi*). Many wars and battles will take place, in which a multitude of warriors and their steeds shall plummet to the ground in their destruction (*Ibn Ezra*). Alternatively, at the time of the ultimate redemption, I will wreak My vengeance upon the nations that have conquered and oppressed you. I shall break their might and destroy them by bringing them to wage war upon one another and decimate one another's ranks (*Abarbanel; Metzudos; R' Eliezer of Beaugency*).

R' Eliezer of Beaugency interprets the first phrase to allude to the overthrow of one empire after the other, with Persia replaced by Greece and Greece in turn by Rome.

23. ... בַּיּוֹם הַהוּא — *On that day ...*

On that day, declares G-d to Zerubbabel, I will bring you close to Me (*Targum Yonasan*) and elevate you to even higher levels than before (*Radak*). Indeed, you will be to Me like a signet ring, which is never removed from one's finger and is thus never forgotten. So, too, shall My Divine Providence focus upon you constantly (*Radak; Mahari Kara*). Thus, all of the wars and battles described above will not bring about your downfall, but will raise you in higher esteem than you are today (*Radak*).

וְשַׂמְתִּיךָ כַּחוֹתָם — *And I shall make you like a signet ring.*

Although Jeremiah had prophesied that Coniah (Jeconiah), the son of Jehoiakim, would be condemned to childlessness (*Jeremiah* 22:24,30), nevertheless, through Jeconiah's repentance, God retracted His oath and granted him children. His great-grandson was Zerubbabel who became *like a signet ring* to the Almighty and led the Babylonian exile back to Israel. Indeed, it is from this verse that our sages learn (*Pesikta DeRav Kahana*), "Great is repentance, for it nullifies the oath" (*Rashi; Radak*).

Others view this verse as a prophecy of the final redemption. At that time your descendant will be the king Messiah, who will rule over My nation and reestablish the Davidic Dynasty (*Abarbanel; Metzudos*).

Abarbanel speculates that it was this prophecy that prompted Zerubbabel to leave Jerusalem after the Temple was rebuilt and to return to Babylonia, for he knew that neither he nor his children would rule over Judah during the era of the Second Temple and his nation will eventually again be exiled.

Zechariah

א בַּחֹדֶשׁ הַשְּׁמִינִי בִּשְׁנַת שְׁתַּיִם לְדָרְיָוֶשׁ הָיָה
דְבַר־יהוה אֶל־זְכַרְיָה בֶּן־בֶּרֶכְיָה בֶּן־עִדּוֹ
ב הַנָּבִיא לֵאמֹר׃ קָצַף יהוה עַל־אֲבוֹתֵיכֶם
ג קָצֶף׃ וְאָמַרְתָּ אֲלֵהֶם כֹּה אָמַר יהוה צְבָאוֹת
שׁוּבוּ אֵלַי נְאֻם יהוה צְבָאוֹת וְאָשׁוּב אֲלֵיכֶם
ד אָמַר יהוה צְבָאוֹת׃ אַל־תִּהְיוּ כַאֲבֹתֵיכֶם

◆§ Introduction

Zechariah was one of the last prophets to deliver God's message to His people. He was a contemporary of Haggai and Malachi and prophesied during the reign of Darius II. He was a member of the אַנְשֵׁי כְּנֶסֶת הַגְּדוֹלָה, the Men of the Great Assembly, the body of Sages who led the Jewish people during the early years of the Second Temple era (*Rambam,* Introduction to *Mishneh Torah*). He exhorts the people to repent their evil ways and chastises them for their lack of alacrity in rebuilding the Temple, even though they had been given permission and support from the Persian king to do so. His prophecies deal with the entire period from his own day until the End of Days. The commentaries agree that Zechariah's prophetic visions are so esoteric that many will not be fully understood until the coming of Elijah the Prophet — see introductory paragraph to *Rashi* 1:1.

I

1. בַּחֹדֶשׁ הַשְּׁמִינִי — *In the eighth month.*

This is the Jewish month of Marcheshvan (*Mahari Kara*). This prophecy took place a short time before the construction of the Second Temple resumed for that did not begin until the twenty-fourth day of the ninth month, the month of Kislev. See *Haggai* 2:18 (*Rashi*).

בִּשְׁנַת שְׁתַּיִם לְדָרְיָוֶשׁ — *In the second year of Darius.*

This is Darius II also referred to as Darius the Persian who, according to the Sages, was the son of King Ahasuerus and Queen Esther (*Rashi* to *Haggai* 1:1). He is not to be confused with Darius I, Darius the Mede, who, together with Cyrus conquered Babylon — see comm. to *Daniel* 9:1, ArtScroll ed. for further study.

The time of Zechariah's prophecy is noted by Scripture in order to indicate that the prophecy was specifically designated for that time. For it was then that the Almighty inspired Darius to allow the rebuilding of the *Beis HaMikdash,* and He therefore sent word to the Jewish people via His prophets that the time had come to build (*Abarbanel*).

זְכַרְיָה בֶּן־בֶּרֶכְיָה — *Zechariah son of Berechiah.*

He is not to be confused with Zechariah son of Jehoiada, the Kohen who prophesied during the days of Joash, king of Judah, and was assassinated by his fellow Israelites in the Holy Temple.

בֶּן־עִדּוֹ הַנָּבִיא — *Son of Iddo the prophet.*

The title *the prophet* refers to Zechariah. However, it is possible that his grandfather Iddo was a prophet as well. Indeed, there are those who say that he is the same as Iddo the Seer (*II. Chron.* 12:15) and Iddo the prophet (ibid. 13:22) (*Radak*). *Abarbanel* suggests that Scripture notes Zechariah's ancestry to teach that Zechariah merited many important prophecies because he descended from prophets.

[1] In the eighth month, in the second year of Darius, the word of HASHEM came to Zechariah son of Berechiah son of Iddo, the prophet, saying: [2] HASHEM became wrathful with your fathers, [a provoked] wrath. [3] Say to [the people]: Thus said HASHEM, Master of Legions: Return unto Me — the word of HASHEM, Master of Legions — and I will return unto you, said HASHEM, Master of Legions. [4] Do not be like your fathers,

Although at times Scripture refers to Zechariah as the son of Iddo (see *Ezra* 5:1; 6:14), it is evident from here that Iddo was the prophet's grandfather. Scripture occasionally identifies people by their grandfather's name rather than their father's, especially when the grandfather was a more famous figure than the father.

לֵאמֹר — *Saying.*

I.e., this is the prophecy that God related to the prophet (*Ibn Ezra*). Alternatively, this is the prophecy that should be said to the Jewish nation (ibid.; *Radak*).

2. קָצַף ה׳ עַל־אֲבוֹתֵיכֶם קָצֶף — *Hashem became wrathful with your fathers, [a provoked] wrath.*

The Almighty vented His wrath upon your ancestors who had witnessed the destruction of the First Temple (*Rashi*), as well as the generations of Jehoiakim, Jeconiah and Zedekiah as a punishment for their wicked deeds (*Mahari Kara*). The prophet warns his generation against committing the very same sins as their predecessors, yet they delayed the construction of the Temple and committed other sins as described in the Book of *Ezra*, Chapter 9 (*Radak*). Therefore, note and consider that which occurred to them as a result of their sins, and you will thereby be moved to repent (*Alshich; Malbim*).

קָצֶף — *[A provoked] wrath.*

Although *Targum* renders *for that which they angered me,* he is actually paraphrasing the text; for the literal translation of the word קָצֶף, a noun, is *anger* or *wrath.* Hence our translation *[a provoked] wrath. Malbim* suggests that the repetition of the word קָצֶף conveys that God's anger had not yet subsided since the destruction of the First Temple because the people had not yet repented their sins.

3. שׁוּבוּ אֵלַי ... — *Return unto Me ...*

Nevertheless, despite the fact that they provoked My wrath, tell the people in My Name that if only they will return to Me I will return to them and have My Divine Presence dwell among them (*Metzudos*).

אָמַר ה׳ צְבָאוֹת — *Said Hashem, Master of Legions.*

Ibn Ezra notes the repetitious mention of Hashem's Name and explains that if the nation will repent their sins and return to Hashem, He will admonish and rebuke them continuously to assist them in their efforts.

In this verse and throughout his prophecies, Zechariah refers to Hashem repeatedly as Hashem, Master of Legions, because the twelve tribes of Israel, who are the legions of Hashem, had been exiled and dispersed, with only a small portion returning to establish the second commonwealth. Therefore, the Almighty continuously reminds and reassures them that He is still the God of all of the tribes of Israel and His Divine Providence still watches over them, and the day will yet come when they will all be returned to their land (*Abarbanel*).

4. אַל־תִּהְיוּ כַּאֲבוֹתֵיכֶם ... — *Do not be like your fathers ...*

Do not follow the ways of your ancestors who lived during the time of the destruction and ignored the prophets of their generation (*Metzudos*).

אֲשֶׁר קָרְאוּ־אֲלֵיהֶם הַנְּבִיאִים הָרִאשֹׁנִים לֵאמֹר
כֹּה אָמַר יְהוָה צְבָאוֹת שׁוּבוּ נָא מִדַּרְכֵיכֶם
הָרָעִים °ומעליליכם הָרָעִים וְלֹא שָׁמְעוּ וְלֹא־
°וּמַעַלְלֵיכֶם ק׳

הִקְשִׁיבוּ אֵלַי נְאֻם־יְהוָה׃ ה אֲבוֹתֵיכֶם אַיֵּה־הֵם
ו וְהַנְּבִאִים הַלְעוֹלָם יִחְיוּ׃ אַךְ | דְּבָרַי וְחֻקַּי
אֲשֶׁר צִוִּיתִי אֶת־עֲבָדַי הַנְּבִיאִים הֲלוֹא הִשִּׂיגוּ
אֲבֹתֵיכֶם וַיָּשׁוּבוּ וַיֹּאמְרוּ כַּאֲשֶׁר זָמַם יְהוָה
צְבָאוֹת לַעֲשׂוֹת לָנוּ כִּדְרָכֵינוּ וּכְמַעֲלָלֵינוּ כֵּן
עָשָׂה אִתָּנוּ׃ ז בְּיוֹם עֶשְׂרִים
וְאַרְבָּעָה לְעַשְׁתֵּי־עָשָׂר חֹדֶשׁ הוּא־חֹדֶשׁ שְׁבָט
בִּשְׁנַת שְׁתַּיִם לְדָרְיָוֶשׁ הָיָה דְבַר־יְהוָה אֶל־
זְכַרְיָה בֶּן־בֶּרֶכְיָהוּ בֶּן־עִדּוֹ הַנָּבִיא לֵאמֹר׃

הַנְּבִיאִים הָרִאשׁוֹנִים — *The prophets of old.* These are the prophets who admonished the nation while Jerusalem and its surrounding cities were settled and peaceful — see 7:7. R' Nachman bar Yitzchak said that the prophets who lived prior to Haggai, Zechariah and Malachi are considered the early prophets (*Sotah* 48b).

מִדַּרְכֵיכֶם הָרָעִים וּמַעַלְלֵיכֶם הָרָעִים — *From your evil ways and from your evil deeds.*

Your evil ways are referring to their bad character traits. *Your evil deeds* are those deeds that were performed as a result of the bad character traits. The prophets had implored them to mend the baseness of their character and improve their wicked deeds (*Malbim*).

5. אֲבוֹתֵיכֶם אַיֵּה־הֵם — *Your fathers, where are they?*

See what has become of your ancestors who had not listened to the words of the prophets. They have died of starvation, been slain by the sword and been cast into captivity (*Rashi*) exactly as the prophets had foretold (*Radak*).

וְהַנְּבִאִים הַלְעוֹלָם יִחְיוּ — *And as for the prophets, could they live forever?*

Zechariah anticipates that the people will object to his use of their fathers' death as proof of heavenly judgment. He therefore declares, "If you counter by asking, 'Where are those prophets, have they not died?', to this I reply, 'Are prophets expected to live forever?' Unlike your fathers, the prophets died a natural death at a ripe old age, but as for your ancestors, all the suffering that had been foretold had in fact occurred" (*Rashi*).

Some see this phrase as a subtle message whereby God is informing the Jewish people that prophecy will soon cease to exist. Therefore, in the future, it will be only through following the laws of the Torah that one will be able to come to true repentance (*Yefes*, cited by *Ibn Ezra*).

6. אַךְ דְּבָרַי וְחֻקַּי ... — *However, My words and My decrees ...*

When your ancestors saw that all the sufferings that had been foretold by the prophets did indeed occur, even they conceded the justice of God and recognized the truth once they were exiled from the Land (*Mahari Kara*). *Malbim* adds that since the people acknowledged the fairness of God's judgment, they would be prepared to achieve righteousness even without the guidance of the prophets.

to whom the prophets of old called out, saying, "Thus said HASHEM, Master of Legions: Return, now, from your evil ways and from your evil deeds," but they did not listen nor pay attention to Me — the word of HASHEM. [5] Your fathers, where are they? And as for the prophets, could they live forever? [6] However, My words and My decrees, which I commanded My servants the prophets, did they not befall your fathers? They repented and said, "Just as HASHEM, Master of Legions, thought to do to us, according to our ways and our deeds, so did He with us."

[7] On the twenty-fourth day of the eleventh month, which is the month of Shevat, in the second year of Darius, the word of HASHEM came to Zechariah son of Berechiah son of Iddo, the prophet, saying.

The Sages interpret these two verses as an actual dialogue which took place between Zechariah and the people. Zechariah asked, "Your fathers, where are they?" and the people responded, "And the prophets — do they live forever?" To this the prophet countered that even the very ancestors whom the prophets rebuked ultimately admitted to the truth of their prophetic words (*Sanhedrin* 105a).

7. בְּיוֹם עֶשְׂרִים וְאַרְבָּעָה לְעַשְׁתֵּי־עָשָׂר חֹדֶשׁ הוּא־חֹדֶשׁ שְׁבָט ... — *On the twenty-fourth day of the eleventh month, which is the month of Shevat.*

On the twenty-fourth day of the month of Shevat, an angel was sent by the Almighty to show Zechariah this vision and impart to him the prophecy that follows (*Radak*).

The names of the months, as used here and in *Megillas Esther*, are not found elsewhere in Scripture and are possibly of Aramaic origin (*Radak*). *Ramban* (*Ex.* 12:2) explains that the Jewish people brought these names with them from Babylonia, and continued their use as a reminder that the Almighty had brought them back to their land and that they were no longer in exile (see *Abarbanel*).

Scripture prefaces this prophecy in a rather unusual manner. It gives a special date on which the prophecy took place, the twenty-fourth day of the eleventh month; it then refers to the eleventh month by its new name, *Shevat*, and it repeats Zechariah's ancestry which had been recorded earlier in this chapter — see 1:1. *Abarbanel* explains that Scripture specified the date because it alludes to the number of years that the Persians dominated Israel. This prophecy took place on the twenty-fourth of *Shevat* exactly fifty-nine days after the construction of the Second Temple had started [the construction of the Second Temple began on the twenty-fourth of *Kislev* — see *Haggai* 1:13; 2:15] corresponding to the fifty-nine years of Persian occupation. This occupation was brought to an end through the rod of Alexander the Great, alluded to by the name of the eleventh month, *Shevat*, hinting to the words שֵׁבֶט, *rod*. Zechariah's ancestry is repeated because the prophetic visions that follow were of great significance for they foretold the entire future and destiny of the Jewish nation. The prophet attributes his receipt of these momentous prophecies to the merit of his ancestors, particularly his grandfather *Iddo*, who was also a prophet.

א/ח ח רָאִ֣יתִי ׀ הַלַּ֗יְלָה וְהִנֵּה־אִישׁ֙ רֹכֵב֙ עַל־ס֣וּס אָדֹ֔ם וְה֣וּא עֹמֵ֔ד בֵּ֥ין הַהֲדַסִּ֖ים אֲשֶׁ֣ר בַּמְּצֻלָ֑ה

The prophecies that follow are very obscure, since they contain visions that resemble a dream and require interpretation. Indeed, the precise meaning of these visions will not become clear until the coming of the Redeemer (*Rashi* to v. 1). *Radak* attempts to explain the reason for this obscurity from a historical perspective. The level of prophecy had been weakening since the nation had been exiled and the era of prophecy was now drawing to a close. *Abarbanel* disagrees because Haggai and Malachi, who also prophesied in the same era, did not express their words in this obscure manner. He contends that it is the lofty nature of these prophecies that required that they be shrouded in mystery.

8. ... רָאִיתִי הַלַּיְלָה וְהִנֵּה־אִישׁ — *I saw [a vision in] the night and behold a man ...*

The man that Zechariah saw was actually an angel (*Rashi; Radak; Ibn Ezra*). Similarly, Scripture refers to the angel Gabriel as הָאִישׁ גַּבְרִיאֵל, the "man" Gabriel — see *Daniel* 9:21. *Rambam* (*Moreh Nevuchim* 2:42) writes that whenever Scripture mentions that one "saw" an angel, it was either in a prophetic vision or a dream.

... וְהִנֵּה־אִישׁ רֹכֵב עַל־סוּס אָדֹם — *And behold a man was riding upon a red horse ...*

Zechariah saw an angel sitting astride a red horse, that was standing among the myrtles of Babylonia. The red horse metaphorically indicates that in the future, God will exact retribution from the Chaldeans, from Persia and from Media with the sword and the sword will shed blood — see v. 15. The "man" was not sent upon this mission by himself for he was followed by other horses of various colors to assist him in carrying out the tasks set by the Almighty (*Rashi*).

Radak understands this vision differently and explains that it parallels the vision of Daniel (*Dan.* Ch. 7), which foretells the future of the four kingdoms that ruled over Israel. The red horse represents Nebuchadnezzar, king of Babylonia, who saw himself in his own dream (*Daniel* 2:38) as a "head of gold." Since gold has a reddish tinge, he is represented in this prophecy by the *red* horse. The angel riding upon this horse symbolizes the angel sent by God to rule over events of this world and carry out His wishes. His position astride the red horse is meant to convey that the destruction of Babylonia which, according to *Radak*, had already occurred prior to this vision, was carried out at the behest of the Almighty through the work of His angels. The angel is standing among the myrtles in a מְצֻלָה, *a pool of water*. The myrtles represent the nation of Israel who, like the fragrant myrtles, were endowed with the pleasant scent of the mitzvos they had observed in the land of Babylonia. The angel is standing there to assist them and redeem them from exile. The horse with the rider is followed by three riderless steeds, indicating that they, too, are guided and ruled by the angel astride the first horse. The first of these three is also red, symbolizing Nebuchadnezzar's son and grandson who ruled after him. The next two horses represent the kingdoms of Persia and Greece. Rome is not represented in this vision because of the long duration of time that was still to precede its rise.

R' Eliezer of Beaugency interprets the three colors as symbolizing the kingdoms of Persia, Greece and Rome [since, as noted above, that of Babylonia had already passed from the scene]. The mightiest of these, at the height of its glory, was Persia, which is represented by the strong color red. Greece was weaker than Persia, and is therefore represented by a hue of red and white. Rome, although it ultimately became the mightiest of all, only reached that power

[8] I saw [a vision in] the night. And behold a man was riding upon a red horse, and he was standing among myrtle bushes that were in a pool of water;

through the combined strength of its many vassals; alone, it was the weakest of the three. It is therefore represented by the color white.

Furthermore, under Persian rule, until the Jewish people rebuilt the Temple, their sins were still "blood red." By the time Greece came to power, their sins had been somewhat lessened through the service in the Temple, but had not yet been thoroughly cleansed. The many years of the Roman exile are to purify the Jewish nation from their sins until they will become totally whitened.

The horses, representing the great powers of Persia, Greece and Rome, related to the angel that each had gone to conquer the entire world and had been successful. Each of these powers had thereby brought peace and tranquility to the entire world, with every nation living peacefully in its own land, under the rule of these great empires: each in its time. Only Israel remained banished in exile, unable to return to its own land. Upon seeing that even after the downfall of Persia the complete redemption of the Jewish nation still did not take place, the angel cried out to God that He have mercy and redeem His people (cf. *Metzudos* to v. 11).

According to *Abarbanel*, the entire prophecy is foretelling events that will occur with Alexander the Great who is represented by the man riding the horse. The red horse is the legendary steed that he is reputed to have tamed and ridden after all who tried to do so had failed and were killed in their effort. He stood among the myrtles in the pool of waters. The pool of waters represented Babylonia and standing indicated that Alexander would conquer Babylonia. The myrtles represented the Nation of Israel. The man [Alexander] was among the myrtles [Israel] which alludes to Alexander's peaceful relationship with the Jewish people that came about through his encounter with Shimon HaTzaddik (see comm. to *Haggai* 2:7). Alexander was followed by three riderless horses, representing the three sections into which his kingdom was divided after his death. These include the Seleucid kingdom of Syria, the Ptolemian kingdom of Egypt and the Antognian kingdom of Persia and did not include the Macedonian and Greek portion which was controlled by his wife and sons. The angel's comment to Zechariah, "I will show you what these are," indicates that Zechariah would live to see the fulfillment of this prophecy (cf. *Malbim*, who follows a similar approach, and *Alshich*, who strongly disputes this view).

The Sages offer the following interpretation to this verse: R' Yochanan said that whenever the word *ish* appears in Scripture, it is a reference to God — see *Exodus* 15:3. The man riding the horse represented God who wanted to turn the entire world to night, i.e., to destroy it because the Jews had submitted to Nebuchadnezzar's command of bowing to the idol at *Bikas Dura*. He was riding upon a *red* horse means that God was ready to turn the world to blood, i.e., to destroy it. But once he looked upon Hananiah, Mishael and Azariah, He was appeased as Scripture states: *and he was standing among the myrtles in the pool of water, the myrtles* refer to the righteous ... and the pool of water refers to Babylonia. Immediately, those that were black[1] became colored and the red turned white (*Sanhedrin* 93a).

However, *Rashi* and *Mahari Kara* (v. 9) note that this is a loose interpretation which does not fit into the flow of these verses.

אֲשֶׁר בַּמְּצֻלָה — *That were in a pool of water.*

The pool of water is referring to Babylon (*Radak*) which was situated near an abundance of water (*Mahari Kara* to *Isaiah* 44:27).

1. This is the reading cited by *Radak*. The reading in our texts of *Sanhedrin* 93a is *immediately those full of anger, which had become colored and red, became white* — see *Maharsha* ibid.

א/ט־יב

ט וְאַחֲרָיו֙ סוּסִ֔ים אֲדֻמִּ֖ים שְׂרֻקִּ֥ים וּלְבָנִֽים׃ וָאֹמַ֖ר מָה־אֵ֣לֶּה אֲדֹנִ֑י וַיֹּ֣אמֶר אֵלַ֗י הַמַּלְאָךְ֙ הַדֹּבֵ֣ר
י בִּ֔י אֲנִ֥י אַרְאֶ֖ךָּ מָה־הֵ֥מָּה אֵֽלֶּה׃ וַיַּ֛עַן הָאִ֥ישׁ הָעֹמֵ֥ד בֵּין־הַהֲדַסִּ֖ים וַיֹּאמַ֑ר אֵ֚לֶּה אֲשֶׁ֣ר שָׁלַ֣ח
יא יְהוָ֔ה לְהִתְהַלֵּ֖ךְ בָּאָֽרֶץ׃ וַֽיַּעֲנ֞וּ אֶת־מַלְאַ֣ךְ יְהוָ֗ה הָעֹמֵד֙ בֵּ֣ין הַהֲדַסִּ֔ים וַיֹּאמְר֖וּ הִתְהַלַּ֣כְנוּ
בָאָ֑רֶץ וְהִנֵּ֥ה כָל־הָאָ֖רֶץ יֹשֶׁ֥בֶת וְשֹׁקָֽטֶת׃
יב וַיַּ֣עַן מַלְאַךְ־יְהוָה֮ וַיֹּאמַר֒ יְהוָ֣ה צְבָא֔וֹת עַד־מָתַ֗י אַתָּה֙ לֹֽא־תְרַחֵ֣ם אֶת־יְרוּשָׁלִַ֔ם וְאֵ֖ת
עָרֵ֣י יְהוּדָ֑ה אֲשֶׁ֣ר זָעַ֔מְתָּה זֶ֖ה שִׁבְעִ֥ים שָׁנָֽה׃

שְׂרֻקִּים — *Sorrel.*

This is the commonly used translation of this word — see *R' Eliezer of Beaugency. Rashi* and *Radak* are uncertain as to the exact color of שְׂרֻקִּים. In *Sanhedrin* (93a) *Rashi* translates שְׂרוּקִים simply as colored. *Malbim* suggests that this color is a mixture of red and white.

אֲדֻמִּים שְׂרֻקִּים וּלְבָנִים — *Red, sorrel and white.* The mention of many colors is actually a means of praising God because it shows that there are many different envoys that carry out His will (*Rashi*).

9. וָאֹמַר מָה־אֵלֶּה אֲדֹנִי וַיֹּאמֶר אֵלַי הַמַּלְאָךְ הַדֹּבֵר בִּי ... — *I said, "What are these, my lord?" The angel who was speaking to me said to me ...*

I inquired of the angel showing me this vision as to the nature of the horses (*Rashi; Radak*). Some identify this angel as the same angel that was riding upon the red horse (*Rashi; Ibn Ezra*). Others say that it was a second angel who was himself standing among the myrtles (*Yafeth*, cited by *Ibn Ezra; Mahari Kara*). According to *Abarbanel*, the angel showing Zechariah the vision was not included within the vision itself, and it was to him that the prophet spoke.

אֲנִי אַרְאֶךָּ מָה־הֵמָּה אֵלֶּה — *"I will show you what these are."*

The words *I will show you* are somewhat puzzling, since the angel did not show him anything. He only explained the vision to him. It is possible, however, that this term is used loosely, referring, in fact, to that which he told him. Alternatively, it alludes to the vision of the four horns of the second chapter (*Radak*).

10. וַיַּעַן הָאִישׁ הָעֹמֵד בֵּין־הַהֲדַסִּים וַיֹּאמַר ... — *And the man who was standing among the myrtles responded and said ...*

The angel who replied to the prophet's question was the same angel to whom the question was addressed: the angel riding the horse [as the horse was standing among the myrtles] (*Ibn Ezra*). *Radak* maintains that although Zechariah had questioned the angel that had related the prophetic vision to him, it was a different angel, the one riding the horse, that had replied. Alternatively, וַיַּעַן may be rendered *and he raised his voice* — see *Deut.* 26:5, for the angel riding the horse did not reply to the prophet's question but asked the others their purpose in traversing the earth (*Radak*).

אֵלֶּה אֲשֶׁר שָׁלַח ה׳ לְהִתְהַלֵּךְ בָּאָרֶץ — *These are the ones whom Hashem has sent to traverse about the earth.*

They have been sent by the Almighty to travel across the earth in order to

behind him were horses: red, sorrel and white. [9] *I said, "What are these, my lord?"*

The angel who was speaking to me said to me, "I will show you what these are!" [10] *And the man who was standing among the myrtles responded and said, "These are the ones whom HASHEM has sent to traverse the earth."*

[11] *Then they responded to the angel of HASHEM who was standing among the myrtles and they said, "We have traversed the earth, and behold all the earth is still and tranquil."*

[12] *The angel of HASHEM responded and said: "HASHEM, Master of Legions, until when will You not have mercy upon Jerusalem and upon the cities of Judah, that You have been wroth for these seventy years?"*

observe the tranquility of the idolatrous nations (*Rashi; Mahari Kara*).

11. וַיַּעֲנוּ אֶת־מַלְאַךְ ה׳ הָעֹמֵד בֵּין הַהֲדַסִּים וַיֹּאמְרוּ ... — *Then they responded to the angel of Hashem who was standing among the myrtles and they said ..."*

Upon the inquiry of the aforementioned angel, the other horsemen told their leader who was standing among the myrtles that they had traveled across the earth and seen that while Jerusalem and the Land of Israel were in ruins, the rest of the world was dwelling in peace and tranquility (*Metzudos*).

12. וַיַּעַן מַלְאַךְ־ה׳ וַיֹּאמַר ה׳ צְבָאוֹת עַד־מָתַי אַתָּה לֹא־תְרַחֵם אֶת־יְרוּשָׁלַםִ ... — *The angel of Hashem responded and said: "Hashem, Master of Legions, until when will You not have mercy upon Jerusalem ...?"*

The angel of Hashem who had been speaking to me (*Rashi; Radak*) turned to the Almighty upon hearing the tidings of the other angels and exclaimed, "Master of the Universe, why are all these gentile nations permitted to live in peace and tranquility in their own lands but the nation of Israel is banished to Babylonia, a foreign land, where they are oppressed? For although this had been decreed upon them for the sins they had committed, the seventy years which were allotted for their punishment have now passed, and the time has come to have mercy upon them and bring them back to their land (*Mahari Kara*). Alternatively, *Radak* suggests that the angel who made this plea may have been the one who was standing among the myrtles to assist the Jewish nation rather than the one who had been speaking to Zechariah. *Metzudos*, as well, follows this approach.

אֲשֶׁר זָעַמְתָּה זֶה שִׁבְעִים שָׁנָה — *That You have been wroth for these seventy years.*

Actually, the Jews had begun rebuilding the Temple during the ninth month, the month of Kislev, and this dialogue took place during the eleventh month, the month of Shevat, but their plight had not yet improved, and their efforts to rebuild were still plagued with harassment from their enemies (*Radak*).

יג וַיַּ֣עַן יהוה אֶת־הַמַּלְאָ֗ךְ הַדֹּבֵ֥ר בִּ֛י דְּבָרִ֥ים טוֹבִ֖ים דְּבָרִ֥ים נִחֻמִֽים׃ יד וַיֹּ֣אמֶר אֵלַ֗י הַמַּלְאָךְ֙ הַדֹּבֵ֣ר בִּ֔י קְרָ֣א לֵאמֹ֔ר כֹּ֥ה אָמַ֖ר יהוה צְבָא֑וֹת קִנֵּ֧אתִי לִירוּשָׁלִַ֛ם וּלְצִיּ֖וֹן קִנְאָ֥ה גְדוֹלָֽה׃ טו וְקֶ֤צֶף גָּדוֹל֙ אֲנִ֣י קֹצֵ֔ף עַל־הַגּוֹיִ֖ם הַשַּׁאֲנַנִּ֑ים אֲשֶׁ֤ר אֲנִי֙ קָצַ֣פְתִּי מְּעָ֔ט וְהֵ֖מָּה עָזְר֥וּ לְרָעָֽה׃ טז לָכֵ֞ן כֹּה־אָמַ֣ר יהוה שַׁ֤בְתִּי לִירוּשָׁלִַ֙ם֙ בְּֽרַחֲמִ֔ים בֵּיתִי֙ יִבָּ֣נֶה בָּ֔הּ נְאֻ֖ם יהוה צְבָא֑וֹת °וקוה יִנָּטֶ֖ה עַל־יְרוּשָׁלִָֽם׃

°וְקָו ק׳

Our translation of וָעַמְתָּה follows *Metzudos* who translates *anger*. Alternatively, *Targum Yonasan* translates לִיָט, *cursed*. According to *Malbim*, it applies specifically to a punishment which results from anger.

13. וַיַּעַן ה׳ אֶת־הַמַּלְאָךְ הַדֹּבֵר בִּי דְּבָרִים טוֹבִים דְּבָרִים נִחֻמִים — *Hashem then answered favorable things to the angel who was speaking to me, words of comfort.*

Zechariah did not actually hear God replying to the angel but from the response that he had received from the angel the prophet understood that God had told the angel favorable and comforting words (*Rashi*). Alternatively, others explain that the prophet did hear God's reply to the angel but only stated in general terms that the words that he had heard were favorable and comforting. The angel specified and elaborated on these words in the verses that follow (*Ibn Ezra; Malbim*). The prophet did not record the exact words that he had heard spoken to the angel because he was not commanded to do so and imparted to the nation only the words subsequently spoken to him by the angel (*Malbim*).

14. וַיֹּאמֶר אֵלַי הַמַּלְאָךְ הַדֹּבֵר בִּי קְרָא לֵאמֹר ... כֹּה אָמַר ה׳ צְבָאוֹת — *The angel who was speaking to me then said to me: Call out, saying: "Thus said Hashem, Master of Legions ...*

The following words are the favorable and comforting words of the previous verse. Zechariah is instructed to call them out loudly and announce them to the people of Judah and Jerusalem (*Radak*).

קִנֵּאתִי לִירוּשָׁלַם וּלְצִיּוֹן קִנְאָה גְדוֹלָה — *I am vengeful for Jerusalem and for Zion, a great vengeance.*

I am vengeful with the nations for that which they have done to Zion and Jerusalem (*Mahari Kara*), and I will exact retribution from them for their deeds (*Rashi* from *Targum Yonasan*).

Others translate קִנְאָה in the positive sense *to be zealous* and render *I have zealously championed [the cause] of Jerusalem and Zion to a great degree* (*Ibn Ezra*). Another interpretation is that קִנְאָה means jealousy: *I am jealous for the honor of Jerusalem and Zion* (*R' Eliezer of Beaugency*); why do the other nations dwell in peace and security whereas Israel is destroyed? (*Alshich*). *Metzudos* maintains that it is used here as a term for anger. "I am furious over that which the Babylonians did to Jerusalem and Zion."

15. וְקֶצֶף גָּדוֹל אֲנִי קֹצֵף עַל־הַגּוֹיִם הַשַּׁאֲנַנִּים ... — *And I am enraged with a great rage upon the complacent nations ...*

I am greatly enraged at the nations regarding whom the angels have reported to be living in peace and tranquility (*Rashi*). According to *Ibn Ezra*, this prophecy was fulfilled during Zechariah's lifetime when various nations of the region engaged in a series of bloody wars.

[13] HASHEM then answered favorable things to the angel who was speaking to me, words of comfort.

[14] The angel who was speaking to me then said to me: Call out, saying, "Thus said HASHEM, Master of Legions: I am vengeful for Jerusalem and for Zion, a great vengeance; [15] and I am enraged with a great rage upon the complacent nations, who, when I became slightly angered, augmented the evil. [16] Therefore, thus said HASHEM: I have returned to Jerusalem in mercy; My Temple will be built in it — the word of HASHEM, Master of Legions — and a plumb line will be stretched out over Jerusalem."

אֲשֶׁר אֲנִי קָצַפְתִּי מְּעָט וְהֵמָּה עָזְרוּ לְרָעָה — *Who, when I became slightly angered, augmented the evil.* I had been angry with Israel to a relatively small degree and therefore I had them exiled from their homeland, but these nations have greatly added to their affliction by harming and oppressing them, and thereby magnifying the ordained punishment many times over (*Radak*). I meant only that they should plunder and humiliate the Jewish people, but they have responded with murder and destruction (*R' Eliezer of Beaugency*). According to *Metzudos*, the verse is referring to the Babylonians for they tortured the Jewish people in a most brutal manner — see *Isaiah* 47:6 (*Radak*). *Malbim* sees the Medes and Persians as the subject of the verse for although they were not involved in the destruction of the First Temple, they hampered the construction of the second. According to *R' Eliezer of Beaugency*, the prophecy described here will not take place until the End of Days.

16. לָכֵן כֹּה־אָמַר ה׳ שַׁבְתִּי לִירוּשָׁלַםִ בְּרַחֲמִים ... בֵּיתִי יִבָּנֶה בָּהּ נְאֻם ה׳ צְבָאוֹת — *Therefore, thus said Hashem: I have returned to Jerusalem in mercy; My Temple will be built in it — the word of Hashem, Master of Legions ...*

Because the angel had challenged God and asked (v. 12), "Until when will You not have mercy upon Jerusalem...?" God now responds that He did indeed return His people to Jerusalem with mercy, for He returned them there even though they have not yet merited that He should do so (*Alshich; Malbim; Metzudos*). Even My Temple will now be built there, for its construction will not be interrupted as it had been during the days of Cyrus (*Metzudos*).

וְקָו יִנָּטֶה עַל יְרוּשָׁלָםִ — *And a plumb line will be stretched out over Jerusalem."*

This is a measuring device used by builders. It will be extended along the walls of the city to measure the length and width in order to repair and rebuild them (*Rashi; Abarbanel; Malbim; Metzudos*), and this work, too, will not be interrupted by the king (*Metzudos*).

R' Eliezer of Beaugency explains the walls of Jerusalem will be measured so that the city limits as established previously by Nehemiah will now be extended. *Malbim* contends that Nehemiah's construction occurred later. Thus, the walls of the city were measured to allow for their actual construction which did not take place until afterward (see also *Alshich*, cited below).

א/יז
ב/א־ד

יז עוֹד ׀ קְרָ֣א לֵאמֹ֗ר כֹּ֤ה אָמַר֙ יְהֹוָ֣ה צְבָא֔וֹת ע֛וֹד תְּפוּצֶ֥ינָה עָרַ֖י מִטּ֑וֹב וְנִחַ֨ם יְהֹוָ֥ה עוֹד֙ אֶת־צִיּ֔וֹן וּבָחַ֥ר ע֖וֹד בִּירוּשָׁלָֽ͏ִם׃ א וָאֶשָּׂ֥א אֶת־עֵינַ֖י ב וָאֵ֑רֶא וְהִנֵּ֖ה אַרְבַּ֥ע קְרָנֽוֹת׃ וָֽאֹמַ֗ר אֶל־הַמַּלְאָ֛ךְ הַדֹּבֵ֥ר בִּ֖י מָה־אֵ֑לֶּה וַיֹּ֣אמֶר אֵלַ֔י אֵ֤לֶּה הַקְּרָנוֹת֙ אֲשֶׁ֣ר זֵר֣וּ אֶת־יְהוּדָ֔ה אֶת־יִשְׂרָאֵ֖ל וִירוּשָׁלָֽ͏ִם׃ ג־ד וַיַּרְאֵ֣נִי יְהֹוָ֔ה אַרְבָּעָ֖ה חָרָשִֽׁים׃ וָאֹמַ֕ר מָ֛ה אֵ֥לֶּה בָאִ֖ים לַעֲשׂ֑וֹת וַיֹּ֣אמֶר לֵאמֹ֡ר אֵ֣לֶּה הַקְּרָנ֞וֹת אֲשֶׁר־זֵ֣רוּ אֶת־יְהוּדָ֗ה כְּפִי־אִישׁ֙ לֹא־

The word וקוה is written with a "ה" (כְּתִיב) but is pronounced קָו, without the "ה" (קְרִי). *Malbim* suggests that קָו is related to תִּקְוָה, *hope*, for *now there may be hope for the nation.*

17. עוֹד קְרָא לֵאמֹר כֹּה אָמַר ה׳ צְבָאוֹת עוֹד תְּפוּצֶינָה עָרַי מִטּוֹב ... — *Call out again, saying: "Thus said Hashem, Master of Legions: My cities will once again spread out with bounty ..."*

Zechariah was instructed by the angel to make yet another proclamation (*Metzudos*): Israel's population will increase due to the blessings that God will bestow upon them. My cities will therefore expand in all directions due to the great increase of its inhabitants (*Ibn Ezra; Radak*). The Almighty will once again comfort Zion from its previous bereavement and choose Jerusalem as the dwelling place of His Divine Presence.

Others interpret this verse as describing two phases in the path toward the ultimate redemption and understand the first part of the verse as saying that those who dwell in My cities will once again be dispersed and will not partake of the city's bounty. Zechariah foresaw the destruction of the Second Temple and its inhabitants again sent into exile. The second part of the verse foretells that God will eventually comfort Zion forever, when He chooses Jerusalem for His dwelling place for eternity (*Abarbanel; Malbim; Metzudos*).

Alshich sees these two verses as contrasting the imminent rebuilding of Jerusalem with its eventual final redemption. Now, a line shall be extended over the city of Jerusalem, for its dimensions shall still be limited. However, the city shall yet expand limitlessly with the final redemption when I comfort Zion and choose Jerusalem for eternity.

II

1. וָאֶשָּׂא אֶת־עֵינַי וָאֵרֶא וְהִנֵּה אַרְבַּע קְרָנוֹת — *Then I raised my eyes and looked, and behold four horns.*

Within the very same puzzling prophecy, Zechariah saw another vision which was not as obscure as the first. He saw four horns,[1] like those that are on the head of a goring animal (*Malbim*). He understood that whoever is represented by these horns will exercise his power and use the horn to gore but he did not know whom the horns represented (*Radak*).

2. ... וָאֹמַר אֶל־הַמַּלְאָךְ הַדֹּבֵר בִּי מָה־אֵלֶּה — *I*

1. A horn is a symbol of strength — see *Metzudas Tzion* to *I Samuel* 2:10. See *Daniel* Chapters 7 and 8 where nations are represented by horns.

1/17 [17]*Call out again, saying, "Thus said* HASHEM, *Master of Legions: My cities will once again spread out with bounty;* HASHEM *will have mercy on Zion once again and He will choose Jerusalem once again."*

2/1-4 [1] *Then I raised my eyes and looked, and behold four horns.* [2]*I said to the angel who was speaking to me, "What are these?"*

And he said to me, "These are the horns that dispersed Judah, Israel and Jerusalem."

[3]HASHEM *then showed me four craftsmen.* [4]*I said, "What are these coming to do?"*

And he spoke, saying, "These are the horns that dispersed Judah, [humiliating them] until no man could

said to the angel who was speaking to me, "What are these?" ...

Wishing to understand the vision he was granted, Zechariah asked the angel with whom he was speaking if he could explain the vision to him. The angel then told the prophet that the horns represented the four kingdoms who conquered the Land of Israel and dispersed the inhabitants of Judah, Israel and Jerusalem (*Radak; Metzudos*).

אֵלֶּה הַקְּרָנוֹת אֲשֶׁר זֵרוּ ... — *"These are the horns that dispersed ..."*

The four kingdoms that afflicted the Jewish people through the ages are Babylonia, Persia, Greece and Rome (*Abarbanel*). Although Persia did not oppress the Jews at first, they nevertheless dealt harshly with them during the days of Artahshasta I and Ahasuerus, until the second year of Darius II (*Radak*).

Although *Mahari Kara* and *Radak* list the four kingdoms differently than cited above, this is obviously due to the censors, who would not have allowed any negative reference to Rome. However, it is clear throughout the writings of the Sages and subsequent Rabbinic literature that these are the four kingdoms intended whenever they are cited.

Rashi explains that the four horns represent the gentile nations who are from the four corners of the heavens that came and gored the people of Judah and Jerusalem until they were dispersed across the globe. *R' Eliezer of Beaugency* interprets this prophecy as referring to the four kingdoms that divided up Alexander the Great's empire. In difficult times, some of the Jewish people fled to all of these four countries.

3. וַיַּרְאֵנִי ה׳ אַרְבָּעָה חָרָשִׁים — *Hashem then showed me four craftsmen.*

Zechariah was now shown a third vision, a vision of four craftsmen. Our translation of חָרָשִׁים follows *Targum Yonasan* who translates אוּמָנִין. *Rashi*, however, specifies that these craftsmen were actually נַגָּרִים, *carpenters*, who were experts in cutting down the horns (*Radak*).

4. וָאֹמַר מָה אֵלֶּה בָּאִים לַעֲשׂוֹת וַיֹּאמֶר לֵאמֹר ... — *I said, "What are these coming to do?" And he spoke, saying ...*

When Zechariah saw the four craftsmen he asked the angel if he could possibly explain to him the reason that they had appeared and what were they coming to do. וַיֹּאמֶר, God then instructed the angel, לֵאמֹר, to interpret the vision for the prophet (*Metzudos*).

נָשָׂא רֹאשׁוֹ וַיָּבֹאוּ אֵלֶּה לְהַחֲרִיד אֹתָם לְיַדּוֹת אֶת־קַרְנוֹת הַגּוֹיִם הַנֹּשְׂאִים קֶרֶן אֶל־אֶרֶץ יְהוּדָה לְזָרוֹתָהּ׃ ה וָאֶשָּׂא עֵינַי וָאֵרֶא וְהִנֵּה־ ו אִישׁ וּבְיָדוֹ חֶבֶל מִדָּה׃ וָאֹמַר אָנָה אַתָּה הֹלֵךְ וַיֹּאמֶר אֵלַי לָמֹד אֶת־יְרוּשָׁלַםִ לִרְאוֹת כַּמָּה־ ז רָחְבָּהּ וְכַמָּה אָרְכָּהּ׃ וְהִנֵּה הַמַּלְאָךְ הַדֹּבֵר ח בִּי יֹצֵא וּמַלְאָךְ אַחֵר יֹצֵא לִקְרָאתוֹ׃ וַיֹּאמֶר אֵלָו רֻץ דַּבֵּר אֶל־הַנַּעַר הַלָּז לֵאמֹר פְּרָזוֹת תֵּשֵׁב יְרוּשָׁלַםִ מֵרֹב אָדָם וּבְהֵמָה בְּתוֹכָהּ׃

וַיָּבֹאוּ אֵלֶּה לְהַחֲרִיד אֹתָם לְיַדּוֹת אֶת קַרְנוֹת הַגּוֹיִם ... — *So these [craftsmen] have come to terrify them, to cast down the horns of the nations ...*

The angel then told Zechariah that the craftsmen represented the nations who were destined to conquer and destroy the four kingdoms who oppressed the Jewish nation, each one overthrowing its predecessor. Thus, Persia conquered Babylonia and was subsequently defeated by Greece, who was humbled, in turn, by the Romans. The fourth craftsman is the Jewish nation, who will ultimately destroy Rome (*Radak*) during Messianic times (*Abarbanel*).

Alternatively, the four craftsmen represent the heavenly angels who are appointed over the aforementioned kingdoms [and will eventually see to their destruction] (*Radak*). According to *R' Eliezer of Beaugency*, that the four horns represent the four Hellenistic kingdoms, the craftsmen are the Hasmoneans who defeated them.

The Sages explain this verse as referring entirely to events that will take place with the advent of the Messiah. The four craftsmen are Mashiach ben Yosef, Mashiach ben David, Elijah the prophet and Kohen Zedek (*Sukkah* 52b). The two Messiahs are depicted as craftsmen because they will rebuild the Temple. Elijah is so represented because of the altar he built upon Mt. Carmel. Kohen Zedek is Shem, the son of Noah, also referred to in the Torah as Malchizedek. He is described as a craftsmen because he assisted Noah in building the ark (*Rashi* ad loc.). These four craftsmen will destroy the might of the four kingdoms described above when the latter will join forces together to attack the Jewish nation in the land of Israel (*Alshich*).

Ibn Ezra interprets this vision as alluding to events which took place during the days of the Second Temple. He translates קַרְנוֹת as *corners* — the four corners of Jerusalem, which was surrounded on all sides by enemies who sought to disperse its inhabitants. The Almighty will send the four craftsmen to destroy these enemies. The rebuilding of the Temple will then proceed unhampered. [He does not specify the identity of the four craftsmen.]

5. וָאֶשָּׂא עֵינַי וָאֵרֶא וְהִנֵּה־אִישׁ וּבְיָדוֹ חֶבֶל מִדָּה — *Then I raised my eyes and looked, and behold, there was a man, and in his hand was a measuring line.*

Within this same prophecy Zechariah was shown yet another vision, in which another angel appeared (*Radak*), holding a measuring line in his hand with which he was to measure the dimensions of Jerusalem (*Rashi*). *Radak* suggests that this vision may be foretelling events that will take place during the days of the Messiah (*Radak*).

6. וָאֹמַר אָנָה אַתָּה הֹלֵךְ ... — *I asked, "Where are you going?" ...*

raise his head — so these [craftsmen] have come to terrify them, to cast down the horns of the nations who raise a horn against the [populace of the] land of Judah, to disperse it."

[5] Then I raised my eyes and looked, and behold, there was a man, and in his hand was a measuring line. [6] I asked, "Where are you going?"

And he answered me, "To measure Jerusalem to see how wide is its breadth and how long is its length." [7] Just then the angel who was speaking to me was going forth, and another angel was going forth toward him. [8] He said to him, "Run, speak to that young man over there, saying:

'Jerusalem will be settled beyond its walls because of the abundance of men and livestock within it.' "

Puzzled, Zechariah asked the "man" where he was going with the measuring line. He answered that he had been sent to measure the length and breadth of Jerusalem, because God had decreed that it be built within these dimensions (*Ibn Ezra*). Alternatively, he was taking these measurements so that he would know how much land must be added to the city's dimensions, for its size will be greatly expanded in the Messianic era (*Radak* to v. 7; *R' Eliezer of Beaugency*). According to a third view, the city of Jerusalem was measured to emphasize the difference between the small size of the city during Zechariah's time and the size of the Jerusalem of the future which will expand in the times of the Messiah (*Abarbanel; Metzudos*).

7. וְהִנֵּה הַמַּלְאָךְ הַדֹּבֵר בִּי יֹצֵא וּמַלְאָךְ אַחֵר יֹצֵא לִקְרָאתוֹ — *Just then the angel who was speaking to me was going forth, and another angel was going forth toward him.*

The angel who had been speaking to Zechariah was either the "man" with the measuring line (*Rashi*) or the angel who had originally spoken to him, the "man" who was standing among the myrtles (*Ibn Ezra; Metzudos*). In any event, a third angel now appeared and approached the angel that had been speaking to Zechariah. This new angel was on a higher spiritual level and came to further explain the prophecy of the measuring line. Since the angel that had been speaking to Zechariah did not fully comprehend the prophecy, he turned to an angel of a higher level to explain it to him so that he may impart it to Zechariah (*Abarbanel*). According to *Metzudos*, the angel that had been speaking to him assumed that measuring the dimensions of Jerusalem meant that the city would always remain that very size even after the coming of the Messiah. He therefore asked the new angel why this would be so.

8. וַיֹּאמֶר אֵלָיו רֻץ דַּבֵּר אֶל־הַנַּעַר הַלָּז לֵאמֹר פְּרָזוֹת תֵּשֵׁב יְרוּשָׁלַםִ מֵרֹב אָדָם וּבְהֵמָה בְּתוֹכָהּ — *He said to him, "Run, speak to that young man over there, saying: 'Jerusalem will be settled beyond its walls because of the abundance of men and livestock within it.' "*

The angel who had just arrived said to the angel who was speaking to me

ט וַאֲנִי אֶהְיֶה־לָּהּ נְאֻם־יהוֹה חוֹמַת אֵשׁ סָבִיב
י וּלְכָבוֹד אֶהְיֶה בְתוֹכָהּ׃ הוֹי
הוֹי וְנֻסוּ מֵאֶרֶץ צָפוֹן נְאֻם־יהוָה כִּי כְּאַרְבַּע
רוּחוֹת הַשָּׁמַיִם פֵּרַשְׂתִּי אֶתְכֶם נְאֻם־יהוָה׃

9. וַאֲנִי אֶהְיֶה־לָּהּ ... חוֹמַת אֵשׁ סָבִיב — *And I will be for it ... a wall of fire all around.*

Although there will be no stone walls surrounding Jerusalem to protect its inhabitants, they will be perfectly safe and secure for God Himself will be as its shield and like a wall of fire He will defend the city from any attacking enemy (*Rashi*). *Radak* adds that just as one does not touch fire for fear of being burned, so too, no one will touch the inhabitants of Jerusalem.

From *Pesikta Rabbasi* it seems that God will place a heavenly fire around the city for R' Shimon ben Lakish taught that all of God's Heavenly hosts will become a protective wall for Jerusalem in the future and He will command His angels to guard it — see *Isaiah* 62:6. But, asks *Pesikta*, if it is surrounded by a wall of fire, how will it be possible to enter the city without being burned? *Pesikta* answers that in the future, the righteous will be capable of walking inside fire, like Chananiah, Mishael and Azariah who were cast into a fiery furnace by Nebuchadnezzar and walked within it like one who "walks in the sun to keep warm on a cold day" — see *Daniel* 3:19-27 (*Pesikta Rabbasi*, cited by *Yalkut*).

The Sages comment: The Torah writes (*Ex.* 22:5): *If a fire will go forth and find thorns* — i.e., it will go forth on its own,

(*Metzudos*), "Stop measuring the walls of the city, for the Almighty has decreed that the city of Jerusalem will not be limited to any set area. Therefore, go and tell Zechariah that Jerusalem shall be settled beyond its walls so that all who wish to come and dwell within it shall do so and thereby increase its population day by day"[1] (*Rashi*). *Radak* interprets: Although you will expand the dimensions of the city, there will still be many who will not fit within its walls. They will, therefore, dwell outside its walls, but without fear, for Hashem will protect them.

According to *Abarbanel* and *Metzudos*, the angel's message was as follows: Although the present dimensions of the city are limited to the measurements that have been taken, this will not be the case after the final redemption for its size will greatly increase.

הַנַּעַר הַלָּז — *That young man.*

The *young man* of this verse is Zechariah, one of three prophets who prophesied while still in their youth; the others were Samuel and Jeremiah (*Ibn Ezra; Radak*). Alternatively, he is referred to as a young man because he still was the disciple of [an unidentified] greater prophet — similar to Joshua, who is also referred to as a נַעַר, *young man*, because he was the disciple of Moses (*Radak*).

1. *Rashi's* interpretation is based on the words of R' Chanina bar Pappa (*Bava Basra* 75b) who said: The Holy One, Blessed is He, intended to give Jerusalem a fixed size as it says, *I asked, "Where are you going?" And he answered me, "To measure Jerusalem to see how wide is its breadth and how long is its length."* Thereupon the ministering angels said before the Holy One, Blessed is He: "Master of the Universe, You created many cities of gentiles in Your world and You did not give any of them a fixed measure for their length or width. Yet with regard to Jerusalem, where Your Name is in its midst and Your Temple is in its midst and righteous men are in its midst, You want to give it a fixed size?" Thereupon, the prophet saw a second angel addressing the first one. *And he said to him, "Run, speak to that young man over there saying, 'Jerusalem shall be settled beyond its walls because of the abundance of men and livestock within it.' "*

[9] *And I will be for it — the word of* HASHEM *— a wall of fire all around and for glory will I be in its midst.* [10] *Ho! Ho! Flee from the land of the north! — the word of* HASHEM *— for I have scattered you like the four directions of the heavens — the word of* HASHEM.

the one who kindled the fire shall surely pay. Therefore, the Holy One, Blessed is He, said that it is incumbent upon Him to pay for the fire that He kindled for it is He Who had set fire to Zion — see *Eichah* 4:11 — and it is He Who will rebuild it with fire in the future, as stated in this verse (*Bava Kamma* 60b).

וּלְכָבוֹד אֶהְיֶה בְתוֹכָהּ — *And for glory will I be in its midst.*

Generally, a city is extolled for its fortifications and protective walls. Nevertheless, although Jerusalem will have no surrounding walls, it will not be denigrated and shamed. It will be honored and held in high esteem for the Divine Presence will dwell in its midst (*Abarbanel; Metzudos*).

10-13. In the following verses, Zechariah's prophecy shifts back and foretells events that will take place during the days prior to the construction of the Second Temple. He describes events of the near future to give validity to all his prophetic words; for when these prophecies will come to pass, all will believe that those concerning the distant future will come true as well (*Alshich*). Others maintain that these verses, too, are discussing events of the final redemption (*Abarbanel; Metzudos*).

10. הוֹי הוֹי וְנֻסוּ מֵאֶרֶץ צָפוֹן — *Ho! Ho! Flee from the land of the north.*

Our translation of הוֹי follows *Targum Yonasan* and *Rashi* who explain that הוֹי is an expression of proclamation and announcement of assembly. The prophet urges the Israelites who are still living in the northern lands of Babylonia and Assyria to return to the Land of Israel (*Rashi*) to participate in the construction of the Temple (*Radak*). Alternatively, the northern lands are Babylonia, Elam, Persia and Media (*Ibn Ezra*).

Others translate הוי as *woe* and explain *woe to anyone who remains in Babylon* for it will be conquered by Greece, Rome and later the Ishmaelites (*Me'am Loez*). According to *Metzudos*, this prophecy concerns the future redemption and is urging the ten tribes who were exiled to Assyria to hasten and return to the Land of Israel.

כִּי כְּאַרְבַּע רוּחוֹת הַשָּׁמַיִם פֵּרַשְׂתִּי אֶתְכֶם — *For I have scattered you like the four directions of the heavens.*

Just as the four corners of the heavens are separate and distinct from one another and cannot be joined together, so have you been dispersed and scattered with no connection between the different groups of your exiles (*Ibn Ezra*). Alternatively, the word רוּחוֹת may be translated *winds*. The verse would then mean, you have been totally banished, as if the four winds of heaven have combined forces to scatter you around (*R' Eliezer of Beaugency*).

According to *Radak*, this phrase contains an entirely new message: My declaration that the exiles shall return applies only to the people of Judah who were banished to Babylonia and are close to the Holy Land. However, the time has not yet arrived for the redemption of those who were exiled from the Kingdom of Israel, who have been dispersed to the four corners of the globe.

The Sages (*Taanis* 3b) interpret this verse homiletically: Just as the world cannot exist without the four winds, so too, it cannot exist without Israel — see *Rashi* to *Taanis* 3b.

יא־יב הוֹי צִיּוֹן הִמָּלְטִי יוֹשֶׁבֶת בַּת־בָּבֶל׃ כִּי
כֹה אָמַר יהוה צְבָאוֹת אַחַר כָּבוֹד שְׁלָחַנִי
אֶל־הַגּוֹיִם הַשֹּׁלְלִים אֶתְכֶם כִּי הַנֹּגֵעַ בָּכֶם נֹגֵעַ
יג בְּבָבַת עֵינוֹ׃ כִּי הִנְנִי מֵנִיף אֶת־יָדִי עֲלֵיהֶם וְהָיוּ
שָׁלָל לְעַבְדֵיהֶם וִידַעְתֶּם כִּי־יהוה צְבָאוֹת
יד שְׁלָחָנִי׃ רָנִּי וְשִׂמְחִי בַּת־צִיּוֹן כִּי הִנְנִי־בָא
טו וְשָׁכַנְתִּי בְתוֹכֵךְ נְאֻם־יהוה׃ וְנִלְווּ גוֹיִם רַבִּים

11. הוֹי צִיּוֹן הִמָּלְטִי יוֹשֶׁבֶת בַּת־בָּבֶל — *Ho, O [exiles of] Zion! Escape, O you who dwell with the daughter of Babylonia.*

The word הוי of this verse is also an expression of announcement (*Rashi*). Scripture repeats it for emphasis (*Radak*). Although the prophet had exhorted the people north of the land of Israel, he did not identify which country he had been addressing. In this verse he clearly identifies Babylonia as that country. The time of their redemption has arrived but not for those who had been exiled to the four corners of the heaven (*Radak*).

As noted above, *Abarbanel* and *Metzudos* interpret these two verses as alluding to the final redemption: Children of the ten tribes, who were exiled to the northern kingdom of Assyria and dispersed to the four corners of the globe, flee from your exile and return to the Holy Land. And children of Zion in the Kingdom of Judah, flee from the lands of your exile and return to Jerusalem. Although Judah had been dispersed to many lands, Scripture refers to them as she *who dwells with the daughter of Babylonia* since they were originally exiled to Babylonia.

12. כִּי כֹה אָמַר ה׳ צְבָאוֹת אַחַר כָּבוֹד ... — *For thus said Hashem, Master of Legions, after glory ...*

This is referring to the prophecy of v.9. After God will give Jerusalem the honor and glory that He had promised, He will send Zechariah to prophesy against the nations that had plundered its people (*Targum Yonasan; Radak*). Alternatively, the phrase אַחַר כָּבוֹד may be interpreted *for the sake of Your glory*, בִּשְׁבִיל כָּבוֹד. For the sake of Your glory God will send me to prophesy to the nations (*Rashi; Mahari Kara*). According to the Midrash, the verse means after I have repaid Esau for the honor he accorded his father Isaac; [I can now punish him for his mistreatment of you] (addendum to *Tanchuma, Buber, Dev.* 4; cited by *Rashi*).

שְׁלָחַנִי אֶל־הַגּוֹיִם הַשֹּׁלְלִים אֶתְכֶם כִּי הַנֹּגֵעַ בָּכֶם נֹגֵעַ בְּבָבַת עֵינוֹ — *He will send me to the nations who despoil you for whoever touches you touches the pupil of his own eye.*

The Almighty will not be satisfied with just compensating the Jewish people for the evil they had suffered while in exile but will also exact vengeance from the nations who mistreated His people. For whoever touches the Children of Israel thereby brings harm upon himself as if he had forcefully struck the pupil of his own eye (*Radak*). Others interpret *His eye* as referring figuratively to the "eye" of the Almighty: He takes their oppression personally, as if it were an attack upon Himself, striking the pupil of His eye (*Abarbanel; Metzudos*).

Minchas Shai notes that this is one of the eighteen variations occurring in Scripture that writers make [תִּיקּוּנֵי סוֹפְרִים] for the purpose of enhancing an expression. See comm. to *Habakkuk* 1:12 for an extensive discussion of this subject.

Alternatively, the prophet may be telling the people who are returning from Babylonia that they have nothing to fear for God has warned the nations not to impede the Israelites as they travel on their way to the Land of Israel (*Ibn Ezra*).

[11] Ho, O [exiles of] Zion! Escape, O you who dwell with the daughter of Babylonia! [12] For thus said HASHEM, Master of Legions, after glory, He will send me to the nations who despoil you, for whoever touches you touches the pupil of his own eye. [13] For behold I am waving My hand against them and they will become spoils to those who served them; then you will know that HASHEM, Master of Legions, has sent me.

[14] Sing and be glad, O daughter of Zion! For behold I am coming, and I will dwell in your midst — the word of HASHEM. [15] Many nations will join themselves

13. כִּי הִנְנִי מֵנִיף אֶת־יָדִי עֲלֵיהֶם וְהָיוּ שָׁלָל לְעַבְדֵיהֶם — *For behold I am waving My hand against them and they will become spoils to those who served them.*

I shall raise My hand against the nations who have oppressed the Jewish people, and they will become prey and plunder to Israel, the very nation who was hitherto forced to serve them (*Rashi*).

וִידַעְתֶּם כִּי־ה׳ צְבָאוֹת שְׁלָחָנִי — *Then you will know that Hashem, Master of Legions, has sent me.*

When this will ultimately occur in Messianic times you will finally come to fully recognize that God had sent me to impart these prophecies to you (*Radak*).

14-17. In the remainder of this chapter, the prophet describes the glory of Israel and the honor of the Almighty which will prevail when the Divine Presence will reside in Jerusalem. Some commentators explain that these verses are referring to the Second Temple era (*Mahari Kara; R' Eliezer of Beaugency*), while others maintain that the prophet is describing events of the final redemption (*Abarbanel*). *Radak*, however, is uncertain and interprets these verses from both perspectives.

There is yet another approach, that the prophet is describing the lot which can be Israel's immediately, if only they will return fullheartedly to the service of G-d (*Ibn Ezra; Alshich*).

14. רָנִּי וְשִׂמְחִי בַּת־צִיּוֹן כִּי הִנְנִי־בָא וְשָׁכַנְתִּי בְתוֹכֵךְ נְאֻם־ה׳ — *Sing and be glad, O daughter of Zion! For behold I am coming, and I will dwell in your midst — the word of Hashem.*

Zechariah turns to the "daughter of Zion" and tells her: Sing and rejoice, O Jerusalem, for God is about to return His Divine Presence to your midst and permit the rebuilding of His Temple (*Mahari Kara; R' Eliezer of Beaugency*).

According to *Abarbanel*, however, this prophecy is foretelling events of the final redemption. Zechariah proclaims, "Well may you rejoice, O daughter of Zion," for unlike the redemption from previous exiles, this redemption will not be dependent upon the whims of man, but rather, God Himself will come and return His glory to Jerusalem because the final redemption will be by the hand of God Himself; it will therefore not be followed by a further exile.

Alshich notes that the words רָנִּי and שִׂמְחִי are stated in the singular form. The Almighty declares to the Jewish nation: If only you will unite fullheartedly and form one unified entity, I will immediately come and restore My glory to your midst.

15. וְנִלְווּ גוֹיִם רַבִּים אֶל־ה׳ בַּיּוֹם הַהוּא — *Many nations will join themselves to Hashem on that day.*

ב/טז־יז
ג/א־ב

אֶל־יהוה בַּיּוֹם הַהוּא וְהָיוּ לִי לְעָם וְשָׁכַנְתִּי בְתוֹכֵךְ וְיָדַעַתְּ כִּי־יהוה צְבָאוֹת שְׁלָחַנִי אֵלָיִךְ: טז וְנָחַל יהוה אֶת־יְהוּדָה חֶלְקוֹ עַל אַדְמַת הַקֹּדֶשׁ וּבָחַר עוֹד בִּירוּשָׁלִָם: יז הַס כָּל־בָּשָׂר מִפְּנֵי יהוה כִּי נֵעוֹר מִמְּעוֹן קָדְשׁוֹ: א וַיַּרְאֵנִי אֶת־יְהוֹשֻׁעַ הַכֹּהֵן הַגָּדוֹל עֹמֵד לִפְנֵי מַלְאַךְ יהוה וְהַשָּׂטָן עֹמֵד עַל־יְמִינוֹ לְשִׂטְנוֹ: ב וַיֹּאמֶר יהוה אֶל־הַשָּׂטָן יִגְעַר יהוה בְּךָ הַשָּׂטָן וְיִגְעַר יהוה בְּךָ הַבֹּחֵר בִּירוּשָׁלִָם הֲלוֹא זֶה

At that time, many nations shall adjoin themselves to God and accept His faith, thereby becoming identified as His people. However, the Divine Presence will dwell only in the midst of Israel (*Abarbanel; Metzudos*). Alternatively, this is referring to the many gentiles who converted to Judaism because of the many miracles they had witnessed when the Temple was rebuilt under the leadership of Zerubbabel (*Mahari Kara*). *R' Eliezer of Beaugency* maintains that this occurred in the times of the Hasmoneans. Alternatively, all that is described in these verses will occur in Messianic times (*Abarbanel; Metzudos*).

וְיָדַעַתְּ כִּי־ה׳ צְבָאוֹת שְׁלָחַנִי אֵלָיִךְ — *Then you will know that Hashem, Master of Legions, has sent me to you.*

Because the Divine Presence will dwell only in your midst and not in the midst of any other nation, you will realize that the prophecies of future glory that I foretold were meant for you and not for any other nation (*Abarbanel; Metzudos*).

16. וְנָחַל ה׳ אֶת־יְהוּדָה חֶלְקוֹ ... — *Hashem will take Judah as His heritage, His portion ...*

The Almighty will then return the people of Judah from exile and implant them once more in the Holy Land, where He will take them as His portion (*Rashi; Ibn Ezra; Radak; Metzudos*) never to be sent into exile again (*Metzudos*). If Scripture is referring to the return of all of Israel at the final redemption, Judah is singled out because it is the tribe that will rule over the nation. If the era of the Second Temple is meant, Judah is mentioned because it was the people of the Kingdom of Judah who returned to the Holy Land from exile (*Radak*).

Others render *Hashem will allot to Judah his portion upon the holy habitation.* This is a reference to the portion of the land that the tribe of Judah will receive in Messianic times — see *Yechezkel* Chapter 45 (*Abarbanel; Malbim*).

וּבָחַר עוֹד בִּירוּשָׁלָם — *And He will choose Jerusalem again.*

God will again choose Jerusalem as the dwelling place for His Divine Presence (*Metzudos*). The city of Jerusalem will not be in the portion of Judah and Benjamin but will be in a separate portion referred to as *Terumah* — see *Yechezkel* Chap. 45 (*Abarbanel*). The history of Jerusalem's troubles will then come to an end (*R' M. Hirsch*).

17. הַס כָּל־בָּשָׂר מִפְּנֵי ה׳ — *Be silent, all flesh, before Hashem.*

Be silent (*Radak*), all nations of the world, in reverent awe (*Rashi*) before Hashem, and never again will you open your mouths against His nation (*Metzudos*).

כִּי נֵעוֹר מִמְּעוֹן קָדְשׁוֹ — *For He is aroused from His holy abode.''* For He has been roused from His heavenly abode to wreak vengeance upon the oppressors of

2/16-17

to HASHEM *on that day, and they will become a people unto Me; and I will dwell in your midst. Then you will know that* HASHEM*, Master of Legions, has sent me to you.* [16] HASHEM *will take Judah as His heritage, His portion upon the Holy Land, and He will choose Jerusalem again.* [17] *Be silent, all flesh, before* HASHEM*, for He is aroused from His holy abode!''*

3/1-2

[1] *Then He showed me Joshua the Kohen Gadol standing before the angel of* HASHEM*, and the Satan was standing on his right to accuse him.* [2] *[The angel of]* HASHEM *said to the Satan, ''May* HASHEM *denounce you, O Satan! May* HASHEM*, Who chooses Jerusalem, denounce you! Indeed, this [man]*

Israel (*Mahari Kara; Radak; Metzudos*). When the Jews are in exile, all the nations think that ''God is asleep'' and they joyously follow their gods. But in the End of Days, when God will be ''roused from His sleep,'' those nations will melt in dread before Him (*Me'am Loez*).

Targum renders הַס כָּל בָּשָׂר as סָפוּ כָּל רַשִׁיעַיָּא, *All the wicked shall be destroyed. R' Eliezer of Beaugency* explains that the rousing of the Almighty is for the sake of saving His nation [rather than punishing their enemies].

III

1. ... וַיַּרְאֵנִי אֶת־יְהוֹשֻׁעַ הַכֹּהֵן הַגָּדוֹל — *Then He showed me Joshua the Kohen Gadol ...*

The prophetic vision continues. Zechariah sees Joshua the Kohen Gadol standing before the angel of God where he was faced by Satan who sought to prosecute him for failing to prevent his children from marrying women who were unfit for Kohanim — see *Ezra* 10:18 (*Rashi; Metzudos*). Alternatively, the confrontation between Joshua and Satan represents the contention between the Jews who were trying to rebuild the Holy Temple, and the local chieftains led by Sanballat the Horonite and his colleagues, who tried to halt its construction — see *Nehemiah* 2:10; 19; 3:33 (*Ibn Ezra; Radak*). In a novel interpretation, *Abarbanel* explains that Zechariah did not actually see a vision of Joshua the Kohen Gadol himself but of his descendants who are called in his name, much as the children of Jacob are often referred to as Jacob [or Israel]. In this vision, Joshua is represented by his descendants Mattisyahu and his sons, and is opposed by the satanic forces of Antiochus and his armies.

2. וַיֹּאמֶר ה׳ — *[The angel of] Hashem said.*

Our translation follows *Radak* and *Metzudos* who say that one of God's angels said this rebuke, for at times, Scripture refers to the angel by the Name of its Master — see *Judges* 6:16. Alternatively, it was God Himself Who spoke these words (*Mahari Kara*).

יִגְעַר ה׳ בְּךָ הַשָּׂטָן ... — *May Hashem denounce you, O Satan ...*

The angel of Hashem (*Radak*) said to Satan: May Hashem, Who has chosen Jerusalem, rebuke you and rebuke you yet again (*Metzudos*) for seeking to prosecute this great man. How dare you prosecute one who is so holy that he was saved miraculously from the flames into which he was cast (*Rashi; Metzudos*).

ג אוּד מֻצָּל מֵאֵשׁ: וִיהוֹשֻׁעַ הָיָה לָבֻשׁ בְּגָדִים ד צוֹאִים וְעֹמֵד לִפְנֵי הַמַּלְאָךְ: וַיַּעַן וַיֹּאמֶר אֶל־הָעֹמְדִים לְפָנָיו לֵאמֹר הָסִירוּ הַבְּגָדִים הַצֹּאִים מֵעָלָיו וַיֹּאמֶר אֵלָיו רְאֵה הֶעֱבַרְתִּי מֵעָלֶיךָ עֲוֺנֶךָ וְהַלְבֵּשׁ אֹתְךָ מַחֲלָצוֹת: ה וָאֹמַר יָשִׂימוּ צָנִיף טָהוֹר עַל־רֹאשׁוֹ וַיָּשִׂימוּ הַצָּנִיף הַטָּהוֹר עַל־רֹאשׁוֹ וַיַּלְבִּשֻׁהוּ בְּגָדִים

The Talmud (*Sanhedrin* 93a) relates that Ahab ben Kolaiah and Zedekiah ben Maaseiah — two false prophets and adulterers (see *Jeremiah* 29:21-23) — were thrown into a fiery furnace together with Joshua the Kohen Gadol. The two false prophets were consumed by the fire but Joshua was miraculously saved; only his clothes were singed. *Rashi* explains that these verses are alluding to this incident.

According to *Ibn Ezra,* this is a prophecy foretelling the downfall and destruction of anyone who will impede or hinder the rebuilding of the Temple. For is it not enough that the people have suffered in the fire of exile from which they have survived? Alternatively, how can you possibly think you will hinder the people who survived the exile and returned to the Land of Israel for the very purpose of constructing the new Temple? Similarly, *Radak* explains that the *firebrand saved from a fire* is referring to the redemption from exile. However, he interprets the phrase as referring specifically to Joshua the Kohen Gadol rather than to the nation as a whole. Although he follows the same approach as *Ibn Ezra* when interpreting this prophecy, he apparently understands the vision of Joshua to symbolize the Kohen Gadol's own personal role in the rebuilding of the Temple as well as the general rebuilding.

Abarbanel maintains that the fire represents Antiochus who would order the persecution of the Kohanim who served in the Temple. The firebrand represents the Hasmoneans who led the battle against the Greek oppressors.

3. וִיהוֹשֻׁעַ הָיָה לָבֻשׁ בְּגָדִים צוֹאִים וְעֹמֵד לִפְנֵי הַמַּלְאָךְ — *But Joshua was dressed in filthy garments as he stood before the angel.*

Joshua appeared in this vision wearing filthy garments, a metaphor for sin. His children had married women who were unfit for the *Kehunah* and because he had not protested, he, too, was held somewhat responsible (*Targum; Rashi; Mahari Kara; Radak; Metzudos*).

Ibn Ezra takes issue with this interpretation, maintaining that the misdeeds of Joshua's children did not occur until after Joshua had passed away. He therefore explains that among other items, the gold garments of the Kohen Gadol were missing at this time. Since Scripture refers to these garments as garments of honor and beauty (see *Exodus* 28:2), the absence of this honor and beauty is represented by the filthy garments (cf. *Abarbanel,* who disputes this view). *Malbim,* however, contends that the verses in *Nehemiah* which discuss the sins of Joshua's descendants may be understood as describing events which had occurred previously, perhaps even during Joshua's lifetime.

4. וַיַּעַן וַיֹּאמֶר אֶל־הָעֹמְדִים לְפָנָיו לֵאמֹר הָסִירוּ הַבְּגָדִים הַצֹּאִים מֵעָלָיו — *[The angel] spoke up and spoke to those standing before him, saying: "Remove the filthy garments from upon him!"*

The angel before whom Joshua stood was greater than those who were standing around him (*Radak*). He raised his voice and instructed the other angels, who were actually his attendants (*Targum Yonasan*), to separate Joshua's children from their forbidden wives so that the righteous Joshua may be forgiven (*Rashi*).

is like a firebrand saved from a fire!" [3]*But Joshua was dressed in filthy garments as he stood before the angel.* [4]*[The angel] spoke up and spoke to those standing before him, saying: "Remove the filthy garments from upon him!" Then he said to [Joshua], "See, I have removed your iniquity from upon you and dressed you in clean attire."* [5]*Then I said: "Let them put a pure turban on his head." So they put a pure turban on his head, and they dressed him in [clean] garments,*

וַיֹּאמֶר אֵלָיו רְאֵה הֶעֱבַרְתִּי מֵעָלֶיךָ עֲוֺנֶךָ — *Then he said [to Joshua], "See, I have removed your iniquity from upon you."*

The angel then turned to Joshua and said (*Metzudos*), "By separating your children from their forbidden wives I have removed from upon you your iniquity of not protesting their misdeeds. You are therefore now cleansed from the sulliness of your sin and you may stand with your honor and dignity intact" (*Rashi; Radak; Metzudos*). *Ibn Ezra* renders: I have removed from you your punishment, pain and humiliation — see *Gen.* 15:16 and *I Samuel* 28:10 where the word עָוֺן is translated *punishment*.

וְהַלְבֵּשׁ אֹתְךָ מַחֲלָצוֹת — *And dressed you in clean attire.*

Lit., a change of clothes (*Ibn Ezra*), beautiful clothes. Since the iniquities are compared to filthy garments, he compares merits to beautiful garments (*Rashi*).

R'. M. Hirsch renders: *clothe yourself* with pure garments, and explains whereas the filthy garments were removed from Joshua by the angels, he had to put the pure ones on himself. God can atone for sins that were committed in the past, but to keep the future free from sin lies solely in the power of the person himself.

5. וָאֹמַר יָשִׂימוּ צָנִיף טָהוֹר עַל־רֹאשׁוֹ — *Then I said: "Let them put a pure turban on his head."*

I, Zechariah, pleaded that the angels should have mercy upon Joshua (*Rashi*) and marry [his sons] to proper women (*Targum Yonasan*). Scripture metaphorically refers to the righteous woman as a turban or crown —see *Proverbs* 12:4: "A righteous woman is the crown of her husband" (*Mahari Kara*).

Others interpret the pure turban as representing the full raiment of the Kohen Gadol. Now that he has been cleansed of his iniquities, initiate him into the position of Kohen Gadol by placing the priestly turban upon his head (*Radak; Metzudos*).

Ibn Ezra understands the word of the prophet to be his own private musings: How appropriate it would be for the garments of the Kohen Gadol to be placed upon Joshua. Alternatively, it refers to his thoughts, with the word וָאֹמַר, *then I said*, alluding to that which he said in his heart.

וַיָּשִׂימוּ הַצָּנִיף הַטָּהוֹר עַל־רֹאשׁוֹ וַיַּלְבִּשֻׁהוּ בְּגָדִים — *So they put a pure turban on his head, and they dressed him in [clean] garments.*

In addition to having already clothed him in clean and beautiful garments as stated in the previous verse, they also placed the holy turban upon his head (*Ibn Ezra; Radak*). Others explain that the words of the previous verse, *and dressed you in clean attire*, refer merely to the angel's command that this be done, but not to its fulfillment. In this verse, the prophet relates how the Kohen Gadol was actually clothed in his turban as well as in his other vestments (*Abarbanel; Metzudos Dovid*).

ו וּמַלְאַךְ יְהֹוָה עֹמֵד: וַיָּעַד מַלְאַךְ יְהֹוָה בִּיהוֹשֻׁעַ
ז לֵאמֹר: כֹּה־אָמַר יְהֹוָה צְבָאוֹת אִם־בִּדְרָכַי תֵּלֵךְ
וְאִם אֶת־מִשְׁמַרְתִּי תִשְׁמֹר וְגַם־אַתָּה תָּדִין אֶת־
בֵּיתִי וְגַם תִּשְׁמֹר אֶת־חֲצֵרָי וְנָתַתִּי לְךָ מַהְלְכִים
ח בֵּין הָעֹמְדִים הָאֵלֶּה: שְׁמַע־נָא יְהוֹשֻׁעַ | הַכֹּהֵן
הַגָּדוֹל אַתָּה וְרֵעֶיךָ הַיֹּשְׁבִים לְפָנֶיךָ כִּי־אַנְשֵׁי
מוֹפֵת הֵמָּה כִּי־הִנְנִי מֵבִיא אֶת־עַבְדִּי צֶמַח:

וּמַלְאַךְ ה׳ עֹמֵד — *While the angel of Hashem [remained] standing.*

In this vision, the angel of Hashem remained standing nearby throughout the time that the Kohen Gadol was clothed in his vestments and turban (*Radak*).

Abarbanel interprets these verses as describing how the descendants of Joshua, the children of the Hasmoneans, sinned by donning the royal garments and retaining the kingship over the Judean state after driving out the Syrian Greeks. Since these garments were reserved for the tribe of Judah, they were considered sullied and soiled — see *Ramban* to *Gen.* 49:10. The angel therefore instructed the people of Judah to remove those soiled garments from upon them by removing them from their position of royalty and returning their pure vestments of *Kehunah* to them. Zechariah urged that the children of Joshua be crowned with the courage and wisdom to return to their proper role and relinquish their power. This finally took place in the days of Herod,[1] when all the descendants of the Hasmoneans were wiped out and the children of Joshua were thus no longer involved in governing the state (see *Bava Basra* 3b).

6. וַיָּעַד מַלְאַךְ ה׳ בִּיהוֹשֻׁעַ לֵאמֹר — *The angel of Hashem then warned Joshua, saying:*

After all the above had transpired, the angel directed his words to Joshua, and issued the following warning to him (*Rashi; Metzudos*).

7. כֹּה־אָמַר ה׳ צְבָאוֹת אִם־בִּדְרָכַי תֵּלֵךְ וְאִם אֶת־מִשְׁמַרְתִּי תִשְׁמֹר ... — *Thus said Hashem, Master of Legions: If you go in My ways and if you will safeguard My watch ...*

Our translation follows *Radak* who understands the entire first portion of this verse as describing the conditions necessary to achieve the great reward of dwelling among the angels (see comm.). Alternatively, *Rashi* explains that Joshua was told, "If you go in My ways and safeguard My charge, then I will respond in kind and grant you the privilege to administer My Holy Temple, guard My courtyards and walk among My angels."[2]

אִם־בִּדְרָכַי תֵּלֵךְ — *If you go in My ways.*

Malbim explains that one goes in God's ways by emulating His acts of graciousness and kindness.

וְנָתַתִּי לְךָ מַהְלְכִים בֵּין הָעוֹמְדִים הָאֵלֶּה — *Then I will grant you strides among these [angels] who stand here.*

You will be granted eternal life among the angels in the afterworld (*Targum Yonasan*). You will be given the legs to walk among them, i.e., you will be given a portion in the World to Come (*Rashi*) because you will achieve a level of sanctity akin to that of angels (*Malbim*). This

1. This point is somewhat puzzling, as the power of the Hasmoneans was taken from them against their will and not due to the donning of wisdom and courage (R' M. Roberts).

2. The word וְגַם, *and also*, is used in this verse to convey: If you, too, shall fulfill these conditions, just as was done by your illustrious father, Jehozadak, who served as Kohen Gadol during the days of the First Temple, then ... (*Ibn Ezra*).

while the angel of HASHEM [remained] standing. [6]*The angel of HASHEM then warned Joshua, saying:* [7]*"Thus said HASHEM, Master of Legions: If you go in My ways, and if you will safeguard My watch, and you also administer My Temple, and you will also guard My courtyards, then I will grant you strides among these [angels] who stand here.* [8]*Listen now, O, Joshua the Kohen Gadol, you and your companions who are sitting before you, for they are men [worthy] of a miracle — for behold I am bringing My servant, Zemah [the flourishing one].*

may also refer to Joshua's descendants (*Rashi*) who will achieve this high level of sanctity in the days of the Messiah (*Malbim*). Alternatively, this alludes to the immortality of the soul which separates from the body upon death. Joshua's soul will dwell among the angels (*Radak; Metzudos*). The angels are referred to as *these who stand here* for they stand and exist forever (*Radak*).

Joshua is to be so totally devoted to the Torah that its spirit which is enthroned in the Temple will penetrate the life of the nation, thereby transforming all their habitations, at whatever distance they may be into "courtyards of the Temple" (*R' M. Hirsch*).

8. שְׁמַע־נָא יְהוֹשֻׁעַ הַכֹּהֵן הַגָּדוֹל אַתָּה וְרֵעֶיךָ הַיֹּשְׁבִים לְפָנֶיךָ כִּי־אַנְשֵׁי מוֹפֵת הֵמָּה — *Listen now O, Joshua the Kohen Gadol, you and your companions who are sitting before you, for they are men [worthy] of a miracle.*

These companions are Hananiah, Mishael and Azariah who, like Joshua, are worthy of having miracles performed on their behalf, and indeed, were all miraculously saved from death in the fiery furnaces of Nebuchadnezzar (*Rashi, Abarbanel, Metzudos,* from *Sanhedrin* 93a, *Bereishis Rabbah* 56:11). The Sages relate that after they were saved, the three migrated to Eretz Yisrael to study Torah under the tutelage of Joshua. Others maintain that Joshua's companions are other Kohanim, who sat before their leader, Joshua the Kohen Gadol. These Kohanim were worthy of having miracles performed on their behalf (*Ibn Ezra*). Alternatively, it alludes to all of the Jewish people who miraculously ascended from Babylonia to resettle the Holy Land (*Mahari Kara*).

כִּי־הִנְנִי מֵבִיא אֶת־עַבְדִּי צֶמַח — *For behold I am bringing My servant, Zemah [the flourishing one].*

The word צֶמַח actually means *sprout.* The prophecy is metaphorically describing Zerubbabel who is now but an insignificant Judean governor in the eyes of the [Persian] king but will soon *grow in stature,* צֶמַח, to the point that his words will be heard by the monarch. It is he who will successfully plead for permission to rebuild the Temple (*Rashi; Radak*). *Mahari Kara* explains that he is referred to as a צֶמַח, *a sprout,* because he is an offshoot of the House of David and is thus fitting to rule over the Jewish nation.

Targum Yonasan identifies this servant as being the Messiah — see *Jeremiah* 23:5. *I will establish for David the righteous Zemah* (*Metzudos*). The Almighty is foretelling that in addition to the redemption that He is about to bring during the days of Zechariah, He will yet bring another redemption during the days of the Messiah that will greatly overshadow the partial redemption of that day

ט כִּי | הִנֵּה הָאֶבֶן אֲשֶׁר נָתַתִּי לִפְנֵי יְהוֹשֻׁעַ עַל־אֶבֶן אַחַת שִׁבְעָה עֵינָיִם הִנְנִי מְפַתֵּחַ פִּתֻּחָהּ נְאֻם יהוה צְבָאוֹת וּמַשְׁתִּי אֶת־עֲוֺן הָאָרֶץ־הַהִיא בְּיוֹם אֶחָד׃ י בַּיּוֹם הַהוּא נְאֻם יהוה צְבָאוֹת תִּקְרְאוּ אִישׁ לְרֵעֵהוּ אֶל־תַּחַת גֶּפֶן וְאֶל־תַּחַת תְּאֵנָה׃

א וַיָּשָׁב הַמַּלְאָךְ הַדֹּבֵר בִּי וַיְעִירֵנִי כְּאִישׁ אֲשֶׁר־יֵעוֹר מִשְּׁנָתוֹ׃

(*Radak*). Indeed, the Sages (*Sanhedrin* 98b) state that the Messiah's name will be Menachem, whose numerical value is the same as the word *Tzemach* [both adding up to the number 138][1] (*Ibn Ezra; Radak*). Furthermore, the Messiah will appropriately be called *Tzemach*, a sprout, since he will be an outgrowth of the Davidic dynasty (*Abarbanel*), concealed at the present like the plant that is buried in the ground, but destined to sprout to full glory when his time arrives (*Malbim*).

9. כִּי הִנֵּה הָאֶבֶן אֲשֶׁר נָתַתִּי לִפְנֵי יְהוֹשֻׁעַ עַל־אֶבֶן אַחַת שִׁבְעָה עֵינָיִם — *For behold the [foundation] stone that I have placed before Joshua — seven eyes upon one stone.*

This stone is the foundation stone of the Temple that was laid immediately after Cyrus permitted the reconstruction of the Temple. This stone seemed small in Joshua's eyes because the enemies of the Jews prevented the people from building upon it. However, it shall now be widened sevenfold: where one stone stood, seven shall appear (*Rashi*). Alternatively: In the eyes of the Almighty it has been seen fit to increase the glory of the Temple by having it rebuilt (ibid.).

Others explain that this stone is the plumb line, the measuring device that Zerubbabel held to make sure that the building was straight (*Ibn Ezra; Radak;* see 4:10). This has been placed in the hands of Joshua, because he has been granted the permission and opportunity to bring it to use. When this will be implemented, every stone in the building will be watched by seven eyes from the Almighty (*Radak*). Alternatively, it is the foundation stone that will be laid in the times of the Third Temple by a Kohen who will be a descendant of Joshua (*Metzudos*).

שִׁבְעָה עֵינָיִם — *Seven eyes.*

The number seven is not meant to be understood literally. It is often used by Scripture to express the concept of many as in *Lev.* 26:18 and *Proverbs* 24:16 (*Radak*). It is also used to show that something is being taken to its full limit (*R' Hirsch, Lev.* ibid.). The angel is saying that God will guard every stone of the Temple very closely. Alternatively, in this verse it is to be understood literally for it is referring to the seven servants of Hashem who will oversee the rebuilding of the Temple: Joshua, Ezra, Zerubbabel, Nehemiah and the three prophets, Haggai, Zechariah and Malachi (*Radak*, citing his father).

הִנְנִי מְפַתֵּחַ פִּתֻּחָהּ — *Behold I am untying its knot.*

Our translation follows *Rashi* who explains that during the years that the Jews were prevented from constructing the Temple, it was as if the Temple stones were bound and could not be moved. God now says that He is untying the knot, i.e., that He will thwart the plans of the gentiles who have campaigned to the king against the reconstruction of the Temple — see *Ezra* 4:6 (*Rashi*). Others render *I am engraving its adornment*. It was customary to decorate the stones of a building with engravings of flowers and knobs upon

1. מנחם - מ=40; נ=50; ח=8; מ=40 = 138.
צמח - צ=90; מ=40; ח=8 = 138.

3/9-10 [9] *For behold the [foundation] stone that I have placed before Joshua — seven eyes upon one stone; behold I am untying its knot — the word of HASHEM, Master of Legions — and I will remove the iniquity of that land on one day.* [10] *On that day — the word of HASHEM, Master of Legions — each man will invite his fellow beneath the vine and beneath the fig tree."*

4/1 [1] *Then the angel who was speaking with me returned and woke me, as a man is awakened from his sleep.*

its completion. Figuratively speaking, God is saying that He will complete the construction of the Temple even to the engravings upon its stones (*Radak*).

וּמַשְׁתִּי אֶת־עֲוֺן הָאָרֶץ־הַהִיא — *And I will remove the iniquity of that land.*

At that time, God will totally obliterate any traces of the sins of the people from the land (*Mahari Kara; Radak*), and they will live in peace and security (*Radak*). Alternatively: God will remove the *punishments* for their sins and the misfortune they experienced as a result of their iniquities (*Ibn Ezra; Radak*).

בְּיוֹם אֶחָד — *On one day.*

Rashi states that he does not know which day is meant. According to *Radak* it refers to the day which had been foretold by the prophets, in which Zerubbabel's stature would achieve its full height (see *Haggai* 2:23). *R' Eliezer of Beaugency* comments: On the day of the building of the Temple, all of its opposition and impediments will be negated altogether.

10. בַּיּוֹם הַהוּא נְאֻם ה' צְבָאוֹת תִּקְרְאוּ אִישׁ לְרֵעֵהוּ אֶל־תַּחַת גֶּפֶן וְאֶל־תַּחַת תְּאֵנָה — *On that day — the word of Hashem, Master of Legions — each man will invite his fellow beneath the vine and beneath the fig tree."*

On the day that the foundations of the Temple will be set (*Ibn Ezra*), from that day peace and tranquility will prevail. You will dwell securely and in peace, and enjoy the benefits of the land and its fruits together (*Ibn Ezra; Radak; Metzudos*).

IV

In this chapter, the angel shows Zechariah yet another vision and engages him in lengthy dialogue concerning its interpretation. According to some commentators, this vision and its meaning apply to the times of the Second Temple (*Ibn Ezra; Radak*). Others see this as a prophecy concerning the final redemption (*Abarbanel; Alshich; Metzudos*). According to *Rashi*, it is basically foretelling events of the Second Temple era, but alludes to the final redemption as well.

1. וַיָּשָׁב הַמַּלְאָךְ הַדֹּבֵר בִּי — *Then the angel who was speaking with me returned.*

Since the angel who had been speaking to Zechariah previously was not the one who spoke to him during the last prophetic vision (see 2:7), Scripture writes that the angel who had been speaking to him previously now returned to speak to him again (*Metzudos*).

וַיְעִירֵנִי — *And woke me.*

The previous vision was introduced with the phrase וָאֶשָּׂא אֶת־עֵינַי וָאֵרֶא, *then I raised my eyes and looked* (2:1). This vision, however, is introduced with the word וַיְעִירֵנִי, *and woke me,* indicating that without the angel's assistance, Zechariah would not have perceived this vision (*Radak*). According to *Mahari Kara,*

ד/ב־ו °וָאֹמַר ק׳

ב וַיֹּאמֶר אֵלַי מָה אַתָּה רֹאֶה °ויאמר רָאִיתִי וְהִנֵּה
מְנוֹרַת זָהָב כֻּלָּהּ וְגֻלָּהּ עַל־רֹאשָׁהּ וְשִׁבְעָה
נֵרֹתֶיהָ עָלֶיהָ שִׁבְעָה וְשִׁבְעָה מוּצָקוֹת לַנֵּרוֹת
ג אֲשֶׁר עַל־רֹאשָׁהּ׃ וּשְׁנַיִם זֵיתִים עָלֶיהָ אֶחָד
ד מִימִין הַגֻּלָּה וְאֶחָד עַל־שְׂמֹאלָהּ׃ וָאַעַן וָאֹמַר
אֶל הַמַּלְאָךְ הַדֹּבֵר בִּי לֵאמֹר מָה אֵלֶּה אֲדֹנִי׃
ה וַיַּעַן הַמַּלְאָךְ הַדֹּבֵר בִּי וַיֹּאמֶר אֵלַי הֲלוֹא יָדַעְתָּ
ו מָה־הֵמָּה אֵלֶּה וָאֹמַר לֹא אֲדֹנִי׃ וַיַּעַן וַיֹּאמֶר אֵלַי
לֵאמֹר זֶה דְּבַר־יהוה אֶל־זְרֻבָּבֶל לֵאמֹר לֹא בְחַיִל
וְלֹא בְכֹחַ כִּי אִם־בְּרוּחִי אָמַר יהוה צְבָאוֹת׃

this vision is an allusion to the situation of the Jewish people during the days of the Second Temple. When the people were forced to stop constructing the Temple, they became forlorn and hopeless, and thought that it would never be rebuilt. Therefore, the angel came to rouse the people from their *slumber of hopelessness and inaction* [to urge them to rededicate themselves to this great task].

Abarbanel interprets the phrase *as a man who is awakened from his sleep* as referring to the vision itself, i.e., the vision appeared to Zechariah in the early morning, when people begin to awaken. Due to the lofty nature of this prophecy, it had to be shown to him at a time when one's faculties are most clear.

2. וַיֹּאמֶר אֵלַי מָה אַתָּה רֹאֶה — *He said to me, "What do you see?"*

When a prophet is inspired and experiences a prophetic vision, he may perceive that God is speaking to him in the vision or he may receive God's message in metaphorical terms. The angel therefore asked Zechariah to describe the vision that appeared in his mind as the expression of this prophecy (*Abarbanel*). [See also *Moreh Nevuchim* 2:43.]

וְהִנֵּה מְנוֹרַת זָהָב כֻּלָּהּ וְגֻלָּהּ עַל־רֹאשָׁהּ — *And behold — there is a menorah [made] entirely of gold with its bowl atop it.*

I saw in my vision a golden menorah with a round bowl atop it (*Rashi*) filled with oil (*Metzudos*), indicating that the Almighty intends to bring light to the children of Israel, in contrast to their present situation of darkness (*Radak*). The Sages (*Pesikta*) explain that Zechariah prophetically foresaw the ultimate destiny of the Jewish people during Messianic times, with the menorah metaphorically representing the Jewish people (*Abarbanel*). It was made of pure gold, symbolizing the good fortune and prosperity that will prevail at that time. Indeed, it was entirely of gold, teaching that in Messianic times the entire nation will share God's blessing, not only those who participated in the Second Commonwealth. The bowl of oil atop the menorah sits as a crown upon its head, indicating the independent sovereignty that the Jewish nation will enjoy (*Abarbanel*). *Alshich* sees the gold as representing the spiritual loftiness of Israel that will prevail at that time. The prophet emphasizes that the entire menorah was made of gold to teach that unity will then exist among the people; the bowl of oil representing the crown of the Messianic king.

וְשִׁבְעָה נֵרֹתֶיהָ עָלֶיהָ — *Its seven lamps are upon it.*

Upon the menorah were seven vessels for the placement of oil and wicks (*Rashi*), like the menorah described in the Torah (*Radak*).

[2] *He said to me, "What do you see?"*

I said, "I see and behold — there is a menorah [made] entirely of gold with its bowl atop it; its seven lamps are upon it, and there are seven ducts for [each of] the lamps atop it. [3] *There are two olive trees upon it, one at the right of the bowl and one on its left."* [4] *I spoke up and said to the angel who was speaking to me, saying, "What are these, my lord?"*

[5] *The angel who was speaking to me answered and said to me, "Do you not know what these are?"*

And I said, "No, my lord!"

[6] *He spoke up and said to me, saying, "This is the word of HASHEM to Zerubbabel saying: 'Not through army nor through strength, but only through My spirit,' said HASHEM, Master of Legions."*

שִׁבְעָה וְשִׁבְעָה מוּצָקוֹת לַנֵּרוֹת אֲשֶׁר עַל־רֹאשָׁהּ — *And there are seven ducts for [each of] the lamps atop it.*

Our translation follows *Rashi* who explains that the oil from the bowl flowed through seven ducts into each of the lamps (*Rashi*). There were thus a total of forty-nine pipes providing oil to the menorah, symbolizing that in future times [during the Messianic era], the light of the sun will be forty-nine times as bright as the light of the seven days of creation (*Rashi* to v. 3).

Radak interprets simply that there were seven pipes through which the oil flowed, one for each lamp.

3. וּשְׁנַיִם זֵיתִים עָלֶיהָ אֶחָד מִימִין הַגֻּלָּה וְאֶחָד עַל־שְׂמֹאלָהּ — *There are two olive trees upon it, one at the right of the bowl and one on its left.*

There were two olive trees alongside the bowl of the menorah, one to its right and one to its left, whose function will be clarified further in the prophecy (*Rashi;* see vs. 11-14).

4. וָאַעַן וָאֹמַר אֶל הַמַּלְאָךְ הַדֹּבֵר בִּי לֵאמֹר מָה אֵלֶּה אֲדֹנִי — *I spoke up and said to the angel who was speaking to me, saying, "What are these, my lord?"*

Zechariah had seen that the olives harvested themselves and the oil flowed into the bowl without any assistance. He therefore asked the angel to explain what the spontaneous production of oil symbolized (*Rashi*).

5. וַיַּעַן הַמַּלְאָךְ הַדֹּבֵר בִּי וַיֹּאמֶר אֵלַי הֲלוֹא יָדַעְתָּ מָה־הֵמָּה אֵלֶּה וָאֹמַר לֹא אֲדֹנִי — *The angel who was speaking to me answered and said to me, "Do you not know what these are?" and I said, "No, my lord."*

The angel wished to know if Zechariah was wise enough to comprehend the meaning of the vision without any assistance but, as he proceeded to answer, he was not (*Ibn Ezra*).

6. וַיַּעַן וַיֹּאמֶר אֵלַי לֵאמֹר זֶה דְּבַר־ה׳ אֶל זְרֻבָּבֶל לֵאמֹר לֹא בְחַיִל וְלֹא בְכֹחַ כִּי אִם־בְּרוּחִי אָמַר ה׳ צְבָאוֹת — *He spoke up and said to me, saying, "This is the word of Hashem to Zerubbabel saying: 'Not through army nor through strength, but only through My spirit,' said Hashem, Master of Legions."*

ז מִֽי־אַתָּ֧ה הַֽר־הַגָּד֛וֹל לִפְנֵ֥י זְרֻבָּבֶ֖ל לְמִישֹׁ֑ר וְהוֹצִיא֙ אֶת־הָאֶ֣בֶן הָרֹאשָׁ֔ה תְּשֻׁא֕וֹת חֵ֥ן חֵ֖ן לָֽהּ׃ ח וַיְהִ֥י דְבַר־יְהוָ֖ה אֵלַ֥י לֵאמֹֽר׃ ט יְדֵ֣י זְרֻבָּבֶ֗ל יִסְּד֛וּ הַבַּ֥יִת הַזֶּ֖ה וְיָדָ֣יו תְּבַצַּ֑עְנָה וְיָ֣דַעְתָּ֔ כִּֽי־יְהוָ֥ה צְבָא֖וֹת שְׁלָחַ֥נִי אֲלֵיכֶֽם׃ י כִּ֣י מִ֣י בַז֮ לְי֣וֹם קְטַנּוֹת֒ וְשָׂמְח֗וּ וְרָא֞וּ אֶת־הָאֶ֧בֶן הַבְּדִ֛יל בְּיַ֥ד זְרֻבָּבֶ֖ל

Just as the olive trees in the vision were harvested spontaneously and produced their own oil without any human involvement or effort for that was the will of God, so too, will Israel rebuild the Temple only when God wills it so. It will not be achieved through military might nor through physical strength. God will inspire Darius with a spirit of kindness that will provide the initiative for its construction and a major part of the needed supplies (*Rashi*). Others interpret this prophecy as referring to the Messianic era when the nations of the world will accept a descendant of Zerubbabel as the Messiah. He will rule the world but not by military might and power, for God will inspire all the nations of the world to accept his authority over them (*Abarbanel; Metzudos*).

7. מִי־אַתָּה הַר־הַגָּדוֹל ... — *Who are you, O Great Mountain ...*

You, Tattenai — the governor of the other side of the [Jordan] River — Shethar Bozenai and their associates (see *Ezra* 6:6), who have stood until now like a great mountain, impeding the work of rebuilding the Temple, shall become like a level plain before Zerubbabel, with no ability whatsoever to hinder his work (*Rashi*).

וְהוֹצִיא אֶת־הָאֶבֶן הָרֹאשָׁה ... — *And He will bring out the stone of the main architect ...*

Our translation follows *Rashi* who understands that the word רֹאשָׁה refers back to the one who will take out the stone rather than to the stone itself. The verse is saying that the main architect will take out the plummet stone for the building of the Temple and will thereby establish himself as the head architect in charge of the construction. He will command them to build a beautiful structure to which the people will cheer and shout, "Grace! Grace! How beautiful is this edifice that is being built with this stone" (*Rashi; Ibn Ezra*). According to some, Zerubbabel himself will be the one who will take out the plummet stone (*Ibn Ezra; Radak*). Others explain that this stone is referring to the cornerstone of the building — the great and beautiful stone upon which the new Temple is to be built (*Mahari Kara; Radak; Metzudos*).

Radak offers a slightly different interpretation of the verse: Just as he took out the main stone when he began building on the twenty-fourth of the ninth month, to the cheers of the people shouting, "Grace! Grace!" so shall he complete his work.

The Sages interpret this verse as referring to the Messiah (*Tanchuma*, cited by *Yalkut*): "Who are you, Messianic king, who, when compared to Zerubbabel, is like a great mountain? For he was merely the governor of Judah whereas you will rule over the entire world." That great king will be like a level, guiding all the nations of the world along the straight path that is the Will of Hashem. He will uncover the cornerstone of the earlier Temples, and build upon them the final, permanent Temple. *Metzudos*, too, explains the verse as discussing the Messiah, but sees Gog as the great

4/7-10 [7] *Who are you, O Great Mountain? Before Zerubbabel [you will] become a plain! And He will bring out the stone of the main architect, with cheers of 'Grace! Grace!' for it."*

[8] *The word of* HASHEM *came to me, saying,* [9] *"The hands of Zerubbabel laid the foundations of this Temple and his hands will complete it; then you will know that* HASHEM, *Master of Legions, has sent me to you.* [10] *For who is scornful on the day of small things? They will rejoice when they see the stone of the plumb line in the hand of Zerubbabel,*

mountain that will be leveled by the descendant of Zerubbabel.

8. וַיְהִי דְבַר־ה׳ אֵלַי לֵאמֹר — *The word of Hashem came to me, saying.*

Having completed his explanation, the angel speaking to Zechariah perceived that the prophet did not yet comprehend the full meaning of his prophecy. He therefore elaborated further (*Abarbanel*).

9. יְדֵי זְרֻבָּבֶל יִסְּדוּ הַבַּיִת הַזֶּה וְיָדָיו תְּבַצַּעְנָה — *The hands of Zerubbabel laid the foundations of this Temple and his hands will complete it.*

Zerubbabel was the one who laid the entire foundation of the Temple during the days of Cyrus I, and he shall now complete its construction (*Rashi*).

וְיָדַעְתָּ כִּי־ה׳ ... — *Then you will know that Hashem ...*

The prophecy is directed to Zerubbabel, *You* will know ..., but it is actually referring to the entire nation. When you, Zerubbabel, will complete the construction of the new Temple, the entire nation whom you represent will clearly recognize that it was the Almighty Himself Who sent me to bring these messages to you (*Ibn Ezra*). Others interpret this verse as foretelling events of the Messianic era. Just as Zerubbabel has laid the foundation for this Temple, so shall his descendant ultimately lay the foundation of the Third Temple (*Abarbanel; Metzudos*).

10. כִּי מִי בַז לְיוֹם קְטַנּוֹת וְשָׂמְחוּ וְרָאוּ אֶת־הָאֶבֶן הַבְּדִיל בְּיַד זְרֻבָּבֶל — *For who is scornful on the day of small things? They will rejoice when they see the stone of the plumb line in the hand of Zerubbabel.*

There were those who bemoaned the smaller size and stature of this Holy Temple when its cornerstone was laid, and wept loudly as they compared it to the more glorious First Temple (see *Ezra* 2:13; *Haggai* 2:3). These people will rejoice when they see the plummet hanging from the plumb line in the hand of Zerubbabel to fix the cornerstone correctly (*Rashi*). Others interpret *the day of small things* as referring to the day that the work of rebuilding the Temple was halted through the efforts of the enemy. That day was commemorated annually as a day of misfortune, scorned by the people for its tragic occurrence. But now those same people shall rejoice over the plummet in the hand of Zerubbabel (*Radak;* cf. *Mahari Kara*).

As noted above, others interpret these verses as describing the ultimate building of the Third Temple in Messianic times. Accordingly, the prophet compares that day to that of the building of the Second Temple. Whereas the people were disappointed with the smaller size and stature of the Second Temple, the final one will be built to the rejoicing of all, when they see the plummet in the hands of the Messiah, the descendant of Zerubbabel (*Metzudos*).

ד/יא־יד

שִׁבְעָה־אֵלֶּה עֵינֵי יהוה הֵמָּה מְשׁוֹטְטִים בְּכָל־ הָאָרֶץ׃ יא וָאַעַן וָאֹמַר אֵלָיו מַה־שְּׁנֵי הַזֵּיתִים הָאֵלֶּה עַל־יְמִין הַמְּנוֹרָה וְעַל־שְׂמֹאולָהּ׃ יב וָאַעַן שֵׁנִית וָאֹמַר אֵלָיו מַה־שְׁתֵּי שִׁבֲּלֵי הַזֵּיתִים אֲשֶׁר בְּיַד שְׁנֵי צַנְתְּרוֹת הַזָּהָב הַמְרִיקִים מֵעֲלֵיהֶם הַזָּהָב׃ יג וַיֹּאמֶר אֵלַי לֵאמֹר הֲלוֹא יָדַעְתָּ מָה־אֵלֶּה וָאֹמַר לֹא אֲדֹנִי׃ יד וַיֹּאמֶר אֵלֶּה שְׁנֵי בְנֵי־הַיִּצְהָר הָעֹמְדִים עַל־אֲדוֹן כָּל־הָאָרֶץ׃

שִׁבְעָה־אֵלֶּה — *[Building] seven times as much [lit., these are seven].*

The foundation will then be seven times the size of the first foundation which was laid in the days of Cyrus (*Rashi; Mahari Kara*) for there will then be seven rows of stones like the stones of the original row (*Targum Yonasan*).

עֵינֵי ה׳ הֵמָּה מְשׁוֹטְטִים בְּכָל־הָאָרֶץ — *The eyes of Hashem — they scan the whole world!"*

The eyes of the Almighty, that scan the whole world and observe all that exists across the globe, have seen fit to bring this about, and have chosen Zerubbabel as the one who is suited to carry it out (*Rashi; Mahari Kara*).

Radak interprets the phrase *these seven* as adjoined to the words that follow it: The seven eyes described above (3:9) as being upon every stone are the eyes of Hashem that scan the entire earth and protect His people. God has seen those who oppress Israel, and will guard His children and prevent those enemies from causing them any more harm. *Malbim* sees this prophecy foretelling events of the final redemption. At that time, God will no longer leave events to their natural destiny but will control all that occurs with direct Divine Providence.

11. וָאַעַן וָאֹמַר אֵלָיו מַה־שְּׁנֵי הַזֵּיתִים הָאֵלֶּה עַל־יְמִין הַמְּנוֹרָה וְעַל־שְׂמֹאולָהּ — *I then spoke up and said to him, "What are these two olive trees to the right of the menorah and on its left?"*

Zechariah inquired of the angel who was speaking to him, "What is the significance of the two olive trees standing alongside the menorah (*Rashi*) and why is it necessary for there to be two when one would seem to suffice?" (*Mahari Kara; Metzudos*).

12. וָאַעַן שֵׁנִית וָאֹמַר אֵלָיו מַה־שְׁתֵּי שִׁבֲּלֵי הַזֵּיתִים ... — *I spoke up a second time and said to him, "What are the two clusters of olives ...?"*

He further inquired concerning the two olive branches which had fallen from the trees into golden presses and they were being pressed without outside assistance, their golden-colored oil flowing into the bowl of oil over the menorah (*Ibn Ezra; Radak*).

שְׁתֵּי שִׁבֲּלֵי הַזֵּיתִים — *Two clusters of olives.*

The prophet describes the branches of olives with the unusual term שִׁבֳּלִים — which literally means *ears of grain* — indicating that the branches were so laden with olives that they resembled ears of grain that are filled with its kernels (*Radak*).

13. וַיֹּאמֶר אֵלַי לֵאמֹר הֲלוֹא יָדַעְתָּ מָה־אֵלֶּה וָאֹמַר לֹא אֲדֹנִי — *He spoke to me, saying, "Do you not know what these are?" And I said, "No, my lord."*

The angel challenged Zechariah and asked him to interpret the vision without being assisted but he was unable to do so (*Metzudos*). According to *Malbim*, Zechariah understood that the olive trees represented those who are

[building] seven times as much. The eyes of HASHEM — they scan the whole world!"

[11] I then spoke up and said to him, "What are these two olive trees to the right of the menorah and on its left?" [12] I spoke up a second time and said to him, "What are the two clusters of olives that are next to the two golden presses, which are pouring golden [oil] from themselves?"

[13] He spoke to me, saying, "Do you not know what these are?"

And I said, "No, my lord!"

[14] He said, "These are the two anointed men who stand before the Lord of the entire earth."

anointed with the anointing oil, but he did not comprehend the reason that they had been placed so close to the menorah.

14. ... אֵלֶּה שְׁנֵי בְנֵי הַיִּצְהָר — *"These are the two anointed men ..."*

The olive trees symbolize the positions of *Kehunah*, priesthood, and *malchus*, royalty, both of which require anointing oil (*Rashi*), i.e., they represent Zerubbabel the governor of Judah and Joshua the Kohen Gadol (*Mahari Kara; Ibn Ezra; Radak*). Although the anointing oil had been hidden during the days of Josiah, they were nevertheless called the *anointed men* because of their lineage from King David and Aaron the Kohen (*Malbim* to *Sifra Lev.* 7:35). *Radak*, however, writes that Zerubbabel and Joshua were actually anointed with anointing oil! The two branches of olives represent the deeds of these great men for it was they who personally began to build the Second Temple. The two presses represent Ezra and Nehemiah, who succeeded Zerubbabel and Joshua as Israel's leaders and continued their work. Between the four of them, the people of Israel were blessed with great light and good, as symbolized by the menorah (*Radak*).

In a metaphorical interpretation of the בְּנֵי הַיִּצְהָר, *Rashi* explains that they represent the two inclinations (יֵצֶר) within a person, both of which can be united to pursue only good through the power of Torah study.

Others interpret the two anointed men as symbolizing the Messianic king and the Kohen Gadol who will both be anointed with the anointing oil (*Metzudos*). They are metaphorically described as emptying themselves of gold, symbolizing that they will shun all forms of material wealth and devote themselves solely to the service of the Almighty (*Abarbanel*). According to the Sages, the anointed men are Aaron and David, who were anointed in this world and will not require anointing in the world of the future, after resurrection (*Toras Kohanim* to *Lev.* 7:35).

הָעֹמְדִים עַל אֲדוֹן כָּל־הָאָרֶץ — *Who stand before the Lord of the entire earth.*

They stand in prayer before the Almighty seeking to be restored to their former glory (*Rashi*) and to be anointed with anointing oil to fill their positions (*Mahari Kara*). *Radak* interprets: They stand before God ready to fulfill His will.

א וָאָשׁוּב וָאֶשָּׂא עֵינַי וָאֶרְאֶה וְהִנֵּה
ב מְגִלָּה עָפָה: וַיֹּאמֶר אֵלַי מָה אַתָּה רֹאֶה וָאֹמַר
אֲנִי רֹאֶה מְגִלָּה עָפָה אָרְכָּהּ עֶשְׂרִים בָּאַמָּה
ג וְרָחְבָּהּ עֶשֶׂר בָּאַמָּה: וַיֹּאמֶר אֵלַי זֹאת הָאָלָה
הַיּוֹצֵאת עַל־פְּנֵי כָל־הָאָרֶץ כִּי כָל־הַגֹּנֵב מִזֶּה
כָּמוֹהָ נִקָּה וְכָל־הַנִּשְׁבָּע מִזֶּה כָּמוֹהָ נִקָּה:
ד הוֹצֵאתִיהָ נְאֻם יהוה צְבָאוֹת וּבָאָה אֶל־
בֵּית הַגַּנָּב וְאֶל־בֵּית הַנִּשְׁבָּע בִּשְׁמִי לַשָּׁקֶר

V

After foretelling that a Second Temple will be built, Zechariah relates a series of prophecies that foretell of the evil that the Jewish people will commit during that time and the punishments that will befall the nation for their evil deeds.

1. וָאָשׁוּב וָאֶשָּׂא עֵינַי וָאֶרְאֶה וְהִנֵּה מְגִלָּה עָפָה — *Once again I raised my eyes, and looked — and behold — a scroll was flying.*

Once again Zechariah raised his eyes heavenward (*Metzudos*) and beheld a prophetic vision of a scroll flying in the air across the sky (*Targum*). According to the simple explanation of the chapter, this scroll was a scroll of retribution, similar to that which was seen by the prophet Ezekiel (see *Ezekiel* 2:10), a scroll containing *lamentations, moaning and woe* (*Rashi; Metzudos*). Our translation of מְגִלָּה עָפָה, *a scroll was flying*, follows *Rashi, Radak, Metzudos* and most other commentaries. An alternative opinion cited by *Rashi* and *Ibn Ezra* translate כְּפוּלָה, *double* or *folded*, i.e., the scroll in the vision was a Torah scroll that was folded or doubled — see comm. to v. 2.

2. וַיֹּאמֶר אֵלַי מָה אַתָּה רֹאֶה וָאֹמַר אֲנִי רֹאֶה מְגִלָּה עָפָה אָרְכָּהּ עֶשְׂרִים בָּאַמָּה וְרָחְבָּהּ עֶשֶׂר בָּאַמָּה — *He said to me, "What do you see?" I answered, "I see a flying scroll; twenty cubits its length and ten cubits its width."*

The angel who had been speaking to Zechariah asked him to describe the prophetic vision that he perceived. Zechariah replied that he saw a scroll flying out from the doorway of the antechamber of the [First] Temple (*Yalkut* from *Vayikra Rabbah* 6). The dimensions of the scroll were the same as that of the Temple antechamber — twenty cubits by ten (*Ibn Ezra; Radak*). These are also the measurements of the Sanctuary doorway from which the scroll was emerging (*Rashi*). The angel will explain the vision to Zechariah in the next verse.

The Sages (*Eruvin* 21a) note that King David described the Torah as being of great breadth, without specifying its dimensions (*Psalms* 119:96). Job went a step further, declaring that the Torah is longer than the world and wider than the sea (*Job* 11:9). Ezekiel described a Torah scroll that appeared to him in a vision as being covered with writing on both sides (*Ezekiel*. 2:10), but did not give any specific dimensions. It was only Zechariah who defined its actual dimensions, twenty by ten cubits.

3. זֹאת הָאָלָה הַיּוֹצֵאת עַל־פְּנֵי כָל־הָאָרֶץ — *This is the curse that is going out over the surface of all the land.*

This scroll contains the curse of retribution for those who have taken false oaths. It is actually emerging from the Holy of Holies from before the *Shechinah* and is traveling across the entire land (*Rashi*) of Israel (*Radak*). Alternatively, it is traveling to all places where Jewish people are to be found, whether they are

[1] **O**nce again I raised my eyes, and looked — and behold — a scroll was flying. [2] He said to me, "What do you see?"

I answered, "I see a flying scroll: twenty cubits its length and ten cubits its width."

[3] He said to me, "This is the curse that is going out over the surface of all the land. For [heretofore] anyone who steals has been absolved of such a curse and anyone who swears [falsely] has been absolved of such a curse. [4] I have taken it out [the curse] — the word of HASHEM, Master of Legions — and it shall enter the house of the thief and the house of the one who swears falsely in My Name,

in Jerusalem, Babylonia, or within the Persian Empire (*Ibn Ezra*).

כִּי כָל־הַגֹּנֵב מִזֶּה כָּמוֹהָ נִקָּה וְכָל־הַנִּשְׁבָּע מִזֶּה כָּמוֹהָ נִקָּה — *For [heretofore] anyone who steals has been absolved of such a curse and anyone who swears [falsely] has been absolved of such a curse.*

Our translation follows *Rashi* who explains that until now, all those who had stolen or had sworn falsely escaped the punishments described in this scroll. God withheld retribution because these laws had been transgressed by only some of the people and He waited until now, when their measure of wickedness had become full. From now on, however, He will exact retribution on a large scale and all will suffer exile and destruction. *Radak* translates נִקָּה, *shall be cut off* (see *Jeremiah* 30:11) and renders *for whoever steals from this side — just like it — will be cut off; and whoever swears falsely from this side — just like it — will be cut off*. He explains that like the scroll that was seen by Ezekiel, there was writing on both sides of the scroll. One side stated that whoever steals will be destroyed and on the other side was written that whoever swears falsely will be destroyed. The words *from this side — just like it* mean just like the retribution inscribed on the other side. God is proclaiming that although He has waited some time to act upon this decree, He will wait no longer for the time has come for the retribution to be meted out.

Radak notes that unlike Ezekiel, Zechariah was unable to read the words written on the scroll. This was due to the declining power of prophecy that was taking place during his day and its visions were therefore perceived with less clarity than in previous times.

Alshich explains that the sin of robbery is of similar severity to false oaths. As noted by the Sages (*Bava Kamma* 79b), one who steals surreptitiously thereby indicates his denial of Hashem, as he fears being observed by human beings but not by the Almighty. Thus, therein, too, lies a desecration of the honor of Hashem, similar to that caused by false oaths.

The Sages, however, understand the mention of this verse of those who steal as those who "steal the minds of others" — i.e., who mislead them — by making false claims against those who owe them nothing and thereby causing them to swear unnecessarily (*Shavuos* 39a).

4. הוֹצֵאתִיהָ נְאֻם ה׳ צְבָאוֹת וּבָאָה אֶל־בֵּית הַגַּנָּב וְאֶל־בֵּית הַנִּשְׁבָּע בִּשְׁמִי לַשָּׁקֶר ... — *I have taken it out [the curse] — the word of Hashem, Master of Legions — and it shall enter the house of the thief and the house of the one who swears falsely in My Name ...*

וְלָנֶה בְּתוֹךְ בֵּיתוֹ וְכִלַּתּוּ וְאֶת־עֵצָיו וְאֶת־אֲבָנָיו׃
ה וַיֵּצֵא הַמַּלְאָךְ הַדֹּבֵר בִּי וַיֹּאמֶר אֵלַי שָׂא נָא
ו עֵינֶיךָ וּרְאֵה מָה הַיּוֹצֵאת הַזֹּאת׃ וָאֹמַר מַה־הִיא
וַיֹּאמֶר זֹאת הָאֵיפָה הַיּוֹצֵאת וַיֹּאמֶר זֹאת עֵינָם
ז בְּכָל־הָאָרֶץ׃ וְהִנֵּה כִּכַּר עֹפֶרֶת נִשֵּׂאת וְזֹאת אִשָּׁה
ח אַחַת יוֹשֶׁבֶת בְּתוֹךְ הָאֵיפָה׃ וַיֹּאמֶר זֹאת הָרִשְׁעָה

God has sent out this curse to travel across the land and exact retribution from those who are guilty of robbery or of taking false oaths in His Name. The curse shall enter the houses of those people and settle there, destroying them together with their houses (*Rashi; Radak*).

וְלָנֶה בְּתוֹךְ בֵּיתוֹ וְכִלַּתּוּ וְאֶת־עֵצָיו וְאֶת־אֲבָנָיו — *And it shall lodge within his house and annihilate him with its wood and stones.*

Alshich notes the singular form of the verb וְכִלַּתּוּ, *and annihilate him* — i.e., the one who swears falsely. The curse shall briefly enter the house of the thief and exact some measure of retribution from him. It will then travel to the house of the one who swears falsely where it will take permanent lodging. There, it will cause its greatest harm, as that is the more severe of the two transgressions.

The Talmud teaches that the transgression of false oaths is different than all other transgressions of the Torah. Generally, punishment for a sin may be suspended by the Heavenly Court for two or three generations if the violator has some merit in his favor. The sin of false oaths, however, is so severe, that retribution is exacted immediately, during the person's lifetime. Furthermore, the destruction caused by this transgression is so great that it destroys even the stones of one's house, that which fire and water cannot do (*Shavuos* 39a). According to the Midrash (*Tanchuma* to *Metzora* Ch. 4), this sin may even cause one's house to be inflicted with *tzaraas* and thereby necessitate its destruction.

5. וַיֵּצֵא הַמַּלְאָךְ הַדֹּבֵר בִּי — *Then the angel who was speaking to me went forth.*

After showing Zechariah the previous vision, the angel disappeared from view. He then reappeared and presented the prophet with a new prophecy (*Radak*). The disappearance of the angel symbolizes the eventual disappearance of prophecy that will take place during the exile (*Abarbanel; Metzudos*). Alternatively, Zechariah observed the angel going forth from among a group of other angels [to address him] (*Ibn Ezra*).

שָׂא נָא עֵינֶיךָ וּרְאֵה מָה הַיּוֹצֵאת הַזֹּאת — *"Raise your eyes and see what this emerging thing is."*

The angel showed Zechariah another vision of something that was emerging from the Holy of Holies (*Rashi*) or from the Holy Land (*Radak*). In addition to the transgressions of false oaths and robbery, there are other sins that the people have transgressed for which God seeks retribution (*Abarbanel; Malbim*).

6. וָאֹמַר מַה־הִיא — *I said, "What is it?"*

What is this object that is emerging, that you instruct me to observe? (*Rashi*).

וַיֹּאמֶר זֹאת הָאֵיפָה הַיּוֹצֵאת וַיֹּאמֶר זֹאת עֵינָם בְּכָל־הָאָרֶץ — *And he said, "This is an ephah that is emerging." And he said, "This is [because] their [greedy] eyes are in all the land."*

The angel told Zechariah that the object emerging is an *ephah*, a large measuring vessel that holds an *ephah*, a dry measure. In the context of the prophecy it symbolized the measure of the Almighty's judgment. With this *ephah*, punishment shall be meted out to all whose greedy eyes rove across the entire land, seeking opportunities to

and it shall lodge within his house and annihilate him, with its wood and stones."

[5] Then the angel who was speaking to me went forth and said to me, "Raise your eyes and see what this emerging thing is."

[6] I said, "What is it?"

And he said, "This is an ephah that is emerging." And he said, "This is [because] their [greedy] eyes are in all the land." [7] And behold! A talent of lead was being lifted, and this one woman was sitting inside the ephah. [8] And he said, "This [woman] is Wickedness,"

rob, plunder and cheat through the use of false measures (*Rashi*). Alternatively, the *ephah* represented the false measures used by the people, rather than the measure of justice to be meted out, for the people had abused the *ephah* measurement in their dealings with one another (*Abarbanel;* ibid. to v. 8; *Metzudos*).

According to *Ibn Ezra,* the *ephah* represented the punishment that would befall those people who remained in Babylonia and ignored the call of the prophet to return to the Land of Israel and rebuild the Holy Temple. Others explain that the *ephah* represented the people who were sent into exile for cheating others with false measures (*Targum; Mahari Kara*). According to *Radak,* it is alluding specifically to the Ten Tribes, who remained in exile even after the tribes of Judah and Benjamin had been returned to the Land. They are symbolized by the *ephah* due to the precise measure of justice that had been meted out to them: Just as they persisted in their wrongdoings for many years, so shall they remain in exile for a very long time.

Although we have translated the phrase וַיֹּאמֶר זֹאת עֵינָם בְּכָל הָאָרֶץ according to *Rashi's* interpretation of the verse, there are various explanations of this phrase. *Targum* renders: *Behold, they are being exiled before [the eyes of] all the inhabitants of the land. Mahari Kara* explains: They are being exiled for that which they set their eyes to distort the measures [i.e., they focused upon that which did not belong to them, seeking to obtain it through dishonest means]. According to *Radak,* the eyes represent the eyes of Divine Judgment watching over them and observing their deeds. These shall be evidenced by the punishment they receive for their wickedness.

7. וְהִנֵּה כִּכַּר עֹפֶרֶת נִשֵּׂאת — *And behold! A talent of lead was being lifted ...*

Zechariah then beheld another vision. He saw a massive lead object weighing a *kikar* rising from the ground into the air. This was followed by a vision of a woman sitting in the midst of the *ephah* described in the previous verse (*Rashi*).

8. וַיֹּאמֶר זֹאת הָרִשְׁעָה — *And he said, "This [woman] is Wickedness,"*

The angel explained that the woman symbolized the wicked ways and character of the evildoers. She was placed — along with her wickedness — within the *ephah,* the very object with which the evildoers commit their thievery, expressing the idea that the measure of retribution that is to be meted out to them is measure for measure (*Rashi*). Because the punishments of the evildoers will be meted out measure for measure, all will recognize that the misfortune that has befallen them is the retribution sent by the Almighty for their wicked deeds. This will move them all to cease their corrupt behavior and bring an end to their afflictions (*Malbim*).

וַיַּשְׁלֵךְ אֹתָהּ אֶל־תּוֹךְ הָאֵיפָה וַיַּשְׁלֵךְ אֶת־אֶבֶן הָעֹפֶרֶת אֶל־פִּיהָ׃ ט וָאֶשָּׂא עֵינַי וָאֵרֶא וְהִנֵּה שְׁתַּיִם נָשִׁים יוֹצְאוֹת וְרוּחַ בְּכַנְפֵיהֶם וְלָהֵנָּה כְנָפַיִם כְּכַנְפֵי הַחֲסִידָה וַתִּשֶּׂאנָה אֶת־הָאֵיפָה בֵּין הָאָרֶץ וּבֵין הַשָּׁמָיִם׃ י וָאֹמַר אֶל־הַמַּלְאָךְ הַדֹּבֵר בִּי אָנָה הֵמָּה מוֹלִכוֹת אֶת־הָאֵיפָה׃ יא וַיֹּאמֶר אֵלַי לִבְנוֹת־לָה בַיִת בְּאֶרֶץ שִׁנְעָר וְהוּכַן וְהֻנִּיחָה שָּׁם עַל־מְכֻנָתָהּ׃

וַיַּשְׁלֵךְ אֹתָהּ אֶל־תּוֹךְ הָאֵיפָה וַיַּשְׁלֵךְ אֶת־אֶבֶן הָעוֹפֶרֶת אֶל־פִּיהָ — *And he threw her into the ephah, and threw the lead weight into her mouth.*

The angel knocked down the woman into the *ephah*, indicating that the wicked are to be subjected to punishment and affliction for their deeds. He then threw the lead weight described above into her mouth in order to weigh her down — for these evildoers shall not rise again nor raise their voices once more to rob and oppress the poor and destitute (*Rashi*). Others understand that when he threw the piece of lead at her mouth, he caused her death either by suffocation (*Metzudos*) or through the hot lead that entered her body and burned her (*Abarbanel*).

According to *Radak*, the woman of these verses represents the wickedness of the Ten Tribes of the Northern Kingdom of Israel who erected the golden calves and introduced Baal worship to Israel. God cast them into the *ephah* to mete out punishment to them according to their measure. He cast the lead into the mouth of the *ephah* to weigh them down and prevent them from returning from exile.

The Sages relate that the Men of the Great Assembly recognized that the inclination in people's hearts toward idolatry that prevailed at that time was responsible for the destruction of the Temple, the death of the righteous and the exile of the people. They therefore pleaded with God to subdue the evil inclination of idolatry once and for all from the psyche of the nation, and the Almighty heeded their plea. In an allegorical description of a prophetic vision seen by members of the Great Assembly (*Yad Ramah*), the Talmud tells that the inclination emerged from the site of the Holy of Holies and was placed in the hands of the Sages. They cast it into a lead container, which they covered with lead so that the evil inclination should not emerge again. The Talmud interprets the words of Zechariah in this verse as describing the evil inclination, זֹאת הָרִשְׁעָה, which was taken and thrown into a container, וַיַּשְׁלֵךְ אֹתָהּ אֶל תּוֹךְ הָאֵיפָה, that was covered with a leadweight וַיַּשְׁלֵךְ אֶת הָאֶבֶן הָעוֹפֶרֶת עַל פִּיהָ (*Sanhedrin* 64a). See *Toras Chaim, Sanhedrin* 64b and *Maharsha* to *Yoma* 69b for interpretations of the allegory.

9. וָאֶשָּׂא עֵינַי וָאֵרֶא וְהִנֵּה שְׁתַּיִם נָשִׁים יוֹצְאוֹת ... — *Then I raised my eyes and looked, and behold two women were emerging ...*

In yet another vision, Zechariah beheld two women emerging from the House (*Rashi*) [i.e., they were emerging from the Holy Temple as in the previous two prophecies]. According to *Metzudos*, they were emerging from the heavens. These women represented the nations of Babylonia and Chaldea, the two nations who were included in the legions of Nebuchadnezzar that vanquished the Jewish people — see *Rashi* to v. 11. Others maintain that the women represent the people who were exiled rather than the nations that vanquished them. According to *Mahari Kara* they represent the two kingdoms of Israel, the Kingdom of Judah and the Kingdom of the Ten Tribes. *Radak*, however, understands that

and he threw her into the ephah, and threw the lead weight into her mouth.

[9] Then I raised my eyes and looked, and behold two women were emerging with wind in their wings, for they had wings like a stork's wings, and they lifted the ephah between the earth and the heavens. [10] I said to the angel who was speaking to me, "Where are they taking the ephah?" [11] He said to me, "To build her a house in the land of Shinar, where it will be established, and she will be set down there on her base."

they represent the tribes of Judah and Benjamin. Although all the Ten Tribes of Israel were symbolically represented by one woman (see v. 7), the Tribe of Judah is nevertheless represented separately due to its prestigious status as the Tribe of Royalty. The Tribe of Benjamin, the one tribe that remained together with Judah, is also represented separately. *Rambam* (*Moreh Nevuchim* 1:49) explains that the two women seen by Zechariah were actually two angels that Zechariah perceived as women. He did not realize that they were angels because of the declining power of prophecy that was taking place and its vision was therefore perceived with less clarity (*Radak*).

וְרוּחַ בְּכַנְפֵיהֶם וְלָהֵנָּה כְנָפַיִם כְּכַנְפֵי הַחֲסִידָה — *With wind in their wings, for they had wings like a stork's wings.*

The women had long wings, like those of the stork, and they flew swiftly with the wind at their wings symbolizing the speed and expediency with which the Jewish people were to be carried into exile (*Radak*) by these two nations (*Rashi*).

וַתִּשֶּׂאנָה אֶת־הָאֵיפָה בֵּין הָאָרֶץ וּבֵין הַשָּׁמָיִם — *And they lifted the ephah between the earth and the heavens.*

The women carried the *ephah* containing the captive Jewish nation between the earth and the heavens, where all flying creatures are to be found. They were suspended in the air symbolizing that unlike the first exiles who were sunk in exile, they would remain airborne ready to return to their land in a short period of time (*Radak*).

According to the Sages, the two women represented the two character traits of sanctimony and arrogance, that descended to Babylonia (*Sanhedrin* 24a). *With wind in their wings* alludes to their arrogance for they were puffed up and arrogant. Their wings resembled those of a *chasidah* bird alluding to their show of [false] piety.

10. וָאֹמַר אֶל־הַמַּלְאָךְ הַדֹּבֵר בִּי אָנָה הֵמָּה מוֹלִכוֹת אֶת־הָאֵיפָה — *I said to the angel who was speaking to me, "Where are they taking the ephah?"*

Due to the swiftness with which they carried the *ephah*, Zechariah was moved to question its destination (*Radak*).

11. וַיֹּאמֶר אֵלַי לִבְנוֹת־לָהּ בַיִת בְּאֶרֶץ שִׁנְעָר וְהוּכַן וְהֻנִּיחָה שָּׁם עַל־מְכֻנָתָהּ — *He said to me, "To build her a house in the land of Shinar, where it will be established and she will be set down there on her base."*

The angel informed Zechariah that the women were going to the land of Babylonia, where they will build a house and prepare it for the *ephah*, which will be placed there and left there upon its base. Thus, the Kingdom of Judah, which had already been exiled to Babylonia, will remain settled there until the preordained duration of their exile has been completed (*Rashi; Mahari Kara*). Alternatively, this prophecy is a criticism leveled against the Jewish exiles. As instructed by the prophet

א וָאָשֻׁב וָאֶשָּׂא עֵינַי וָאֶרְאֶה וְהִנֵּה אַרְבַּע מַרְכָּבוֹת יֹצְאוֹת מִבֵּין שְׁנֵי הֶהָרִים ב וְהֶהָרִים הָרֵי נְחֹשֶׁת: בַּמֶּרְכָּבָה הָרִאשֹׁנָה סוּסִים אֲדֻמִּים וּבַמֶּרְכָּבָה הַשֵּׁנִית סוּסִים ג שְׁחֹרִים: וּבַמֶּרְכָּבָה הַשְּׁלִשִׁית סוּסִים לְבָנִים וּבַמֶּרְכָּבָה הָרְבִעִית סוּסִים בְּרֻדִּים אֲמֻצִּים:

Jeremiah, the people built houses for themselves in Babylonia in which they could dwell throughout the course of the exile. However, they extended their stay. They ignored the call of the prophet to return to Jerusalem and remained settled in their Babylonian dwellings and failed to return to their Land (*Radak*).

According to *Ibn Ezra*, the two women represent the two officers of Artashasta, king of Babylonia, who persecuted those Jewish families who remained in Babylon after being exhorted by the prophet to return and build the Holy Temple. Even after they sought to return, they were prevented from doing so by these officers, who forced them to settle permanently in the land of Babylonia.

Abarbanel contends that the two women represent the two Kingdoms of the Tribes of Israel: the Kingdoms of Israel and Judah, both of whom were sent into exile for many generations; the Ten Tribes were exiled sometime prior to the destruction of the First Temple, the Kingdom of Judah, after its destruction. Upon seeing this vision, the prophet inquired as to the destination of this exile: Where will they dwell while they are banished from their Land? To this the angel responded that they will build houses in a land of upheaval — שִׁנְעָר, from the root לְנַעֵר, *to shake*. They shall not succeed in establishing permanent roots in any one land but will wander from country to country in the course of their exile. This came to pass after the destruction of the Second Temple.

VI

1. וָאָשֻׁב וָאֶשָּׂא עֵינַי וָאֶרְאֶה וְהִנֵּה אַרְבַּע מַרְכָּבוֹת... — *Once again I raised my eyes and saw, and behold, four chariots ...*

Zechariah saw a prophetic vision of four chariots emerging from between two mountains of copper. According to most commentators, the four chariots represent the four great empires of the world, i.e., Babylonia, Persia, Greece and Rome (*Radak; Abarbanel*). According to *Rashi*, the chariots represent the heavenly emissaries of the Almighty through whom these nations were granted supremacy. Although the prophet had previously been granted a prophetic vision of four horns which represented the same four kingdoms (see 2:1), that vision was too fleeting to reveal the nature and identity of those kingdoms. He was therefore granted this vision which is more detailed (*Abarbanel*).

אַרְבַּע מַרְכָּבוֹת — *Four chariots*

Each chariot was drawn by four horses (*Ibn Ezra; Radak*), to emphasize its great power (*Radak*), as well as its dominion over the four ends of the earth (*Malbim* to v. 5). Alternatively, it symbolizes that each empire will reign over a multitude of nations (*Abarbanel*).

וְהֶהָרִים הָרֵי נְחֹשֶׁת — *And the mountains were mountains of copper.*

These chariots were seen as emerging from between two mountains of copper, a tough and hard metal, indicating that the four empires were to enjoy the great power of mighty mountains and the toughness of strong, hard metal (*Rashi; Radak*).

Abarbanel sees the two mountains as symbolizing the two "ends of the earth." These empires would rule over the entire known world, from end to end. Alternatively, they

[1] Once again I raised my eyes and saw, and behold, four chariots were emerging from between two mountains, and the mountains were mountains of copper. [2] In the first chariot [there were] red horses, and in the second chariot [there were] black horses, [3] and in the third chariot [there were] white horses, and in the fourth chariot [there were] spotted [and] ash-colored horses.

represent the two Temples of Israel. The reign of these empires would begin during the downfall of the First Temple and extend through the era of the Second Temple. *Yalkut,* followed by *Mahari Kara,* interprets the two mountains as representing the two Kingdoms of Israel and Judah. Although they had once been strong and tough like metal, they were nevertheless conquered and exiled by the aforementioned empires. Alternatively, they were steadfast like copper in their resistance to the rebuke of the prophets.

2. בַּמֶּרְכָּבָה הָרִאשֹׁנָה סוּסִים אֲדֻמִּים — *In the first chariot [there were] red horses.*

The first chariot was drawn by red horses and represented the Babylonian Empire, which was described by *Daniel* (2:38) as being of gold (*Rashi*) — a color with a somewhat reddish appearance (*Metzudos*). In addition, the color red also symbolizes the abundant Jewish blood that had been shed by the Babylonians as they slaughtered the people of Judah (*Yalkut*).

וּבַמֶּרְכָּבָה הַשֵּׁנִית סוּסִים שְׁחֹרִים — *And in the second chariot [there were] black horses.*

The second chariot was drawn by black horses which represented the second empire, the kingdom of the Medes (*Rashi*) or the Persians (*Metzudos*), for they enacted evil decrees during the days of Haman that blackened the faces of the Jewish people (ibid.). Some suggest that they were accustomed to wearing black clothing (*Radak; Abarbanel*). *Radak* sees these verses as paralleling the four horses described in the first chapter (v. 8). The second horse is described there as being שְׂרֻקִּים, *sorrel* [see comm. ad loc.], because the Persian Empire was in actuality the combined kingdom of the separate nations, Persia and Media, and is therefore depicted by horses of two different colors, sorrel and black. Possibly, these two colors were those of the customary garb worn by the members of the two nations (ibid.).

3. וּבַמֶּרְכָּבָה הַשְּׁלִישִׁית סוּסִים לְבָנִים — *And in the third chariot [there were] white horses.*

The third chariot was drawn by white horses. *Rashi* and *Mahari Kara,* who perceive Persia and Media as two separate kingdoms, maintain that the white horses represent the Persian Empire for it was they who granted the Israelites permission to rebuild the Temple that brought light to the world. *Radak,* who explained that the black horses represented the Persian Empire that consisted of both the kingdoms of Persia and Media, interprets the white horses as representing the Greeks; either because Alexander the Great, their first monarch, was a wise philosopher, and the color white symbolizes wisdom (*R' Saadiah Gaon*) or because the ancient Greeks were noted for the white finery of their apparel (*Metzudos*).

Malbim sees the white horses representing the rulers of the present era, who in general have shown more tolerance toward the Jewish people than the leaders of medieval or ancient times.

וּבַמֶּרְכָּבָה הָרְבִיעִית סוּסִים בְּרֻדִּים אֲמֻצִּים — *And in the fourth chariot [there were] spotted [and] ash-colored horses.*

The fourth chariot was drawn by spotted and ash-colored horses. The spotted horses represent the Greeks for they subjugated and oppressed Israel with various kinds of decrees [like many

ד וָאַעַן וָאֹמַר אֶל־הַמַּלְאָךְ הַדֹּבֵר בִּי מָה־אֵלֶּה
ה אֲדֹנִי׃ וַיַּעַן הַמַּלְאָךְ וַיֹּאמֶר אֵלָי אֵלֶּה אַרְבַּע
רֻחוֹת הַשָּׁמַיִם יוֹצְאוֹת מֵהִתְיַצֵּב עַל־אֲדוֹן
ו כָּל־הָאָרֶץ׃ אֲשֶׁר־בָּהּ הַסּוּסִים הַשְּׁחֹרִים
יֹצְאִים אֶל־אֶרֶץ צָפוֹן וְהַלְּבָנִים יָצְאוּ אֶל־
אַחֲרֵיהֶם וְהַבְּרֻדִּים יָצְאוּ אֶל־אֶרֶץ הַתֵּימָן׃

spots on a solid background]. The ash-colored horses represent Edom [Rome] and the Ishmaelites [Arabs] (*Rashi; Mahari Kara*).

Radak relates the word בְּרֻדִּים to בָּרָד, *hail*, and explains that these horses have white spots similar to hailstones and represent the Roman Empire [who adopted Christianity as their state religion]. They claim that they follow the principles of the Torah which is "white as hail" but actually they "spotted it" by incorporating other ideals and beliefs into their faith. Although this chariot represents Rome which vanquished Greece and ruled the world, it is accompanied with the kingdom of Ishmael represented by the ash-colored horses because the area occupied by the Roman Empire eventually split into two [religions, Christianity and Islam] — see also commentary of *Abarbanel* to this verse.[1]

Metzudos maintains that the spotted horses represent the kingdom of Ishmael for as descendants of the Patriarch Abraham who follow the commandment of circumcising the males, they have some degree of merit. The Romans, who destroyed the Second Temple and reduced it to ashes, are represented by the ash-colored horses.

Others interpret this prophecy as referring only to those foreign nations that were to hold power from the time of Zechariah and onward. They are described as emerging from the mountains of copper, because the first empire, the Greek Empire, is described in the visions of Nebuchadnezzar as the color of copper (*Malbim;* see *Daniel* 2:39). Thus, the first chariot, led by red horses, is that of Greece, the copper kingdom itself. It is not described later, in v.6 as going out with the other chariots since it is the original power from which the others "emerged." The chariot with the black horses represents the Roman Empire who, like the Greeks, spilled much blood and caused darkness to fall on Israel. The chariot with the white horses represents the many peaceful kings who reigned after the downfall of the Roman Empire. These are followed by a chariot with spotted and ash-colored horses, symbolizing an empire that emerged from the peaceful kingdoms of the "white empire" but was spotted with "black and white spots," for they too waged war. It is from them that Gog and Magog will come forth to battle over Israel (*Malbim*).

Quoting *Pesikta Rabbasi, Yalkut* offers an entirely different approach. The four chariots symbolize the four encampments of the Israelite nation during their travels through the desert. The red horses represent the camp of Judah, the black that of Reuven, the white that of Ephraim and the final chariot the camp of Dan. Scriptural verses are cited explaining the reason that each color horse represents that particular camp. These are the counterparts of the four great empires, for when the former transgress the will of Hashem, the latter are given the power to conquer them.

4. וָאַעַן וָאֹמַר אֶל־הַמַּלְאָךְ הַדֹּבֵר בִּי מָה־אֵלֶּה אֲדֹנִי — *I spoke up and said to the angel who was speaking to me, "What are these, my lord?"*

1. We have followed *Radak's* explanation of this verse found in the Mechon Moar edition of *Mikraos Gedolos Navi.* Earlier printings seem to have been tampered by censors as they have the spotted horses representing Ishmael who claim to follow the principles of the Torah etc. This contradicts *Radak* to v.6 where he writes that the spotted horses represent Rome.

[4] I spoke up and said to the angel who was speaking to me, "What are these, my lord?"

[5] The angel answered and said to me, "These are the four ends of the heavens emerging from standing before the Lord of the entire earth. [6] [The chariot] within which are the black horses ... they are going forth to the land of the north, and the white ones went forth after them; the spotted ones went forth to the land of the south.

Upon witnessing this vision, Zechariah realized that it was related to the previous visions that had been granted to him: the vision of the four horses (1:8-11) and the vision of the four horns (2:1-4). He therefore asked the angel to explain the reason for this vision, i.e., what did this vision come to add to the other visions (*Radak*).

5. וַיַּעַן הַמַּלְאָךְ וַיֹּאמֶר אֵלָי אֵלֶּה אַרְבַּע רֻחוֹת הַשָּׁמַיִם יוֹצְאוֹת מֵהִתְיַצֵּב עַל־אֲדוֹן כָּל־הָאָרֶץ — *The angel answered and said to me, "These are the four ends of the heavens emerging from standing before the Lord of the entire earth.*

These are the heavenly officers of four empires that are destined to rule over the four ends of the earth. They are emerging from before the Almighty for He has just given them their mandate to rule (*Rashi*). Alternatively, these are the four chariots that are going to *the four corners* (*Radak; Ibn Ezra*) of the heavens to permit the four empires to rule over the four corners of the earth, each in its appointed time (*Radak*).

6. אֲשֶׁר־בָּהּ הַסּוּסִים הַשְּׁחֹרִים יֹצְאִים אֶל־אֶרֶץ צָפוֹן — *[The chariot] within which are the black horses ... they are going forth to the land of the north.*

The chariot led by the black horses represents the kingdom of Media (*Rashi; Mahari Kara*) and is followed by the white horses of Persia. Together they traveled northward to jointly conquer the forces of Babylonia (*Rashi*). Alternatively, the chariot with the black horses represents the kingdoms of Persia and Media that have gone northward to conquer the kingdom of Babylonia (*Metzudos*) and to subsequently rule the entire world (*Radak*). They are followed by the white horses of Greece and Macedonia, who, led by Alexander the Great, are destined to wrest power from the Persians and replace them as the supreme world power.

וְהַבְּרֻדִּים יָצְאוּ אֶל־אֶרֶץ הַתֵּימָן — *The spotted ones went forth to the land of the south.*

According to *Rashi,* the spotted horses represent the kingdom of Greece which replaced Persia as the leading world power. Alternatively, it is the spotted horses of Rome that are seen heading south from their land, en route to vanquish the Greek Empire. Their first destination is Egypt, far to the south, where Lulianus Caesar was to vanquish the Hellenist forces and begin the chain of Roman conquest (*Radak; Abarbanel*). According to *Metzudos,* the spotted horses represent the kingdom of Ishmael. Scripture writes that these horses *went forth,* יָצְאוּ, *to the land of the south,* and does not write *they went forth after them,* יָצְאוּ אֶל אַחֲרֵיהֶם, as it does regarding the white horses because the kingdom of Ishmael did not come to power by conquering the empire of Greece which had already been conquered by Rome.

The red horses — representing Babylonia — are not mentioned here, as the Babylonian Empire had already been destroyed at the time of this prophecy, and there was thus no need to elaborate upon its destiny (*Rashi; Radak*).

ז וְהָאֲמֻצִּים יָצְאוּ וַיְבַקְשׁוּ לָלֶכֶת לְהִתְהַלֵּךְ בָּאָרֶץ וַיֹּאמֶר לְכוּ הִתְהַלְּכוּ בָאָרֶץ וַתִּתְהַלַּכְנָה בָּאָרֶץ: ח וַיַּזְעֵק אֹתִי וַיְדַבֵּר אֵלַי לֵאמֹר רְאֵה הַיּוֹצְאִים אֶל־ ט אֶרֶץ צָפוֹן הֵנִיחוּ אֶת־רוּחִי בְּאֶרֶץ צָפוֹן: וַיְהִי י דְבַר־יְהוָה אֵלַי לֵאמֹר: לָקוֹחַ מֵאֵת הַגּוֹלָה מֵחֶלְדַּי וּמֵאֵת טוֹבִיָּה וּמֵאֵת יְדַעְיָה וּבָאתָ אַתָּה בַּיּוֹם הַהוּא וּבָאתָ בֵּית יֹאשִׁיָּה בֶן־צְפַנְיָה אֲשֶׁר־ יא בָּאוּ מִבָּבֶל: וְלָקַחְתָּ כֶסֶף־וְזָהָב וְעָשִׂיתָ עֲטָרוֹת וְשַׂמְתָּ בְּרֹאשׁ יְהוֹשֻׁעַ בֶּן־יְהוֹצָדָק הַכֹּהֵן הַגָּדוֹל:

7. וְהָאֲמֻצִּים יָצְאוּ וַיְבַקְשׁוּ לָלֶכֶת לְהִתְהַלֵּךְ בָּאָרֶץ — *The ash-colored ones went forth and asked to go to traverse the earth.*

The nation represented by the ash-colored horses asked God to extend the length of their rule over the earth (*Rashi*).

וַיֹּאמֶר לְכוּ הִתְהַלְּכוּ בָאָרֶץ וַתִּתְהַלַּכְנָה בָּאָרֶץ — *He said, "Go traverse the earth." So they traversed the earth.*

This is referring to the kingdom of Edom (*Rashi; Mahari Kara*), the mighty Roman Empire whose power extended across the earth and remained supreme for a uniquely long period of time (*Rashi; Mahari Kara; Metzudos*). Alternatively, this is referring to the kingdom of Ishmael, the Arab peoples, who girded themselves with strength to attain dominion wherever they could achieve it. They sought permission [from the Almighty] to carve out their empire and were granted the right to do so (*Radak; Abarbanel*).

8. וַיַּזְעֵק אֹתִי וַיְדַבֵּר אֵלַי לֵאמֹר רְאֵה הַיּוֹצְאִים אֶל־אֶרֶץ צָפוֹן הֵנִיחוּ אֶת־רוּחִי בְּאֶרֶץ צָפוֹן — *He then summoned me and he spoke to me, saying, "See, the ones going out to the land of the north have allayed My anger in the land of the north."*

The angel who was speaking to me called me with a loud voice (*Radak*) and said, "Look at the chariots with the black horses: Persia and Media are going northward to conquer and destroy Babylonia. In so doing they have [satisfied and thereby] quelled My wrath against the Babylonians for the evil they have brought upon My people (*Rashi; Radak; Abarbanel*). Although I decreed that Israel should be punished, the Babylonian hordes far exceeded My wishes with the severity and vigor which they displayed toward My people" (*Radak*).[1]

10. לָקוֹחַ מֵאֵת הַגּוֹלָה מֵחֶלְדַּי וּמֵאֵת טוֹבִיָּה וּמֵאֵת יְדַעְיָה — *Take from the exiles — from Heldai and from Tobijah and from Jedaiah.*

When these individuals return from the exile in Babylonia and wish to donate gifts of gold and silver for the building of the Temple, accept their offering and use it to make crowns, as described below (see v. 11) (*Radak*).

1. *Ramban* (*Genesis* 15:13) discusses this concept in great detail, particularly regarding the enslavement of the Israelite nation in Egypt. Although God had decreed that Israel would be subjected to servitude and affliction in Egypt, the Egyptians overzealously executed God's decree and were therefore subject to punishment. Nebuchadnezzar, too, although called upon by the prophets to destroy Jerusalem, and though his people knew that they were fulfilling God's command, they were nevertheless punished because Nebuchadnezzar had his own personal glory in mind and because his people overzealously perpetrated evil against Israel — see ArtScroll *Genesis* pp. 528-529, Egypt as God's agent.

[7] *The ash-colored ones went forth and asked to go to traverse the earth. He said, "Go traverse the earth." So they traversed the earth.*

[8] *He then summoned me and he spoke to me, saying, "See, the ones going out to the land of the north have allayed My anger in the land of the north."*

[9] *The word of* H*ASHEM came to me, saying,* [10] *"Take from the exiles — from Heldai and from Tobijah and from Jedaiah. Come on that day; come to the house of Josiah son of Zephaniah, who have come from Babylonia,* [11] *and take silver and gold and make crowns, and place [one of them] on the head of Joshua son of Jehozadak, the Kohen Gadol.*

Although you hesitate to accept offerings for the Temple from those who refused to leave Babylonia and return to the Holy Land, these individuals did return, are righteous and upright, and are therefore worthy of having their offering accepted (*Abarbanel*).

Abarbanel suggests that the names of these individuals reflect their high esteem: חֶלְדַּי, *Heldai*, was possibly the son of Huldah the prophetess [and followed in her ways]. טוֹבִיָּה, *Tobijah*, is a form of the word טוֹב, *good*, for he enjoyed good relations with both God and man. יְדַעְיָה, *Jedaiah*, is derived from the word יְדִיעָה, *knowledge*, indicating his knowledge and understanding of the ways and wisdom of Hashem.

וּבָאתָ אַתָּה בַּיּוֹם הַהוּא וּבָאתָ בֵּית יֹאשִׁיָּה בֶן־צְפַנְיָה — *Come on that day; come to the house of Josiah son of Zephaniah.*

On the day of their arrival to the Land of Israel (*Abarbanel; Metzudos David*) you shall meet with them in the home of Josiah son of Zephaniah. *Abarbanel* postulates that this may be Zephaniah the prophet.

אֲשֶׁר בָּאוּ מִבָּבֶל — *Who have come from Babylonia.*

This refers to all four individuals mentioned in this verse. They have all come from Babylonia to the Holy Land (*Rashi; Radak*). Others contend that only the three mentioned at the beginning of the verse came at that time from Babylonia. Josiah, however, was already a resident of Jerusalem (*Ibn Ezra; Abarbanel*).

11. וְלָקַחְתָּ כֶסֶף־וְזָהָב וְעָשִׂיתָ עֲטָרוֹת — *And take silver and gold and make crowns.*

Take the silver and gold that these individuals brought with them from Babylonia and make two crowns (*Radak; Metzudos*), one of silver and one of gold (*Abarbanel; Metzudos*). Some explain that the עֲטָרוֹת were not actually crowns but were the windows of the Temple, which were rounded like crowns. Joshua the Kohen Gadol was to head the construction of these windows (*Mahari Kara*). Others explain that the עֲטָרוֹת were domes that were built above the Temple windows (*Tosafos — Gittin* 7a). Alternatively, these are the crowns that were later hung in the windows of the Temple — see *Middos* 3:8 (*Rashi* to v. 14).

וְשַׂמְתָּ בְּרֹאשׁ יְהוֹשֻׁעַ בֶּן־יְהוֹצָדָק הַכֹּהֵן הַגָּדוֹל — *And place [one of them] on the head of Joshua son of Jehozadak, the Kohen Gadol.*

Take one of the crowns and place it upon the head of Joshua son of Jehozadak (*Radak; Metzudos*), symbolizing his inauguration to the position of Kohen Gadol (*Ibn Ezra; Radak; Metzudos*). In all probability, it was the silver crown that was placed upon the

יב וְאָמַרְתָּ אֵלָיו לֵאמֹר כֹּה אָמַר יהוה צְבָאוֹת לֵאמֹר הִנֵּה־אִישׁ צֶמַח שְׁמוֹ וּמִתַּחְתָּיו יִצְמָח וּבָנָה אֶת־הֵיכַל יהוה: יג וְהוּא יִבְנֶה אֶת־הֵיכַל יהוה וְהוּא־יִשָּׂא הוֹד וְיָשַׁב וּמָשַׁל עַל־כִּסְאוֹ וְהָיָה כֹהֵן עַל־כִּסְאוֹ וַעֲצַת שָׁלוֹם תִּהְיֶה בֵּין שְׁנֵיהֶם: יד וְהָעֲטָרֹת תִּהְיֶה לְחֵלֶם וּלְטוֹבִיָּה וְלִידַעְיָה וּלְחֵן בֶּן־צְפַנְיָה לְזִכָּרוֹן בְּהֵיכַל יהוה:

head of the Kohen Gadol, for the golden crown had been set aside for a descendant of King David who will reign when the dynasty of the House of David will be reestablished (*Metzudos*). According to *Abarbanel*, both crowns were symbols of the monarchy. The silver one was placed upon the head of the Kohen Gadol to indicate that in the times of the Hasmoneans his descendants would assume the monarchy over the nation. However, since the monarchy was not rightfully theirs for it belonged to the tribe of Judah, the golden crown was not placed upon the head of Joshua (cf. *Ramban* to *Genesis* 48:10).

Some maintain that both crowns were placed upon the head of the Kohen Gadol (*Ibn Ezra; R' Eliezer of Beaugency*). Although one of the crowns represents royalty, royalty, too, is linked to the Kohen, since the king is anointed under his direction. Furthermore, the king receives his instructions concerning warfare and matters of state from the *Urim VeTumim*, the breastplate which was worn upon the chest of the Kohen Gadol (*R' Eliezer of Beaugency*).

12-15. The prophecy in this chapter concludes with the foretelling of the rebuilding of the Temple and the restoration of the authority of monarchy in Israel. The commentators disagree as to whether it refers to the building of the Second Temple and the establishment of the Jewish commonwealth under the leadership of Zerubbabel or to the restoration of the full glory of the Kingdom of Israel that will occur in the time of the Messiah.

12. וְאָמַרְתָּ אֵלָיו לֵאמֹר כֹּה אָמַר ה׳ צְבָאוֹת לֵאמֹר הִנֵּה־אִישׁ צֶמַח שְׁמוֹ — *You shall speak to him, saying, "So said Hashem, Master of Legions, saying: Behold, there is a man, his name is Zemah.*

[Upon placing the crown on the head of Joshua you shall say to him] (see *Ibn Ezra*), "Behold, Zerubbabel shall stand together with you to lead the nation, and he shall be called Zemah, the flourishing one, for his honor and stature shall grow little by little until he shall attain great heights of glory (*Rashi; Radak;* cf. *Ibn Ezra; Mahari Kara;* see also above 3:8; *Haggai* 2:23). Upon his head shall be placed the second crown, which is reserved for the monarchy of Israel. Although he is now merely a governor, he shall eventually attain the stature of royalty" (*Radak* to v. 11; cf. *Mahari Kara* to v. 13). *Abarbanel* (v. 9) strongly disagrees with *Radak* and notes that there is no record whatsoever of Zerubbabel having ruled over the Judean commonwealth after the Temple was built. He maintains that, in fact, after having built the Temple, Zerubbabel returned to Babylonia where he remained until his death (cf. comm. to *Haggai* 2:23).

Targum Yonasan interprets this verse as referring to the Messianic king and renders: *Behold a man whose name is the Messiah shall be revealed in the future and he shall become great and build the Temple of Hashem.*

Others see the verse as alluding both to Zerubbabel and to the Messiah. Although

[12]You shall speak to him, saying, "So said HASHEM, Master of Legions, saying: Behold, there is a man, his name is Zemah, and he will flourish in his place; he will build the Sanctuary of HASHEM. [13]He will build the Sanctuary of HASHEM; he will bear majesty and he will sit and rule upon his throne. The Kohen will be upon his own throne and there will be a disposition of peace between the two of them. [14]The crowns will be a remembrance for Helem, for Tobijah, for Jedaiah and for Hen son of Zephaniah in the Sanctuary of HASHEM.'

Zerubbabel was the leader of the Jewish people at that time, he was not given the golden crown designated for the monarchy because he was yet only a shoot in the process of growing. He was merely a satrap under Persian rule. However, from among his descendants an individual will rise and sprout who will attain the full glory of the Kingdom of Israel and upon his head alone shall be placed the golden crown. Nevertheless, since this greatness will come through Zerubbabel he shall merit building the sanctuary of Hashem at this time (*Abarbanel;* cf. *Malbim; Metzudos*), signifying that it will be his descendant who will build the Third Temple at the time of the final redemption (*Metzudos*).

וּמִתַּחְתָּיו יִצְמָח — *And he will flourish in his place.*

He shall sprout from the seed of the Davidic dynasty (*Rashi; Mahari Kara*). Alternatively: From the city of Jerusalem where he lives he shall achieve this greatness (*Radak*). *R' Eliezer of Beaugency* sees this phrase as evidence that the person under discussion was already born but had been demeaned and demoted from his proper stature. Thus the prophet states that he will be raised from his degradation and restored to his appropriate heights of glory.

13. וְהוּא יִבְנֶה אֶת־הֵיכַל ה׳ וְהוּא־יִשָּׂא הוֹד וְיָשַׁב וּמָשַׁל עַל־כִּסְאוֹ — *He will build the Sanctuary of Hashem; he will bear majesty and he will sit and rule upon his throne.*

Zerubbabel shall rebuild the Temple (*Radak*) and assume the majesty of his sovereignty (*Rashi; Radak*). With the royal crown placed upon his head (*Mahari Kara*) he shall sit upon the throne, ruling over the nation (*Radak*). According to *Metzudos* who maintains that this prophecy alludes to the Messianic king, the verse is to be understood as follows: The descendant of Zerubbabel who will be the Messiah will build the Temple at that time and sit upon his throne with the crown of glory upon his head.

וְהָיָה כֹהֵן עַל־כִּסְאוֹ וַעֲצַת שָׁלוֹם תִּהְיֶה בֵּין שְׁנֵיהֶם — *The Kohen will be upon his own throne and there will be a disposition of peace between the two of them.*

Joshua the Kohen Gadol will sit on his own throne, the exalted seat of the high priesthood (*Rashi; Mahari Kara*). Indeed, the two will carry out their roles in perfect harmony, with no dissension or jealousy between them (*Rashi; Mahari Kara; Ibn Ezra; Radak*), and they will confer together on all major issues and policies, standing united behind all decisions (*Radak*). In an alternative explanation, *Radak* renders: *And the Kohen shall be before his throne* — the Kohen Gadol shall come before the king to advise him and guide him in carrying out the will of G-d.

14. וְהָעֲטָרֹת תִּהְיֶה לְחֵלֶם וּלְטוֹבִיָּה וְלִידַעְיָה וּלְחֵן בֶּן־צְפַנְיָה לְזִכָּרוֹן בְּהֵיכַל ה׳ — *The crowns will be a remembrance for Helem, for Tobijah, for Jedaiah and for Hen son of Zephaniah in the Sanctuary of Hashem.'*

טו וּרְחוֹקִים | יָבֹאוּ וּבָנוּ בְּהֵיכַל יהוה וִידַעְתֶּם
כִּי־יהוה צְבָאוֹת שְׁלָחַנִי אֲלֵיכֶם וְהָיָה אִם־
שָׁמוֹעַ תִּשְׁמְעוּן בְּקוֹל יהוה אֱלֹהֵיכֶם׃

א וַיְהִי
בִּשְׁנַת אַרְבַּע לְדָרְיָוֶשׁ הַמֶּלֶךְ הָיָה דְבַר־יהוה
אֶל־זְכַרְיָה בְּאַרְבָּעָה לַחֹדֶשׁ הַתְּשִׁעִי בְּכִסְלֵו׃
ב וַיִּשְׁלַח בֵּית־אֵל שַׂרְאֶצֶר וְרֶגֶם מֶלֶךְ וַאֲנָשָׁיו
לְחַלּוֹת אֶת־פְּנֵי יהוה׃ ג לֵאמֹר אֶל־הַכֹּהֲנִים
אֲשֶׁר לְבֵית־יהוה צְבָאוֹת וְאֶל־הַנְּבִיאִים

After being placed upon the heads of Joshua the Kohen Gadol and Zerubbabel (*Radak;* see comm. to v. 11), the crowns shall be hung in the windows at the top of the sanctuary (*Rashi* from *Middos* 3:8). Golden chains were fastened to the ceiling of the Temple, and the young Kohanim would climb up and view the crowns in the windows (*Middos* ibid.). This will serve as a memorial to the generosity of Helem,[1] Tobijah, Jedaiah and Hen,[1] who donated the gold and silver for the crowns. Thus their gift will stand forever before "the eyes of Hashem" and evoke His beneficence upon them. Alternatively: They will thereby be remembered by future generations, for their names will be carved on the crowns (*Radak*). *R' Eliezer of Beaugency* interprets: The crowns will serve as a remembrance for the Jews still in exile, so that no one would be able to deny them their share in the Holy Temple.

15. וּרְחוֹקִים יָבֹאוּ וּבָנוּ בְּהֵיכַל ה' וִידַעְתֶּם כִּי־ה' צְבָאוֹת שְׁלָחַנִי אֲלֵיכֶם — *People will come from far away and build the Sanctuary of Hashem and then you will know that Hashem, Master of Legions, has sent me to you.*

The Children of Israel shall come from their distant dwellings in exile to participate in the rebuilding of the Sanctuary (*Mahari Kara; Ibn Ezra*). Alternatively: The gentiles shall come from their distant lands to assist in the building of the Sanctuary and to offer materials for its construction. This actually occurred in the days of King Herod, when the entire Temple was reconstructed (*Radak*).

וְהָיָה אִם־שָׁמוֹעַ תִּשְׁמְעוּן בְּקוֹל ה' אֱלֹהֵיכֶם — *This will happen if you will truly listen to the voice of Hashem your God.*

All of this shall come to pass only if you will hearken to the voice of Hashem your God (*Rashi; Radak*).

Others see this verse, too, as describing the building of the final Temple: At that time, the dispersed of Israel will come from across the entire globe to assist and participate in its construction. If you will truly hearken to the words of Hashem and return to his ways wholeheartedly, this will take place during this era — indeed during your own lifetime (*Metzudos*).

VII

The present chapter finds Zechariah prophetically reviewing the events that led to the destruction of the First Temple. This prophecy was prompted by a question asked by the princes of Judah who remained in Babylonia and did not ascend to Jerusalem with the others. They wanted to know if they should continue to observe the fast days that had been established to commemorate the destruction.

1. Helem is the same individual as Heldai in verse 10 (*Rashi*) and Hen is another name for Josiah (*Radak; Ibn Ezra*).

6/15 [15] *People will come from far away and build the Sanctuary of* HASHEM *and then you will know that* HASHEM, *Master of Legions, has sent me to you. This will happen if you will truly listen to the voice of* HASHEM *your God."*

7/1-3 [1] *It happened in the fourth year of King Darius [that] the word of* HASHEM *came to Zechariah on the fourth day of the ninth month, in Kislev.* [2] *Sarezer, as well as Regem-melech and his men, had sent [a message] to Beth-el to beseech* HASHEM, [3] *[and] to speak [their question] to the Kohanim of the Temple of* HASHEM, *Master of Legions, and to the prophets,*

1. וַיְהִי בִּשְׁנַת אַרְבַּע לְדָרְיָוֶשׁ הַמֶּלֶךְ הָיָה דְבַר־ה׳ אֶל־זְכַרְיָה בְּאַרְבָּעָה לַחֹדֶשׁ הַתְּשִׁעִי בְּכִסְלֵו — *It happened in the fourth year of King Darius [that] the word of Hashem came to Zechariah on the fourth day of the ninth month, in Kislev.*

While the Temple was being rebuilt (*Ibn Ezra*) [which began in the second year of Darius' reign (see *Haggai* 1:14, 15)], Zechariah received a prophecy from G-d. This is the prophecy recounted below (vs. 4-9), following the description of the events that precipitated it (*Metzudos*).

Malbim notes that this was the first prophecy Zechariah received since those that he had received during the second year of Darius' reign.

2. וַיִּשְׁלַח בֵּית־אֵל שַׂרְאֶצֶר וְרֶגֶם מֶלֶךְ וַאֲנָשָׁיו לְחַלּוֹת אֶת־פְּנֵי ה׳ — *Sarezer, as well as Regem-melech and his men, had sent [a message] to Beth-el to beseech Hashem.*

Sarezer, Regem-melech and his associates were righteous men who resided in Babylonia. They sent a message to their relatives who resided in the city of Beth-el beseeching them to go to Jerusalem on their behalf. The purpose of this mission was twofold: to pray to God on their behalf; and to ask the Kohanim to resolve an uncertainty of the Babylonians [see next verse] (*Rashi*). Some explain that Beth-el is referring to the House of G-d, the Holy Temple in Jerusalem. The Babylonian Jews sent these men to pray at the Temple and beseech God to bestow His prophetic spirit upon the Kohanim and prophets so that they may find a reply to their question (*Metzudos*). Others contend that Beth-el was the name of one of the leaders of Babylonia (*Ibn Ezra; R' Eliezer of Beaugency*).

3. לֵאמֹר אֶל־הַכֹּהֲנִים אֲשֶׁר לְבֵית־ה׳ צְבָאוֹת — *[And] to speak [their question] to the Kohanim of the Temple of Hashem, Master of Legions.*

These emissaries were sent to seek guidance from the Kohanim who were to be found in the Temple and who were designated to convey the rulings of the Torah to the people (*R' Eliezer of Beaugency;* see *Deut.* 17:9).

וְאֶל־הַנְּבִיאִים — *And to the prophets.* The emissaries were also to ask Haggai, Zechariah and Malachi, the prophets of G-d for their guidance (*Radak; Metzudos*). *Targum* understands וְאֶל הַנְּבִיאִים as referring to the סַפְרַיָּא, the Torah Sages.

לֵאמֹר הַאֶבְכֶּה בַּחֹדֶשׁ הַחֲמִשִׁי הִנָּזֵר כַּאֲשֶׁר
ד עָשִׂיתִי זֶה כַּמֶּה שָׁנִים: וַיְהִי
ה דְּבַר־יהוה צְבָאוֹת אֵלַי לֵאמֹר: אֱמֹר אֶל־כָּל־
עַם הָאָרֶץ וְאֶל־הַכֹּהֲנִים לֵאמֹר כִּי־צַמְתֶּם
וְסָפוֹד בַּחֲמִישִׁי וּבַשְּׁבִיעִי וְזֶה שִׁבְעִים שָׁנָה

הַאֶבְכֶּה בַּחֹדֶשׁ הַחֲמִשִׁי הִנָּזֵר כַּאֲשֶׁר עָשִׂיתִי זֶה כַּמֶּה שָׁנִים — *"Should I weep in the fifth month, abstaining [from pleasures] as I have done these many years?"*

Now that the Holy Temple is in the process of being rebuilt, should we continue to mourn over the destruction of the original Temple that had been destroyed during the month of Av? Shall we continue to abstain from those pleasures prohibited by the mourning of that day of destruction, just as we have been doing during the seventy years of exile? (*Rashi*). Shall we continue to weep and fast on the ninth day of Av?[1] (*Mahari Kara; R' Eliezer of Beaugency; Metzudos*).

The question of the emissaries included the three[2] other fasts that commemorate related tragedies that occurred during the time of the destruction and exile but only the day of the worst tragedy is mentioned (*Metzudos*).

Alternatively, the people of Babylonia inquired regarding the fast of the ninth of Av, but not about the other three fast days. Unlike the fast of the ninth of Av that was instituted to commemorate the destruction of the Temple and the city of Jerusalem, these fast days commemorate the conquest of the Jewish people and their exile from the Land. The renewal of the Jewish Commonwealth in Eretz Yisrael, although inferior to that which was during the days of the First Temple, obviated the need for these lesser days of mourning (*Abarbanel*).

Radak explains that the Jews of Babylon were not convinced that the efforts to rebuild the Temple would prevail against the evil designs of their enemies. Indeed, it was for this reason that they hesitated to join their brethren who had migrated from Babylonia to the Holy Land.

Abarbanel [followed by *Metzudos*] explains that the Babylonian Jews did not realize the importance and significance of the rebuilding of the Temple and therefore raised their question of fasting and mourning on the ninth of Av. This was due to seven factors: First, they knew that the Divine Presence would not reside in this Temple as it had in the first. Second, they feared that the community in Israel would not last, and would again be driven out by the Persian government in just a matter of days. Third, there was no significant ingathering of the exiles for it was only the Jews of Babylon who returned to Israel, restricted [primarily] to the exiles of the Kingdom of Judah. Those of the Ten Tribes of Israel did not return with them. Fourth, the land no longer gave forth its fruits as it had in the past. This was seen as a sign that the unique level of Divine Providence that was previously prevalent in the Holy Land was not to be restored. Fifth, the Jewish people living there were still despised

1. *Ibn Ezra* maintains that unlike the Second Temple that was destroyed on the ninth of Av, the First Temple was actually destroyed on the tenth of Av. The Talmud (*Taanis* 29a), however, states that both Temples were actually destroyed on the ninth of Av.

2. The three other fast days are:

A. The fast of the tenth of Teves at which time Nebuchadnezzar king of Babylonia besieged Jerusalem (see *II Kings* 25:1).

B. The fast of the seventeenth of Tamuz which commemorates the breaching of the walls of Jerusalem prior to the destruction of the Temple (see *Jeremiah* 52:6,7 and explanation of *Tos. Rosh Hashanah* 18b).

C. The fast of Gedaliah, on the third of Tishrei when Gedaliah ben Ahikam, governor of the Jewish community after the destruction, was assassinated (see *Jeremiah* 41:2).

saying, "Should I weep in the fifth month, abstaining [from pleasures] as I have done these many years?"

[4] So the word of HASHEM, Master of Legions, came to me, saying:

[5] Speak to all the people of the land and to the Kohanim, saying, "When you fasted and lamented in the fifth [month] and in the seventh for these seventy years,

and threatened by the other nations, indicating that the time for their redemption had not yet arrived. Sixth, the Cuthites and other nations still held the majority of the Land of Israel. The Jewish people, who numbered a mere forty thousand (see *Ezra* 2:60), were clearly only a small minority in their own land. Finally, no king from the House of David had arisen to lead the nation. This was ample evidence that the redemption was not at hand.[1]

4. וַיְהִי דְּבַר־ה׳ צְבָאוֹת אֵלַי לֵאמֹר — *So the word of Hashem, Master of Legions, came to me, saying.*

The Kohanim were unable to respond to this question, and it therefore fell to Zechariah to provide the answer by means of prophecy (*Ibn Ezra*). This is the prophecy alluded to in the first verse of this chapter (*Metzudos*).

5. אֱמֹר אֶל־כָּל־עַם הָאָרֶץ — *Speak to all the people of the land.*

Convey this prophecy to all of the Jewish people, those in Jerusalem as well as those in Babylonia (*Ibn Ezra*). Others contend that this prophecy was directed only to the people dwelling in the Holy Land; those who had refused to ascend were shunned by the Almighty and received no direct response (*Abarbanel; Metzudos*).

וְאֶל־הַכֹּהֲנִים — *And to the Kohanim.* Direct this prophecy to the Kohanim as well, since they were unable to respond to the question (*Ibn Ezra*).

כִּי־צַמְתֶּם וְסָפוֹד בַּחֲמִישִׁי וּבַשְּׁבִיעִי — *When you fasted and lamented in the fifth [month] and in the seventh.*

The fifth [month] is referring to the fast of the ninth of Av and the seventh [month] is referring to the Fast of Gedaliah which is in the month of Tishrei (*Rashi*, et al.).

Although there are four fast days that had been proclaimed to commemorate the destruction of the Temple and its related tragedies (see v. 3 fn. 2), only these two are mentioned by the prophet because of their distinct status. The ninth of Av was the actual day of the destruction of the Holy Temple and had therefore been designated as a day of fasting and mourning. The Fast of Gedaliah actually commemorates the culmination of that destruction. For after Gedaliah was assassinated, the poor who had remained in the land as vinedressers and farmers, and worked the land preventing its total devastation, were finally driven out (*Radak*).

Abarbanel sees this as a response to the emissaries who had made a distinction between the ninth of Av and the other three fast days. Zechariah is told to inform the people that the Fast of Gedaliah must be viewed on a par with the ninth of Av, since it, too, commemorates the destruction of the Jewish settlement in the land. *Metzudos* adds that he wished to impress upon them the concept stated by the Sages (*Rosh Hashanah* 18b) that the death of the righteous is comparable to the destruction of the Temple.

וְזֶה שִׁבְעִים שָׁנָה — *For these seventy years.*

Actually, it had been seventy-two years since the destruction of the Temple, for the seventy years of exile

1. [This follows *Abarbanel's* view that Zerubbabel never achieved the status of king, for he left Eretz Yisrael soon after the Temple had been rebuilt (see comm. to 6:13).]

ו הֲצ֖וֹם צַמְתֻּ֣נִי אָ֑נִי׃ וְכִ֤י תֹֽאכְלוּ֙ וְכִ֣י תִשְׁתּ֔וּ הֲל֤וֹא אַתֶּם֙ הָאֹ֣כְלִ֔ים וְאַתֶּ֖ם הַשֹּׁתִֽים׃
ז הֲל֣וֹא אֶת־הַדְּבָרִ֗ים אֲשֶׁ֨ר קָרָ֤א יְהוָה֙ בְּיַ֙ד הַנְּבִיאִ֣ים הָרִאשֹׁנִ֔ים בִּהְי֤וֹת יְרוּשָׁלַ֙ם֙ יֹשֶׁ֣בֶת וּשְׁלֵוָ֔ה וְעָרֶ֖יהָ סְבִיבֹתֶ֑יהָ וְהַנֶּ֥גֶב וְהַשְּׁפֵלָ֖ה יֹשֵֽׁב׃
ח וַֽיְהִי֙ דְּבַר־יְהוָ֔ה אֶל־זְכַרְיָ֖ה לֵאמֹֽר׃
ט כֹּ֥ה אָמַ֛ר יְהוָ֥ה צְבָא֖וֹת לֵאמֹ֑ר מִשְׁפַּ֤ט אֱמֶת֙ שְׁפֹ֔טוּ וְחֶ֣סֶד וְרַחֲמִ֔ים עֲשׂ֖וּ אִ֥ישׁ אֶת־אָחִֽיו׃
י וְאַלְמָנָ֧ה וְיָת֛וֹם גֵּ֥ר וְעָנִ֖י אַֽל־תַּעֲשֹׁ֑קוּ וְרָעַת֙ אִ֣ישׁ אָחִ֔יו אַֽל־תַּחְשְׁב֖וּ בִּלְבַבְכֶֽם׃

ended during the second year of Darius' reign (see preface to *Haggai* 1:1), and this prophecy took place during the fourth year of his reign, one full year plus some portion of another. Nevertheless, the prophet uses the approximate number of seventy (*Ibn Ezra*).

הֲצוֹם צַמְתֻּנִי אָנִי — *Was the fasting that you fasted for My honor? [Was it] for Me?*

The "ה" of הֲצוֹם is vowelized with a חֲטַף פַּתַח because it denotes that a question is being asked. It is the "ה" הַשְּׁאֵלָה, the interrogative "ה" (*Rashi*). God replies that it really doesn't matter to Him whether the people continue to fast and mourn or whether they don't. He points out that the fasting that had been observed by the people since the destruction of the First Temple had not been for His honor and therefore has no more meaning to Him than their eating and drinking [as put forth in the next verse] (*Targum Yonasan; Rashi*).

Others render הֲצוֹם צַמְתֻּנִי, *Is it for My sake that you fast?* אָנִי — *Did I [command you to do so]?* Zechariah is told to inform the people that their fasting is a result of their sins, which brought about the destruction of the Temple and their exile from the land. If the people would only pursue righteousness and justice there would be no need for them to fast, for the Temple would be rebuilt and they would all return to their land. Thus, it is really for their own sins that they fast, just as it is for their own benefit and pleasure that they eat and drink; neither is done for the sake of My honor (*Radak;* cf. *Mahari Kara*).

7. הֲלוֹא אֶת־הַדְּבָרִים אֲשֶׁר קָרָא ה׳ בְּיַד הַנְּבִאִים הָרִאשׁוֹנִים — *Are these not the words that Hashem pronounced through the earliest prophets ...?*

God emphasizes that their fasting and mourning came about only because the people did not heed the words of warning and rebuke that He sent them through His prophets (*Rashi*).

בִּהְיוֹת יְרוּשָׁלַםִ ... — *When Jerusalem ...*

God sent the prophets to rebuke and warn His people when peace and tranquility reigned throughout the entire land (*Radak*). But because the people spurned God's admonition and continued to sin, the land was destroyed and its people were banished from their homes (*Mahari Kara; Radak*). *Malbim* adds: If this was sufficient cause to bring about the destruction of the people of Israel while they still lived in peace, it will certainly prevent the restoration of

was the fasting that you fasted for My honor? [Was it] for Me? [6] *And when you eat and when you drink, is it not you who are the eaters and you who are the drinkers?* [7] *Are these not the words that* HASHEM *pronounced through the earliest prophets, when Jerusalem and its surrounding cities were settled and peaceful, and the south and the lowlands were settled?"*

[8] *The word of* HASHEM *came to Zechariah, saying:* [9] *So said* HASHEM, *Master of Legions, saying: "Judge with truthful justice, and perform kindness and mercy towards one another.* [10] *Do not oppress the widow and the orphan, the stranger and the poor, and do not think in your hearts of wronging one another."*

their former tranquility if they do not mend their ways.

Others follow a different approach to these three verses: What God desires from His nation is to follow in His ways and to emulate the characteristics evidenced through His dealings with His people. Thus, it is not their fasting and mourning that He seeks but rather their adherence to the ways of righteousness and justice. Is fasting an emulation of God's ways? Does God fast or eat and drink that your doing so should resemble His actions and thereby fulfill His wishes? These are not the paths God seeks. His desire is that His people follow in the ways that were taught by His prophets, when Israel yet dwelled securely in the Holy Land (*Abarbanel*).

8. וַיְהִי דְּבַר־ה׳ אֶל־זְכַרְיָה לֵאמֹר — *The word of Hashem came to Zechariah, saying.*

Although this introductory clause generally marks the beginning of a topic, the verses that follow reiterate God's words of rebuke that were addressed to an earlier generation. Zechariah is told to repeat these messages to his generation (*Rashi; Radak*). *Alshich* adds: Just as the previous generation was rebuked in this manner by the earlier prophets, so, too, is the nation now admonished through the prophecies of Zechariah.

9. כֹּה אָמַר ה׳ צְבָאוֹת לֵאמֹר — *So said Hashem, Master of Legions, saying.* So did Hashem speak to the earlier prophets to say to you (*Metzudos*). When judging cases between two litigants, you must always execute true justice and at times, you must extend yourselves beyond the letter of the law with acts of benevolence and mercy (*Radak*). Only then will God execute justice against your enemies and bestow upon you His Divine benevolence and mercy (*Malbim*).

10. וְאַלְמָנָה וְיָתוֹם גֵּר וְעָנִי אַל־תַּעֲשֹׁקוּ ... — *Do not oppress the widow and the orphan, the stranger and the poor...*

Make certain never to oppress the weak and downtrodden among you, neither in monetary matters nor with words of cruelty. Be careful, as well, never even to consider wronging one another. Such thoughts are forbidden in and of themselves (see *Lev.* 19:17), aside from the evil deeds to which they tend to lead (*Radak*).

יא וַיְמָאֲנוּ לְהַקְשִׁיב וַיִּתְּנוּ כָתֵף סֹרָרֶת וְאָזְנֵיהֶם הִכְבִּידוּ מִשְּׁמוֹעַ: יב וְלִבָּם שָׂמוּ שָׁמִיר מִשְּׁמוֹעַ אֶת־הַתּוֹרָה וְאֶת־הַדְּבָרִים אֲשֶׁר שָׁלַח יהוה צְבָאוֹת בְּרוּחוֹ בְּיַד הַנְּבִיאִים הָרִאשֹׁנִים וַיְהִי קֶצֶף גָּדוֹל מֵאֵת יהוה צְבָאוֹת: יג וַיְהִי כַאֲשֶׁר־קָרָא וְלֹא שָׁמֵעוּ כֵּן יִקְרְאוּ וְלֹא אֶשְׁמָע אָמַר יהוה צְבָאוֹת: יד וְאֵסָעֲרֵם עַל כָּל־הַגּוֹיִם אֲשֶׁר לֹא־יְדָעוּם וְהָאָרֶץ נָשַׁמָּה אַחֲרֵיהֶם מֵעֹבֵר וּמִשָּׁב וַיָּשִׂימוּ אֶרֶץ־חֶמְדָּה לְשַׁמָּה:

11. וַיְמָאֲנוּ לְהַקְשִׁיב וַיִּתְּנוּ כָתֵף סֹרָרֶת וְאָזְנֵיהֶם הִכְבִּידוּ מִשְּׁמוֹעַ — *But they refused to heed and they turned a rebellious shoulder and made their ears hard of hearing.*

Your forefathers of that generation did not heed the rebuke of the prophets but instead, defiantly turned away from them. Indeed, they presented the prophets with only their turned shoulder, refusing even to listen to their words (*Ibn Ezra; Mahari Kara; Radak*).

12. וְלִבָּם שָׂמוּ שָׁמִיר — *They made their hearts [like a] shamir.*

The *shamir* is described by *Ezekiel* (3:9) as *stronger than flint. Ibn Ezra* and *Radak* say that it is a very hard type of stone. *Metzudos* translates *shamir* as *hard iron* and *Rashi* explains that it is a special worm that had the ability to split stones. This worm was used by Moses to engrave the stones of the *ephod* of the Kohen Gadol and King Solomon employed it for cutting the stones of the Temple since they may not be cut with any metal tool — see *Gittin* 68. All three of these views are cited by *Rashi* in his commentary to *Ezekiel* (ad loc.). In any event, the prophet is metaphorically describing the stubbornness of the people. They made their hearts so hard that the teachings of the Torah and the messages of prophetic rebuke could not penetrate their hearts (*Ibn Ezra; Radak*). As a result, God's rage was provoked against them (*Mahari Kara; Metzudos*). Alternatively, *Abarbanel* renders שָׁמִיר to mean *a guard*, from the word שׁוֹמֵר. They guarded their hearts against being moved to heed the words of the Torah and the prophets.

אֲשֶׁר שָׁלַח ה׳ צְבָאוֹת בְּרוּחוֹ — *That Hashem, Master of Legions, sent by His spirit.*

This is the spirit of prophecy that would come to the prophet (*Radak*). Alternatively, *His spirit* is referring to the angels through whom God conveyed His words to the prophets (*Metzudos*).

13. וַיְהִי כַאֲשֶׁר־קָרָא וְלֹא שָׁמֵעוּ כֵּן יִקְרְאוּ וְלֹא אֶשְׁמָע אָמַר ה׳ צְבָאוֹת — *And it happened that just as He called but they did not listen, so will they call out and I will not listen, said Hashem, Master of Legions.*

This verse is problematic as it changes from third person [קָרָא — *He called*] to first person [וְלֹא אֶשְׁמָע — *I will not listen*]. According to *Rashi*, the prophet is speaking and declaring, "Just as it was that G-d called to them but they did not listen, so too, did G-d say at that time, 'When they will call to Me, I will not listen

7/11-14

[11]*But they refused to heed and they turned a rebellious shoulder and made their ears hard of hearing.* [12]*They made their hearts [like a] shamir, rather than hear the teaching and the words that* HASHEM, *Master of Legions, sent by His spirit through the earliest prophets, and there was a great rage from* HASHEM, *Master of Legions.* [13]*And it happened that just as He called but they did not listen, 'So will they call out and I will not listen, said* HASHEM, *Master of Legions;* [14]*'and I will cause them to be storm tossed among all the nations that they did not know.' After that the land became deserted from any who come and go; they made an exquisite land into a desolation.*

to them.'" The other commentators don't seem to address this problem. *Mahari Kara* renders: Just as they did not heed the word of G-d when He called to them to repent while they still dwelled in their land, so shall He deal with them when they cry out to Him in their exile. Others understand that God is the speaker of the entire verse: Just as My prophets called to them in My name but they did not hear, etc. (*Targum; Radak*).

14. וְאֵסָעֲרֵם עַל כָּל־הַגּוֹיִם אֲשֶׁר לֹא־יְדָעוּם ... — *And I will cause them to be storm tossed among all the nations that they did not know ...*

This is a continuation of the prophecy that was foretold by the earlier prophets (*Rashi; Metzudos Dovid*). God said He would scatter them forcefully across the globe and exile them to the lands of foreign nations with whom they were not even familiar (*Rashi*).

Radak is puzzled by the contradictory grammatical form of the word וְאֵסָעֲרֵם. If Scripture would have written וְאֵסָעֵר, it would mean *and I will be a storm* or *I will be scattered by storm*. If it would have written וְאֶסְעָרֵם, it would mean *and I will scatter them by storm. Ibn Ezra* therefore interprets וְאֵסָעֲרֵם as a combined word having a dual connotation: I will *storm them* with the tempest of My spirit, which will *disperse* them among all the nations. *Radak* cites his father as interpreting: *And I will be scattered with them* [i.e., the Almighty will join them in their exile (cf. *Deut.* 30:3, *Rashi* ad loc.)].

וַיָּשִׂימוּ אֶרֶץ־חֶמְדָּה לְשַׁמָּה — *They made an exquisite land into a desolation.*

Thus, declares the Almighty [to the generation of Zechariah]: The people who lived at that time were themselves responsible for the destruction of the land, for it was their sin that brought about its desolation. And this is the reason for their fasting and mourning, not My desire that they do so (*Rashi; Metzudos;* cf. comm. to v. 6).

Others say that the subject of this phrase is the nations who conquered the land and exiled the Jewish people: They utterly destroyed and laid waste the once-desirable land (*Mahari Kara; Alshich*).

וַיְהִי דְּבַר־יהוה צְבָאוֹת לֵאמֹר׃ כֹּה אָמַר יהוה צְבָאוֹת קִנֵּאתִי לְצִיּוֹן קִנְאָה גְדוֹלָה
ג וְחֵמָה גְדוֹלָה קִנֵּאתִי לָהּ׃ כֹּה אָמַר יהוה שַׁבְתִּי אֶל־צִיּוֹן וְשָׁכַנְתִּי בְּתוֹךְ יְרוּשָׁלָםִ וְנִקְרְאָה יְרוּשָׁלַםִ עִיר הָאֱמֶת וְהַר־יהוה צְבָאוֹת הַר
ד הַקֹּדֶשׁ׃ כֹּה אָמַר יהוה צְבָאוֹת עֹד יֵשְׁבוּ זְקֵנִים וּזְקֵנוֹת בִּרְחֹבוֹת יְרוּשָׁלָםִ וְאִישׁ
ה מִשְׁעַנְתּוֹ בְּיָדוֹ מֵרֹב יָמִים׃ וּרְחֹבוֹת הָעִיר יִמָּלְאוּ יְלָדִים וִילָדוֹת מְשַׂחֲקִים בִּרְחֹבֹתֶיהָ׃

VIII

1. וַיְהִי דְּבַר־ה׳ צְבָאוֹת לֵאמֹר — *The word of Hashem, Master of Legions, came [to me] saying:*

Because Zechariah had described the Land of Israel as a desolation (see 7:14) (*Ibn Ezra*) and had admonished the nation for ignoring the exhortations of the prophets (*Malbim*), he now comforts them (*Ibn Ezra*) and informs them that if they will rectify their deeds and will execute true justice and righteousness, then God's Divine Presence will dwell in the new Temple as it had dwelt in the First Temple (*Malbim*). Alternatively, these words of comfort are foretelling events that will occur in Messianic times. God will then defend Jerusalem from the armies of Gog and Magog, whom He will destroy with great vengeance and fury (*Radak*).

Radak notes that the word אֵלַי, *to me*, has been omitted from the text of the verse but is understood from its context. *Minchas Shai* records that some ancient manuscripts do indeed include the word אֵלַי as part of the text.

2. כֹּה אָמַר ה׳ צְבָאוֹת קִנֵּאתִי לְצִיּוֹן קִנְאָה גְּדוֹלָה — *Thus said Hashem, Master of Legions: I have become vengeful for Zion, a great vengeance.*

God expresses His great love for His people and declares that His vengeance is upon the nations (*Rashi*) because of the suffering that they caused His beloved Zion (*Metzudos*). Then, when this prophecy will be fulfilled, you will no longer have reason to fast and mourn for the fast days will be transformed into occasions of *joy and gladness and happy festivals* (see v. 8:19) (*Rashi*). Alternatively, this prophecy is referring to Messianic times. When Gog and Magog will rise against Jerusalem, God will defend His Holy City and with great fury destroy all the nations who gathered to destroy her (*Radak*).

וְחֵמָה גְדוֹלָה קִנֵּאתִי לָהּ — *And with great fury have I become vengeful for her.*

The word לָהּ means on her behalf — *for her* [and not *to her*] (*Rashi*). חֵמָה is an anger which is contained. It is an inner resentment, a wrath that boils inside (*R' Hirsch, Genesis* 49:7; *Psalms* 37:8). [God will allow this wrath to burst forth with great fury on behalf of His people and His Holy City.]

3. שַׁבְתִּי אֶל־צִיּוֹן ... — *I have returned to Zion ...*

The prophecy continues: Just as God has already returned the exiles to Zion, so too, will He have His Divine Presence dwell in the midst of Jerusalem if the people will continue to hearken to His voice (*Abarbanel*).

וְנִקְרְאָה יְרוּשָׁלַםִ עִיר הָאֱמֶת — *Jerusalem will be called "The City of Truth."*

[1] *The word of HASHEM, Master of Legions, came [to me] saying:*

[2] *Thus said HASHEM, Master of Legions: I have become vengeful for Zion, a great vengeance; and with great fury have I become vengeful for her.* [3] *Thus said HASHEM: I have returned to Zion, and I have made My dwelling in the midst of Jerusalem; Jerusalem will be called "The City of Truth" and the mountain of HASHEM, Master of Legions, "The Holy Mountain."*

[4] *Thus said HASHEM, Master of Legions: Old men and old women shall yet sit in the streets of Jerusalem, each with his staff in his hand because of advanced age;* [5] *and the streets of the city will be filled with boys and girls playing in its streets.*

At that time Jerusalem will be called "The City of Truth" for it will be inhabited by people who seek to do the truth (*Metzudos*). Alternatively, it is not only the city of Jerusalem that will be called "The City of Truth" but all the cities of the Land of Israel for God promised that *the remnant of Israel will not commit corruption, they will not speak falsehood and a deceitful tongue will not be found in their mouths* (*Zephaniah* 3:13). Only Jerusalem is mentioned because it is the capital city (*Radak*).

וְהַר־ה׳ צְבָאוֹת הַר הַקֹּדֶשׁ — *And the mountain of Hashem, Master of Legions, "The Holy Mountain."*

The Temple site will then be called "The Holy Mountain" because the Divine Presence will once again reside in the Temple (*Metzudos*).

4. כֹּה אָמַר ה׳ צְבָאוֹת עֹד יֵשְׁבוּ זְקֵנִים וּזְקֵנוֹת בִּרְחֹבוֹת יְרוּשָׁלָםִ... — *Thus said Hashem, Master of Legions: Old men and old women shall yet sit in the streets of Jerusalem ...*

The streets of Jerusalem will be filled with many old people because all who will dwell there will be blessed with longevity (*Ibn Ezra*). Alternatively, this is referring to Messianic times. Normally, the young people sit in the streets and the old people who are frail and debilitated are confined to their homes but in Messianic times, people will no longer become weak in their old age and will sit in the streets as do the young (*Metzudos*).

מִשְׁעַנְתּוֹ בְּיָדוֹ... — *Each with his staff in his hand ...*

Since they are old, they will each need their staff for support (*Rashi*). But they will not be confined to their homes (*Metzudos*). *Targum Yonasan*, however, understands this phrase metaphorically: The good deeds [תַקְנַיָא] that the people have done will protect them during their old age.

5. וּרְחֹבוֹת הָעִיר יִמָּלְאוּ יְלָדִים וִילָדוֹת מְשַׂחֲקִים בִּרְחֹבֹתֶיהָ — *And the streets of the city will be filled with boys and girls playing in its streets.*

The population of the nation will increase until the streets will be filled with children playing and rejoicing due to the good times [with which the nation will be blessed] (*Metzudos*). It will be a peaceful time — so peaceful that even the weakest of the nation will sit tranquilly in the streets of the city (*Malbim*).

ו כֹּה אָמַר יהוה צְבָאוֹת כִּי יִפָּלֵא בְּעֵינֵי שְׁאֵרִית הָעָם הַזֶּה בַּיָּמִים הָהֵם גַּם־בְּעֵינַי יִפָּלֵא נְאֻם ז יהוה צְבָאוֹת: כֹּה אָמַר יהוה צְבָאוֹת הִנְנִי מוֹשִׁיעַ אֶת־עַמִּי מֵאֶרֶץ מִזְרָח וּמֵאֶרֶץ מְבוֹא ח הַשָּׁמֶשׁ: וְהֵבֵאתִי אֹתָם וְשָׁכְנוּ בְּתוֹךְ יְרוּשָׁלָ͏ִם וְהָיוּ־לִי לְעָם וַאֲנִי אֶהְיֶה לָהֶם לֵאלֹהִים ט בֶּאֱמֶת וּבִצְדָקָה: כֹּה־אָמַר יהוה צְבָאוֹת תֶּחֱזַקְנָה יְדֵיכֶם הַשֹּׁמְעִים בַּיָּמִים הָאֵלֶּה אֵת הַדְּבָרִים הָאֵלֶּה מִפִּי הַנְּבִיאִים אֲשֶׁר בְּיוֹם יֻסַּד בֵּית־יהוה צְבָאוֹת הַהֵיכָל לְהִבָּנוֹת:

6. כֹּה אָמַר ה׳ צְבָאוֹת כִּי יִפָּלֵא בְּעֵינֵי שְׁאֵרִית הָעָם הַזֶּה בַּיָּמִים הָהֵם... — *Thus said Hashem, Master of Legions: Just as it will be wondrous in the eyes of the remnants of this people in those days ...*

Just as the remnant of the nation will marvel at the great loving-kindness that God will do for them, so too will God Himself be "amazed" at how He restrained His great wrath from them (*Rashi*). Alternatively, the great miracles that God will perform for them at that time will far surpass anything that the world has ever seen that even God Himself will consider them incredible (*Ibn Ezra*).

R' Yehudah HaLevi understands this verse as if the interrogative "ה" ["ה" הַשְּׁאֵלָה] is written before the word גַּם and renders: *Will it also be wondrous in My eyes?* (quoted and rejected by *Ibn Ezra*).

Our Sages (*Succah* 52a) write that at a future time, God will take the evil inclination and slaughter it before the righteous and the wicked. The righteous will view it as a great mountain; the wicked as a thin hair. Both will weep: The righteous wondering how they were able to conquer such a lofty mountain and the wicked wondering how they were unable to conquer such a thin hair. God, too, will wonder with them as Scripture writes, "*so will it be wondrous in My eyes.*"

7. כֹּה אָמַר ה׳ צְבָאוֹת הִנְנִי מוֹשִׁיעַ אֶת־עַמִּי מֵאֶרֶץ מִזְרָח וּמֵאֶרֶץ מְבוֹא הַשָּׁמֶשׁ — *Thus said Hashem, Master of Legions: Behold I am saving My people from the land of the east and from the land where the sun sets.*

God will gather His [exiled] people[1] who have been scattered from east to west, i.e., who have been scattered over the entire populated world (*Radak*). Alternatively, the land of the east refers to Babylonia and Persia and the land of the west refers to Egypt and Assyria (*Ibn Ezra*).

The Ten Tribes of Israel had been exiled to the east and the tribes of Judah and Benjamin had been exiled to the west (*Abarbanel; Malbim*).

8. וְשָׁכְנוּ בְּתוֹךְ יְרוּשָׁלָ͏ִם — *And they will dwell within Jerusalem.*

When one considers the small size of the Holy City and the large number of people who will be returning from exile, it is evident that this verse is not to be understood literally for it would be impossible to fit all those returnees into a city that size. The prophet is saying that unlike Jerusalem of old which was located in the portions of Judah and Benjamin, the Holy City of the

1. The term עַמִּי — *My people* is used to express God's affection for His people (*Rashi, Numbers* 11:1).

[6]*Thus said* H*ASHEM*, *Master of Legions: Just as it will be wondrous in the eyes of the remnant of this people in those days, so will it be wondrous in My eyes — the word of* H*ASHEM*, *Master of Legions.*

[7]*Thus said* H*ASHEM*, *Master of Legions: Behold I am saving My people from the land of the east and from the land where the sun sets;* [8]*and I will bring them and they will dwell within Jerusalem. They will be a people unto Me, and I will be a God unto them, in truth and in righteousness.*

[9]*Thus said* H*ASHEM*, *Master of Legions: Let your hands be strong; you who hear these days these words from the mouths of the prophets, which [were spoken] on the day that the foundation was laid for the Temple of* H*ASHEM*, *Master of Legions — the Sanctuary — to be built.*

future will belong to all the tribes of Israel as foretold by the prophet Ezekiel [Chap. 48] (*Abarbanel; Metzudos*). Alternatively, Scripture does not mean that the returnees will dwell in the city of Jerusalem exclusively for they will actually dwell in all the cities of Israel. Jerusalem is singled out because it is the capital city and the site of the Holy Temple to which all of Israel would come on Festivals (*Radak*).

וַאֲנִי אֶהְיֶה לָהֶם לֵאלֹהִים — *And I will be a God unto them.*

God will protect them with His Divine Providence (*Malbim*), and He will be their Helper and Savior (*Metzudos*).

בֶּאֱמֶת וּבִצְדָקָה — *In truth and in righteousness.* All the aforementioned goodness will come about only if there is truthfulness and righteousness among the people (*Metzudos; Malbim*).

9. תֶּחֱזַקְנָה יְדֵיכֶם ... — *Let your hands be strong; ...*

The Jews living in Israel were facing great difficulties in completing the Temple — see *Ezra* 4:4,5. Furthermore, they had perceived from the question that the messengers had asked (see 7:1-3), that the Jews of Babylon did not really believe that the Temple would actually be erected. God, therefore, instructed Zechariah to encourage the Jews living in Israel. He is to tell them that they should resolve to build and complete the Temple and they should not fear those who have been hindering them and disrupting its construction. They should realize that just as the prophecies that were foretold on the day that the foundation of the Temple was laid were proven true [see next verse], so too, will the words of comfort uttered by those very same prophets concerning the present time be proven true, as well (*Rashi*).

The prophets Haggai and Zechariah (*Ibn Ezra*) had prophesied for the nation during the second year of King Darius' reign (*Rashi*) and God's blessings then came upon them (*Radak*).

The people must not let their resolve weaken because of the attitude of the exiles living in Babylonia; they must understand that abundant goodness awaits them as was foretold by the prophets (*Abarbanel; Metzudos*).

י כִּי לִפְנֵי הַיָּמִים הָהֵם שְׂכַר הָאָדָם לֹא נִהְיָה וּשְׂכַר הַבְּהֵמָה אֵינֶנָּה וְלַיּוֹצֵא וְלַבָּא אֵין־שָׁלוֹם מִן־הַצָּר וַאֲשַׁלַּח אֶת־כָּל־הָאָדָם אִישׁ בְּרֵעֵהוּ׃ יא וְעַתָּה לֹא כַיָּמִים הָרִאשֹׁנִים אֲנִי לִשְׁאֵרִית הָעָם הַזֶּה נְאֻם יְהוָה צְבָאוֹת׃ יב כִּי־זֶרַע הַשָּׁלוֹם הַגֶּפֶן תִּתֵּן פִּרְיָהּ וְהָאָרֶץ תִּתֵּן אֶת־יְבוּלָהּ וְהַשָּׁמַיִם יִתְּנוּ טַלָּם וְהִנְחַלְתִּי אֶת־שְׁאֵרִית הָעָם הַזֶּה אֶת־כָּל־אֵלֶּה׃ יג וְהָיָה כַּאֲשֶׁר הֱיִיתֶם קְלָלָה בַּגּוֹיִם בֵּית יְהוּדָה וּבֵית יִשְׂרָאֵל כֵּן אוֹשִׁיעַ אֶתְכֶם וִהְיִיתֶם בְּרָכָה אַל־תִּירָאוּ תֶּחֱזַקְנָה יְדֵיכֶם׃ יד כִּי כֹה אָמַר יְהוָה צְבָאוֹת כַּאֲשֶׁר זָמַמְתִּי לְהָרַע לָכֶם בְּהַקְצִיף אֲבֹתֵיכֶם אֹתִי אָמַר יְהוָה צְבָאוֹת וְלֹא נִחָמְתִּי׃ טו כֵּן שַׁבְתִּי זָמַמְתִּי בַּיָּמִים הָאֵלֶּה לְהֵיטִיב אֶת־יְרוּשָׁלִַם

10. כִּי לִפְנֵי הַיָּמִים הָהֵם שְׂכַר הָאָדָם לֹא נִהְיָה... — *For before those days, people had no earnings ...*

Before Darius gave permission to resume construction of the Temple and the foundations of the Temple were not yet laid, people were unable to earn any profit from working their land or from leasing their animals, for there was a curse in the land (*Radak; Mahari Kara*), but as soon as construction began, the handiwork of the people became blessed as was foretold by the prophets (*Rashi*).

Although this is a description of the period prior to the building of the Second Temple, R' Elazar (*Sanhedrin* 98a) assumes that the same economic conditions will take place before the final redemption and is a sign that the coming of the Messiah is imminent.

11. וְעַתָּה לֹא כַיָּמִים הָרִאשֹׁנִים אֲנִי לִשְׁאֵרִית הָעָם הַזֶּה נְאֻם ה׳ צְבָאוֹת — *But now, not as in earlier days am I toward the remnant of this people — the word of Hashem, Master of Legions.*

But now since the people have started construction and have begun rebuilding the Temple (*Metzudos*), I do not cause strife among them (*Ibn Ezra*).

12. כִּי־זֶרַע הַשָּׁלוֹם — *For [now] the seed is of peace.*

[Unlike the earlier days when there was strife among the people] now they will sow and harvest in peace (*Ibn Ezra*). Their sowing will bring peace and blessing to the extent that the seed will be called "the seed of peace" (*Radak*) for when there is a shortage of food, jealousy and hatred prevail but when there is a blessing of plenty, there is no jealousy and no hatred (*Metzudos*).

וְהִנְחַלְתִּי אֶת־שְׁאֵרִית הָעָם הַזֶּה אֶת־כָּל־אֵלֶּה — *I have bestowed all of these upon the remnant of this people.*

All this goodness did not come upon the people coincidentally but was due to the blessing that God had bestowed upon the people (*Metzudos*).

This prophecy may be referring to the days of the Second Temple at which time the nation will be blessed if they obey God's commandments, or it may be referring to Messianic times. *Radak* is inclined to the

[10] *For before those days, people had no earnings, nor were there earnings from animals; those who travel back and forth had no peace because of the enemy; and I set everyone, man against his neighbor.* [11] *But now, not as in earlier days am I toward the remnant of this people — the word of* HASHEM, *Master of Legions.* [12] *For [now] the seed is of peace: The vine gives forth its fruit, the land gives forth its produce, and the heavens give forth their dew. I have bestowed all these upon the remnant of this people.* [13] *And it shall be that just as you were a curse among the nations, O House of Judah and House of Israel, so will I save you and you will be a blessing. Do not fear, and let your hands be strong!* [14] *For thus said* HASHEM, *Master of Legions: Just as I had planned to bring misfortune upon you when your forefathers angered Me — said* HASHEM, *Master of Legions — and I did not relent [from doing so],* [15] *so have I turned back these days and planned to benefit Jerusalem*

latter, because the following verse mentions that the House of Israel will be blessed together with the House of Judah. The House of Israel did not return from exile during the days of the Second Temple.

13. וְהָיָה כַּאֲשֶׁר הֱיִיתֶם קְלָלָה בַּגּוֹיִם — *And it shall be that just as you were a curse among the nations.*

In the past, the gentile nations would blame the Jewish citizens among them for their misfortunes (*Radak; Ibn Ezra*). Alternatively, when the gentile nations wished to curse others, they would use the Jews as an example: "May you be as accursed as the unfortunate Jews" (*Metzudos*).

כֵּן אוֹשִׁיעַ אֶתְכֶם — *So will I save you.*

To the extent of the distress that the nation experienced, so will be the extent of the salvation (*Metzudos*).

וִהְיִיתֶם בְּרָכָה — *And you will be a blessing.*

This is similar to the blessing God gave Abraham (*Gen.* 12:2) וֶהְיֵה בְּרָכָה, *and you shall be a blessing.* You will be the standard of blessing by which the gentile nations will bless themselves (*Radak*). When they wish to bless others they will say, "May God make you like the blessed Jews" (*Metzudos*).

אַל־תִּירָאוּ תֶּחֱזַקְנָה יְדֵיכֶם — *Do not fear, and let your hands be strong.*

Zechariah instructs the nation to draw strength from these favorable prophecies (*Radak*) and encourage the people living in Israel to continue with the construction of the Temple and not to be discouraged by the attitude of the exiles living in Babylonia (*Metzudos*).

14-15. כִּי כֹה אָמַר ה׳ צְבָאוֹת כַּאֲשֶׁר זָמַמְתִּי לְהָרַע לָכֶם ... כֵּן שַׁבְתִּי זָמַמְתִּי בַּיָּמִים הָאֵלֶּה לְהֵיטִיב אֶת־יְרוּשָׁלַיִם ... — *For thus said Hashem, Master of Legions: Just as I had planned to bring misfortune upon*

טז וְאֶת־בֵּית יְהוּדָה אַל־תִּירָאוּ: אֵלֶּה הַדְּבָרִים אֲשֶׁר תַּעֲשׂוּ דַּבְּרוּ אֱמֶת אִישׁ אֶת־רֵעֵהוּ אֱמֶת
יז וּמִשְׁפַּט שָׁלוֹם שִׁפְטוּ בְּשַׁעֲרֵיכֶם: וְאִישׁ | אֶת־רָעַת רֵעֵהוּ אַל־תַּחְשְׁבוּ בִּלְבַבְכֶם וּשְׁבֻעַת שֶׁקֶר אַל־תֶּאֱהָבוּ כִּי אֶת־כָּל־אֵלֶּה אֲשֶׁר שָׂנֵאתִי נְאֻם־
יח־יט יְהוָה: וַיְהִי דְּבַר־יְהוָה צְבָאוֹת אֵלַי לֵאמֹר: כֹּה־אָמַר יְהוָה צְבָאוֹת צוֹם הָרְבִיעִי וְצוֹם הַחֲמִישִׁי

you ... so have I turned back, these days, and planned to benefit Jerusalem ...

Just as God did not relent and carried out His plan [of punishment] to make the people return to Him, so too, will He surely carry out His plan and not relent from doing good to them (*Rashi*). The people should therefore not fear the emissaries of the Babylonians (*Metzudos*) or Sanballat and His cohorts who conspire to stop that which they are doing (*Radak*) [see *Nehemiah* 2:10; 19; 3:33; 34].

Ibn Ezra notes that Scripture mentions only the House of Judah and not the House of Israel in this verse and suggests that this is because Judah was both the majority and the royal family. *Abarbanel* maintains that only the House of Judah had been granted permission by Cyrus to return and build the Temple. The House of Israel, the Ten Tribes, who had been exiled earlier, were not granted this permission and did not return. They are therefore not mentioned here [see *Ramban, Sefer HaGeulah*].

16. אֵלֶּה הַדְּבָרִים אֲשֶׁר תַּעֲשׂוּ דַּבְּרוּ אֱמֶת אִישׁ אֶת־רֵעֵהוּ — *These are the things that you should do: Speak the truth with each other.*

This is how the people should conduct themselves (*Metzudos*) to keep this Temple from being destroyed (*Malbim*). They must be sincere with each other and should not say anything that they do not really feel or believe (*Radak*).

אֱמֶת וּמִשְׁפַּט שָׁלוֹם שִׁפְטוּ בְּשַׁעֲרֵיכֶם — *And in your gates judge with truth, justice and peace.*

Throughout Scripture we find that the "gate" was the meeting place of the elders and judges. See *Deuteronomy* 22:15, 25:7, *I Samuel* 4:18. When judging the people, the courts must execute their judgments with truth for this will bring peace among the litigants (*Radak*).

The Sages (*Sanhedrin* 6b) find the combination of *justice and peace* to be contradictory, for judgment implies a strict application of the law which usually means that the court favors one litigant over the other; a situation where it is unlikely for peace to prevail. They therefore explain that this verse is advocating that the judges should arbitrate a פְּשָׁרָה, *a compromise* between the litigants satisfying both parties, and peace will prevail. Indeed, *Rambam* rules (*Mishnah Torah Hil. Sanhedrin* 22:4): Praiseworthy is the court that generally arbitrates a compromise.

17. וְאִישׁ אֶת־רָעַת רֵעֵהוּ אַל־תַּחְשְׁבוּ בִּלְבַבְכֶם וּשְׁבֻעַת שֶׁקֶר אַל־תֶּאֱהָבוּ ... — *Do not think evil toward each other in your hearts; and do not love false oaths ...*

The prophet now warns them against the sin of שִׂנְאַת חִנָּם, *gratuitous hatred*.[1] Indeed, this was the sin that eventually brought about the destruction of the Second Temple (*Rashi*). In addition, he warns them regarding the sin of false oaths as well [see 5:4]. God

1. This is hatred directed toward individuals who have not committed any action for which it would be justifiable to hate them — see *Rashi* to *Shabbos* 32b ד"ה וְשִׂנְאַת.

and the House of Judah. Do not fear! [16]*These are the things that you should do: Speak the truth with each other; and in your gates judge with truth, justice and peace.* [17]*Do not think evil toward each other in your hearts; and do not love false oaths — for all these are what I hate — the word of* HASHEM.

[18]*The word of* HASHEM, *Master of Legions, came to me, saying:*

[19]*Thus said* HASHEM, *Master of Legions: The fast of the fourth [month], the fast of the fifth [month],*

says that since He hates all the sins mentioned in these two verses (*Radak*), the people should surely not show any kind of love for them (*Radak; Metzudos*).

19. ... כֹּה־אָמַר ה׳ צְבָאוֹת ... — *Thus said Hashem, Master of Legions ...*

In the previous chapter, the Jews of Babylonia had sent emisaries to the Kohanim in Jerusalem, inquiring whether or not they should continue fasting and mourning on the fast days that commemorate the destruction of the Temple and Jerusalem — see 7:2,3. God now replies through His prophet (*Mahari Kara; Ibn Ezra*): If the people will do all that God commanded and repent their ways (*Malbim*), then they will not need to fast on these days for they will now become days of joy celebrating the abundant goodness that they will receive (*Radak*).

צוֹם הָרְבִיעִי — *The fast of the fourth [month].*

This is the fast of the seventeenth of Tammuz (*Mahari Kara; Radak; Metzudos*) which is the fourth month [counting from Nissan] (*Rashi*). It was on this day that the walls of Jerusalem were breached by the Babylonians prior to the destruction of the First Temple. *Ibn Ezra* maintains that the fast was on the ninth of Tammuz and it was on that day that the walls were breached.

Ibn Ezra's view is seemingly corroborated by *Jeremiah* 52:6,7: בַּחֹדֶשׁ הָרְבִיעִי בְּתִשְׁעָה לַחֹדֶשׁ ... וַתִּבָּקַע הָעִיר, *In the fourth month on the ninth of the month ... the city was breached.*

Actually, the Babylonian Talmud and the Palestinian Talmud dispute this very question. According to the Babylonian Talmud (*Taanis* 28b), the walls were breached on the ninth of Tammuz as described by Jeremiah. The fast of the seventeenth of Tammuz commemorates the breaching of the walls by the Romans prior to the destruction of the Second Temple. According to the Palestinian Talmud (*Taanis* 4:5), the Babylonians also breached the city walls on the seventeenth. As for the verse in *Jeremiah*, there was a קִלְקוּל חֶשְׁבּוֹנוֹת, *a mistaken reckoning* by the people, due to the troubles the Jews had experienced and they had mistakenly believed that the walls had been breached on the ninth although it actually occurred on the seventeenth and Scripture wrote the date that had been the belief of the people. [See *Tos. Rosh Hashanah* 18b and *Korban HaEdan* to *Talmud Yerushalmi*.]

וְצוֹם הַחֲמִישִׁי — *The fast of the fifth [month].*

This is the fast of the ninth (*Mahari Kara; Radak; Metzudos*) of Av (*Rashi*), the day that the Temple was destroyed (*Taanis* 29a). *Ibn Ezra* maintains that the First Temple was actually destroyed on the tenth of Av and the people, therefore, fasted on the tenth of Av and not on the ninth. It was only the Second Temple that was destroyed on the ninth.

וְצ֨וֹם הַשְּׁבִיעִ֜י וְצ֣וֹם הָעֲשִׂירִ֗י יִהְיֶ֤ה לְבֵית־יְהוּדָה֙ לְשָׂשׂ֣וֹן וּלְשִׂמְחָ֔ה וּֽלְמֹעֲדִ֖ים טוֹבִ֑ים
כ וְהָאֱמֶ֥ת וְהַשָּׁל֖וֹם אֱהָֽבוּ׃ כֹּ֥ה אָמַ֖ר יְהוָ֣ה צְבָא֑וֹת עֹ֚ד אֲשֶׁ֣ר יָבֹ֣אוּ עַמִּ֔ים וְיֹשְׁבֵ֖י עָרִ֥ים
כא רַבּֽוֹת׃ וְֽהָלְכ֡וּ יֹשְׁבֵ֣י אַחַת֩ אֶל־אַחַ֨ת לֵאמֹ֜ר נֵלְכָ֣ה הָל֗וֹךְ לְחַלּוֹת֙ אֶת־פְּנֵ֣י יְהוָ֔ה וּלְבַקֵּ֖שׁ
כב אֶת־יְהוָ֣ה צְבָא֑וֹת אֵלְכָ֖ה גַּם־אָֽנִי׃ וּבָ֨אוּ עַמִּ֤ים רַבִּים֙ וְגוֹיִ֣ם עֲצוּמִ֔ים לְבַקֵּ֛שׁ אֶת־יְהוָ֥ה צְבָא֖וֹת בִּירוּשָׁלִָ֑ם וּלְחַלּ֖וֹת אֶת־פְּנֵ֥י
כג יְהוָֽה׃ כֹּֽה־אָמַר֮ יְהוָ֣ה צְבָאוֹת֒ בַּיָּמִ֣ים הָהֵ֔מָּה

וְצוֹם הַשְּׁבִיעִי — *The fast of the seventh [month].*

This is the fast of Gedaliah (*Mahari Kara; Radak; Metzudos*) which is observed on the third of Tishrei [the seventh month counting from Nissan] when Gedaliah was assassinated (Rashi). *Radak* [7:5] maintains that Gedaliah was actually assassinated on the first of Tishrei, but since that day is the holiday of Rosh Hashanah, the fast commemorating his death was postponed until the third.

Gedaliah ben Ahikam was the governor of the remnant Jewish community in Israel after the destruction of the First Temple. He was assassinated by Ishmael ben Nathaniah upon the urging of Baalis, king of Ammon. This resulted in the subsequent flight of all the remaining Jews to Egypt. [See *Jeremiah* Chap. 41.]

The Sages (*Rosh Hashanah* 18b) write that the fast of Gedaliah is enumerated among the fasts that commemorate the destruction of the Temple to teach us that the death of the righteous is as tragic as the burning of the Temple.[1]

וְצוֹם הָעֲשִׂירִי — *And the fast of the tenth [month].*

This is the fast of the tenth of Teves (*Mahari Kara; Radak; Rashi; Metzudos*), the day that Nebuchadnezzar, king of Babylonia, besieged Jerusalem [*II Kings* 25:1] (*Radak*) prior to the destruction of the First Temple.

יִהְיֶה לְבֵית־יְהוּדָה ... — *Will be for the House of Judah ...*

Each one (*Radak*) of these fast days will eventually become days of joy and happiness provided that you love truth and peace (*Metzudos*).

The prophet states that these fast days will be days of joy and happiness only for the *House of Judah* and does not mention the House of Israel for they did not return from exile during the days of the Second Temple (*Radak*). Alternatively, all these fast days had been proclaimed to commemorate the tragedies that had befallen the House of Judah [for the Ten Tribes of Israel had already been exiled]. Surely, the House of Israel had instituted their own fast days to commemorate the tragedies that had befallen them in their exile (*Abarbanel*). Those fast days will also become days of joy and happiness strictly for the House of Israel (*Metzudos*).

1. Years of great effort are needed to build a sanctuary, and its benefits to the world are immense; but even more effort must be expended to develop a truly righteous man (*Torah Nation*).

the fast of the seventh [month] and the fast of the tenth [month] will be for the House of Judah for joy and for gladness and for happy festivals. [Only] love truth and peace!

[20] *Thus said* H*ASHEM*, *Master of Legions: [There will] yet [be a time] that peoples will come as well as inhabitants of many cities.* [21] *The dwellers of one [city] will go to [those of] the other, saying, "Let us go and supplicate before* H*ASHEM and seek out* H*ASHEM*, *Master of Legions!" [They will answer,] "I, too, will go!"* [22] *Many peoples and mighty nations will come to seek out* H*ASHEM*, *Master of Legions, in Jerusalem and to supplicate before* H*ASHEM*.

[23] *Thus said* H*ASHEM*, *Master of Legions: In those days*

20-23. *Radak* followed by *Malbim* views the remainder of this chapter as a prophecy foretelling events of the Messianic era. *Abarbanel*, however, sees this prophecy as a continuation of the description of events that took place during the Second Temple era. God is informing the Jewish people that if they better their deeds then the Temple, the city of Jerusalem and the nation will be revered by the gentile nations.

20. כֹּה אָמַר ה׳ צְבָאוֹת עֹד אֲשֶׁר יָבֹאוּ עַמִּים וְיֹשְׁבֵי עָרִים רַבּוֹת — *Thus said Hashem, Master of Legions: [There will] yet [be a time] that peoples will come as well as inhabitants of many cities.*

Although the Jewish people will yet be despised by the gentile nations at this time, the city of Jerusalem will nevertheless be held in esteem and will be recognized as the city of holiness. The nations will journey there to pray and to seek the truth of God's existence (*Malbim*).

21. וְהָלְכוּ יוֹשְׁבֵי אַחַת אֶל־אַחַת לֵאמֹר ... — *The dwellers of one [city] will go to [those of] the other, saying ...*

The inhabitants of one city will say to the inhabitants of another, "Let us go together to pray before God and beg His forgiveness so that He may pardon our sins" (*Metzudos*).

אֵלְכָה גַּם־אָנִי — *"I, too, will go."*

According to *Metzudos*, the inhabitants of the city making the proposal are saying this to encourage and convince the others to go. *Malbim*, however, understands this phrase as the response of the people of the other city.

22. וּבָאוּ עַמִּים רַבִּים וְגוֹיִם עֲצוּמִים לְבַקֵּשׁ אֶת־ה׳ צְבָאוֹת בִּירוּשָׁלָםִ וּלְחַלּוֹת אֶת־פְּנֵי ה׳ — *Many peoples and mighty nations will come to seek out Hashem, Master of Legions, in Jerusalem and to supplicate before Hashem.*

At first only the inhabitants of one city will meet with the inhabitants of other cities and journey to Jerusalem to seek out and to pray to G-d but eventually multitudes of nations will gather there to do the same (*Malbim*).

23. בַּיָּמִים הָהֵמָּה ... — *In those days ...*

Ultimately, during the Messianic era the gentile nations will not go to Jerusalem to search for the true faith but will go directly to the Jewish nation, for they will all realize that the true faith is only with Israel (*Malbim*).

אֲשֶׁר יַחֲזִיקוּ עֲשָׂרָה אֲנָשִׁים מִכֹּל לְשֹׁנוֹת הַגּוֹיִם
וְהֶחֱזִיקוּ בִּכְנַף אִישׁ יְהוּדִי לֵאמֹר נֵלְכָה עִמָּכֶם
ט/א־ג א כִּי שָׁמַעְנוּ אֱלֹהִים עִמָּכֶם׃ מַשָּׂא דְבַר־
יהוה בְּאֶרֶץ חַדְרָךְ וְדַמֶּשֶׂק מְנֻחָתוֹ כִּי לַיהוה
ב עֵין אָדָם וְכֹל שִׁבְטֵי יִשְׂרָאֵל׃ וְגַם־חֲמָת תִּגְבָּל־
ג בָּהּ צֹר וְצִידוֹן כִּי חָכְמָה מְאֹד׃ וַתִּבֶן צֹר מָצוֹר
לָהּ וַתִּצְבָּר־כֶּסֶף כֶּעָפָר וְחָרוּץ כְּטִיט חוּצוֹת׃

עֲשָׂרָה אֲנָשִׁים מִכֹּל לְשֹׁנוֹת הַגּוֹיִם ... — *Ten men of all the [different] languages of the nations.*

Ten men from each of the seventy nations of the world[1] (*Rashi; Mahari Kara*). I.e., seven hundred gentiles will take hold of each corner of the *tallis* [garment] which has four corners, totaling two thousand eight hundred men [10 x 70=700; 700 x 4=2800] (ibid.), and will come to you when they will see your *tzitzis* (thereby recognizing that you are a Jew) to learn the true faith (*Malbim*).

Since Scripture uses the expression *will take hold* and it is impossible for 2800 men to actually take hold of one's garment (*Maharsha*), the Talmud (*Shabbos* 32b) explains the passage as the reward for one who diligently fulfills the mitzvah of *tzitzis*: He will merit to have 2800 servants who will cater to him.

IX

1. מַשָּׂא דְבַר־ה׳ ... — *The prophecy of the word of Hashem ...*

מַשָּׂא, lit., *burden*, is used synonymously for prophecy because the prophet *carries* the prophetic word in his mouth (*Metzudos* to *Isaiah* 13:1). The prophecy of the previous chapter continues. When the vast numbers of gentile nations will turn to the Jewish people for spiritual guidance and to learn the true faith (*Malbim*), the prophetic word of God will then not only be heard in the Land of Israel but will also be heard in the distant land of Hadrach as well. At that time the borders of the Land of Israel will expand and will include Hadrach and Damascus, cities that will be incorporated into the Land of Israel (*Metzudos*).

Alternatively, *Ibn Ezra* sees this prophecy foretelling events of the Second Temple era. *Abarbanel* vehemently rejects this explanation for none of these events occurred during the Second Temple era — see *Abarbanel* to v. 8.

בְּאֶרֶץ חַדְרָךְ — *In the land of Hadrach.*

Hadrach is either the name of a kingdom or of a particular king (*Ibn Ezra*). It is an area near Damascus (*Metzudos*).

R' Yehudah bar Ilai taught that Hadrach is not the name of a city but is a reference to the Messiah for He is sharp (חַד) against the gentile nations and soft (רַךְ) to Israel. R' Yose the son of a Damascene mother sharply disagreed and accused R' Yehudah of distorting Scripture's meaning. He then testified that there is indeed a city with the name Hadrach (Rashi from Sifre).

וְדַמֶּשֶׂק מְנֻחָתוֹ — *With Damascus His resting place.*

God's *Shechinah* will rest in Damascus for it, too, will become a city of Israel (*Metzudos*). Alternatively, the [influence of the] Temple in which God rests His *Shechinah* will extend to Damascus (*Mahari Kara*).

1. There are seventy nations in the world each with its own specific language. See *Rashi, Deuteronomy*, 32:8; *R' Bachya, Genesis* 10:1.

it will happen that ten men of all the [different] languages of the nations will take hold, they will take hold of the corner of the garment of a Jewish man, saying, "Let us go with you, for we have heard that God is with you!"

9/1-3 [1] *The prophecy of the word of HASHEM in the land of Hadrach, with Damascus His resting place: Toward HASHEM will be the eyes of mankind and all the tribes of Israel.* [2] *Also Hamath will be in its borders, as well as Tyre and Sidon, though she is very wise.* [3] *Tyre built a fortification for herself; she amassed silver like dust, and fine gold like the mud of the street.*

כִּי לַה׳ עֵין אָדָם וְכֹל שִׁבְטֵי יִשְׂרָאֵל — *Toward Hashem will be the eyes of mankind and all the tribes of Israel.*

The nations will no longer worship idols as in the past for there will come a time when not only Israel but all mankind will recognize that Hashem is the true God and will therefore desire to serve Him. Although Israel is included in all mankind, Scripture sets Israel apart from the other nations to teach that God regards and loves Israel more than any other nation (*Radak*). In an alternative explanation, *Radak* renders the eyes of mankind will be toward Hashem and also toward all the tribes of Israel for all the nations will turn toward the tribes of Israel for spiritual guidance as they wish to follow in their ways.

2. וְגַם־חֲמָת תִּגְבָּל־בָּהּ ... — *Also Hamath will be in its borders ...*

Since there will be many Jews now living in the Land of Israel, its borders will spread out to nearby lands (*Mahari Kara*) with Hamath, Tyre and Sidon being within its borders (*Radak; Metzudos*). *Rashi* explains that these cities will border Jerusalem. *Malbim* cites *Yechezkel* 47:15,16,17 where Scripture implies that these cities will actually border Israel's northern border.

כִּי חָכְמָה מְאֹד — *Though she is very wise.*

This is referring specifically to Tyre who considers herself too wise to be conquered (*Radak*). She thought that through her wisdom she will always remain the city of beauty and wealth — see *Yechezkel* Chs. 26,27 (*Radak*), the mistress of cities (*Rashi*). During the Messianic era she will no longer rely on her wisdom but will subjugate herself to Israel (*Radak*).

3. וַתִּבֶן צוֹר מָצוֹר לָהּ וַתִּצְבָּר־כֶּסֶף כֶּעָפָר וְחָרוּץ כְּטִיט חוּצוֹת — *Tyre built a fortification for herself; she amassed silver like dust and fine gold like the mud of the street.*

Although Tyre had built a fortification to protect herself from the Jewish nation (*Mahari Kara*), amassed great wealth and boasted that she wouldn't be overthrown (*Rashi*), it was all to no avail (*Radak*).

וְחָרוּץ — *And fine gold.*

This is a very high-quality gold (*Metzudos*) and is identified by its specific color (*Rashi, Psalms* 68:14).

The word חָרוּץ actually means "sharp." When used in connection with mental ability it means "industrious" or "diligent." It is also used as an adjective denoting the quality of a precious metal (*R' Hirsch, Psalms* ibid.).

ד הִנֵּה אֲדֹנָי יוֹרִשֶׁנָּה וְהִכָּה בַיָּם חֵילָהּ וְהִיא
ה בָּאֵשׁ תֵּאָכֵל: תֵּרֶא אַשְׁקְלוֹן וְתִירָא וְעַזָּה
וְתָחִיל מְאֹד וְעֶקְרוֹן כִּי־הֹבִישׁ מֶבָּטָהּ וְאָבַד
ו מֶלֶךְ מֵעַזָּה וְאַשְׁקְלוֹן לֹא תֵשֵׁב: וְיָשַׁב מַמְזֵר
ז בְּאַשְׁדּוֹד וְהִכְרַתִּי גְּאוֹן פְּלִשְׁתִּים: וַהֲסִרֹתִי
דָמָיו מִפִּיו וְשִׁקֻּצָיו מִבֵּין שִׁנָּיו וְנִשְׁאַר
גַּם־הוּא לֵאלֹהֵינוּ וְהָיָה כְּאַלֻּף בִּיהוּדָה

4. הִנֵּה אֲדֹנָי יוֹרִשֶׁנָּה — *Behold, the Lord will impoverish her.*

Our translation of יוֹרִשֶׁנָּה follows *Rashi* who relates it to the phrase מוֹרִישׁ וּמַעֲשִׁיר, *impoverishes and makes rich* (see *I Samuel* 2:7). God Who rules over everything will impoverish her from all her greatness (*Radak*). Other translations are: He will drive her away (see *Joshua* 23:9) (*Targum Yonasan; Metzudos*). He will cause [Israel] to inherit her (*Ibn Ezra; Mahari Kara*).

וְהִכָּה בַיָּם חֵילָהּ — *And He will strike her wealth with the sea.*

Tyre will be inundated by the sea and all her wealth will be carried away (see *Ezekiel* 27:34) (*Rashi; Radak*).

וְהִיא בָּאֵשׁ תֵּאָכֵל — *And it will be consumed by fire.*

The city — its buildings and fortified towers that were relied on for protection — will be destroyed by fire (*Radak*).

5. תֵּרֶא אַשְׁקְלוֹן וְתִירָא וְעַזָּה וְתָחִיל מְאֹד וְעֶקְרוֹן ... — *Ashkelon will see [this] and fear, and Gaza [will see] and tremble greatly, and Ekron ...*

Ashkelon, Gaza and Ekron were three of the largest Philistine cities. When they will see the destruction of Tyre, the one in whom they had placed their trust and hope for protection, they will humble themselves before Israel (*Rashi; Radak*).

Tyre was the premier city of Edom, the nation which was founded by Esau. Ekron, Caesarea, was originally a Philistine city (*Rashi*) and was later conquered by the Greeks and eventually by Rome[1] (*Maharsha, Megillah* 6a). Ashkelon and Gaza were also Philistine cities and were all allies of Tyre (see *Jeremiah* 47:4; *Joel* 4:4) (*Malbim*).

וְאָבַד מֶלֶךְ מֵעַזָּה ... — *A king will perish from Gaza ...*

Gaza will lose its king and its land will be overtaken by Israel. Ashkelon will no longer be inhabited by its former inhabitants for now Israel will dwell there (*Radak*). Alternatively, people will inhabit Gaza, but without their king; Ashkelon will be void of its inhabitants (*Malbim*).

6. וְיָשַׁב מַמְזֵר בְּאַשְׁדּוֹד — *A stranger will dwell in Ashdod.*

Our translation of מַמְזֵר follows *Rashi* who relates the word מַמְזֵר to זָר, *strange* (*Metzudos*). A strange nation, Israel, whom the Philistines had derided as foreigners, will dwell in Ashdod (*Targum Yonasan; Rashi*). Other interpretations are: The Philistines will be strangers in Ashdod because they will be under Israelite rule (*Radak*). Some say that מַמְזֵר is the name of a nation (*R' Yehudah Ibn Balaam* quoted by *Ibn Ezra*).

Ibn Ezra interprets it according to its usual definition: one who is born of an adulterous or incestuous union. These Jews will be segregated from the Jews of proper lineage and will dwell in Ashdod.[2]

1. Rome is regarded as the heir to the Biblical nation of Edom.

2. See *Kiddushin* 72b where the interpretation of this verse is the topic of a dispute between

[4] *Behold, the Lord will impoverish her, and He will strike her wealth with the sea, and it will be consumed by fire.* [5] *Ashkelon will see [this] and fear, and Gaza [will see] and tremble greatly, and Ekron, for the one to whom she looked [for protection] has been humiliated. A king will perish from Gaza, and Ashkelon will not be inhabited.* [6] *A stranger will dwell in Ashdod, and I will cut off the pride of the Philistines.* [7] *I will remove his blood from his mouth and his abominations from between his teeth, and then he, too, will remain for our God. He will be like a master in Judah,*

וְהִכְרַתִּי גְּאוֹן פְּלִשְׁתִּים — *And I will cut off the pride of the Philistines.*

The pride of the Philistines will be cut off because their city will be inhabited by Israelites even if they are of questionable lineage (*Ibn Ezra*).

7. ... וַהֲסִרֹתִי דָמָיו מִפִּיו וְשִׁקֻּצָיו מִבֵּין שִׁנָּיו — *I will remove his blood from his mouth and his abominations from between his teeth ...*

Although *Rashi* sees the Edomites as the subject of this verse, most commentaries (*Ibn Ezra; Radak; Metzudos; Abarbanel; Malbim*) maintain that the verse is referring to the Philistines. In any event, the point of this prophecy is that ultimately, even this nation will cease its repulsive practices and turn to worship the true God.

The basis for *Rashi's* interpretation is the Talmud *Megillah* 6a where this verse is expounded. *Rashi* there ד״ה וַהֲסִירוֹתִי writes that this verse is referring to Tyre, the premier city of Edom and not to Ashkelon and Gaza. [Accordingly, Ekron is mentioned here because although it had originally been a Philistine city, it was later overtaken by Edom, as explained earlier.]

דָמָיו, *his blood,* is referring to the house of Bamaya, one of the main idols worshiped by the Edomites, where they would sprinkle the blood of their sacrifices (*Rashi*), וְשִׁקֻּצָיו, *and his abominations,* is referring to the house of Galaya, another Edomite deity (*Megillah* 6a). The mouth of Esau [Edom] will not mention the names of these idols again (*Rashi*). Alternatively, this is referring to the Israelite blood that the Edomites shed (*Rashi; Mahari Kara*).

Abarbanel explains that the Philistines, who had praised their idols for the victories they had triumphed over Israel, will never do so again. Alternatively, the Philistines will cease their repulsive practice of drinking the blood of the victims they had murdered for they will now follow the true God (*Ibn Ezra*).

וְנִשְׁאַר גַּם־הוּא לֵאלֹהֵינוּ — *And then he too will remain for our God.*

These are the synagogues and the study halls where the Jews would pray and study during the exile (*Rashi*). Alternatively, only Philistines who would serve the true God will remain (*Ibn Ezra*) for I will destroy the wicked among them (*Radak*).

וְהָיָה כְּאַלֻּף בִּיהוּדָה — *He will be like a master in Judah.*

The Philistines will be as the most prominent of Judah in their service of G-d (*Ibn Ezra; Radak*). Alternatively, *Rashi* translates אַלֻּף as an expression of study and learning, as in *Proverbs* 22:25 (*Metzudos*), and explains that the amphitheaters and circuses will be used by the princes of Judah to teach Torah [from *Megillah* 6a].

R' Meir and R' Yose hinging on whether or not Eliyahu the prophet will purify *mamzerim* in the Messianic era.

ח וְעֶקְרוֹן כִּיבוּסִי: וְחָנִיתִי לְבֵיתִי מִצָּבָה מֵעֹבֵר וּמִשָּׁב וְלֹא־יַעֲבֹר עֲלֵיהֶם עוֹד נֹגֵשׂ כִּי עַתָּה רָאִיתִי בְעֵינָי: ט גִּילִי מְאֹד בַּת־צִיּוֹן הָרִיעִי בַּת יְרוּשָׁלַםִ הִנֵּה מַלְכֵּךְ יָבוֹא לָךְ צַדִּיק וְנוֹשָׁע הוּא עָנִי וְרֹכֵב עַל־חֲמוֹר וְעַל־עַיִר בֶּן־אֲתֹנוֹת: י וְהִכְרַתִּי־רֶכֶב מֵאֶפְרַיִם וְסוּס מִירוּשָׁלַםִ

וְעֶקְרוֹן כִּיבוּסִי — *And Ekron [will be] like the Jebusite.* The inhabitants of Ekron will pay tribute to Israel as did the Jebusites, the inhabitants of Jerusalem, during the reign of King David (*Ibn Ezra; Radak*) (See comm. to *Radak* to *II Samuel* 24:23). Alternatively, Ekron will be filled with houses of study (*Rashi, Megillah* 6a) and pure-minded men (*Metzudos*) like the city of Jerusalem [which was originally a Jebusite city] (*Rashi*).

8. וְחָנִיתִי לְבֵיתִי מִצָּבָה — *I will encamp at My house [to protect it] against any army.*

God refers to His nation as His *house* and declares that He will be as a great army and will camp near His house, the House of Israel (*Radak*). He will protect them so they will not need to fear anyone who will rise against them. Alternatively, *My house* is referring to Jerusalem (*Ibn Ezra*) or to the Holy Temple where God will rest His Divine Presence (*Targum Yonasan*).

Although the word מִצָּבָה is written with a *hei* [ה], it is translated army, as if it would be written with an *alef* [א] (*Ibn Ezra; Radak; Rashi, second interpretation; Abarbanel; Metzudos; Malbim*). Alternatively, it is related to the word מַצָּב, *a garrison stationed to besiege a city*, similar to צֹבֶיהָ (*Isaiah* 29:7) [and הַמַּצָּב — *I Samuel* 14:15] (*Rashi; Mahara Kara*).

כִּי עַתָּה רָאִיתִי בְעֵינָי — *For now I have seen [their suffering] with My eyes.*

Although God has concealed His countenance from them, He has now seen their distress with His eyes (*Rashi; Metzudos*).

When Israel sins, God figuratively "turns His eyes" away from the nation. Zechariah foretells that a day will come when God will turn "His eyes toward" Israel and show concern for their welfare.

Alternatively, this phrase is not part of the prophecy but is Zechariah's own words. I have seen all these prophetic visions through prophetic eyes (*Ibn Ezra*).

9. גִּילִי מְאֹד בַּת־צִיּוֹן ... — *Rejoice greatly, O daughter of Zion ...*

Upon seeing the following vision, Zechariah instructs Israel to shout for joy for their victorious king is coming before them. Traditionally (see *Sanhedrin* 98a), this prophecy is describing the arrival of the Messianic king. In fact, *Rashi* maintains that it is impossible to explain this prophecy as referring to any other king for we do not find any ruler of Israel during the Second Temple era that ruled from *the sea to the end of the world* — see *Rashi* to v. 10. Nevertheless, others interpret this prophecy as referring either to the Messiah son of Joseph, or to Nehemiah, whom Scripture calls "a king in Judah" — see *Nehemiah* 6:7, or to the Hasmonean leader Judah Maccabee (*Ibn Ezra*). *Abarbanel* strongly rejects all of these interpretations.

גִּילִי מְאֹד — *Rejoice greatly.*

Rejoice at the continuous miracles that you will experience at that time. Scripture chose the word גִּילָה rather than שִׂמְחָה or רִנָּה etc. because גִּילָה is the joy one experiences over something that is newly acquired (*Malbim*).

בַּת־צִיּוֹן ... בַּת יְרוּשָׁלַםִ — *O daughter of Zion ... O daughter of Jerusalem.*

and Ekron [will be] like the Jebusite. [8] *I will encamp at My house [to protect it] against any army and from any [enemy] who comes and goes, and an oppressor will never again pass through them; for now I have seen [their suffering] with My eyes.*

[9] *Rejoice greatly, O daughter of Zion! Shout for joy, O daughter of Jerusalem! For behold your king will come to you, righteous and victorious is he, a humble man and riding on a donkey, on a foal, a calf of she-donkeys.* [10] *I will cut off any [battle] chariot from Ephraim and any [war] horse from Jerusalem,*

Targum Yonasan translates בַּת as כְּנִשְׁתָּא — *Congregation* of Zion, *congregation of* Jerusalem. It is a poetic form meaning the inhabitants of ... They are told to shout for joy, because Samaria will rival you no more for you alone will be the royal city (*Abarbanel*).

הִנֵּה מַלְכֵּךְ יָבוֹא לָךְ — *For behold your king will come to you.*

Your true king, a scion of the House of King David, will come to you; not a descendant of Aaron the Kohen [referring to the Hasmoneans] nor a descendant of any other family (*Abarbanel*).

צַדִּיק וְנוֹשָׁע הוּא — *Righteous and victorious is he.*

He will be righteous in his deeds and victorious in battle (*Abarbanel; Metzudos*). He will be victorious not because of any great army but because he is righteous (*Malbim*). Alternatively, the literal translation of וְנוֹשָׁע is he will be *saved*. The Messiah will be saved from the sword of Gog and Magog because of his righteousness (*Radak*).

עָנִי וְרֹכֵב עַל־חֲמוֹר ... — *A humble man and riding on a donkey ...*

Our translation of עָנִי, *humble*, follows *Targum Yonasan* who translates עִנְוְתָן and not עַנְיָא, *a poor man*. This is similar to the description of the Messiah foretold by *Isaiah* 42:2,3, *he will not shout nor raise his voice... He will not break even a bruised reed ...* (*Radak*). Because of his deep humility, he will choose to ride on a donkey rather than on a horse, a more stately animal (*Rashi; Radak*). Furthermore, explains *Maharal*, the word חֲמוֹר, *donkey*, is derived from חוֹמֶר, *raw material*, which lacks final form and finish. This is the opposite of spirituality, because spirituality is the ultimate in final form and finish. One who rides an animal is seen as totally separated from it, but yet in control of it. Thus, the Messiah, as a rider of a donkey, is portrayed in complete opposition to חוֹמֶר, *gross physicality*. He is the closest among men to pure spirituality. Riding the donkey symbolizes his preeminence over all earthly life (*Gevuros Hashem* — Chapter 29.).

As a beast of burden, the donkey signifies that the Messiah will come as a result of the harsh and heavy burden of exile. It may also signify that he will come in the merit of our father Abraham who *saddled his [own] donkey* (*Genesis* 22:3) as he prepared to obey God's command to sacrifice his son Isaac (*Iyun Yaakov, Sanhedrin* 98a).

10. וְהִכְרַתִּי־רֶכֶב מֵאֶפְרַיִם וְסוּס מִירוּשָׁלַםִ — *I will cut off any [battle] chariot from Ephraim and any [war] horse from Jerusalem.*

At that time, God will eliminate all battle chariots, war horses, bows of war (*Metzudos*) and archers (*Abarbanel*)

וְנִכְרְתָה קֶשֶׁת מִלְחָמָה וְדִבֶּר שָׁלוֹם לַגּוֹיִם וּמָשְׁלוֹ מִיָּם עַד־יָם וּמִנָּהָר עַד־אַפְסֵי־אָרֶץ:
יא גַּם־אַתְּ בְּדַם־בְּרִיתֵךְ שִׁלַּחְתִּי אֲסִירַיִךְ מִבּוֹר אֵין מַיִם בּוֹ: יב שׁוּבוּ לְבִצָּרוֹן אֲסִירֵי הַתִּקְוָה גַּם־הַיּוֹם מַגִּיד מִשְׁנֶה אָשִׁיב לָךְ:

from all of Israel (*Radak*) for they will no longer be needed (*Rashi*); because the Messiah will speak to the nations to grant peace to Israel (*Mahari Kara*) and there will be no more wars (*Radak, Micah* 5:9).[1]

מֵאֶפְרַיִם ... מִירוּשָׁלַם — *From Ephraim ... from Jerusalem.* Ephraim is a reference to the Ten Tribes, the Northern Kingdom of Israel (*Abarbanel*). Scripture separates Ephraim and Jerusalem because their kingdoms had been divided in earlier times but in Messianic times, all Israel will be united (*Radak*).

וְדִבֶּר שָׁלוֹם לַגּוֹיִם — *And he will speak peace to the nations.*

He will not humble the nations through war but through words of peace (*Metzudos*). Since all nations will accept his decisions, his orders will be executed (*Radak*).

מִיָּם עַד־יָם — *From the sea to the west.*

Our translation of עַד יָם, *to the west,* follows *Targum Yonasan* and *Rashi.* The idea portrayed is that the Messiah will rule to the end of the world [i.e., from the Reed Sea westward]. Others translate from sea to sea — from the Reed Sea to the Sea of the Philistines [who dwelled along the Mediterranean coast] (*Ibn Ezra*) or from the southern sea — the Reed Sea to the northern sea — the Atlantic ocean (*Radak*).[2]

וּמִנָּהָר עַד־אַפְסֵי־אָרֶץ — *And from the river to the ends of the earth.*

Rashi and *Ibn Ezra* say that this is referring to the Euphrates. Alternatively, *Radak* explains that it is the river that flows from Eden (*Genesis* 2:10,) which is at the extreme east, and he will rule to the end of the earth on the west. He will rule over the entire world (*Radak*).

11. גַּם־אַתְּ בְּדַם־בְּרִיתֵךְ — *Also you, through the blood of your covenant.*

Not only will the Messiah be saved by his merit — because he is righteous, but Israel, too, will be saved together with him by their merit — the blood of the covenant (*Rashi; Radak*). It is with the merit of this covenant that God had His prophets prophesy regarding the future redemption and He had them prophesy to the people now as well. The merit of this covenant will redeem the people from the Babylonian exile in which they are now found (*Rashi*). According to *Rashi,* Scripture is referring to the covenant that was sealed at Sinai when the blood of the sacrifices was sprinkled upon the people. It was at that time that the Jewish people consented to adhere to all the commandments of the Torah (see *Exodus* 24:8). Alternatively, Scripture is referring to the covenant of ritual circumcision — (see *Genesis* 17:1-14) (*Radak; Ibn Ezra*).

The Jewish people have conscientiously adhered to the commandment of circumcision throughout the exile, more so than any other commandment (*Radak*). Indeed, it was in the merit of the blood of the covenant

1. The prophet Micah similarly foretold: *And it will be on that day, declares Hashem, that I will cut your [war] horses from your midst and I will destroy your [battle] chariots* (*Micah* 5:9) (*Radak*).

2. See *Gittin* 8a רש״י ד״ה ר׳ יְהוּדָה אוֹמֵר where *Rashi* refers to the Atlantic ocean as the end of the world.

and the bow of warfare will be eliminated; and he will speak peace to the nations. His dominion will be from the sea to the west and from the river to the ends of the earth. [11] *Also you, through the blood of your covenant I will have released your prisoners from a pit in which there was no water.* [12] *Return to the fortress, O prisoners of hope! Today, too, a second announcement, "I will return to you."*

of circumcision that God redeemed us from Egypt and in that merit will also redeem us at the end of the exile brought about by the fourth kingdom (*Pirkei D'Rabbi Eliezer* Chap. 29).

Another interpretation is that Scripture is referring to the Jewish blood that the nation shed during the years of exile when the Jewish people would sanctify God's Name rather than turn away from God and abandon His covenant (*Mahari Kara*).

שִׁלַּחְתִּי אֲסִירַיִךְ מִבּוֹר אֵין מַיִם בּוֹ — *I will have released your prisoners from a pit in which there was no water.*

Scripture metaphorically describes the exile as a waterless pit. Like the pit into which Joseph was thrown (see *Rashi* to *Genesis* 37:24), it was empty of water but filled with dangerous snakes and scorpions; representing the nations that have caused Israel to suffer greatly during her exile (*Abarbanel; Metzudos*). At that time, God will have redeemed the nation from exile (*Rashi; Mahari Kara*). Alternatively, since Haggai, Zechariah and Malachi were the last of the prophets, the exile would be devoid of prophecy which is metaphorically compared to water (see *Isaiah* 55:1) (*Radak*).

Malbim renders *because the blood of your covenant is not mixed with water, I will release your prisoners from a pit;* i.e., since you faithfully gave your life to sanctify God's Name rather than replace the blood of the covenant of circumcision with the waters of baptism and sprinkling, I will redeem you from exile.

12-17. Most commentators explain that the following verses are foretelling events of the Second Temple era. *Abarbanel* (v. 13) and *Metzudos*, however, maintain that it is foretelling events of the future redemption of the Messianic era.

12. שׁוּבוּ לְבִצָּרוֹן ... — *Return to the fortress ...*

Zechariah tells the people, "You, who have hoped for God's salvation until now, i.e., that His words would be fulfilled at the end of seventy years, return to your strength and glory, although you are yet under the rule of the Persian kings" (*Rashi*). Alternatively, return to God Who is a fortress and tower of strength (*Radak*) to those who place their trust in Him (*Abarbanel*); or return to Jerusalem, your fortress city (*Ibn Ezra; Metzudos*).

גַּם־הַיּוֹם מַגִּיד מִשְׁנֶה אָשִׁיב לָךְ — *Today, too, a second announcement, "I will return to you."*

Besides the message of rebuilding the Temple that I have already conveyed to you, I have a second message to repeat to you (*Rashi*). Alternatively, the first tidings were regarding the future [redemption] (*Radak*). This message is regarding the salvation that will take place during the Second Temple era (*Rashi; Radak*).

Another interpretation is that this is a הַגָּדָה כְּפוּלָה, *a double prophecy*, a prophecy that foretells both the redemption of Israel and the destruction of her enemies. Just as in Egypt the nation was redeemed and the Egyptians were dealt retribution, so too, at the future redemption, the nation will be redeemed and their enemies will suffer retribution (*Metzudos*).

יג כִּי־דָרַכְתִּי לִי יְהוּדָה קֶשֶׁת מִלֵּאתִי אֶפְרַיִם
וְעוֹרַרְתִּי בָנַיִךְ צִיּוֹן עַל־בָּנַיִךְ יָוָן וְשַׂמְתִּיךְ
יד כְּחֶרֶב גִּבּוֹר׃ וַיהוה עֲלֵיהֶם יֵרָאֶה וְיָצָא
כַבָּרָק חִצּוֹ וַאדֹנָי יֱהוִה בַּשּׁוֹפָר יִתְקָע וְהָלַךְ
טו בְּסַעֲרוֹת תֵּימָן׃ יהוה צְבָאוֹת יָגֵן עֲלֵיהֶם
וְאָכְלוּ וְכָבְשׁוּ אַבְנֵי־קֶלַע וְשָׁתוּ הָמוּ כְּמוֹ־יָיִן

Although according to the simple meaning, the verse is foretelling the return of Israel during the Second Temple era, the Talmud (*Sanhedrin* 22a) nevertheless expounds the latter part of the verse to mean that God promised to return on this day "that which had been altered" referring to the scripts that the Torah had foretold would be changed — מִשְׁנֵה הַתּוֹרָה — i.e., forgotten (*Deuteronomy* 17:18). Now that Israel has repented and merited to return to their Land, they have also merited to relearn their original *Ashuri* script.

13. כִּי־דָרַכְתִּי לִי יְהוּדָה קֶשֶׁת — *For I will bend Judah as a bow for Me.*

This is the second message. *Rashi* and *Radak* understand that this prophecy is referring to the war that Judah will wage against the Greeks who will eventually conquer Persia and oppress Israel. God will then use Judah and Ephraim as His weapons against the Greeks and send victory to Israel during the days of the Hasmoneans. *Abarbanel, Metzudos and Malbim,* however, explain this verse as referring to the war of Gog and Magog at which time Ephraim, i.e., the Ten Tribes of the Northern Kingdom, will return to Israel.

Metzudos notes that the root of the word דָרַכְתִּי is דָרַךְ, *to step.* One would step on the bow to bend it so that the string would pull back further giving more power for the arrow to shoot farther.

מִלֵּאתִי אֶפְרַיִם — *I will fill [the hand of] Ephraim [with a bow].*

Although the word קֶשֶׁת is connected to the first phrase of the verse — דָרַכְתִּי לִי יְהוּדָה קֶשֶׁת — *for I will bend Judah as a bow for Me,* this is an elliptical verse and it is as if Scripture also wrote קֶשֶׁת מִלֵּאתִי אֶפְרַיִם, *I will fill [the hand of] Ephraim with a bow* (*Rashi*).

To fill the hand with a bow means to put all of one's strength into bending the bow so that it would shoot the arrows (*Radak*).

Although the tribe of Ephraim did not return to the Land of Israel during the days of the Second Temple, there were nevertheless some members of Ephraim who were not exiled with the Ten Tribes but remained in the land. When Judah and Benjamin were exiled, they were exiled together with them. When Judah and Benjamin returned to Israel, they too, returned (*Radak*).

וְעוֹרַרְתִּי ... — *And I will arouse ...*

God will arouse the Israelites and give them strength and power to wage war against the Greek army that will be led by Antiochus to invade the Land of Israel. They were eventually defeated by the Israelites during the Hasmonean revolt (*Rashi*). According to *Abarbanel* and *Metzudos* the verse is referring to the war of Gog and Magog who were from the same ancestral lineage as Yavan (Greece).

וְשַׂמְתִּיךְ כְּחֶרֶב גִּבּוֹר — *And I will make you like the sword of a mighty warrior.*

God says that He will make Israel like the sword of a mighty man which strikes down and destroys the enemy (*Metzudos*)

14. וַה׳ עֲלֵיהֶם יֵרָאֶה ... — *Hashem will appear to them ...*

God will reveal His Divine Presence upon Judah and Ephraim by waging war for them against their enemies (*Radak*). His arrow will then swiftly flash forth toward the enemy like a bolt of lightning (*Metzudos*).

[13] *For I will bend Judah as a bow for Me; I will fill [the hand of] Ephraim [with a bow]; and I will arouse your children, O Zion, against your children, O Greece; and I will make you like the sword of a mighty warrior.* [14] *HASHEM will appear to them, and His arrow will go forth like the lightning; and the Lord HASHEM/ELOHIM will blow with a shofar and He will go forth in southern tempests.* [15] *HASHEM, Master of Legions, will protect them, and they will devour and conquer the "stones of the slingshot." They will drink and be boisterous as [from] wine;*

Rashi cites *Yossipon* [Chap. 18] who writes that when Antiochus was preparing to attack Israel, for forty days the people of Jerusalem saw a vision in the likeness of two groups of horses with armed riders stationed for battle against each other. The Sages interpreted this vision as a sign that God will wage war for them against their enemies with the wicked Antiochus falling to the sword of Israel.

וַה׳ אֱלוֹקִים בַּשּׁוֹפָר יִתְקָע — *And the Lord Hashem/Elokim will blow with a shofar.*

It will appear as if God is sounding the shofar as warriors do in battle (*Radak; Metzudos*).

תקע actually means to ram or drive an object into something, as a nail into the wall or a peg into the ground. When used in the sphere of music it designates the forceful or prolonged blowing of a column of air into a wind instrument or the strong prolonged note produced thereby penetrating the ear (*R' Hirsch, Numbers* 10:3).

וְהָלַךְ בְּסַעֲרוֹת תֵּימָן — *And He will go forth in southern tempests.*

God will go forth to storm the people of the south: the Greeks (*Rashi*) who dwelt south of the Land of Israel (*Mahari Kara*). Alternatively, God will storm the Greeks as a tempest of the south, the area from where tempests originate (*Radak*).

Although *Rashi* explains this verse as a continuation of the prophecies pertaining to the era of the Second Temple, he adds that there are some Sages who interpret this phrase as referring to *Edom* (see *Bereishis Rabbah* 56:13). *Sifre, Behaaloscha,* also understands this verse as referring to the future redemption.

One of the special blessings of the *Rosh Hashanah Mussaf* prayers is the blessing of *"Shofaros."* It consists of ten Scriptural verses that are related to the theme of the revelation of God's presence that is announced by the sounding of the shofar. This verse is one of the three verses selected from the books of the Prophets to express this concept.

15. ה׳ צְבָאוֹת יָגֵן עֲלֵיהֶם — *Hashem, Master of Legions, will protect them.*

God will protect the Hasmoneans (*Ibn Ezra*) or Judah and Ephraim (*Radak*) in their battle against the Greeks (*Mahari Kara*) or He will protect Israel [during the war of Gog and Magog] (*Abarbanel; Metzudos*).

וְאָכְלוּ וְכָבְשׁוּ אַבְנֵי־קֶלַע — *And they will devour and conquer the "stones of the slingshot."*

They will conquer the Greeks who were skilled in the use of the bow and slingshot and they will devour the spoils of their enemies (*Rashi*). *Radak* adds they will enslave those enemies who survive. Alternatively, Judah and Ephraim will capture the Greek fortresses and the "stones of the slingshot"; the Greek officers will be unable to save their people (*Ibn Ezra*).

וְשָׁתוּ הָמוּ כְּמוֹ־יָיִן — *They will drink and be boisterous as [from] wine.*

They will revel as do those who drink an abundance of wine (*Rashi*).

ט/טז־יז

טז וּמָלְאוּ כַּמִּזְרָק כְּזָוִיּוֹת מִזְבֵּחַ: וְהוֹשִׁיעָם יהוָה אֱלֹהֵיהֶם בַּיּוֹם הַהוּא כְּצֹאן עַמּוֹ כִּי אַבְנֵי־נֵזֶר יז מִתְנוֹסְסוֹת עַל־אַדְמָתוֹ: כִּי מַה־טּוּבוֹ וּמַה־יָּפְיוֹ דָּגָן בַּחוּרִים וְתִירוֹשׁ יְנוֹבֵב בְּתֻלוֹת:

י/א־ב

א שַׁאֲלוּ מֵיהוָה מָטָר בְּעֵת מַלְקוֹשׁ יהוָה עֹשֶׂה חֲזִיזִים וּמְטַר־גֶּשֶׁם יִתֵּן לָהֶם לְאִישׁ עֵשֶׂב ב בַּשָּׂדֶה: כִּי הַתְּרָפִים דִּבְּרוּ־אָוֶן וְהַקּוֹסְמִים חָזוּ שֶׁקֶר וַחֲלֹמוֹת הַשָּׁוְא יְדַבֵּרוּ הֶבֶל יְנַחֵמוּן

Alternatively, they will "drink" the blood of their enemies, i.e., they will vanquish them (*Radak*).

וּמָלְאוּ כַּמִּזְרָק כְּזָוִיּוֹת מִזְבֵּחַ — *They will be filled like the bowl, and like the corners of the altar.*

They will be so "filled" with the blood of their enemies, like the bowls used to collect the blood for the sacrificial offerings, and like the corners of the altar that are filled with the blood of the sacrifices (*Radak*). Alternatively, they will be filled with such an abundance of good (see v. 17), as full as the bowls by the altar that are filled with blood and like the corners of the altar that are filled with wine from the libations (*Rashi*).

16. וְהוֹשִׁיעָם ה׳ ... כְּצֹאן עַמּוֹ — *Hashem ... will save them ... like the sheep of His people.*

God will save His people as He saved the "flocks of sheep" that He brought out of Egypt to become His nation (*Rashi*). At that time the Israelites were under the care of Moses who tended to them as a shepherd tends to his flocks (see *Psalms* 77:21) (*Ibn Ezra*).

כִּי אַבְנֵי־נֵזֶר מִתְנוֹסְסוֹת עַל־אַדְמָתוֹ — *For the "stones of the crown" will be exalted on His land.*

The Hasmoneans, who were Kohanim and prided themselves with the stones of the breastplate and *Ephod*, will be exalted through the miracles that will occur on their land (*Rashi*). Although the word אַדְמָתוֹ actually means his land, *Rashi* understands that it is referring to the land of the people, it is their land. Alternatively, *Radak* renders Judah and Ephraim who are like the stones of the crown will be exalted on His land, i.e., the Holy Land (*Radak*).

17. כִּי מַה־טּוּבוֹ — *How good.*

How abundant is the goodness that is reserved for that generation (*Rashi*)! Alternatively, how good will the produce of your land be (*Radak*)! A third explanation is: How great will be the beauty of your young men and maidens *because of* their grain and wine (*Mahari Kara*)!

The word מַה denotes astonishment and wonder at the great abundance [of goodness and beauty that has been set aside for the nation] (*Metzudos*).

וְתִירוֹשׁ יְנוֹבֵב בְּתֻלוֹת — *And the wine that will make maidens sing.*

יְנוֹבֵב is related to נִיב שְׂפָתַיִם [*Isaiah* 57:19] (*Ibn Ezra*) or יָנוּב חָכְמָה [*Proverbs* 10:31], *to speak* (*Metzudos*); the wine will cause the maidens to speak in song and joy (*Rashi*); hence, our translation, *to sing*.

In alternative interpretations, *Rashi* and *Ibn Ezra* translate יְנוֹבֵב as *fruitful*, relating it to יְנוּבוּן בְּשֵׂיבָה, *to bear fruit even in old age* (*Psalms* 92:14) (*Ibn Ezra*), and render wine that is fruitful and grows in virgin soil, קַרְקַע בְּתוּלָה — superior wine.

Actually, the translation of יְנוֹבֵב as *speech* originates from the translation *fruitful*, for "speech is the fruit of the tongue" — הַדִּיבּוּר הוּא פְּרִי הַלָּשׁוֹן (*Metzudos, Isaiah* 57:19).

they will be filled like the bowl, and like the corners of the Altar. [16] *HASHEM their God will save them on that day like the sheep of His people, for the "stones of the crown" will be exalted on His land.* [17] *How good and how beautiful will be the grain of young men and the wine that will make maidens sing.*

[1] *Request rain of HASHEM in the season of the late rains, [of] HASHEM Who makes rainclouds; and He will provide them a shower of rain, for each person, herbage in the field.* [2] *For the teraphim speak words of nothingness, and the diviners see falsehoods and the dreamers speak lies; they comfort with meaningless words.*

X

1. ... שַׁאֲלוּ מֵה׳ מָטָר בְּעֵת מַלְקוֹשׁ ... — *Request rain of Hashem in the season of the late rains ...*

The time of which the prophet is speaking in the previous chapter will be a time of Divine favor. Even if one will entreat God for unusually heavy rain at the very end of the rainy season and it is required for the growth of the crops (*Rashi; Mahari Kara*), God will provide it and the crops will grow quickly (*Radak*).

The early rains, יוֹרֶה, fall during the month of Marchesvhan; the late rains, מַלְקוֹשׁ, fall during the month of Nissan (*Taanis* 6a). Our translation of חֲזִיזִים follows *Rashi* who translates *rain clouds*. Other translations are *strong winds* (*Targum Yonasan*) or lightning (*Radak*). According to *Taanis* 9b they are *flying clouds*, i.e., clouds that are thinner and lower in the sky than the heavier clouds and therefore seem to fly by faster. R' Yochanan said they are a sign of impending rain.

לְאִישׁ עֵשֶׂב בַּשָּׂדֶה — *For each person, herbage in the field.*

At this time of extraordinary Divine Providence, God will provide rain even if it is necessary for only one individual (אִישׁ) and even if it is necessary for only one of his fields (בַּשָּׂדֶה) and even if it is necessary for only one plant (עֵשֶׂב). He will have the rain fall only on that plant (*Radak* from *Taanis* 9b).

2. כִּי הַתְּרָפִים דִּבְּרוּ־אָוֶן וְהַקּוֹסְמִים חָזוּ שֶׁקֶר וַחֲלֹמוֹת הַשָּׁוְא יְדַבֵּרוּ הֶבֶל יְנַחֵמוּן — *For the teraphim speak words of nothingness, and the diviners see falsehoods and the dreamers speak lies; they comfort with meaningless words.*

At that future time, the people will realize that those who misled their forefathers, and encouraged them to rebel against God, spoke words of nothingness, falsehood and lies by predicting a peace that did not come (*Rashi*) and declaring that the destruction of the Temple would never take place (*Radak*). They will see that only the prophecies of the true prophets have been realized (*Radak*).

כִּי הַתְּרָפִים דִּבְּרוּ־אָוֶן — *For the teraphim speak words of nothingness.*

Some commentators understand this literally and explain that the *teraphim* were images made by astrologers which at certain times had the power of speech (see *Ibn Ezra, Genesis* 31:19). *Metzudos*, however, writes that they had human form but were made to speak through *sorcery*. Although from *Genesis* 31:30 it would appear that *teraphim* were idols,

עַל־כֵּן נָסְעוּ כְמוֹ־צֹאן יַעֲנוּ כִּי־אֵין רֹעֶה׃ **ג** עַל־הָרֹעִים חָרָה אַפִּי וְעַל־הָעַתּוּדִים אֶפְקוֹד כִּי־פָקַד יהוה צְבָאוֹת אֶת־עֶדְרוֹ אֶת־בֵּית יְהוּדָה וְשָׂם אוֹתָם כְּסוּס הוֹדוֹ בַּמִּלְחָמָה׃ **ד** מִמֶּנּוּ פִנָּה מִמֶּנּוּ יָתֵד מִמֶּנּוּ קֶשֶׁת מִלְחָמָה מִמֶּנּוּ יֵצֵא כָל־נוֹגֵשׂ יַחְדָּו׃ **ה** וְהָיוּ כְגִבֹּרִים בּוֹסִים בְּטִיט חוּצוֹת בַּמִּלְחָמָה וְנִלְחֲמוּ כִּי יהוה עִמָּם וְהֹבִישׁוּ רֹכְבֵי סוּסִים׃ **ו** וְגִבַּרְתִּי | אֶת־בֵּית יְהוּדָה וְאֶת־בֵּית יוֹסֵף אוֹשִׁיעַ

Ramban (*Genesis* 31:19) writes that they were not necessarily worshiped as idols but were oracles used to magically foretell the future. The word *teraphim* is derived from the root רפה, *weak*, and alludes to the weakness of their prognostications. [For extensive treatment of *teraphim*, see ArtScroll *Bereishis* 31:19.]

וְהַקּוֹסְמִים חָזוּ שֶׁקֶר — *And the diviners see falsehoods.*

Although generally translated as *diviners* [one who consults a stick and asks, "Shall I go or shall I not go" — *Rashi, Deuteronomy* 18:10], *Metzudos* translates stargazers, i.e., astrologers.

Unlike the major commentators, *Abarbanel* maintains that the prophet is not referring to Jewish diviners but to the enemies of the Jews who would consult the diviners before going to battle against Israel.

עַל־כֵּן נָסְעוּ ... כִּי־אֵין רֹעֶה — *Therefore they have wandered off ... for there is no shepherd.*

They were exiled from their land [because they followed the advice of the diviners] as sheep that have no shepherd (*Radak*) for they had no leader that was capable of guiding them on the proper path and ultimately were humbled by their enemy (*Metzudos*).

3. עַל־הָרֹעִים חָרָה אַפִּי וְעַל־הָעַתּוּדִים אֶפְקוֹד ... — *My wrath is kindled against the shepherds, and I will punish the he-goats ...*

The shepherds and he-goats are metaphoric references to the kings of Greece and their officers (*Rashi*) (see *Daniel* 8:21 where the kingdom of Greece is metaphorically referred to as he-goats). *Radak* identifies the shepherd as the kings of Greece who oppressed Israel until they were overpowered by the Hasmoneans. At the time that God will remember His flock, He will punish the kingdom of Greece.

Because Israel was metaphorically likened to sheep, the prophet likened the kings who ruled over her to shepherds or to the he-goats that go before the sheep and the sheep follow them (*Radak*).

וְשָׂם אוֹתָם כְּסוּס הוֹדוֹ בַּמִּלְחָמָה — *And He will make them like a horse whose glory is in war.*

At that time Israel will show its power and strength in battle as does the horse. See *Job* 39:21: "He [the horse] rejoices in [his] strength, he goes out to face weapons" (*Radak*).

Malbim explains these two verses as foretelling events pertaining to Messianic times. God will then take to task the shepherds who misled His flock through their *teraphim*, divinations and dreams. Instead of being like the meek lamb, Israel will then become like the brave horse and display its strength in the war of Gog and Magog.

4. מִמֶּנּוּ פִנָּה מִמֶּנּוּ יָתֵד מִמֶּנּוּ קֶשֶׁת מִלְחָמָה — *From themselves [will come forth] the cornerstone; from themselves [will come forth] the peg; from themselves [will come forth] the bow of war.*

This entire verse is a metaphoric description of the Israelite leaders. Until

Therefore, they have wandered off like sheep; they are humbled, for there is no shepherd.

[3]My wrath is kindled against the shepherds, and I will punish the he-goats. For HASHEM, Master of Legions, has remembered his flock, the House of Judah, and He will make them like a horse whose glory is in war. [4]From themselves [will come forth] the cornerstone; from themselves [will come forth] the peg; from themselves [will come forth] the bow of war; from themselves all the leaders will come forth together. [5]They will be like mighty warriors trampling [their enemies] in the mud of the streets in war; they will wage war, for HASHEM will be with them; and the [enemy] riders of horses will be put to shame. [6]I will give power to the House of Judah and I will save the House of Joseph;

now, the Israelite nation was ruled by foreign kings; now their rulers will come forth from themselves (*Mahari Kara*), from the tribe of Judah (*Metzudos*). The פִּנָּה, *the cornerstone,* is the most unique stone of a structure for it is the only stone visible from two sides (*Metzudos*). It therefore symbolizes the king, the most esteemed person of the nation (*Rashi; Metzudos*). Alternatively, it may be referring to the leaders of the nation (*Radak*). The יָתֵד, *the peg,* is symbolic of the princes (*Rashi*) or the officers (*Radak; Metzudos*) upon whom the entire nation depend [all the burdens of the nation are "hung" on them] like the peg upon which all vessels are hung (see *Radak* to *Isaiah* 23). The קֶשֶׁת מִלְחָמָה, *the bow of war,* symbolizes the warrior who will lead the nation in battle (*Rashi*) without the assistance of other nations (*Radak*).

מִמֶּנּוּ יֵצֵא כָל־נוֹגֵשׂ יַחְדָּו — *From themselves all the leaders will come forth together.*

Our translation follows *Targum Yonasan* who translates נוֹגֵשׂ as פַּרְנְסוֹהִי. *Radak*, however, translates נוֹגֵשׂ literally, *oppressors,* and explains that Scripture refers to the leaders as oppressors because they will oppress their enemies.

5. וְהָיוּ כְגִבֹּרִים בּוֹסִים בְּטִיט חוּצוֹת בַּמִּלְחָמָה — *They will be like mighty warriors trampling [their enemies] in the mud of the streets in war.*

The phrases of this verse are reversed and should be understood: In war they will walk and trample people [i.e., their enemies] as mighty men trample the mud of the streets (*Rashi*). Israel will be mighty, like the men of Greece had formerly been and will trample their enemies in the mud of the streets (*Radak*).

וְנִלְחֲמוּ כִּי ה׳ עִמָּם ... — *They will wage war, for Hashem will be with them ...*

Although they are unfamiliar with the tactics and strategies of war, they will battle as seasoned soldiers for G-d will be with them (*Metzudos*). The horsemen of the enemy will be put to shame for Israel will defeat them while battling only on foot (*Radak*).

6. וְגִבַּרְתִּי אֶת־בֵּית יְהוּדָה וְאֶת־בֵּית יוֹסֵף אוֹשִׁיעַ — *I will give power to the House of Judah and I will save the House of Joseph.*

God will strengthen the House of Judah and give them the power to defeat their enemies (*Radak*) in their war against the Greeks (*Rashi*). And He will

וְהוֹשְׁבוֹתִים כִּי רִחַמְתִּים וְהָיוּ כַּאֲשֶׁר לֹא־
ז זְנַחְתִּים כִּי אֲנִי יהוה אֱלֹהֵיהֶם וְאֶעֱנֵם: וְהָיוּ
כְגִבּוֹר אֶפְרַיִם וְשָׂמַח לִבָּם כְּמוֹ־יָיִן וּבְנֵיהֶם יִרְאוּ
ח וְשָׂמֵחוּ יָגֵל לִבָּם בַּיהוה: אֶשְׁרְקָה לָהֶם וַאֲקַבְּצֵם
ט כִּי פְדִיתִים וְרָבוּ כְּמוֹ רָבוּ: וְאֶזְרָעֵם בָּעַמִּים
וּבַמֶּרְחַקִּים יִזְכְּרוּנִי וְחָיוּ אֶת־בְּנֵיהֶם וָשָׁבוּ:
י וַהֲשִׁיבוֹתִים מֵאֶרֶץ מִצְרַיִם וּמֵאַשּׁוּר אֲקַבְּצֵם

save the House of Joseph, the Ten Tribes of the Northern Kingdom (*Mari Kara*), who had been exiled during the days of Sennacherib to the cities of Halah and Habor. These cities were situated on the Gozan River far removed from civilization (see *II Kings* 17:6, ArtScroll edition). They will remain there and dwell safely in those cities (*Rashi*).

Ibn Ezra explains that Judah and Joseph are referring to those Israelites who had *returned from Assyria* to the Land of Israel during the days of the Second Temple. He is sharply criticized by *Abarbanel* who maintains that there is no recorded evidence of any member of the House of Joseph who returned to the Land of Israel from Assyria during the Second Temple era. Because of this, *Radak* (v. 12) writes that although he explained this chapter like most commentators, that it is referring to the Second Temple era, he feels that the true explanation is that it is referring to Messianic times.

וְהוֹשְׁבוֹתִים — *I will settle them.*

Our translation follows *Rashi* who explains וְהוֹשְׁבוֹתִים as וְהוֹשַׁבְתִּים, an expression of *settling*, לְשׁוֹן יְשִׁיבָה. *Ibn Ezra* and *Radak*, however, see וְהוֹשְׁבוֹתִים, as a combination of וַהֲשִׁיבוֹתִים, *and I will return them*, and וְהוֹשַׁבְתִּים, *and I will settle them.* During Messianic times, God will do both: return them to their land and settle them to live tranquilly and securely (*Radak*).

וְהָיוּ כַּאֲשֶׁר לֹא־זְנַחְתִּים ... — *And they will be as if I had not rejected them ...*

As the mighty God, He will bestow goodness upon them, at that time, so much so, that they will forget all the misery that they had suffered in exile (*Radak; Metzudos*). They will then live in honor and peace as though G-d had never forsaken them (*Radak*).

7. ... וְהָיוּ כְגִבּוֹר אֶפְרַיִם — *Ephraim will be like a mighty warrior ...*

Although the people of Ephraim have no military experience, they will nevertheless battle their enemies and strike them down as mighty warriors (*Metzudos*). They will then rejoice over having defeated their enemies (*Radak*).

וְשָׂמַח לִבָּם כְּמוֹ־יָיִן — *And their heart will be happy as [with] wine.*

Our translation follows *Ibn Ezra* who translates the verse as if it would read כְּמוֹ בְּיַיִן. Alternatively, *Targum Yonasan* renders and their heart will be happy as a *person who drinks* wine.

וּבְנֵיהֶם יִרְאוּ וְשָׂמֵחוּ יָגֵל לִבָּם בַּה׳ — *Their children will see and be happy; their heart will rejoice in Hashem.*

The children who are not accustomed to waging war will rejoice in the victory of their father (*Radak*) and in God's salvation (*Metzudos*).

Alshich sees Ephraim as alluding to the tradition that there will be a Messiah descended from Joseph who will lead Israel in battle *like a mighty warrior* (וְהָיוּ כְגִבּוֹר אֶפְרַיִם). However this Messiah is destined to eventually be killed in battle and the happiness brought by his victories will only be temporary — *like the happiness brought by wine* (וְשָׂמַח לִבָּם כְּמוֹ יָיִן). [After that, the events will be set in motion for the rule of the Davidic Messiah] at which time *their heart will rejoice in Hashem* (יָגֵל לִבָּם בַּה׳). (For more information on this subject see ArtScroll *Yechezkel* 37:8.)

I will settle them, for I will have mercy upon them, and they will be as if I had not rejected them; for I am HASHEM *their God, and I will answer them.* [7] *Ephraim will be like a mighty warrior, and their heart will be happy as [with] wine. Their children will see and be happy; their heart will rejoice in* HASHEM. [8] *I will whistle to them and gather them, for I have redeemed them; and they will become as numerous as they had been numerous.* [9] *I will sow them among the nations, and they shall remember Me in far-away places; they will live with their children and they will return.* [10] *I will bring them back from the land of Egypt; I will gather them in from Assyria;*

8. אֶשְׁרְקָה לָהֶם וַאֲקַבְּצֵם כִּי פְדִיתִים — *I will whistle to them and gather them, for I have redeemed them.* God addresses the Jews of the Messianic era and, figuratively speaking, tells that at the time of the future redemption He will whistle to those who have strayed from Him during their stay in exile as one whistles to get the attention of a lost person (*Rashi*). This will serve as a signal that those in exile should gather to the Land of Israel (*Metzudos*). Alternatively, because of the suffering inflicted upon them by the heathen kings, many Jews had been scattered among the nations. They returned to the Land of Israel during the days of the Hasmoneans (*Radak*).

וְרָבוּ כְּמוֹ רָבוּ — *And they will become as numerous as they had been numerous.*

They will become as numerous in exile as they had been in Egypt (*Rashi*). Alternatively, because of the plots and pogroms that the Jews suffered in exile their numbers diminished. At the time of the future redemption they will become as numerous as they were previously (*Malbim*).

9. ... וְאֶזְרָעֵם בָּעַמִּים — *I will sow them among the nations ...*

Our translation follows *Rashi* and *Ibn Ezra* who relate וְאֶזְרָעֵם to זוֹרֵעַ, *to seed*, and explain that just as one sows a small amount of seed so that he may reap a larger crop, so too, will God sow Israel among the nations to increase their number. Alternatively, *Targum Yonasan* followed by *Radak*, *Mahari Kara* and *Metzudos* translate *scatter*. God had scattered them among the nations because of the suffering inflicted upon them by the heathen kings but they nevertheless remembered God and kept His commandments, wherever they were.

וְחָיוּ אֶת־בְּנֵיהֶם וָשָׁבוּ — *They will live with their children and they will return.*

They will live there with their children (*Rashi*). They will return to their land in the days of the Hasmoneans (*Radak*).

Radak quotes others who explain this entire verse as taking place *after* the nation had been saved during the days of the Hasmoneans. When the Jewish people will travel among the nations, they will be held in high esteem because of the victory that God wrought for them and they will return to their land with great wealth.

10. וַהֲשִׁיבוֹתִים מֵאֶרֶץ מִצְרַיִם וּמֵאַשּׁוּר אֲקַבְּצֵם — *I will bring them back from the land of Egypt; I will gather them in from Asssyria.*

י/יא־יב

וְאֶל־אֶרֶץ גִּלְעָד וּלְבָנוֹן אֲבִיאֵם וְלֹא יִמָּצֵא
יא לָהֶם׃ וְעָבַר בַּיָּם צָרָה וְהִכָּה בַיָּם גַּלִּים
וְהֹבִישׁוּ כֹּל מְצוּלוֹת יְאֹר וְהוּרַד גְּאוֹן אַשּׁוּר
יב וְשֵׁבֶט מִצְרַיִם יָסוּר׃ וְגִבַּרְתִּים בַּיהוָה וּבִשְׁמוֹ
יִתְהַלָּכוּ נְאֻם יְהוָה׃

יא/א־ב

א פְּתַח לְבָנוֹן דְּלָתֶיךָ
ב וְתֹאכַל אֵשׁ בַּאֲרָזֶיךָ׃ הֵילֵל בְּרוֹשׁ כִּי־נָפַל אֶרֶז

I will bring them back from Egypt and Assyria[1] to the Land of Israel but because of their great number they will be too numerous to settle there (*Radak*) and will find it necessary to conquer the surrounding lands (*Mahari Kara*).

וְאֶל־אֶרֶץ גִּלְעָד וּלְבָנוֹן אֲבִיאֵם ... — *I will bring them to the land of Gilead and Lebanon ...*

The land of Gilead is the area east of the Jordan River and Lebanon is the entire area of Israel on its west (*Radak*). It is referred to as Lebanon because of the forest situated there that was so named (*Metzudos*) or since the forest consisted of cedar trees that stand taller than any other trees, it is a symbol for the entire Land of Israel which is "higher" than any other land (*Radak, Ezekiel* 17:3).

Alternatively, Lebanon is another name for the Holy Temple (*Targum Yonasan; Rashi*) because it whitened [לָבָן] the stains of Israel's sins (*Yoma* 39b).

11. וְעָבַר בַּיָּם צָרָה וְהִכָּה בַיָּם גַּלִּים — *Misfortune will pass through the sea, and [God] will strike the waves in the sea.*

Zechariah foresees the destruction of Tyre, the leading city of Edom which is situated in the midst of the sea. God will strike the waves of the sea to inundate *Tyre* (*Rashi*). [See commentary to 9:4.]

Mahari Kara maintains that this prophecy is specifically foretelling the destruction of the Romans. Alternatively, it is referring to the heathen nations in general who are likened to the seas and deep rivers. Misfortune will pass through the nations who are as numerous as the waters of the seas and rivers. God will strike their high-ranking officers and princes — *the waves of the sea* — and annihilate the people of these nations — *the deep waters* (*Metzudos*).

Scripture chose to mention Assyria and Egypt because they did more harm to Israel than any other nation (*Radak*).

וְהֹבִישׁוּ כֹּל מְצוּלוֹת יְאֹר — *All the deep waters of the river will dry up.*

This is referring to Egypt (*Rashi*) for its entire sustenance was dependent on the Nile river (*Mahari Kara*).

וְהוּרַד גְּאוֹן אַשּׁוּר ... — *The pride of Assyria will be brought down.*

The Assyrians will not dominate Israel for the fear of the Hasmoneans will be upon them[2] (*Ibn Ezra*).

12. וְגִבַּרְתִּים בַּה׳ ... — *I will give them power through Hashem ...*

God will give Israel power through His salvation (*Metzudos*). Although God is the speaker, He refers to Himself in the third person (*Radak; Metzudos*).

XI

1. פְּתַח לְבָנוֹן דְּלָתֶיךָ וְתֹאכַל אֵשׁ בַּאֲרָזֶיךָ — *Open your doors, O Lebanon, and let fire consume your cedars.*

The commentators differ in their interpretation of this prophecy. *Targum Yonasan*, followed by *Rashi* understands

1. The Ten Tribes had been exiled to Assyria by Sennacherib and most did not return when he was defeated. At the advent of the Messiah, all twelve tribes will meet in Egypt and will then be gathered to the Land of Israel (*Radak* to *Isaiah* 27:12).

2. See commentary to v.6.

10/11-12

I will bring them to the land of Gilead and Lebanon; there will not be enough [room] for them. [11] *Misfortune will pass through the sea, and [God] will strike the waves in the sea; all the deep waters of the river will dry up; the pride of Assyria will be brought down, and the staff of Egypt will depart.* [12] *I will give them power through* HASHEM, *and they will walk with His Name — the word of* HASHEM.

11/1-2

[1] *Open your doors, O Lebanon, and let fire consume your cedars!* [2] *Wail, O cypress, for the cedar has fallen,*

לְבָנוֹן, *Lebanon,* as representing the nations of the world who are as numerous as the trees of the mighty forest of Lebanon. The prophet calls out to the nations, "Open your gates so the fire may consume the aggressors among you who have oppressed the people of Israel." Within this interpretation, *Abarbanel* suggests that Scripture is referring to the destruction of Edom and Ishmael who will dominate the Land of Israel for many hundreds of years. The prophet calls to the Land of Israel to open its gates so that these powerful nations may be destroyed. Alternatively, *Ibn Ezra* maintains that the prophet is lamenting the future downfall of the Hasmonean Dynasty. Others say that לְבָנוֹן, *Lebanon,* is referring to the Land of Israel (see commentary to 10:10), and explain that Zechariah foresaw that the Second Temple which was not yet constructed will eventually be destroyed. He instructs the Land of Israel to open its gates so that the enemy may enter and destroy the Land and the Temple.

Although Zechariah had been granted prophecies foretelling events of the future redemption, he had not been told when in the future the redemption would take place. Now that he foresaw the destruction of the Second Temple and the tragedies that will occur during that era, he realized that the prophecies of the future redemption will not be fulfilled during the Second Temple era (*Malbim*). Indeed, the Talmud (*Yoma* 39b) writes that for forty years prior to the destruction of the Temple, the doors of the הֵיכָל, *the Sanctuary,* would swing open by themselves, a portentous sign for the enemies of Israel to enter the Temple and destroy it (*Rashi* ibid.) until R' Yochanan ben Zakkai rebuked them and said "Sanctuary, Sanctuary, why do you terrify us?"[1] I know that you will be destroyed, for Zechariah son of Iddo[2] had already prophesied concerning you, *Open your doors, O Lebanon,* foretelling that the spontaneous opening of the Temple's doors would signify the impending fiery destruction of the Temple (see *Rashi* to v. 3).

2. הֵילֵל בְּרוֹשׁ כִּי־נָפַל אֶרֶז ... — *Wail, O cypress, for the cedar has fallen ...*

The prophecy metaphorically describes the leaders of the nations as trees of the forest. Wail, O cypress tree, and wail, O oak tree, for the cedar tree has fallen and both of you are sure to fall (*Rashi; Mahari Kara; Abarbanel*). The cypress tree represents the rulers of the foreign nations and the cedar tree represents their kings (*Rashi*). The oak tree, which is smaller than the cypress tree, represents the princes and the king's

1. This translation follows *Maharsha*. Our text is: "will terrify *yourself*." In any event, R' Yochanan ben Zakkai scolded the doors because the doors were opening forty years prematurely and it is enough that the misfortune be suffered in its time.

2. Zechariah was actually the son of Berechiah and the grandson of Iddo.

אֲשֶׁר אַדִּרִים שֻׁדָּדוּ הֵילִילוּ אַלּוֹנֵי בָשָׁן כִּי יָרַד
ג יַעַר °הבצור: קוֹל יִלְלַת הָרֹעִים כִּי שֻׁדְּדָה
אַדַּרְתָּם קוֹל שַׁאֲגַת כְּפִירִים כִּי שֻׁדַּד גְּאוֹן
ד הַיַּרְדֵּן: כֹּה אָמַר יהוה אֱלֹהָי רְעֵה אֶת־צֹאן
ה הַהֲרֵגָה: אֲשֶׁר קֹנֵיהֶן יַהַרְגֻן וְלֹא יֶאְשָׁמוּ וּמֹכְרֵיהֶן
יֹאמַר בָּרוּךְ יהוה וַאעְשִׁר וְרֹעֵיהֶם לֹא יַחְמוֹל
ו עֲלֵיהֶן: כִּי לֹא אֶחְמוֹל עוֹד עַל־יֹשְׁבֵי הָאָרֶץ נְאֻם־
יהוה וְהִנֵּה אָנֹכִי מַמְצִיא אֶת־הָאָדָם אִישׁ בְּיַד־
רֵעֵהוּ וּבְיַד מַלְכּוֹ וְכִתְּתוּ אֶת־הָאָרֶץ וְלֹא אַצִּיל
ז מִיָּדָם: וָאֶרְעֶה אֶת־צֹאן הַהֲרֵגָה לָכֵן עֲנִיֵּי הַצֹּאן

°הַבָּצִיר ק׳

servants (*Mahari Kara*). Alternatively, when the enemy will enter the Land, he will cut down its leaders (*Metzudos*).

כִּי יָרַד יַעַר הַבָּצִיר — *Because the impregnable forest has come down.*

The glory of the impregnable forest, i.e., the kings of the foreign nations, has gone down (*Mahari Kara*). *Rashi* translates יָרַד as broken (נִשְׁבַּר) and renders the fortified forest, i.e., *the strong walled cities have been broken.*

3. קוֹל יִלְלַת הָרֹעִים כִּי שֻׁדְּדָה אַדַּרְתָּם — *There is a sound of the shepherds' wailing, for their power has been vanquished.*

After foretelling the destruction of the foreign nations and their leaders, the prophet describes the cries and shouts of the kings, metaphorically described as shepherds, as they see their dominion being removed (*Targum Yonasan; Rashi*). Alternatively, the shepherds are the Israelite leaders who wail and lament the loss of their fortified strongholds that have fallen to the enemy (*Metzudos*).

קוֹל שַׁאֲגַת כְּפִירִים ... — *There is a sound of young lions' roar ...*

The princes, metaphorically represented by the roaring young lions, will wail for their palaces have been destroyed (*Metzudos*).

The heights of the Jordan were inhabited by lions (*Rashi; Metzudos*) (see *Jeremiah* 49:19).

The following prophecy is difficult to fully comprehend because its ideas are very deep and enigmatic (*Abarbanel*). There are two divergent approaches offered by the commentators. *Targum Yonasan, Rashi* and *Radak* [first explanation] understand that this prophecy is recalling events that occurred during the First Temple era. *Ibn Ezra, Radak* and others explain that the prophet is foretelling events that will take place during the Second Temple era.

4. כֹּה אָמַר ה׳ אֱלֹהָי רְעֵה ... — *Thus said Hashem, My God: Tend ...*

Zechariah is instructed to prophetically speak about those who will now lead and provide for Israel in the future (*Rashi*).

צֹאן הַהֲרֵגָה — *The flock meant to be slain.* This is referring to Israel, who had been slain and devoured by her shepherds (*Rashi*). Alternatively, the prophet refers to Israel as *the flock meant to be slain* for whenever they transgress God's commandments they are delivered into the hands of their enemies to be slaughtered (*Radak*).

for the mighty ones have been vanquished; wail, O oaks of Bashan, because the impregnable forest has come down. [3]*There is a sound of the shepherds' wailing, for their power has been vanquished; there is a sound of young lions' roar, for the heights of the Jordan have been vanquished.*

[4]*Thus said HASHEM, My God: Tend the flock meant to be slain,* [5]*whom their buyers slay and they are not guilty and those who sell them say, "Blessed be HASHEM! Now I am rich!" and whose shepherds do not pity them.* [6]*For I will no longer pity the inhabitants of the land — the word of HASHEM. Behold, I am giving over the people, each one into the hand of his fellow and into the hand of his king; they will crush the land, and I will not save [them] from their hand.* [7]*I had tended the flock meant to be slain because they were the meekest of the flock.*

5. אֲשֶׁר קֹנֵיהֶן יַהַרְגֻן וְלֹא יֶאְשָׁמוּ — *Whom their buyers slay and they are not guilty.*

Zechariah foretells that Israel will be sold, bought and murdered by the kings of the nations to whom they will be exiled and no one will have any feelings of guilt for doing so (*Rashi*).

וּמֹכְרֵיהֶן יֹאמַר בָּרוּךְ ה׳ וַאעְשִׁר — *And those who sell them say, "Blessed be Hashem! Now I am rich!"*

Instead of feeling guilty, they thank God for assisting them in the sale of an unprofitable item and making them wealthy through the sale of the Jews (*Rashi*), for they erroneously think that they are fulfilling God's will by doing this (*Radak*). See *Isaiah* 36:10 where Sennacherib also felt that he fulfilled God's will when he destroyed the Land of Judah.

וְרֹעֵיהֶם לֹא יַחְמוֹל עֲלֵיהֶן — *And whose shepherds do not pity them.*

The kings of the foreign nations have no mercy upon Israel (*Mahari Kara*). Alternatively, God Who is their shepherd has no mercy on them and will deliver them into the hands of their enemies (*Radak*).

6. כִּי לֹא אֶחְמוֹל עוֹד עַל־יֹשְׁבֵי הָאָרֶץ נְאֻם־ה׳ ... — *For I will no longer pity the inhabitants of the land — the word of Hashem ...*

If the inhabitants of the Land of Israel will not improve their ways, God will no longer show them any mercy. They will destroy one another and both the Israelite king and the gentile king who rules over them will destroy them. Ultimately, they will destroy the land and because they sinned against Him, God will not save them (*Radak*). *Metzudos* notes that this did indeed occur at the end of the Second Temple era.

7. וָאֶרְעֶה אֶת־צֹאן הַהֲרֵגָה לָכֵן עֲנִיֵּי הַצֹּאן — *I had tended the flock meant to be slain because they were the meekest of the flock.*

The imagery of Israel as *the flock meant to be slain* continues. God tells Zechariah that in the early days when His relationship with Israel first began, it was He Who tended the flock; indeed, they were the meekest of the flock when He began to tend them (*Rashi*).

וָאֶקַּח־לִי שְׁנֵי מַקְלוֹת לְאַחַד קָרָאתִי נֹעַם וּלְאַחַד קָרָאתִי חֹבְלִים וָאֶרְעֶה אֶת־הַצֹּאן:
ח וָאַכְחִד אֶת־שְׁלֹשֶׁת הָרֹעִים בְּיֶרַח אֶחָד וַתִּקְצַר נַפְשִׁי בָּהֶם וְגַם־נַפְשָׁם בָּחֲלָה בִי:

וָאֶקַּח־לִי שְׁנֵי מַקְלוֹת ... — *I took for Myself two staffs ...*

Shepherds lead their sheep with staffs; the two staffs represent the two kingdoms that lead the Israelite nation (*Rashi; Mahari Kara*). The Northern Kingdom of Israel is called "Noam," *pleasantness,* because its king Jeroboam used pleasant words to lure ten of the tribes into his camp. The Kingdom of Judah is called "Hobelim," *destroyers,* because its king, Rehoboam, told the nation that he would *chastise them with scorpions* and ruled with a destructive iron hand (*I Kings* 12:11) (*Rashi; Mahari Kara*).

Alternatively, *Radak* maintains that the two staffs represent God's fluctuating relationship with the people of Israel. When Israel followed in His ways and observed the laws of the Torah and its kings led the nation and taught them to do what is proper and right, then God acted with "pleasantness" and the nation enjoyed peaceful and plentiful times. But when the nation sinned and corrupted its ways and violated the laws of the Torah, God dealt with them as a "destroyer"; He did not protect them from their enemies and destruction took place. Others explain that it is not God Who is the shepherd but it is Zechariah. God had instructed the prophet (v.4) to *tend the flock;* He now replies that He tended the flock because He had pity on them for they were the meekest, alluding to the righteous of the nation (*Abarbanel*). Zechariah took two staffs to lead his flock representing the Hasmoneans. Noam, *pleasantness,* represents Judah, Jonathan and Simeon, the sons of Matathias, God-fearing people who guided and led the nation with righteousness. Hobelim, *destroyers,* represent their descendants who ruled with an iron fist and with wickedness and destroyed the nation (*Abarbanel; Metzudos*). *Ibn Ezra* explains that the staffs that were used to tend the flock represent Zerubbabel and Nehemiah. Since they were not kings but governors, they are referred to as staffs and not shepherds.

The *Talmud* (*Sanhedrin* 24a) sees the two staffs as alluding to the Torah scholars of the Land of Israel and to their counterparts, the Torah scholars of Babylonia. נֹעַם represents the scholars of the Land of Israel, for they would conduct themselves graciously with one another and work together and try to understand the words of each person. By contrast, the scholars of Babylonia would sharply refute each other's words with stinging retorts and are therefore represented by חֹבְלִים.

In summary, the different opinions of Noam and Hobelim are:

	Noam	**Hobelim**
Rashi	Kingdom of Israel	Kingdom of Judah
Radak	God's Rule through peace	God's Rule with destruction
Abarbanel	Hasmoneans — Judah, Simeon, Jonathan	Later Hasmonean Rulers
Ibn Ezra	Zerubbabel	Nehemiah
Talmud — *Sanhedrin* **24a**	Torah Scholars of the Land of Israel	Torah Scholars of Babylonia

וָאֶרְעֶה אֶת הַצֹּאן — *And I tended the flock.*

God protects His people from the nations both in good times and bad (*Radak*).

8. וָאַכְחִד אֶת־שְׁלֹשֶׁת הָרֹעִים בְּיֶרַח אֶחָד — *I removed the three shepherds in one month.*

11/8 *I took for Myself two staffs — one I called "Noam" and the other I called "Hobelim" and I tended the flock.* [8] *I removed the three shepherds in one month, and My soul became impatient with them, for their soul also found Me repulsive.*

The three shepherds are King Jehoram of the Northern Kingdom, King Ahaziah of Judah, and Ahaziah's potential successors, all murdered by Jehu at the same time (*II Kings* 9,10). God had them slain because they had exceedingly corrupted their ways (*Rashi*).

Other interpretations of the three shepherds are: the three sons of Josiah, king of Judah: Jehoahaz, Jehoiakim and Zedekiah, who died at the hands of their enemies within several years of one another (*II Kings* 23-25). Accordingly, in one month [בְּיֶרַח אֶחָד] is figurative (*Radak*).

Ibn Ezra suggests that they may represent Joshua the Kohen Gadol, the כֹּהֵן הַמָּשׁוּחַ, the Kohen anointed for the task of admonishing the nation before going to battle, and the כֹּהֵן מִשְׁנֶה, the assistant Kohen Gadol. Alternatively, they may be the prophets Haggai, Zechariah and Malachi, for prophecy terminated with their death.

Abarbanel and *Metzudos* see the three sons of Matathias — Judah, Simeon and Jonathan — as the three shepherds. They led the nation for a total of thirty years, alluded to by the thirty days of "one month" [בְּיֶרַח אֶחָד].

Malbim understands that the three shepherds may be the three Persian kings who were gracious toward Israel: Cyrus, Artahshasta (Artaxerxes) and Darius. Their reign ended abruptly when Alexander the Great conquered Persia and destroyed their entire empire. After his death, the Greeks dealt harshly and cruelly with Israel.

The Sages (*Taanis* 9a) interpret this verse homiletically and maintain that the three shepherds are Moses, Aaron and Miriam, the three who led Israel during their sojourn in the desert before they entered the Land of Canaan. In their merit, three special gifts were bestowed upon Israel. The manna was granted in the merit of Moses, the cloud of glory in the merit of Aaron and the well in the merit of Miriam. When Miriam died, the well disappeared but returned in the combined merit of Moses and Aaron. When Aaron died, the cloud of glory disappeared but returned in the merit of Moses. When Moses died, all three disappeared. The three gifts that were bestowed on Israel in the merit of the three shepherds all disappeared at one time.

וַתִּקְצַר נַפְשִׁי בָּהֶם — *And My soul became impatient with them.*

God removed the three kings because He could not tolerate them (*Rashi*). According to *Radak's* interpretation this symbolizes the destruction of the Land of Israel that took place during the days of Zedekiah [see *Jeremiah* Ch. 52].

וְגַם־נַפְשָׁם בָּחֲלָה בִי — *For their soul also found Me repulsive.*

It was as if even the memory of the three kings was too repulsive for God to handle (*Rashi*). Alternatively, *Radak* explains that God did not reject His nation until they rejected Him.

In summary, the different opinions of the three shepherds are:

Rashi	King Jehoram, King Ahaziah, the descendants of King Ahaziah
Radak	The three sons of King Josiah
Ibn Ezra	The Kohen Gadol, the Kohen of battle, the assistant Kohen Gadol or the prophets Haggai, Zechariah and Malachi
Abarbanel	Hasmoneans — Judah, Simeon, Jonathan
Metzudos	Hasmoneans — Judah, Simeon, Jonathan
Malbim	Cyrus, Artahshasta, Darius
Talmud — *Taanis* **9a**	Moses, Aaron, Miriam

ט וָאֹמַ֕ר לֹ֖א אֶרְעֶ֣ה אֶתְכֶ֑ם הַמֵּתָ֨ה תָמ֜וּת וְהַנִּכְחֶ֣דֶת תִּכָּחֵ֗ד וְהַ֨נִּשְׁאָר֔וֹת תֹּאכַ֕לְנָה אִשָּׁ֖ה אֶת־בְּשַׂ֥ר רְעוּתָֽהּ׃ י וָאֶקַּ֤ח אֶת־מַקְלִי֙ אֶת־נֹ֔עַם וָאֶגְדַּ֖ע אֹת֑וֹ לְהָפֵיר֙ אֶת־בְּרִיתִ֔י אֲשֶׁ֥ר כָּרַ֖תִּי אֶת־כָּל־הָעַמִּֽים׃ יא וַתֻּפַ֖ר בַּיּ֣וֹם הַה֑וּא וַיֵּדְע֨וּ כֵ֜ן עֲנִיֵּ֤י הַצֹּאן֙ הַשֹּׁמְרִ֣ים אֹתִ֔י כִּ֥י דְבַר־יְהֹוָ֖ה הֽוּא׃ יב וָאֹמַ֣ר אֲלֵיהֶ֗ם אִם־ט֧וֹב בְּעֵינֵיכֶ֛ם הָב֥וּ שְׂכָרִ֖י וְאִם־לֹ֣א ׀ חֲדָ֑לוּ וַיִּשְׁקְל֥וּ אֶת־שְׂכָרִ֖י שְׁלֹשִׁ֥ים כָּֽסֶף׃ יג וַיֹּ֨אמֶר יְהֹוָ֜ה אֵלַ֗י הַשְׁלִיכֵ֙הוּ֙ אֶל־הַיּוֹצֵ֔ר אֶ֣דֶר הַיְקָ֔ר אֲשֶׁ֥ר יָקַ֖רְתִּי מֵעֲלֵיהֶ֑ם וָאֶקְחָה֙ שְׁלֹשִׁ֣ים הַכֶּ֔סֶף וָאַשְׁלִ֥יךְ אֹת֛וֹ בֵּ֥ית יְהֹוָ֖ה אֶל־הַיּוֹצֵֽר׃

9. וָאֹמַר לֹא אֶרְעֶה אֶתְכֶם הַמֵּתָה תָמוּת וְהַנִּכְחֶדֶת תִּכָּחֵד וְהַנִּשְׁאָרוֹת תֹּאכַלְנָה אִשָּׁה אֶת־בְּשַׂר רְעוּתָהּ — *I said, "I will not tend you. Let the dying one die and let the decimated one be decimated. And as for the remaining ones, let each devour the other's flesh."*

In the days of the three shepherds, Jehoahaz, Jehoiakim and Zedekiah, prior to the destruction of the Temple, God declared that He would no longer tend them because He saw that they acted wickedly and there would not arise among them a righteous king to lead the people. God will therefore remove His protection from them. The one who is destined to die will then die by pestilence, the decimated one will be killed by the sword and those who remain will die from hunger (*Radak*).

Ibn Ezra explains: After the death of the prophets Haggai, Zechariah and Malachi or the pious Kohanim, God said that He will not tend the people.

10. וָאֶקַּח אֶת־מַקְלִי אֶת־נֹעַם וָאֶגְדַּע אֹתוֹ לְהָפֵיר אֶת־בְּרִיתִי אֲשֶׁר כָּרַתִּי אֶת־כָּל־הָעַמִּים — *And I took My staff [called] Noam and I broke it to annul My covenant that I had sealed with all the peoples.*

God broke the staff that represented the Northern Kingdom of Israel by delivering Jehoahaz, son of Jehu, into the hands of Aram (*II Kings* 13:7) and Hoshea, son of Eilah, into the hands of Sennacherib (ibid. 17:6). God had given the Torah to the people of Israel conditionally, that if they follow its ways, then the nations will not harm them. The people, however, had betrayed God and violated the laws of His Torah so He nullified the covenant that He had sealed with the nations and removed His protection from them (*Rashi*). Indeed, during the days of Josiah, no foreign king harmed Israel and it was as if God had sealed a covenant with the nations that Israel should not be harmed. But God saw that no righteous king would rise after him so He had him removed by Pharaoh-neco [*II Kings* 23:29] so that the foreign nations could then have the power to rule over Israel (*Radak*).

Abarbanel and *Metzudos* explain that this verse refers to the demise of the Hasmonean dynasty. After the death of Matathias' three sons, God did not wish to lead the Jewish people בְּנוֹעַם, with *pleasantness*, but בְּחֹבְלִים, with *destroyers*, who oppressed them with a strong hand.

Ibn Ezra suggests that the subject of the verse is Zerubbabel. He is represented by the staff "Noam" for he had made peace with all the nations who dwelt near Jerusalem. The prophet is foretelling the death of this righteous leader.

[9]I said, "I will not tend you! Let the dying one die and let the decimated one be decimated. And as for the remaining ones, let each devour the other's flesh!"

[10]And I took My staff [called] Noam and I broke it to annul My covenant that I had sealed with all the peoples. [11]So it became annulled on that day; and the meek of the flock, who paid heed to Me, recognized that it was so, that it was the word of HASHEM. *[12]I said to [the people], "If it is proper in your eyes, give Me My fee, and if not, refrain." So they weighed out My fee: thirty silver coins.*

*[13]*HASHEM *said to me, "Throw it to the treasurer of the Precious Stronghold, which I have divested from them." So I took the thirty silver coins and I threw it into the Temple of* HASHEM, *to the treasurer.*

11. וַתֻּפַר בַּיּוֹם הַהוּא ... — *So it became annulled on that day ...*

The covenant was annulled on the day that Josiah died, for the three shepherds that succeeded him [see v.8] were dominated by the foreign nations who plundered, slew and exiled them (*Radak*). Alternatively, *that day* is the day the Ten Tribes were exiled (*Mahari Kara*) or the day Zerubbabel died (*Ibn Ezra*) or when the Hasmonean dynasty ended (*Abarbanel*).

The righteous among them realized that this decree fulfilled the prophecy of *Deut.* 28:36: *Hashem will lead you and your king ... to a nation you never knew ...* (*Rashi*).

12. וָאֹמַר אֲלֵיהֶם אִם־טוֹב בְּעֵינֵיכֶם הָבוּ שְׂכָרִי וְאִם־לֹא חֲדָלוּ — *I said to [the people], "If it is proper in your eyes, give Me My fee, and if not, refrain."*

As a shepherd demanding payment from the owner of the flock, God addresses the remaining kings of Judah (*Rashi*) or the people themselves through His prophets (*Radak*). He rhetorically asks them that if they wish that He should continue to be their shepherd, then they must pay His fee, i.e., they must righteously obey His commandments (*Rashi*), repent and do good deeds (*Radak*). If they will not comply, then God will reciprocate by refraining from protecting them (*Rashi*).

וַיִּשְׁקְלוּ אֶת־שְׂכָרִי שְׁלֹשִׁים כָּסֶף — *So they weighed out My fee: thirty silver coins.*

Metzudos suggests that this was the standard wage for a shepherd in those days. The thirty silver coins represent the small number of thirty truly righteous men (*Rashi*), the very small number of people who repented (*Radak*). Among the righteous were הֶחָרָשׁ וְהַמַּסְגֵּר, the Torah scholars and leaders (*Rashi*), Daniel, Hananiah, Mishael, Azariah, Jeremiah, Ezekiel, Zephaniah (*Radak*).

The *Midrash Aggadah* explains that God had assured the patriarch Abraham that there would be at least thirty truly righteous men in every generation corresponding to the numerical value of the word יִהְיֶה in the verse כֹּה יִהְיֶה זַרְעֶךָ, *so will your offspring be* (*Gen.* 15:5) (*Rashi*).

13. וַיֹּאמֶר ה׳ אֵלַי הַשְׁלִיכֵהוּ אֶל־הַיּוֹצֵר אֶדֶר הַיְקָר אֲשֶׁר יָקַרְתִּי מֵעֲלֵיהֶם ... — *Hashem said to me, "Throw it to the treasurer of the Precious Stronghold which I have divested from them." ...*

יד וָאֶגְדַּע אֶת־מַקְלִי הַשֵּׁנִי אֵת הַחֹבְלִים לְהָפֵר
טו אֶת־הָאַחֲוָה בֵּין יְהוּדָה וּבֵין יִשְׂרָאֵל: וַיֹּאמֶר
טז יְהוָה אֵלָי עוֹד קַח־לְךָ כְּלִי רֹעֶה אֱוִלִי: כִּי
הִנֵּה־אָנֹכִי מֵקִים רֹעֶה בָּאָרֶץ הַנִּכְחָדוֹת
לֹא־יִפְקֹד הַנַּעַר לֹא־יְבַקֵּשׁ וְהַנִּשְׁבֶּרֶת לֹא
יְרַפֵּא הַנִּצָּבָה לֹא יְכַלְכֵּל וּבְשַׂר הַבְּרִיאָה
יז יֹאכַל וּפַרְסֵיהֶן יְפָרֵק: הוֹי רֹעִי הָאֱלִיל

Zechariah was instructed to take the thirty pieces of silver and throw it to the treasurer of the Temple. This is to be understood figuratively: The righteous individuals are to separate themselves from the common masses of people and seclude themselves in God's Temple so that they will not be together with the evil populace (*Radak*). Alternatively, they should write down the deeds of these righteous people on a scroll and preserve them in the Temple until the end of the Babylonian exile, symbolizing that the Temple will be rebuilt due to their righteous deeds (*Rashi*).

14. וָאֶגְדַּע אֶת־מַקְלִי הַשֵּׁנִי אֵת הַחֹבְלִים לְהָפֵר אֶת־הָאַחֲוָה בֵּין יְהוּדָה וּבֵין יִשְׂרָאֵל — *Then I broke My second staff, Hobelim, to annul the brotherhood between Judah and Israel.*

The breaking of the second staff symbolizes the exile of King Zedekiah (*Rashi*) and the ultimate destruction of the Kingdom of Judah and the Holy Temple (*Radak*) through Nebuchadnezzar, king of Babylonia (*Targum Yonasan*). This ended the brotherhood of idolatry that the Kingdoms of Judah and Israel maintained between themselves (*Radak; Rashi*).

Alternatively, this is referring to the cessation of the Hasmonean monarchy (*Abarbanel; Metzudos*) or to the death of Nehemiah (*Ibn Ezra*). Some say that the verse is referring to the appointment of Herod, a gentile, as king over the people of Israel. This violates the teaching of the Torah that only one of their brethren may be appointed as king (*Metzudos*).

15. וַיֹּאמֶר ה׳ אֵלָי עוֹד קַח־לְךָ כְּלִי רֹעֶה אֱוִלִי — *Hashem said to me: Again take for yourself the implement[s] of a foolish shepherd.*

The foolish shepherd does not guide his sheep with his staff; instead he strikes them and beats them with it and thereby causes them injury (*Metzudos*). This symbolizes that the wicked shepherds, the wicked gentile nations, will rule over Israel (*Mahari Kara*) or it alludes to Herod, the wicked and cruel ruler who succeeded the Hasmonean dynasty (*Radak*). Alternatively, it is referring to the prophecy of v. 4, *Tend the flock meant to be slain*, that Israel will be delivered into the hands of Esau at the destruction of the Second Temple (*Rashi*).

16. כִּי הִנֵּה־אָנֹכִי מֵקִים רֹעֶה בָּאָרֶץ — *For behold, I am setting up a shepherd in the land.*

This verse describes the foolish shepherd of the previous verse and is actually referring to a wicked king (*Metzudos*). *Rashi* and *Mahari Kara* maintain that it is referring to Edom (the Roman Empire) in whose land the exiled Jews will settle and be maltreated. Alternatively, it is referring to Herod, the notorious king who ruled over Israel toward the end of the Second Temple era, and figuratively describes his evil deeds (*Metzudos*).

[14] *Then I broke My second staff, Hobelim, to annul the brotherhood between Judah and Israel.*

[15] *HASHEM said to me:*

Again take for yourself the implements of a foolish shepherd. [16] *For behold, I am setting up a shepherd in the land: He will not pay attention to the decimated ones; he will not seek out the youth; he will not heal the broken one; and he will not nurture the weak one; but he will eat the flesh of the healthy one and break their hooves.* [17] *Woe to the worthless shepherd*

הַנִּכְחָדוֹת לֹא־יִפְקֹד ... — *He will not pay attention to the decimated ones ...*

Unlike the shepherd who is concerned and pays attention to his flock, the Edomites will show no concern nor pay any attention to the people of Israel to see if any are lost or missing (*Mahari Kara*). Neither will they look out for the young, as do the shepherds, to check that none have strayed.

Our translation of הַנַּעַר, *the youth,* follows *Radak, Ibn Ezra, Mahari Kara* and *Metzudos. Rashi,* however, translates הַשּׁוֹטוֹת, *the foolish ones who do not know to enter the stall.*

וּבְשַׂר הַבְּרִיאָה יֹאכַל — *But he will eat the flesh of the healthy one.*

Just as the shepherd chooses a healthy lamb and consumes it, so too, will the nations consume the property of the wealthy Jews (*Mahari Kara*).

וּפַרְסֵיהֶן יְפָרֵק — *And break their hooves.*

These shepherds are not only negligent in the care of their flock, but even beat the legs of their sheep with their shepherd's staff until their hooves are broken (*Mahari Kara; Radak; Metzudos*). Similarly, the nations will attempt to destroy Israel (*Mahari Kara*).

Targum Yonasan followed by *Rashi* translates *he will totally destroy that which remains.* He will consume the lamb until the last morsel is finished.

17. הוֹי רֹעִי הָאֱלִיל — *Woe to the worthless shepherd.*

Our translation of the word הוֹי, *woe,* follows *Metzudos.* God turns to this foolish shepherd and declares, "Woe to these foolish, i.e., wicked, shepherds who will be severely punished when I will demand retribution from them" (*Mahari Kara*). This is referring either to Edom or the wicked gentile nations — see comm. to v. 15. Some commentators maintain that this wicked shepherd is Herod or Agrippas, the last king of the house of Herod. He was a traitor to his nation and joined with the Romans by inviting Vespasian and Titus to come to the Land of Israel. Shortly after their arrival, the Second Temple was destroyed (*Radak*). *Rashi* quotes others who see King Zedekiah as this shepherd for he had been blinded (see *II Kings* 25:7) as stated at the end of this verse. But this opinion is refuted by *Rashi,* (v. 16) *for behold, I am setting up a shepherd in the land* cannot be referring to Zedekiah who had died seventy years earlier.

רֹעִי הָאֱלִיל — *The worthless shepherd.*

The word אֱלִיל is related to אַל, *not.* He is not a shepherd; he is a shepherd of nothing, a worthless shepherd (*Rashi*).

עֹזְבִי הַצֹּאן חֶרֶב עַל־זְרוֹעוֹ וְעַל־עֵין יְמִינוֹ זְרֹעוֹ
א יָבוֹשׁ תִּיבָשׁ וְעֵין יְמִינוֹ כָּהֹה תִכְהֶה׃ מַשָּׂא
דְּבַר־יְהוָה עַל־יִשְׂרָאֵל נְאֻם־יְהוָה נֹטֶה שָׁמַיִם
ב וְיֹסֵד אָרֶץ וְיֹצֵר רוּחַ־אָדָם בְּקִרְבּוֹ׃ הִנֵּה אָנֹכִי
שָׂם אֶת־יְרוּשָׁלַםִ סַף־רַעַל לְכָל־הָעַמִּים סָבִיב
וְגַם עַל־יְהוּדָה יִהְיֶה בַמָּצוֹר עַל־יְרוּשָׁלָםִ׃
ג וְהָיָה בַיּוֹם־הַהוּא אָשִׂים אֶת־יְרוּשָׁלַםִ אֶבֶן
מַעֲמָסָה לְכָל־הָעַמִּים כָּל־עֹמְסֶיהָ שָׂרוֹט יִשָּׂרֵטוּ

חֶרֶב עַל־זְרוֹעוֹ ... — *A sword upon his arm ...*

Scripture continues to describe the shortcomings of the wicked shepherd. He carries a knife to slaughter the healthy sheep upon which he cast his right eye. The healthy sheep refer to the wealthy people who were chosen to be plundered and destroyed (*Rashi*).

Alternatively, this verse is describing the punishment that will be meted out to the wicked shepherd. May a sword come upon his right arm and his right eye. *Radak* explains that this does not mean that a sword will actually destroy his arm for the verse continues to explain that his arm will wither and his eye will go blind. The prophet figuratively foretells that the wicked shepherd will lose his strength.

XII

1. מַשָּׂא דְבַר־ה׳ עַל־יִשְׂרָאֵל — *The prophecy of the word of Hashem concerning Israel.*

מַשָּׂא, lit., *burden*, is often used by Scripture as a synonym for the prophetic word of God — see commentary to 9:1. Because of its transgressions during the Second Temple era, Israel did not merit God's benevolence and kindness and did not merit redemption. Instead, it suffered exile and destruction through the hands of the Edomites (*Abarbanel*). The prophet now speaks of the retribution that will be wrought upon the nations of the world (*Radak*), particularly the Edomites (*Rashi*),[1] for all they had caused Israel to endure during their long exile. He foretells that Israel will indeed merit God's favor at a future time (*Abarbanel*). *Ibn Ezra* writes that the punishment of the nations will take place when Israel will return to Jerusalem under the leadership of מָשִׁיחַ בֶּן יוֹסֵף, *Messiah the son of Joseph.*

נֹטֶה שָׁמַיִם וְיֹסֵד אָרֶץ ... — *Who stretches out the heavens and lays the foundation of the earth ...*

Zechariah teaches that God is in total control of the entire universe. Since it is God Who created the heavens and the earth, it is only He Who has the power to uproot and destroy, to build and to plant (*Radak*). He mentions that God created man to teach that since it is God Who created man and it is He Who has sent Israel into exile, it is He Who has the power to redeem them from their exile (*Radak*). The prophet is also stressing that the purpose of the future redemption is the perfection of all mankind:

1. We have followed the text of *Rashi* as it appears in the Machon HaMaor edition of *Mikraos Gedolos* which reads עֵשָׂיו אוֹכֵל יִשְׂרָאֵל וּכְיוֹצֵא בוֹ, *Esau, the progenitor of those who devour Israel ... and those like him*, the Edomites (Romans). The standard edition of *Mikraos Gedolos* reads בָּבֶל וּכְיוֹצֵא בוֹ, *the Babylonians*, an obvious change due to censorship.

who abandons the flock! A sword upon his arm and upon his right eye! May his arm utterly wither and his right eye go completely blind!

12/1-3 [1] *The prophecy of the word of* HASHEM *concerning Israel:*

The word of HASHEM*, Who stretches out the heavens and lays the foundation of the earth, and Who fashions the spirit of man within him:* [2] *Behold! I am making Jerusalem a cup of poison for all the peoples all around; and also Judah will take part in the siege of Jerusalem.* [3] *It shall be on that day that I will make Jerusalem a burdensome stone for all the peoples, all whose bearers become lacerated;*

that all of mankind should throw away their false beliefs and believe only in the true God (*Abarbanel*).

2. הִנֵּה אָנֹכִי שָׂם אֶת־יְרוּשָׁלַםִ סַף־רַעַל לְכָל־הָעַמִּים סָבִיב — *Behold! I am making Jerusalem a cup of poison for all the peoples all around.*

The nations will march against Jerusalem and try to besiege the Holy City but they will meet death and perish, for Jerusalem will be a cup of poison that brings death upon all who drink it (*Radak; Abarbanel; Metzudos*).

Radak identifies these *peoples* as the armies of Gog and Magog. They will attempt to besiege Jerusalem, confidently believing that if that great city is conquered, the remainder of the Land of Israel will automatically fall. According to *Malbim*, the armies of Gog and Magog are the Edomites. They will attempt to wrest Jerusalem from the Ishmaelites (Arabs) who will be in control of the city at that time. God will wage war with them both and repay them for the suffering they caused the Jewish people while they were in exile.

סַף־רַעַל — *A cup of poison.*

Our translation of the word סַף, a *cup* or *basin*, follows most commentators (see *Exodus* 12:22). Alternatively, *Mahari Kara* translates סַף as *threshold* and explains that Jerusalem will be like a high threshold that the nations wish to jump over and cross but they will trip, stumble and fall. The city will be a *threshold of poison for all the peoples* who come to wage war against her.

וְגַם עַל־יְהוּדָה יִהְיֶה בַמָּצוֹר עַל־יְרוּשָׁלָםִ — *And also Judah will take part in the siege of Jerusalem.*

These nations will force Judah to participate with them in their siege of Jerusalem (*Targum Yonasan; Rashi*). At first, Judah too, will "drink the cup of poison" (*Radak; Abarbanel*) and suffer retribution with the nations (*Metzudos*). According to *Malbim*, the prophet is foretelling that on their way to Jerusalem, the armies of Gog and Magog will lay a siege around the cities of Judea. They will conquer them all and cause their inhabitants great suffering.

3. וְהָיָה בַיּוֹם־הַהוּא אָשִׂים אֶת־יְרוּשָׁלַםִ אֶבֶן מַעֲמָסָה לְכָל־הָעַמִּים כָּל־עֹמְסֶיהָ שָׂרוֹט יִשָּׂרֵטוּ — *It shall be on that day that I will make Jerusalem a burdensome stone for all the peoples, all whose bearers become lacerated.*

Zechariah describes the punishment of those who will attack Jerusalem. The prophet had previously likened the

ד וְנֶאֶסְפוּ עָלֶיהָ כֹּל גּוֹיֵי הָאָרֶץ׃ בַּיּוֹם הַהוּא
נְאֻם־יהוה אַכֶּה כָל־סוּס בַּתִּמָּהוֹן וְרֹכְבוֹ
בַּשִּׁגָּעוֹן וְעַל־בֵּית יְהוּדָה אֶפְקַח אֶת־עֵינַי
ה וְכֹל סוּס הָעַמִּים אַכֶּה בַּעִוָּרוֹן׃ וְאָמְרוּ אַלֻּפֵי
יְהוּדָה בְּלִבָּם אַמְצָה לִי יֹשְׁבֵי יְרוּשָׁלִַם
ו בַּיהוה צְבָאוֹת אֱלֹהֵיהֶם׃ בַּיּוֹם הַהוּא אָשִׂים
אֶת־אַלֻּפֵי יְהוּדָה כְּכִיּוֹר אֵשׁ בְּעֵצִים וּכְלַפִּיד
אֵשׁ בְּעָמִיר וְאָכְלוּ עַל־יָמִין וְעַל־שְׂמֹאול
אֶת־כָּל־הָעַמִּים סָבִיב וְיָשְׁבָה יְרוּשָׁלִַם עוֹד
ז תַּחְתֶּיהָ בִּירוּשָׁלִָם׃ וְהוֹשִׁיעַ יהוה אֶת־אָהֳלֵי
יְהוּדָה בָּרִאשֹׁנָה לְמַעַן לֹא־תִגְדַּל תִּפְאֶרֶת
בֵּית־דָּוִיד וְתִפְאֶרֶת יֹשֵׁב יְרוּשָׁלִַם עַל־יְהוּדָה׃

Holy City to a *cup of poison* to those besieging it; he now refers to it as a *burdensome stone.* Just as one who lifts a heavy stone suffers scratches and gashes on his hands and body, so too, will those who attack Jerusalem suffer severe injury (*Rashi; Radak*).

The prophet is pointing out the contrast between the siege of Jerusalem that will then take place and those of earlier times. When the nations captured Jerusalem from the Romans and then from the Arabs, they conquered it with relative ease, but this time it will be most difficult — as *a burdensome stone* (*Abarbanel*).

Just as the carrier of the burdensome stone calls to others for assistance for the stone is too heavy for him to lift alone, so too, will it be with the nations attacking Jerusalem; no nation will have the ability to conquer Jerusalem unassisted and will therefore call to others for aid (*Alshich*).

וְנֶאֶסְפוּ עָלֶיהָ כֹּל גּוֹיֵי הָאָרֶץ — *And all the nations of the world will gather against it.*

The armies of Gog and Magog will gather together to capture Jerusalem from the Arabs who will be in control of the city. Jerusalem will become a burdensome stone for them for they will have to protect the city from the powerful armies of Gog and Magog (*Malbim*).

4. בַּיּוֹם הַהוּא נְאֻם־ה׳ אַכֶּה כָל־סוּס בַּתִּמָּהוֹן וְרֹכְבוֹ בַּשִּׁגָּעוֹן — *On that day — the word of Hashem — I will strike every horse with confusion and its rider with madness.*

Zechariah describes the confusion and panic that will take place among the besieging nations. God will smite every horse of the nations that have gathered against Jerusalem with confusion and blindness and their riders with madness rendering them incapable of battle (*Rashi; Mahari Kara*).

According to *Ibn Ezra* the horses will be blind with hysteria. According to *Abarbanel* their blindness will be caused by terror.

וְעַל־בֵּית יְהוּדָה אֶפְקַח אֶת־עֵינַי ... — *But I will open My eyes to the House of Judah ...*

Although the House of Judah has gathered against Jerusalem together with the enemy nations, I will open My eyes to protect the Judean warriors (*Radak*) for they had been forced by the nations to join the siege (*Mahari Kara*).

5. וְאָמְרוּ אַלֻּפֵי יְהוּדָה בְּלִבָּם אַמְצָה לִי יֹשְׁבֵי יְרוּשָׁלִַם בַּה׳ צְבָאוֹת אֱלֹהֵיהֶם — *Then the captains of Judah will say in their hearts, "The inhabitants of Jerusalem*

and all the nations of the world will gather against it. [4]On that day — the word of HASHEM — I will strike every horse with confusion and its rider with madness. But I will open My eyes to the House of Judah, while I strike every horse of the peoples with blindness. [5]Then the captains of Judah will say in their hearts, "The inhabitants of Jerusalem are a source of strength for me [in their prayers] to HASHEM, Master of Legions, their God!"

[6]On that day I will make the captains of Judah like a stove [with] fire [burning] wood and like a fiery torch [burning] sheaf, and they will consume on the right and on the left all the peoples all around; and Jerusalem will again settle in its place, in Jerusalem. [7]HASHEM will save the tents of Judah first, so that the splendor of the House of David and the splendor of the inhabitants of Jerusalem should not overwhelm Judah.

are a source of strength for me [in their prayers] to Hashem, Master of Legions, their God."

At this point, Zechariah describes the reaction of the captains of Judah who will lay siege to Jerusalem together with the enemy forces. When the captains of Judah see that they had been spared the punishments of the nations who had gathered with them against Jerusalem, they will realize that they were saved only in the merit of the prayers of the inhabitants of Jerusalem who knew that Judah had been coerced and gathered there against their will (*Rashi; Mahari Kara, Metzudos*).

6. בַּיּוֹם הַהוּא אָשִׂים אֶת־אַלֻּפֵי יְהוּדָה כְּכִיּוֹר אֵשׁ בְּעֵצִים וּכְלַפִּיד אֵשׁ בְּעָמִיר... — *On that day I will make the captains of Judah like a stove [with] fire [burning] wood and like a fiery torch [burning] sheaf ...*

Zechariah continues his prophecy and foretells that the Judeans will then turn against their enemies — the nations who had forced them to gather against Jerusalem (*Rashi*) — and like a great fire they will consume and destroy them (*Rashi; Mahari Kara*). Alternatively, the Judean leaders who are *outside* the city of Jerusalem will join forces with the Jerusalemites and destroy the enemy (*Radak*).

וְיָשְׁבָה יְרוּשָׁלַםִ עוֹד תַּחְתֶּיהָ בִּירוּשָׁלָםִ — *And Jerusalem will again settle in its place, in Jerusalem.*

Although the nations had attempted to destroy Jerusalem so that it will never again be a city, it will nevertheless continue to exist and remain standing on its original place (*Radak*).

Abarbanel and *Metzudos* maintain that the current city of Jerusalem was not built on the site of the original city for after it was destroyed by Titus, it was rebuilt by Hadrian on a different site. Therefore, the prophet writes that Jerusalem will eventually be rebuilt on its original site, in Jerusalem.

7. ...וְהוֹשִׁיעַ ה׳ אֶת־אָהֳלֵי יְהוּדָה בָּרִאשֹׁנָה — *Hashem will save the tents of Judah first...*

ח בַּיּוֹם הַהוּא יָגֵן יהוה בְּעַד יוֹשֵׁב יְרוּשָׁלַםִ וְהָיָה הַנִּכְשָׁל בָּהֶם בַּיּוֹם הַהוּא כְּדָוִיד וּבֵית דָּוִיד כֵּאלֹהִים כְּמַלְאַךְ יהוה לִפְנֵיהֶם׃ ט וְהָיָה בַּיּוֹם הַהוּא אֲבַקֵּשׁ לְהַשְׁמִיד אֶת־כָּל־הַגּוֹיִם הַבָּאִים עַל־יְרוּשָׁלָםִ׃ י וְשָׁפַכְתִּי עַל־בֵּית דָּוִיד וְעַל | יוֹשֵׁב יְרוּשָׁלַםִ רוּחַ חֵן וְתַחֲנוּנִים וְהִבִּיטוּ אֵלַי אֵת אֲשֶׁר־דָּקָרוּ וְסָפְדוּ עָלָיו כְּמִסְפֵּד עַל־הַיָּחִיד וְהָמֵר עָלָיו כְּהָמֵר עַל־הַבְּכוֹר׃ יא בַּיּוֹם הַהוּא יִגְדַּל הַמִּסְפֵּד בִּירוּשָׁלַםִ כְּמִסְפַּד הֲדַדְרִמּוֹן בְּבִקְעַת מְגִדּוֹן׃

The tents of Judah refers to the Judeans who had been coerced to participate in the siege against Jerusalem and had therefore pitched their tents outside the city (*Radak*). They will be granted salvation first, before the inhabitants of Jerusalem — for if the inhabitants of Jerusalem and the members of the House of David were saved first, they would arrogantly declare that the Judeans were saved only in their merit (*Rashi; Radak*).

8. בַּיּוֹם הַהוּא יָגֵן ה׳ בְּעַד יוֹשֵׁב יְרוּשָׁלַםִ — *On that day Hashem will protect the inhabitant of Jerusalem.*

When the battle will reach the gates of Jerusalem (*Abarbanel*), its inhabitants will go out and battle the armies of Gog and Magog, and God will protect them (*Metzudos*).

וְהָיָה הַנִּכְשָׁל בָּהֶם בַּיּוֹם הַהוּא ... — *On that day even the weakest among them ...*

The weakest fighter among them will be as valiant and mighty as King David, who was known as a fierce warrior (*Radak*) who overcame all his enemies (*Metzudos*).

וּבֵית דָּוִיד כֵּאלֹהִים ... — *And the House of David will be like Divine Beings ...* This is referring to the Messianic king (*Radak*) who is a descendant of the House of David. He will lead the nation in battle and will be victorious like an avenging angel of God (*Rashi*).

Abarbanel understands the next few verses as referring to מָשִׁיחַ בֶּן יוֹסֵף, the Messiah son of Joseph. See comm. to v. 10.

9. וְהָיָה בַּיּוֹם הַהוּא אֲבַקֵּשׁ לְהַשְׁמִיד אֶת־כָּל־הַגּוֹיִם הַבָּאִים עַל יְרוּשָׁלָםִ — *It shall be on that day that I will seek to destroy all the nations that come upon Jerusalem.*

Zechariah continues to describe the destruction of the nations who will attempt to destroy the Holy City of Jerusalem. On that day God will be determined to destroy all the nations who have come upon Jerusalem. He will seek their destruction and He will accurately judge their sins with the full measure of Divine Judgment (*Rashi*).

The *Talmud* (*Avodah Zarah* 3a) wonders from whom or what must Hashem the Omnipotent God seek permission when He wishes to destroy the nations. R' Alexandri explained that God will examine their chronicles which contain a history of their actions. If they do indeed possess merit, then God will redeem them. If not, then He will destroy them.

Ibn Ezra and *Malbim* explains that God will seek to destroy these nations for they had killed מָשִׁיחַ בֶּן יוֹסֵף, the Messiah son of Joseph — see comm. to next verse.

10. וְשָׁפַכְתִּי עַל־בֵּית דָּוִיד וְעַל יוֹשֵׁב יְרוּשָׁלַםִ רוּחַ חֵן וְתַחֲנוּנִים — *I will pour out upon the House of David and upon the inhabitant of Jerusalem a spirit of grace and supplications.*

[8]*On that day* HASHEM *will protect the inhabitant of Jerusalem; on that day even the weakest among them will be like David, and the House of David will be like Divine Beings, like an angel of* HASHEM *before them.* [9]*It shall be on that day that I will seek to destroy all the nations that come upon Jerusalem.* [10]*I will pour out upon the House of David and upon the inhabitant of Jerusalem a spirit of grace and supplications. They will look toward Me because of those whom they have stabbed; they will mourn over him as one mourns over an only [child], and be embittered over him like the embitterment over a [deceased] firstborn.* [11]*On that day the mourning will become intense in Jerusalem, like the mourning of Hadadrimmon [and the mourning] at the Valley of Megiddon.*

God will inspire all of Israel, the Judeans of the House of David and the other tribes, the inhabitants of Jerusalem (*Abarbanel*), with a desire to pray to Him and they will find favor in His eyes and He will be gracious to them (*Rashi*) and will save them from the nations that come upon them (*Radak*).

וְהִבִּיטוּ אֵלַי אֵת אֲשֶׁר־דָּקָרוּ — *They will look toward Me because of those whom they have stabbed.* The Israelites will look toward God and grieve over their fellow Jews who have been slain by the nations during their long exile (*Rashi; Mahari Kara*).

וְסָפְדוּ עָלָיו כְּמִסְפֵּד עַל־הַיָּחִיד ... — *They will mourn over him as one mourns over an only [child] ...*

The salvation will be so complete that people will look toward God in astonishment if even one common man is killed by the enemy. They will mourn for him as one mourns for his only son (*Radak*).

According to the Talmudic Sages (*Sukkah* 52a), the words *those whom they have stabbed* is referring to מָשִׁיחַ בֶּן יוֹסֵף, to the Messiah son of Joseph, who is destined to be slain in this battle (*Rashi*). *Radak* questions this interpretation for nowhere does Scripture ever mention a tradition of a Messiah son of Joseph. Although shrouded in mystery, the tradition of *Mashiach ben Yosef* is nevertheless discussed extensively in *Kabbalah* literature such as the *Zohar* and *Arizal.* It is mentioned in many Midrashim and in the writings of *R' Saadiah Gaon, Emunos V'Dei'os* (*Maamar* 8), *Vilna Gaon* and others. (See ArtScroll *Yechezkel* page 578 for further discussion.) *Abarbanel, Metzudos* and *Malbim* explain this verse according to the view of the Sages:

Upon the death of *Mashiach ben Yosef,* God will seek to avenge his death (v. 9) by destroying all the nations who will seek to lay siege to the Holy City of Jerusalem. The Jewish people, understanding that the death of their leader was due to their sins, will be inspired to truly repent and will pray to God Who will answer their prayers graciously.

11. בַּיּוֹם הַהוּא יִגְדַּל הַמִּסְפֵּד בִּירוּשָׁלַם כְּמִסְפַּד הֲדַדְרִמּוֹן בְּבִקְעַת מְגִדּוֹן — *On that day the mourning will become intense in Jerusalem, like the mourning of Hadadrimmon [and the mourning] at the Valley of Megiddon.*

יב/יב־יד

יב וְסָפְדָה הָאָרֶץ מִשְׁפָּחוֹת מִשְׁפָּחוֹת לְבָד מִשְׁפַּחַת בֵּית־דָּוִיד לְבָד וּנְשֵׁיהֶם לְבָד מִשְׁפַּחַת בֵּית־נָתָן לְבָד וּנְשֵׁיהֶם לְבָד: יג מִשְׁפַּחַת בֵּית־לֵוִי לְבָד וּנְשֵׁיהֶם לְבָד מִשְׁפַּחַת הַשִּׁמְעִי לְבָד וּנְשֵׁיהֶם לְבָד: יד כֹּל הַמִּשְׁפָּחוֹת הַנִּשְׁאָרוֹת מִשְׁפָּחֹת מִשְׁפָּחֹת לְבָד וּנְשֵׁיהֶם לְבָד:

יג/א־ב

א בַּיּוֹם הַהוּא יִהְיֶה מָקוֹר נִפְתָּח לְבֵית דָּוִיד וּלְיֹשְׁבֵי יְרוּשָׁלָם לְחַטַּאת וּלְנִדָּה: ב וְהָיָה בַיּוֹם הַהוּא נְאֻם | יהוה

The grief and mourning that will be expressed for those who had been slain by the nations will be so intense that it will resemble the mourning of Hadadrimmon at the valley of the Megiddon (*Mahari Kara*). Alternatively, the prophet is describing the grief that will be expressed for the loss of *Mashiach ben Yosef* (*Metzudos; Ibn Ezra*).

By writing *like the mourning of Hadadrimmon at the Valley of Megiddon*, Scripture would seem to be referring to one incident; actually, it is alluding to two events: the mourning over Ahab son of Omri, king of Israel, who was killed in battle (*I Kings* Ch. 22) by Hadadrimmon son of Tabrimmon; and the mourning for Josiah, king of Judah, who was slain in the Valley of Megiddon (*II Chronicles* 35:20-25) (*Rashi* from *Targum Yonasan* and *Moed Katan* 28b).

Alternatively, Scripture is referring to an incident that was well known during the days of Zechariah but is not recorded in Scripture and is unknown to us (*Ibn Ezra; Radak; Metzudos*).

12. וְסָפְדָה הָאָרֶץ מִשְׁפָּחוֹת מִשְׁפָּחוֹת לְבָד — *The land will mourn, each of the families by itself.*

When the people of the land will mourn for the one who was stabbed [v.10] (*Radak*), each family will mourn separately (*Metzudos*) in its own specific place (*Radak*), thereby increasing the public display of grief and mourning to many different areas (*Metzudos*).

מִשְׁפַּחַת בֵּית דָּוִיד לְבָד — *The family of the House of David by itself.*

The family of the House of David will mourn for their kingdom that had been discontinued for so many years (*Mahari Kara*). *Abarbanel* explains that they will mourn the death of the Messiah son of Joseph as if he were a member of their family.

13. מִשְׁפַּחַת בֵּית־לֵוִי לְבָד — *The family of the house of Levi by itself.*

Among the mourners will be the priests and the Levites (*Rashi*) and the prominent families of Nathan and Shimei (*Ibn Ezra; Radak*). According to *Rashi*, Nathan and Shimei are the sons of King David mentioned in *II Sam.* 5:14 — *Shammua and Shobab and Nathan and Solomon.* Alternatively, Nathan may be Nathan the Prophet.

וּנְשֵׁיהֶם לְבָד ... — *And their wives by themselves ...*

The women will not mourn together with the men for in observance of the laws of modesty and decency (*Rashi; Radak*) or since women mourn and lament exceedingly more than men, they are more comfortable if they are together with other women than with men (*Radak*).

14. כֹּל הַמִּשְׁפָּחוֹת הַנִּשְׁאָרוֹת ... — *All the families who remain ...*

I.e., all the surviving families of the House of David will mourn and lament: each family separately (*Rashi*).

12/
12-14

[12]*The land will mourn, each of the families by itself: the family of the House of David by itself, and their wives by themselves; the family of the house of Nathan by itself and their wives by themselves;* [13]*the family of the house of Levi by itself and their wives by themselves; the family of Shimei by itself and their wives by themselves;* [14]*all the families who remain, each of the families by itself and their wives by themselves.*

13/1-2

[1] *On that day there will be a spring opened up for the House of David and for the inhabitants of Jerusalem for cleansing and for purification.* [2]*It will happen on that day — the word of* HASHEM,

XIII

1. בַּיּוֹם הַהוּא יִהְיֶה מָקוֹר נִפְתָּח ... — *On that day there will be a spring opened up...*

Zechariah prophetically describes events of Messianic times and foretells of a spring that will flow from Jerusalem (*Radak*). This parallels the prophecies of Joel and Ezekiel who also experienced a prophetic vision of a spring emerging from the Holy Temple (see *Joel* 4:18 and *Ezekiel* 47:1). According to the Talmud (*Yoma* 78a; *Shekalim* 17a), the water will emerge as a trickle from under the threshold of the Sanctuary and will progressively grow wider and stronger. Alternatively, some commentators understand this prophecy metaphorically: Because of the Torah and true beliefs that will flow from Jerusalem, God will cleanse the people of their sins (*Targum Yonasan; Rashi; Mahari Kara; Abarbanel*).

לְבֵית דָּוִיד וּלְיוֹשְׁבֵי יְרוּשָׁלָם לְחַטַּאת וּלְנִדָּה — *For the House of David and for the inhabitants of Jerusalem for cleansing and for purification.* The spring will be used to purify the members of the House of David and the inhabitants of Jerusalem. They will no longer need to leave the city to obtain spring water for purification (*Radak*). בֵּית דָּוִיד, *the House of David*, is the area of Mt. Zion which is located outside of Jerusalem (*Rashi* to *Yoma* 77b). When the trickle of water will reach this area it will become a swift stream (*Radak*).

לְחַטַּאת — *For cleansing.*

This is referring to the purification of one who had become contaminated by touching a corpse and must be sprinkled with a mixture of spring water and the ashes of a red heifer (see *Numbers* Ch. 19).

וּלְנִדָּה — *And for purification.*

This is either referring to the same process of purification as above, for the Torah refers to the water used for sprinkling as מֵי נִדָּה (see *Numbers* 19:9), or it refers to the purification process of one who is *tamei* and must immerse in either a stream or *mikveh* (*Metzudos*).

2. וְהָיָה בַיּוֹם הַהוּא נְאֻם ה׳ צְבָאוֹת אַכְרִית אֶת־שְׁמוֹת הָעֲצַבִּים מִן־הָאָרֶץ וְלֹא יִזָּכְרוּ עוֹד — *It will happen on that day — the word of Hashem, Master of Legions — that I will cut off the names of the idols from the land, and they will not be mentioned again.*

צְבָאוֹת אַכְרִית אֶת־שְׁמוֹת הָעֲצַבִּים מִן־הָאָרֶץ וְלֹא יִזָּכְרוּ עוֹד וְגַם אֶת־הַנְּבִיאִים ג וְאֶת־רוּחַ הַטֻּמְאָה אַעֲבִיר מִן־הָאָרֶץ: וְהָיָה כִּי־יִנָּבֵא אִישׁ עוֹד וְאָמְרוּ אֵלָיו אָבִיו וְאִמּוֹ יֹלְדָיו לֹא תִחְיֶה כִּי שֶׁקֶר דִּבַּרְתָּ בְּשֵׁם יהוה וּדְקָרֻהוּ אָבִיהוּ וְאִמּוֹ יֹלְדָיו בְּהִנָּבְאוֹ: ד וְהָיָה | בַּיּוֹם הַהוּא יֵבֹשׁוּ הַנְּבִיאִים אִישׁ מֵחֶזְיֹנוֹ בְּהִנָּבְאֹתוֹ וְלֹא יִלְבְּשׁוּ אַדֶּרֶת ה שֵׂעָר לְמַעַן כַּחֵשׁ: וְאָמַר לֹא נָבִיא אָנֹכִי אִישׁ־עֹבֵד אֲדָמָה אָנֹכִי כִּי אָדָם הִקְנַנִי ו מִנְּעוּרָי: וְאָמַר אֵלָיו מָה הַמַּכּוֹת הָאֵלֶּה בֵּין יָדֶיךָ וְאָמַר אֲשֶׁר הֻכֵּיתִי בֵּית מְאַהֲבָי:

Zechariah foretells that in Messianic times, God will destroy all forms of idolatry that had been worshiped by the gentiles through the ages (*Abarbanel*); utterly so, that even their names will be forgotten (*Malbim*). Included in this prophecy is the removal of the Christian shrines of Jerusalem (*Abarbanel*) and the idolaters of India, China and Japan (*Malbim*).

וְגַם אֶת־הַנְּבִיאִים ... — *I will also remove the [false] prophets ...*

There will be no more false prophets (*Rashi; Metzudos*) *and the spirit of impurity*, the evil inclination, will be removed from the Land (*Rashi; Radak; Metzudos*), for the world will be filled with knowledge and will distinguish truth from falsehood (*Metzudos*).

Idols are referred to as עֲצַבִּים (עָצֵב, *sad*) for they sadden the hearts of their worshipers who cry out to them and are unanswered (*Metzudos*).

3. וְהָיָה כִּי־יִנָּבֵא אִישׁ עוֹד וְאָמְרוּ אֵלָיו אָבִיו וְאִמּוֹ יֹלְדָיו לֹא תִחְיֶה ... — *It will happen if a man will still prophesy [falsely], that his father and mother — those who bore him — will say to him, "You should not live ..."*

Although God will indeed remove the false prophets, there may yet occasionally be an individual who will falsely claim to prophesy in God's Name. That person will surely receive his due. His parents will either beat him (*Radak*) or, because of their strong love for God (*Ibn Ezra*), even slay him (*Radak; Ibn Ezra*), for a false prophet does not deserve to live (*Metzudos*).

4. וְהָיָה בַּיּוֹם הַהוּא יֵבֹשׁוּ הַנְּבִיאִים אִישׁ מֵחֶזְיֹנוֹ בְּהִנָּבְאֹתוֹ — *It will happen on that day, the prophets will be ashamed, each one of his vision when he prophesies it,*

When these false prophets will see that their prophecies have not been fulfilled, they will be ashamed of their past and will no longer prophesy falsely.

וְלֹא יִלְבְּשׁוּ אַדֶּרֶת שֵׂעָר לְמַעַן כַּחֵשׁ — *And they will no longer wear the hairy cloak in order to lie.*

They will remove the hairy cloak that they wore to deceive the people into thinking that they were true prophets (*Radak*).

It was the custom of true prophets to wear an expensive (*Metzudos*) robe or cloak (see *I Kings* 19:19). Others explain that it was like sackcloth (*Radak; Ibn Ezra; Malbim*). In any event, it was a garment signifying piety

Master of Legions — that I will cut off the names of the idols from the land, and they will not be mentioned again; I will also remove the [false] prophets and the spirit of impurity from the land. [3] *It will happen if a man will still prophesy [falsely], that his father and his mother — those who bore him — will say to him — "You should not live, for you have spoken falsehood in the name of* HASHEM*!" His father and mother — those who bore him — will stab him when he prophesies.* [4] *It will happen on that day, the prophets will be ashamed, each one of his vision when he prophesies it, and they will no longer wear the hairy cloak in order to lie.* [5] *Rather, he will say, "I am not a prophet! I am a worker of the land for a person took me as a herdsman since my youth."* [6] *And [if] someone will say to him, "What are these wounds between your arms?" He will say, "It is from when I was beaten in the house of those who loved me."*

which the false prophets wore to give their messages an aura of acceptability (*Rashi*).

5. וְאָמַר לֹא נָבִיא אָנֹכִי אִישׁ־עֹבֵד אֲדָמָה אָנֹכִי כִּי אָדָם הִקְנַנִי מִנְּעוּרָי — *Rather, he will say, "I am not a prophet! I am a worker of the land for a person took me as a herdsman since my youth."*

When the false prophet will be asked what ever became of his prophecies (*Radak*) or to describe his occupation (*Ibn Ezra*) or the reason he secludes himself in the fields (*Metzudos*), he will be forced to admit that he is nothing more than a mere shepherd and farmer and was never a prophet (*Radak; Mahari Kara; Metzudos*).

The word הִקְנַנִי is related to the word מִקְנֶה, *flocks of sheep* or *herds of cattle* (*Rashi*); הִקְנַנִי, *he took me as a herdsman*. Alternatively, it is *an expression of purchase*, קִנְיָן (*Metzudos*).

6. וְאָמַר אֵלָיו מָה הַמַּכּוֹת הָאֵלֶּה בֵּין יָדֶיךָ וְאָמַר אֲשֶׁר הֻכֵּיתִי בֵּית מְאַהֲבָי — *And [if] someone will say to him, "What are these wounds between your arms?" He will say, "It is from when I was beaten in the house of those who loved me."*

It was the custom of the false prophets to beat and gash themselves thinking that self-flagellation will cause the spirit of prophecy to rest upon them (see *I Kings* 18:28). In essence, the questioner is accusing the false prophet of continuing his false prophecies, as indicated by the cuts on his back. The false prophet then replies that his wounds are from the beatings that he received from *the house of those who loved me*, the rabbinical court, as its members reproved him to return to God (*Metzudos*).

Other interpretations of his reply are: He had been sporting with friends who had mistakenly wounded him (*Ibn Ezra*), or that he had not occupied himself with his farming, so his friend bound his hands and feet so that he should not run away (*Radak*).

ז חֶ֗רֶב ע֚וּרִי עַל־רֹעִי֙ וְעַל־גֶּ֣בֶר עֲמִיתִ֔י נְאֻ֖ם יְהוָ֣ה צְבָא֑וֹת הַ֤ךְ אֶת־הָֽרֹעֶה֙ וּתְפוּצֶ֣יןָ הַצֹּ֔אן וַהֲשִׁבֹתִ֥י יָדִ֖י עַל־הַצֹּעֲרִֽים׃ ח וְהָיָ֤ה בְכָל־הָאָ֙רֶץ֙ נְאֻם־יְהוָ֔ה פִּֽי־שְׁנַ֣יִם בָּ֔הּ יִכָּרְת֖וּ יִגְוָ֑עוּ וְהַשְּׁלִשִׁ֖ית יִוָּ֥תֶר בָּֽהּ׃ ט וְהֵבֵאתִ֣י אֶת־הַשְּׁלִשִׁית֮ בָּאֵשׁ֒ וּצְרַפְתִּים֙ כִּצְרֹ֣ף אֶת־הַכֶּ֔סֶף וּבְחַנְתִּ֖ים כִּבְחֹ֣ן אֶת־הַזָּהָ֑ב ה֣וּא ׀ יִקְרָ֣א בִשְׁמִ֗י וַאֲנִי֙ אֶעֱנֶ֣ה אֹת֔וֹ אָמַ֙רְתִּי֙ עַמִּ֣י ה֔וּא וְה֥וּא יֹאמַ֖ר יְהוָ֥ה אֱלֹהָֽי׃

א הִנֵּ֥ה יוֹם־בָּ֖א לַיהוָ֑ה וְחֻלַּ֥ק שְׁלָלֵ֖ךְ בְּקִרְבֵּֽךְ׃

7. חֶרֶב עוּרִי עַל־רֹעִי וְעַל־גֶּבֶר עֲמִיתִי ... — *O sword, arouse yourself against My shepherd and against the man who is My colleague.*

The prophet foretells that many wars will break out among the nations of the world during the era of *Mashiach ben Yosef* (*Ibn Ezra*). God's shepherds and colleagues are the gentile kings and leaders to whom He entrusted the fate of His "flock" Israel. When they harm instead of help, God will unleash the sword against them (*Rashi*). *Abarbanel* suggests that *My shepherd* is referring to Mohammed and *My colleague* is referring to Yeshu for their followers referred to them in this manner. Zechariah is foretelling the downfall of the Arabs and Christians who were their followers.

הַךְ אֶת־הָרֹעֶה וּתְפוּצֶיןָ הַצֹּאן — *Strike the shepherd and let the flock disperse.*

Israel (the flock) will then be free to scatter and God will turn His vengeance against the subordinates of those kings (*Mahari Kara*). Alternatively, the flock is referring to the rulers. When the kings are slain, their rulers will scatter (*Targum Yonasan*).

Targum Yonasan renders *O sword, reveal yourself against the king of Babylon* ... and again later in the verse הַךְ אֶת הָרֹעֶה, *slay the king of Babylon.* Now, Zechariah was a post-exilic prophet and would not be foretelling the downfall of a king who no longer existed! In the Malbim edition of *Rashi*, there is no mention of the king of *Babylon*. It has been suggested that *Babylon* was inserted by certain publishers due to the fear of censors. The Machon HaMaor edition deletes בָּבֶל from *Rashi's* quote of *Targum* and adds עֵשָׂיו to *Rashi* s.v. ... חֶרֶב רֹעִי.

8. וְהָיָה בְכָל־הָאָרֶץ נְאֻם־ה׳ פִּי־שְׁנַיִם בָּהּ יִכָּרְתוּ יִגְוָעוּ וְהַשְּׁלִשִׁית יִוָּתֶר בָּהּ — *There will be in all the land — the word of Hashem — [that] two portions [of the population] will be cut off and perish, and the third will remain in it.*

Zechariah foretells of great destruction that will take place before the coming of the Messiah. At that time, two thirds of [those residing in] the Land of Israel will perish; some by the sword and some by a plague and one third of the people will survive (*Radak*). Alternatively, two thirds of the entire world population will perish at that time. The two thirds that will perish are the Edomites and Ishmaelites [Christians and Moslems] and the third that will survive are the Israelites (*Metzudos*). Alternatively, one third of the nations will convert to Judaism and thereby survive (*Rashi*).

According to *Reish Lakish*, this verse means that only one third of the Jewish nation will survive these days. *R' Yochanan* disagrees and interprets that all the Jewish people will survive (see *Sanhedrin* 111a).

9. וְהֵבֵאתִי אֶת־הַשְּׁלִשִׁית בָּאֵשׁ וּצְרַפְתִּים כִּצְרֹף אֶת־הַכֶּסֶף — *I will bring that third into fire and purify it as one purifies silver.*

[7] O sword, arouse yourself against My shepherd and against the man who is My colleague! — the word of HASHEM, *Master of Legions. Strike the shepherd and let the flock disperse! And I will turn My hand against the lesser leaders. [8] There will be in all the land — the word of* HASHEM *— [that] two portions [of the population] will be cut off and perish, and the third will remain in it. [9] I will bring that third into fire and purify it as one purifies silver, and I will refine it as one refines gold; it will call out in My Name, and I will answer it. I have said, "It is My people," and it will say, "*HASHEM *is my God."*

[1] Behold, a day is coming for HASHEM, *when your spoils will be divided in your midst.*

Even the surviving third will suffer greatly as God purifies them, refines them and separates them from those who sin and rebel against Him (*Metzudos*). Alternatively, God will test the sincerity of the new converts who have joined the Jewish people by subjecting them to the suffering that will take place during the wars of Gog and Magog. Many will fail the test and return to their former religion and join with Gog and Magog, but the true converts will remain faithful to God (*Rashi*).

XIV

Zechariah now foretells events that will take place during the war of Gog and Magog. The Sages speak of three separate wars that will be fought (*see Midrash Tehillim to Psalms* 118). According to *Malbim*, the first two of these wars are discussed in the Book of *Ezekiel* (Chs. 38-39). The final war, when Gog will actually break into Jerusalem, is the subject of this chapter.

As *R' Mendel Hirsch*, eldest son of Rabbi S. R. Hirsch writes in his commentary on the *Haftaros*: "This chapter ... presents difficulties which certainly require explanations. Many of them will only be fully understood when the actual time arrives ... but the basic thought and the great truths which were to be revealed by the historical events prophesied, only shine through to us the brighter, out of the darkness of the historical background."

[See ArtScroll *Yechezkel*, introduction to Chapter 38 for background information regarding the wars of Gog and Magog.]

1. הִנֵּה יוֹם־בָּא לַה׳ וְחֻלַּק שְׁלָלֵךְ בְּקִרְבֵּךְ — *Behold, a day is coming for Hashem, when your spoils will be divided in your midst.*

Behold, a day that is dear to Hashem (*Rashi*) is coming. A day that the entire world will realize His might and glory (*Radak*). A time when He alone

יד/ב־ה

ב וַאֲסַפְתִּי אֶת־כָּל־הַגּוֹיִם | אֶל־יְרוּשָׁלִַם לַמִּלְחָמָה
וְנִלְכְּדָה הָעִיר וְנָשַׁסּוּ הַבָּתִּים וְהַנָּשִׁים °תשגלנה
וְיָצָא חֲצִי הָעִיר בַּגּוֹלָה וְיֶתֶר הָעָם לֹא יִכָּרֵת
ג מִן־הָעִיר: וְיָצָא יהוה וְנִלְחַם בַּגּוֹיִם הָהֵם כְּיוֹם
ד הִלָּחֲמוֹ בְּיוֹם קְרָב: וְעָמְדוּ רַגְלָיו בַּיּוֹם־הַהוּא
עַל־הַר הַזֵּיתִים אֲשֶׁר עַל־פְּנֵי יְרוּשָׁלִַם מִקֶּדֶם
וְנִבְקַע הַר הַזֵּיתִים מֵחֶצְיוֹ מִזְרָחָה וָיָמָּה גֵּיא
גְּדוֹלָה מְאֹד וּמָשׁ חֲצִי הָהָר צָפוֹנָה וְחֶצְיוֹ נֶגְבָּה:
ה וְנַסְתֶּם גֵּיא־הָרַי כִּי־יַגִּיעַ גֵּי־הָרִים אֶל־אָצַל

°תִּשָּׁכַבְנָה ק׳

will be recognized as the victor (*R' M. Hirsch*). But that will not come easily; it will not arrive without heavy fighting (ibid.) for this is the day Gog and Magog will march on the Land of Israel as prophesied by Ezekiel [38:18-39:16] (*Radak*).

וְחֻלַּק שְׁלָלֵךְ בְּקִרְבֵּךְ — *When your spoils will be divided in your midst.*

Israel will divide the spoils that she will plunder from her enemies (*Targum Yonasan; Rashi*). She will divide the spoils that the nations originally had plundered from her (*Abarbanel; Metzudos*). Alternatively, some commentators maintain that this verse is not bringing good tidings. The nations that will attack Jerusalem will seize the possessions of its inhabitants as they plunder the city (*Ibn Ezra; Radak*).

2. וְאָסַפְתִּי אֶת־כָּל־הַגּוֹיִם אֶל יְרוּשָׁלִַם לַמִּלְחָמָה — *I will gather all the nations to Jerusalem for the war.*

God will inspire the armies of Gog and Magog to wage war against Jerusalem (*Metzudos*). He will lure Gog into thinking that he can wage a successful war against Israel. He will capture the city and plunder the houses etc., but his success will be his downfall (*Mahari Kara*) [see *Ezekiel* 39:2].

וְנִלְכְּדָה הָעִיר ... — *And the city will be captured ...*

All these troubles will befall Israel so that the remaining third may be refined (*Radak*). Regarding this period, the prophet Daniel foretold "there will be a time of trouble such as there had never been since there was a nation until that time" [*Daniel* 12:1] (*Radak*).

וְיָצָא חֲצִי הָעִיר בַּגּוֹלָה — *Half of the city will go out into exile.*

Zechariah foretells that Gog and Magog will take half of the inhabitants of Jerusalem captive and lead them to their encampment that will be situated outside the city (*Radak*).

וְיֶתֶר הָעָם לֹא יִכָּרֵת מִן־הָעִיר — *But the rest of the people will not be eliminated from the city.*

However, God will stop the enemy before he manages to capture the remainder of the city.

3. וְיָצָא ה׳ וְנִלְחַם בַּגּוֹיִם הָהֵם כְּיוֹם הִלָּחֲמוֹ בְּיוֹם קְרָב — *Hashem will go out and wage war with those nations, as He waged war on the day of the battle.*

Then God will "come forth from the heavens" and battle the enemies and destroy them (*Metzudos*). As long as Israel, supported by its own strength, stands against them, it, as always, will be overcome, until God emerges from His apparent retirement and takes up the fight (*R' Mendel Hirsch*).

בְּיוֹם קְרָב — *On the day of the battle.*

[2] *I will gather all the nations to Jerusalem for the war; and the city will be captured, the houses will be pillaged and the women will be violated; half of the city will go out into exile, but the rest of the people will not be eliminated from the city.* [3] *HASHEM will go out and wage war with those nations, as He waged war on the day of the battle.* [4] *His feet will stand on that day on the Mount of Olives, which faces Jerusalem on the east, and the Mount of Olives will split open at its middle, east to west, [forming] a very wide valley; half of the mountain will move to the north and half of it to the south.* [5] *And you will flee to the valley of the mountains, for the valley of the mountains will reach to Azal,*

God will wage war with those nations as He waged war at the Reed Sea (*Targum Yonasan*). At that time, the Israelite nation was in a perilous state for the Egyptians were pursuing them. Moses told the nation, "God will wage war for you ..." (*Radak*).

Malbim differentiates between קְרָב and מִלְחָמָה. קְרָב is a battle fought between two parties that are in close proximity to each other i.e., wrestling. A מִלְחָמָה, however, is fought from a distance, shooting arrows, etc. This battle will not be fought from a distance but close by, through God's miracles.

4. וְעָמְדוּ רַגְלָיו בַּיּוֹם־הַהוּא עַל־הַר הַזֵּיתִים אֲשֶׁר עַל־פְּנֵי יְרוּשָׁלַםִ מִקֶּדֶם — *His feet will stand on that day on the Mount of Olives, which faces Jerusalem on the east.*

The word רֶגֶל, *foot*, when used in reference to God expresses the idea that God is the cause of that which is occurring (*Rambam, Moreh Nevuchim* 1:28), He is the cause of the great miracles that will come about at that time (*Radak*). He will be revealed in His might at that time (*Targum Yonasan*).

וְנִבְקַע הַר הַזֵּיתִים ... — *And the Mount of Olives will split open ...*

The mountain will split apart creating a great gorge going from east to west with the two halves of the mountain on the north and south of the gorge. These two sections of mountain will move northward and southward respectively leaving a wide valley between them (*Rashi*).

Although *Rashi* and *Ibn Ezra* interpret the splitting of the mountain literally, *Radak* suggests that it is metaphorically describing the total routing of the invading armies. Just as God split the mountain and moved the two halves apart, so will He split the ranks of the enemy's army and cast their soldiers to the sides. *Abarbanel*, too, understands this prophecy figuratively and argues that it is foretelling of a battle between the descendants of Edom,the Christians, and the descendants of Ishmael, the Moslems.

5. וְנַסְתֶּם גֵּיא־הָרַי כִּי־יַגִּיעַ גֵּי־הָרִים אֶל־אָצַל — *And you will flee to the valley of the mountains, for the valley of the mountains will reach to Azal,*

Zechariah foresees the fear and panic that will overtake the people when they will hear the sound of the mountain splitting. They will flee[1] from the mountainous region that surrounds Jerusalem

1. Due to an alternative reading of the verse — [וְנִסְתַּם instead of וְנַסְתֶּם] — *Rashi*, following *Targum Yonasan*, explains that an additional miracle will take place at that time.

וְנַסְתֶּם כַּאֲשֶׁר נַסְתֶּם מִפְּנֵי הָרַעַשׁ בִּימֵי עֻזִּיָּה מֶלֶךְ־יְהוּדָה וּבָא יהוה אֱלֹהַי כָּל־קְדֹשִׁים עִמָּךְ׃ ו וְהָיָה בַּיּוֹם הַהוּא לֹא־יִהְיֶה אוֹר יְקָרוֹת °יקפאון׃ ז וְהָיָה יוֹם־אֶחָד הוּא יִוָּדַע לַיהוה לֹא־יוֹם ח וְלֹא־לָיְלָה וְהָיָה לְעֵת־עֶרֶב יִהְיֶה־אוֹר׃ וְהָיָה | בַּיּוֹם הַהוּא יֵצְאוּ מַיִם־חַיִּים מִירוּשָׁלַםִ חֶצְיָם אֶל־הַיָּם הַקַּדְמוֹנִי וְחֶצְיָם אֶל־הַיָּם הָאַחֲרוֹן

°וְקִפָּאוֹן ק׳

into the valley that was created when the Mount of Olives split in half. They will flee all the way to a place called Azal for the valley formed will extend past the mountain to that location (*Radak; Abarbanel*).

וְנַסְתֶּם כַּאֲשֶׁר נַסְתֶּם מִפְּנֵי הָרַעַשׁ בִּימֵי עֻזִּיָּה מֶלֶךְ־יְהוּדָה — *And you will flee as you fled from the earthquake that was in the days of Uzziah, king of Judah.*

The people will flee because of this earthquake as their ancestors had fled (*Radak*) when an earthquake occurred during the days of Uzziah, king of Judah, as he was stricken with *tzaraas* (*Rashi*).

Uzziah had entered the Temple illicitly to burn incense, a service reserved for the Kohanim and was stricken with *tzaraas* for his terrible misdeed (*II Chronicles* 26:16-21). The Sages (*Yalkut Shimoni, Isaiah* Chap. 6) explain that this caused the earthquake mentioned here [see *Amos* 1:1; *Isaiah* 6:4]. While the earth and the Sanctuary shook to its very foundations, Isaiah's prophetic eye saw the סִילּוּק הַשְּׁכִינָה — that God's glorious presence was removing itself from the Sanctuary. The nation, terrified at the earthquake, fled from the proximity of the Temple. Now, during the wars of Gog and Magog, again there is an earthquake as the mountains split, but it is not a sign of the departure of God's glory but of its return. Again the nation flees because of the earthquake, but this time not away from the Temple but toward it! (*R' Mendel Hirsch*).

וּבָא ה׳ אֱלֹהַי כָּל־קְדֹשִׁים עִמָּךְ — *And Hashem my God, will come; all [of His] Holy Ones will be with you.*

At this time, God will come with His angels and will protect the city of Jerusalem (*Radak*). Alternatively, the קְדֹשִׁים, *Holy Ones*, are God's prophets; all the promises that God assured His nation through His prophets will now be fulfilled (*Rambam, Moreh Nevuchim* 1:22).

6. וְהָיָה בַּיּוֹם הַהוּא לֹא־יִהְיֶה אוֹר יְקָרוֹת וְקִפָּאוֹן — *It will be on that day, the light will not be very bright nor very dim.*

Our translation follows *Metzudos. Rashi*, following *Targum Yonasan*, explains that there won't be any bright light at that time, only a faint glimmer similar to the light that appears in the morning over the mountains and slowly disappears [יְקָרוֹת], and a darkness that is concealed and thick [קִפָּאוֹן].

The commentators explain this verse figuratively. After these awesome events, Israel will experience a mixture of blessing and distress (*Rashi*). The people will be confused and perplexed wondering whether this is a prelude to victory or destruction (*Metzudos*). The nation will be unable to celebrate the victory that God's vengeance had wrought upon the enemy for they will still be stricken with fear of them (*Abarbanel*).

The mountain that had been split in two will move back to its original place and the valley that had been formed will become *stopped up*. The height of the valley will then be the height of the mountaintop (אָצַל).

and you will flee as you fled from the earthquake that was in the days of Uzziah, king of Judah. And H*ASHEM, my God, will come; all [of His] Holy Ones will be with you.* [6]*It will be on that day, the light will not be very bright nor very dim.* [7]*It will be a unique day; it will be known as* H*ASHEM's [day], neither day nor night, but it will happen toward evening time that there will be light.* [8]*It shall be on that day, spring water will flow out of Jerusalem; half of it [will flow] to the Eastern Sea and half of it toward the Western Sea.*

7. וְהָיָה יוֹם־אֶחָד הוּא יִוָּדַע לַה׳ לֹא־יוֹם וְלֹא־לָיְלָה וְהָיָה לְעֶת־עֶרֶב יִהְיֶה־אוֹר — *It will be a unique day; it will be known as Hashem's [day], neither day nor night, but it will happen toward evening time that there will be light.*

That day will become famous as the unique day when God revealed His might and His wonders. It will be neither day, i.e., entirely "day," completely free of troubles nor night, i.e., entirely "night," completely beset with troubles. But toward evening — as the troubles and tragedies of v. 2 approach — there will be light: God's salvation of v. 3 will begin (*Radak*).

Alternatively, on the day that God will reveal His might, the world will be in such turmoil that people won't realize whether it is day or night due to the clouds, rain, fire and winds that will engulf the land (*Abarbanel*).

Rashi's explanation of this verse is vague and enigmatic for he explains:

This thing will be one day of the days of God; it will be known that it is for the preparation of the salvation by God. It will not be like the World to Come — a bright light — but it will not be a time of trouble either; it will not be a time of dominion of foreign kingdoms; for this will take place just prior to the coming of the Messiah, a time when foreign kingdoms will dominate the Jewish people. But it will occur toward evening time; before the thousand years are up, there will be a bright light.

Abarbanel maintains that *Rashi's* explanation is based on *Pesikta Rabbasi* and *Pirkei D'Rabbi Eliezer* (Chap. 29) where this verse is cited as proof that the four foreign kingdoms will not dominate Israel for more than one day — *toward evening time there will be light* — the light of Israel. God's day is one thousand years [see *Psalms* 90:1]. Accordingly, *Rashi's* interpretation is that the foreign dominion of the Jewish people will be less than one thousand years, a calculation refuted by *Abarbanel* for in his day one thousand nine hundred and forty years of foreign dominion had already passed. [May we merit to see the coming of מָשִׁיחַ soon and in our days.]

8. וְהָיָה בַּיּוֹם הַהוּא יֵצְאוּ מַיִם־חַיִּים מִירוּשָׁלַםִ — *It shall be on that day, spring water will flow out of Jerusalem.*

On the day that the Mount of Olives will split from east to west, spring water will flow from Jerusalem by way of the valley eastward. This is the same spring that was already mentioned in 13:1. It is also mentioned in *Joel* 4:18 and *Ezekiel* Chap. 47.

חֶצְיָם אֶל־הַיָּם הַקַּדְמוֹנִי וְחֶצְיָם אֶל־הַיָּם הָאַחֲרוֹן — *Half of it [will flow] to the Eastern Sea and half of it toward the Western Sea.*

It will flow toward the Eastern Sea which is situated at the east end of the world, and half will flow westward toward the Western Sea (*Rashi*). The Eastern Sea is either the Kinneret or the Dead Sea. The Western Sea is the Mediterranean Sea (see *Radak* to *Joel* 2:20).

ט בַּקַּיִץ וּבַחֹרֶף יִהְיֶה׃ וְהָיָה יהוה לְמֶלֶךְ עַל־כָּל־הָאָרֶץ בַּיּוֹם הַהוּא יִהְיֶה יהוה אֶחָד וּשְׁמוֹ אֶחָד׃ י יִסּוֹב כָּל־הָאָרֶץ כָּעֲרָבָה מִגֶּבַע לְרִמּוֹן נֶגֶב יְרוּשָׁלָ͏ִם וְרָאֲמָה וְיָשְׁבָה תַחְתֶּיהָ לְמִשַּׁעַר בִּנְיָמִן עַד־מְקוֹם שַׁעַר הָרִאשׁוֹן עַד־שַׁעַר הַפִּנִּים וּמִגְדַּל חֲנַנְאֵל עַד יִקְבֵי הַמֶּלֶךְ׃ יא וְיָשְׁבוּ בָהּ וְחֵרֶם לֹא יִהְיֶה־עוֹד וְיָשְׁבָה יְרוּשָׁלַ͏ִם לָבֶטַח׃

בַּקַּיִץ וּבַחֹרֶף יִהְיֶה — *This will be in summer and in winter.*

This spring will flow both in the summer, when springs usually dry up, and in the winter, when their waters usually freeze (*Ibn Ezra*)

This verse may be understood both literally and figuratively, i.e., that the belief in God and in His Torah will flow forth from Jerusalem to the entire world as a spring flows from its source (*Abarbanel*).

9. וְהָיָה ה׳ לְמֶלֶךְ עַל־כָּל־הָאָרֶץ — *Hashem will be the King over all the world.*

All the surviving nations that attacked Jerusalem will acknowledge that God is the King over the entire world once they have seen the great miracles that He has performed for His nation (*Radak; Abarbanel*). His kingship will no longer be recognized only by Israel but by all the nations (*Abarbanel*).

בַּיּוֹם הַהוּא יִהְיֶה ה׳ אֶחָד — *On that day Hashem will be One.*

All the nations will abandon their false deities and acknowledge that Hashem is the only God and does not share His mantle with any other power (*Rashi*).

The Talmud (*Pesachim* 50a) questions the meaning of this verse for it implies that God's unity will not be absolute until the ultimate redemption will have taken place [on *that* day Hashem will be One — implying *not before that day*]. R' Acha bar Chanina explained that unlike in this world where upon hearing good things one relates the blessing of *"Who is good and does good"* — הַטּוֹב וְהַמֵּטִיב — and upon hearing bad tidings *"The true Judge"* — דַּיַּין הָאֱמֶת [which may cause one to believe in a plurality in God for it is difficult to reconcile suffering and tragedy with God's attributes of mercy and kindness], in the World to Come, all of the blessings will be *"Who is good and does good"* for at that time there will be no bad tidings [and the unity of God will be fully acknowledged and appreciated].

וּשְׁמוֹ אֶחָד — *And His Name will be One.*

God's Name will be One because no one will mention the names of other gods; only the Name of Hashem will be mentioned (*Radak*). Alternatively the respected Name of Hashem, the Tetragrammaton [י־ה־ו־ה], will then be pronounced as it is written (*Ibn Ezra*).

The Rabbis [see *Pesachim* 50a; *Kiddushin* 71a] ruled that due to the sanctity of this Name, it is not to be read as it is written but is to be read *Adonoy* instead. Only in the Temple during the Yom Kippur service and during the daily Priestly Blessing was it pronounced as it is written. Indeed, among those who are excluded from a share in the World to Come is one who pronounces the Name according "to its letters" (*Mishneh, Sanhedrin* 90a — see *Tosafos Avodah Zarah* 18a s.v. הוגה). After the ultimate redemption, this Name will be read as it is written.

All the Names of God other than the Four-letter Ineffable Name [the Tetragrammaton] are descriptions of the different ways mortal man perceives God: through His actions. The frequent use of these Names led to the belief of a plurality in God. In future times, only one Name of God will be used, the Tetragrammaton, God's actual Name, not derived from His actions (*Rambam, Moreh Nevuchim* 1:61).

This will be in summer and in winter. [9] *HASHEM will be the King over all the world; on that day HASHEM will be One and His Name will be One.* [10] *The entire land will change to a plain, from the Hill of Rimmon, south of Jerusalem, and [Jerusalem] will become lofty and it will be settled in its place, from the Gate of Benjamin to the place of the first gate, to the Corner Gate, and [from] the Tower of Hananel up to the king's winery.* [11] *People will dwell in it, and there will be no more devastation; and Jerusalem will dwell in security.*

10. יִסּוֹב כָּל־הָאָרֶץ כָּעֲרָבָה — *The entire land will change to a plain.*

God will transform the entire world into a flat plain (*Rashi*). *Radak* maintains that it is only the mountains surrounding Jerusalem that will be leveled transforming the area into a flat plain giving Jerusalem a towering appearance (*Radak; Rashi*).

מִגֶּבַע לְרִמּוֹן — *From the Hill of Rimmon.*

Our translation follows *Rashi* and *Metzudos* and is supported by *Tosefta, Sotah* (11:14): *"the Hill of Rimmon is rugged and stony." Targum Yonasan* followed by *Malbim* translate from Geba to Rimmon.

The plain will start from the Hill of Rimmon which is south of Jerusalem (*Metzudos*) or the Hill of Rimmon will be flattened to a plain and will be like the south of Jerusalem which is a plain (*Rashi from Tosefta, Sotah* 11:4). Alternatively, after the Mountain of Olives will split in two, the valley formed will widen to a plain stretching from Geba which is in the south of Jerusalem to Rimmon (*Malbim*).

וְיָשְׁבָה תַחְתֶּיהָ — *And it will be settled in its place.*

The city of Jerusalem will then be rebuilt on its original site, for after it had been destroyed by Titus, it had never been rebuilt on its original site (*Abarbanel; Metzudos*).

לְמִשַּׁעַר בִּנְיָמִן ... עַד יִקְבֵי הַמֶּלֶךְ — *From the Gate of Benjamin ... up to the king's winery.*

Not only will Jerusalem be rebuilt on its original site but it will be greatly expanded (*Abarbanel*). The Gate of Benjamin and the place of the first gate are the city's original boundaries. The Corner Gate, the Tower of Hananel and the king's winery are the boundaries of the expanded city (*Malbim*); the Corner Gate in the north and the Tower of Hananel in the south with the boundary extending eastward to the king's winery (*Metzudos*).

Targum Yonasan translates יֶקֶב as שִׁיחַ, *a ditch*, referring to the ditch of the winepress into which the wine flows (*Rashi*). *Midrash Aggadah* interprets יִקְבֵי הַמֶּלֶךְ, *the ditches of the king*, as the Atlantic Ocean, the ditch that was dug by the King of kings. Accordingly, Jerusalem of the future will expand its borders to the distant shores of the Atlantic Ocean.

11. וְיָשְׁבוּ בָהּ וְחֵרֶם לֹא יִהְיֶה־עוֹד וְיָשְׁבָה יְרוּשָׁלַםִ לָבֶטַח — *People will dwell in it, and there will be no more devastation, and Jerusalem will dwell in security.*

The prophet foretells that the Jewish people will permanently return to their Holy City. Jerusalem will then be inhabited forever (*Radak; Metzudos*) and will never be destroyed. Its people will dwell there securely because the Divine Presence will then dwell among them. It is then that the Messiah will reveal himself to the people (*Ibn Ezra*).

יב וְזֹאת | תִּהְיֶה הַמַּגֵּפָה אֲשֶׁר יִגֹּף יהוה אֶת־כָּל־הָעַמִּים אֲשֶׁר צָבְאוּ עַל־יְרוּשָׁלָםִ הָמֵק | בְּשָׂרוֹ וְהוּא עֹמֵד עַל־רַגְלָיו וְעֵינָיו תִּמַּקְנָה בְחֹרֵיהֶן וּלְשׁוֹנוֹ תִּמַּק בְּפִיהֶם׃ יג וְהָיָה בַּיּוֹם הַהוּא תִּהְיֶה מְהוּמַת־יְהוָה רַבָּה בָּהֶם וְהֶחֱזִיקוּ אִישׁ יַד רֵעֵהוּ וְעָלְתָה יָדוֹ עַל־יַד רֵעֵהוּ׃ יד וְגַם־יְהוּדָה תִּלָּחֵם בִּירוּשָׁלָםִ וְאֻסַּף חֵיל כָּל־הַגּוֹיִם סָבִיב זָהָב וָכֶסֶף וּבְגָדִים לָרֹב מְאֹד׃ טו וְכֵן תִּהְיֶה מַגֵּפַת הַסּוּס הַפֶּרֶד הַגָּמָל וְהַחֲמוֹר וְכָל־הַבְּהֵמָה אֲשֶׁר יִהְיֶה בַּמַּחֲנוֹת הָהֵמָּה כַּמַּגֵּפָה הַזֹּאת׃ טז וְהָיָה כָּל־הַנּוֹתָר מִכָּל־הַגּוֹיִם הַבָּאִים עַל־יְרוּשָׁלָםִ וְעָלוּ מִדֵּי שָׁנָה בְשָׁנָה לְהִשְׁתַּחֲוֺת לְמֶלֶךְ יְהוָה צְבָאוֹת וְלָחֹג אֶת־חַג הַסֻּכּוֹת׃

12. וְזֹאת תִּהְיֶה הַמַּגֵּפָה אֲשֶׁר יִגֹּף ה׳ אֶת־כָּל־הָעַמִּים אֲשֶׁר צָבְאוּ עַל יְרוּשָׁלָםִ — *This will be the plague with which Hashem will strike all the peoples who have organized against Jerusalem.*

After describing the victory and salvation that God will perform for His nation, the prophet describes the punishments that will befall their enemies (*Abarbanel*). These enemies are the armies of Gog and Magog for it was they who gathered together and waged war against Jerusalem (*Ibn Ezra*).

הַמַּגֵּפָה — *The plague.*

This plague will be unlike any other plague ever experienced and will not be viewed as a natural occurrence. Everyone will realize that it was God Who sent this plague against the nations (*Me'am Loez*). *Midrash Tanchuma* (*Tazria* v. 11), however, identifies this plague as *tzaraas.*

הָמֵק בְּשָׂרוֹ וְהוּא עֹמֵד עַל־רַגְלָיו ... — *Each one's flesh will melt away while he is standing on his feet ...*

God will strike all these nations with a plague that will cause their flesh to melt away and their limbs to suddenly fall off their bodies (*Rashi; Radak*). This will occur while they are *still standing on their feet,* physically perfectly healthy and strong, without any illness (*Radak*), as a sign to the nations that this has come from God, the protector of His nation [see *Isaiah* 66:19].

R' Mendel Hirsch notes that although punishment of the nations is taking place, Scripture uses the Name ה׳, the Name denoting God's attribute of love and compassion, rather than the name אֱלֹהִים which describes God as the Demander of Justice. He explains that the downfall of those who are incorrigible and irreclaimable up to the "eleventh hour" is not viewed as punishment but rather as protection of the pure mankind which henceforth is blossoming up on earth.

13. וְהָיָה בַּיּוֹם הַהוּא תִּהְיֶה מְהוּמַת־ה׳ רַבָּה בָּהֶם ... — *It shall be on that day that there will be a great panic of Hashem among them ...*

The prophet foretells that God will cause a great panic to befall the enemy and they will be unable to discern between friend and foe. Therefore, when one will stretch forth his hand to assist his fellow, the friend will

[12]This will be the plague with which HASHEM will strike all the peoples who have organized against Jerusalem: Each one's flesh will melt away while he is standing on his feet; each one's eyes will melt away in their sockets; and each one's tongue will melt away in their mouths. [13]It shall be on that day that there will be a great panic of HASHEM among them; each one will grab the hand of his fellow, and his hand will be raised up against the hand of his fellow. [14]Also Judah will wage war against Jerusalem; and the wealth of all the nations all around will be gathered: gold, silver and garments in great abundance. [15]And similarly will be the plague of the horse, the mule, the camel and the donkey, all the animals that will be in those camps, just like this plague.

[16]It shall be that all who are left over from all the nations who had invaded Jerusalem will go up every year to worship the King, HASHEM, Master of Legions, and to celebrate the festival of Succos.

think that he is being attacked and will therefore raise up his hand against the outstretched hand of his fellow (*Abarbanel; Metzudos*). Alternatively, *Radak*, following *Targum Yonasan*, renders *his hand will be torn off by the hand of his fellow*. When a victim of the plague will support himself by holding on to his fellow's hand, his entire arm will fall off.

14. וְגַם־יְהוּדָה תִּלָּחֵם בִּירוּשָׁלָםִ ... — *Also Judah will wage war against Jerusalem ...*

The nations had forced Judah to assist them in their siege against Jerusalem (*Rashi; Radak; Metzudos*) [see 12:2]; when Judah will witness the plague that God will send against these nations, it will gather the wealth of these nations (*Radak*).

Alternatively, the confusion and panic that will take place among the nations (v. 13) will be caused by the Judeans who had been forced to assist the nations, for when one will stretch forth his hand to assist his fellow, the fellow will suspect that he is a Judean who has become his enemy (*Metzudos*).

15. וְכֵן תִּהְיֶה מַגֵּפַת הַסּוּס ... — *And similarly will be the plague of the horse ...*

God will not only strike Jerusalem's attackers with a plague but He will do the same to their animals (*Metzudos*) for they are the bearers and instruments of the enemy's might (*R' Mendel Hirsch*). It is for this reason, i.e., that they will be destroyed in the plague, that the animals are not mentioned among the spoils of v. 14 (*Abarbanel*).

16. וְהָיָה כָּל־הַנּוֹתָר מִכָּל־הַגּוֹיִם הַבָּאִים עַל־יְרוּשָׁלָםִ ... — *It shall be that all who are left over from all the nations who had invaded Jerusalem ...*

יז וְהָיָה אֲשֶׁר לֹא־יַעֲלֶה מֵאֵת מִשְׁפְּחוֹת הָאָרֶץ אֶל־יְרוּשָׁלִַם לְהִשְׁתַּחֲוֺת לְמֶלֶךְ יהוה צְבָאוֹת וְלֹא עֲלֵיהֶם יִהְיֶה הַגָּשֶׁם׃ יח וְאִם־מִשְׁפַּחַת מִצְרַיִם לֹא־תַעֲלֶה וְלֹא בָאָה וְלֹא עֲלֵיהֶם תִּהְיֶה הַמַּגֵּפָה אֲשֶׁר יִגֹּף יהוה אֶת־הַגּוֹיִם אֲשֶׁר לֹא יַעֲלוּ לָחֹג אֶת־חַג הַסֻּכּוֹת׃ יט זֹאת תִּהְיֶה חַטַּאת מִצְרָיִם וְחַטַּאת כָּל־הַגּוֹיִם אֲשֶׁר לֹא יַעֲלוּ לָחֹג אֶת־חַג הַסֻּכּוֹת׃ כ בַּיּוֹם הַהוּא יִהְיֶה עַל־מְצִלּוֹת הַסּוּס קֹדֶשׁ לַיהוה וְהָיָה הַסִּירוֹת בְּבֵית יהוה כַּמִּזְרָקִים לִפְנֵי הַמִּזְבֵּחַ׃

The people who repented, when they saw the catastrophe that was befalling their camp, will mark the anniversary of the miracles they had witnessed during the war by going up to Jerusalem and offering sacrifices (*Metzudos*) on the Succos festival, for it is during the season of Succos that the war of Gog and Magog will have taken place (*Radak*).

The Talmud (*Avodah Zarah* 3a) states that God will concede to the wishes of the gentile nations and offer them a final chance to accept His Torah. To test their sincerity, He will ask them to perform the commandment of *succah* and each one will immediately respond by eagerly building a *succah* atop his roof. God will then cause the sun to blaze on them and each of them will kick over his *succah* proving his insincerity and lack of commitment.

R' Hirsch (*Numbers* 29:13) notes that "all the efforts of the nations using their powers to fight against connections with God and His laws end with their acknowledging God as King (v.9) and coming to Jerusalem to celebrate the festival of Succos each year." What connection is there between Gog and Magog and Succos?

R' Hirsch relates the name Gog (גוֹג) to the word גַּג, *roof*, which is in contrast to the *succah*, the weak, unstable covering of foliage. This contrast actually sums up the entire history of mankind, who think that just as they have the ability to build דְּפָנוֹת, strong walls to protect them from their earthly contemporaries, so too do they imagine that they have the power to protect themselves from that which comes from above: God and His power to direct matters. They imagine that they can build a "roof" and take their fate in their own hands and render themselves independent of God.

The war of Gog and Magog is the battle of גַּג against סוּכָּה: the fight of the "roof" illusion of human greatness which never allows man to rest against the "*succah*" truth of cheerful confidence and serenity which is the result of placing one's trust in God's protection.

17. וְהָיָה אֲשֶׁר לֹא־יַעֲלֶה מֵאֵת מִשְׁפְּחוֹת הָאָרֶץ אֶל־יְרוּשָׁלִַם ... — *And it shall be that whichever of the families of the land does not go up to Jerusalem ...*

On Succos, judgment is passed in regard to water and rain for the entire year (*Mishnah, Rosh Hashanah* 1:2). Indeed, the Torah's commandments of the four species and the water libations are performed on the festival of Succos to entreat God and invoke His blessing on the year's rainfall. Therefore, those nations who do not go up to Jerusalem to pray for rain will be punished by not having any rainfall (*Rashi; Mahari Kara*).

18. וְאִם־מִשְׁפַּחַת מִצְרַיִם לֹא־תַעֲלֶה וְלֹא בָאָה ... — *But if it is the family of Egypt that does not go up and does not come [to Jerusalem] ...*

[17] *And it shall be that whichever of the families of the land does not go up to Jerusalem to bow down before the King, HASHEM, Master of Legions, there will be no rain upon them.* [18] *But if it is the family of Egypt that does not go up and does not come [to Jerusalem], there will be no [water] for them; the same plague will come to pass with which HASHEM will strike the nations that do not go up to celebrate the festival of Succos.* [19] *This will be the punishment of the Egyptians and the punishment of all the nations that will not go up to celebrate the festival of Succos.*

[20] *On that day will be [written] on the horse's bells, "Holy unto HASHEM"; and the pots in the Temple of HASHEM will be as [numerous] as the bowls before the Altar.*

But if it be the Egyptians (who do not require rainfall to irrigate their land, for the flooding Nile supplies its water) (*Rashi*) who will not come to celebrate the festival of Succos in Jerusalem, they will be deprived of "their rain" — the waters of the flooding Nile (*Targum Yonasan*) — and will suffer with famine (*Rashi*). Alternatively, since they do not require rain for their water supply, they will be stricken with the same plague as the nations who attacked Jerusalem: their flesh will melt away [see v. 12] (*Radak*).

Egypt is specifically mentioned for it personifies the nation that finds its pride solely in its might. In the end, it will meet the same fate as the other nations who refused to acknowledge God (*R' Mendel Hirsch*).

19. זֹאת תִּהְיֶה חַטַּאת מִצְרָיִם וְחַטַּאת כָּל־הַגּוֹיִם אֲשֶׁר לֹא יַעֲלוּ לָחֹג אֶת־חַג הַסֻּכּוֹת — *This will be the punishment of the Egyptians and the punishment of all the nations that will not go up to celebrate the festival of Succos.*

Our translation of the word חַטַּאת, *punishment*, and not sin follows *Radak*, *Ibn Ezra* and *Metzudos*.

As noted earlier (v. 18), *Rashi* maintains that both Egypt and the other nations will be punished in the same manner, i.e., that rain will be withheld from them. *Radak*, however, maintains that although the other nations will suffer from the lack of rain, Egypt will be punished with a plague.

20. בַּיּוֹם הַהוּא יִהְיֶה עַל מְצִלּוֹת הַסּוּס קֹדֶשׁ לַה׳ — *On that day will be [written] on the horse's bells, "Holy unto Hashem."*

The sacrifices will be so numerous at that time that even the metal bells that were hung on the horses for ornamentation will be used to produce vessels with which to bring offerings to God and pots in which to cook them (*Rashi*). The words קֹדֶשׁ לַה׳, *Holy unto Hashem*, will not actually be written on the bells. Scripture's intent is that the consecration of the horse's bells will be so widely known that it would be *as if* the very words inscribed on the template of the Kohen Gadol will be inscribed on the horse's bells as well (*Radak*).

The Sages (*Pesachim* 50a) relate מְצִלּוֹת to צֵל, *a shadow*, and explain that Jerusalem will be expanded to the extent that it would take a horse until midday, when it casts a shadow, צֵל, directly under it, to run its length.

כא וְהָיָה כָּל־סִיר בִּירוּשָׁלַם וּבִיהוּדָה קֹדֶשׁ לַיהוָה צְבָאוֹת וּבָאוּ כָּל־הַזֹּבְחִים וְלָקְחוּ מֵהֶם וּבִשְּׁלוּ בָהֶם וְלֹא־יִהְיֶה כְנַעֲנִי עוֹד בְּבֵית־יְהוָה צְבָאוֹת בַּיּוֹם הַהוּא׃

21. וְהָיָה כָּל־סִיר בִּירוּשָׁלַם וּבִיהוּדָה קֹדֶשׁ לַה׳ צְבָאוֹת — *And it will happen that every pot in Jerusalem and in Judah will be holy unto Hashem, Master of Legions.*

The number of pots of the Temple will be insufficient to accommodate the increase of sacrifices now brought by the nations and therefore it will be necessary to consecrate all the pots of Jerusalem and Judah so that they may be used for the peace-offerings being offered (*Radak; Metzudos*).

Alternatively, Scripture is referring to the vessels used for removing the ashes from the altar which will now be made of gold and silver, like the sprinkling basins (*Rashi*).

וְלֹא יִהְיֶה כְנַעֲנִי ... — *And there will no longer be any merchants ...*

[21] *And it will happen that every pot in Jerusalem and in Judah will be holy unto* HASHEM, *Master of Legions; all those who sacrifice will come and take from them and cook in them; and there will no longer be any merchants in the Temple of* HASHEM, *Master of Legions, on that day.*

Since many people will be donating items to the Temple, the treasurer will no longer need to purchase necessities for the Temple service (*Radak*).

Our translation of כְּנַעֲנִי as *merchants* follows *Targum Yonasan*. Others see this as a reference to the Gibeonites who served as woodchoppers and water carriers in the Temple. Their services will no longer be needed for the distinguished leaders of all the nations will now serve the Kohanim (*R' Joseph Kimchi; Metzudos*).

Thus, Zechariah ends his prophecy with the redemption of Jerusalem and a description of its elevated status. The spirit of the Sanctuary will have penetrated the entire life of the people and will have raised them to a stage where selfishness and self-interests have been completely overcome and each person will perform his duty for the sole purpose of fulfilling God's will (*R' Mendel Hirsch*).

MALACHI

א/א־ד

א־ב מַשָּׂא דְבַר־יְהוָה אֶל־יִשְׂרָאֵל בְּיַד מַלְאָכִי: אָהַבְתִּי אֶתְכֶם אָמַר יְהוָה וַאֲמַרְתֶּם בַּמָּה אֲהַבְתָּנוּ הֲלוֹא־אָח עֵשָׂו לְיַעֲקֹב נְאֻם־יְהוָה וָאֹהַב אֶת־יַעֲקֹב:
ג וְאֶת־עֵשָׂו שָׂנֵאתִי וָאָשִׂים אֶת־הָרָיו שְׁמָמָה וְאֶת־
ד נַחֲלָתוֹ לְתַנּוֹת מִדְבָּר: כִּי־תֹאמַר אֱדוֹם רֻשַּׁשְׁנוּ וְנָשׁוּב וְנִבְנֶה חֳרָבוֹת כֹּה אָמַר יְהוָה צְבָאוֹת

☙ Introduction

Malachi prophesied during the Second Temple era and was a contemporary of the prophets Haggai and Zechariah. However, the exact time of his prophecies is unclear. *Radak* notes that although Scripture (*Ezra* 5:1;6:14) clearly states that Haggai and Zechariah prophesied prior to the rebuilding of the Temple, Malachi is not mentioned together with them nor does he mention the rebuilding of the Temple in any of his prophecies. *Radak* therefore feels that Malachi was the very last prophet and prophesied *after* the Temple had been rebuilt. *Ibn Ezra,* too, is of the opinion that Malachi was the last prophet to prophesy for Israel for at the end of his prophecies, Malachi exhorts Israel to *remember the Torah of Moses My servant* (3:22), which, according to *Ibn Ezra,* implies that in the future there will be no more prophets to chastise Israel regarding their observance of the mitzvos. [See also *Mahari Kara* to 3:22.]

Malachi's identity is shrouded in mystery. The Talmud (*Megillah* 15a) discusses this and quotes various opinions: R' Nachman said that Malachi was actually Mordechai [of *Megillas Esther*] but his opinion is refuted. R' Yehoshua ben Korcha suggested that Malachi was actually Ezra, to which R' Nachman agreed and even offered Scriptural support from the similarity of their prophetic messages [see *Malachi* 2:11 and *Ezra* 10:2]. The Sages held that there was a prophet whose real name was Malachi who prophesied at that time. *Targum Yonasan ben Uziel* (*Malachi* 1:1) and *Meiri* (introduction to *Avos)* identify Malachi as Ezra.

But *Rambam* (introduction to *Yad HaChazakah)* writes that Malachi [and Mordechai] were both members of the *Beis Din* of Ezra, i.e., the *Anshei Knesses HaGedolah* (Men of the Great Assembly). This would seem to concur with the opinion of the Sages that Malachi, Mordechai and Ezra were separate individuals. *Radak* and *Abarbanel* also maintain that Malachi was not Ezra but an individual named Malachi who prophesied at that time.

I.

1. מַשָּׂא דְּבַר־ה׳ — *The prophecy of the word of Hashem.*

מַשָּׂא, lit., *burden,* is one of the ten expressions of prophecy enumerated in *Bereishis Rabbah* (44:7) and generally introduces a fateful and foreboding prophecy [see *Nahum* 1:1]. In this particular instance, it designates the fate of the word of Hashem which Israel is appointed to bear throughout the world, and the degree of Israel's understanding and devotion to His word (*R' Mendel Hirsch*). It may also be referred to as a burden because the nation at that time viewed the exhortations of the prophets as a burden (*Abarbanel*).

אֶל־יִשְׂרָאֵל — *To Israel.*

Actually, Scripture is referring specifically to the people of Judah for the other ten tribes had been exiled by the Assyrians many years earlier (*Ibn Ezra*).

[1] The prophecy of the word of H*ASHEM to Israel, through Malachi:*

[2] I loved you, says H*ASHEM; but you say, "How have You loved us?" Was not Esau the brother of Jacob — the word of* H*ASHEM — yet I loved Jacob. [3] But I hated Esau; I made his mountains a desolation and [gave] his heritage to the desert serpents. [4] Though Edom will say, "We have become destitute, but we will return and rebuild the ruins," thus says* H*ASHEM, Master of Legions:*

2. אָהַבְתִּי אֶתְכֶם אָמַר ה׳ ... וָאֹהַב אֶת־יַעֲקֹב — *"I loved you," said Hashem ... — "yet I loved Jacob."*

God confirms that He has loved the Jewish nation from bygone days by expressing His love for Jacob. Although Esau and Jacob were both sons of Isaac, He nevertheless chose Jacob to receive the Land that He had promised to Abraham and Isaac (*Radak; Rashi*).

וַאֲמַרְתֶּם בַּמָּה אֲהַבְתָּנוּ — *But you say, "How have You loved us?"*

Most commentators (*Radak; Mahari Kara; Metzudos*) explain that the nation did not actually challenge the word of God and ask, *"How have You loved us?"* but it is the prophetic word of God stating, *And if you will say, "How have You loved us?"* then I answer you, *"Was not Esau ..."*

Alternatively, *Abarbanel* explains that although the nation had sinned and had been punished by God, it had been the punishment of a father, with love; and yet the nation was ungrateful and asked, "How have You loved us?" However, even *Abarbanel* maintains that the nation never denied that God loved them. They felt that God showered His kindness upon them not because of any particular love for them but because He loved their forefathers. They wanted proof that God had a particular love for *them.*

3. וְאֶת־עֵשָׂו שָׂנֵאתִי וָאָשִׂים אֶת־הָרָיו שְׁמָמָה וְאֶת־נַחֲלָתוֹ לְתַנּוֹת מִדְבָּר — *But I hated Esau; I made his mountains a desolation and [gave] his heritage to the desert serpents.*

Generally, when one has two sons, he gives the firstborn son a double portion (*Mahari Kara*) or a nicer portion than he gives his younger son; but God says, "I hated Esau and pushed him off to the land of Seir whose mountains do not compare to those of Israel, the beautiful land that I gave Jacob" (*Rashi*).

Abarbanel finds this explanation difficult to incorporate into the text and maintains that the prophet is stating that Esau is hated by God to the degree that He will continuously destroy his land.

Alternatively, I gave him Mount Seir because I did not want him to share the Land of Canaan with his brother Jacob. When his descendants acted wickedly toward Israel and rejoiced at Israel's destruction and exile, I expressed My hatred toward them by making his mountains a desolation never to be resettled. It will remain a heritage to the desert serpents (*Radak*).

Our translation of לְתַנּוֹת מִדְבָּר as desert serpents follows *Metzudos Tzion* and *Malbim* who relate תַּנּוֹת to the word תַּנִּין, a *serpent*. In modern Hebrew a תַּן is a *jackal*. For further discussion of תַּן, see ArtScroll *Eichah* 4:3.

4. כִּי־תֹאמַר אֱדוֹם רֻשַּׁשְׁנוּ וְנָשׁוּב וְנִבְנֶה חֳרָבוֹת — כֹּה אָמַר ה׳ צְבָאוֹת הֵמָּה יִבְנוּ וַאֲנִי אֶהֱרוֹס — *Though Edom will say, "We have become destitute, but we will return and rebuild the ruins," thus says Hashem, Master of Legions: They may build, but I will tear down!*

If Edom will say, "We have become

הֵ֤מָּה יִבְנוּ֙ וַאֲנִ֣י אֶהֱר֔וֹס וְקָרְא֤וּ לָהֶם֙ גְּב֣וּל רִשְׁעָ֔ה
ה וְהָעָ֛ם אֲשֶׁר־זָעַ֥ם יְהוָ֖ה עַד־עוֹלָֽם׃ וְעֵינֵיכֶ֖ם
תִּרְאֶ֑ינָה וְאַתֶּ֤ם תֹּֽאמְרוּ֙ יִגְדַּ֣ל יְהוָ֔ה מֵעַ֖ל לִגְב֥וּל
ו יִשְׂרָאֵֽל׃ בֵּ֛ן יְכַבֵּ֥ד אָ֖ב וְעֶ֣בֶד אֲדֹנָ֑יו וְאִם־אָ֣ב
אָ֡נִי אַיֵּ֣ה כְבוֹדִ֩י וְאִם־אֲדוֹנִ֨ים אָ֜נִי אַיֵּ֣ה מוֹרָאִ֗י
אָמַ֣ר ׀ יְהוָ֣ה צְבָא֗וֹת לָכֶם֙ הַכֹּֽהֲנִים֙ בּוֹזֵ֣י שְׁמִ֔י
ז וַאֲמַרְתֶּ֕ם בַּמֶּ֥ה בָזִ֖ינוּ אֶת־שְׁמֶֽךָ׃ מַגִּישִׁ֤ים עַֽל־
מִזְבְּחִי֙ לֶ֣חֶם מְגֹאָ֔ל וַאֲמַרְתֶּ֖ם בַּמֶּ֣ה גֵֽאַלְנ֑וּךָ

destitute and our land is in ruins, but we will yet return and rebuild our land as did Israel," God answers, "If they will build, I will tear it down never to be rebuilt as punishment for the wickedness they had exercised against Israel" (*Radak*).

וְקָרְאוּ לָהֶם גְּבוּל רִשְׁעָה — *They will be called "the boundary of wickedness."*

All the nations of the world will refer to the land of Edom as *"the boundary of wickedness"* and to its people as *"the people whom Hashem has condemned forever"* because it will be obvious to all that God has despised them because of their wickedness (*Abarbanel; Metzudos*).

וְהָעָם אֲשֶׁר־זָעַם ה׳ עַד־עוֹלָם — *And "the people whom Hashem has condemned forever."*

Although God had commanded Israel, *"Do not despise an Edomite for he is your brother"* [see *Deuteronomy* 23:8], Edom harmed Israel at every opportunity and rejoiced at the destruction of their land and their Temple, forever incurring God's wrath (*Radak*).

5. וְעֵינֵיכֶם תִּרְאֶינָה וְאַתֶּם תֹּאמְרוּ יִגְדַּל ה׳ מֵעַל לִגְבוּל יִשְׂרָאֵל — *And your eyes will see [it] and you will say, "May Hashem be glorified beyond the boundary of Israel."*

Upon witnessing the destruction of Edom (*Radak*) the people will realize that God is displaying His greatness even beyond the borders of the Land of Israel, thereby announcing to the world that the Children of Israel are His people (*Rashi*). Alternatively, give praise to God because He has restored the people of Israel to their borders while the borders of Edom lay in ruins (*Radak*). It would seem that the prophet is referring to events of the Second Temple era for at that time the land of Edom was in ruins and the people of Judah dwelt peacefully in their land (*Abarbanel*). Nevertheless, *Abarbanel* followed by *Metzudos* suggests that this prophecy will take place *when you will be beyond the boundary of Israel*, i.e., at the time of the future redemption, when Israel's borders will be widened. At that time, the people will praise God for His continuous revenge against Edom.

6. בֵּן יְכַבֵּד אָב וְעֶבֶד אֲדֹנָיו וְאִם־אָב אָנִי אַיֵּה כְבוֹדִי וְאִם־אֲדוֹנִים אָנִי אַיֵּה מוֹרָאִי אָמַר ה׳ צְבָאוֹת — *A son will honor his father and a slave his master. Now, if I am a Father, where is My honor? And if I am a Master, where is My reverence? says Hashem, Master of Legions.*

After describing the special love God has for His nation, Israel is taken to task for not reciprocating this love. It is universally accepted that it is proper for a son to honor his father and for a slave to respect his master. The prophet therefore declares in the name of God, "If you consider Me your Father, then

They may build, but I will tear down! They will be called "the boundary of wickedness" and "the people whom HASHEM *has condemned forever."* [5] *And your eyes will see [it] and you will say, "May* HASHEM *be glorified beyond the boundary of Israel."*

[6] *A son will honor his father and a slave his master. Now, if I am a Father, where is My honor? And if I am a Master, where is My reverence? says* HASHEM, *Master of Legions, to you, O Kohanim who scorn My Name. Yet you say, "How have we scorned Your Name?"* [7] *You present on My Altar loathsome food, and you say, "How have we loathed You?"*

where is the honor due Me? If you consider Me your Master, then where is the respect and reverence due Me?" (*Rashi; Metzudos*).

אַיֵּה כְבוֹדִי ... אַיֵּה מוֹרָאִי — *Where is My honor? ... Where is My reverence?*

This verse seems problematic for it starts by stating that the son gives honor to his father and the slave gives honor to his master but continues to ask, "If I am a master, where is my reverence" — *reverence?* We are discussing the *honor* due the master, not the *reverence*! R' Yaakov Kaminetzky solves this problem and explains that the honor that a slave is obligated to give his master springs from his obligation to revere and respect him and is therefore categorized as reverence (*Emes L'Yaakov, Devarim* 10:20).

הַכֹּהֲנִים בּוֹזֵי שְׁמִי — *O Kohanim who scorn My Name.*

Malachi rebukes the Kohanim first for they are the leaders of the nation (*Abarbanel*) and it is incumbent upon them to teach the people the laws of the Torah. Instead, not only do they neglect to teach the people, but they even scorn My Name (*Radak*).

וַאֲמַרְתֶּם בַּמֶּה בָזִינוּ אֶת־שְׁמֶךָ — *Yet you say, "How have we scorned Your Name?"*

Our translation follows *Rashi* who explains that instead of admitting their guilt, the Kohanim added to their wrongdoings and denied it (*Abarbanel*) by answering God's reproof and saying, *"How have we scorned Your Name?"* Alternatively, *Targum Yonasan* followed by *Metzudos* renders, *"And if you will say* ... i.e., implying that the Kohanim did not actually ask, *"How have we scorned Your Name?"* Accordingly, these are the prophetic words of God Who is anticipating the response of the Kohanim.

7. מַגִּישִׁים עַל־מִזְבְּחִי לֶחֶם מְגֹאָל — *You present on My Altar loathsome food.*

The prophet proceeds to describe the manner in which the Kohanim have scorned God's Name: by offering sacrifices that are unfit to be offered on His Altar. The word לֶחֶם, *bread,* is a general term that Scripture uses for all types of sacrifices [see *Leviticus* 21:21; 3:11 and *Numbers* 28:2] (*Radak; Metzudos*).

וַאֲמַרְתֶּם בַּמֶּה גֵאַלְנוּךָ — *And you say, "How have we loathed You?"*

Malachi addresses the Kohanim who wonder and ask, *"How have we loathed God?"* What is wrong with bringing these animals as sacrifices? Why are they deemed unfit to be offered?

ח בֶּאֱמָרְכֶם שֻׁלְחַן יהוה נִבְזֶה הוּא: וְכִי־תַגִּשׁוּן
עִוֵּר לִזְבֹּחַ אֵין רָע וְכִי תַגִּישׁוּ פִּסֵּחַ וְחֹלֶה אֵין
רָע הַקְרִיבֵהוּ נָא לְפֶחָתֶךָ הֲיִרְצְךָ אוֹ הֲיִשָּׂא פָנֶיךָ
ט אָמַר יהוה צְבָאוֹת: וְעַתָּה חַלּוּ־נָא פְנֵי־אֵל וִיחָנֵנוּ
מִיֶּדְכֶם הָיְתָה זֹּאת הֲיִשָּׂא מִכֶּם פָּנִים אָמַר יהוה
י צְבָאוֹת: מִי גַם־בָּכֶם וְיִסְגֹּר דְּלָתַיִם וְלֹא־תָאִירוּ
מִזְבְּחִי חִנָּם אֵין־לִי חֵפֶץ בָּכֶם אָמַר יהוה צְבָאוֹת
יא וּמִנְחָה לֹא־אֶרְצֶה מִיֶּדְכֶם: כִּי מִמִּזְרַח־שֶׁמֶשׁ וְעַד־
מְבוֹאוֹ גָּדוֹל שְׁמִי בַּגּוֹיִם וּבְכָל־מָקוֹם מֻקְטָר מֻגָּשׁ

בֶּאֱמָרְכֶם שֻׁלְחַן ה׳ נִבְזֶה הוּא — *By your saying, "The table of Hashem is repulsive."*

The table of Hashem is a prophetic idiom for the Altar of the Temple upon which the sacrifices were offered [see *Ezekiel* 41:22]. Malachi charges that the Kohanim found the Altar repulsive. Because they did not attempt to fully comprehend the spiritual significance of the sacrifices, they viewed the sprinkling of the blood contemptuously. The sight of the Altar covered with blood and animal fats revolted them. They therefore saw nothing wrong with bringing unfit animals as sacrifices (*Radak; Metzudos*). Since those services are performed upon the commandment of God, in essence you have despised God Himself (*Radak*). Alternatively, the Kohanim scorned God's Name by looking contemptuously at the small portions of sacrificial meat and meal-offerings (*Rashi*). *Mahari Kara* suggests that this is referring to the showbread that would be apportioned to each Kohen of that particular weekly group [מִשְׁמָר]. Accordingly, *the table of Hashem* is not referring to the Altar but the golden table of the Sanctuary on which the showbread was placed each Sabbath day.

8. וְכִי־תַגִּשׁוּן עִוֵּר לִזְבֹּחַ אֵין רָע וְכִי תַגִּישׁוּ פִּסֵּחַ וְחֹלֶה אֵין רָע — *When you present a blind [animal] for sacrifice, is nothing wrong? And when you present a lame or sick [animal], is nothing wrong?*

Our translation of אֵין רָע, *is nothing wrong?*, follows *Rashi* who translates it interrogatively. Alternatively, *Radak* and *Ibn Ezra* translate it declaratively: There is nothing wrong [in your view] with presenting a blind, lame or sick animal as a sacrifice, since the Altar has already been made repulsive with animal blood and fats.

Actually, this is in violation of *Lev.* 22:22. *One that is blind or broken, etc. you shall not offer these to Hashem* (*Radak*) [see also *Deut.* 15:21].

הַקְרִיבֵהוּ נָא לְפֶחָתֶךָ — *Present it, please, to your governor.*

Malachi continues to challenge the Kohanim and asks, "How can you possibly say that there is nothing wrong with presenting these deformed animals as sacrifices? How would your governor react if you presented these animals to him as a gift? Would he be pleased or show you favor because of it? He would hate you and vent his anger upon you for presenting him with this sort of gift! Surely then, it is scornful to bring them to God" (*Radak*).

The Talmud (*Succah* 50a) teaches that anything repulsive to humans is forbidden to be used in God's service and quotes this verse as its source.

9. וְעַתָּה חַלּוּ־נָא פְנֵי־אֵל וִיחָנֵנוּ מִיֶּדְכֶם הָיְתָה זֹּאת הֲיִשָּׂא מִכֶּם פָּנִים אָמַר ה׳ צְבָאוֹת — *And now, if you entreat God, will He be gracious unto us? This [sin] comes*

By your saying, "The table of H*ASHEM is repulsive."* [8]*When you present a blind [animal] for sacrifice, is nothing wrong? And when you present a lame or sick [animal], is nothing wrong? Present it, please, to your governor: Would he be pleased with you or show you favor? said* H*ASHEM, Master of Legions.* [9]*And now, if you entreat God, will He be gracious unto us? This [sin] comes from your hand; will He show you favor? says* H*ASHEM, Master of Legions.*

[10]*If only there were someone among you who would shut the [Temple] doors, so that you could not kindle [a fire] upon My Altar in vain! I have no desire for you, said* H*ASHEM, Master of Legions, and I will not accept an offering from your hand.* [11]*For, from the rising of the sun until its setting, My Name is great among the nations, and in every place [where offerings] are presented*

from your hand; will He show you favor? says Hashem, Master of Legions.

Malachi reprimands the Kohanim for assuming that God will accept their service. He wonders: How can the Kohanim possibly expect to be the messengers of Israel to beseech God to be compassionate to them after committing these sins? Will He show any of them favor and listen to any of their prayers? (*Rashi*).

Alternatively, the prophet is demanding that the Kohanim repent their evil ways. If they return to God and pray to Him sincerely, He will still be gracious to them and will not bring the curse (see 2:2) that is coming because of them. But if they do not return with all their heart, He will not show them favor and will continue to reprove them for their evil ways (*Radak; Ibn Ezra*).

10. מִי גַם־בָּכֶם וְיִסְגֹּר דְּלָתַיִם וְלֹא־תָאִירוּ מִזְבְּחִי חִנָּם ... — *If only there were someone among you who would shut the [Temple] doors, so that you could not kindle [a fire] upon My Altar in vain! ...*

God wishes that there were someone among the Kohanim who would be good enough to shut the doors of His Temple so that His Altar would not be defiled by unsuitable sacrifices (*Rashi*), for God would rather have no sacrifices at all than invalid ones (*Radak*). Even if they would offer a valid sacrifice, God would not accept it from them for He has no desire for them since their ways are evil. The fire that they kindle on His Altar is therefore unnecessary and useless (*Radak*).

11. כִּי מִמִּזְרַח־שֶׁמֶשׁ וְעַד־מְבוֹאוֹ גָּדוֹל שְׁמִי בַּגּוֹיִם — *For, from the rising of the sun until its setting, My Name is great among the nations.*

Malachi continues to admonish the Kohanim for offering blemished and unsuitable sacrifices, something that even the gentile nations of the world would never do. He points out that from east to west (*Radak*), from one end of the world to the other (*Mahari Kara*), God's Name is held in esteem among the nations of the world for even though they are steeped in idolatry, they nevertheless recognize that He is the Supreme Being and refer to Him as God of the gods (*Rashi* from *Menachos* 110a). They

לִשְׁמִי וּמִנְחָה טְהוֹרָה כִּי־גָדוֹל שְׁמִי בַּגּוֹיִם אָמַר
יְהוָה צְבָאוֹת׃ יב וְאַתֶּם מְחַלְּלִים אוֹתוֹ בֶּאֱמָרְכֶם
שֻׁלְחַן אֲדֹנָי מְגֹאָל הוּא וְנִיבוֹ נִבְזֶה אָכְלוֹ׃
יג וַאֲמַרְתֶּם הִנֵּה מַתְּלָאָה וְהִפַּחְתֶּם אוֹתוֹ אָמַר
יְהוָה צְבָאוֹת וַהֲבֵאתֶם גָּזוּל וְאֶת־הַפִּסֵּחַ וְאֶת־
הַחוֹלֶה וַהֲבֵאתֶם אֶת־הַמִּנְחָה הַאֶרְצֶה אוֹתָהּ
מִיֶּדְכֶם אָמַר יְהוָה׃ יד וְאָרוּר נוֹכֵל וְיֵשׁ בְּעֶדְרוֹ זָכָר
וְנֹדֵר וְזֹבֵחַ מָשְׁחָת לַאדֹנָי כִּי מֶלֶךְ גָּדוֹל אָנִי

view Him as the First Cause and worship the heavenly bodies as intermediaries between God and His creatures (*Radak; Rambam, Moreh Nevuchim* 1:36).

The entire populated world is described as spanning from east to west rather than from north to south because some areas in the north and south are uninhabited (*Radak*).

Alternatively, through Israel, God's Name is great among the nations; for God has placed His love and affection upon them that wherever they may pray to Him, even if it be in exile, it is considered as if sacrifices and pure meal-offerings have been presented to Him. Why then do they profane God's Name among the nations (Rashi)?

Rashi and *Targum Yonasan* base their explanation of the verse on *Midrash Tanchuma (Acharei* 8) and *Menachos* (110a) where the words, *"And in every place [where offerings] are burnt and presented to My Name,"* are interpreted to mean either the prayers of Israel (*Tanchuma*) or Torah scholars who study the laws of the Temple service (*Menachos*). God considers both as worthy as sacrifices.

12. וְאַתֶּם מְחַלְּלִים אוֹתוֹ בֶּאֱמָרְכֶם שֻׁלְחַן אֲ־דֹנָי מְגֹאָל הוּא — *But you defile it by your saying, "The table of the Lord is loathsome."*

The gentile nations, without following the Torah, honor and magnify God's great Name. But, the Kohanim, the servants of God, desecrate it and defile it for is there a greater desecration of His Name than to say that the table of Hashem is loathsome (*Radak; Abarbanel*)!

וְנִיבוֹ נִבְזֶה אָכְלוֹ — *And by [your] description of it as "Its food is repulsive."*

The word נִיבוֹ means speech or words as in *Isaiah* 57:19: נִיב שְׂפָתַיִם, *speech of the lips* (*Radak; Metzudos*). The words that are continuously on their lips to describe the altar are "its food is repulsive" (*Rashi*). Others relate נִיבוֹ to תְּנוּבָה, *fruit* or *produce*. נִיב שְׂפָתַיִם — speech is *the fruit of the lips* (*Ibn Ezra*). In our verse it is referring to the אֹכֶל — *food* (ibid.); the portion that the Kohanim receive from each sacrifice. It is this that the Kohanim say is repulsive (*Malbim*).

13. וַאֲמַרְתֶּם הִנֵּה מַתְּלָאָה — *You say, "Behold this [offering] is so burdensome."*

Malachi now turns to the nation and rebukes them for bringing inferior and blemished animals for their sacrifices (*Radak*). They bring weak, thin animals as sacrifices and falsely explain that even this is beyond their financial means (*Rashi*). Alternatively, they falsely claim that they have struggled to carry fat and heavy lambs to the Temple as sacrifices and they have become fatigued and worn out (*Radak*).

וְהִפַּחְתֶּם אוֹתוֹ — *And so you vex Him.*

The lies of the people (*Metzudos*) [if one may say regarding Hashem] cause God pain or cause God's Altar to be pained (*Rashi*).

The verse should actually read וְהִפַּחְתֶּם אוֹתִי, *and so you vex Me.* This is one of the variations occurring in Scripture, such as

to My Name, and also pure meal-offerings; for My Name is great among the nations, says HASHEM, Master of Legions. [12]*But you defile it by your saying, "The table of the Lord is loathsome"; and by [your] description of it as "Its food is repulsive."* [13]*You say, "Behold this [offering] is so burdensome," and so you vex Him, says HASHEM, Master of Legions. You bring the stolen and the lame, and the sick [animal], and you bring [it] as an offering — shall I accept it from your hand? says HASHEM.* [14]*Cursed be the charlatan who has a [superior] ram in his flock, but vows and sacrifices a blemished [animal] to the Lord! For I am a great King,*

writers make for the purpose of enhancing an expression — תִּיקּוּנֵי סוֹפְרִים, lit., *emandations of the scribes. Minchas Shai* (*Zechariah* 2:12) explains that in order to avoid writing an irreverent expression, God substituted a more reverent term than the text would seem to have required. See ArtScroll *Habakkuk* 1:12 for further study of תִּיקּוּנֵי סוֹפְרִים.

Alternatively, *Abarbanel* relates the word וְהִפַּחְתֶּם to נוֹפֵחַ, *to inflate* or *blow up*. The people would inflate their thin animals with air so that they would appear as fat, meaty animals.

וַהֲבֵאתֶם גָּזוּל ... — *You bring the stolen ...*

The people wish to offer stolen animals as sacrifices but they are unacceptable for they are considered a מִצְוָה הַבָּאָה בְּעֲבֵרָה, *a mitzvah made possible by a transgression.*

The Talmud (*Succah* 30a) uses this verse as the source of this invalidating principle and notes Scripture's comparison of the stolen and the lame. Just as the lame is permanently invalid for a sacrifice, so too, is the stolen permanently unacceptable.

וַהֲבֵאתֶם אֶת־הַמִּנְחָה — *And you bring [it] as an offering.*

Our translation follows *Targum Yonasan* and *Metzudos* who understand that the word מִנְחָה is referring to the stolen, lame and sick animal that was to be brought as the actual sacrifice. Alternatively, *Abarbanel* and *Malbim* maintain that it is referring to the מִנְחַת נְסָכִים, *the meal-offering of libations,* that accompanied any animal-*olah* or *shelamim*-offering [See *Numbers* 15:1-16]. Since the animal-offering is unacceptable, the meal-offering that accompanies it is also unacceptable.

14. וְאָרוּר נוֹכֵל וְיֵשׁ בְּעֶדְרוֹ זָכָר וְנֹדֵר וְזֹבֵחַ מָשְׁחָת לַא־דֹנָי — *Cursed be the charlatan who has a [superior] ram in his flock, but vows and sacrifices a blemished [animal] to the Lord!*

Cursed be the one who has perfectly fit animals in his flock and intentionally dedicates a blemished animal to God with the false claim that he hasn't anything better (*Rashi; Metzudos*).

A נוֹכֵל is one who conspires deceitfully (*Rashi*). He attempts to do harm to the highest interests of others in a secret and hidden manner (*R' Hirsch, Genesis* 37:18).

Our translation of זָכָר as *a ram* follows *Rashi* who translates *a ram fit for an olah-sacrifice* — see *Rosh Hashanah* 26b, *Rashi* ד״ה בְּשֶׁל זְכָרִים. Alternatively, *Radak* and *Ibn Ezra* render *a perfect male* — without a blemish.

כִּי מֶלֶךְ גָּדוֹל אָנִי ... — *For I am a great King ...*

Therefore, only the most perfect animals should be offered before Me

א אָמַר יְהוָה צְבָאוֹת וּשְׁמִי נוֹרָא בַגּוֹיִם: וְעַתָּה
ב אֲלֵיכֶם הַמִּצְוָה הַזֹּאת הַכֹּהֲנִים: אִם־לֹא תִשְׁמְעוּ
וְאִם־לֹא תָשִׂימוּ עַל־לֵב לָתֵת כָּבוֹד לִשְׁמִי
אָמַר יְהוָה צְבָאוֹת וְשִׁלַּחְתִּי בָכֶם אֶת־הַמְּאֵרָה
וְאָרוֹתִי אֶת־בִּרְכוֹתֵיכֶם וְגַם אָרוֹתִיהָ כִּי אֵינְכֶם
ג שָׂמִים עַל־לֵב: הִנְנִי גֹעֵר לָכֶם אֶת־הַזֶּרַע וְזֵרִיתִי
פֶרֶשׁ עַל־פְּנֵיכֶם פֶּרֶשׁ חַגֵּיכֶם וְנָשָׂא אֶתְכֶם
ד אֵלָיו: וִידַעְתֶּם כִּי שִׁלַּחְתִּי אֲלֵיכֶם אֵת הַמִּצְוָה
הַזֹּאת לִהְיוֹת בְּרִיתִי אֶת־לֵוִי אָמַר יְהוָה צְבָאוֹת:

(*Metzudos*). It would never enter one's mind to offer such gifts to the governor of his province [see v. 8]. How then can the nation offer them to Me, a great King? (*R' Mendel Hirsch*).

וּשְׁמִי נוֹרָא בַגּוֹיִם — *And My Name is awesome among the nations.*

All the nations fear Me (*Metzudos*) but Israel, the nation I love more than any other, does not fear Me (*Radak*).

II.

1. וְעַתָּה אֲלֵיכֶם הַמִּצְוָה הַזֹּאת הַכֹּהֲנִים — *And now, this commandment is upon you, O Kohanim.*

God charges the Kohanim with the commandment of not sacrificing these inferior animals on His Altar (*Rashi*). It is their responsibility to teach the people that they should not consecrate blemished animals, for the Torah prohibits offering them as sacrifices (*Radak*). Furthermore, the Kohen who performs the sacrificial services is a greater transgressor than the owner, for the Kohen transgresses three negative commandments while the owner of the animal only transgresses one (*Rambam, Mishneh Torah, Hil. Isurei Mizbe'ach* 1:1,2,4).

2. אִם־לֹא תִשְׁמְעוּ וְאִם־לֹא תָשִׂימוּ עַל־לֵב לָתֵת כָּבוֹד לִשְׁמִי אָמַר ה׳ צְבָאוֹת וְשִׁלַּחְתִּי בָכֶם אֶת־הַמְּאֵרָה וְאָרוֹתִי אֶת־בִּרְכוֹתֵיכֶם — *If you will not listen and will not take it to heart to render honor to My Name, says Hashem, Master of Legions, I will send the curse among you and I will curse your blessings.*

When the nation had started to rebuild the Temple, God bestowed special blessings upon them [see *Haggai* 2:19] (*Metzudos*). The prophet now warns the people that if they will not heed God's commandment and will profane His Name by bringing unfit sacrifices (*Metzudos*), then He will send a curse upon them in place of the blessings that they currently enjoy (*Radak*). Alternatively, the verse is referring to the Priestly Blessings (*Numbers* 6:27) that were uttered after sacrifices were offered. Since the Kohanim were profaning God's Name, their blessings will be converted to curses (*Malbim*).

Ramban (*Genesis* 4:11) notes that the curse is that the people will plant much seed but it will only bring forth a small amount.

וְגַם אָרוֹתִיהָ — *Indeed I have [already] cursed it.*

God foresees that the people will ignore His warning and will not obey His commandment and therefore has already cursed their blessings (*Rashi*). Alternatively, God has sent a curse the people when they started to offer blemished animals as sacrifices. If they

says HASHEM, *Master of Legions, and My Name is awesome among the nations.*

2/1-4

[1] *And now, this commandment is upon you, O Kohanim.* [2] *If you will not listen and will not take it to heart to render honor to My Name, says* HASHEM, *Master of Legions, I will send the curse among you and I will curse your blessings. Indeed I have [already] cursed it, for you do not take it to heart.* [3] *Behold! I will rebuke the seed because of you; and I will scatter dung upon your faces, the dung of your offerings; [the sins] will carry you to this.*

[4] *Know that I have sent this commandment to you so that My covenant should be with Levi, says* HASHEM, *Master of Legions.*

do not change their ways and continue to disobey His commandment, then the existing curse will intensify (*Radak*).

3. הִנְנִי גֹעֵר לָכֶם אֶת־הַזֶּרַע — *Behold! I will rebuke the seed because of you.*

Our translation of גֹעֵר, *rebuke*, follows *Metzudos* who renders, "Because of you, God will rebuke the seed and command it not to sprout." *Radak* (*Psalms* 9:6), however, differentiates between ... גָּעַר בְּ which he translates *rebuke* and גָּעַר, without the ב, which he translates *destroy*. He therefore renders: God will *destroy* the seeds (*Radak; Abarbanel*). The intent of the verse is when the people offered unfit animals on the Altar, it was as if they had left the Altar empty (*Ibn Ezra*). God will therefore punish them measure for measure by causing their table to remain empty (*Radak*).

וְזֵרִיתִי פֶרֶשׁ עַל־פְּנֵיכֶם פֶּרֶשׁ חַגֵּיכֶם — *And I will scatter dung upon your faces, the dung of your offerings.*

Offerings are referred to as חַגִּים, *festivals*, because it was on the festivals that most sacrifices were brought [see *Exodus* 23:18; *Isaiah* 29:1; *Psalms* 118:27] (*Radak; Metzudos*). God will scatter the filth and waste of your invalid offerings in your faces. This is symbolic of the disgrace and humiliation that the people will experience because they disgraced God (*Rashi; Metzudos*).

וְנָשָׂא אֶתְכֶם אֵלָיו — *[The sins] will carry you to this.*

Our translation follows *Radak* and *Metzudos* who explain that all this will be brought about by your own sins. *Rashi*, however, renders: you will become lowly and repugnant as the dung of your sacrificial animals.

4. וִידַעְתֶּם כִּי שִׁלַּחְתִּי אֲלֵיכֶם אֵת הַמִּצְוָה הַזֹּאת לִהְיוֹת בְּרִיתִי אֶת־לֵוִי אָמַר ה׳ צְבָאוֹת — *Know that I have sent this commandment to you so that My covenant should be with Levi, says Hashem, Master of Legions.*

The prophet declares that God wants everyone to realize that He is so emphatic regarding this commandment so that the covenant that He had made with the *tribe of Levi* may be perpetuated (*Radak*). *Metzudos* explains that Scripture is referring to Aaron, the head

ה בְּרִיתִ֣י ׀ הָיְתָ֣ה אִתּ֗וֹ הַֽחַיִּים֙ וְהַשָּׁל֔וֹם וָאֶתְּנֵֽם־לוֹ מוֹרָ֖א וַיִּֽירָאֵ֑נִי וּמִפְּנֵ֥י שְׁמִ֖י נִחַ֥ת הֽוּא׃ ו תּוֹרַ֤ת אֱמֶת֙ הָיְתָ֣ה בְּפִ֔יהוּ וְעַוְלָ֖ה לֹא־נִמְצָ֣א בִשְׂפָתָ֑יו בְּשָׁל֤וֹם וּבְמִישׁוֹר֙ הָלַ֣ךְ אִתִּ֔י וְרַבִּ֖ים הֵשִׁ֥יב מֵעָוֺֽן׃ ז כִּֽי־שִׂפְתֵ֤י כֹהֵן֙ יִשְׁמְרוּ־דַ֔עַת וְתוֹרָ֖ה יְבַקְשׁ֣וּ מִפִּ֑יהוּ כִּ֛י מַלְאַ֥ךְ יהוה־צְבָא֖וֹת הֽוּא׃ ח וְאַתֶּם֙ סַרְתֶּ֣ם מִן־הַדֶּ֔רֶךְ הִכְשַׁלְתֶּ֥ם רַבִּ֖ים בַּתּוֹרָ֑ה שִֽׁחַתֶּם֙ בְּרִ֣ית הַלֵּוִ֔י אָמַ֖ר יהוה צְבָאֽוֹת׃

of the tribe of Levi, for God made a covenant with him, that the *Kehunah* will belong to Aaron and his descendants [see *Numbers* 18:7].

5. בְּרִיתִי הָיְתָה אִתּוֹ הַחַיִּים וְהַשָּׁלוֹם — *My covenant of life and peace was with him.*

God made a covenant with Aaron, the holy one of Hashem, and with his great-grandson Phinehas, the one who was zealous on God's behalf (*Radak*).

Phinehas turned back God's wrath from upon the Israelite nation when he took vengeance for Hashem and slew the Israelite man and the Midianites who publicly sinned before the nation. God therefore gave him His covenant of peace and granted his offspring a covenant of eternal *Kehunah* (*Numbers* 25:10-15). Not only will the Kohanim be granted life and peace but Israel, too, will partake in this covenant through the sacrifices offered by the Kohanim (*Ibn Ezra*).

Phinehas was granted a special gift of life as is evident from *Judges* 20:28 where he is mentioned, indicating that he lived to be more than three hundred years old (*Radak*).

וָאֶתְּנֵם־לוֹ מוֹרָא וַיִּירָאֵנִי — *I gave them to him for the sake of the fear with which he feared Me.*

Our translation follows *Radak*. Alternatively, I gave him life and peace conditionally: that he fear Me; and indeed he did fear Me (*Rashi*).

וּמִפְּנֵי שְׁמִי נִחַת הוּא — *For he shuddered before My Name.*

The word נִחַת is related to חִתַּת (*Genesis* 35:5): חִתַּת אֱלוֹקִים, a Godly terror (*Metzudos*). It means to be broken and crushed before God's Name (*Radak*); to be shattered, to tremble (*R' Mendel Hirsch*).

R' Mendel Hirsch notes that this awesome fear of God was later characteristic of the entire tribe of Levi. The Levites were the only ones who possessed no part of the land and their existence depended entirely on the good will of their propertied brethren. Nevertheless, they feared no one but God. They did not speak to the people regarding that with which they would agree; they only feared God.

6. תּוֹרַת אֱמֶת הָיְתָה בְּפִיהוּ וְעַוְלָה לֹא־נִמְצָא בִשְׂפָתָיו — *The teaching of truth was in his mouth, and injustice was not found on his lips.*

According to *Radak*, the subject of the verse is Phinehas and according to *Metzudos* and *Abarbanel*, it is Aaron. *Rashi* explains that the verse is referring to Aaron, Phinehas, Elazar and their descendants (*Ibn Ezra*), who taught God's Torah with sincerity (*Radak*) and guided the nation with true Torah decision (*Mahari Kara*). According to *Yerushalmi Peah* 1:1, תּוֹרַת אֱמֶת, *the teaching of truth*, is referring to the teachings that Aaron received from Moses who had received them directly from the Almighty. וְעַוְלָה לֹא נִמְצָא בִשְׂפָתָיו, *and injustice was not found on his lips*, is referring to the teachings that he did not receive from his teacher.

בְּשָׁלוֹם וּבְמִישׁוֹר הָלַךְ אִתִּי — *In peace and in fairness he walked with Me.*

[5] My covenant of life and peace was with him; I gave them to him for the sake of the fear with which he feared Me, for he shuddered before My Name. [6] The teaching of truth was in his mouth, and injustice was not found on his lips; in peace and in fairness he walked with Me, and brought back many from iniquity.

[7] For the lips of the Kohen should safeguard knowledge, and teaching they should seek from his mouth; for he is an agent of HASHEM, Master of Legions. [8] But you have veered from the path; you have caused many people to stumble through [your] teaching. You have corrupted the covenant of Levi, says HASHEM, Master of Legions.

Phinehas walked with Me in peace and in fairness — with the qualities that I cherish — to do loving-kindness, justice and charity (*Radak*). Alternatively, Scripture is referring to Aaron for it was he who promoted peace between a man and his wife and between man and his fellow (*Yerushalmi Peah* 1:1).

וְרַבִּים הֵשִׁיב מֵעָוֺן — *And brought back many from iniquity.*

Our translation of this phrase follows *Rashi* who explains that after the nation sinned with the golden calf (*Exodus* Chapter 32), Aaron, Elazar and Phinehas brought back their entire tribe from iniquity (*Rashi*). According to *Yerushalmi Peah* 1:1, through his reproof, Aaron brought back many from the ways of iniquity to the ways of the Torah. Alternatively, many were *kept* from sinning because Phinehas continuously taught the people God's Torah (*Radak*).

7. כִּי־שִׂפְתֵי כֹהֵן יִשְׁמְרוּ־דַעַת וְתוֹרָה יְבַקְשׁוּ מִפִּיהוּ כִּי מַלְאַךְ ה׳־צְבָאוֹת הוּא — *For the lips of the Kohen should safeguard knowledge, and teaching they should seek from his mouth; for he is an agent of Hashem, Master of Legions.*

The Kohen must safeguard the knowledge of the Torah because he is God's agent to teach His Torah to Israel [see *Deut.* 33:10] (*Rashi; Radak*). *Rashi* adds, like the ministering angels, the Kohen Gadol ministers before the Divine Presence when he performs the Yom Kippur service in the Holy of Holies. Furthermore, according to *Midrash Rabbah* (*Leviticus*, end of Chap. 21), when the holy spirit rested upon the Kohen Gadol, his face flamed like torches about him as it is written, *for the lips of the Kohen etc. Matnos Kehunah* (131a) comments that the Kohen Gadol was raised to such a level of spirituality that he could be regarded as an angel rather than a human.

R' Yochanan taught: From this verse we learn that one should study Torah only from a teacher who can be compared to an angel of God (*Moed Katan* 17a), i.e., the teacher must view himself as one who is fulfilling a mission with which he was entrusted by God (*Me'am Loez*).

8. וְאַתֶּם סַרְתֶּם מִן־הַדֶּרֶךְ הִכְשַׁלְתֶּם רַבִּים בַּתּוֹרָה שִׁחַתֶּם בְּרִית הַלֵּוִי אָמַר ה׳ צְבָאוֹת — *But you have veered from the path; you have caused many people to stumble through [your] teaching. You have corrupted the covenant of Levi, says Hashem, Master of Legions.*

But you Kohanim of this generation

ט וְגַם־אֲנִי נָתַתִּי אֶתְכֶם נִבְזִים וּשְׁפָלִים לְכָל־הָעָם כְּפִי אֲשֶׁר אֵינְכֶם שֹׁמְרִים אֶת־דְּרָכַי וְנֹשְׂאִים פָּנִים בַּתּוֹרָה׃ י הֲלוֹא אָב אֶחָד לְכֻלָּנוּ הֲלוֹא אֵל אֶחָד בְּרָאָנוּ מַדּוּעַ נִבְגַּד אִישׁ בְּאָחִיו לְחַלֵּל בְּרִית אֲבֹתֵינוּ׃ יא בָּגְדָה יְהוּדָה וְתוֹעֵבָה נֶעֶשְׂתָה בְיִשְׂרָאֵל וּבִירוּשָׁלִָם כִּי | חִלֵּל יְהוּדָה קֹדֶשׁ יהוה אֲשֶׁר אָהֵב וּבָעַל בַּת־אֵל נֵכָר׃ יב יַכְרֵת יהוה לָאִישׁ אֲשֶׁר יַעֲשֶׂנָּה עֵר וְעֹנֶה מֵאָהֳלֵי יַעֲקֹב

(*Abarbanel*) have turned away from the path of the earlier Kohanim (*Radak*). Instead of bringing back many from iniquity, through your teachings you have caused many people to stumble (ibid.). Instead of keeping the covenant that God made with the tribe of Levi, you corrupted it (ibid.) by misrepresenting the laws of the Torah and accepting inferior animals for sacrifices (*Mahari Kara*).

The Sages (*Bechoros* 26b) taught: If a Kohen or Levi assists a farmer at the threshing floor so that he may receive the *terumah* or *maaser*, he has corrupted the covenant of Levi [for *terumah* and *maaser* are to be given to them as their due and not as payment].

9. וְגַם־אֲנִי נָתַתִּי אֶתְכֶם נִבְזִים וּשְׁפָלִים לְכָל־הָעָם כְּפִי אֲשֶׁר אֵינְכֶם שֹׁמְרִים אֶת־דְּרָכַי — *[Therefore] I have also made you repulsive and lowly to all the people in the same measure that you do not observe My ways.*

Just as the Kohanim have made God's Name repulsive before the nation (*Radak*) by saying that His Altar is repulsive (*Ibn Ezra*) [see 1:7], so too, has God made them repulsive and lowly before those very same people: measure for measure (*Radak*). *Metzudos* notes that this is in contrast to the covenant of life and peace that God had made with the tribe of Levi; for a life filled with shame is not considered living and lacks tranquility and peace of mind.

וְנֹשְׂאִים פָּנִים בַּתּוֹרָה — *And you show favoritism in [your] teaching.*

When the wealthy of the nation brought blemished animals for sacrifices, the Kohanim did not object nor did they rebuke them for they were afraid to tell them that their animal was unfit (*Radak*). Similarly, when the Kohanim judged a monetary dispute, they would rule in favor of the wealthier litigant (*Metzudos*).

10. הֲלוֹא אָב אֶחָד לְכֻלָּנוּ — *Have we not all one father?*

Malachi now addresses the men of his day and rebukes them for betraying their Jewish wives during the exile and marrying local heathen women [see *Ezra* Chap. 9]. He declares that since all Israelites, both men and women, are descendants of one father, the patriarch Jacob, it is wrong for the Israelite men to cast aside their Jewish wives who are their next of kin (*Radak*).

הֲלוֹא אֵל אֶחָד בְּרָאָנוּ — *Did not one God create us [all]?*

Do not all Israelites believe in the same One God Who created every one of its people? Why then do they marry heathen women who believe in several deities? (*Radak*).

לְחַלֵּל בְּרִית אֲבֹתֵינוּ — *In order to defile the covenant of our forefathers.*

The covenant of our forefathers is referring to the covenant that God made with our forefathers at Mount Sinai [when they agreed to uphold all the laws of the Torah] (*Rashi; Ibn Ezra*). Alternatively, the Patriarchs — Abraham, Isaac and Jacob — had each made a covenant not to betray his wife by marrying a second one without the consent of the first (*Radak*).

[9] [Therefore] I have also made you repulsive and lowly to all the people in the same measure that you do not observe My ways and you show favoritism in [your] teaching.

[10] Have we not all one Father? Did not one God create us [all]? Why, then, is one person betrayed by another, in order to defile the covenant of our forefathers? [11] Judah has betrayed, and an abomination has been done in Israel and in Jerusalem. For Judah has defiled the holy [nation] of HASHEM *which He loved, and has taken in marriage the daughter of a foreign god. [12] May* HASHEM *cut off from the man who does this any child and descendant from the tents of Jacob,*

According to *Abarbanel,* this verse is not the rebuke of the prophet but the attempt of the people to justify their heathen marriages. If all people are descendants of one father, Adam, and were created by the same God, there is no reason to distinguish between Jews and non-Jews for ultimately all people are really brothers!

11. בָּגְדָה יְהוּדָה וְתוֹעֵבָה נֶעֶשְׂתָה בְיִשְׂרָאֵל וּבִירוּשָׁלָם — *Judah has betrayed, and an abomination has been done in Israel and in Jerusalem.*

Had the Israelites traveled to a different country and married gentile wives there, that would have been a grievous sin. But that they dared to commit this sin in the Land of Israel, in the Holy City of Jerusalem, aggravated their sin even more (*Metzudos*).

כִּי חִלֵּל יְהוּדָה אֶת קֹדֶשׁ ה׳ אֲשֶׁר אָהֵב — *For Judah has defiled the holy [nation] of Hashem which He loved.*

Our translation follows *Radak* and *Mahari Kara* who translate the verse according to its cantillations. Alternatively, *Metzudos* renders: Judah, who was the holy one of God, has defiled his own holiness by loving and marrying the daughter of a nation that worships foreign gods.

Israel's control of promiscuous relationships is a manifestation of its sanctity. By marrying foreign wives, Judah defiled the sanctity of the nation, i.e., the Jewish wives (*Radak*).

בַּת אֵל נֵכָר — *The daughter of a foreign god.*

Scripture refers to the followers of foreign gods as its son, daughter or nation (*Ramban, Numbers* 21:29). The Talmud (*Sanhedrin* 82a) notes that Scripture surely cannot mean that he actually married the daughter of a foreign god for foreign gods don't have daughters with whom marriage can be performed! Rather the intent of the verse is that one who cohabits with a non-Jewish woman is considered as if he married the idol itself.

12. יַכְרֵת ה׳ לָאִישׁ אֲשֶׁר יַעֲשֶׂנָּה עֵר וְעֹנֶה מֵאָהֳלֵי יַעֲקֹב — *May Hashem cut off from the man who does this any child and descendant from the tents of Jacob.*

Malachi warns that God will cut off the descendants of the man who sins by cohabiting with an idolatress. According to *Targum Yonasan,* He will specifically eliminate his son and grandson, בַּר וּבַר בַּר. *Radak,* however, translates עֵר as *awake,* and עוֹנֶה as *one who answers* and renders: *no living offspring of this man will remain;* for one who is dead is asleep: not awake and cannot answer when called upon.

יג וּמַגִּ֥ישׁ מִנְחָ֖ה לַיהוָ֥ה צְבָאֽוֹת׃ וְזֹאת֙ שֵׁנִ֣ית תַּֽעֲשׂ֔וּ כַּסּ֤וֹת דִּמְעָה֙ אֶת־מִזְבַּ֣ח יהוה בְּכִ֖י וַֽאֲנָקָ֑ה מֵאֵ֣ין ע֗וֹד פְּנוֹת֙ אֶל־הַמִּנְחָ֔ה וְלָקַ֥חַת רָצ֖וֹן מִיֶּדְכֶֽם׃ יד וַאֲמַרְתֶּ֖ם עַל־מָ֑ה עַ֗ל כִּֽי־יהוה֩ הֵעִ֨יד בֵּינְךָ֜ וּבֵ֣ין ׀ אֵ֣שֶׁת נְעוּרֶ֗יךָ אֲשֶׁ֤ר אַתָּה֙ בָּגַ֣דְתָּה בָּ֔הּ וְהִ֥יא חֲבֶרְתְּךָ֖ וְאֵ֥שֶׁת בְּרִיתֶֽךָ׃ טו וְלֹא־אֶחָ֣ד עָשָׂ֗ה וּשְׁאָ֥ר ר֙וּחַ֙ ל֔וֹ וּמָה֙ הָֽאֶחָ֔ד מְבַקֵּ֖שׁ זֶ֣רַע אֱלֹהִ֑ים וְנִשְׁמַרְתֶּם֙ בְּר֣וּחֲכֶ֔ם וּבְאֵ֥שֶׁת נְעוּרֶ֖יךָ אַל־יִבְגֹּֽד׃

From the Talmud (*Sanhedrin* 82a), it appears that this verse is referring to one who cohabits with a gentile woman and was not apprehended during the evil deed [one who is, may be executed by zealots]. If he is a Talmudic scholar who frequents the אָהֳלֵי יַעֲקֹב, *the study halls of Jacob*, where Torah is studied [see *Metzudos*], he will not have a son who will initiate learned discussions among the disciples [עֵר] or is qualified to answer the questions of the Sages [עוֹנֶה].[1]

וּמַגִּישׁ מִנְחָה לַה׳ צְבָאוֹת — *And anyone who may present an offering to Hashem, Master of Legions.*

If the sinner is a Kohen, he will not be privileged to have a son who will present an offering to God (*Rashi, Sanhedrin* 82a).

13. וְזֹאת שֵׁנִית תַּעֲשׂוּ — *And this is a second [sin] that you commit.*

The sin of taking gentile women is indeed very grave but the people have committed a second sin which is much worse. They have chosen their gentile wives as their primary wives and have given them control over the household. The Jewish wives have thereby become the inferior wives and are bound in "living widowhood." Alternatively, offering blemished animals for sacrifices [see 1:13] (*Radak*) or describing God's Altar as loathsome [see 1:12] (*Metzudos*) is a grave sin but tormenting your Jewish wives through your taking gentile wives and causing them to cover God's Altar with their tears (*Radak; Metzudos*) is much worse.

כַּסּוֹת דִּמְעָה אֶת־מִזְבַּח ה׳ בְּכִי וַאֲנָקָה — *Covering the Altar of Hashem with tears, weeping and moaning.*

They have caused the Jewish wives to weep before the Altar and plea to drink the bitter waters [מֵי סוֹטָה — see *Numbers* 5:11-29] so they may prove that they have not sinned against their husbands as adulteresses (*Rashi*).

מֵאֵין עוֹד פְּנוֹת אֶל־הַמִּנְחָה וְלָקַחַת רָצוֹן מִיֶּדְכֶם — *So that He will no longer turn to [your] offering or take it with favor from your hand.*

God will no longer accept the sacrifices of the people for they offer blemished and stolen animals. The tears of the women attest to the evil of their husbands and encourage Him not to accept their offerings (*Rashi*).

14. וַאֲמַרְתֶּם עַל־מָה — *You say, "Why [is this]?"*

The people will ask in feigned innocence, "Can it truly be that God has found our offerings unacceptable because of our behavior toward our wives?" (*Radak*) "Are not are wives to blame for our behavior?" (*Metzudos*)

עַל כִּי־ה׳ הֵעִיד בֵּינְךָ וּבֵין אֵשֶׁת נְעוּרֶיךָ ... — *It is*

1. *Radak* and extant editions of the Talmud read: a son who will initiate learned discussions among the *Sages* or is qualified to answer the questions of the *disciples.*

and anyone who may present an offering to HASHEM, Master of Legions. [13] *And this is a second [sin] that you commit: covering the Altar of HASHEM with tears, weeping and moaning, so that He will no longer turn to [your] offering or take it with favor from your hand.* [14] *You say, "Why [is this]?" It is because HASHEM has testified between you and the wife of your youth whom you have betrayed, though she is your companion and the wife of your covenant.* [15] *[You ask,] "But did not the unique one do [so], and he had an extraordinary spirit?" And what did the unique one seek? Godly offspring! However, you should guard your spirit and let it not betray the wife of your youth!*

because Hashem has testified between you and the wife of your youth ...

The prophet sternly replies that God bears witness between the people and their wives and declares that the men are guilty for they have betrayed the wives of their youth, but the women have remained faithful to the sacred covenant that had been made at the time of their marriage (*Metzudos*). It is the men who no longer love their wives and their hearts are no longer with them (*Radak*).

אֵשֶׁת נְעוּרֶיךָ ... וְהִיא חֲבֶרְתְּךָ — *The wife of your youth ... she is your companion.*

Radak notes that Scripture describes their wives as אֵשֶׁת נְעוּרֶיךָ — *the wife of your youth* — and חֲבֶרְתְּךָ — *your companion* — and explains that because this woman has been your wife and your companion since your youth you should therefore have had feelings of love toward her. In a second explanation, he explains that if this woman were simply your companion and had not been the wife of your youth, that would have been enough reason for you to love her. Surely, then, if she is both your companion and the wife of your youth, how much more reason is there for you to love her, but you betrayed and rejected her.

The Talmud (*Sanhedrin* 22a) expounds this verse to illustrate the undesirability of divorcing one's first wife; for this even God's Altar weeps.

15. וְלֹא־אֶחָד עָשָׂה וּשְׁאָר רוּחַ לוֹ וּמָה הָאֶחָד מְבַקֵּשׁ זֶרַע אֱלֹהִים וְנִשְׁמַרְתֶּם בְּרוּחֲכֶם וּבְאֵשֶׁת נְעוּרֶיךָ אַל־יִבְגֹּד — *[You ask,] "But did not the unique one do [so], and he had an extraordinary spirit?" And what did the unique one seek? Godly offspring! However, you should guard your spirit and let it not betray the wife of your youth.*

Most commentators explain that אֶחָד, *the unique one*, is referring to the patriarch Abraham [see *Ezekiel* 33:24]. The treacherous husbands retorted, "Did not the exalted Abraham do the same: Did he not take Hagar while he was married to Sarah?" To this God responded through the words of the prophet, "Abraham's motive was holy, for he had not had any children with Sarah and his only reason for taking Hagar was to raise a family faithful to God. But you have no such higher purpose; how dare you betray your Jewish wives and deal treacherously with the wife of your youth?" (*Mahari Kara; Metzudos*).

טז כִּי־שָׂנֵא שַׁלַּח אָמַר יהוה אֱלֹהֵי יִשְׂרָאֵל וְכִסָּה חָמָס עַל־לְבוּשׁוֹ אָמַר יהוה צְבָאוֹת וְנִשְׁמַרְתֶּם
יז בְּרוּחֲכֶם וְלֹא תִבְגֹּדוּ׃ הוֹגַעְתֶּם יהוה בְּדִבְרֵיכֶם וַאֲמַרְתֶּם בַּמָּה הוֹגָעְנוּ בֶּאֱמָרְכֶם כָּל־עֹשֵׂה רָע טוֹב | בְּעֵינֵי יהוה וּבָהֶם הוּא חָפֵץ אוֹ

ג/א

א אַיֵּה אֱלֹהֵי הַמִּשְׁפָּט׃ הִנְנִי שֹׁלֵחַ מַלְאָכִי וּפִנָּה־דֶרֶךְ לְפָנָי וּפִתְאֹם יָבוֹא אֶל־הֵיכָלוֹ הָאָדוֹן | אֲשֶׁר־אַתֶּם מְבַקְשִׁים וּמַלְאַךְ הַבְּרִית אֲשֶׁר־אַתֶּם

Radak and *Rashi* (second explanation) offer similar interpretations, all based on *Targum Yonasan's* translation of this verse. In an alternative interpretation, *Rashi* explains וְלֹא אֶחָד עָשָׂה: Did He not create Adam and Eve as one couple — not one man with two wives? וּשְׁאָר רוּחַ לוֹ — and the rest of the spirits and souls, i.e., mankind, were from him — from Adam. Therefore, וּמָה הָאֶחָד מְבַקֵּשׁ — why does one member of the couple seek accusations; זֶרַע אֱלֹקִים — against his wife who is a "child of God"?

This is *Abarbanel's* understanding of *Rashi*. Another understanding of *Rashi* may be וְלֹא אֶחָד עָשָׂה: Did He not create Adam and Eve originally as one being and then separated them? [See Yiddish translation to Lublin edition.]

16. כִּי־שָׂנֵא שַׁלַּח אָמַר ה׳ אֱלֹהֵי יִשְׂרָאֵל וְכִסָּה חָמָס עַל־לְבוּשׁוֹ אָמַר ה׳ צְבָאוֹת וְנִשְׁמַרְתֶּם בְּרוּחֲכֶם וְלֹא תִבְגֹּדוּ — *For he who hates [his wife] should divorce [her], says Hashem, God of Israel! He covers injustice with his garment, says Hashem, Master of Legions! Guard your spirit and do not commit betrayal.*

A man who hates his wife should divorce her so that she may marry someone else who truly loves her. He will then be free to find a woman who is more to his liking. But under no circumstances should he remain married to this woman and conceal his dislike for her, for that is considered an act of treachery and is as if he is covering injustice with his garment (*Rashi; Metzudos*). Alternatively, *Radak* understands the garment figuratively: representing one's wife to whom he clings as a garment clings to his body.

Actually, the meaning of this verse is debated by the Sages (*Gittin* 90b). R' Yehudah explains that Scripture is stating that one is permitted to divorce his wife even if she merely loses favor in his eyes [as *Rashi* to our verse explains]. R' Yochanan interprets שָׂנוּי הַמְשַׁלֵּחַ — God despises one who sends away his wife without a compelling reason. The Talmud there continues to explain that the two opinions do not conflict.

17. הוֹגַעְתֶּם ה׳ בְּדִבְרֵיכֶם וַאֲמַרְתֶּם בַּמָּה הוֹגָעְנוּ בֶּאֱמָרְכֶם כָּל־עֹשֵׂה רָע טוֹב בְּעֵינֵי ה׳ וּבָהֶם הוּא חָפֵץ אוֹ אַיֵּה אֱלֹהֵי הַמִּשְׁפָּט — *You have wearied Hashem with your words, but you say, "How have we wearied Him?" By your saying, "Everyone who does wrong is good in the eyes of Hashem, and He favors them; or else where is the God of justice?"*

Until now, the prophet rebuked the nation — Kohen and common person alike — for their unacceptable deeds. He now takes the nation to task for their unacceptable beliefs (*Abarbanel*). The people had seen that wicked people prosper and concluded that either God loves the wicked or that there is no justice in the world (*Rashi*).

Radak notes the anthropomorphism in this verse, *you have wearied Hashem*, for God does not weary. He explains that Scripture writes allegorically regarding God as people speak regarding one another.

2/16-17

[16] *For he who hates [his wife] should divorce [her], says* HASHEM, *God of Israel! He covers injustice with his garment, says* HASHEM, *Master of Legions! Guard your spirit and do not commit betrayal.*

[17] *You have wearied* HASHEM *with your words, but you say, "How have we wearied Him?" By your saying, "Everyone who does wrong is good in the eyes of* HASHEM, *and He favors them; or else where is the God of justice?"*

3/1

[1] *Behold, I am sending My messenger, and he will clear a path before Me; suddenly, the Lord Whom you seek will come to His Sanctuary, and the messenger of the covenant for whom you*

III.

1. הִנְנִי שֹׁלֵחַ מַלְאָכִי — *Behold, I am sending My messenger.*

At the end of the previous chapter, the people had asked about the judgment of the wicked in this world. God now answers that there will yet be a time when justice will indeed be executed upon all the wicked. However, it will not be until the day that I send My messenger to you, in the era preceding the final redemption (*Metzudos*).

מַלְאָכִי — *My messenger.*

The messenger is either an angel of God (*Radak; Metzudos*) or Messiah the son of Joseph — מָשִׁיחַ בֶּן יוֹסֵף (*Ibn Ezra*). *Malbim* explains that God will send a prophet who will clear the way of all obstacles by bringing everyone to repentance. *Mahari Kara* [to v. 23] identifies this messenger as Elijah the prophet.

וּפִנָּה־דֶרֶךְ לְפָנָי — *And he will clear a path before Me.*

In preparation for the Messianic era, God's messenger will clear a path for Divine revelation by destroying all the wicked among the people (*Rashi*) or by inducing them to repent their sins (*Malbim*). According to *Radak*, He will clear the road of all obstacles so that the people will be unhindered when they return to Israel at the time of the ingathering of the exiles.

וּפִתְאֹם יָבוֹא אֶל־הֵיכָלוֹ הָאָדוֹן אֲשֶׁר־אַתֶּם מְבַקְשִׁים — *Suddenly, the Lord Whom you seek will come to His sanctuary.*

The Lord Whom you seek, the God of Justice, will suddenly come to His sanctuary (*Rashi*). Alternatively, *Radak* identifies the אָדוֹן as the Messianic king. Since the time of his arrival is obscured in Scripture, his coming is considered of a sudden nature. [Accordingly, *lord* would be spelled with a lower case "l."]

וּמַלְאַךְ הַבְּרִית ... — *And the messenger of the covenant ...*

This is either referring to the Messianic king, and is the אָדוֹן mentioned earlier in the verse (*Radak*), or to Elijah the prophet who was given the title of the *Angel of the Covenant*, for his zealousness in reaffirming the covenant of circumcision (*Radak; Metzudos*). The people long and yearn for Elijah's arrival because he will announce the onset of the final redemption and will revive the dead prior to the arrival of the Messiah (*Metzudos*).

ב חֲפֵצִים֙ הִנֵּה־בָ֔א אָמַ֖ר יְהוָ֥ה צְבָאֽוֹת׃ וּמִ֤י מְכַלְכֵּל֙ אֶת־י֣וֹם בּוֹא֔וֹ וּמִ֥י הָעֹמֵ֖ד בְּהֵרָאוֹת֑וֹ כִּֽי־הוּא֙ כְּאֵ֣שׁ ג מְצָרֵ֔ף וּכְבֹרִ֖ית מְכַבְּסִֽים׃ וְיָשַׁ֨ב מְצָרֵ֤ף וּמְטַהֵר֙ כֶּ֔סֶף וְטִהַ֤ר אֶת־בְּנֵֽי־לֵוִי֙ וְזִקַּ֣ק אֹתָ֔ם כַּזָּהָ֖ב וְכַכָּ֑סֶף ד וְהָיוּ֙ לַֽיהוָ֔ה מַגִּישֵׁ֥י מִנְחָ֖ה בִּצְדָקָֽה׃ וְעָֽרְבָה֙ לַֽיהוָ֔ה מִנְחַ֥ת יְהוּדָ֖ה וִירוּשָׁלִָ֑ם כִּימֵ֣י עוֹלָ֔ם וּכְשָׁנִ֖ים ה קַדְמֹנִיֹּֽת׃ וְקָרַבְתִּ֣י אֲלֵיכֶם֮ לַמִּשְׁפָּט֒ וְהָיִ֣יתִי ׀ עֵ֣ד מְמַהֵ֗ר בַּֽמְכַשְּׁפִים֙ וּבַֽמְנָ֣אֲפִ֔ים וּבַנִּשְׁבָּעִ֖ים לַשָּׁ֑קֶר וּבְעֹשְׁקֵ֣י שְׂכַר־שָׂ֠כִיר אַלְמָנָ֨ה וְיָת֤וֹם וּמַטֵּי־גֵר֙ וְלֹ֣א

After fleeing from the wrath of King Ahab, Elijah declared to God that he had zealously defended the Divine honor against those of Israel who had abandoned the covenant of ritual circumcision. To this God replied that as a reward for his zealousness henceforth, Jews will perform the mitzvah of circumcision only when Elijah is present to witness it with his own eyes. It is for this reason that the Sages instituted that a seat of honor is prepared for Elijah on which the infant is placed prior to his circumcision (*Radak*, see *Pirkei DeRabbi Eliezer* Chap. 29).

2. וּמִי מְכַלְכֵּל אֶת־יוֹם בּוֹאוֹ וּמִי הָעֹמֵד בְּהֵרָאוֹתוֹ כִּי־הוּא כְּאֵשׁ מְצָרֵף וּכְבֹרִית מְכַבְּסִים — *Who can bear the day of his coming and who can survive when he appears? For he will be like the smelter's fire and like the launderers' soap.*

Who will be able to bear the day that the angel will arrive and clear the path? For like the smelter's fire and the launderers' soap, this angel will purify and cleanse the world of its wicked and rebellious (*Metzudos*). Alternatively, the day [not the angel] will be like the smelter's fire and the launderers' soap for the wicked will be separated from the righteous and will meet their end on that day (*Radak*).

The prophet Zechariah similarly foretold: *And I will bring that third into fire and purify it as one purifies silver* [see *Zechariah* 13:9] (*Radak; Ibn Ezra*).

3. וְיָשַׁב מְצָרֵף וּמְטַהֵר כֶּסֶף וְטִהַר אֶת־בְּנֵי־לֵוִי וְזִקַּק אֹתָם כַּזָּהָב וְכַכָּסֶף — *He will sit smelting and purifying silver; he will purify the children of Levi and refine them like gold and like silver.*

As a judge sits in judgment and carefully examines the deeds of the litigants to determine who is guilty and who is innocent, so too, will God's messenger sit and carefully examine the deeds of the Kohanim, the descendants of Levi. As one who smelts and purifies silver, he removes those who wickedly presented loathsome sacrifices and thereby scorned God's Name (*Metzudos*). *Mahari Kara* suggests that to temper the harsh rebuke of 2:8, *You have corrupted the covenant of Levi,* the prophet now states that God will purify the children of Levi.

וְהָיוּ לַה׳ מַגִּישֵׁי מִנְחָה בִּצְדָקָה — *And they will be for Hashem presenters of offerings in righteousness.*

After God's messenger will purify the tribe of Levi, the Kohanim will strictly observe the laws of sacrificial animals and will no longer offer blemished animals as they had during the generation of Malachi. Alternatively, the prophet had cursed those who had taken foreign wives by stating *May Hashem cut off from the man who does this any child ... who may present an offering to Hashem* [see trans. 2:12]. He now foretells that in the future their children will indeed present offerings in Hashem's Holy Temple (*Mahari Kara*).

yearn, behold, he comes, says HASHEM, *Master of Legions.* [2]*Who can bear the day of his coming and who can survive when he appears? For he will be like the smelter's fire and like the launderers' soap.* [3]*He will sit smelting and purifying silver; he will purify the children of Levi and refine them like gold and like silver, and they will be for* HASHEM *presenters of offerings in righteousness.* [4]*Then the offering of Judah and Jerusalem will be pleasing to* HASHEM *as in the days of old and in former years.* [5]*I will draw near to you for the judgment, and I will be a swift witness against the sorcerers; against the adulterers; against those who swear falsely; against those who extort the wage of the worker, the widow and the orphan; and [against] those who wrong the stranger and do not fear Me,*

4. וְעָרְבָה לַה׳ מִנְחַת יְהוּדָה וִירוּשָׁלָם — *Then the offering of Judah and Jerusalem will be pleasing to* HASHEM.

After the tribe of Levi will be purified and only pure hands will offer the sacrifices to God, only then will the offerings be pleasing to Him as in the days of old (*R' Mendel Hirsch*).

כִּימֵי עוֹלָם וּכְשָׁנִים קַדְמוֹנִיּוֹת — *As in the days of old and in former years. The days of old* are the days of the First Temple (*Ibn Ezra; Abarbanel*) and the *former years* are the days of Moses when the Tabernacle was erected (*Abarbanel*) and God willingly accepted Israel's offerings (*Metzudos*). Alternatively, *the days of old* refer to the days of Moses and the *former years* to the era of King Solomon [the First Temple] when a fire descended from heaven and consumed the offerings that were on the Altar, demonstrating that God had willingly accepted their sacrifices. [See *Lev.* 10:24 and *II Chronicles* 7:1.] Unlike the Second Temple, the Temple that will eventually be established in the future will also merit the heavenly fire as a demonstration of God's willingness to accept the offerings of the Jewish people (*Abarbanel; Malbim*). Rebbi [R' Yehudah Hanasi] explains that *the days of old* refer to the days of Noah[1] and the *former years* are the days of Abel, before idolatry had been introduced to the world (*Sifra — Lev.* 10:23).

5. וְקָרַבְתִּי אֲלֵיכֶם לַמִּשְׁפָּט ... — *I will draw near to you for the judgment ...*

Do not think that there is no God of justice [see 2:17], for on that day God will draw closer to Israel to judge the deeds of every individual (*Metzudos*) so that a purer nucleus will be formed for the nation (*R' M. Hirsch*). He will be a swift witness against the wicked for He knows their inner thoughts and will therefore immediately pay them their due (*Radak*).

בַּמְכַשְּׁפִים ... וְלֹא יְרֵאוּנִי — *Against the sorcerers ... and do not fear Me.*

1. Here, too, God accepted the sacrifice by consuming it with a heavenly fire (*Radak, Genesis* 8:21).

ו יִרְאוּנִי אָמַר יהוה צְבָאוֹת׃ כִּי אֲנִי יהוה לֹא שָׁנִיתִי
ז וְאַתֶּם בְּנֵי־יַעֲקֹב לֹא כְלִיתֶם׃ לְמִימֵי אֲבֹתֵיכֶם
סַרְתֶּם מֵחֻקַּי וְלֹא שְׁמַרְתֶּם שׁוּבוּ אֵלַי וְאָשׁוּבָה
אֲלֵיכֶם אָמַר יהוה צְבָאוֹת וַאֲמַרְתֶּם בַּמֶּה נָשׁוּב׃
ח הֲיִקְבַּע אָדָם אֱלֹהִים כִּי אַתֶּם קֹבְעִים אֹתִי
וַאֲמַרְתֶּם בַּמֶּה קְבַעֲנוּךָ הַמַּעֲשֵׂר וְהַתְּרוּמָה׃
ט בַּמְּאֵרָה אַתֶּם נֵאָרִים וְאֹתִי אַתֶּם קֹבְעִים הַגּוֹי
י כֻּלּוֹ׃ הָבִיאוּ אֶת־כָּל־הַמַּעֲשֵׂר אֶל־בֵּית הָאוֹצָר

The people commit these sins because they do not fear God. Sorcery and adultery are committed clandestinely. People swear falsely because their lies can go undetected. They oppress the widow, orphan and stranger because these people are weak and have no one to protect them. If they would fear God Who views all their deeds, they would surely not commit these sins (*Metzudos*).

6. כִּי אֲנִי ה׳ לֹא שָׁנִיתִי וְאַתֶּם בְּנֵי־יַעֲקֹב לֹא כְלִיתֶם — *For I, Hashem, have not changed; and you, the sons of Jacob, you have not perished.*

Although God lets the wicked prosper, it is not because He has changed and now cherishes evildoers and hates that which is good, but because He is merciful and patient with sinners; if the sinner won't receive retribution in this world, he is sure to receive it in the World to Come (*Rashi*). Alternatively, all that God has foretold through His prophets will eventually occur, for God's will does not change. Similarly, the existence of the sons of Jacob as a nation is guaranteed forever (*Radak*).

Our translation of לֹא שָׁנִיתִי, *I have not changed*, follows *Rashi, Radak* and *Ibn Ezra*. The Sages (*Sotah* 9a), however, translate *I did not repeat* [related to שֵׁנִי, *a second time*] and render "when the nations of the world sinned, God struck them only once and did not repeat the blow and yet they have disappeared but the sons of Jacob have repeatedly been smitten, yet they have remained and will never perish" (*Rashi; Mahari Kara*).

7. לְמִימֵי אֲבֹתֵיכֶם סַרְתֶּם מֵחֻקַּי וְלֹא שְׁמַרְתֶּם — *Since the days of your forefathers you have veered away from My laws and you have not observed them.*

God tells the people through His prophet that it had been an extremely long time since they last kept His laws and that He has meted out to them the punishment that they deserve (*Radak*).

שׁוּבוּ אֵלַי וְאָשׁוּבָה אֲלֵיכֶם — *Return to Me and I will return to you.*

God promised that if the people will return to Him and once again observe the laws of the Torah, He will restore the same blessings that He had bestowed upon them in the past (*Targum Yonasan; Metzudos*).

וַאֲמַרְתֶּם בַּמֶּה נָשׁוּב — *But you say, "For what should we repent?"*

But the people respond by boldly and impudently denying that they have sinned (*Metzudos*). Alternatively, they wonder what additional sins have they committed besides those for which they have been rebuked, i.e., the sins of the sacrifices and the gentile wives (*Radak*).

8. הֲיִקְבַּע אָדָם אֱלֹהִים כִּי אַתֶּם קֹבְעִים אֹתִי וַאֲמַרְתֶּם בַּמֶּה קְבַעֲנוּךָ הַמַּעֲשֵׂר וְהַתְּרוּמָה — *Should a person steal from God, as you steal from Me? And you say, "How have we stolen from You?" [By withholding] the tithes and the terumah-offerings.*

The prophet continues and informs the people of their additional sins. He

says HASHEM, Master of Legions. [6] *For I, HASHEM, have not changed; and you, the sons of Jacob, you have not perished.*

[7] *Since the days of your forefathers you have veered away from My laws and you have not observed them. Return to Me and I will return to you! says HASHEM, Master of Legions; but you say, "For what should we repent?"* [8] *Should a person steal from God, as you steal from Me? And you say, "How have we stolen from You?" [By withholding] the tithes and the terumah-offerings!* [9] *You are cursed with a curse, yet you [continue to] steal from Me, the entire nation!* [10] *Bring all the tithes into the storage house*

asks on God's behalf, "Is it proper for a person to steal from God? Of course not, yet you steal from Him by not giving His attendants, the Kohanim and Levites, their due, for God considers the tithes His own property" (*Metzudos*). In an alternative interpretation of this verse, *Targum Yonasan* translates הֲיִקְבַּע as הֲיַרְגֵז, *will one anger,* and אֱלֹהִים as דַיָּנָא and renders *will a man anger a judge that you should anger Me.* The Sages (*Rosh Hashanah* 26b), however, explain that הֲיִקְבַּע is an Aramaic word that means *steal* (*Rashi*). See *Proverbs* 22:23 (*Radak*).

9. בַּמְּאֵרָה אַתֶּם נֵאָרִים וְאֹתִי אַתֶּם קֹבְעִים — *You are cursed with a curse, yet you [continue to] steal from Me.*

Because you have not given the Kohanim and Levites their due, I have sent a curse upon the work of your hands, but you nevertheless continue to steal their *terumah* and *maaser* tithes (*Rashi*). Alternatively, *Radak* explains that the curse was the result of the sins mentioned earlier, i.e., sacrificing inferior and blemished animals [1:13] and marrying foreign wives [2:11] [see 2:2 where the curses were foretold]. By refusing to give the Kohanim and Levites their due, they added to their sins.

הַגּוֹי כֻּלּוֹ — *The entire nation.*

Unlike the sins mentioned until now, i.e., sacrificing blemished animals and marrying foreign wives, which were committed by groups of individuals, the sin of withholding the tithes and *terumah* offerings were committed by the entire populace (*Radak*).

The curses will be on the grain for the rain will not fall (*Radak*) and the land will not give forth its produce (*Metzudos*). You will plant much seed but it will yield little (*Ramban, Gen.* 4:11).

10. הָבִיאוּ אֶת־כָּל־הַמַּעֲשֵׂר אֶל־בֵּית הָאוֹצָר וִיהִי טֶרֶף בְּבֵיתִי — *Bring all the tithes into the storage house and let it be sustenance in My Temple.*

Since the entire nation has been guilty of withholding their tithes, they will now be required to bring all the tithes to the storage house of the Temple [see *Nehemiah* 10:39] (*Metzudos*), so that food will be available for the Kohanim and Levites who minister before Me (*Rashi; Radak*). If you will bring the tithes and *terumah* as required and give them wholeheartedly (*Abarbanel*), I swear that I will reward you by opening the windows of the heavens and rain blessing upon you without end (*Metzudos*).

וִיהִ֥י טֶ֙רֶף֙ בְּבֵיתִ֔י וּבְחָנ֤וּנִי נָא֙ בָּזֹ֔את אָמַ֖ר יְהוָ֣ה צְבָא֑וֹת אִם־לֹ֧א אֶפְתַּ֣ח לָכֶ֗ם אֵ֚ת אֲרֻבּ֣וֹת הַשָּׁמַ֔יִם
יא וַהֲרִיקֹתִ֥י לָכֶ֛ם בְּרָכָ֖ה עַד־בְּלִי־דָֽי׃ וְגָעַרְתִּ֤י לָכֶם֙ בָּֽאֹכֵ֔ל וְלֹֽא־יַשְׁחִ֥ת לָכֶ֖ם אֶת־פְּרִ֣י הָאֲדָמָ֑ה וְלֹא־תְשַׁכֵּ֨ל לָכֶ֤ם הַגֶּ֙פֶן֙ בַּשָּׂדֶ֔ה אָמַ֖ר יְהוָ֥ה צְבָאֽוֹת׃
יב וְאִשְּׁר֥וּ אֶתְכֶ֖ם כָּל־הַגּוֹיִ֑ם כִּֽי־תִהְי֤וּ אַתֶּם֙ אֶ֣רֶץ חֵ֔פֶץ אָמַ֖ר יְהוָ֥ה צְבָאֽוֹת׃
יג חָזְק֥וּ עָלַ֛י דִּבְרֵיכֶ֖ם
יד אָמַ֣ר יְהוָ֑ה וַאֲמַרְתֶּ֕ם מַה־נִּדְבַּ֖רְנוּ עָלֶֽיךָ׃ אֲמַרְתֶּ֕ם שָׁ֖וְא עֲבֹ֣ד אֱלֹהִ֑ים וּמַה־בֶּ֗צַע כִּ֤י שָׁמַ֙רְנוּ֙ מִשְׁמַרְתּ֔וֹ
טו וְכִ֤י הָלַ֙כְנוּ֙ קְדֹ֣רַנִּ֔ית מִפְּנֵ֖י יְהוָ֥ה צְבָאֽוֹת׃ וְעַתָּ֕ה

טֶרֶף — *Sustenance.*

The word טֶרֶף is related to טְרֵיפָה, *a torn animal.* It is a borrowed term used for food and sustenance [see *Proverbs* 30:8; *Psalms* 111:5], because the beast sustains itself by tearing apart weaker animals and feeding on them (*Metzudos*).

וּבְחָנוּנִי נָא בָּזֹאת — *Test Me, if you will, with this.*

Although it is generally prohibited to test G-d [see *Deut.* 6:16], the case of separating tithes is an exception to this rule (*Taanis* 9a) for our verse clearly sets forth a challenge to test God to see whether a reward will be forthcoming (*Chinuch, Mitzvah* 424).

עַד־בְּלִי־דָי — *Without end.*

Your yield will be so abundant that your vessels and storage houses will not suffice to contain it (*Radak; Metzudos*). The Talmud (*Taanis* 9a) quotes Rav who interprets these words homiletically relating בְּלִי to the phonetically similar בָּלָה, *to wear out.* He explains that God will pour out blessing upon you until you wear out from saying "enough."

Malbim notes that a *blessing without end,* an unlimited blessing, comes directly from God and is not governed by the laws of nature; for anything that is governed by the laws of nature is limited.

The Talmud (*Makkos* 23b) quotes R' Yehoshua ben Levi who stated that the enactment of הָבִיאוּ אֶת כָּל הַמַּעֲשֵׂר, *bring all the tithes,* was one of three things that were innovated by the earthly *beis din* and were ratified by the heavenly *beis din.* *Rivan* (ibid.) explains that the enactment included three new laws: a. מַעֲשֵׂר רִאשׁוֹן, *the first tithe,* normally given to the Levi will now be shared with the Kohen. b. Special chambers were set aside by King Hezekiah in the Temple for the storage of the tithes and *terumah* and were distributed there. c. Tithes must be set aside from fruits and vegetables even though they are not included in the Scriptural command.

11. וְגָעַרְתִּי לָכֶם בָּאֹכֵל וְלֹא־יַשְׁחִת לָכֶם אֶת־פְּרִי הָאֲדָמָה — *And I will rebuke the devourer for you, and it will not destroy for you the produce of the ground.*

God will rebuke the locusts and other crop-destroying creatures and they will stop devouring the produce of the land as they had been doing previously (*Rashi; Radak*).

12. וְאִשְּׁרוּ אֶתְכֶם כָּל־הַגּוֹיִם כִּי־תִהְיוּ אַתֶּם אֶרֶץ חֵפֶץ אָמַר ה׳ צְבָאוֹת — *All the nations will praise you, for you will be a land of delight, says Hashem, Master of Legions.*

In contrast to its previously disgraceful status, the nations will now praise

and let it be sustenance in My Temple. Test Me, if you will, with this, says HASHEM, Master of Legions, [see] if I do not open up for you the windows of the heavens and pour out upon you blessing without end. [11] *And I will rebuke the devourer for you, and it will not destroy for you the produce of the ground, and the vine will not cast off its fruit for you in the field, says HASHEM, Master of Legions.* [12] *All the nations will praise you, for you will be a land of delight, says HASHEM, Master of Legions.*

[13] *Your words have become harsh against Me, says HASHEM; but you say, "How have we spoken against You?"* [14] *You have said, "It is useless to serve God! What gain is there for us that we have kept His charge, and that we walk submissively before HASHEM, Master of Legions?* [15] *So now*

the people of Israel because of their increased success (*Radak; Metzudos).* The Land of Israel will now be a land that I desire (*Rashi*), producing much grain (*Radak*), lacking nothing, making it a land of delight to its inhabitants (*Metzudos*). According to *Targum Yonasan,* this prophecy foretells that the people of Israel will follow God's commandments and that the Divine Presence will once again reside in the Temple.

13. חָזְקוּ עָלַי דִּבְרֵיכֶם אָמַר ה׳ וַאֲמַרְתֶּם מַה־נִּדְבַּרְנוּ עָלֶיךָ — *Your words have become harsh against Me, says Hashem; but you say, "How have we spoken against You?"*

The prophet again takes the nation to task for their unacceptable beliefs: that there is no justice in the world [see 2:17] (*Radak*). He reviews their questions a second time for he is about to answer them (*Abarbanel*).

14. אֲמַרְתֶּם שָׁוְא עֲבֹד אֱלֹהִים וּמַה־בֶּצַע כִּי שָׁמַרְנוּ מִשְׁמַרְתּוֹ וְכִי הָלַכְנוּ קְדֹרַנִּית מִפְּנֵי ה׳ צְבָאוֹת — *You have said, "It is useless to serve God! What gain is there for us that we have kept His charge and that we walk submissively before Hashem, Master of Legions?*

The prophet replies: You have said, "We have served God in vain for we receive no reward" (*Rashi*). The people thought that the deeds of lowly man are meaningless to God Who is so eminently exalted (*Metzudos*).

R' Mendel Hirsch notes that the nation had not broken away from observing the laws of the Torah; but what they did practice, they did solely in the expectation of immediate reward. When this did not materialize, they concluded that those who did not observe the laws of the Torah at all were wiser and more clever than they.

קְדֹרַנִּית — *Submissively* [lit., blackened — see *Joel* 4:15].

Our translation follows *Metzudos.* Alternatively, *Rashi* translates *with low spirits. Mahari Kara* explains that the people said that they had been darkened because they had suffered much in exile.

אֲנַחְנוּ מְאַשְּׁרִים זֵדִים גַּם־נִבְנוּ עֹשֵׂי רִשְׁעָה גַּם
טז בָּחֲנוּ אֱלֹהִים וַיִּמָּלֵטוּ: אָז נִדְבְּרוּ יִרְאֵי יהוה אִישׁ
אֶל־רֵעֵהוּ וַיַּקְשֵׁב יהוה וַיִּשְׁמָע וַיִּכָּתֵב סֵפֶר זִכָּרוֹן
יז לְפָנָיו לְיִרְאֵי יהוה וּלְחֹשְׁבֵי שְׁמוֹ: וְהָיוּ לִי אָמַר
יהוה צְבָאוֹת לַיּוֹם אֲשֶׁר אֲנִי עֹשֶׂה סְגֻלָּה וְחָמַלְתִּי
עֲלֵיהֶם כַּאֲשֶׁר יַחְמֹל אִישׁ עַל־בְּנוֹ הָעֹבֵד אֹתוֹ:
יח וְשַׁבְתֶּם וּרְאִיתֶם בֵּין צַדִּיק לְרָשָׁע בֵּין עֹבֵד
יט אֱלֹהִים לַאֲשֶׁר לֹא עֲבָדוֹ: כִּי־הִנֵּה הַיּוֹם
בָּא בֹּעֵר כַּתַּנּוּר וְהָיוּ כָל־זֵדִים וְכָל־עֹשֵׂה רִשְׁעָה
קַשׁ וְלִהַט אֹתָם הַיּוֹם הַבָּא אָמַר יהוה צְבָאוֹת

15. וְעַתָּה אֲנַחְנוּ מְאַשְּׁרִים זֵדִים ... — *So now we praise the wicked ...*

Now that the people feel that it is useless to serve God, they praise the wicked for disregarding the laws of the Torah (*Metzudos*). They tempt and test God with their evil deeds waiting to see whether He will punish them, but they escape unharmed and go unpunished (*Rashi; Mahari Kara*).

16. אָז נִדְבְּרוּ יִרְאֵי ה׳ אִישׁ אֶל רֵעֵהוּ — *Then those who fear Hashem spoke to each other.*

As the wicked pursue their evil ways, the God-fearing men have spoken to each other and affirmed that they will never adopt the evil deeds of the wicked (*Rashi*). They converse and discuss the blasphemies of the wicked until they are utterly refuted (*Radak*).

וַיַּקְשֵׁב ה׳ וַיִּשְׁמָע ... — *And Hashem listened and heard ...*

God hearkens to the words of the wicked and the righteous and has them written in a book of remembrance so that each may receive his due at a future time (*Mahari Kara; Rashi*).

וַיִּכָּתֵב סֵפֶר זִכָּרוֹן לְפָנָיו — *And a book of remembrance was written before Him.*

This is clearly a metaphoric expression used to portray how every single deed is seen by God (*Abarbanel*), for it is obvious that God does not forget and needs no reminder (*Radak*).

Alternatively, *Abarbanel* relates נִדְבְּרוּ to דֶּבֶר, a *plague*, and explains that the wicked are pointing to the tragedies with which the righteous have been stricken and plagued, as if God pays no attention to their righteousness. To this the prophet responds that everyone's deeds are *written in a book of remembrance* until the time of reward and retribution will arrive for He has heard and listened to everything.

לְיִרְאֵי ה׳ ... — *For those who fear Hashem ...*

Abarbanel explains that יִרְאֵי ה׳, *those who fear Hashem*, are the ones who perform His commandments; the חֹשְׁבֵי שְׁמוֹ, *those who give thought to His Name*, are those who have perfected their beliefs and understanding of the knowledge of God.

17. וְהָיוּ לִי אָמַר ה׳ צְבָאוֹת לַיּוֹם אֲשֶׁר אֲנִי עֹשֶׂה סְגֻלָּה — *They will be a precious treasure for Me, says Hashem, Master of Legions, on the day which I bring about.*

On the day that God will bring about judgment on the wicked, the God-fearing people will be like a precious treasure to Him for He will guard and protect them from any harm (*Radak*). At that time the difference between a righteous man and a wicked man will clearly be seen (*Rashi*). *Radak* explains

we praise the wicked. Evildoers are built up; they have even tested God and escaped.'' [16] *Then those who fear* HASHEM *spoke to each other, and* HASHEM *listened and heard, and a book of remembrance was written before Him for those who fear* HASHEM *and those who give thought to His Name.* [17] *They will be a precious treasure for Me, says* HASHEM, *Master of Legions, on the day which I bring about; and I will have mercy on them as a man has mercy on his son who serves him.* [18] *Then you will return and see the difference between the righteous and the wicked, between one who serves God and one who does not serve Him.*

[19] *For behold, the day is coming, burning like an oven, when all the wicked people and all the evildoers will be like straw; and that coming day will burn them up, says* HASHEM, *Master of Legions,*

that Malachi is referring to the God-fearing people of the generation who will be resurrected together with the righteous of the generation of the resurrection. *Metzudos* understands that their *words* will be precious and will be preserved until the time of reward.

... כַּאֲשֶׁר יַחְמֹל אִישׁ ... — *As a man has mercy ...*

A father has mercy on all his sons (see *Psalms* 103:13), but will forever shower his mercy on the son who serves him (*Radak*).

18. וְשַׁבְתֶּם וּרְאִיתֶם בֵּין צַדִּיק לְרָשָׁע — *Then you will return and see the difference between the righteous and the wicked.*

Everyone will then see the difference between the righteous and the wicked, and no one will again say that God favors the wicked and that it is useless to serve God (*Radak*).

בֵּין עֹבֵד אֱלֹהִים לַאֲשֶׁר לֹא עֲבָדוֹ — *Between one who serves God and one who does not serve Him.*

This is synonymous with the previous clause (*Metzudos*). Alternatively, Scripture may be making a distinction between one who fulfills God's commandments purely out of devotion to God — לִשְׁמָהּ, and one who serves Him for ulterior motives — שֶׁלֹּא לִשְׁמָהּ (*R' Mendel Hirsch*). One who serves God for ulterior motives in truth is in service of himself, not of God! (*R' Mendel Hirsch*).

19. ... כִּי־הִנֵּה הַיּוֹם בָּא בֹּעֵר כַּתַּנּוּר — *For behold, the day is coming, burning like an oven ...*

The word יוֹם in this verse is a metaphoric reference to the sun. At a future time, God will remove the sun from its case and thereby the wicked will be punished and the righteous will be healed (*Rashi* from *Nedarim* 8b). You will then be able to discern who are the wicked and who are the righteous (*Mahari Kara*). Alternatively, *Radak* translates יוֹם as the day of final judgment. Scripture compares this day of judgment to a burning fire.

וְלִהַט אֹתָם הַיּוֹם הַבָּא — *And that coming day will burn them up.*

The sun will be burning like an oven

כ אֲשֶׁר לֹא־יַעֲזֹב לָהֶם שֹׁרֶשׁ וְעָנָף: וְזָרְחָה לָכֶם יִרְאֵי שְׁמִי שֶׁמֶשׁ צְדָקָה וּמַרְפֵּא בִּכְנָפֶיהָ וִיצָאתֶם
כא וּפִשְׁתֶּם כְּעֶגְלֵי מַרְבֵּק: וְעַסּוֹתֶם רְשָׁעִים כִּי־יִהְיוּ אֵפֶר תַּחַת כַּפּוֹת רַגְלֵיכֶם בַּיּוֹם אֲשֶׁר אֲנִי עֹשֶׂה
כב אָמַר יהוה צְבָאוֹת: זִכְרוּ תּוֹרַת מֹשֶׁה עַבְדִּי אֲשֶׁר צִוִּיתִי אוֹתוֹ בְחֹרֵב עַל־כָּל־יִשְׂרָאֵל
כג חֻקִּים וּמִשְׁפָּטִים: הִנֵּה אָנֹכִי שֹׁלֵחַ לָכֶם אֵת אֵלִיָּה הַנָּבִיא לִפְנֵי בּוֹא יוֹם יהוה הַגָּדוֹל וְהַנּוֹרָא:

and will consume the wicked who are compared to straw (*Mahari Kara*). *Rambam* [Introduction to *Cheilek, Sanhedrin,* Chapter 11) writes that some Sages understand that this verse is describing Gehinnom: a term used for the suffering and punishment that will be inflicted upon [the souls of] the wicked. The sun will come close to them and burn them. *Ramban* [discourse on *Rosh Hashanah; Shaar HaGemul*], however, explains that it is referring to the day of judgment that will take place at the advent of the resurrection. See *Abarbanel* who discusses this at length.

אֲשֶׁר לֹא־יַעֲזֹב לָהֶם שֹׁרֶשׁ וְעָנָף — *So that it will not leave them a root or branch.*

The wicked will perish leaving neither son nor grandson [root or branch] (*Targum Yonasan*). Alternatively, the *root and branch* are the few good deeds performed by the wicked for which they will be rewarded in this world and not in the World to Come, after the dead are resurrected. They therefore will be left without root or branch, i.e., good deeds that need to be rewarded (*Abarbanel*).

20. וְזָרְחָה לָכֶם יִרְאֵי שְׁמִי שֶׁמֶשׁ צְדָקָה — *But a sun of righteousness will shine for you who fear My Name.*

But the very same sun that will burn the wicked will heal the righteous (*Rashi*). It will shine upon those who fear God's Name and will deliver them from all evil (*Radak*). Alternatively, their righteous deeds will shine for them as the sun shines (*Metzudos*) and will heal them from the effects of the blazing heat on the Day of Judgment (*Malbim*).

וּמַרְפֵּא בִּכְנָפֶיהָ — *With healing in its rays* (lit., *wings*).

Scripture refers to the rays of the sun as *wings* because the sun spreads its light over the earth as the bird spreads its wings (*Radak; Ibn Ezra*).

וּפִשְׁתֶּם כְּעֶגְלֵי מַרְבֵּק — *And flourish like calves [fattened] in the stall.* Our translation is a composite of *Rashi* who translates וּפִשְׁתֶּם as *fattened* and *Radak* who translates *increase.*

An alternative explanation is: and you will go forth like calves that "have been shut in their stalls and are now being let out into the meadows" (*R' Mendel Hirsch*).

21. וְעַסּוֹתֶם רְשָׁעִים כִּי־יִהְיוּ אֵפֶר תַּחַת כַּפּוֹת רַגְלֵיכֶם — *And you will trample the wicked, for they will be ashes under the soles of your feet.*

Unlike the present time that the wicked rule over the righteous, in the future their roles will reverse and the righteous will trample the wicked for they will have become ashes from the heat of the burning sun (*Mahari Kara*). Although the prophet had foretold that the wicked will be destroyed on the Day of Judgment, *burned up on that day*, this will not occur in just one single day but will be a continuous process of destruction. During that time the wicked will be trampled by the righteous (*Radak*).

so that it will not leave them a root or branch. [20]*But a sun of righteousness will shine for you who fear My Name, with healing in its rays, and you will go out and flourish like calves [fattened] in the stall.* [21]*And you will trample the wicked, for they will be ashes under the soles of your feet, on that day that I bring about, says* HASHEM, *Master of Legions.* [22]*Remember the Torah of Moses My servant, which I commanded him at Horeb for all of Israel — [its] decrees and [its] statutes.*

[23]*Behold, I send you Elijah the prophet before the coming of the great and awesome day of* HASHEM.

22. זִכְרוּ תּוֹרַת מֹשֶׁה עַבְדִּי — *Remember the Torah of Moses My servant.*

Observe the Torah for it will teach you the way to fear God so that you may be spared on the day of judgment (*Ibn Ezra*). Alternatively, Malachi is informing Israel that there will be no more prophets to admonish them for their sins but if they will adhere to the Torah of Moses and observe its commandments, they will speed up the redemption (*Mahari Kara*).

אֲשֶׁר צִוִּיתִי אוֹתוֹ ... — *Which I commanded him ...*

This is the Torah that I commanded Moses to give to all of Israel so that they may observe it in its entirety. He did not invent any part of it[1] (*Metzudos*). Alternatively, *Radak* renders "remember the Torah of Moses *exactly* as I commanded him ..." without any changes or differences from that which I commanded Moses.[2]

חוֹרֵב — *Horeb.*

This is Mount Sinai (*Metzudos; Ibn Ezra, Deut.* 1:6). Alternatively, *Ramban* (*Deut.* 1:6; *Leviticus* 7:38) explains that Horeb is not synonymous with Mount Sinai but is the entire area around Mount Sinai, where the nation camped and erected the *Ohel Moed*, the Tent of Meeting, from which many laws were taught to them. Scripture is therefore instructing the nation to observe the commandments that were taught on Sinai and in the *Ohel Moed* which were both situated in Horeb.

חֻקִּים וּמִשְׁפָּטִים — *[Its] decrees and [its] statutes.*

חֻקִּים, *decrees*, are laws for which the reasons are unknown to us. מִשְׁפָּטִים, *statutes*, are laws for which the reasons are known to us (*Metzudos*).

23. הִנֵּה אָנֹכִי שֹׁלֵחַ לָכֶם אֵת אֵלִיָּה הַנָּבִיא לִפְנֵי בּוֹא יוֹם ה׳ הַגָּדוֹל וְהַנּוֹרָא — *Behold, I send you Elijah the prophet before the coming of the great and awesome day of Hashem.*

Although I admonish you to keep the commandments of the Torah so that

1. If one says that Moses wrote it [the Torah] on his own, then he denies the Torah (*Rambam, Yad HaChazakah, Hil. Teshuvah* 3:8; see also Commentary on the *Mishneh*, Introduction to *Sanhedrin* Chapter *Cheilek — Eighth Principle*).
2. The Torah clearly states that its commandments will remain binding forever, with neither change, addition or subtraction... We see, then, that we are commanded to keep the words of the Torah forever (*Rambam, Yad HaChazakah, Hil. Yesodei HaTorah* 9:1 — see also Comm. on the *Mishneh* — Introduction to Chap. *Cheilek — Ninth Principle*).

ג/כד

כד וְהֵשִׁיב לֵב־אָבוֹת עַל־בָּנִים וְלֵב בָּנִים עַל־אֲבוֹתָם פֶּן־אָבוֹא וְהִכֵּיתִי אֶת־הָאָרֶץ חֵרֶם:
הִנֵּה אָנֹכִי שֹׁלֵחַ לָכֶם אֵת אֵלִיָּה הַנָּבִיא לִפְנֵי בּוֹא יוֹם יהוה הַגָּדוֹל וְהַנּוֹרָא:

סכום פסוקי תרי עשר: הושע מאה ותשעים ושבעה. ורגלך לא בצק״ה סימן. יואל שבעים ושלשה. שלחו מג״ל סימן. עמוס מאה וארבעים וששה. קמ״ו בניה סימן. עובדיה עשרים ואחד. א״ך טוב לישראל סימן. יונה ארבעים ושמנה. ישראל עושה חי״ל סימן. מיכה מאה וחמשה. על״ה אלקים בתרועה סימן. נחום ארבעים ושבעה. יז״ל מים סימן. חבקוק חמשים וששה. ול״ך תהיה צדקה סימן. צפניה חמשים ושלשה. ג״ן נעול סימן. חגי שלשים ושמנה. כי אם גל״ה סודו סימן. זכריה מאתים ואחד עשר. אשרי כל יר״א ה׳ סימן. מלאכי חמשים וחמשה. ויעקב הל״ך לדרכו סימן. סכום הפסוקים של כל שנים עשר נביאים אלף וחמשים כ״י שרי״ת ע״ם אלהים סימן.

you may be saved on the day of judgment, I will nevertheless send Elijah the prophet to warn Israel to repent and to return to God wholeheartedly before the day of judgment arrives (*Radak*). *Metzudos* understands that it will be only through the merit of the Torah that God will send Elijah.

When Elijah ascended to heaven in a whirlwind (*II Kings* 2:1,11), a fiery chariot and fiery horses appeared. He was taken into the chariot where his body and clothes were consumed by the fire (excluding his mantle) and his soul returned to its maker (*Radak, II Kings* 2:1,11). Before the great and awesome day of Hashem, God will create a body in the likeness of Elijah's original one and place his soul in that body and send him to rebuke the nation to return to God (*Radak*). Accordingly, Elijah will be the first to be resurrected from the dead, at that time (*Abarbanel*).

The Sages (*Derech Eretz Zuta*, Chapter 1), however, write that Elijah was one of the nine who entered Gan Eden with both body and soul together. Accordingly, God will send him back in that state prior to the judgment day (*Abarbanel*) [see also *Moed Katan* 26a where Reish Lakish states that Elijah is still alive, i.e., that his soul did not part from his body. This seems to be the accepted view — see *Kuzari* 1:115].

אֵלִיָּה — *Elijah.*

In addition to our verse, there are four places in *II Kings* (1:3,4,8 and 1:12) where the name אֵלִיָּהוּ is written with its ו missing. *Rashi* (*Lev.* 26:42) notes that there are also five places where the name יַעֲקֹב is written with a ו added, יַעֲקוֹב (*Lev.* 26:42, *Jeremiah* 30:18, 33:26, 46:27 and 51:19). He midrashically explains that Jacob took the ו from Elijah's name as security that Elijah will come and herald the redemption of the children of Jacob (see *Midrash Chaseiros V'Yeseiros*).

R' Yaakov Kamenetsky *zt''l* suggests that Elijah's original name was אֵלִיָּה, without the ו [see *Radak I Chron.* 8:27 and *Tos. Bava Metzia* 114b בד״ה מהו], but was changed to אֵלִיָּהוּ, with the ו, when he became the leading prophet of the nation; for it was customary to add to the name of one who attended kings or leaders [see *Rashbam, Numbers* 13:16 regarding Joshua's change of name from Hoshea to Yehoshua]. Therefore, after Elisha had been appointed as Elijah's successor as the leading prophet of the nation, Elijah was only referred to as אֵלִיָּה [*II Kings* 1:3,4,8,12], his original name, and not אֵלִיָּהוּ, his acquired name (*Emes L'Yaakov, Lev.* 26:42).

יוֹם ה׳ הַגָּדוֹל וְהַנּוֹרָא — *The great and awesome day of Hashem.*

This is the day of judgment that will precede the resurrection (*Ramban, Shaar HaGemul; Ritva, Rosh Hashanah* 16b). Alternatively, *Rambam* (*Yad*

[24] *And he will turn back [to God] the hearts of fathers with [their] sons and the hearts of sons with their fathers, lest I come and strike the land with utter destruction.*

Behold, I send you Elijah the prophet before the coming of the great and awesome day of HASHEM.

HaChazakah, Hil. Melachim 12:2) explains that this is the war of Gog and Magog that will usher in the Messianic age. Elijah will arise to rectify the ways of the Jewish people. *Rambam* concedes that there are Sages who opine that Elijah will come immediately before the coming of the Messiah after the war of Gog and Magog. [For further study of this topic see Appendix to ArtScroll *Sanhedrin* 3.]

24. וְהֵשִׁיב לֵב־אָבוֹת עַל־בָּנִים וְלֵב בָּנִים עַל־אֲבוֹתָם פֶּן־אָבוֹא וְהִכֵּיתִי אֶת־הָאָרֶץ חֵרֶם — *And he will turn back [to God] the hearts of fathers with [their] sons and the hearts of sons with their fathers, lest I come and strike the land with utter destruction.*

Elijah will draw the hearts of all the people back to God: fathers together with their sons and sons together with their fathers, for if they will not repent at that time, G-d will utterly destroy the land (*Radak; Mahari Kara*).

Alternatively, Elijah will turn the hearts of the fathers back to God *through* their sons and the hearts of the sons *through* their fathers (*Rashi; Metzudos*). He will speak to the sons with love and favor that they in turn should speak to their fathers that they should follow in God's ways. The same explanation applies to the second part of the verse (*Rashi*). *Abarbanel* and *Metzudos* explain that since the resurrection of the dead will take place through Elijah, he will cause the hearts of the fathers to turn back to God through their sons who had died and are now being resurrected during their father's lifetime. When these fathers will see their resurrected sons and listen to their report of the just reward and retribution that their souls had received, they will immediately return to God. The same applies to the second part of the verse.

According to the Sages (*Eduyos* 8:7), Elijah will come to make peace in the world. *Tos. Yom Tov* explains that he will make peace between Israel and the nations and inform them that the Messiah will imminently arrive. He will unite the fathers and sons who fled to various areas and countries because of their sufferings in exile. All this will occur on the day prior to the arrival of the Messiah [as per *Eruvin* 43b].

הִנֵּה אָנֹכִי שֹׁלֵחַ לָכֶם אֵת אֵלִיָּה הַנָּבִיא לִפְנֵי בּוֹא יוֹם ה׳ הַגָּדוֹל וְהַנּוֹרָא — *Behold, I send you Elijah the prophet before the coming of the great and awesome day of HASHEM.*

It is customary to repeat this verse so that we may conclude on a positive note. May הקב״ה send His prophet speedily in our days.

This volume is part of
THE ARTSCROLL SERIES®
an ongoing project of
translations, commentaries and expositions
on Scripture, Mishnah, Talmud, Halachah,
liturgy, history, the classic Rabbinic writings,
biographies and thought.

For a brochure of current publications
visit your local Hebrew bookseller
or contact the publisher:

Mesorah Publications, ltd
4401 Second Avenue
Brooklyn, New York 11232
(718) 921-9000
www.artscroll.com

MW00861906